ASPECTS OF EDUCATIONAL TECHNOLOGY

Aspects
of Educational Technology
Volume XII

Educational Technology
in a Changing World

*Edited for the Association for Programmed Learning
and Educational Technology by*
David Brook and Philip Race

General Editor:
R E B Budgett *Department of Teaching Media,
University of Southampton*

Kogan Page

First published 1978
by Kogan Page Limited,
120 Pentonville Road, London N1 9JN

Printed in Great Britain by
T. J. Press (Padstow) Ltd, Padstow, Cornwall

ISBN 0 85038 137 1
ISSN 0141-5956

Distributed in the USA by Nichols Publishing Co
PO Box 96, New York, NY 10024

Contents

Editorial   9

Keynote Address   11

Chapter 1: Educational Technology and Developing Countries   15

1. The Role of the Educational Consultant in Developing Countries
   R McAleese 17

2. Have Senate — Will Travel: A Study of the Adaptation and
   Application of a Case Study/Simulation from a British Context
   to Use in the United States, Canada and Nigeria *L F Evans* 21

3. Curriculum Development at the Fiji Technical College
   E E Green 29

4. Developing a Large-Scale Modularized Training System for Brazilian
   Telecommunications *N H S Machado and A J Romiszowski* 39

5. Individualized Instruction and the Mature Student
   A J Romiszowski 48

Chapter 2: Propagating Educational Technology — 'Training the Trainers'   59

6. The Propagation of Educational Innovations *D G Hawkridge* 61

7. An Exercise in the Development of Support Materials to Facilitate
   Internal Training in Schools and Colleges *W J K Davies* 67

8. City and Guilds of London Institute Course No 731-3 Certificate
   in Educational Technology: A Description of the Pilot Scheme
   operated in the Department of Educational Technology at Coventry
   Technical College 1975-76 and 1976-77 *J E Hills* 76

9. Developing Strategies for In-Service Training in Educational
   Technology *C Neville* 85

10. Use of a Two-Tier Training Strategy in Technical Education
    R Ward 94

11. Reflections on the Course Development Team Organization in the
    Technician Education Council External Student Pilot Project
    J Coffey 100

12. The Primary Extension Programme as a Strategy for Training
    in Educational Technology *J Cooper* 108

Chapter 3: Commercial and Industrial Applications   117

13. MAVIS: A Case History of Educational Technology in Industry
J M Moffatt 119

14. Design of Package Training Materials for Accountancy Firms
D M Tyrrell 126

15. Utilization of the Programmed Learning Technique in Management
Development *C H Mason* 132

16. Programmed Learning in the Footwear Industry *K H Westley* 136

17. Some Applications of Educational Technology in Agricultural
Training *J R S Bulford, A R G Tallis and P W J Howard* 149

Chapter 4: 'Ways and Means' — The Instructional Media   157

18. Appropriate Educational Technology *A M Stewart* 159

19. Social Perception: Designing Mixed-Media Instruction
in a Polytechnic *I Winfield* 164

20. An Integrated Learning System for Technician Education
P A I Davies, J F Jarvis, J G Kelly, D T Rees and K R Webber 171

21. Teaching a Graphics Course through Programmed Instruction
C Y Oh 177

22. A Comparison of the Effectiveness of Teaching: (1) In the Traditional
Classroom Situation and (2) By Cine Film *C M Bird* 182

23. A Facility for Self-Paced Instruction using Tape/Slide Programmes
A G Stephens 190

24. Microfiche: A New Medium for Audiovisual Instruction
G Murza 195

25. Ten Years of Closed Circuit Television in the Royal Navy
Lt Comdr B A Brooking 201

26. Levels of Use of Educational Broadcasting in Britain and West Africa:
A Study of Rejection of an Innovation *P Hurst* 206

27. A Survey and Evaluation of Teleconferencing *A D Becker* 212

28. Satellites in Education: Experimenting for Ever? *J S Daniel* 219

29. The Use of a Communications Satellite and Interactive Colour
Television in Simulation Teaching of Fire Suppression Skills
W D Robertson 225

Chapter 5: Applications in Science Education   231

30. Identification of Educational Needs: Diagnostic Testing
R A Sutton 233

31. A Three-Tier Approach to First-Year Physics *W S Telfer* 241

32. The Use of Video-Tape Recordings as an Aid to Teaching in an
Undergraduate Course *B G M Jenkins* 244

33. Teaching Physical Chemistry Objectively — Extension to Laboratory
Work *W P Race* 247

34. Design and Production of Self-Instructional Learning Packages in Biochemistry using the Philips PIP System *C F A Bryce and A M Stewart* 256

35. Building Science-Based Educational Games into the Curriculum *H I Ellington, F Percival and E Addinall* 263

36. Communication of Scientific Information *E Bardell* 269

Chapter 6: Applications in Medical and Paramedical Education   277

37. Relevance in Medical Education: An Evaluation of Students' Introduction to Clinical Medicine *C R Coles and B Mountford* 279

38. Applications of Educational Technology to Dietetic Education *P Fieldhouse and M Shaw* 287

39. Simulation in Health Education *A Taylor* 293

40. Training Family Planning Field-Workers by Behaviour Modelling *P M J Hancock* 302

41. Applications of Educational Technology for Community Health Workers in Developing Countries *A C L Zelmer and A E Zelmer* 309

Chapter 7: The Computer and Educational Technology   315

42. Opportunities and Pitfalls in Computer-Based Education Networks *H F Rahmlow* 317

43. A Survey of the Development, Application and Evaluation of Computer-Based Learning in Tertiary Education in the UK, the USA, the Netherlands and Canada *C A Hawkins* 323

44. Structuring Computer-Assisted Learning in a University Environment *M Leiblum* 330

45. A Modular CAI System *C van der Mast* 336

46. The CAIPE Project — Aims, Development and Assessment; Computer-Aided Instruction Programs in Economics at the Northern Ireland Polytechnic *D W McCulloch* 345

47. Resources for an Independent Study Course *A Brew* 350

Chapter 8: Learning and Perception   359

48. The Shared Understanding of Human Action: A More Appropriate Goal for Educational Technology? *W G Fleming* 361

49. Understanding Learning: A Case Study in Student and Staff Development *C R Coles and W G Fleming* 367

50. The Effect of Adjunct Question Position, Type and the Presence or Absence of Feedback on Learning from a Video-Taped Lesson *P A Kirschner and H J van der Brink* 373

51. Searching Tables in the Dark: Horizontal vs Vertical Layouts *J Hartley and K L Davies* 384

Chapter 9: Resourcing Educational Technology   391

52.   Some Low-Budget Assessment Procedures *E W Anderson* 393

53.   Librarians' Needs in Relation to Teaching and Learning in Higher Education *P J Hills* 401

54.   Encouraging Freedom in Learning: Implications for Cataloguing and Retrieval of Resource Materials *A L Barker and E G Bingham* 406

55.   Progress with Programmed Learning 1968-78: The Development of the Longman Group Reading Programme *J Leedham* 418

Chapter 10: Additional Contributions and Delegates' Forum Review   425

Chapter 11: Workshop Sessions   431

    Workshop Review *D M Wharry* 433

56a.   Semi-Programmed Group Instruction: An Appropriate Technology for Developing Countries *J G Barker* 438

56b.   Workshop Transcript: Problems in the Design of Training Packages for Developing Countries *J G Barker* 444

57.   Analysing Lecture Styles *D M Wharry* 452

Appendices   461

List of Exhibitors   463

Sponsorship   464

List of Delegates   465

Closing Address   469

Keyword Index   471

Author Index   473

Editorial

Educational Technology in a Changing World

The theme of ETIC '78 was intended to embrace a wide variety of the roles of educational technology at the present time. It was particularly intended to broaden the content of the conference to include educational technology developments in developing countries, and to re-establish the relevance of the conference to industrial and commercial organizations both by encouraging relevant papers and by increasing the scope of the trade exhibition.

Inevitably, with a collection of papers ranging over the whole field of educational technology, it has been difficult to decide on the most logical way to arrange them in this volume. Many papers could have been placed equally well under two or three chapter headings. We have therefore attempted to balance the content of chapters, trusting that the reader will also check chapters other than those most directly relevant. The 'subject keywords' index is designed to be of particular use here.

We have tried to make this a 'usable' book, both by indexing and by commenting briefly on the content of each chapter in turn. Inevitably, the 'subject keywords' index cannot cover every view of what are the most important keywords in every paper, but the index is intended to *help*, at least, in the reader's location of relevant material. Sadly, it was not possible to include in the volume the often 'riveting' discussions which followed many presentations (and which have often proved most illuminating to us when we have listened to the audio recordings of the sessions). The discussions are often so far-ranging, that it would require a second volume to do them justice.

The Conference

ETIC '78 was organized in four parallel streams made up of 40-minute presentations. Chairmen were asked to ensure that each 40 minutes was about equally divided between presentation and discussion. The workshop programme ran parallel to the streams, and was organized by Dr D.M. Wharry of University College, Cardiff. A 'Delegates' Forum' intended for post-deadline presentations and impromptu contributions was organized by Dr D.I. Trotman-Dickenson of the Polytechnic of Wales. In addition, the Trade and Members' exhibitions occupied two whole floors of the main conference building, and an interesting range of seminars about educational television were presented by HTV (Wales).

It was unavoidable that even the most dedicated delegates could only attend about one-sixth of the total conference (though many made use of the reprographic facilities to compensate for presentations they were unable to attend). Attendance figures for the presentations varied widely, but very often a small audience produced the most stimulating discussions.

The issue of 'which type of conference structure is the most appropriate for ETICs' remains. The multi-stream format adopted for ETIC '78 had the advantage that it allowed a wide range of subjects to be covered, and it enabled about 70 contributors to talk about their work. The disadvantages were the impossibility of any delegate doing more than 'dip into' the whole conference, and discouragingly small audiences for some excellent presentations. Furthermore, with such a wide subject spectrum, levels of excellence necessarily are variable!

A conference on a much 'tighter' theme, and with only one main stream would allow much firmer control of the standard of work accepted, but a much lower proportion of the APLET membership might find any such conference relevant. We feel it is important to optimize the standard of the content of the conference, whilst at the same time maintaining the conference as 'the time when the ordinary member of APLET can take the floor'. In these times of economic constraint, it has to be said that many delegates can obtain funding to attend the conference only if they are contributing work. Perhaps, then, despite the drawbacks, we are stuck with a 'supermarket' conference?

Acknowledgements

We thank particularly Conference Secretary Miss Beverly Ryan (now Mrs John Hart, and resident in Australia) and Conference Chairman John Hanson, for organizing a conference which attracted such an interesting variety of contributions. We express our appreciation to Robin Budgett, Leo Evans and Aled Rhys Wiliam for invaluable advice in the planning stages of the conference. We are much indebted to many people from various departments of the Polytechnic, in particular Jeff Farrow (who performed myriad tasks of all sorts as well as handling all financial aspects of the conference) and Glen Jenkins, who ably assisted Beverly. Under duress (of being beaten about our heads with this volume) we thank our wives for their endurance of our seemingly endless 'being-unavailable' for normal domestic duties!

Phil Race
David Brook

The Polytechnic of Wales, May 1978

Keynote Address

G. Hubbard
Director, Council for Educational Technology for the United Kingdom, London

The theme of this conference is 'Educational technology in a changing world'. I do not dispute that it is necessary to ask in what way it is changing, and which of those changes most affect educational technology.

I am going to single out three changes, which I see as by any criteria significant, but particularly significant for us and our activities.

The first is the fall in the birth rate. For the first time since we had universal education, there is a shortfall in the supply of the raw material of education — children. Already there is a convenient euphemism — the problem of falling rolls. But let me say clearly, firstly, that I do not believe any but the lowest of the official demographic predictions, and, secondly, that I believe this to be one of the best pieces of news we have had this century. In human terms the babies we are not having are the babies we did not want, and anyone concerned with education should rejoice at the thought of fewer children with the disadvantages that follow from being unwanted. In economic terms, I shall be going on to discuss structural unemployment, which makes a nonsense of the spectre of an ageing population sitting on the backs of an inadequate force of young workers. No, the problems are not grave social problems, but simple organizational and logistic problems concerned with adapting a system which has flourished on continuous expansion to manage in a steady state or to cope with a decline. But remember that it is only the numbers which are in decline; it is not a necessary consequence that the quantity of education purveyed must fall also. And even the fall in numbers applies only to the compulsory years. Beyond that, in further and higher education, there is the prospect of variation in numbers, of bulges and troughs, such as we have been accustomed to in the past. The major social problem — so major that in my view the survival of our society in its present form may well depend on what we do about it — is structural unemployment. I do not need to explain this to you; you all know well enough that because of new technologies efficient competitive industries do not use as many workers per unit of output as inefficient, under-capitalized, old-fashioned industries. So, with every step to make our industry competitive more jobs disappear. The prospect is a division of the country into the elite who have jobs and the rest who have not — a recipe it seems to me for conflict — or a radical change in the way we use work.

We are used to work having two functions: to create the goods and services we need and to redistribute wealth. We may have to find different mechanisms for these two functions; there is still, hovering over us, an absolute limitation of energy and a finite availability of easily won materials. We cannot go on making things to be thrown away just so as to provide jobs.

Now I believe the immediate sensible course is to share the available work. We have been accustomed to divide our time into three roughly eight-hour sections each day — for work, leisure and sleep. I believe we will have to try a new division,

11

say, into four. Keep, if you need it, eight hours for sleep, but then have a division into three — work, learning, leisure. The difference between the last two need not be clear cut; the learning will not always or necessarily be institutional, but there is an important difference in attitude. Because, as I have said before, education is a socially acceptable form of unemployment, and this learning not only enriches the learner but helps to maintain his sense of his own value, so easily diminished in the absence of the work which society recognizes.

I would like to see us moving to genuine work sharing — a shorter working day for all — and the development of continuing education as a universally accepted element in a normal life. I fear, however, that on the way to that end we must expect a fairly harrowing period when the work sharing is in the form of periods of unemployment, and the self-esteem generated by self-improvement will be all the more necessary.

The third major change we will see is in the third stage of the industrial revolution. The first stage was the revolution based on power; the second stage on communication; the third stage will be based on control. It is the revolution of micro-electronics; it is hammering at our door, and we do not know, cannot see, what its consequences will be.

Now, what do these changes mean for educational technology? Well, as always, the technological development is in advance of our usage; we have always picked up existing technology. But the problems to which we need to apply it seem likely to be:

As a consequence of falling rolls — the teaching of uneconomic small groups.
As a consequence of structural changes in industry — requirements for flexible training and retraining arrangements.
And continuing education provision, both formal and informal, as an essential strand in life.

Thus we can see easily enough that the main line of response will be through the application of individualized learning methods and the continued development of various forms of open and distant learning.

Equally, we can foresee the development of the techniques and methods currently used, together with systems taking advantage of, and coupling together, narrow-band and wide-band communications (using the massive existing investment in a nationwide broadcasting system and a nationwide telephone system), the existing domestic TV in its emergent role as a visual display unit, audio-recording equipment as stores for digital information which can drive that display unit, and the computer, small in size, cheap and ubiquitous, as an aid to learning.

But as we go into this period we need to prepare ourselves by improving our conceptual understanding. We have lived, for a number of years, on a basic input of ideas which has not been added to; the linking of the systems approach, founded in behavioural psychology and cybernetics, with the technology of communications and reprographics.

We have run into certain problems, particularly in relation to the effective evaluation of the educational consequences of particular innovations, and the particular difficulty therefore in justifying a particular choice of mode or media. My general feeling is that we need to offer our own views on these problems, and not, as we have tended to, to leave it to academic research workers in established disciplines. Research is needed, but it should be in the context of the ideas which those working in the field see as important.

I would like to put forward four propositions for discussion.

The first is that educational technology is essentially one part, alongside curriculum development, staff development and the development of student learning, of the wider process that might be called 'educational development' and that we need therefore to strengthen the links between these different aspects of the process.

The second I have to explain carefully. I believe the educational process is generally at a low level of efficiency. This is not a criticism, not to say that things are getting worse, only a statement about the improvability of the situation. You can arrive at it, if you like, by saying that the educational process is remarkably unresponsive to small changes. This suggests that it is either very near the peak of perfection, or at a rather low level of efficiency. It then follows that the difference between very efficient systems and very inefficient systems is that in the former most changes make things worse and in the latter most changes makes things better. So, my second proposition is that almost any considered innovation aimed at improving the effectiveness of the educational process is worth a try. I am not arguing for change for the sake of change — I am suggesting that, if a little thought suggests that it will be beneficial, it's probably not necessary to set up an elaborate initial controlled trial.

My third proposition is that technology is in advance of our capacity to use it. More than ever, we do not get what we like in the way of technology, so we might as well like what we get. But we should note that, while this is the case in relation to major equipment and systems, the links between systems, being increasingly based on microelectronics, are something we can have tailored to suit our needs at a reasonable price. Dr Boris Townsend pointed out that, in the last 30 years, the £100 car has become the £2,000 car, but the £70 black and white TV set is still (though rather superior in quality) £70.

My fourth proposition is that we, those of us concerned with educational technology, have to build the bridge between the available technology and the learner's needs by initiating discussion of possible ways of learning. It was a notable omission from the Great Debate, a notable omission from the Secretary of State's recent set of questions for discussion relating to higher education. How can we get the idea across that education and training need not be constrained, as it has been so often in the past, by the requirement that teacher and learner must be in the same place at the same time for any effect to arise? There will be a statement by CET shortly which will set out this case; I hope you will help us by using it as a text whenever possible.

Those are my four propositions for discussion. I know that you will have much else to discuss and that the next few days will be the usual headlong rush from session to session. In wishing you a good conference, may I finally say that I believe the educational technology community has come through the economic blizzard of the last few years in remarkably good shape, and that the education and training services need your skills and your abilities more now than ever before.

Chapter 1:
Educational Technology
and Developing Countries

Educational changes occurring in developing countries throughout the world require many of the skills and tools which educational technology may provide. In several such countries, education is changing at an unprecedented rate, often assisted by personnel from developed nations serving as instructors, field-workers or consultants. The call for papers preceding ETIC '78 asked for papers referring to education in such developing countries, and in several chapters in this volume these papers may be found. In particular, many of the papers on media applications and development, communications, and health education were submitted with some reference to developing nations; however, we think it most appropriate to place these papers in the relevant chapters alongside complementary papers relating to the developed world.

It is appropriate, however, to open this volume with a cross-section of papers presenting work of relevance directly to developing countries, and illustrating the role played by experts from the developed world in adapting materials and providing advice and help for 'younger' nations.

Mr McAleese (1), questioning whether money being spent to assist educationally underdeveloped countries is being spent wisely, examines the role of the media consultant. In a humorous manner, he raises many very valid criticisms of the way consultants are likely to 'intervene' rather than promote beneficial change.

Professor Evans (2) directed a project aiming to study the meetings of formally established committees in universities, in order to provide a training package to help academic and administrative staff gain the skills requisite to their committee activities. His paper describes the extension of this simulation study to relate to situations in other educational establishments in Britain, North America, and a developing country: Nigeria.

Dr Green (3) gives a description of course development and evaluation of courses connected with industrial and business studies at Fiji Technical College. He illustrates the evaluation of students' performance, instructional materials, and course programmes (referring in detail to a cabinetmaking course).

In two papers describing work relating to Brazil, Dr Romiszowski (4), (5) refers respectively to the production of a training system for telecommunications personnel, and training of adolescents and adults in mathematics. Both projects are presented with detailed consideration of the needs for which they were developed, production of materials, and organization and operation of the schemes. It may be interesting (even provocative) to analyse these applications of educational technology in a developing nation in terms of the ideals proposed earlier (1).

1. The Role of the Educational Consultant in Developing Countries

R. McAleese *University of Aberdeen*

Abstract: The role of the media consultant is ill defined and consultants may be ill equipped to meet the problems encountered. This paper discusses the interaction of the consultant with clients, his mediation of educational technology knowledge, and the degree to which change is effected.

Prologue

This paper had an unlikely origin. Firstly, an 18-hour flight to South East Asia. It is remarkable what one does to pass the time! The reason for my flight was a two-week seminar in Java that I was helping to organize. To pass the time I tried to think what the British Council would get out of my visit and how the Indonesian Ministry of Education would benefit. Secondly, and acting as a background to this self-investigation, I was still thinking about some work I had been doing in Aberdeen. I had been working as a 'consultant' in a medical faculty department and my 'clients' had just made a few changes to their practical classes. Somewhere over Mecca (I'm only guessing) an idea struck me that what I was doing in my staff development work had a parallel in Java. Further introspection and an earlier attempt (McAleese, 1978) has led to this paper.

Background

There are 25 Least Developed Countries (LDC) according to a World Bank classification (1974). Such countries have a GNP of $120 per capita. Taking a higher per capita GNP (less than $750) then 88 of the family of nations (about 70 per cent) are 'developing countries'. Even if one rejects GNP as an indicator and takes illiteracy rate, then a similar number of such countries exist. Such countries receive development aid from the most developed countries (USA, UK, etc.), part of this aid is manpower. In 1974, some 38,000 experts were working in LDCs under the aegis of the OECD. If one counts in other international and national bodies (UNESCO, WHO, ILO, IMTEC and the British Council) then about 50,000 such experts are in post each year. At a conservative estimate such development aid represents about $1,000m per annum. Recent criticisms of development aid manpower have called into question whether such money is well spent (Bousquet, 1976; McAleese, 1978). This paper takes a look at the role that media consultants play in providing aid to developing countries.

The Consultant

Experts, advisers or consultants are terms that are not easy to define (Bolam, 1975). Catalyst, change agent (Hoyle, 1970) or problem solver (Havelock, 1971) are still unsatisfactory. Catalyst is used in a pejorative and misleading sense and others imply a prejudging of the nature of the job, i.e. a change agent *does* something to a client. Curle suggests:

> It is an unspoken statement of superiority, it implies the survival of intellectual imperialism after political manifestations have disappeared (Curle, 1968).

However, in order to say something I will use the term 'consultant' to cover all those who go abroad to work, give advice, teach or administer development aid.

The Problem

Bousquet (1976) in a swingeing attack on experts suggests that the 'indictment' to be met by consultants is that they are deficient in three ways. Their private lives; their work; and their comprehension of their host country. They are accused of earning more than the people of the country they are in; some of them are more concerned with 'seeing' the host country, further that they do not do any work, and lastly

> If they had their own way they would change everything. They would try and sell new-fangled ideas which are not necessarily what the country needs (Bousquet, 1976).

The basic problem with consultants is that they are often unsuited to the job they have to do. McAleese (1978) suggests that consultants among other things trivialize knowledge and apply culture — dependent ideas. Donovan (1972) writing about the US Consultant in Library Science seems to fall into this trap.

> His [the consultant's] objective is to develop people ... his goal is to *leave behind* something lasting ... he should be able to *transfer* to a developing country all the knowledge and skills needed at a particular time... (my emphasis).

Many authors recognize the problem. Bousquet (1976) emphasizes his point by saying:

> An expert is not only a professional, he belongs to a country and to a culture. He has his own habits and ways of seeing and feeling.

Sherrington (1977) discussing audiovisual consultations sees the danger:

> British professionals who carry their British standards and expectations abroad to an alien administrative structure can be hopelessly frustrated and cause great offence.

A very good example of the culture specific nature of consultancy is in the work of the *media* consultant. Media (all forms of audiovisual technology) is by its nature culture based. Western (developed) society has sought a dependency on heavy technology, some developing countries 'ape this posture' (McAleese, 1978). The OECD (1975) recognizes this problem in relation to technology-linked educational innovations, for example microteaching. This report acknowledges that the international transfer of learning systems involves a process whereby an educational practice is introduced in a cultural setting other than that for which it was originally intended. It does, however, say that such transfers have been *successful!* I saw such an 'international transfer package' lying on the floor of a room in Java. The six films were useless as the 16mm projector wasn't working. The electricity supply was not reliable enough! Many developing countries have been trapped by the super hardware salesman of the developed world. Many such countries have obsolete language laboratories without either the technical know-how or the willingness to learn foreign languages using outdated language teaching ideas. Spicer (1972) emphasizes this point when he says that change agents work across barriers of language belief and customs stemming from cultural backgrounds. The dominant

18

Western (i.e. Developed) cultural background is that of 'heavy technology dependency'. There is a danger that I may be seen to be arguing for a value-free form of consultation, akin to the Weber idea of value-free sociology. Not so; I am simply observing the lack of awareness of the problem shown by consultants.

If we accept that there is a problem but acknowledge that consultancy work does continue, what role should such consultants play in developing countries?

The Role of the Consultant

A number of authors have attempted to conceptualize the consultant's role. Juarez (1969) and Gallagher and Stantofolo (1968) saw the consultant in terms of being an Adviser, an Advocate, an Analyst etc. — terms that seem to describe a dimension relating to the 'Degree of Intervention' by the consultant. For example, in the distinction between 'Adviser' and 'Advocate'. Juarez saw the Adviser *presenting* alternatives, whereas the Advocate *recommended* alternatives. Presenting has a degree of neutrality whereas, recommending has a degree of becoming involved — a difference of commitment or degree of consultant *intervention*. McAleese, (1978) listing the roles of Organizer, Teacher, Resource Person, Evaluator and Facillitator, emphasizes the importance of the type and nature of the consultant's knowledge (probabalistic, conditional, culture specific, etc.). Another dimension that can be detected is the degree of change required or effected. These three dimensions can be used to construct a model of the consultant and his role in innovation.

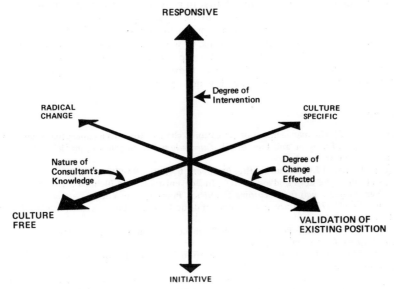

Figure 1. *Model for the role of the consultant (three orthogonal dimensions)*

Figure 1 shows a simple way of thinking of the consultant's role. Consultants can vary their intervention from being Responsive to showing Initiative (Resource Person to 'Expert' Teacher). The knowledge that the consultant uses can vary depending on its degree of culture specificity. The third dimension indicates the degree of change effected by the consultant (and his knowledge).

19

In some cases clients want validation of extant policies, in others they want genuine change and new 'knowledge'.

It is possible using this model to construct a consultancy typology. Two types will suffice for examples:

Type A: Responsive; Culture Free; Radical Change. In this type of work, the consultant would be acting as a 'Problem Solver' (Havelock, 1971). His role, in the developing country, would be to act as a 'Resource Person' (McAleese, 1978); he would be aware of the cultural assumptions in his 'knowledge', yet he would be involved in real change. A very rare breed!

Type B: Interventionist; Culture Specific; Validating present position. A more typical (at least according to Bousquet, 1976) position. This is the specialist sent abroad to give a course. He is asked to go at one week's notice. He is totally unaware of the problems in the host country, tries to transplant Western practice (his undergraduate course), and, without knowing it, is irrelevant as the host government have already decided against 'an open-plan primary school system'.

Conclusion

This paper has the limited aim of presenting evidence on the role of the consultant. Two conclusions merit further study and need only be mentioned here. First, the lack of training provided for consultants. In general such training is meagre and often dispensed with by consultants. Further, training such as it is, tends to be the presenting of 'tourist' information, not preparing a consultant for his work (e.g. 'Don't make political speeches'). Second, to what extent is a *media* consultant more at risk than others? One would hope that the consultant described by one client as 'someone we have to put up with for two months to obtain £10,000 worth of equipment, that we don't really need' is not attending this conference!

References

Bolam, R. (1975) The management of educational change: towards a conceptual framework. In Harris, A., Lawn, M. and Prescott, W. *Curriculum Innovation.* Croom Helm and Open University Press, London.

Bousquet, J. (1976) Experts under fire. *Prospects,* 6,4, pp. 595-602.

Curle, A. (1968) The devil's advocate view. In Benveniste, G. and Illchman, W.F. *Agents of Change: Professionals in Developing Countries.* Praeger, New York.

Donovan, D.G. (1972) Library development and the US consultant overseas. *Library Trends,* 20, 3, pp. 506-14.

Gallagher, A. and Stantofolo, F. A. (1969) Perspectives on agent roles. *Journal of Co-operative Extension,* 4, pp. 223-9.

Havelock, R.G. (1971) The utilisation of educational research and development. *British Journal of Educational Technology,* 2,2, pp. 84-97.

Hoyle, E. (1970) Planned organisation change in education. *Research in Education,* 3, pp. 1-22.

Juarez, L. J. (1969) *The Technical Advisor as a Cross Cultural Change Agent.* Occasional Paper Number 7, University of Kentucky, ERIC ED 040 488.

McAleese, R. (1978) The media consultant's role in innovation. *Educational Broadcasting International,* 10, 4, pp. 182-6.

OECD (1975) *The International Transfer of Microteaching Programmes for Teacher Education,* OECD, Paris.

Sherrington, R. (1977) Media expertise for export. *The Media Reporter,* 3, pp. 12-13.

Spicer, E.H. (1972) *Human Problems in Technological Change.* Russell Sage, New York.

2. Have Senate – Will Travel: A Study of the Adaptation and Application of a Case Study/Simulation from a British Context to Use in the United States, Canada and Nigeria

L.F. Evans *Centre for Educational Technology, City University, London*

Abstract: Can committee members working in formalized committees in educational establishments be taught the skills required in their committee work? This paper describes a training package produced for this purpose, and the adaptation of this package for use in different situations, including work in developing countries.

In 1971, in the halcyon days when the University Grants Committee had financial reserves and made funds available for 'The Training and Development of University Teachers and Administrators', The City University received a grant to carry out a study and training programme on 'The Conduct of Meetings'. The agreed purposes of the project were:

(1) To study the function of all types of meetings in universities, particularly those of formally established committees
(2) To train academic and administrative staff in the skills requisite to their activities in organizing, directing, contributing to and reporting on meetings
(3) To provide a 'package' of exercises, video-tapes, case studies and other training materials
(4) To provide means for the operation of the training programme at a number of universities.

The author was designated to direct this project and has, since the initial 'Meetings Workshop' held at The City University in September 1973, described elsewhere (Evans, 1975), extended the work to include the 'public' sector of higher education, the training of university administrators from African universities and, more recently, faculty and administrators in North American universities.

This account is primarily concerned with the development of one exercise in the package, 'Senate in Action', and the use of that experience in producing analogous exercises for use in universities in North America and in further education colleges in England and Wales.

The exercise referred to involves participants in a preparatory paper reading activity, and then in carrying out designated tasks related to their viewing of a video recording abstracted from a 'live' recording of a senate meeting, and is extensively described elsewhere (Evans, 1975; Evans and Cowan, 1977).

As far as the author was able to ascertain, there existed no video recording of 'real' meetings of major university committees at the inception of the study. A scripted and rehearsed meeting of one university senate had been video recorded, and meetings of major committees of the Open University had been broadcast. None of these, however, was suitable for an exercise in which recognizable relevance to common experience, and a sense of actuality, were of importance in producing the intended learning outcome. Consequently, permission was sought, and granted, to make video recordings of meetings of the Council, the Senate and a number of the Boards of Study in The City University, and from these to abstract study material. In all, a total of 14½ hours of material was recorded, with a minimum of disturbance of the business of the meetings. The recordings were reviewed with the purpose of identifying an incident or incidents which would fulfil the following conditions:

(1) Show a large proportion of members participating in the discussion.
(2) Show an experienced chairman in action.
(3) Involve relevant activity by the committee secretary.
(4) Include the taking of a decision or decisions.
(5) There should be a subsequent, agreed, minute of those decisions.
(6) There should be observable effects of 'non-verbal' communication.
(7) The seating arrangements, surroundings, etc., should have some discernible effects on the discussion process;
(8) be comprehensible to 'outsiders';
(9) have the consent of the participants to its use.

In the event, a 'short list' of three incidents was produced, all of which were reviewed by the author with two collaborators, Ron Glatter and David Warren Piper, who were currently directing the 'Staff Development in Universities' programme. Unanimously, the incident in a senate meeting, showing the discussion of an ordinance and regulations for the award of a DSc was chosen as meeting most, if not all, of the conditions.

It was then possible to prepare a set of working papers which included the minutes of the previous meeting of Senate which had 'referred back' the item, the agenda and relevant documentation of the recorded meeting, and the minutes of that meeting adopted at the subsequent meeting.

In addition to these 'working papers', a set of tasks, to be carried out by individuals within a group but to be the joint responsibility of that group, was prepared.

In the first run of the exercise, these tasks were as follows:

Tasks
Agree on the allocation of these tasks within your group, where there is an individual responsibility.
1) Write, on the acetate sheet provided, using script 1.0 – 1.5 cms in height, a minute of the discussion, appropriate for submission to the next meeting of Senate.
2) Record the progress of the discussion on the topic/time grid provided.
3) Comment on the role the Chairman played in the discussion, and indicate how you would consider this should be modified.
4) Comment on the role the Chairman of Ordinances and Regulations Committee played in the discussion, and suggest ways in which his presentation could be modified to improve effective discussion.
5) Comment on the efficacy of the discussion process observed, in producing a 'better' draft.

The 'topic/time' grid shown in Figure 1 was reproduced, on acetate sheet, for marking up by the designated participants.

A standard feedback evaluation form, as shown in Figure 2, was completed by participants. Two major modifications were made after the first two runs of the exercise, in response to this feedback. Firstly, it became apparent that not all observers were clear as to the particular agenda item being dealt with, and as to the essential differences between the previous and the newly revised ordinance and regulations. Secondly, the tasks were somewhat overdirective, and restrictive of broad discussion.

TOPIC	MINUTES													
	0	2	4	6	8	10	12	14	16	18	20	22	24	26 →
Work not subject of previous award														
External assessors only for Internal Candidates														
Provision for former Northampton students														
External assessors from University of London														
Eligibility of external & internal London degrees														
Length of time on staff 3 years. 4 years														
Regulations generally														
Declaration of work for previous degree														
Declaration of previous submissions														
Number and status of internal assessors														
Number and status of external assessors														
Does Science include Engineering?														
Can the regulations cover LLD?														

Figure 1. *'Topic/time' grid*

Consequently, a 'mini objective test' was prepared as follows:

1. What is the agenda item number and subsection of the incident you are about to see?
2. What is the reference number of the relevant report?
3. What is the reference number of the relevant draft?
4. What are the major differences between the present and the preceding draft?

and administered after a 'paper reading' period, the answers being displayed on an overhead projector before proceeding to the next stage. The tasks were modified to the following:

Tasks to be carried out by group

1. Prepare a minute of the Item discussed, suitable for submission to the next meeting of Senate. Write the minute, using script 1.0-1.5 cm high, on the acetate sheets provided.

2. Prepare analytical and constructive comment on the chairman's role in the discussion.

3. Prepare analytical and constructive comment on the secretarial role in the discussion.

4. Prepare comment on the discussion as a whole, and the discernible outcomes.

5. Prepare comment on the physical surroundings and facilities as they may have affected the discussion process.

23

6. Record the progress of discussion on the grid provided.

7. Discuss and agree the reports on each topic, and agree on separate individuals to present each of them in the plenary session.

Please complete this form, in order to assist in the evaluation of this course, and to use the information in planning future activities.

Ring round the response which most nearly corresponds to your opinion, using the scale +3 to −3 given, 0 indicating 'no opinion', and inserting further comment in the space provided.

Session	Interest							Usefulness							Effectiveness						
	+	+	+		−	−	−	+	+	+		−	−	−	+	+	+		−	−	−
	3	2	1	0	1	2	3	3	2	1	0	1	2	3	3	2	1	0	1	2	3

Further comments on session

Session	Interest							Usefulness							Effectiveness						
	+	+	+		−	−	−	+	+	+		−	−	−	+	+	+		−	−	−
	3	2	1	0	1	2	3	3	2	1	0	1	2	3	3	2	1	0	1	2	3

Further comments on session

Session	Interest							Usefulness							Effectiveness						
	+	+	+		−	−	−	+	+	+		−	−	−	+	+	+		−	−	−
	3	2	1	0	1	2	3	3	2	1	0	1	2	3	3	2	1	0	1	2	3

Further comments on session

Session	Interest							Usefulness							Effectiveness						
	+	+	+		−	−	−	+	+	+		−	−	−	+	+	+		−	−	−
	3	2	1	0	1	2	3	3	2	1	0	1	2	3	3	2	1	0	1	2	3

Further comments on session

Figure 2. *Meetings Workshop — evaluation of course*

In this form, the exercise was used in the regular 'Meetings Workshops' held at The City University. The first two of these workshops were limited to participants from United Kingdom universities, but subsequently extended to include academic and administrative staff from polytechnics, colleges of education and similar organizations.

The rating of this exercise on the evaluation form referred to above, which was used throughout the project, was uniformly high, with additional comments such as: 'Most effective as it dealt with a real-life situation', 'Very relevant', 'There but for the grace of God goes our Academic Board', 'So true, it hurts', 'Boring at times'.

Having established its usefulness, the exercise was used as the 'core' of a shorter workshop package.

During the time that these developments were taking place, the University of

Manchester Department of Administrative Studies had initiated a course for university administrators from overseas, and the organizers, having experienced the 'Meetings Workshop', decided that much of the material, in particular 'Senate in Action', could be used for participants in their programme. Some small adaptation was needed, including an extension of the paper reading phase of the exercise, a 'note for information' (see below), and some informal briefing on the role and status of a vice-chancellor. The exercise, in this form, was used in a workshop provided for the course by the Centre for Educational Technology, The City University, and used regularly in subsequent courses in Manchester.

Note for information to participants in 'Senate in Action' exercise

In order to appreciate some aspects of the discussion on the status of past students of The City University, the following historical background may be of use:

The Institution which received its charter as The City University in 1966 was founded at the end of the 19th century and, following a grant of land by the Marquis of Northampton, became the Northampton Polytechnic Institute.

From the beginning of this century, full-time and part-time students attending the Polytechnic sat the examination for the degree of Bachelor of Science (Engineering) of the University of London. By virtue of the presence of recognised teachers, many of these sat as internal candidates, a lesser number as external candidates.

In 1957, the Polytechnic was designated a College of Advanced Technology, and students on full-time courses sat their examinations for the Diploma in Technology. A number continued courses leading to the London Bachelor of Science Degree, which continued until 1966.

In parallel with the Overseas Development Ministry-supported scheme at Manchester, involving the travel of participants to the United Kingdom, the anglophone African universities had initiated a course for university administrators to be held in West Africa. This course was planned by a steering group led by Dr Kofi Edzii, Registrar of the University of Ghana, and provided in the Department of Public Administration, University of Ife, Nigeria. Through the good offices of the Inter-University Council, the author was invited to direct a 'Meetings Workshop' in Ife as part of this course. Compatibility of playback facilities was ensured on the advice of Dr Harry Creaser of the University of York, who had superintended the original television installation at Ife, and comprehensibility of exercise material from its use on the 'Manchester' course. The workshop was presented first in 1976 and, with some additional material but with the 'Senate in Action' exercise unchanged, in 1977, in both cases with commendatory comment from participants.

It has, so far, not been possible to record and use material from meetings of senate or other committees in West African universities, but it is hoped that this may eventually prove possible particularly in the light of the experience gained in the recording and use of indigenous material in North America.

In this latter connection, there had been some participation from academic staff of the United States and Canadian universities in the Meetings Workshops held at The City University. In addition to this, in the course of visits to the United States during 1974 and 1976, primarily concerned with academic staff development in their teaching role, the author had described and discussed the 'Conduct of Meetings' with senior academics and administrators. He was therefore able, as part of his sabbatical programme at West Virginia University, to observe and record faculty meetings of many kinds, and to prepare an exercise similar in character to 'Senate in Action' using material entirely apposite to North American practice.

'Senate in Action', USA, was based on an incident during a meeting of the senate

SPEAKER	MINUTES												
	0	1	2	3	4	5	6	7	8	9	10	11	12→
Budig													
Watts													
Foster													
Meitzen													
Singer													
Holten													
Lorenson													
Barton													

Figure 3a. *'Speaker/time' grid*

TOPIC	MINUTES														
	0	1	2	3	4	5	6	7	8	9	10	11	12	13	14→
Introduction of Subject															
Explanation of Alternative Schemes															
Reasons for 'Time Lag' on Results															
Disadvantages of 'Batch Processing'															
Effects of Completion Dates															
Significance in Promotion and Tenure															
Availability of Computer Facilities															
Voting on Proposals															

Figure 3b. *'Topic/time' grid*

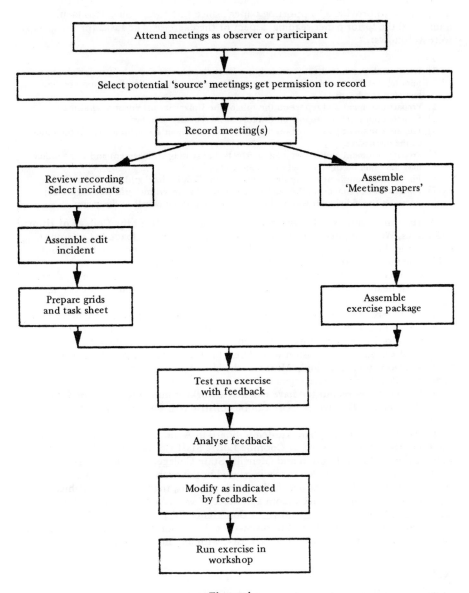

Figure 4

of West Virginia University. The item arose under 'any other business' and concerned the timing of the publication of the responses to faculty evaluation questionnaires. The incident met the conditions listed previously, except that it was not possible to provide a 'supporting paper', since there was none. This lacuna minimized the 'prior paper reading' aspect of the exercise. The tasks for the groups were as follows:

Tasks
1) Write on the acetate sheet provided, in a large clear, script about half an inch high, a minute, suitable for adoption at the next Senate meeting, of the discussion you have just seen and heard.
2) Prepare comment and report on the role of the University president as chairman.
3) Prepare comment and report on the role of the Faculty secretary.
4) Prepare comment and report on the effects of participants' contributions to the outcome of the discussion.
5) Prepare comment and report on any effects that seating arrangement and surroundings may have had on the conduct of the meeting.
6) Fill out and comment on the significance of the 'Topic/time' grid [see Figure 3b].
7) Fill out and comment on the significance of the 'Speaker/time' grid [see Figure 3a].
8) Agree on the individuals who will present each report on behalf of the group.

A trial run of this exercise was made, with colleagues from the College of Human Resources, West Virginia University, as participants. This feedback led to some very minor changes in the wording of the tasks and the listing of the topics, but otherwise indicated that the package was entirely acceptable.

The exercise was then used in a series of workshops for university and college presidents, deans, department Chairpersons and other senior administrators and faculty.

The standard evaluation form referred to previously was used throughout, and ratings were highly comparable with those obtained on the United Kingdom version. 'Additional comments' were plentiful, some archetypical examples being: 'Originally I thought this session would be a bust, but I was pleasantly surprised', 'The behaviour was revealing', 'Most worthwhile session', 'Difficult, but good, exercise', 'Possibly a shorter segment?'

The experiences recounted have enabled a working model to be devised, on the basis of which an effective exercise can be constructed. The 'model' is shown in Figure 4.

Using this, an exercise, 'An Academic Board in Action', has been prepared and used successfully by the staff of Coombe Lodge Staff College, and others by the Polytechnic of North London and Glenville State College, Glenville, West Virginia.

An excerpt from the video recordings used in the exercises, and of material recorded, but unsuitable for use, follows this account, together with graphical representation of the feedback from a number of workshops in which the exercises were used. [A video-tape was shown to Conference Ed.]

The author would be pleased to discuss the development of an exercise using the given model, or the use of existing exercises, with any interested persons.

References

Evans, L. F. (1975) *Issues in Staff Development.* SDU/UTMU. The Cavendish Press, Kent.
Evans, L. F. and Cowan, J. (1977) *'Senate in Action': An experience in workshop developments.* Staff Development in Higher Education, Society for Research into Higher Education, London.

3. Curriculum Development at the Fiji Technical College

E.E. Green, *Brigham Young University, Utah, USA*

Abstract: The paper describes work at the Fiji Technical College. It shows how research, development and evaluation can be integrated to produce effective materials and methods to teach industrial and business courses to form 5 level students.

Introduction

The LDS Fiji Technical College, located near Suva, Fiji, is one of the many schools built by the Church of Jesus Christ of Latter-day Saints and administered by its Church Education System. Its new facilities were completed in 1977; now the important work of preparing curriculum materials and methods for vocational courses has begun. Those who have been given this assignment are members of the David O. McKay Institute, a development, research, and evaluation organization at Brigham Young University in Provo, Utah.

The purpose of the Fiji Technical College is to prepare students either (1) to enter the Derek Technical Institute where they will gain further technical skills or (2) to enter the full-time job market as skilled workers in Fiji. Job opportunities in that country have been identified in blocklaying, welding, carpentry, sheetmetal work, cabinetmaking, office practice and book-keeping; general courses therefore have been included to meet these specific needs. Since industrial growth in Fiji is progressing more rapidly than in any other part of the South Pacific, the future looks very bright for the school's graduates.

Curriculum work is now progressing at the forms 5 and 6 levels within the technical college programme because of the close correlation these have with the government certification tradesman Class III examinations. The academic preparation also provides an internship programme whereby students are able to work with local contractors and businessmen to improve the skills which they are taught in course work. After students demonstrate competency at the form 5 level they are given the opportunity to pass the government-administered Class III apprenticeship exam in their particular trade area. Those who pass are permitted to continue to work in an internship experience and gain credit at the form 6 level within the school. Those who fail are given remedial instruction in weak areas and then allowed to re-challenge the apprenticeship exams.

One of the strengths of the curriculum developed by the McKay Institute has been the integration of development, research, and evaluation efforts. Whereas these disciplines are often segregated in developing a project, we have found that they can profitably be coordinated.

This paper will briefly investigate those three areas to show what has been done.

Design of the Instructional Materials

The Fiji Project is instructionally sound and at the same time simple to understand and administer. For each of the seven vocational courses, materials have been prepared which can be used in classes, small groups, or by individuals. The materials include: a guidance presentation, a student manual, and a teacher's guide.

The guidance materials, which are introduced to the student first, are part of a career education programme, through which students can determine the career best suited to them. This initial focus on guidance is a result of concern expressed by Brigham Young University President Dallin Oaks over the number of students changing majors. At BYU more than 80 per cent of the students shift to another major during their undergraduate work at enormous costs to the university and the students.

The guidance materials consist of a slide/tape presentation and a brochure describing job opportunities in the trades taught by the school as well as a brief account of the curriculum. It is recommended that the students and their parents attend a 'trade fair' at the school one evening prior to registration so that they can decide together which vocation is most compatible with student talents and interests.

The student manual which is carefully organized into units, presents prerequisite skills first and then progresses to task-oriented skills. Each unit contains a listing of the tasks required, the competency level to be achieved by each student, and a brief introduction to the unit (see Figure 1). Next is given a complete written and illustrated description of further detail for each task (see Figure 2). After the written instruction there is space for practice on each particular task (see Figure 3).

The teacher's guide consists of the student manual together with explanatory notes to the teacher. At the beginning of each unit the notes recommend learning sequences, indicate time expected to complete a task, and point out any difficulties students might experience. It is most important for instructors to anticipate problems because students are not allowed to leave a unit until they have demonstrated their competence in all the tasks listed there. The notes to the teacher also include scripts to slide/tape presentations.

The materials, though very simple, are based on sound instructional principles among which are the following:

(1) Presentation form — (rules, examples and practice forms which have been defined by content experts).
(2) Sequencing of subject-matter materials and learner experiences.
(3) Level of difficulty of instructional materials.
(4) Message design considerations — (clarity, accuracy, conciseness, and appropriateness of the materials and their visual portrayal to students).
(5) Learner control of feedback and help devices.

Research

Research should be an integral part of development work. Developers, from the beginning of the Fiji project found it easy to evolve real-life research questions by analysing the above principles of instructional design. Some of these questions were as follows:

(1) Is the 'storyboard format' of the instructional materials an adequate aspect of message design?
(2) Could the materials be used independently of a tutor? Do they provide more efficient instruction than the normal textbook now being used?

UNIT 6:   ORIGINS AND FLAWS
IN TIMBER

TASKS:

1.   *Identify the flat grain, end
grain, and edge grain of a
piece of timber*

2.   *Explain five reasons why
moisture must be extracted
from newly cut timber.*

3.   *Explain the difference between
air drying and kiln drying.*

4.   *Define five major flaws of
timber and give their causes.*

INTRODUCTION

Timber goes through number
of different processes before you
are able to buy it.   The reasons
it must go through the processes
are described in this unit.   You
need to know about the flaws
timber has so you can order the
quality of timber you need.

Figure 1

TASK 1: WOOD STRUCTURE

Wood is one of our greatest natural resources. When cut into pieces that are uniform in thickness, width, and length, it becomes timber.

Timber is the name given to products of the sawmill and includes all sorts of boards used in doors, drawers, table tops, legs, etc.

There are thousands of different sorts of timber trees and they are grouped into <u>open</u> seeded timber trees and <u>enclosed</u> seeded timber trees.

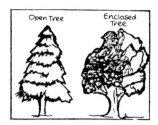

Figure 2

Practice

1. Identify the flat grain, end grain, and edge grain on the following diagram.

2. Why does moisture have to be extracted from timber (five reasons)?

_____

_____

_____

_____

_____

3. Explain the difference between air drying and kiln drying.

Air Drying	Kiln Drying

Figure 3

(3) Could the elements of the visual and verbal displays be portrayed in a more effective and efficient manner?

(4) What effect does the inclusion of advanced organizer 'tasks' or introductions have upon the learning experience?

(5) Are the real photographs utilized in the demonstration techniques more effective than simple line drawings?

(6) What effect do proper implementation procedures have upon the success rate of the materials and methods involved?

(7) Of what value are guidance materials and do they affect the achievement, affective, or cognitive objectives?

These are just a few of the questions that might be asked. As the course progresses undoubtedly more questions will evolve.

Evaluation

The three types of evaluation typically used on McKay Institute development projects fall within the three categories: *student* evaluation, *product* evaluation, and *programme* evaluation. *Student* evaluations deal with the construction, administration, and reporting of examinations or questions to measure student attitude, knowledge, and/or behaviour. *Product* evaluations test the effect of individual products produced for a particular system of instruction. These usually consist of questions about the physical characteristics, utility, and effect of the individual products. *Programme* evaluations deal with the total integration of product and student evaluations in order to decide whether the programme as a whole is effective and whether additional time and money should be spent improving a particular programme or in initiating others.

What follows is a more detailed description of each of these three types of evaluations as they are being applied to the Fiji Curriculum Project.

Student Evaluation

Pre-test and post-test scores for each course are kept on Personal Achievement Records (PAR sheets) (see Figure 4). The tasks on this sheet correspond to the tasks in the instruction and on the Class III Trade Examinations. The pre-test is given at the beginning of each unit of instruction to determine what the student already knows or can do. (Previously designed forms incorporated the level of achievement, such as retention, identification and problem solving. However, this system proved to be too complicated for most administrators of the exam and therefore a simple checklist was made such as that indicated on the Personal Achievement Record. The teacher merely checked those items which the student could demonstrate or recite back to him.) The information on the Personal Achievement Record is used mostly to determine which students can help others in the performance of the required tasks. It meant the elimination of certain tasks only if all of the students indicated prior achievement of the tasks listed.

After the instruction for each unit the students were again tested and a similar evaluation method was used. A check mark indicated that the student could demonstrate mastery to the level required in the specific task. A gain in instruction as a result of the pre-test and post-test examination, was indicated in the third column under 'Gain in Instruction'. This information will be used to help the developers know which specific tasks will require either better or more personalized instruction. It will help in the elimination of certain tasks if they are found to have been covered in previous grade levels. The information will also assist the

34

CABINETMAKING

PERSONAL ACHIEVEMENT RECORD

STUDENT Unit Task	Pre-test	Post-test	Gain in Instruction
1 State major tasks of cabinetmaker.		✓	✓
Give schooling and experience requirements to pass Class III Apprenticeship Exam.	✓	✓	
2 Know difference between 'three-view', oblique, perspective and isometric drawings by identifying and drawing one example of each.		✓	✓
Give two reasons for the cabinetmaker to be able to read drawings.		✓	✓
3 Define basic arithmetic terms used in construction drawings.		✓	✓
Add, subtract, multiply, and divide fractions, whole numbers and decimals.	✓	✓	
Use basic arithmetic to estimate materials needed in a typical job.		✓	✓
Use basic arithmetic for measuring and laying out cabinetmaking.		✓	✓
Describe various cuts of wood that equal a board foot.		✓	✓
Work board foot problems using the foot formula.		✓	✓
Work board foot problems using the inch formula.		✓	✓
4 Be aware of and apply safety rules required in cabinetmaking.	✓	✓	
Know why the cabinetmaker should be concerned about safety.		✓	✓
Know protective measures for the eyes, feet, hands and head.		✓	✓
Know how to prevent falls.		✓	✓
Know how to clean up after working.	✓	✓	
5 Identify and use the 20 major hand tools used in cabinetmaking.	✓	✓	
Identify and properly use the machine tools used in cabinetmaking.		✓	✓
6 Identify the flat grain, end grain, and edge grain of a piece of timber.		✓	✓
Explain five reasons why moisture must be extracted from newly cut timber.		✓	✓
Explain the difference between air drying and kiln drying.	✓	✓	
Define five major flaws of timber and give their causes.		✓	✓
7 State different characteristics of wood with respect to planed surfaces received from the timber merchant.		✓	✓
Give the commercial forms of timber usually available from the timber merchant.	✓	✓	
Fill out a timber order form for a class project.		✓	✓
Give the steps for preparing each member of materials to be used as your first class project.	✓	✓	
8 Identify eight types of nails; give their use and any special caution in pounding them.		✓	✓
Explain how to order nails and know quantities per 500 gm package.		✓	✓
Identify three types of screws; give their use and any special caution in driving them in.		✓	✓
		✓	✓

Figure 4

35

administrators who are funding this project to know which instructional procedures resulted in a gain in instruction. Figure 4 indicated that there was a gain in instruction in 35 out of the 42 tasks listed. These gains correlate somewhat to the scores the students achieve on the Class III Tradesman Examination.

The Personal Achievement Record will be kept in the central office of the school so that the principal will be aware of both teacher and student progress. By this means he can continually be informed of activities and problems associated with each course. He will thus be available to assist instructors and/or students as the need arises. This information is recorded and filed in his office and is reported quarterly to the central administration in Salt Lake City.

The Personal Achievement Record enables the teacher to (1) pre-assess each student before a unit of study and (2) diagnose at the end of the instruction and demonstration any particular strengths and weaknesses of each student. Classes are small enough to allow individual attention for those students who need tutoring.

Product Evaluation

Developers will need to know what changes must be made in the instructional materials. Therefore the teacher will be required to keep an annotated copy of all materials used and answer the questions shown in Figure 5. They will also be asked to give special attention to the teacher suggestion sheets which accompany each unit because these were developed without the benefit of previous teaching experience. Therefore it is hoped that their daily schemes will be incorporated into the teacher suggestions.

Programme Evaluation

The administrators will also be responsible for answering the questions indicated in Figure 5. These questions, which are very general, consider the level of difficulty of the materials, their sequence, and any other overall recommendations. In these questions special attention is given to implementation.

Through these three types of evaluation it is hoped that relatively unbiased data will be gathered. Although these evaluation procedures are primitive in design and implementation, we hope to gain much experience that will be useful in improving future evaluation methods.

Conclusion

Although our data is limited, the Fiji instructional materials appear to be appropriate to the needs of the students and the culture.

What effect, then, will this development experience have in similar underdeveloped countries served by the Church Educational System? Answers to the evaluation and research questions mentioned earlier will help the administrators of the educational system for the South Pacific determine whether or not similar efforts in instructional design should be carried out at other elementary and secondary schools under their direction. There is also some hope of tying in the requirements for the secondary schools within the LDS Church Education System with the requirement of the BYU – Hawaii campus and Brigham Young University. The competency levels required at BYU in general education, for example, could be taught and monitored within the academic programme of the secondary schools in all of the Church-sponsored schools in underdeveloped countries. This would assist students who have a desire to attend the Provo campus because they would be able to meet some of the entrance and general education requirements before they reach

1. Are the goals and objectives of the product stated clearly, with sufficient detail to determine success or failure? Yes   No
   If 'no', explain which goals and objectives should be explained more clearly.

2. Does the content possess sufficient coverage and detail to serve the purposes and needs of the intended users? Yes   No
   If 'no', explain.

3. Do you feel that prospective users would find the materials easy to read and understand? (Are the vocabulary and writing style appropriate for the audience?)
   Yes   No
   If 'no', please explain.

4. Does the content of the product match up with its goals and objectives?
   Yes   No
   If 'no', please explain.
   Guidance materials? Yes   No
   Student booklets? Yes   No

5. Is there any material which should be added or eliminated in this product?
   Yes   No
   If 'yes', explain what materials should be added or eliminated.

6. Does the product adequately consider the important characteristics of those people with whom it will be used? Yes   No
   If 'no', please explain.

7. Is the material appropriately sequenced within this product? Yes   No
   If 'no', please explain.

8. Does the table of contents as shown provide a detailed and easy reference to sections of this piece? Yes   No
   If 'no', please explain.

9. Are the headlines and titles satisfactory for helping to organize and reference the contents sections? Yes   No
   If 'no', please explain.

10. Are the assessment tools included in this product appropriate in number and kind?
    Yes   No
    If 'no', please explain.

11. What is your overall recommendation concerning this product?
    A. I consider the changes I have suggested relatively minor and would recommend that this product be included in the total product pretty much as it is.
    B. I consider that some of the changes I have suggested are rather major and I would recommend that this piece be significantly revised.
    C. I recommend that the development of the entire product be ceased.

Figure 5

the BYU campus. So it is hoped that other data will soon become available to judge the long-range effects as well as the relative short-range effects of the total programme.

4. Developing a Large-Scale Modularized Training System for Brazilian Telecommunications

N.H.S. Machado, *Telebras* and **A.J. Romiszowski,** *ITU*

Abstract: Some of the tasks of TELEBRAS are to plan, promote and in part execute the training and development of the human resources required by this vast and rapidly expanding telecommunications network.

To assist this task, a project was planned in 1974, with the cooperation of the International Telegraphic Union (ITU) and the United Nations Development Programme (UNDP).

1. Introduction

The Brazilian telecommunications system is composed of 25 state-based companies, a national company in charge of inter-state and international networks (EMBRATEL) and a holding company (Telecomunicações Brasileiras S/A — TELEBRÁS), which is supervised by the Ministry of Communications. Project BRA/74/010 got under way in 1975, its main objectives being to develop job performance standards, training standards, training materials and methodologies (including new methodologies such as self-paced instruction) for the human resources needs of the telecommunications network, and to set up an instructional technology/training research unit in TELEBRÁS.

2. The Problem and the Proposed Solution

2.1. The Human Resources Needs

These needs are very variable from one state to another, both in quantity and in the type of specialist skills required.

Thus TELEBRÁS was faced with the problem of achieving a reasonable level of standardization of methods and practices throughout the group of companies. Part of the solution to this problem is to standardize training methods and standards throughout the group. This has to be done in a way which can cope with the variety of local conditions (different recruitment, existence or absence of training centres, quality of instructors, etc.). It also has to be done in a hurry due to the enormous expansion of demand for telephones that the country's industrialization and development plans are creating.

Thus the total of 80,000 — plus personnel currently employed by the telephone companies, apart from being dispersed over a country of some eight million square kilometres, is expected to grow rapidly in numbers for many years to come.

2.2. The Modular System

During 1975-77, a team of trainers at TELEBRÁS, in close cooperation with

39

international experts from the ITU, developed a methodology and an implementation plan to cope with the human resources training problem. To cope with local variety, training materials should be modularized, enabling course content to be adapted to local needs whilst maintaining standardization of methods. In order to control training standards, the philosophy of training by objectives was adopted as a general guide.

The overall plan bears some conceptual resemblance to the 'modules of employable skill' concept, promoted for some years now by the International Labour Office (ILO, 1973) and to such systems as developed by the Engineering Industry Training Board (EITB) in the UK. A module is a self-contained set of training materials and procedures, designed to achieve a specified set of training objectives associated with a specified definable task. Thus, modules can be combined with other prerequisite and associated modules, to produce a course which reflects the real job situation in a particular locality, including training in only those tasks which the trainee will perform. The same modules may, however, be used in different combinations to match the needs of a different group of trainees in a different locality.

The overall methodology of module development is very much based on current objectives-based training philosophies and on the systems approach.

Details of the methodology will not be described here. An account has appeared elsewhere (Almeida, Machado, Daffix and Blanquart, 1978). In general it follows established practices of educational technology and owes much to the early work of Mager (1962) and Bloom (1956) on objectives and test design, Mager and Beach (1969) on task analysis and training design, Gagné (1965) on instructional methods and media, and to many other writers. However, the approach is eclectic and has adapted imported techniques to local needs and traditions, attempting to simplify, where possible, the procedures of course design and developing new techniques (e.g. of course sequencing) where necessary.

2.3. Structure and Use of a Module

The overall structure of a module is governed by two factors. Firstly, a module is task-based. As the necessary knowledge and skills required to execute one task may be very different from another, the size of modules varies considerably. The typical range encountered so far is from about 20 to about 200 hours of study time (naturally a module of 200 hours is mainly practical and may contain only 30 or 40 hours of formal instruction).

Secondly, the modules are designed to be instructor-led. Although a given module may contain self-instructional materials (texts or practical exercises) as some of its components, it is not entirely self-instructional. A module is divided into a series of learning steps (or 'progressions'). The principal component of any step is the 'instructional procedure' which tells the instructor exactly how to plan, execute and evaluate the training, when and how to use the other module components (texts, slide sequences, transparencies, etc.).

Thus the modular concept of this project should not be confused with the alternative current concepts of 'A/V modules', or 'multi-media modules' which imply a self-contained set of instructional materials (usually self-instructional and using a variety of media but not the instructor), of short duration, often forming only one lesson or study session (or even only part of a lesson).

The modules are instructor-led for two practical reasons. One reason is economic. Much of the training, particularly at craftsman level, takes place in the various state companies, which are not equipped with the necessary training infrastructure and equipment to mount a course which is intensely media-based and individualized.

But, more importantly, the training needs are so great and growing so rapidly that there is no time to develop systematic individualized training. One must rely on the knowledge of existing personnel to train new human resources. However, there are not, in general, large numbers of trained instructors. One aim of the modules is to enable an experienced worker, with reasonable communication skills, to become (with a minimum of training) an effective instructor. For this reason, the modules contain detailed procedures for each progression. The instructor receives all his lesson plans, all his tests and all his support materials ready. The trainee receives all necessary study and reference materials and copies of all exercises. The course manager, or coordinator receives all necessary control documents to enable him to exercise a 'management by training objectives' function.

Thus the principal physical components of any module are three manuals:

— the instructor's manual
— the trainee's manual, and
— the training coordinator's manual.

Associated with the instructor's manual are the training resources or media, which typically include slides, transparencies, texts, reference charts and diagrams, audiovisual slide/tape presentations, posters, flip charts, and occasionally models, simulation exercises, special equipment, etc.

3. Implementing the Solution

3.1. The Locale

Until recently, all training took place at the individual company level. Some of this would be on-the-job training of a relatively organized type, but much would be 'sitting next to Nellie'. Some (but not all) companies had training centres for off-the-job training. These varied in size and quality.

Current efforts have focused on the creation of effective local training centres in all the 25 companies of the group. These local centres will provide systematic training at the operative and craftsman levels (both on and off the job) which will be based on the standard training modules currently being produced by the Project.

In addition, four regional training centres are in construction at Recife (North East), Brasilia (Centre), Rio de Janeiro and São Paulo (South — South East). These regional centres will execute much of the training at the technician and technologist levels, in conditions allowing direct 'hands-on' or simulated experience of all equipment used in the region, under systematically controlled training conditions. The Brasilia centre will also act as a national centre, concentrating on training policy, training design and materials production and distribution, as well as attending to special training needs at the management level. Once again, much of the training in these centres will be based on the modular system. It is expected also to introduce, at first experimentally, the use of individualized, self-paced, training plans, enabling trainees to enter and exit a course independently of the group and possibly to study particular course options especially relevant to their job.

Thus both at the regional and at the local levels, there will be a developing demand for systematic training modules. Many local centres are already operating and ready to absorb the modules. The Recife and Brasilia regional centres will commence operation in early 1979. Module preparation is well under way. A total of 260 training modules are projected for 1978 and several productions teams have been created to produce them.

3.2. Module Production — Quantitative Aspects

The total amount of training materials to be generated by the Project is extremely large. The 260 modules currently contracted are not the total of the training needs foreseen, but merely the priorities. Even if all the modules are ready for implementation by the end of 1978, much of the training during 1979/80 will still be of a more traditional type. This will be particularly true at the regional centre level where new techniques will continually create new and immediate training needs (for which modules will not exist) and where specialist skills will require to be learnt by only small numbers of trainees (rendering the production of elaborate training modules uneconomical).

Thus 'modularization' is seen to be an ongoing and growing process throughout the years to come, but will never become the only methodology of training to be employed.

The current batch of modules is sufficient to keep the Project busy for some time both in the task of production and in the solution of a variety of problems generated, in part, by its sheer size. Based on already completed modules and on task analyses for others in the planning stages, the size of the production task for 1978 appears as follows:

- ☐ 260 modules, requiring 260 task analyses to be performed (in the main, these have been completed)
- ☐ 3 x 260 = 780 separate manuals to be written, edited, printed and reproduced.
- ☐ Between 500 and 750 study texts (programmed or traditional) to be written (or selected and adapted from existing materials).
- ☐ Up to 50,000 different slides or photographs to be taken, edited and organized into instructional sequences.
- ☐ Up to 5,000 different overhead projector transparencies to be originated.
- ☐ Up to 1,000 different commentaries or scripts to be written, to accompany slide and transparency sequences, about half of which would be recorded on cassettes as self-contained slide/tape presentations.
- ☐ A smaller (unpredictable) quantity of other instructional media, such as posters, large network diagrams, models and simulation exercises.

3.3. Module Production — Organizational Aspects

The problem of getting this vast amount of training materials produced was not an easy one to solve. The solution adopted was a process of sub-contracting certain groups of modules to certain of the companies in the TELEBRÁS Group best equipped to prepare them. Thus a given company may contract to produce 60 or 40 modules (or no modules) and will receive 260 modules (or whichever of the 260 are relevant to the company's training needs) — 'from each according to his capacities, to each according to his needs'.

Each of the five companies contracted to date have formed (or are still forming) module production teams, composed of task analysts and module designers, together with ancillary support staff. Already, over 70 full-time analysts and designers are working in the companies and this number is now climbing to over 100.

The training of these teams and the supervision and validation of their products are tasks of the main project team, based in TELEBRÁS, in Brasilia. In order to facilitate the training, four modules were developed early on in the Project, utilizing the Project's methodology in order to teach the methodology. These modules deal with task analysis, module design, module utilization, and course coordination. The first two have been extensively used in the training of the teams so far, being progressively revised and improved in the light of experience.

4.   Progress and Problems

4.1.   Results So Far

As can be expected in a Project adopting a new approach on a large scale, a number of operational difficulties and attitudinal obstacles have been encountered. These have conspired to somewhat delay the production of the training modules. This is partly due to some of the teams only now reaching their full numerical strength. But other sources of difficulties have been encountered. These include difficulties in obtaining the information required to perform a task analysis. This is caused partly by administrative or attitudinal obstacles which render it difficult to obtain as much contact with relevant technical experts as the task analyst requires. Analysts have in part created or aggravated this situation, by the disruptive effects of their presence in operational departments. Also, the pioneering nature of the Project has taken it into technical areas where operational procedures and standards have not as yet been defined at the national level. Thus technical experts are sometimes reluctant to commit themselves in the absence of some official specification of norms and standards. These problems are multiplied by the variety of local differences in equipment, procedures and technical language to create a complex decision-making situation which the recently trained and relatively inexperienced task analyst finds difficult to face.

In addition to the above-mentioned factors influencing the quantitative progress of the Project, factors exist which affect the quality of the task analyses and the modules. Some of these factors are operational; the difficulties encountered in some of the companies in preselecting the production personnel and the relative inexperience of the production teams. Other factors are attitudinal: the general clash between the academically oriented, content-based traditions of Brazilian education and training and the task-oriented, objectives-based methodology of the Project have led to some difficulties in the acceptance of the methodology or in its complete implementation. Brazilian education, in common with most Latin cultures, has a strong tradition of academic formalism, which adapts with difficulty to current training philosophy.

One further source of lost time has no doubt been the failure to apply a rigorous management-by-objectives approach to the work of the production teams.

The picture is not all that grim however. On the positive side, at least one of the companies has applied the Project methodology to some of its own internal courses and has demonstrated training-time savings of the order of 66 per cent coupled to improved post-course performance. This is a sample of what can be expected once the Project is fully implemented — a gain due almost entirely to the elimination of the academic 'nice to know' content from courses and concentration on the 'need to know'. Furthermore, the problems indicated above have been identified and solutions have been, or are being, developed. It is expected that further module production will continue more smoothly. A sign that this is indeed so, is the more recent experience with one company which entered the Project later. In the light of experiences with the three companies previously contracted, more attention was paid to recruitment and selection of personnel, to preparation of supervision staff, to execution and follow-up of the training, with the result that the team is maintaining a satisfactory level of productivity and is well on original schedule.

Some of the most important problems and their proposed solutions are discussed in more detail below.

4.2.   Specific Problems and Proposed Solutions

(a) THE TRAINING-BY-OBJECTIVES PHILOSOPHY. The companies in which the modules are being developed are not in the main objectives-oriented, certainly not in the area of training (a newly developing area) which is very much influenced by the academic subject-based philosophies of the formal educational systems. Thus a training-by-objectives Project has been injected into an environment which does not think or operate by objectives. Hence spring many problems of mutual understanding between the Project team, production teams and the human resources management of the various companies.

A viable solution to this problem area is to extend the Project's activities higher up the organizational ladder, to instil the management with objectives philosophy in training departments in general, whereby the Project's methodology becomes a special case: the management (of learning) by (performance) objectives. This process has to some extent begun, through visits and discussions prompted by the production problems which have been encountered.

(b) THE MODULE – PRODUCTION METHODOLOGY. The very same cultural difference can be seen at the back of some of the problems that have been experienced in the production teams. There has been an overemphasis on the process, as opposed to the desired products of this process – a result of the predominance of the content-based tradition over the performance-based tradition.

It is common for analysts and designers to concentrate attention on the detail of the steps in the process, rather than to consider the desired outputs of these steps and evaluate for themselves the relative importance of each step in a given situation. Equal effort is often given to the analysis of operations which, it is immediately obvious, have very different levels of importance from a training point of view. Enormous pains are taken to complete one stage of the design process 'as per the book' only to find later that little use of that particular step will be made, due to specific peculiarities of the module in preparation.

A possible solution to this problem area would be to revise the module design methodology, emphasizing yet more strongly the use of objectives and objectives-based tests, whilst playing down the lesson-design process, leaving this as an empirical, semi-intuitive process.

(c) IMPLEMENTATION OF THE METHODOLOGY. At key points (for example completion of task analysis, specification of objectives, first drafts of module, prototypes of auxiliary resources) there is a need for validation and cross checking by technical experts, training experts, media experts, etc. To date, much of this checking has been performed by the Project team at TELEBRÁS. It will, however, become necessary to delegate much of the validation to the production teams in the contracted companies. This depends on the prior solution of problem areas (a) and (b): the establishment of an objectives-based approach to project management both within the production teams and their organizational environment. This is likely to be a difficult task.

It appears on reflection that a more viable way to implement the Project would have been to 'start small' and to grow within the producing companies, attacking obvious training needs and carrying the process through from task analysis to course implementation and evaluation. The advantages of this approach are many:

— Analysts and designers learn-by-doing, receiving real feedback on their performance, in the short term.
— The methodology is under constant revision and scrutiny, adapting itself to the realities of the situation. The teams develop their own analysis and synthesis tools, through experience, rather than having the tools 'thrust upon them'. They would not become 'slaves to the process'.
— New analysts and designers may always be trained by 'attachment' to existing teams. The need for formal training and supervision by the TELEBRÁS team would be diminished. The team could concentrate on the control of the final products produced by the teams.
— Right from the beginning, usable products would be available, demonstrating in practice the benefits of the training-by-objectives approach. Training management would have evidence of efficiency to convince them, and to convince other departments to support the Project. Many of the problems of lack of support and understanding, or of low priority for the Project, would be diminished.
— The experience, right from the early stages of the Project, of working with objectives-based materials, of systematic evaluation of results and of continuous formative evaluation, would do much to make the Project's environment receptive to the management-by-objectives approach.

(d) WORKING METHODS OF THE PRODUCTION TEAMS. Training design is a complex, organic, interactive and iterative process, despite the fact that it is often pictured as a set of sequential steps. As Leonard Silvern (1964) put it:

> The Human Race is composed of analysts, synthesists, and knuckleheads. The ability required by the training designer to both analyse and synthesise at one and the same time — anasynthesis — is rarely encountered in one person.

This is one reason why teamwork — close teamwork — often produces better results in training design. The size of a Project such as the TELEBRÁS Project renders this 'anasynthesis' process difficult, as it becomes necessary to separate in time-scale the preparation of the task analysis and the use of the task analysis for training design. Inevitably, some 'noise' creeps into the system. The analyst does not always predict what information the training designer will require. The designer does not always interpret the task analysis perfectly. Due to the size and structure of the Project it is difficult to arrange for close cooperation between analyst and designer.

This has been difficult in the early stages of the Project, due to the enormous amount of analyses to be prepared and the time-lapse between analyst training and designer training. As a result some designers have now to work with analyses prepared months before, so that even the analyst sometimes cannot remember exactly why he made a particular comment.

This problem is currently being solved by insistence on closer cooperation and teamwork. Once again exhortation is not enough, planned experience through Project-Team/Production-Team cooperation is necessary.

However, once again, with hindsight, one feels that a different approach to implementing the Project might have avoided or eased the current problems. The small-scale, step-by-step implementation of the Project, suggested in (c) above, may have made it easier to avoid the separation of the analysis and synthesis stages.

— Right from the beginning, small, embryonic production teams, would be 'seeing-through' the production of modules through all their stages. Each

45

team member would be involved in analysis and synthesis and formative evaluation of the results.

— The need for a massive short time-scale programme of task analysis would be avoided. This would be produced piecemeal, as required for module design. The large stock of completed task analyses, waiting for module designers would not be created. The time-gap between analysis and synthesis would not exist.

— Incidentally, the disruptive effect of task analysts entering and working in operational departments would be much reduced. The need for expert advice would be spread out more evenly, at much less intensity over a longer period. Operational departments would also be more receptive to task analysts once they could see the beneficial results of their work, in the form of rapidly and effectively trained personnel exiting from previously prepared courses.

5. Conclusion — Lessons for Developing Countries

The TELEBRAS Project has some characteristics which are of interest to other large-scale projects, particularly in countries which are in a stage of rapid development.

It is unlikely that a Project of this size and scope would be necessary in any highly developed country. The problems of innovation there are different. Generally the problem is to change an entrenched system. This has its difficulties, as by their nature systems are self-conserving and tend to resist change. Much has been written on the problems of innovation in existing systems. Particularly in education and training, innovations have often failed because they clashed with existing procedure and hierarchical structures. The need to implement innovations in a careful step-by-step way, from within the system rather than from outside, has often been stressed.

The TELEBRÁS case, however, is one of installing a system where no entrenched system existed. It has often been felt that this should be easier, as one avoids the disruption of an existing system. But this is not necessarily the case. One has to consider possible clashes between the new system and its environment. If the new system is too alien, it will be rejected by the environment, just as a transplanted organ is rejected unless the receiving organism has been prepared to accept it.

In the case of this Project, the alien element was the objectives-based approach. Until the total environment in the company uses, or at least genuinely feels the need, for this approach, it proves difficult to inject a new sub-system which is totally based on objectives. We feel that the injection of embryonic sub-systems, which would then grow within the company and in so doing influence and change its environment, would stand a greater chance of being accepted without reactions. It so happens that this approach would also probably facilitate the construction and functioning of the training sub-system — both the training of production teams and their methods of working.

Whether the step-by-step, evolutionary approach would carry an impossible time-penalty is not clear. The wide-front attack adopted should, in theory, produce rapid results, as required by the demands for human resources. But in practice, the planning and development stages have taken a long time, and few results are as yet achieved. The step-by-step approach would produce some results at an early stage, and there is nothing, in principle, to prevent the long-term, large-scale planning from occurring in parallel with the embryonic implementation. Indeed, the long-term planning would benefit immensely from the feedback it would receive from the small-scale implementation.

The history of technical development projects has amply demonstrated the folly of adopting imported systems wholesale. It is becoming rarer to encounter African children learning British geography, rather than their own, or a factory producing products for which there is no demand. One can see the shift in the change of emphasis in UNDP (and other agencies) projects from 'technical assistance', through 'development' to 'joint-venture'.

The current Project has avoided this pitfall. The methodology and the Project content are well tailored to Brazilian needs. The Project is being executed by Brazilian personnel, the problems which have been described are not due to the importation of a totally alien system. The system appears to be just what is required.

However, the environment into which the system is being implanted was not quite ready. Some rejection symptoms are being observed. Steps are being taken to alleviate these symptoms, and total rejection is not likely. However, the assimilation process might have been quicker and less painful if greater attention had been paid to preparing the environment. The first maxim of the systems approach is 'study the wider system, the environment'.

In an age when many nations are entering an accelerated industrialization and development process, the situation encountered by TELEBRÁS is not unique. For example, several of the newly oil-rich countries of the Middle East are contracting with outside consultancy agencies for complete education and training systems, from elementary to university, and technical/industrial training as well. All of these are cases of implanting a system where no system existed before. The problems of this type of innovation have not been studied very closely. However, it would be wise for the contracting nations and the contracted agencies to remember the maxim 'study the environment'.

If the environment needs to change in order to assimilate the new system, it will only do so when it *feels the need to do so* in order to survive. Therefore the problem of the innovator is twofold: firstly to adapt the originally implanted system to the actual state of development of the environment, and secondly to create the conditions necessary for both the system and its environment to develop, in unison, in the desired direction.

References

Almeida, R., Machado, N., Daffix, R. and Blanquart, C. (1978) A Practical example of training by objectives: project BRA/74/010. *Telecommunication Journal,* ITU, January 1978.

Bloom, B.S. *et al.* (1956) *Taxonomy of Educational Objectives, Handbook 1 Cognitive Domain.* Longmans, London and New York.

Gagné, R.M. (1965) *The Conditions of Learning.* Holt, Rinehart and Winston, London and New York.

ILO (1973) *Introduction of a Vocational Training System Using Modules of Employable Skill.* ILO, Geneva.

Mager, R.F. (1962) *Preparing Instructional Objectives.* Fearon, Palo Alto.

Mager, R.F. and Beach, K.M. (1969) *Developing Vocational Instruction.* Fearon, Palo Alto.

Silvern, L. (1964) *The Systems Engineering of Learning.* Audio-Visual — Silvern Associates, California.

5. Individualized Instruction and the Mature Student

A J Romiszowski

Abstract: This paper presents a study of two varieties of self-instructional materials used in three different instructional plans with adult and adolescent students of mathematics in Brazil. The paper compares information mapping approaches with conventional linear programmed texts.

1. Introduction

The research reported here was carried out during the months of August to December 1976 in Salvador, the capital of the state of Bahia in Brazil. The study involved both adults and upper secondary schoolchildren of 15 or 16 years of age studying the same material, namely, a 'modern' mathematics approach to arithmetic. The upper secondary school students were participating in the first year of the *segundo grau* which is the 15 to 18 years of age section of the secondary educational system of Brazil. The adults involved in the study were participating in adult continuing education programmes of evening classes designed to bring them up to the standard of the secondary school leaving certificate. As adults are not permitted to take the secondary school certificate on this supplementary continuing education basis until they reach the age of 21, it is normal that they are accepted in these evening classes only after they have passed the age of 19 or even 20. The college at which the present study was based is a very large secondary and upper primary school, state-owned, with upwards of 8,000 students and the year group with which this study dealt had 600 students in 16 parallel forms.

All these students were in the 15 to 16 years of age bracket, and had entered the *segundo grau* directly after their completion of the 15 + or *primeiro grau* certificate. The standard for this certificate is not exceptionally high and it is common for a large number of those entering the *segundo grau* to have large gaps in their primary education and lower secondary education, which creates problems in their upper secondary school career.

As Salvador was at one time the capital of Brazil, it has a level of cultural development which is higher than exists in neighbouring north-eastern states. There is reasonably adequate provision of school places in the urban area and its closer rural districts, so that the problem of plain 'non-availability' of education is not as serious as in many other states. However, teacher shortages, specifically *qualified* teacher shortages, are much more acute than in, for example, the highly industrialized state of São Paulo and very much more acute than the situation that we know in the United Kingdom. Equipment is also scarce as are textbooks and many practising teachers are untrained; so the educational system although it 'exists', hardly becomes functional. In the college used in this investigation it was common for children to turn up for a day's work and receive only one or two supervised lessons due to lack of teachers for the other four or five lessons. It is not surprising that many children give up attending school, not due to lack of interest but on the grounds that they are not receiving much education in return for the trouble of attending. This then is the general climate into which the BASG-M materials were injected in 1976. A full account of this project, of all the research studies so far performed, of others still under way and all related statistical results are available elsewhere (Romiszowski, 1977). This account is limited to a summary of the project and the results of the four main experiments.

2. The Birth of the BASG-M Project

The learning materials used as a basis for this study are a series of self-instructional texts which were developed in a project termed BASG-M, which stands in Portuguese for 'Bases for Access to the Segundo Grau-Mathematics'. This was a project of the Federal Ministry of Education, designed to deal with the above-mentioned problems of poor teaching in the earlier grades (or no teaching), resulting in serious gaps in the learning of children on entry to the *segundo grau*. The mathematical content, the sequence of this content and the general treatment given to it was dictated by the standard *primeiro grau* curriculum of the state of Bahia and by teacher/consultants supplied by the state's secretariat for education. The author's responsibilities were limited to the design of the materials, to the training and supervision of the materials production team and to the development of the systems for implementing the materials in the schools.

The basic design was a modularized 'revision' course of the mathematics normally taught in the *primeiro grau*, together with diagnostic instruments to enable the *segundo grau* mathematics teacher to identify the weaknesses of individual students and to prescribe appropriate self-instructional assignments.

The materials were therefore totally programmed, utilizing several programmed instruction techniques. These included fairly rigorously programmed 'mathetics-based' materials for some modules and less rigorous, student-controlled materials utilizing 'information mapping' techniques, for others.

As an integral part of the BASG-M project, a programme of research was planned to investigate the different techniques used for structuring the materials, their effects on different age-groups and alternative systems for the utilization and control of the modularized course.

3. The Subjects

Eight groups of students were supplied for these experiments, four groups of adult learners and four groups of schoolchildren. Group size was in each case about 30 to 33 students. For the purpose of this study the groups have been designated A, B, C, and D for the adult groups and P, Q, R, and S for the schoolchildren groups. Details of these eight groups are shown in Table 1.

Group	Type	Mean age	Range of ages	Number participating in study
A	Adults continuing education	28.4	18-40	30
B	,,	25.8	18-43	33
C	,,	26.8	18-38	33
D	,,	24.5	18-38	31
P	Schoolchildren — segundo grau, first year	15.4	14-16	30
Q	,,	15.5	14-16	33
R	,,	15.2	14-16	33
S	,,	15.1	14-16	32

Table 1. *The eight groups of subjects*

4. The Experimental Design

4.1 The Three Sections of the Course

The course materials were administered in three major sections, between each of which an examination-type test was taken.

The experimental design is summarized in Table 2 which shows the instructional plans adopted for each section of the course, at which points evaluation tests were administered and during which periods learning times were measured. The design contains four distinct experiments which will be described more fully below.

4.2 The Experiments

4.2.1 EXPERIMENT 1 – HYPOTHESIS.

That there is no difference between the results achieved by groups studying from the self-instructional texts on their own without any tutorial assistance, and groups receiving normal classroom-based group instruction.

This experiment was repeated three times. The comparisons were only made on the basis of test scores at the ends of the course sections, as the learning times under group instruction cannot be meaningfully compared with the learning time under the self-instructional system, because we have no measure of how much homework time was given to problems set by the teacher.

The three comparisons made were: (1) the adult groups C and D during section 1 of the course, (2) the adult groups A and D on section 2 of the course, and (3) the schoolchildren groups P/Q combined with the group R/S combined on section 1 of the course. Thus we are comparing an 'independent study plan' with 'traditional instruction' in each case (see Table 2).

4.2.2 EXPERIMENT 2 – HYPOTHESIS.

That no differences exist in the amount of learning, or in the learning time, between adults and youths when utilizing the programmed instructional materials (with or without tutorial assistance).

This may be investigated by comparison of the scores and the learning rates of group C (adults) with those of groups P and Q (schoolchildren), on each of the three sections of the course, as these three groups received similar treatments section by section. This experiment thus compared the performances of adults and youths under an 'independent study' plan, under the 'Keller' plan and under an intermediate 'student-directed' plan of course implementation.

4.2.3. EXPERIMENT 3 – HYPOTHESIS.

That the more frequent the tutorial intervention, the more efficient the learning (as measured by scores on section tests and learning time to complete a section).

The design of this experiment is shown more clearly in Table 3. Principally, this experiment is comparing groups A, B and C of the adults under the three study plans used in the study; the independent study plan, the student-directed plan and the tutor-directed 'Keller' plan. The experimental design, statistically, was a 3 x 3 square comparing groups and sections.

4.2.4 EXPERIMENT 4 – HYPOTHESIS.

That the *information mapping* format of presentation is more effective than the *mathetical programmed instruction* format (in both levels of achievement and learning time) and that this benefit to the information-mapping format is more pronounced in the case of adult learners than in the case of youths.

Pre/Post Test | Test (I - III) | Test (IV - V) | Questionnaire Pre/Post Test

Group	Section 1 (Mods. I - III)	Section 2 (Mods. IV - V)		Section 3 (Mods. VI - VII)			
				VIa	VIb	VII	
Adults							
* A	*Student-directed Plan* (Tutor intervention between modules only)	*Independent Study Plan*	A1	Inf.Map	Prog.Inst.	P.I.	*Keller Plan*
			A2	Prog.Inst.	Inf.Map	P.I.	
* B	*Keller Plan* (Tutor intervention between each lesson)	*Student-directed Plan*	B1	Inf.Map	P.I.	P.I.	*Indep. Study Plan*
			B2	P.I.	Inf.Map	P.I.	
* C	*Independent Study Plan* (No planned tutorial intervention)	*Keller Plan*	C1	Inf.Map	P.I.	P.I.	*Student-directed Plan*
			C2	P.I.	Inf.Map	P.I.	
D	'Traditional' (classroom group instruction, using the same course content/sequence)		D	Control Group for Tests			
School							
* P	*Independent Study Plan*	*Keller Plan*	P	Inf.Map	P.I.	P.I.	*Student-directed Plan*
* Q			Q	P.I.	Inf.Map	P.I.	
R	'Traditional' (classroom group instruction, using the same course content/sequence)		R	Control Group			
S							

Note: * indicates that learning times were measured for this group.

Table 2. *The overall experimental design*

51

The experimental design here involves two separate experiments, one for adults, utilizing groups A, B, C on section 3 of the course and the other one for school-children, utilizing groups P and Q on the same course section. In the case of the three adult groups, each one worked on section three of the course under a different study plan. The groups were therefore treated separately, each one being sub-divided into two sub-groups receiving the two alternative formats of the modules (see Table 4).

	Section 1	*Section 2*	*Section 3*
Group A	Student-directed plan 49.7/36	Independent study plan 67.3/25	Keller plan 85/1.3
Group B	Keller plan 63.6/22.7	Student-directed plan 71/19	Independent study plan 77/1.4
Group C	Independent study plan 49.4/49.7	Keller plan 76/18.6	Student-directed plan 77/1.4

NOTE: The figures shown in each cell of the table indicate: mean score (%)/mean study time (hours).

Table 3. *Experiment 3: design and summary of results*

Experiment 4(a) (Adult groups)

		Module VIa	*Module VIb*
Group A (Keller plan)	A1	Information maps 7.7/41	Linear programme 6.8/38
	A2	Linear programme 6.9/4.5	Information maps 7.6/32
Group B (Independent study)	B1	Information maps 6.5/43	Linear programme 6.0/41
	B2	Linear programme 6.4/46	Information maps 7.0/36
Group C (Student-directed)	C1	Information maps 6.7/46	Linear programme 5.9/43
	C2	Linear programme 6.2/48	Information maps 7.5/35

Experiment 4(b) (Schoolchildren groups)

	Module VIa	*Module VIb*
Group P	Information maps 6.0/39	Linear programme 5.7/35
Group Q	Linear programme 5.8/45	Information maps 6.3/33

NOTE: The figures shown in each cell of the table indicate: Mean gain score (max. 10)/ Mean study time (min.).

Table 4. *Experiment 4: design and summary of results*

5. Conclusions from the Experiments

5.1 The First Experiment

The results of this experiment supported fairly strongly the null hypothesis that there are no differences in the amount of learning achieved by students using the

BASG-M materials (quite independently of tutorial interaction) and students receiving equivalent classroom instruction (in groups of about 30).

Clearly this conclusion is subject to various critical comments particularly on the grounds discussed by Hartley (1972) that there are so many undefined and uncontrolled factors in the 'classroom-instruction' mode as to render it impossible to generalize any conclusion. The most that can be said with certainty is that in this particular experiment, with the particular students and teachers used, the learning levels achieved were equivalent in terms of final test scores and pre-test/post-test gains.

However, for the purposes of this study, this first experiment serves mainly to establish a 'base-line'. Once satisfied that the materials *by themselves* are reasonably effective, we may proceed to comparisons of alternative plans for their utilization and alternative formats for their presentation.

5.2 The Second Experiment

The second experiment yielded results which suggested that under the highly prescriptive 'Keller' plan, adults learn somewhat better than do younger students. They also appear to work faster under this plan. But, on the other hand, they appear to work better, but work slower under the student-directed plan (in which the tutor rarely imposes help or evaluation on the learner, but is always available at the student's request).

Statistically, these results were significant, although in real terms they may not signify anything of great value. Particularly in the case of study times, the real differences in mean study times between groups are not very large (although statistically significant).

However, trends in the direction indicated are very interesting and somewhat surprising from a theoretical point of view. If, as much industrial training experience suggests (Belbin and Belbin, 1972), adults are slower learners, are more conscientious, and have more learning difficulties, one would expect him to do less well or at least to take more time to reach the same level of proficiency. There is perhaps some reason to believe that, due to the adult's higher level of conscientiousness and self-evaluation he may eventually do better than the school-child but in so doing would require a considerably greater learning time. This was not so in these experiments. The adults generally did considerably better and in a somewhat shorter (or much equivalent) learning time.

One possible explanation for the generally better performance of the adults in our experiments may well be that the effects of a higher level of motivation more than counterbalanced any greater learning difficulties that they may have had. After all, the adults were attending a continuing education course quite voluntarily whilst the schoolchildren were attending the *segundo grau* (which is not compulsory by law) perhaps as much due to family and external pressures as to internal self-motivation.

However, there were no other obvious signs of vastly different levels of motivation between adults and youths involved in the experiments (indeed, the truancy rates in the experimental groups of schoolchildren were well below those of other groups in the same school and showed a steady decline during the period of the experiments, until unexplained absenteeism almost vanished from the experimental groups — in other classes it could reach 30 or 40 per cent on occasions).

The stronger advantage to the adults (in both test scores and learning time) when working under the Keller plan is particularly interesting as it goes against one of Belbin and Belbin's (1972) other assertions that adults learn better when they have more complete and direct control over their own learning process.

The Keller plan is the most prescriptive, most 'tutor-led' of the three study plans used in the experiments. Yet adults seemed to prefer the Keller plan and took to it more readily than did the younger students, as shown by responses to a questionnaire and by the already quoted results.

It has become highly fashionable to promote the 'learner-controlled' model for adult education. A new science of adult learning — 'andragogy' — has even been launched on this bandwagon (andragogy purports to deal with 'the learner learning' as opposed to pedagogy which supposedly is more concerned with 'the teacher teaching').

However, not all the evidence points in this direction. One should take note of, for example, the survey of adult independent study projects performed by Tough (1967) which showed that adults experienced the greatest difficulties with decision-making (concerning the learning goals to adopt, the learning methods to use, and how to overcome the learning problems they encounter). This was where they sought more help from others and 'would have used more help if they could have got it'.

Tough's findings, as well as the author's, do not support the view that adults are able or indeed willing to exert more control over their learning than are younger learners. Of course, both these studies were concerned with adults in continuing education of a remedial nature. The situation may be different in the case of adults who have already experienced success as learners and have 'learnt to learn'. Some inkling of such a trend was noticed in the author's experiments. The adult group B did only a little worse on the second section of the course than did adult group C and in a time which was not much longer. But on part 1 of the course, group B did much better and in a much shorter time (see Table 3). One possible explanation is that on part 1 of the course, studied under the Keller plan, this group learnt to organize its learning and therefore 'did for itself' on section 2 what the tutor was doing for group C. This suggestion would require a more detailed study in order to control other possible sources of difference (for example, an inherent imbalance between the groups).

5.3 The Third Experiment

On all three sections of the course, the Keller plan appeared as the most effective study plan in terms of *final test scores*. The 'student-directed' and the 'independent' study plans were not very different from each other in this respect.

The author has already commented (when discussing experiment 2) that this finding is somewhat at odds with currently held views on adult learning. One needs to distinguish here between the different types of adult learner — Lewis Elton's 'Martha's and Mary's' of post-secondary education (Elton, 1975). Whereas the university undergraduate, or the adult participating in continuing education for its own sake, may well be both skilled and interested in taking decisions concerning the course of study he is following; the typical vocationally oriented student (be he interested in obtaining specific job skills or merely a paper qualification) is neither skilled nor interested in taking over the decision-making role which was traditionally the teacher's. The adult students in this study most certainly fall into this second category. The Brazilian adult student, repeating (or taking for the first time) the basic school curriculum is almost exclusively seeking a paper qualification, necessary (often by law) in order to hold down a job at a certain level, quite irrespective of the relevance of the course to the job or of whether his abilities and experience are already sufficient for the job. He wishes to finish the course and get the qualification in the most rapid and painless manner possible. He exhibits no desire to question the course content, objectives, materials or teaching methods. To what extent this is a general phenomenon of the type described by Lewis Elton, and to what extent a cultural trait reinforced by existing social customs and educational methods, is not as yet clear.

As concerns *learning time* under the three study plans, the results are less clear-cut. In general, the independent study plan required the largest amount of time. This was almost certainly due to the lack of tutor guidance and control. Procrastination was quite common in groups working under this plan. The Keller plan emerges as the fastest of the three plans. The extra tutorial time in this plan seems to be more than compensated by the reduction in study time between tutorials. Also, as mentioned above, there is some reason to believe that experience of studying under the Keller plan at the beginning of the experiment, contributed to a reduction of the study time for later parts of the course, studied under the more independent, less tutor-led plans (a possible learning-to-learn effect which requires further study).

5.4 The Fourth Experiment

The results of this experiment, which compared a linear-programmed learning technique (based on mathetics), with a student-controlled random-access programming technique (based on information mapping), appeared strongly in favour of the information-mapping format, both in terms of reduced learning time and increased final test score. These conclusions are in accordance with the author's previous findings when studying alternative versions of a course on matrices (with polytechnic undergraduates in the United Kingdom) and with similar studies performed in the United States (Romiszowski and Ellis, 1974).

The results in this case, though highly significant statistically, must however be qualified. *Firstly,* one must note that the comparison involved only Module VI of the course, which is quite a small module requiring only a few hours of study. Thus the experiment was necessarily short, particularly as any given student only studied a half of Module VI in the information-mapping format (see Table 4). Furthermore, the information-mapping technique was new to the learners, whereas they had been using linear programmes almost daily for several months. There must surely be a strong 'Hawthorne' effect favouring the 'new' technique. The experiment was so short that it would be unlikely that a Hawthorne effect would have time to die away. It is difficult in this experiment to separate the effects that may be due to genuine differences between the techniques of programming from the Hawthorne effects. *Secondly,* the differences noted, though statistically significant are not very large in absolute terms, being of the order of 5 to 10 percentage points on gain scores and about 10 per cent saving in learning time. In the author's opinion, and based on other experiments, if the use of the information-mapping technique were to be extended to larger sections of the course, then the difference in test scores as compared to linear programmes would continue to be rather small and unimportant in practical terms (both techniques of presentation are effective). But the difference in learning time would increase, becoming more favourable for the information-mapping format as the size of the learning task increased. Further modules are now being written in the information-mapping format and this new hypothesis will be put to the test.

6. Conclusions and Suggestions for Further Work

6.1. The experiments so far have suggested that information-mapping may be a more effective technique for the presentation of mathematical content than are linear-programmed texts. However, there are certain weaknesses in the present study which render generalization dangerous. The study will be repeated on a larger scale with more inbuilt controls. Also other possible presentation formats should be considered (for example, 'structural communication'), as well as non-print media.

6.2. The study has also revealed some interesting trends concerning the efficiency of learning that mature and adolescent learners achieve in individualized, largely self-instructional courses. The present study has considered only one type of mature learner, in one type of socio-educational system, studying one type of mathematical content. In this context the results are at odds with some currently held theories concerning the mature learner. The research could well be extended to other types of learners in other situations, to establish whether the greater benefit to adults of prescriptive individualized courses (noted here) is a general phenomenon.

6.3. The study has also suggested that the more prescriptive approach of the Keller plan is more efficient than more student-directed or teacher-independent modes of course implementation. Whilst this was a more strongly marked trend with the adult learners, it was also observed as a general trend for adult and schoolchildren groups alike. The author feels that both the content of the course (introduction to modern mathematics — largely involving the learning of concepts and standard procedures) and the socio-cultural traditions of Brazilian education (much more formal, autocratic, unquestioning, content-oriented and preoccupied with paper qualifications than is the Anglo-Saxon tradition) would tend to influence the results in the direction noted. It would be interesting to replicate the experiments in different situations with students who are more questioning, more sophisticated learners and more aware of their specific learning objectives, and also with different subject matter which requires more creative, 'productive' responses from the learner, rather than merely a 'reproductive' repetition and application of concepts and procedures. In the area of mathematics, this would involve the teaching of problem solving and (more importantly) problem formulation — the building of mathematical models for new problem situations. In short, are the instructional plans here shown effective for the teaching of algorithmic procedures, equally effective for the teaching of heuristical procedures, and if not, how should our instructional plans be modified?

Can individualized, self-instructional techniques be effectively applied where a vast majority of teachers of mathematics, the world over, have failed?

References

Belbin, E. and Belbin, R. M. (1972) *Problems in Adult Retraining*. Heinemann, London.

Elton, L. R. B. (1975) Mature students: OU and non-OU. In Evans, L. and Leedham, J. (eds.) *Aspects of Educational Technology IX*. Kogan Page, London.

Hartley, J. (1972) Evaluating instructional methods. In Davies, I. K. and Hartley, J. (eds.) *Contributions to an Educational Technology*. Butterworth, London.

Romiszowski, A. J. (1977) *A Study of Individualized Systems for Mathematics Instruction at the Post-Secondary Levels*. Unpublished doctoral thesis available in the library, University of Technology, Loughborough.

Romiszowski, A. J. and Ellis, P. (1974) *Interim Report on Research into Alternative Programming Styles for the Presentation of the Correspondence Course Sections of the Proposed Multi-Media Course in Vectors and Matrices*. Report to the Council of Europe Committee for Cultural Cooperation, Strasbourg, March 1973.

Tough, A. M. (1967) *Learning Without a Teacher: A study of Tasks and Assistance during*

Adult Self-Teaching Projects. Educational Research Series Number 3, Ontario Institute for Studies in Education, Toronto.

Chapter 2:
Propagating Educational Technology
– 'Training the Trainers'

Last year's conference had the theme 'The Spread of Educational Technology'. Many kinds of courses at all levels from university to primary education continue to be designed to up-date and develop the way teaching takes place. This chapter, after commencing with an informative review of the way educational innovations have been propagated in the USA, presents a number of papers relating to various types of in-service training in Britain.

Professor Hawkridge (6) gives a fluent account of the policies adopted in recent years by the United States Office of Education, to propagate advances in education primarily at school level. The performance of the National Diffusion Network is reviewed and assessed. The Project Information Packages (PIPs) developed from the NDN are described and their adoption and adaptation by local schools reviewed.

Mr Davies (7) describes the development of support materials for the 'Certificate in Educational Technology' course run by the City and Guilds of London Institute. The course is considered in terms of the subject material, the 'target population' and the need for local colleges to be able to mount the course using their own resources. Various problems identified and lessons learnt in the development exercise are presented.

Mr Hills (8) continues the discussion of the course mentioned above in terms of a pilot course run at Coventry Technical College, for in-service teacher education. The account includes the design of the course, how it was advertised and conducted, and a detailed evaluation.

Mr Neville (9) presents an account of the general strategies for in-service educational technology training from the 'Council for Educational Technology's' point of view. Describing educational technology as neither science nor art, he points out that it is an area where it is impossible to formulate a specific body of knowledge. The recent trend moving from approaches centred on 'a taught course' towards supported 'on-the-job' training is welcomed.

There follow two papers particularly welcome at the present time when many colleges are 'gearing-up' in readiness to run courses leading to Technician Education Council (TEC) qualifications. Mr Ward (10) gives some background to the formation of TEC, and describes the two-tier workshop system designed in response to CET's commission for training packages for college lecturers. He provides a useful list of recommendations for future designers of such training materials.

Mr Coffey (11) gives an account of the organization and work of a course development team in the TEC external student pilot project. He provides valuable suggestions about how such teams may best be set up, including the skills likely to be required in the teams. This should be of considerable help to those initiating similar teams in technical education institutions.

Finally, Miss Cooper (12) takes us to a very different (and no less important) sector of education, describing the 'Primary Extension Programme'. This centres on the needs of the young, disadvantaged child, and involves the propagation of teacher-designed, 'low-technology' materials.

6. The Propagation of Educational Innovations

D.G. Hawkridge, *The Open University*, Milton Keynes*

Abstract: The paper reviews strategies for dissemination of educational innovations as developed by the US Office of Education, particularly Project Information Packages (PIPs) and the National Diffusion Network, both of which have been fully evaluated. The question is posed: Which strategies are likely to be most effective in the British context?

Introduction

Educational reformers believe in propagating successful innovations. To improve education, spread the good news well — but cheaply. How to do so nationally is a problem faced by organizations such as the Council for Educational Technology and the Schools Council that believe they have a duty to propagate successful innovations in their own fields of endeavour. In this context, the experience of the Federal Government of the United States is worth examining closely.

First, it is important to understand the nature of national education policies emanating from Washington, DC. Then I shall describe to you the dissemination strategies of the US Office of Education (USOE). Two recent strategies are particularly interesting. One is based on a labour-intensive network of human agents. The other employs packages developed at high initial cost and in accord with many of the tenets of American educational technologists. I shall summarize evaluations of these strategies. Finally, I shall leave you with a question or two for discussion.

Nature of Federal Policies in Education

Over the past 25 years USOE has intervened more and more directly in American education. In particular it has aimed at bringing about improvements rather than simply maintaining the *status quo*.

Congress first charged USOE with promoting education more than 100 years ago (Hutchins and Clemens, 1976), but until about 25 years ago USOE operated on a small budget (House, 1974). The Cooperative Research Act of 1954 marked the beginning of major changes in federal educational policy (Clark, 1974). Successive Acts have rested on common assumptions we should note: *that American education can do better, with the existing structure, and that Federal money will enable selected Local Education Agencies (LEAs) to demonstrate improved methods, later to be adopted by other LEAs* (Berman and McLaughlin, 1975).

---

* This paper is based on work carried out at the American Institutes for Research by the author on behalf of the Office of Planning, Budgeting and Evaluation of USOE. Views expressed herein are those of the author and do not necessarily reflect policy of the US Government.

The nature of federal policy in education is determined by three factors: the constitution, the focus on national rather than regional or local goals, and USOE's philosophical viewpoint.

The constitution assigns different roles in education to government at federal, state and local levels. The powers of state and local agencies have always constrained federal intervention in education. Thus USOE is usually persuader, advocate and provider, rather than dictator, censor or inspector.

National problems are USOE's concern. You may think, with House (1974), that the nature of educational problems is locally determined and so should be the solutions, yet USOE must deal with national problems. In turn, it must seek national solutions that can be widely applied. Economies of scale then look very attractive.

What about USOE's philosophical viewpoint? USOE cannot adopt a coercive stance towards LEAs, except in a few matters such as desegregation. It does not have the resources to try a re-educative approach involving widespread personal persuasion and re-training (Chin and Benne, 1969). It is obliged to adopt a rational and empirical viewpoint. It bases its programmes on the assumption that people are rational and will follow their self-interest once it is revealed to them. This philosophy fits well a technologically oriented society whose members believe they have benefited greatly from the application of knowledge discovered through rational development and empirically designed experimentation. USOE has employed the Research, Development and Diffusion model in education, articulated by Havelock (1971). This model embodies many of the values of American industrial society, being derived from studies of modernization of American agriculture, industry and commerce. It demands a rational sequence of activities: research to development to packaging to dissemination, planned and executed on a grand scale and employing division of labour among the activities. The consumers of the products are seen as essentially passive. High initial costs are justified by planners in terms of anticipated long-term benefits.

Gideonse's (1972) 'market model' underlies more recent USOE thinking. He claims that traditional views of research and development are counter-productive in education. Consumers must be taken into account in setting goals. Client satisfaction is the criterion of success. Studies of transfer of technology indicate that dissemination may depend more on 'market pull' than 'technology push' (Baer *et al.* 1976), but educational innovations differ radically from those of technology, and may require different dissemination strategies (Baldridge, 1974).

In summary, USOE sees dissemination of knowledge about successful practices in education as one of its tasks, and employs a rational and empirical approach to this task.

History of USOE Dissemination Strategies

Twenty years ago, USOE lacked a plan for using results of educational research and development (R&D) activities (Rogers *et al.*, 1976). There was no explicit mandate to disseminate R&D products to the nation's schools until the National Defense Act of 1958. Since then, every act authorizing R&D has also mandated dissemination (Hutchins and Clemens, 1976).

Strategies employed by USOE have been progressively developed. I list six in Table 1. Let me say something about each.

ERIC (Educational Resources Information Center) is a network of clearinghouses first funded in 1965. The clearinghouses are far apart and are not funded to send out agents to promote the use of effective practices. They depend on indirect means of influence, such as brochures, indexes and computer print-outs. Many of

Educational Resources Information Center (ERIC)	USOE set up a network of clearinghouses linked to a computerized search system. Intended mainly for educational research and development reports.
Publication of descriptions of successful projects	USOE published compendia, pamphlet series and periodicals to publicize successes.
Educational extension agents	USOE funded the Pilot State Dissemination Project, in which agents linked schools to information sources such as ERIC.
Devolution to states	USOE devolved some dissemination functions to State Education Agencies.
National Diffusion Network (NDN)	USOE set up a network of agents linking Federal, State and Local Education Agencies (LEAs), linking LEAs having successful projects (developer-LEAs) with LEAs wanting to replicate these.
Project Information Packages (PIPs)	USOE funded packaging of successful projects, the packages to be used by LEAs wanting to replicate these projects without help from developer-LEAs.

Table 1. *Six major dissemination strategies of the US Office of Education (USOE)*

you are familiar with *Research in Education,* the monthly catalogue based on ERIC.

USOE's second major strategy was to publish descriptions of successful projects. A monthly publication, *Putting Research into Educational Practice,* was sent to State Education Agencies for distribution to LEAs. Later, the *It Works* pamphlets came out. These described exemplary projects for educating disadvantaged children (Hawkridge, *et al.*, 1968; Hawkridge *et al.*, 1969). Other series followed, such as *Modern Programs, Childhood Education, ALERT* (Hall and Alford, 1976), and *Product Development Reports* (Crawford *et al.*, 1974).

The third major strategy was derived explicitly from agricultural extension work. Agricultural extension agents visit farmers to inform them about and persuade them to adopt practices based on research and development. In education, educational extension agents roamed the schools in three states looking for teachers who had problems for which there might be research solutions. This was called the Pilot State Dissemination Program and ran for two years from 1970. ERIC was the main source of solutions (Sieber, 1973).

A fourth major strategy stemmed from changes in policy during the Nixon administration. Dissemination was devolved partially to State Education Agencies, but few of these were qualified or equipped to do the work (Rogers *et al.*, 1976).

The fifth major strategy, establishment of the National Diffusion Network (NDN), was a compromise based on earlier experience. The NDN (Emrick, 1976; Emrick *et al.*, 1977) was aimed at linking federal, state and local agencies for the purpose of exchanging successful ideas, materials and projects (Hall and Alford, 1976). In particular, it complemented the Dissemination Review Panel of USOE (now the Joint Dissemination Review Panel of USOE and National Institute of Education). This panel approved certain projects as successful and worth disseminating. The NDN had an expensive network of agents, known as facilitators, who acted as links between LEAs developing successful projects and those wishing to adopt successes for themselves. In addition, developer-LEAs were paid to assist adopter-LEAs to replicate successful projects.

The sixth major strategy of USOE involved Project Information Packages (PIPs). It was launched at the same time as the NDN in 1974. Project information packaging was not simply a new name for the old business of publishing accounts

63

of successful projects. The original reason for developing PIPs was that LEAs found reports being passed to them by the Dissemination Review Panel to be inadequate for guiding them as they attempted to replicate successful projects. Personal guidance for all adopters from developers did not appear feasible. Costs would be prohibitive, the load on developers would be too great, and the number of adoptions would be limited by developers' capacity to provide services. Thus a basic concept of PIPs was that they would obviate the need for expensive personal technical assistance from developers. PIPs would have a management-oriented approach and would pay great attention to detail. PIPs would permit LEAs to by-pass years of costly development activities. USOE would see some return for capital invested in educational research and development as adoptions multiplied through use of PIPs. PIPs would be complementary to the NDN, whose agents would use PIPs without resorting to expensive developers' assistance for adopters. PIPs would increase efficiency in the NDN. These were the expectations.

Development of PIPs was expensive, thorough and in accord with many of the tenets of American educational technologists. The first six, describing projects for disadvantaged children (Tallmadge, 1974), were field-tested in 19 LEAs and then revised (Stearns, 1975 and 1977). The second edition was published and disseminated during the 1976-77 school year by a special network of eight agents spread across the country. Four more PIPs were developed for exemplary bilingual education projects, three Spanish/English, one French/English. These are under field-test at the moment. A further six PIPs were prepared for exemplary projects for disadvantaged children, making 14 PIPs now available altogether.

Evaluation of these Strategies

How effective were these different strategies? Did they spread the good news well and cheaply? We know some of the answers. There have been no studies of the effects of disseminating booklets or of devolving dissemination to State Education Agencies, but ERIC, the Pilot State Dissemination Projects, the National Diffusion Network and PIPs have all been evaluated. I want to say nothing about the first, a little about the second, and a good deal about the NDN and PIPs.

The Pilot State Dissemination Project was evaluated by Sieber (1973) and others. His report offered three views of the practitioner in the schools: as rational man, as cooperator, and as powerless functionary. Strategies that require the practitioner to be rational produce dismal results, claimed the team. Strategies that *demand* innovation, with sanctions for non-compliance, are most effective in producing change. Strategies that expect practitioners to be cooperative by nature, willing to work with change agents, hold out most hope. The Pilot Project's success — and it was judged successful — depended on a combination of strategies that required both rational and cooperative practitioners. The agents' success depended upon each being a generalist without power or authority; the agents' presence in the schools was legitimated by their capacity to provide information. Why did the Project disappear? The reasons were political, related to NIE's creation.

In 1974 the NDN began. It was evaluated over the first two years by Emrick *et al.* (1977). His team found that NDN agents used both printed materials and personal contact, and encouraged developers and adopters to get together. While Pilot Project agents were primarily information sources, NDN agents passed this role to developers. Adoptions were not evenly distributed: no less than 80 per cent occurred in rural or suburban LEAs, and 72 per cent were at the pre-school and primary levels. Almost every adoption involved *adaptation* of the original model, sometimes to the point where it was scarcely recognizable. In spite of this, the study took a very positive view of the NDN. As a major dissemination strategy, it worked, said the report without providing full evidence of the extent to which this was true. In political terms, the first NDN's success was confirmed when a second and even more expensive NDN was set up in 1977, authorized directly by Congress.

What about the PIPs? Two reports by Stearns (1975 and 1977) covered field-testing of the first six PIPs. Stearns observed that the effectiveness criteria used to select projects for packaging in PIPs were not widely acceptable even within USOE, let alone among LEAs. In other words, were these really successes that were being packaged? The cost to LEAs that wished to adopt PIP projects was too high unless they had extra funding, usually from federal sources. If an adopter-LEA was markedly different from the developer-LEA, say in its size or ethnic make-up, chances of successful replication were diminished. Replication implied repeating essential features of the original, but there were difficulties in discerning what was essential.

Stearns praised the PIPs' management orientation. Details about how to get the projects started and how to operate them appealed to potential adopters. On the other hand, the first version of the PIPs was thin on curriculum and instructional methods.

Stearns raised the question of how much technical assistance might be needed when PIPs became generally available (as they are now). She thought that LEAs would go on asking for personal help from developers and would not be satisfied with PIPs alone.

Were the PIP-transplanted projects as successful as the originals in raising student achievement? The answer provided by standardized tests during the two-year field-test was negative. Stearns recommended against making norm-referenced tests (of the type used) the main criterion of success. She believed that the measures of success of dissemination activity should be the rate of adoption of projects and satisfaction of users' criteria. She recommended that USOE should continue to use packaging, but not merely in the PIP format, which was unsuitable for some projects

In 1976 a further evaluation began of the first six PIPs, now revised. I was personally involved in the first year of this study, which was aimed at finding out the best way to disseminate the packages, and whether LEAs followed the processes and achieved the outcomes described in the PIPs. In 1977, the four bilingual PIPs went into field-testing. Results of these studies will appear in 1978 and 1979.

In the meantime, the highly rational and empirical approach adopted by USOE in developing PIPs has been only partially successful. So far, PIPs have needed a network of disseminators. LEAs have not exactly rushed to seize the packages from the shelves. On the other hand, adopter-LEAs have been able to select and set up PIP projects with little help from developer-LEAs. Surprisingly, they have done so without referring much to the packages. They have short-circuited the comprehensive decision-making procedures laid down in the PIPs and gone straight for the parts of the packages they felt they needed. They have certainly *adapted* the projects to suit their own circumstances (Campeau *et al.*, in press).

I view these developments with considerable interest. Will the NDN, with its high recurrent costs and its human approach, gain a place in history as the most successful dissemination strategy? Or will PIPs, developed at great expense to fit into a consumer society in a rational, mechanistic way, win in the long run? The new NDN employs an expensive but probably effective mixture of strategies: disseminators tell LEAs about PIPs *and* put them in touch with developers — packages plus people.

What should Britain learn from American experience? Or, to make the question more personal, what strategies should we adopt ourselves to propagate successes? Will we opt for capital-intensive packaging? For labour-intensive networks of dissemination agents? Or for some combination of the two? These are the questions I put forward for discussion.

Acknowledgements

I should like to thank the following for their helpful comments on a draft of this paper: Peggie Campeau, American Institutes for Research; Robert Nicodemus, The Open University; Derek Rowntree, The Open University.

References

Baer, W., Johnson, L. L. and Merrow, E.W. (1976) *Analysis of Federally Funded Demonstration Programs.* Executive Summary. Rand, Santa Monica, California.

Baldridge, J. V. (1974) Political and structural protection of educational innovations. In Temkin, S. and Brown, M.V. (eds.) *What Do Research Findings Say about Getting Innovations into Schools?* Research for Better Schools, Inc. Philadelphia.

Berman, P. and McLaughlin, M. W. (1975) *Federal Programs Supporting Educational Change,* 4. Rand, Santa Monica, California.

Campeau, P. L., Brinkley, J. L., Hawkridge, D. G., and Treadway, P. G. (in press) *First-Year Report: Evaluation of Project Information Package (PIP) Dissemination and Implementation.* American Institutes for Research, Palo Alto, California.

Chin, R. and Benne, K. D. (1969) General strategies for effecting change in human systems. In Bennis, W. G., Benne, K. D. and Chin, R. (eds.) *The Planning of Change.* Holt, Rinehart and Winston, New York.

Clark, D. L. (1974) *Federal Policy in Educational Research.* Indiana University Research Foundation, Bloomington, Indiana.

Crawford, J. J., Kratochvil, D. W. and Wright, C. E. (1974) *Evaluation of the Impact of Educational Research and Development Products.* American Institutes for Research, Palo Alto, California.

Emrick, J. A. (1976) *Evaluation of the National Diffusion Network: Study Design and Analysis Plan.* Stanford Research Institute, Menlo Park, California

Emrick, J. A., Peterson, S. M. and Agarwala-Rogers, R. (1977) *Evaluation of the National Diffusion Network: Final Report,* 1. Stanford Research Institute, Menlo Park, California.

Gideonse, H. (1972) R&D for education; a market model. In Schalock, H. D. and Sell, G. R. (Eds.) *Conceptual Frameworks for Viewing Educational RDD&E.* The Oregon Studies in educational research, development, diffusion and evaluation, 30. Oregon State System of Higher Education, Monmouth, Oregon. ED 066840.

Hall, C. E. and Alford, S. E. (1976) *Evaluation of the National Diffusion Network: Evolution of the Network and overview of the Literature on Diffusion of Educational Innovations.* Stanford Research Institute, Menlo Park, California.

Havelock, R.G. (1971) *Planning for Innovation Through Dissemination and Utilization of Knowledge.* Institute for Social Research, University of Michigan, Ann Arbor.

Hawkridge, D. G., Campeau, P. L., DeWitt, K. M. and Trickett, P. K. (1969) *A Study of Further Exemplary Programs for the Education of Disadvantaged Children.* American Institutes for Research, Palo Alto, California.

Hawkridge, D. G., Chalupsky, A. B. and Roberts, A. O. H. (1968) *A Study of Selected Exemplary Programs for the Education of Disadvantaged Children.* American Institutes for Research, Palo Alto, California.

House, E. R. (1974) *The Politics of Educational Innovation.* McCutchan, San Francisco.

Hutchins, C. L. and Clemens, T. D. (1976) Information utilization and dissemination. In *Catalog of NIE Products.* National Institute of Education, Washington, DC.

Rogers, E. M., Eveland, J. D. and Bean, A. S. (1976) *Extending the Agricultural Extension Model.* Institute for Communications Research, Stanford University, Stanford, California.

Sieber, S. D. (1973) The Pilot State Dissemination Program. *Journal of Research and Development in Education,* 6, 4.

Stearns, M. S. (1975) *Evaluation of the Field Test of Project Information Packages.* 1: Viability of packaging. Stanford Research Institute, Menlo Park, California.

Stearns, M. S. (1977) *Evaluation of the Field Test of Project Information Packages.* 1 Summary report. Research Institute, Menlo Park, California.

Tallmadge, G. K. (1974) *The Development of Project Information Packages for Effective Approaches in Compensatory Education.* RMC Research Corporation, Mountain View, California.

7. An Exercise in the Development of Support Materials to Facilitate Internal Training in Schools and Colleges

W.J.K. Davies, *St. Albans College, Herts*

Abstract: The paper describes a venture in educational technology course design which has particular relevance to changing conditions in in-service training. It relates to the development of the Certificate in Educational Technology of the City and Guilds of London Institute and to a cooperative exercise which resulted from it.

1. Genesis of the Course

The course to be discussed in this paper is the 'Certificate in Educational Technology' of the City and Guilds of London Institute. CGLI is essentially an examining body, best known for its wide range of skill-based courses at craft and technician level but with an expanding stake in teacher education especially in the further education sector. Its 730 Initial Teacher Training Course is well known in its field and the Institute is also developing a series of more advanced Teacher Development Courses — in Administration; in Achievement Testing; in Teaching of the Handicapped; and in Educational Technology — though this title is something of a misnomer since the course is essentially one in the systematic management of learning. The media aspect of educational technology plays a very small part.

The Educational Technology Course was originally envisaged as a 'Part III' to an existing two-part course in Programmed Learning which, by 1972, had been run for a number of years; the writer was involved in running and assessing this and thence became involved in the design stage of 'Part III'. The first intention was to train educational technology specialists for institutions but design studies showed that, on the part-time basis characteristic of City and Guilds courses, this would take three years: the Institute's Education Committee quite rightly felt this was too long for a development course, and charged the advisory panel with the job of redesigning the course to provide educational technology expertise for the classroom teacher.

At this point three criteria were overtly or tacitly established:

(1) The course must be able to be completed in, at most, two years part-time study

(2) The premise was taken that 'AV' or media elements at classroom level were already being adequately covered by local in-service courses and media service units.

(3) As might be expected from their background, the bias of the panel members was towards the 'structured' or 'systematic' learning approach.

Although the 'level' might be thought to have dropped and the range narrowed, the course was considerably more difficult to design because a defined *job* no longer existed as an end product. It was instead intended to provide the teacher with a battery of skills to apply to his/her own work and the target population was very wide: it might range from the part-time teacher of art, taking one or two lessons a week, to a polytechnic lecturer in degree-level science. The model shown in Figure 1 was therefore taken as the basis, establishing a methodical system which appeared to be that taken by many effective teachers, and the course was predicated as providing skills to help teacher performance both in components of the system and in the complete system.

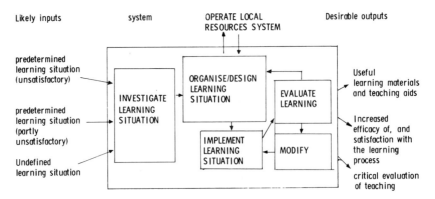

Figure 1. *Outline systems model for course design in management of learning*

To enable these differing objectives to be achieved as far as possible, the course structure was designed according to the theory postulated by T. F. Gilbert's 'Demonstrate, Prompt, Release' model (Figure 2) and studies indicated that transfer of skills could be accomplished in the time at lesson level (DPR); design of courses or projects level (DP); and much more superficially at institution level (Demonstrate only). This could, moreover, be done while allowing the course to be split into two single years to accommodate those who only wanted an introduction to the skills.

At this point the design panel encountered another problem inherent in CGL1 courses in that they are not 'institutionalized' in the manner of most major in-service courses. All students take the same *examination* and are expected to attain similar standards, but the courses are run by a number of individual colleges who can adopt their own teaching methods and timetables within the constraints imposed by course objectives and assessment procedures.

It was anticipated from the start that in this field many of the colleges wishing to offer the course would not have tutors with the overall expertise required to carry out the work as defined by the three major elements: model; general goals derived from the model; the content syllabus arising from the formulation of these goals. Nonetheless under CGLI regulations any approved college wishing to run a course is permitted to do so and it was therefore hypothesized that tutor-support materials at local levels would be very desirable. After some discussion, the Council for Educational Technology (UK) (CET) and CGLI between them agreed to sponsor a collaborative exercise in materials development: a group of tutors from colleges selected to pilot the course, together with the writer as examiner and part-designer, and an HMI was to design and produce support materials to help less experienced college tutors. The hoped-for advantages of the exercise were that:

(1) A concentration of expertise would result in good-quality materials.
(2) The development in parallel with the course itself would give constant feedback and keep the writers in touch with reality — most of the tutors confessed to some weaknesses in expertise so could authenticate their colleagues' efforts at help!
(3) The interlinks between the exercise and the concurrent development of the course and its assessment procedures would give possibilities of refinement in both directions — at the cost of having to try to avoid self-fulfilling prophecies!

	'Lesson' Level	'Course' Level	Institution Level
YEAR 1	Demonstrate, Prompt and release components Demonstrate & prompt synthesis	Demonstrate	
YEAR 2	Release synthesis through project	Prompt, in context of course project & student's institution	Demonstrate

NOTE: DEMONSTRATE is, typically, done by introduction to the topic or concept and by study of it.
PROMPT is, typically, done by guided practice.

Figure 2. *Demonstrate, Prompt, Release sequence for the course*

Some control over the whole process was expected by selecting colleges known to have adequate expertise to pilot the course in its first two years.

2. The Collaborative Workshops

The collaborative exercise was intended to start a little in advance of the first pilot courses, but various administrative and other constraints made the start of both almost simultaneous. As a stimulus, tutors from all colleges concerned were invited to a meeting bringing with them any support materials they already had and which they felt to be useful. These were then sorted, classified into one (or more) of the existing 'syllabus sections' defined by the CGLI course pamphlet, and offered for inspection to all present. It soon became plain:

(1) That the materials offered varied greatly both in quality and in degrees of individual idiosyncrasy.
(2) That some syllabus sections were apparently well provided for while others

— inevitably the most difficult ones — had little or no materials available. On examination even the apparently 'rich' sections often proved to contain much material that either duplicated other work or was rejected by a majority of those present.

It was therefore clear that much of the intended support material for tutors would have to be created virtually from scratch. Accordingly, it was agreed that the CET and CGLI would fund a series of weekend workshops specifically to develop such material. The actual pattern of work was decided largely by two factors:

(1) The nature of the 'team' available, consisting mainly of tutors who were heavily committed in their own colleges and who, because the pilot experiment was partly geographical, came from all parts of the country.

(2) The desire for formative development and evaluation in parallel with the course itself. If the materials could be written, tried out and revised under real conditions they were likely to be of more use.

The composition of the original team included tutors from colleges hoping to run the course, an HMI, a representative from the armed services, a member of CET staff, and the writer as general coordinator. The exact membership changed slightly as one or two colleges dropped out and others entered the scheme, but on average a working party of 12-14 members was available and the CGLI provided administrative support.

To quantify the operation, a 'weekend' normally consisted of total commitment by members from lunch-time on Friday to mid-afternoon on Sunday, working day and evening with a break of two to three hours for relaxation at some point. Various combinations of working were tried — plenary sessions, in fours, in threes, eventually in pairs. The plenary sessions, normally called at beginning and end of sessions — and at other times if a common problem arose — were extremely useful in sorting out such items as objectives and material format, but most of the work was done in groups. Groups of three and four proved of some value in the initial discursive stages, but for the final writing and revising, pair-groups appeared to be the most effective. During the first two years the course ran, six full weekends were arranged and reasonably effective material was produced for some two-thirds of the course syllabus. The stumbling block, as might be expected, turned out to be in the areas of assessment and evaluation which proved to be extremely intractable. Even the various 'authorities' consulted were often at variance and the sections of the syllabus as written proved to be difficult to interpret in practical terms. Thus of the total eight-weekend allocation to date, two and a half, plus a considerable amount of extra time by individuals, have been devoted to this area. In passing it may be said that the writer, who had the task of coordination, was surprised by the dedication which members of the team brought to the task and by the amount of extra work they were prepared to put in to complete allotted tasks, considering that they were paid only out-of-pocket expenses and gave up weekends of their own time. Partly this was no doubt because the material was needed for their own courses, partly it may have been that, as a matter of policy, they were housed in reasonable comfort and provided with separate working facilities.

3. The Materials

Initially the intention was that student learning materials should be the main product, but it became clear early on that a great deal of basic analysis would have to be undertaken before these could be produced on other than a random basis. The design panel clearly identified that the main priority was to give *tutors* support in areas where their own expertise might be defective, and the content and format of the materials was therefore evolved to fit this need.

The content and format were eventually determined by several criteria:

(1) They were to be tutor-support materials and therefore did not need to be self-instructional. They should not be too prescriptive but should basically provide 'back-up' knowledge of specific content areas with suggestions on how to handle work in which the tutor might not feel too confident.

(2) They were to be organized as flexibly as possible, so that parts could be extracted for use in other courses, and so that tutors could re-organize them to suit their own needs and methods of working (e.g. to extract all the course objectives and put them together).

(3) Ease of retrieval of individual items was to be an important factor since the whole corpus of material promised to reach something like 350-400 sheets of A4 paper (any 'visual' elements were included as black/white masters for copying, to simplify distribution).

The resulting format appeared as a series of 'tutor guides' each covering one or more parts of the syllabus (e.g. Aims & Objectives) so that syllabus sections could be extracted for use alone (transferability). Each guide, in turn, was divided into sections containing, respectively, background information for the tutor; hints on teaching and assessing; a collection of materials (handouts, etc.) not otherwise obtainable but felt to be useful. Figure 3 shows the eventual content breakdown of tutor guides.

1. Investigating Learning (methods and factors)
2. Student Characteristics
3. Curriculum
4. Constraints & Resources
5. Aims & Objectives
6. Teaching Techniques
7. Learning Situation Design
8. Structuring the Environment
9. Communicating Information
10. Acquiring Resources
11. Creating Materials
12. Managing Learning ⎫ combined
13. Managing Learning ⎭
14. Obtaining and Interpreting Data ⎫ exact pattern
to   and   ⎬ not finalised
18. Assessing and Evaluating   ⎭
19. Ways of Modifying Learning Situations
20. Producing Reports

Figure 3. *Content of tutor guides*

All guides were produced to a standard format, so that corresponding parts of each one could be collected to form a different bank of information (e.g. all objectives could be withdrawn for overall study) and then easily returned to their right place. Figure 4 shows the overall concept. To facilitate this, each individual item took the form of an information map with specific headings relating it to its place in the scheme.

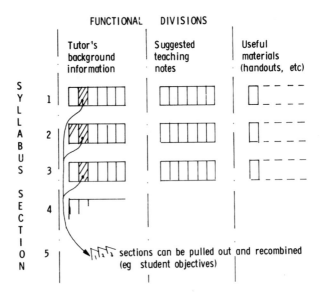

Figure 4. *Overall concept of tutor guide organization*

The content, in its turn, was divided up to cover the different aspects of information a tutor might need. Thus in the background information section he had a description of intended student goals, with amplifying notes where needed; a brief description of the required entry behaviour for a student; a set of key reading references he could use to improve his own knowledge; an annotated list of materials included in the guide. Figure 5 shows the content breakdown of a tutor guide.

The result, achieved only after a great deal of discussion and experiment, was a set of materials that could be extremely versatile if used as they were intended in the form of a resource bank from which a tutor could select. The major disadvantage was that, to achieve this flexibility, there was a certain amount of duplication of material; that (to allow for the needs of copying and rearrangement) materials could be printed only on one side of a sheet, thus substantially increasing the bulk; and that, if read from cover to cover as a textbook, the advantages of the format become liabilities.

4. Lessons to be Learnt

These can be divided roughly into 'operational' (i.e. the materials produced, and their problems), and 'administrative' (what we learnt about the advantages and disadvantages of running a cooperative of the type described above).

```
Pt 1:    Overview
         Student entry behaviour
         Student objectives              TUTOR
         Notes on objectives             INFORMATION
         Key references for tutor
         Annotated list of integral materials


Pt 2:    Overview
         Student objectives
         Assessing achievement of objectives    TEACHING
         Tutor activities (suggestions)         NOTES
         Student activities (suggestions)
         Notes on useful material


Pt 3:    Overview
         Materials as listed in the overview,
            all printed as masters on good      INTEGRAL
            quality A4 paper                     MATERIALS
```

Figure 5. *Layout of tutor guide*

In dealing with the materials themselves, the overall effectiveness can only be judged from use over a period of years, although a small-scale formative evaluation exercise is being undertaken at the present time. Initial reactions to the *format* are mixed since the method of presentation is novel to many people and its success may well depend on whether tutors want to treat the materials flexibly or stick to using them simply as an indivisible reference book: in the latter case the format might be intrusive and its potential advantages would be outweighed by its bulk. Initial results from use of the *information* contained in the guides indicates that they are a powerful tool — so powerful in fact that considerable care is clearly needed by anyone contemplating an exercise of this sort. Analysis of the first two years' course work and formal examination answers which are derived from course objectives shows clearly that the guidelines have proved effective: the problem is illustrated by the fact that, in the early stages, some inappropriate information was included and that this appeared, very well assimilated, in a wide range of students' work, before it was noticed and edited out. This problem is, of course, of particular importance if support materials are being produced for tutors in any course who are not wholly familiar with what they are doing — and who, hence, will tend to depend on the support provided.

In detail, four major problems arose:

(1) The advantages and disadvantages of the 'step-by-step' approach necessitated by working in parallel with on-going courses. It meant that syllabus sections were treated individually or in small groups rather than starting by examining and writing detailed goals for the course as a whole. This had a number of advantages, and in practice the major perceived disadvantage — that it was not possible to co-relate all objectives to each other until the materials were almost complete — does not seem to have

proved significant. Analysis of the required entry behaviour for each section has showed that the goals do interrelate in practice.

(2) The problems involved in defining general goals, rather than behavioural objectives, given that standards were established by course assessment. It was very interesting to note the difficulty found by experienced practitioners of educational technology in actually formulating clear goals rather than partly 'fuzzy' aims. They also had severe problems in agreeing commonly acceptable goals in several areas, with the inevitable resort to compromises which will not please some people.

(3) The problems caused by working to a predetermined — and apparently acceptable — syllabus, notwithstanding the fact that the course design panel had laboured for a long time over this and paid particular attention to the semantics. In detailed analysis, alas, both the breakdown of syllabus content and the semantics themselves proved defective when considered in the light of sectional objectives, entry behaviour and course teaching experience. It is also interesting that this analysis exposed a weakness common to many educational technology courses, the lack of help in the actual *implementation* process — the management of learning once all the designing, materials, production evaluation procedures, etc., have been done. The latter are comparatively easily taught discreet procedures. Synthesizing and using them is a much more difficult thing to teach and this was reflected in an initial lack of material. Fortunately, the omission was redeemed by the inclusion in the main course of parallel course work that made the student use the techniques in his own work — thus fulfilling the 'implement teaching/learning' criterion. It is, however, very difficult to put this concept into physical support materials since the reader is inevitably going to see 'implementation' as one section among many (i.e. Figure 6 (i)). Whereas the systems diagram is really more like that in Figure 6 (ii).

9	10	11	12	13	14	15	16	17	18

Figure 6 (i). *User's likely perception of module on 'Implementation' in a collection of tutor's guides*

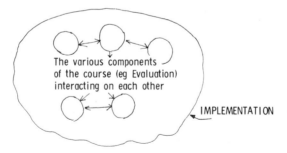

Figure 6 (ii). *Course designer's perception of the position of 'Implementation' in a total course concept*

(4) The design and adoption of a format proved to be a fairly protracted business and undoubtedly added considerably to the work in producing early sections of material since these had to be rewritten two or even three times. It is easy to say that one should start with a predetermined format. The team did so, but the need for modification became apparent early on and the writer suspects that the same would apply to similar exercises in other subject areas.

As regards the *administrative* lessons, these focus on the advantages and disadvantages of using a series of widely spaced workshops, bringing together widely scattered experts. The 'wide-spaced' workshop concept appears to work fairly well. Certainly two full days of concentrated work of this nature was as much as any of the group could take and, subjectively, it appears fairly certain that less would have been achieved, for example, in two consecutive weeks than in five groups of two days. It had the additional advantages of allowing uncompleted work to be finished at leisure; of allowing ideas and materials to be tried out before revision; and of allowing modifications to be incorporated as and when found necessary. Operationally it undoubtedly provided considerable advantages; ideas could be 'bounced' off other members of the group, criticism could be provided from a wide range of experience, and work on any one section could readily be related to that going on elsewhere. It was, however, more expensive than working locally in that extensive travelling and subsistence had to be covered, whereas local groups might have been able to work 'by the day'. In retrospect it was an interesting exercise and one which will hopefully produce support for a number of courses. Under such circumstances the advantages are likely to outweigh the cost and administrative complications, but only under such circumstances. What is clear is that to provide tested and finished materials a succession of concentrated bouts of work is needed. The odd occasional 'workshop' can do little more than provide a stimulus, and is likely to lead to materials which may be defective but whose defects may not be recognized owing to lack of trial and revision.

8. City and Guilds of London Institute Course No 731-3 Certificate in Educational Technology

J.E. Hills, *Coventry Technical College*

Abstract: Introducing a new course into further education is sometimes a rather traumatic experience. When the course is a Certificate in Educational Technology course, one can expect problems, stemming from ignorance of the concepts of educational technology. The time is right for all teachers to make an appraisal of their function. What better way than through a systematic approach.

With schools and colleges alike feeling the impact of the cutbacks in educational spending, it is perhaps fortunate that the academic session of 1975-76 saw the introduction on a pilot scheme basis of a new in-service development course for teachers. The course, the City and Guilds of London Institute Course No. 731-3 Certificate in Educational Technology, aims at producing teachers who are skilled in using a systematic approach to solving educational problems. This includes applying systematic techniques to the design and organization of a teaching/ learning situation so as to maximize the use of appropriate available resources. By doing so, it is expected that the teachers will be able to minimize the impact of the many constraints that the financial cutbacks have imposed, whether at classroom or institutional level. It is hoped that as a direct result of applying techniques taught on the course, teachers from all areas of the profession will become more effective managers of learning situations.

The pilot scheme as operated in the Department of Educational Technology at Coventry Technical College is outlined in the following paragraphs.

Why does an Institution decide to operate a Pilot Scheme?

The staff of the Department of Educational Technology had what it considered to be a varied range of experience in such areas as programmed learning, achievement testing, in-service and pre-service teacher training for further education, and staff development. It also ran a variety of short courses encompassing modern thinking in the organization and management of learning. Because of these types of courses being operated in the Department, the CGLI approached the College with a view to operating a pilot scheme for the new Educational Technology Certificate course. In fact, a member of the department, through his APLET connections was a member of the original City and Guilds Panel which drew up the syllabus for the course.

The department appeared to have two major assets necessary for operating a pilot scheme, namely the physical resources in terms of manpower and space, and an enthusiasm for the solving of educational problems through a systematic approach.

What Initial Preparation was required?

The syllabus for this course is a fairly broad one and from the outset it was recognized that high demands would be made of the tutors who were running pilot schemes. A natural approach to the preparation for any new course is to examine the syllabus and the objectives, and decide on any areas of overlap with existing or previously operated courses. This move was undertaken at Coventry and overlap areas with other courses were identified. However, due to the rather diverse nature of this new syllabus there were some quite significant areas which appeared to be almost entirely new, for example syllabus sections 1,2,8,11 and 19 (see Appendix A). Resource materials were already in existence for many areas of the syllabus, for example syllabus sections 5,6,10 and 15 (see Appendix A).

In anticipation of the problems of design and production of new resource materials for the course, a joint City and Guilds Council for Educational Technology Working Party was commissioned to produce objectives and learning materials for each syllabus section. However, the pilot scheme at this College was to commence in September 1975, almost three months before the working party had its first production meeting in December of 1975.

In the first term of the course at Coventry the syllabus sections covered were those with which the tutors were familiar and for which resource materials existed. Throughout the operation of the full two-year pilot scheme, and indeed to date, some of the areas of the syllabus are still lacking in adequate resource material.

How was the Course advertised?

The course is intended for practising teachers, full-time or part-time, from all areas of education. It is expected that course members have previously obtained an initial teaching qualification. There are approximately 3,500 teachers who come into this category in the City of Coventry.

It was anticipated, based on previous experience, that it would be desirable to make the course available to the West Midlands region within a 20 miles radius of Coventry.

Blanket advertising was planned to cover all educational establishments within this area including secondary, further and higher, industrial and commercial training centres, but excluding the primary sector for the time being. A market research exercise as such was not undertaken but extensive enquiries were made of the likely needs of various institutions and individuals. The results of this survey indicated a need for a course whose main aim was to improve the effectiveness of the classroom teacher.

Advertising literature was drafted, printed and distributed before the end of the Summer term of 1975. This timing is important because Autumn term timetables for schools are planned well before the summer break. The LEA 'free postbag' was used for distribution of the literature in Coventry; other establishments had the literature mailed direct to them. This system of flooding the area with advertising is not too expensive and it has been used by the department very successfully in the past. Literature was addressed to each institution head and to each named head of department or section within the institution. This method enables the publicity to have a better chance of reaching all teachers. Former students and current students on courses in the department who were eligible for the new course were also informed. Approximately 400 leaflets and application forms were sent out. It was not considered necessary to advertise in the national or local press.

What Response came from Advertising?

As a direct result of the advertising 41 completed application forms were returned and a further 15 telephone enquiries were received. Of the 41 applicants, six were ruled out on the grounds of being either not qualified or lacking sufficient experience to benefit from the course. The 30 or so remaining applications were analysed for such factors as subject taught, teaching area, post held, teaching qualifications and teaching experience. The general intention was to have a suitable mixture of types of teacher, and hopefully to have a balanced group of people who would mutually benefit from an exchange of ideas and methods, techniques and procedures. Each applicant was sent a copy of the syllabus, course aims and major objectives and notes for guidance. Fourteen applicants were selected to attend an informal interview prior to being invited to enrol for the course. All 14 appeared to be satisfactory potential course members and were duly enrolled.

In What Form was the Course offered?

The City and Guilds do not specify exactly how the course should be operated by colleges, but it is fairly obvious from the course structure how they intend it to run.

The course is in two parts, Part 1 and Part 2. Each part has a specified syllabus content, compulsory coursework, a recommended number of hours to be spent on each Part of the course, and an examination. It is intended that this course should follow a similar pattern to several other courses for teachers which are offered by the City and Guilds. At Coventry Technical College the course is offered on a part-time evening basis, one evening per week for two academic sessions for full completion of the course. Part 1 and Part 2 are completed in year 1 and year 2 respectively. A certificate is awarded for each Part on the successful completion of the compulsory coursework and the written examination. Attendance for one evening per week for one academic session is not expecting too much from practising teachers, knowing that many teachers have evening commitments with extra curricula activities. For many teachers evening study is the only time that the they could possibly attend a course, the likelihood of day release being quite remote.

What Factors encouraged Teachers to apply?

In all 14 cases, candidates when asked a specific question at the informal interview responded by indicating that they were looking for a course which was intended to help teachers to be more effective in the classroom. While not all of them understood the implications of the aims of the course as stated in the literature, they were looking for a course that would at least bring them up to date with current educational practice.

They all accepted that this course was:

(1) not a course on how to make and use visual aids,
(2) a course which would demand the application of the principles of educational technology in their own teaching,
(3) a genuine in-service course for teachers which would be recognized as such.

There was some confusion among candidates regarding the concept of educational technology. The definition of it as 'a systematic approach to the solving of learning problems' was given as being appropriate for the purposes of the course. Many of the course members, particularly those in secondary education, had never heard of the City and Guilds of London Institute.

What Staff were involved in the Operation of the Course?

Four full-time members of the Coventry Technical College staff taught on the pilot course. Each staff member had experience and expertise for use in certain syllabus areas. This experience and expertise had been gained over several years of operating other City and Guilds courses in education.

One member of staff specialized in the writing and use of educational aims and objectives. See syllabus section 5 (Appendix A). One specialized in the general area of achievement testing. See syllabus sections 14 to 18 (Appendix A). One specialized in information classification, storage and retrieval. See syllabus section 9 (Appendix A). The fourth lecturer and course tutor covered all the other aspects of the course including the following (a) advertising, (b) recruitment, (c) lecturing, (d) directing and monitoring the compulsory coursework and (e) marking the coursework on behalf of the City and Guilds.

Which Teaching and Learning Methods were used?

Before deciding on any specific teaching or learning methods a close examination was made of the following: the target population; the topic to be learned; relevance of topic to coursework; the resources which were available; and also the problems of adults learning. This last item, the problems of adults learning, was scrutinized particularly carefully. Teachers do not make the best students.

Throughout the course emphasis was placed on the development of teacher effectiveness and wherever possible, student participation was planned for in the selection of teaching and learning methods. Consequently the main methods used, relied less on tutor presentation and more on student activity. The teaching methods used included short lecture presentations, demonstrations and visual presentations.

Student activities were in the main based on group discussions, classroom and homework assignments and projects. There was little scope in the pilot scheme for much individualized resource-based learning.

All the course members had more than four years full-time teaching experience and several had had upwards of fifteen years full-time teaching experience. This range of experience coming from secondary, and further and higher education teachers is a very valuable asset for such a course.

Wherever possible course members were expected to relate the topic being taught to their own day-to-day classroom teaching. When it was appropriate, course members were referred to key references in textbooks. The number of textbook references were kept to a working minimum due to lack of availability or prohibitive price. There are no textbooks which cover the entire course and this puts the responsibility on the tutor to provide alternative materials. An unexpected benefit from the course has been the opportunity created for course members to meet colleagues from quite different sectors of education. The heterogeneous nature of the group at Coventry made for a lively and useful exchange of ideas on problems of teaching and classroom organization.

What caused some Students to drop out?

One of the main problems with a course of this kind is maintaining student numbers to provide a viable working group. The drop-out rate for this pilot scheme was higher than this department had experienced in the past with similar part-time

79

courses. The College has to specify a minimum viable course number and for this type of course the minimum number was ten. Six course members dropped out for a variety of reasons during the first year and one dropped out during the second year. Because of the nature of the pilot scheme special permission was obtained from the College authorities to continue into the second year with only eight course members enrolled (see Appendix B).

What Use was made of the Tutor Guide?

The author was an invited participant on the joint CGLI—CET working party for the production of objectives and learning materials. Several other working party members were also operating pilot schemes and it proved invaluable to all of them to be closely collaborating on the production of the Tutor Guide and operating pilot schemes at the same time. Unfortunately the pace of the production of the contents of the Guide was considerably slower than the pace of the course. This meant that much of the work on the Tutor Guide was done in retrospect, and consequently there was a tendency to look back at what had been taught and compare what had to be produced for the Tutor Guide. As far as the pilot scheme at Coventry was concerned the Guide provided little more by way of guidance than the objectives. But it must be pointed out that on subsequent courses the contents of the Tutor Guide have been invaluable.

The Tutor Guide contains much useful information for each syllabus section, such as learning objectives, key references, suggested activities and useful resource materials, e.g. extracts, handouts, paper copies of transparencies and student exercises. The Guide is intended to be used particularly in those areas of the syllabus in which the course tutors feel in need of support.

What Feedback became available from the Course?

One of the main reasons for operating courses on a pilot scheme basis is so that any areas of weakness can be isolated and corrective measures can be taken before the course is allowed into widespread use. The tutors operating the pilot schemes were encouraged to confer during the working party meetings and every opportunity for discussion of points arising from the pilot schemes was taken. The exchange of ideas and experiences between tutors proved to be of great value. Because many of the sections in the Tutor Guide were being designed 'after the event' it was not uncommon to find the tutor responsible for designing a syllabus section consulting in depth with those tutors who had already taught that section. Operating the pilot schemes alongside the design of the Tutor Guide also meant that new resource materials were being designed, used and evaluated and then in many cases, incorporated into the Guide. Each pilot course tutor made time to confer with colleagues on other aspects of the course, such as the design and production of the compulsory coursework items. Other areas of the course were discussed such as advertising and recruitment methods, and the general standards of student performance. Valuable feedback was made available from pilot course tutors to the examiner and the coursework assessor.

In some instances, but particularly at Coventry, time was allocated on the course for course members to express their views on all aspects of the course, including course content, teaching and learning methods, coursework and the style of the examination. Once again this was a useful source of feedback to the course operators and designers.

How was the Course monitored and evaluated?

On-going assignments throughout the first and second year of the course provided a satisfactory monitoring system. The assignments, whether compulsory or otherwise, provided feedback to the course tutor who in turn was asked to advise the course examiner and coursework assessor. Eventually, feedback via the monitoring system may result in changes in the syllabus and in the general operating of the course. One of Her Majesty's Inspectors visited at least three colleges including Coventry Technical College. He made a survey of the operating of the courses at first hand. Both the lecturing staff and course members were consulted by the Inspector regarding such items as staffing difficulties, student expectations and institutional needs.

One of the senior members of the working party was made responsible for evaluation of the pilot courses. Two questionnaires were designed by him, one for completion by the students and one by the pilot course tutor. These questionnaires were completed anonymously at the end of the first and second years of the course. Topics covered by the evaluation questionnaires included aspects of time allocation, teaching and learning methods, use of textbooks, assessment procedures and the examination.

What Progress has been made since the Pilot Schemes?

One of the main benefits of the operating of pilot schemes has been the production of the invaluable Tutor Guide. Pilot course tutors contributing to the design of the Guide have made significant modifications and changes in its content. Many of the syllabus sections were over endowed with higher level objectives which proved quite unrealistic in practice. Changes have been introduced in the light of experience. It is expected that further changes will be necessary when feedback is obtained from a wider field. An editing process was built into the initial design of the Guide, but provision will always exist for additions and modifications to be made.

The course at Coventry Technical College continues to be well supported. This current academic year 1977-78 has seen the introduction of infant and junior school teachers to the course and they are proving to be very useful course members.

The staff are now more experienced in operating this course, much additional resource material has been produced and specimen samples of compulsory coursework items have been prepared for future use. The current first-year group has 18 regular attenders, comprising polytechnic lecturers, secondary school teachers, infant and junior school teachers, further education lecturers and an industrial trainer. With the anticipated forthcoming increase in the in-service training of teachers at all levels the continued operation of the course at Coventry Technical College seems assured.

Appendix A

SYLLABUS

731-3 — EDUCATIONAL TECHNOLOGY

Note: the syllabus and objectives apply to both Part I and Part II. In Part I the techniques are to be studied in their application to small-scale situations, e.g. lessons, topics. In Part II they are to be studied in their application to larger scale situations, e.g. projects, courses, schemes of work.

INVESTIGATION OF LEARNING SITUATION
1 Methods of identifying, examining and correlating the factors which influence a learning situation.
2 Students: educational and environmental background, achievement levels, learning skills and abilities.
3 Curriculum and sources of curriculum: review of local curriculum in operation, internal and external curricula.
4 Constraints and resources including teachers, time, physical conditions, finance.

DESIGN OF LEARNING SYSTEM
5 Aims and objectives: classification, analysis and formulation of objectives and techniques for achieving them. The uses and limitations of objectives in defining an educational situation.
6 Identification of appropriate techniques of teaching: possible criteria for the selection of techniques, materials and hardware applicable to the results of the analysis; use of theoretical models and simulations as a means of investigating teaching situations.
7 Ways of applying systematic procedure to the design of learning situations.

PHYSICAL ORGANIZATION OF THE LEARNING SITUATION
8 Structuring of physical environment: deployment of materials and hardware.
9 Methods of signposting and labelling the learning environment. Communicating to students, including displays, procedural guides, and instructions in various media. Storage and retrieval systems for information, materials and equipment.

MATERIALS AND HARDWARE
10 Sources of existing materials and hardware: means of obtaining them.
11 Principles and problems of design and production of materials: worksheet, display and guideline materials; response structured materials on paper and in visual and audio-visual format. Simple games and simulations.

OPERATION OF THE LEARNING SYSTEM
12 Management of learning and teaching: student control and guidance. Feedback to students. Student records.
13 Monitoring: methods of assessment; continuous appraisal and adaptation to changing situations.

EVALUATION OF THE LEARNING SYSTEM
14 Purpose of evaluation as applied to individual pieces of learning and to the overall success of the learning situation.
15 Types of evaluation: their uses and limitations, observation of behaviour; types of testing; questionnaires.
16 Criteria for judging performance.
17 Basic techniques of obtaining and processing the data.

MODIFICATION OF THE LEARNING SYSTEM
18 Techniques of interpretation of processed data including pre- and post-situation comparison.

19 Methods of modification
  (a) to the evaluated learning system, e.g. detailed revision of techniques, material and hardware used, physical organization, administrative systems.
  (b) to curriculum externally imposed, e.g. ways of securing change.

REPORTING
20 Design, construction and presentation of oral and written reports to provide
  (a) a justification for a project to modify an existing situation, or to make an innovation
  (b) an account of an implemented project with a discussion of its findings and implications for future developments.

OBJECTIVES

731-3 — EDUCATIONAL TECHNOLOGY

See introductory note to the syllabus for application of objectives at Part I/Part II levels. At the end of a course, the course member should be able to carry out systematically the following tasks.

	Relevant Syllabus Sections
1 Define a teaching situation in terms of the students, the learning required and the means of assessing it.	1, 2, 3, 5
2 Identify the factors affecting that situation and say how these would affect what he wants to do; determine which can be altered and which cannot.	1, 2, 3, 4
3 Identify techniques, materials and equipment appropriate to the situation.	3, 4, 5, 6, 10
4 Prepare an initial design for a lesson, topic or course and provide a reasoned justification.	5, 6, 7, 11
5 Modify the lesson design taking into account material and equipment which is available, or which can be produced.	4, 6, 7, 8, 10, 11, 19
6 Produce simple items of learning material to meet specified requirements.	5, 6, 11, 12, 14
7 Set up, operate and monitor the learning system he has devised.	8, 9, 12
8 Use appropriate techniques to evaluate the effectiveness of (a) the individual items and techniques used (b) the overall success of the designed learning system.	13, 14, 15, 16, 17, 18
9 Produce a written report on the implementation of objectives 1 — 8, specifying to what extent he departed from the original design, detailing the results, with reasons for any modifications proposed and be prepared to explain these verbally.	20

#	Teaching area (Secondary/FE/HE/Other)	Technical qualifications	Teaching qualification	Male/female	Part 1 *		Part 2 *		Withdrawal reason
					Exam	C'Work	Exam	C'Work	
1	Secondary		Cert Ed	F					Illness
2	Other FE	SRN, RMN RNMS	C&G FETC, Adv FETC	M	F	F			
3	Secondary	HNC	Cert Ed (Technical)	M	P	P	C	C	
4	Other FE	SRN, SCM	Midwifery tutor's diploma	F	P	P	P	P	
5	Secondary	BA (Hons)	PGCE	M					Teaching duties
6	HE	BSc PhD FInstP	Short course only	M	P	P	D	C	
7	Other FE	Home Office exams	Police Instructor's Cert	M	P	P			Examination only
8	FE	MHCIMA	C&G FETC	M	P	P	C	P	
9	Secondary		Cert Ed	F					Personal reasons
10	Secondary	BSc (Hons)	Cert Ed	F	P	P	C	D	
11	Secondary	C&G FTC	Cert Ed	M	P	P	P	P	
12	Secondary	BA	Cert Ed	F					Teaching duties
13	Secondary		Cert Ed	F					Moved from area
14	Other FE	SRN, SCM, NDNC	C&G FETC	F	P	P			Family reasons

Note: *

Part 1
Exam Grades and   P= Pass   F= Fail
C'Work Grades   P= Pass   F= Fail

Part 2
Exam Grades and   P= Pass   C= Credit   D= Distinction
C'Work Grades   P= Pass   C= Credit   D= Distinction

Appendix B

9. Developing Strategies for In-Service Training in Educational Technology

C. Neville, *Council for Educational Technology, London*

Abstract: The paper explains the way in which new strategies for providing in-service training are developing. It discusses their suitability for training in educational technology, and attempts to characterize them in terms of their orientation towards successful conveying of knowledge, management of materials production skills, interaction skills or curriculum development.

Introduction

If there is one area of education where there appears to be universal agreement, between systems as diverse as those in the UK, France, Sweden and the communist bloc, it is that the quality of education provided will depend increasingly on the in-service training offered to teachers throughout their careers. Where there is little agreement, of course, is in what the aims and content of that training should be and how most effectively it might be undertaken.

It is not my intention in this paper to argue the case that training in educational technology should form a major part of in-service provision. The case I would make, for those who are interested, is available in a recent CET publication (Neville, 1977a). My intention here, assuming that some in-service training in educational technology will take place, is to explore a variety of common and novel strategies for achieving in-service training and to discuss their suitability for training in educational technology. The title I have chosen — 'Developing strategies of in-service training' — is deliberately ambiguous. Strategies of training have been 'developing', under the influence of the usual mixture of constraints, accident and insight, but I hope to show that it is possible to consider the various forms of training provision in a way which should allow us to 'develop' new patterns from old in a systematic way.

Problems of In-Service Training specific to Training in Educational Technology

Educational technology is, as its name implies, neither a science nor an art. Thus it does not comprise an accepted body of knowledge (not yet at least) nor an agreed epistemology. It is not a 'discipline' in the academic sense, yet it requires self-discipline for its successful practice. Educational technology is a state of mind, and one not readily acceptable to a large number of practising teachers who have been encouraged to see teaching as an art. It follows that much in-service training in educational technology must be aimed at achieving changes of attitude and of habits of thought. Yet it must do so often without the support of rigorously tested theory or incontrovertible demonstrations of the effectiveness of the educational technology approach. The teacher in training must be put in a position to convince himself of the worth of the approach, to himself and to his learners.

85

If educational technology argues for a systems approach to educational problem solving then it must concern itself with whole systems, not with 'bleeding chunks' of such systems — and with systems over which the teacher in training feels he stands a reasonable chance of maintaining control. It follows that successful courses are likely to be comprehensive in coverage and designed to accord closely with the situations in which trainees find themselves professionally.

The practice of educational technology is the application of an iterative process to educational situations. Many such situations require much time to carry through, particularly through two or more cycles of the iterative process. It follows that the trainee teacher attempting to apply educational technology will need long-term support.

No practising teacher makes decisions on how to teach without considering what is to be taught, and vice versa. It follows that courses in educational technology are likely to be less successful if they attempt to teach the application of the techniques of educational technology in a 'content free' way, or otherwise fail to recognize the interaction between methodology and the curriculum.

Recent Trends in In-Service Provision

The bold generalizations made above have to some extent been validated by recent developments in patterns of in-service provision and the successes and limitations which they display. I will describe a number of these approaches, with examples of the less familiar ones in practice, and attempt generally to characterize them. Throughout I shall use the terms 'trainer' for the person who provides training in educational technology, 'practitioner' for the person he trains and who is to practise the application of educational technology, and 'learner' for the subject on whom the practitioner practises, with, we hope, beneficial effects.

1. The Taught Course

DESCRIPTION. Practitioners, usually not more than one per school, or teaching institution, attend the centre for a course, of short duration but full-time, and are taught by one or more trainers.

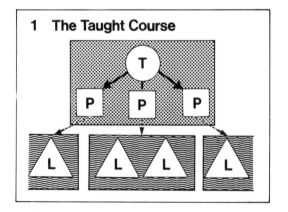

CHARACTERISTICS. The taught course is:

(1) Intensive, and can therefore be economical, but is limited in coverage and tends to have only short-term effects on return to practitioners' teaching institutions.

(2) It is demanding of both trainers' time and (particularly where travel is involved) practitioners' time.

(3) It tends to be trainer-centred (didactic rather than practical) and so is effective in communicating knowledge, but not skills and attitudes.

(4) It takes place out of the teaching institution, encouraging concentration without distraction, but it may need to be content non-specific to cope with participating practitioners from various disciplines and situations. This encourages a 'theoretical' approach to problem solving.

This form of in-service training is probably the most common. In fact there is every tendency to respond to a recognized training need by unthinkingly mounting a course. Courses may be an effective, and in some cases economic, way of conveying knowledge to a chosen group of practitioners, but such research as there is indicates that taught in-service courses seldom result in any long-term change in classroom practice. This is partly due to the pressures faced by the 'lone innovator' in any institution, but equally important is the difficulty that the practitioner has in converting the theory learnt on the course into a practical scheme of actions in the classroom. The trainer's support is withdrawn at the time when it is most needed.

Some form of continuing support can be provided by independent study materials.

2. Independent Study Materials

DESCRIPTION. The trainer 'packages' the course for study by individual practitioners, or institution-based groups of practitioners.

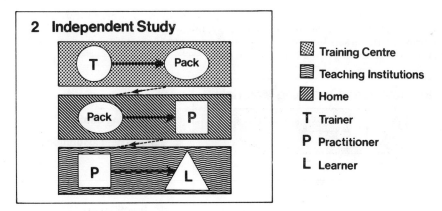

CHARACTERISTICS.

(1) The preparation of successful materials for independent study requires the trainer to have considerable skills in structuring and 'packaging' his course. It often requires a considerable change of perceived role for the trainer.

(2) Once materials are made they can be validated and improved, and possibly meet the needs of a larger number of practitioners than can be met by taught courses, etc.

(3) Learning materials are convenient to the practitioner, cheap to administer but expensive to produce.
(4) It is difficult to build into the materials all the forms of support and additional help that will be needed by practitioners from widely differing circumstances.
(5) Materials lend themselves to the provision of modular courses, providing practitioners with individualized programmes of study.
(6) Since materials may be used in the teaching institution they lend themselves to 'classroom focused' study, integrating practice with theory.

In practice, the provision of in-service training in educational technology extensively through the use of learning packages will depend on establishing the criteria for successful transfer of good materials from one situation to another. Presently, trainers tend to prefer their own packages, however inadequate, to recommending those produced by others, and practitioners find that such materials as are available have usually been produced for so specific a context that they are invalid in other circumstances.

CET is currently financing a study into these problems of transfer, using mainly the materials created at Jordanhill and Dundee Colleges of Education for their distance learning courses in educational technology.

Although independent study materials overcome a number of the (largely administrative) problems of the taught course, notably that of integrating theory with practice, they are probably still largely limited to the conveying of knowledge, rather than the acquisition of new skills and attitudes.

A strategy related to the provision of independent study material for the practitioner is the provision of 'good examplars' in the form of teaching materials for use by the practitioner or his learners.

2A. Provision of Teaching Materials

DESCRIPTION. The trainer prepares materials for use by the learner in learning something other than educational technology, but which in their construction and use provides the practitioner with a practical example of the application of educational technology to a learning situation.

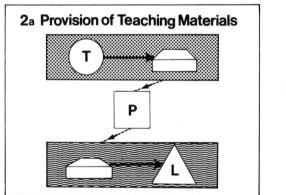

2a Provision of Teaching Materials

Training Centre
Teaching Institutions
Home
T Trainer
P Practitioner
L Learner

CHARACTERISTICS.

(1) The trainer must also have expertise in the subject of the materials, or work in collaboration with a subject expert.
(2) Extensive use requires widely accepted curricula.
(3) The materials must be 'teacher proof' to be convincing.
(4) The materials generally need to be accompanied by a guide to the practitioner encouraging him to separate the process by which the materials work from their content and context, and enabling him to apply the process, appropriately, to new content and new contexts.
(5) Can lead to successful teaching by the practitioner producing a positive attitude to the application of educational technology.

The main limitation to this strategy lies in ensuring that, despite the practitioner's efforts, the materials teach effectively. Extensive experience from, for example, Schools Council projects, from the Colleges of Education Learning Programmes Project (CELPP) (Neville, 1976) and from other national and regional schemes for the production of learning materials, indicates that practitioners who are not involved in the production of the materials tend to make ineffective use of them. Generally they try to impose different modes of use, thereby implying different attitudes to teaching and learning than those inherent in the materials.

CET has adopted a related strategy, which might not be as liable to this failing. The Council has encouraged three LEAs to attempt to provide a considerable proportion of the in-service training to teachers through packaged learning (Neville, 1977b). The in-service training is not itself in educational technology, and the Council is primarily concerned to identify those factors which support and those which militate against effective in-service provision this way, but it is hoped that the teachers who learn successfully from packaged materials will become interested in and able to apply the principles of effective package learning to the needs of their learners.

To overcome the difficulties experienced in endeavouring to train practitioners through good example, attempts have been made to involve the practitioner in the production of learning materials as a method of training in the principles of educational technology.

3. Workshops for Practitioners

DESCRIPTION. A group of practitioners, usually not more than one per teaching institution, meet at the centre and under the guidance of a trainer, jointly practice skills on problem solving.

CHARACTERISTICS.

(1) Workshops in centres share many of the advantages and disadvantages of taught courses, but they place greater emphasis on practical work, and encourage practitioners to learn from each other, as well as from the trainer.
(2) However, the 'problems' tackled still tend to be generalized rather than specific to the current circumstances of practitioners, and are often dealt with in a 'content free' way.

Workshops do appear to have more effect on classroom practice than taught courses, but, again because trainer support is usually not available after the workshop, and because the practitioner finds no mutual support from others in his institution, the effects are often short term. The next stage in developing effective in-service training strategies therefore would appear to be to carry out workshops for all, or a large number of the staff, of one institution. There are two problems here: not all of the staff may share a common curriculum, so that even in-institution workshops tend to be 'content free', and secondly there are not enough trainers available to carry out in-institution workshops on any scale.

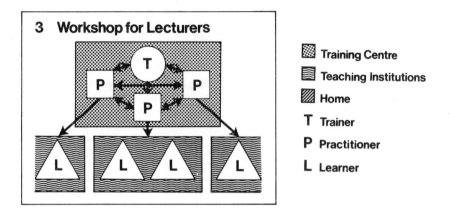

To overcome these problems CET has experimented with a modification of this strategy, the training of staff development tutors.

3A. Workshops for Staff Development Tutors

DESCRIPTION. Specially selected practitioners, designated 'staff development tutors' attend a workshop at the centre. There they receive training from the trainer in the skills of running institution-based workshops. On return to their institutions, they run workshops for colleagues, in groups with common concerns. The staff development tutors may be provided with workshop materials.

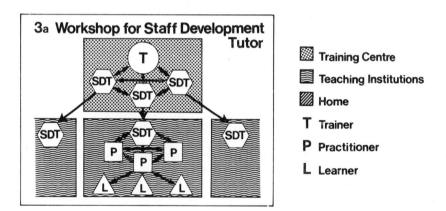

CHARACTERISTICS.

(1) These 'two-tier' workshops have the advantages of workshops for practitioners, namely active participation and ability to learn from other practitioners, together with the fact that the second level, in-institution workshops, can be institution, department or curriculum group-based as required.

(2) Practitioners on the second-level workshops have continuing support from both their colleagues and their staff development tutor. This support encourages the practitioners to adopt an experimental, empirical approach to improving learning, and may lead to improvement of skills, responsiveness to changing situations and possibly changing attitudes. However, the staff development tutor may not have continuing support from the trainer and may need periodic retraining.

The multiplier effect built into this strategy makes it particularly attractive when in-service training in one or more aspects of educational technology is widely and immediately needed. Such was the case when the Technician Education Council (TEC) required that lecturers in further education submit courses for validation in the form of behavioural objectives with related assessment procedures and teaching methods. CET responded by producing a two-part pack of materials — one to provide basic training in the required skills and a second to support staff development tutors in running workshops using the first part. The materials and their validation are described in the paper by Robert Ward (1978).

4. Supported On-the-Job Training

DESCRIPTION. Practitioners, working singly or in groups in their teaching institutions, are released at regular (say weekly) intervals to attend one-day workshops, supervised by a trainer. At these they produce learning materials or plan activities relevant to their perceived needs and for use in the teaching institution before the subsequent workshop. At this they discuss with the trainer and other practitioners the reactions to the materials or activities, with a view to improving their effectiveness. Between workshops the trainer is available to provide in-institution support to individual practitioners.

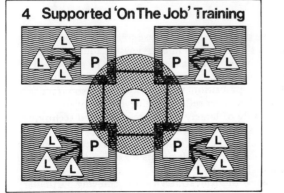

4 Supported 'On The Job' Training

▨ Training Centre
▤ Teaching Institutions
▨ Home
T Trainer
P Practitioner
L Learner

CHARACTERISTICS.

(1) Supported on-the job training requires a heavy commitment of trainers' time.

(2) It combines the advantages of being institution-focused with access to outside support. It therefore encourages the practitioner in the process of on-going curriculum development and evaluation, and provides opportunity for the improvement of diagnostic skills by the practitioner and consultancy skills by the trainer.

(3) It is supportive of the innovating practitioner.

This strategy is the one which was developed by the Primary Extension Programme (PEP). The aim of the programme is to train teachers in the systematic design of independent study materials to meet the needs of children at a disadvantage in the classroom. The starting point of that training is the problems which teachers can themselves identify as existing for individuals in their classroom. The key agent, the trainer, in this programme is the teacher/leader. Each local authority operating the programme appoints one or more teachers (or an adviser) to lead the group of teachers working on the scheme.

The teacher/leaders are experienced primary teachers who are then trained at a national level in such matters as group leadership, the diagnosis of learning problems and the characteristics of the low-level technologies. Each teacher/leader then returns to his or her local authority and organizes courses for other teachers. The courses normally last about 10 weeks, operating one day each week. To the course, teachers are asked to bring problems which they have with particular children in the classes. These are discussed by the group of teachers. Suggestions are made for ways in which learning materials might be used to overcome these problems, and how the equipment could be exploited to give the individual child the attention he or she needs. Then the teachers prepare the materials, learning the machine skills as they need them. The materials are tried by the teacher back in the classroom and later she reports back to the group on the practical difficulties and on the successful and unsuccessful aspects of the materials, which may then be modified.

The method adopted means that the practitioner develops the curriculum, the teaching and learning skills and the organizational system together in an integrated fashion. The PEP is described in the paper by Joyce Cooper (1978).

Conclusion

The strategies described above have developed in response to both recognition of the limitations of previous strategies and changes in our views of educational technology and of teachers' roles. The move from taught courses to supported on-the-job training certainly reflects a search for strategies which will not only bring about long-term improvements in the practitioners' behaviour but also effect changes in attitudes. However, the move also reflects the development of educational technology from the study of largely hardware-orientated techniques to the management of interactive systems for learning and teaching. Thirdly, it reflects the recognition that the teacher, the practitioner, is central to the process of innovation, and does not in practice separate decisions regarding the process of education and the content of education.

Our knowledge of the effectiveness of given strategies for achieving particular aims in in-service training in educational technology is very limited, and choices are often made more on the grounds of expediency than likely effectiveness. However, the development process that I have outlined would suggest that certain strategies could be said to have their inherent orientation. Some seem to have a potential for conveying knowledge efficiently to those who need it, but not to encourage the development of management skills — or positive attitudes. Others seem best fitted to teaching such skills as the production of learning materials but not to achieving the successful adoption of methods requiring personal interaction skills.

The, admittedly scanty, information available would suggest a first rough classification as in Figure 5, but we must await much research, such as that being

```
5  Strategy              Orientation


   1 Taught Course      ⎤
                        ⎥  Knowledge
   2 Independent Study  ⎦

   2a Teaching Materials    Management Skills

   3 Lecturer Workshops ⎤   Materials Skills

   3a S.D.T. Workshops  ⎥   Interaction Skills

   4 Supported 'On Job' ⎦   Curriculum development
```

undertaken by Bristol University on school-based, in-service training, before we can attempt the truly systematic design of in-service training programmes in educational technology.

References

Cooper, J. (1978) The Primary Extension Programme as a strategy for training in educational technology. APLET 1978, reproduced as Paper 12 in this volume.

Neville, C. (May 1976) The colleges of education learning programmes project — an experiment in long term innovation. *Programmed Learning and Educational Technology,* 13, 2.

Neville, C. (ed.) (1977a) *The Role of Educational Technology in Teacher Education.* Council for Educational Technology of the United Kingdom, London.

Neville, C. (1977b) *The Generation and Use of Learning Materials for the In-service Training of Teachers.* Council for Educational Technology of the United Kingdom, London.

Ward, R. (1978) Use of a two-tier training strategy in technical education. APLET paper 1978.

10. Use of a Two-Tier Training Strategy in Technical Education

R Ward, *Harrow College of Technology and Art*

Abstract: Lecturers in further education faced problems of adapting to new-style courses introduced by the Technician Education Council. The development and use of a two-stage training package is described, where workshops are used to train staff development tutors who would then run workshops for their colleagues.

Introduction

Educational change always calls for some redevelopment of the teachers who will make the new systems work. Although in Britain many agencies may contribute to in-service training, such provision is apt to be haphazard, merely available for those who want it once a need has become recognized. In this paper I will discuss one training project designed to help technical college lecturers cope with what they felt to be a major innovation. Also I shall consider whether the strategy might be applicable to other circumstances.

Background to the Project; the Training of Technicians

In the 1960s it became clear that there was a need to review the national pattern and organization of technician courses and examinations. These were being supervised by an uncoordinated tangle of boards which were having to adapt to developments in professional requirements, industrial training and higher education. The Secretary of State for Education and Science set up a committee to conduct the review and its report recommended a complete restructuring of course provision (Haslegrave, 1969). In future a new body, the Technician Education Council (TEC), should assume policy and planning responsibility for all technician courses in the fields of science, engineering and allied subjects. Similarly a new Business Education Council (BEC) should coordinate business training at a comparable level.

The first of these bodies to be set up was TEC, which, after widespread consultations, issued its *Policy Statement* in June, 1974. This introduced a new scheme in which students would follow programmes of study based on a modular system. The advantages promised to be greater coherence and flexibility. Future courses would be made up from a mixture of standard study units, provided by TEC itself, and units designed by colleges acting in conjunction with employers to meet specific industrial needs. At this stage there was but a comment that syllabuses might be couched in the form of a 'statement of learning objectives' but no hint that this would become prescriptive.

A year later the policy crystallized (TEC, 1975a). Standard units would be issued in a learning objective format derived from Bloom's taxonomy (Bloom, 1956). Colleges, in putting up their course programmes for validation, were allowed to submit them in a traditional descriptive format but only on an interim basis. A

Guidance Note was issued by the Council just ten months before the first wave of TEC courses was due to start (TEC, 1975*b*).

What were the problems for ordinary college lecturers? First of all, relatively few of them had gone through professional teacher training so although the approach was well established, and readily accessible in Open University course materials for example, it was unfamiliar. Lecturers were not only faced with translating learning objectives into teaching strategies, but they were being required to devise and to operate complex assessment schedules. To make matters worse many lecturers were sceptical of the need for change, apparent more at a managerial than a grass-roots level, particularly when they would be expected to bring in the new with very little time to spare from phasing out the old. Fortunately the TEC scheme would be introduced in stages over several years.

Design of a Training Package

In these circumstances the Council for Educational Technology (CET) was approached from various quarters with requests to provide suitable training. The most powerful constraint was that whatever form the training should take, it had to be available quickly to large numbers and not last very long. CET therefore commissioned Rodney Battey of the Middlesex Polytechnic Learning Systems Group to create an appropriate learning package.

The main factors which Battey found that he must take into consideration were as follows:

(1) The maximum training period in which it could be hoped to involve hard-pressed lecturers was 14 working hours, split between two consecutive weeks or on four half days.

(2) TEC policy called for *course team* procedures. Independent study packages would fall short in this essential.

(3) In training groups, the participants would most likely be drawn from varied disciplines.

(4) The package should be capable of ready duplication by whoever wanted to make use of it.

Since many colleges have now a person functioning as a professional tutor/training officer, it seemed possible that such people could attend workshop sessions based on the learning package, then take the materials away to use with their colleagues.

CET LEARNING PACKAGE
    ↓
TUTORS/TRAINERS   — first generation workshops
    ↓   (run by the package designer initially)
COLLEGE LECTURERS   — second generation workshops
                                      (run for local groups by those who had
                                      attended the first generation workshops)

In the light of these considerations, Battey produced his learning materials in the following form:

Part I. Workshop Package
— one copy to be given to each participant. It comprised four parts, each requiring roughly half a day's work in groups, together with exercises to be undertaken by individuals on return to their own institution. 82 pages overall.
Section A: writing objectives (three exercises)
Section B: devising teaching strategies from stated objectives (two exercises)
Section C: assessment scheme analysis (four exercises)

Section D: instruments of assessment (three exercises)

At the end of Section D was a workshop evaluation questionnaire to be completed anonymously by the participants and returned to the organizer.

Part II. Instructor's Manual

— issued as a prize to those graduating from the first generation workshops who intended to train others in their turn. It comprised:

(1) suggestions for a timetable and organization;
(2) detailed guidance on running the individual exercises;
(3) white master sheets of tables and diagrams suitable for reproduction either as class handouts or overhead projector transparencies, 26 in all;
(4) a questionnaire for return to CET by the organizer at the completion of every college workshop based on the package materials.

The principal method to be used in running a workshop was to provide information leading up to an exercise in which the group would break up into syndicates charged with the task of reporting back to a plenary session. The exercises were intended to model as closely as possible the tasks that lecturers would be involved in when handling TEC courses.

Implementation: How has the Package been used?

After pilot trials with the materials, Battey staged an initial round of three first generation workshops in the early months of 1977. Note that this was after some colleges had actually started to teach the lower level TEC courses. Altogether 97 people, drawn from 39 different colleges in the London area or the Midlands, participated in these workshops. On the whole they considered that the package was extremely well presented, relevant and potentially useful back in their own colleges.

Of course, the real test of the package came at the next stage, when people came to present workshops of their own. I was invited to evaluate the effectiveness of the learning package out in the field, largely because I was one of the few people to return a workshop questionnaire promptly — I knew I'd forget if I didn't! By the end of 1977 in spite of the apparent enthusiasm for the package and the continuing alarm at the difficulties raised by the TEC development, I had received information about only seven second generation workshops, involving a total of a further 132 lecturers. It was evident nevertheless that these had proved satisfactory. Five of the seven people who tackled the presentation of a workshop themselves were not engaged in regular in-service training and they did not admit to any more difficulty than the need for some solid homework beforehand. (Working with a partner seemed to help.)

What also emerged was that the package had circulated widely, functioning to some extent as a means of independent learning for those unable to attend a workshop. Two colleges of education (technical) had introduced modified forms of the package into their pre-service training programmes. A third, however, was severely critical of what they saw as an approach which appeared to be transmitting TEC dogma without subjecting it to scrutiny.

This leaves us with finding the reasons why so few people put the package to work. A few confessed to lacking the confidence to appear before colleagues in circumstances where they might be master neither of the content nor the appropriate teaching techniques. Then in several colleges the duplication of an 82-page document was no light matter. It is possible to run a workshop by issuing to participants only those papers essential to the exercises but this deprives lecturers of a useful source of reference afterwards. The most common excuse for failing to stage workshops was the difficulty of finding both the time to do it and the opportunity to bring staff together. With the shadow of educational thrift falling upon them, it would seem that all too few colleges could spare staff from on-going commitments. Somewhere the plan for change has neglected sufficient consideration of the means by which it should be brought about.

Though late on the scene, the Further Education Advisory Service in Liverpool have recently shown one way of rising to the situation. I was invited to run a first generation workshop at which all four of the local college vice-principals would be present. They were intending to give a joint training programme every support and insist that the resources be found. I suspect that elsewhere it has been left to the heads of department to take advantage of any training available and they have received only token backing at a higher management level.

Strengths and Limitations of the Learning Package

Criticism of the package materials had to be teased out from everybody by a variety of routes: questionnaires, reminders, letters asking for comment and a day conference for those who had presented workshops.

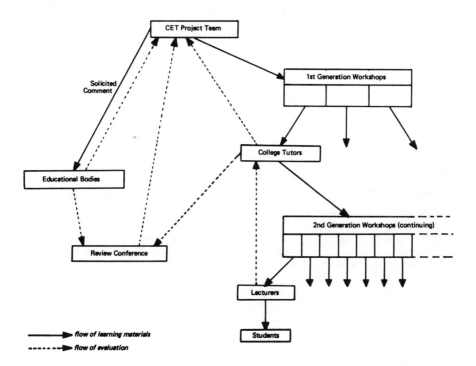

Figure 1. *Flow chart*

The great merit of the package was that it did represent a constructive attempt to cope with the demands being made by TEC. Participants in the workshops often found afterwards not that they had learned all the essential new skills but that they had *gained in confidence*. A 14-hour spell of study should be seen as no more than an introduction, giving lecturers enough substance to develop without overwhelming them.

Three weaknesses emerged from using the package in its original form. In an attempt to provide exercises sufficiently general to be tackled by any group of lecturers, there was a danger of losing relevance in some cases. Also there needed to be a wider range of alternative exercises available to meet the requirements of syndicate groups working in specific subject areas. Both of these points are being met by issuing supplementary material rather than redrafting the whole package. Another kind of limitation was that the material tended to fall between the requirements of the senior lecturer, wrestling in the coils of administration, and those of the bloke faced with the students. For the latter it is planned to produce a model scheme whereby learning objectives are translated into teaching strategies and methods of assessment. Finally, everyone complained that the workshop exercises were expecting them to tackle too much in too little time. In this, perhaps the workshops merely reflect the TEC developments.

Here, of course, we see one of the recurrent dilemmas of the education system. The Haslegrave Committee reported in 1969, and it may be another five years before the TEC schemes are fully implemented and years beyond that before they are evaluated. One reason for scepticisim in the staff room is that the older hands have known earlier schemes ripe for change barely after they had become established. We must find ways of enabling necessary innovations to occur smoothly and rapidly. In this case, the body initiating the new scheme, namely TEC, was not expected to be responsible for all the consequences of its actions. Although it must have been clear that substantial in-service training would be essential, the matter was left for such agencies as chose to take initiatives. The greatest shortcoming of the CET learning package is that it arrived on the scene a year too late for those who had to start off the first of the new courses. I would like to recommend strongly that in any future curriculum development mounted on this scale, the in-service training implications should be regarded as a vital part of the overall design and not merely allowed to emerge from the bushes once the carnival has begun.

Could the Two-tier Workshop Strategy be applied elsewhere?

One can see ways now in which news of the package could have been made to penetrate the further education system more effectively. Better information could have been issued and first generation workshops staged deliberately in all the main regions of the country. (The South-West is getting going now but the North-East has missed out apparently.) But in answering the above question the issue to be cleared is whether or not the second generation workshops do their job. My evidence is that they do. Provided that the package is put together scrupulously, there can be few schools or colleges without a member of staff who has the nerve, adequate background, and the enthusiasm to accept the challenge of using it.

For any organizations likely to consider a two-tier training strategy I suggest that they bear the following points in mind:

(1) Time scale: unless working on a local basis, allow a year for the package to make its way into the field.
(2) Package designer(s): a short secondment to do the job is essential.
(3) First generation workshops: ensure that these are staged throughout the region in need of the training. If there were, say, two package designers working jointly, then they could provide a reasonable coverage between them. (This would have been an advantage in the present instance.)

(4) Information: take pains to engage the support of school heads/college principals.

(5) Reprography: ensure either that a supply of the package materials is provided centrally at modest cost, or that local copying systems will not be expected to overreach themselves.

(6) Feedback: do not rely solely on people returning questionnaires, however simple.

Acknowledgements

I wish to record the pleasure it has been collaborating with Rodney Battey and with the staff of the Council for Educational Technology.

References

Battey, R. (1977) *Learning Package for TEC Unit Syllabus Writers' Workshop.* Council for Educational Technology, London.

Bloom, B. S. (1956 and subsequent revisions) *Taxonomy of Educational Objectives: the Classification of Educational Goals.* Longmans, London.

Haslegrave, H. L. (chairman) (1969) *Report of the Committee on Technician Courses and Examinations.* National Advisory Council on Education for Industry and Commerce, HMSO.

Technician Education Council (1974) *Policy Statement.* TEC, London.

Technician Education Council (1975a) *Circular No.6.* TEC, London.

Technician Education Council (1975b) *Guidance Note No. 1.* TEC, London.

11. Reflections on the Course Development Team Organization in the Technician Education Council External Student Pilot Project

J. Coffey, *Council for Educational Technology for the United Kingdom (CET), London*

Abstract: In addition to producing materials for the independent study of telecommunications, the Technician Education Council (TEC) external student pilot project has helped to identify various factors important in course development team organization. To illustrate the points raised the process of course development adopted by the team is described.

Introduction and Overview

In their June 1974 policy statement the Technician Education Council (TEC) recognized the need to provide facilities for external students. TEC wrote:

> There will no doubt continue to be many potential students seeking technician education who cannot attend college regularly and the Council intends to provide adequately for their needs (TEC 1974).

Accordingly, TEC set up a working party in June 1975 to examine the needs of external students and to make recommendations. In January 1976 this working party received proposals from the Post Office to develop a structured correspondence course. In May 1976 the working party accepted a modified form of these proposals and a course development team was formed under the chairmanship of Professor G. Holister (Open University). Work began in July 1976, and the learning package produced is at present undergoing trials in colleges prior to publication in 1978.

Team Membership

It would be nice to be able to say that team members were chosen because of their outstanding and known expertise in a subject or in teaching. In fact, things were more haphazard. We were chosen largely because, like Everest, we were there. The team comprised 14 members: five full-time staff from the Post Office team of correspondence course writers, seven staff for (on average) one half-day per week from colleges of technology and the Ministry of Defence (MOD), an educational technologist for three days a week from the Council for Educational Technology (CET), and the team chairman.

The writers for the most part worked in pairs, one member of each pair from the PO correspondence course team and one member from a college. (One section of the course, radar, was written by a college member in conjunction with an officer from MOD.) Each pair worked on one section of the course, the bulk of the writing being done by the PO member. The college member took much of the responsibility for developing assessment material and field-testing components of the package. This arrangement worked well because the college members have not been able to give sufficient time to the project to undertake much writing, while PO staff have not had ready access to students willing to try out the material.

Course Development

After a false start which involved the use of some of the Open University course development procedures, the team adopted a simple, four-stage model of development comprising analysis of objectives, design of appropriate learning materials, testing materials with students, and revision where necessary.

Analysis of Objectives

The TEC standard unit, *Telecommunications Systems 1*, like other TEC standard units, is published in the form of lists of behavioural statements which are intended to indicate clearly to someone familiar with the subject what a student is expected to learn. From such a list, a competent teacher should be able to work out exactly the content and the depth of treatment he should attempt in his teaching. That is the theory!

But the lists are produced by programme committees which represent industrial and academic interests; not all of these committees are equally skilful in their work. Similarly, the teachers who have to work with the objectives vary in their approach to interpretation. In many cases these teachers may be unfamiliar with the TEC method of presenting curriculum statements.

So it was with the course development team. A simple statement such as '. . . draw a block diagram of a commercial broadcast system showing relevant waveforms', was seen to have very many levels of interpretation. These varied from 'a block diagram consisting of two boxes labelled respectively transmitter and receiver', at one end of a spectrum, to 'a complex set of boxes including transducers, amplifiers, modulators, etc' at the other. TEC objectives, unfortunately, do not specify standards and consequently lack the information necessary to prevent such wide interpretation.

Another feature of the standard units is the use of three levels of statements to describe a course. Aims specify a context, the general objectives specify teaching goals, and specific objectives specify the means by which a student demonstrates his attainment of teaching goals. All three are important in defining a course programme. The order of these various statements in no way indicates a preferred sequence for teaching. Unfortunately, the temptation to treat the specific objectives as a conventional syllabus is very strong, and in the early stages of the project the writing teams tended to focus exclusively on their own sections, ignoring the context and accepting the sequence given in the unit.

It was obvious, after early attempts to develop ideas about content, that the team needed to examine the objectives in great detail. To ensure that the whole team shared a common language about objectives, a training workshop on the subject was undertaken in which the relationships between aims, general objectives and specific objectives were discussed. The team then examined each of the objectives in the *Telecommunications Systems 1* unit and agreed a team interpretation. An example of such a team interpretation is given below.

TEC objective:

States that primary radar is a measuring system which enables range, bearing and height to be assessed.

Team interpretations:

(1) Explains that range is the distance between two points on the earth's surface measured in statute miles (5,280 ft), nautical miles (6,080 ft) or kilometres (1,000 metres).

(2) Explains that a bearing is the angle (θ) (measured in degrees) subtended from some fixed reference direction, zero bearing OA, by the rotation of a straight line OB extending from the measuring device (O) through the point P whose bearing is being measured.

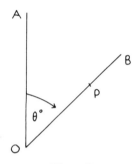

Figure 1

(3) Explains that height, measured in feet or metres, is the distance NH of an object (H) above a point (N) on the earth's surface as part of a radial line extending from the centre of the earth through the point N and the object H.

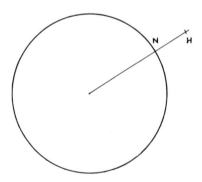

Figure 2

(4) Explains that primary radar is used on ships to assess the range and bearing to known landmarks, buoys and other ships.

(5) Explains that primary radar is used on aircraft to assess the range and bearing to known landmarks and assess the height above the earth's surface.

The interpretations were very detailed and in some cases, such as the example given, were close in sequence and content to the final form of the written material. But even these interpretations make assumptions about the conditions under which the student's mastery of the subject matter will be tested.

The important thing, from the team organization point of view, was to clarify the task in hand sufficiently well to ensure that individual writers knew what they were doing in relation to others.

Designing the Learning Materials

Analysis of objectives identified much of the content of the package, but writing should not have proceeded until a teaching strategy had been decided. Unfortunately a lot of time had been lost (or so it seemed to the participants) in the false start and the analysis of objectives. Writing teams were reluctant to spend more time, at this stage of the work, which seemed to postpone the writing task. The result, in spite of a study workshop on methods and media, was a return to established habits. That is, the initial drafts were extended pieces of technical prose with little thought for the student. Preliminary tests showed that those few students who were able to read through the material did not learn very much from it.

It was necessary therefore to reconsider the writing format to ensure that important aspects of teaching strategy should not be overlooked again. Though the points had been discussed in detail at team meetings and workshops, it was necessary to reassert that:

(1) Students needed to be involved in their own learning. They cannot be regarded as passive receptacles for knowledge.
(2) The powers of concentration of most students are limited and the material should be broken up into short segments.
(3) Variety of approach, including visual and aural material as well as the more usual print, would help increase motivation.
(4) The student would be greatly helped if he could measure his own progress in some way. Self-assessment material for this purpose should be included in the package at regular and frequent intervals and the student should be able to check his responses immediately.

To ensure that these principles were adopted by all the writers, a standard format for segments (components of the package representing about 20 minutes of study) was agreed. Each segment includes:

(1) A cover which states the topic to be studied as well as its context; i.e. it reminds the student of the previous topic and gives the title of the next. Also on the cover is a complete list of the material contained in the segment (the numbers of words, of pictures, of diagrams, of audio tapes, of self-assessment questions and of answers).
(2) A text on average less than 500 words, or an audio tape and transcript with study notes.
(3) Figures and diagrams.
(4) One or more self-assessment questions (SAQs) and, on a separate page, answers to these.

With so many hands contributing to one package it was inevitable that there would be a major editing problem. Not only did writers have individual styles, but they also had individual approaches to the use of non-print material. To exacerbate the problem the team did not include anyone with prior editorial experience. The team educational technologist, as someone not directly concerned with the writing and perceived by the team as being in the best position to review the whole package, undertook the task. But this was one area of the project which needed help, but could not get it in the time available.

Another problem was production. Team members were widely dispersed and had conflicting loyalties. This led to a management structure which left no one with overall authority to make necessary arrangements. Also, there was no stated budget. This resulted, to one's great surprise, in delays and confusion when the time came to print. The Post Office team coordinator, R. Odell, to his great credit, managed somehow to overcome all these difficulties and produce an attractive package.

The Teaching System

The package has been designed to fit into the 'exporting' and 'importing' college system described by Frank Fidgeon (1977). In this system a college having special expertise in a subject (the exporting college) produces distance learning materials for use by its own external students and by the students of other (importing) colleges. The importing colleges supply tutorial help, opportunities for practical work, and library facilities, but it is not regarded as essential that they have a high degree of expertise in the subject of the distance learning package. An important requirement in this system is a tutor guide for tutors in importing colleges.

Students work for most of the time independently away from a college but attend tutorials during the course. This college attendance is seen as essential in most cases though the idea has not been critically examined.

Testing the Package and the Teaching System

I use the word testing rather than evaluation or validation to suggest that the procedures we adopted were not highly sophisticated. Given the constraints it was never reasonable to expect to be able to state an exact performance criterion for the course. What we decided to do, therefore, was find, remove and replace with something better those parts of the course which went badly wrong, ensure that most students would not drop out, and ensure that most students would pass a test comparable to conventional tests.

The types of testing procedure we adopted were as follows:

(1) Accuracy of content was reviewed by other teachers and subject experts.
(2) Gross errors in presentation were removed by trying some of the early production material on small groups of volunteer students from colleges of further education.
(3) A 'real-life' test of the materials is now taking place in 15 colleges with 135 students. 12 of these colleges were not involved in the materials development phase and can be regarded for the test as importing colleges. Evidence for revision of the course materials will be drawn from pre-test/ post-test differences and feedback questionnaires (Henderson and Nathenson, 1976).
(4) Tutors in importing and exporting colleges comment on the course from the administrative point of view. They will also log student difficulties and special features of their own tutorials.

Preliminary results from these tests show that students are highly motivated and for the most part successful. (Hawthorn effect?) Where difficulties have been encountered there has been a marked reluctance to contact tutors and ask for help. The reasons for this are not yet clear and it is too early to say whether this will continue to be a feature of their approach to the course.

Tutors, on the other hand, have been concerned about the lack of contact with students and have said that the tutor guide, comprehensive though it is, has not prepared them properly for their task. They have asked for, and agreed to contribute, case studies of tutorials showing the variety of approach which can be adopted. The original tutor guide went no further than listing the essential elements of a tutorial. It has to be remembered, however, that many of the apparent problems derive from novelty and anxiety rather than inherent difficulty. It is not easy to decide what sort of things will be needed in tutor guides if an exporting/importing system is widely adopted.

The materials and the tutor support system are now beginning to be revised for an Autumn 1978 publication.

Discussion

I have given these details of the development of the package in an attempt to identify important features of team organization. Other teams may well be established by colleges or industry and face similar problems. They will probably be, as we were, under pressure to produce something quickly. Our experience suggests a clear analysis of the task is important before embarking on it. This may seem very obvious, but one wonders how many organizations would do this in more than general terms. At least two things are necessary: a clear and complete list of the skills required for package production before selecting team members, and a recognition that there will be probably a need for some skills training.

Job Description

There are various approaches to formation of working groups. The one currently in fashion in education is one based on a caricature of management. . . first we have a leader, then two under him, etc. I believe this approach is mistaken because it presumes that the given task is already well understood. It may be in some cases, but there is too little published experience to assume that this is true for course development.

An approach to team formation which I think should be tried is one based on analysis of course development skills. This would have three stages:

(1) Identify the appropriate course development skills.
(2) Select personnel to ensure a good balance of these skills.
(3) Develop an appropriate team management structure to suit the particular balance of team personnel and the task.

During the telecommunications course development project the need for a number of key skills emerged. While it is probably true that future teams will identify other important skills, the bulk of skills required will be common to all engaged in the systematic development of learning materials. I believe the following skills to be most important:

(1) *Working with objectives* — Identification of teaching goals and specific outcomes are essential if the team members are required to communicate with precision about their teaching intentions. Skill is therefore required *to relate* aims and objectives, *to write* objectives, *to design* appropriate assessment material, *to order* implied teaching points in a suitable study sequence, and *to evaluate* learning materials.
(2) *Being a wordsmith* — Skill is required *to write* and *edit* clearly, concisely and to a set of objectives.

105

(3) *Media and teaching method skills* — What media and methods should be used in a given situation? This requires knowledge of what is available, what is possible, and what is appropriate. *Knowledge* of production processes is also essential.

(4) *Subject expertise* — A *sine qua non!*

(5) *Management skills* — A team needs clear leadership, good internal communications and good relations with outside bodies.

This list needs further development, particularly in the area of production skills, but demonstrates that there is more to package production than subject expertise. It will not always be possible when forming course development teams to match personnel to all the skills involved, and there will be a need for on-the-job training or advice from external sources. The skills listed in (1) and (2) above are essential for all team members but they are also the skills at present in short supply in many training establishments. While it may not be reasonable to attempt training in the skills of 'wordsmithing' in the sort of time-scale which might be available to a project, training in (1) is certainly possible.

Use of Consultants

The telecommunications project made use of outside consultants and the team educational technologist to provide appropriate training. Good consultants not only have knowledge and expertise in a field of endeavour but they also recognize that it is essential to understand the problems of a client before attempting to find solutions. Above all they recognize that the solutions must be workable for the client. The project was very fortunate in the choice of its consultants, all of whom were very sensitive to the problems the team faced at different times, and very constructive and positive in their advice. It may not be possible for all teams to have a resident educational technologist but consultants can be used for advice, skills training, and problem solving.

The real problem for teams is recognizing the need for skills. It is to be hoped that, as experience is gained in this type of course development project, information will be published on which future teams can build.

A Note on Costs

There is no doubt that the telecommunications project has been very expensive in real terms and that the same work could have been done in less time by fewer people if problems of membership and organization had been more carefully considered in the early stages. But it must be recognized that team members have gained considerably in experience — they have in fact been involved in a process of in-service training, albeit incidental to the main purpose of the project. In addition, something has been learned about team organization which may help future teams to be more efficient. It is too early to demand very high standards of cost effectiveness unless they take into account these spin-offs.

Summary

I have described briefly the development of a learning package for the TEC *Telecommunications Systems 1* project and tried to identify some of the mistakes that were made in the team's establishment and work. The team was not a high-powered group of professional course designers backed by a sophisticated production unit. It was probably typical of many teams that will be formed in colleges of further education and industrial concerns in the future. Its experience is therefore of value to such teams and managers who set them up. Lest I be considered too negative, and in fairness to my colleagues on the course team, I must add that in the later stages of the project, work was efficiently done. The package is proving to be a success with students.

References

Fidgeon, F. (1977) TEC's proposals for the external student. In a symposium on *Independent Learning Systems for Technicians.* Society of Electronic and Radio Technicians, London.

Henderson, E. S. and Nathenson, M. B. (1976) Development testing, an empirical approach to course improvement. *PLET,* 13, 4. Kogan Page, London.

Technician Education Council (1974) *Policy Statement.* TEC, London.

12. The Primary Extension Programme as a Strategy for Training in Educational Technology

J. Cooper, *St Christopher Infants School, Coventry*

Abstract: The Primary Extension Programme aims to encourage teachers of children between four and eight, to develop learning materials for use by the children, singly or in groups, using simple audiovisual equipment. Training is provided in the diagnosis of learning difficulties, the design and production of materials to resolve these, and in classroom management.

The primary extension programme (PEP) was introduced in 1973 to meet the needs of the young disadvantaged child by creating special teacher-designed material for use with low-level technology — a term used to describe simple machines like Language Masters, cassette tape recorders, the Audio Page and the camera, which can be operated by children and are easily portable. The term 'disadvantaged' can be applied to any child who, as a member of a class, is in need of particular and individual attention because of some learning difficulty, which can be social, emotional or intellectual. PEP recognized the need to provide the necessary training for teachers wishing to use these materials and methods and suggested to local authorities that weekly workshop courses extending over a period of one term would be the most satisfactory means of training.

With funding from the Bernard Van Leer Foundation and the Council for Educational Technology, ten widely dispersed local authorities were invited to make a three-year commitment to PEP and provide a training base in their teachers' centres under the supervision of newly appointed teacher/leaders. The following areas were chosen for their varied locations and contrasting problems:

Devon — rural county
Southampton — large seaport in the south
Croydon — outer London residential area
ILEA — densely populated inner city area
Coventry — Midlands industrial city
Nottinghamshire — Midlands industrial county
Leeds — North-eastern industrial city
Cleveland — Northern industrial port
Lancashire - Northern manufacturing district
Aberdeenshire — remote rural fishing villages

The pattern of the 10-week courses varied slightly to meet local needs, but followed a general pattern. In the discussion with the teacher/leader and other members of the course, teachers identified a specific curriculum or organizational problem concerning their own children, and, with help, devised a programme of work, using one of the child-operated machines, and linking visual and aural experience. During the following week the particular children used this material and the teachers evaluated its success at the next course meeting. Amendments, developments or progressions were effected during the workshop period and the reappraised programmes used in school again the following week.

The selection of teachers to attend these courses varied from one authority to another. Devon and Aberdeenshire, because of their many scattered rural two-teacher schools, considered it advantageous to 'in-service' as many schools as possible. Two teacher/leaders were appointed in each of these counties and courses were held in several centres, with teachers travelling many miles each week to attend. In contrast to this organization, Cleveland adopted a policy of 'saturation' in selected EPA schools, with the express intention of training every member of staff and supplying sufficient hardware to ensure the smooth running of this resource-based learning.

In Lancashire, headteachers of schools in designated towns were invited to an initial PEP meeting when the aims and objectives of the programme were explained in detail, and an exhibition of material shown. Those headteachers who wished to take advantage of PEP training for their staff were asked to release two teachers each week to attend for 10 consecutive weeks on any two of the 'three-term' courses which the authority would provide.

In ILEA, the teacher/leader organized school-based courses, where all the members of the staff were trained at fortnightly meetings within the school. These schools then acted as consultative schools for teachers in the neighbourhood and always provided a display of teachers' and children's work.

Several areas — Croydon, Coventry and Nottinghamshire — issued open invitations to schools, and 12-15 teachers were selected by advisers and teacher/leaders. Each term, courses were oversubscribed and teachers who were not accepted for the first term were given priority for the subsequent courses. Since PEP was first introduced in 1973 many hundreds of teachers have benefited from these intensive workshop courses.

At the outset of the programme, it was considered important that a training pack of software would be created from materials which had been piloted and thoroughly tested in schools in three widely separated areas of the country. These materials were designated 'Starter Packs' and were distributed to the teacher/leader in each of the 10 original areas. Their main purpose was to get people moving in the general direction of PEP curriculum change, but to leave the particular choice of route to them. It was obvious that it would be an impossible task to supply a standard pack of materials or a standard policy for training which would suit everyone, as the very nature of the geographical spread of the areas chosen meant that there would be localized demands, differing approaches, and different problems and expectations. Consequently, localities were left free to tackle the organizational implications which suited them best, and teachers' attitudes and relationships could take on an individual character within the broad framework of the PEP.

As successful material was replicated and exchanged between teachers, not only in their particular town, but between teachers in all areas of the UK who are involved in mediated learning, a large bank of software was quickly accumulated. This could be made use of in its original form, or it might require alteration to suit local conditions, or the needs of individual children. Examples of materials devised for a variety of skills are now included in the PEP Pattern Packs for Training which can be obtained from Educational Productions Ltd, East Ardsley, Wakefield. These Pattern Packs, intended for use by children aged three to eight years, give ideas to students and teachers for the development of their own requirements. The basic material has been well tested and evaluated so it can be used with confidence, but its presentation is deliberately simple to encourage teachers to produce their own material of a superior quality.

The original material which was devised for the pilot scheme was also thoroughly tested and evaluated and one example of this is given below: A class of 40 five-year olds was selected in a Midlands school and the children were carefully divided into two equal groups, by an educational psychologist and the class teacher. Twenty children formed the control group and 20 the experimental group. The school was asked to prepare a reading programme based on the television series 'The Magic Roundabout', using support material created for use on a Language Master machine.

Software was prepared so that the group using the machine could work unaided for quite long periods. At this stage, only one track of the tape was used. It was quickly realized that a booth in the classroom would help to lessen the noise, and earphones were also incorporated; the additional equipment in the classroom was quickly accepted by all the children and those in the experimental group used the Language Master during some part of each day.

A graded series of 20 small reading books had been prepared and when the children reached Book 7, a second track was introduced, giving an activity which would test their comprehension, e.g. 'On this card is written "Dougal is going to write a book".' This sentence appears on the master track of the tape, and on the student track is recorded 'You write a book about yourself'. Here is another card which says 'Do you know who has eaten the leaves? said Florence', and on the student track 'Draw a picture of the animal who has eaten the leaves'. All these activities helped the child's understanding of his reading and released the teacher for other forms of classroom teaching. The teacher could quickly check each child's progress at the end of the day because each taped card had the appropriate activity written on the reverse. As each child completed a book, he took it along to the teacher and read aloud from beginning to end.

The children's reading progress was tested every six months, by the educational psychologist, using the Burt Reading Test. At the end of the two years there was significantly little difference between the control and experimental groups in Word Recognition Age, but the teacher, with 40 children in her class, was convinced that she could not have given them *all* the necessary attention to attain the very high standard which had then been achieved. The chronological ages of the 40 children ranged from 6.6 to 7.2 and the last assessment on the Burt Test ranged from 6.0 to 10.2 giving an excellent picture over a full range of ability.

When the Language Master had been in use two terms, it became obvious that it had potential in other fields connected with the teaching of reading. Some of the older Infants, whose reading progress was slow, found great difficulty in mathematics, because the assignment cards were too difficult for them to read. They consequently presumed that they were failures at mathematics. It was decided to put a selection of assignments on to taped cards.

Groups of six children worked with the Language Master in a mathematical environment for an hour each day and the resultant improvement in maths was obvious. These children were a success. As you know, success breeds success and before long their newly found confidence was making itself evident in their reading and writing skills. The length of their periods of concentration improved and their general enthusiasm for work was remarkable.

Several aspects of Infant maths were covered — both tracks were used and the questions were either open-ended or self-corrective. Here are two examples of assignments:

1st track   Make a ball of plasticine and put it on the scales.
2nd track   How many shells will balance the plasticine?

1st track   Draw a long straight line with chalk in the playground. Measure it in strides.
2nd track   Write 'My line is . . . strides long'.

Without the aid of the Language Master, the slow-learning child would have needed to ask the teacher several times what was required of him. With this aid, a group of children could be self-employed outside the classroom, while the teacher concentrated on teaching particular skills to the rest of the class.

The ideas and materials which were so extensively tested and evaluated during this early period were eventually incorporated into the 'Starter Packs' which were distributed to the original areas.

It should be stressed from the outset that PEP, through its materials, has aimed to try to create a climate whereby teachers bring about *their own* curriculum development, rather than a curriculum development dependent upon PEP materials. Achievement of curriculum change depends most upon the enlargement of the teacher's understanding and judgement of children's needs and the responsibility for meeting these requirements.

Since the beginning of the programme, several other local authorities have become associated with PEP and have developed a different pattern of training. Teachers' centre courses have been organized by an adviser or the centre warden and have been linked with consultative schools which would act as 'shop windows' for PEP activities and also provide some in-depth study into particular aspects of the curriculum. The schools chosen are well equipped with hardware, with staff fully committed to individualized learning linked with low-level technology, and generously staffed to allow for preparation and discussion time.

Several examples of specific subject study by certain areas are as follows:

Coventry PEP headteachers have been determining at which stage in the young child's development of mathematical thinking, human intervention is essential, and at which stage, teacher-prepared software for machines can more effectively be used. A handbook of examples of intervention in the early mathematics scheme has been circulated to all the primary schools in the city and interested teachers can see examples of children's work at any of the consultative schools.

In ILEA, one primary school was involved in the study of the effects of art on the rest of the curriculum. The teacher/leader has introduced pattern, symmetry and line drawing linked with maths, using the Audio Page machines, tape recorders and Language Masters; imaginative painting has been linked with taped stories and poetry; and craft modelling has been introduced on tape and Audio Page. Teachers with little or no artistic ability have found the programme extremely helpful and the stimulation they have provided for the children has produced lively original art and given some impetus to language and mathematical development.

Whereas in 1972 very few primary schools were equipped with the simple devices of low-level technology, it has now been established that hardware, in the form of cassette tape recorders, Language Master machines, cameras, projectors, viewers and Audio Page machines, are either in infrequent use in many classrooms, or are gathering dust on the shelves of stock rooms. Consequently, a large part of the financial outlay, for either individual schools or the local authorities, has already been made, and the importance of the daily use of the equipment has become more imperative. If teachers are to be made more aware of the rate and quality of their intervention in the curriculum, they need to learn which sections of the curriculum can only be effectively taught by a teacher, which sections require an adult and a machine, and which can give the child the necessary 'learning' experience with a machine alone.

Although the largest financial outlay on PEP courses is the salary of the teacher/ leader, it has been realized that the success of this type of workshop/discussion approach can only be successful with the appointment of a seconded teacher/ adviser to organize the courses and give 'follow-up' support to teachers in the classroom. Experience has shown that the title of 'teacher/leader' has been a

Figs. 1 & 2 are important awareness and familiarisation stages for teachers, so that they can attend courses at least aware of the basic operating instructions of these machines, and are then competent to begin the exciting work of diagnosing their problems and preparing solutions, not just tool training.

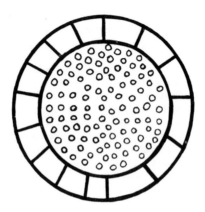

Figure 1. *PEP Awareness — 100 teachers visit exhibition of PEP materials*

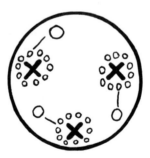

Figure 2. *FAMILIARIZATION — Hardware Potential — one-day workshop courses for 30 teachers on use of specific machines*

Figs. 3 & 4 show the advantages of the discussion sessions for exchange of ideas on curriculum development, the problems of "disadvantaged" children within the normal school, classroom organisation, and of the workshop course for encouraging corporate problem solving in a practical context.

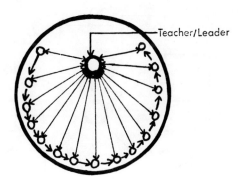

Figure 3. *PEP In-service Course (10 sessions) — discussion of problems in class management, curriculum and organization. (15 teachers)*

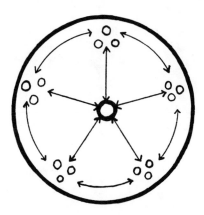

Figure 4. *Workshop Situation (15 teachers — 1 teacher/leader)*

Figs. 5 & 6 illustrate the importance of the 'follow-up' support given
by the Teacher Leader at the school of every course member. Classroom
organisation can often be transformed by an unbiased suggestion from a
visiting leader. Head Teachers welcome the opportunity to discuss the
impact which these new developments are having on the school in general,
and how best to disseminate PEP ideas among other members of staff,
using the trained teacher as a 'leader' within the school. Some areas have
found that concentrating on one machine only (e.g. tape recorder) has more
immediate impact with promotion of ideas to the whole staff.

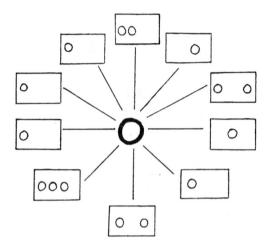

Figure 5. *Teacher/leader Support and Follow-up in Schools. (Number of schools involved is dependent on local patterns of in-service training)*

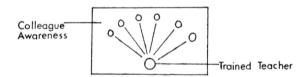

Figure 6. *Mini-PEP within each school*

particularly wise one — the leader 'leads' rather than 'teaches' and encourages the development of each teacher's ideas. Teachers often find difficulty in communicating with their peers, so consequently the policy of small group discussions with the teacher/leader and other members of the course has proved particularly successful.

The pattern of teacher/leader, workshop/discussion-type PEP course is shown in Figures 1-6. Figures 1 and 2 are important awareness and familiarization stages for teachers, so that they can attend courses at least aware of the basic operating instructions of these machines, and are then competent to begin the exciting work of diagnosing their problems and preparing solutions, not just tool training. Figures 3 and 4 show the advantages of the discussion sessions for exchange of ideas on curriculum development, the problems of 'disadvantaged' children within the normal school, classroom organization, and of the workshop course for encouraging corporate problem solving in a practical context. Figures 5 and 6 illustrate the importance of the 'follow-up' support given by the teacher/leader at the school of every course member. Classroom organization can often be transformed by an unbiased suggestion from a visiting leader. Head teachers welcome the opportunity to discuss the impact which these new developments are having on the school in general, and how best to disseminate PEP ideas among other members of staff, using the trained teacher as a 'leader' within the school. Some areas have found that concentrating on one machine only (e.g. tape recorder) has more immediate impact with promotion of ideas to the whole staff.

PEP does not expect to produce revolutionary changes overnight, but we are convinced we have been able to do three things:

(1) Show how teacher-prepared material for use with simple machines can help children to help themselves with their learning.
(2) That through children using these devices, we can help adults rethink their role in education.
(3) That through adults, and particularly teachers, rethinking their role in education, more appropriate curricula arise.

Chapter 3:
Commercial and Industrial Applications

The reader may recollect that we have already made mention of the ETIC '78 Organizing Committee's desire to encourage the participation of industry in the conference.

As the dust of ETIC '78 settled on the Welsh hillsides, your editors launched into the task of reading in detail and discussing the many papers presented at the conference in order to assemble this volume. The compilation of this chapter resulted from such discussion (as indeed did the others), but in the above connection it gave us particular pleasure to be able to present the following collection of material which describes educational technology so truly 'at work'.

Mr Moffatt (13), Managing Director of Malt Keyboard Ltd, Oxford, opens the chapter with a very readable and succinct account of the development, implementation and evaluation of a 'stand-alone' programmed audiovisual system, designed for 'Linotype' keyboard operators retraining in the printing industries. His evaluation of the scheme should be of particular interest to other industries with similar retraining problems.

Dr Tyrrell (14) follows with an equally interesting history of the development of packaged learning materials for use in the accountancy profession. The materials, which are designed for use by inexperienced tutors whenever and wherever a need for instruction arises, have been developed over a five-year period since 1972. A mixed-media approach to package design has been adopted; the first packages based solely on print-support materials and OHP slides appearing in 1977.

Still on the theme of professional training, Mr Mason (15) makes a strenuous case for the application of programmed learning techniques to the field of management development — 'The exercise of good management in the teaching of management.'

Mr Westley (16) presents a well-illustrated 'no-nonsense' account of a systems approach to the training of operatives and technicians in the British footwear industry. A mixture of programmed learning strategies are employed to solve the various training problems encountered — the effective use of the learner-centred 'Guided Discovery' approach being particularly well exemplified. The reader who is searching for an effective strategy to deal with technician/operative training problems, particularly where numbers are small and scattered and training is required at variable times, is advised to refer to this paper.

Similar problems to those found above are encountered in agriculture in Britain and perhaps worldwide. Mr Bulford et al. (17) of the Agricultural Training Board (ATB) describe the rapidly changing world of agriculture in the UK and highlight the need for a responsive system of training and retraining for the industry's labour force. The authors go on to describe the development of various training schemes produced by the ATB in response to identified needs in the industry.

Mr Bulford and colleagues believe that 'educational technology has a vital part to play in both the UK and throughout the world in assisting with change and with meeting the ever-increasing demand for food production'. We trust their felt need for 'a section to be devoted to agriculture at a future conference', in order to encourage an international exchange of ideas in this important area will be explored.

13. MAVIS: A Case History of Educational Technology in Industry

J. M. Moffat, *Managing Director of Malt Keyboard Ltd, Oxford*

Abstract: The Malt method of keyboard operator training was developed very successfully in the 1960s, but unsuitable for conventional classroom application.

MAVIS (Malt Audio-Visual Instruction Service) now provides Malt training by Audiovisual package. This paper describes the problems of conversion; and the results achieved.

Introduction

Our experience with MAVIS is of interest in the subject area 'Industrial Applications of Educational Technology' for two main reasons:

(1) It is possible to give a comprehensive case history from the start. I do not intend to say 'from start to finish' because the story is by no means finished.

(2) The case history sheds light on some questions that may be asked on how far it is practical to train complex manual skills with a stand-alone or nearly stand-alone audiovisual training system.

Well, what is MAVIS? MAVIS means the Malt Audio Visual Instruction Service. The audiovisual bit — AVIS — is easy to grasp, but what is Malt? To answer that I have to go back to the sixties.

In the early sixties, a new technology in printing, and more particularly in composing, began to be introduced in the UK. As almost always, the technology came first, and the human problems were only considered late in the day. Operators, often with half a lifetime of experience behind them on linotype machines, needed to learn to operate keyboards with a totally different keyboard layout. How could they be trained in the new skills?

A skills analysis consultant called Lillian Malt was called in. She looked closely at the requirement for teaching what was essentially the typewriter keyboard, and found that most teaching methods, like the typewriter keyboard itself, had remained unchanged since the nineteenth century. So she set about developing a method of training based on modern understanding of skills analysis and learning theory. The result was the Malt method. This is widely recognized, if perhaps not quite universally, as the most advanced and effective method of training keyboarders there is.

The Malt method originally involved a normal classroom teaching situation with instruction by carefully trained Malt tutors. Classes were held not only for the printing industry but also for anyone else — data prep. operators or typists for instance — for whom speed and accuracy were important.

The Need for a System

B. F. Skinner in a recent TV interview declared that the idea behind his teaching

119

machines was simply to give everyone the opportunity to receive the same kind of instruction he had himself received as a boy from a few dedicated teachers in his small Pennsylvania home town. In the same way MAVIS was designed to give more people the opportunity to receive the kind of instruction that too few had been able to receive from Malt tutors.

Behind the conversion from tutor to audiovisual system were very practical considerations. These considerations appeared to us under a commercial guise, for we were and are a commercial organization. But they were considerations which would carry equal weight with any type of organization or institution.

There were two main considerations:

(1) The economics of time and place. It can be economic to provide instruction in a big city for a sizeable class at a regular time. It is quite uneconomic to provide it in a small town — perhaps in remoter Wales — for one or two lino operators at hours that vary as their present duties allow, and disappear altogether if there is an industrial dispute.

(2) The control and maintenance of the quality of instruction. It is essential, even with carefully selected, carefully trained, responsible tutors (as ours are), to be able to supervise instruction quality. Where instruction itself is uneconomic, supervision is even more so.

These two considerations virtually forced us into contemplating a stand-alone audiovisual system. I think this is the point to mention that we knew, of course, that there had already been in existence for some time a form of automated keyboard instruction: 'Sight and Sound'. The philosophy behind 'Sight and Sound' was so different, however, from our own that, so far as I know, there is no element in their system which was or could have been embodied in ours. I intend to ignore 'Sight and Sound' from here on, not because I think it is altogether a bad system, but because it is not relevant to our story: the story of how a particular skills-analysed training procedure was converted into a programmed audiovisual system.

Problems

In making the conversion we had one in-built advantage. In converting normal material to programmed form there is much preliminary work to do: the definition of objectives; the breakdown of the material into small manageable and logically related steps; the establishment of quantitative measures of success. With the Malt method much of this had already been done. The objective was defined at every point; and each step was a manageable progression from the previous step, and could be assessed in quantitative terms. Nonetheless there were considerable problems to face:

(1) The target audience was very mixed. We could not economically justify creating a programme for only, say, the printing industry; let alone separate and different programmes for every category of potential user. So we had to write for a target audience ranging from teenage girls on typewriters to men in their fifties or even sixties who had operated linotype machines for perhaps 30 or 40 years. The machines that these different groups would have to learn on would be equally or even more varied: manual typewriters; electric typewriters; punch-card machines; other data prep. keyboards producing punched tape, or magnetic tape or cassettes — or operating VDUs; and an equally wide range of keyboards in the print industry.

(2) The objective was a manual skill. Most PL experience is related to the imparting of information. The end product is a right answer. In branched

120

programmes, for instance, the whole structure is related to the giving of answers. The end product in our case was a skill not an answer, so we had to devise a different dynamic. (I know you can say that giving an answer is a skill, and so it is, but it is a very different skill.)

(3) Further, the skill was a particular kind of skill. It involved the development of neuro-muscular pathways, operating not consciously but in the near-conscious. With a skilled keyboarder, the message travels from the eyes through to the fingers by-passing the higher regions of the brain. He or she can happily key — or type — while talking or attending to something else. The development of such a skill involves more than, for instance, learning to strip and repair a piece of machinery (important though that may be).

(4) The scale of the whole operation was therefore considerable. The face-to-face instruction course lasted, for beginners or retrainees, for five weeks with sessions of 3½ hours every morning, often plus extra practice, etc. in the afternoons and totalling at least 87½ hours. MAVIS can in theory be completed in 17 sessions of about the same length and under 60 hours in all: but in practice, with repeats, this often mounts up, especially in industrial retraining situations, to something like the original period.

Of course, the larger part of the time on the course is spent with trainees doing the work set them in the programme, but this programme if played without interruption, would nonetheless run for some 9 or 10 hours. That is as long as *Hamlet* and then *Macbeth* and then most of *King Lear*. On the subject of Shakespeare, Ben Jonson said of him: 'He never blotted out a line . . . would he had blotted a thousand.' We certainly did a lot of blotting. We wrote and rewrote and re-rewrote many hundreds of lines. But that is the only favourable comparison I claim!

Solutions

How did we go about creating the programme to overcome these and many other difficulties? As in any project there was much concurrent action, and much interaction, but for this paper I have set things out in sequence.

(1) We needed to provide the equivalent of a Malt tutor giving his or her professional best. We settled for, so to speak, putting the tutor in a box — the 'La Belle Courier' box.
A tutor needs to demonstrate posture and actions. The Courier shows still pictures — in colour — on a film strip. The strip is advanced by pulsed audiotape in a neat, self-contained cassette or cartridge. It is easy to operate and acceptably like a familiar old TV set.

(2) We needed a production company. Once settled on the Courier, we appointed Talking Pictures Ltd through their subsidiary Training and Education Associates Ltd. They provided professional photography and artwork, and casting and recording facilities, as well as supplying all the necessary equipment.

(3) We concentrated on the standard QWERTY keys only. A face-to-face Malt tutor course includes instruction on peripheral keys and command keys, often specially developed for the installation concerned. We made MAVIS deal with the standard keys only.
Special instruction could, of course, be added to MAVIS on a custom basis later, but we refused to be distracted from the main job in hand at that stage.
Incidentally we solved the problem of the diversity of the target audience

by using a male voice for the instructor, but a girl as the model trainee. Neither men nor girls should resent the male voice: and the girls can *identify* with the trainee while we hope the men can *enjoy looking* at her.

(4) Applying the principles of programmed learning to inculcation of manual skills was not easy. What we principally did was as follows:

    (a) We developed a series of short test pieces.

    (b) We built in daily testing on these pieces right from the third day on.

    (c) The tests were designed to be self-timed against a taped lead-in.

    (d) We provided specially designed 'results records' in which the trainee was to enter times taken and could easily read off the speed attained.

    (e) Personnel from the trainee's own organization were scheduled to perform a few minutes' supervisory work daily in checking the short test pieces for errors.

    (f) The work to be done every day was varied according to the speed and accuracy achieved the previous day.

    Throughout the course step-by-step explanation and the frequent involvement of the trainee in actually doing something were the rule of the day.

(5) Scripting and visualization went hand in hand. Fortunately we had some experience of film scripting, and in the art of thinking in parallel in pictures as well as script.

(6) We developed special training aids and special stationery. Some items under this general head we inherited from the face-to-face training service: the all-important manual of keyboard exercises for instance, and the finger guide. Some items we developed for MAVIS, and our tutors subsequently adapted them for face-to-face instruction; the rubber practice mats, for instance.

Some items were designed for MAVIS and MAVIS only: for instance, the 'results record' which is referred to in relation to the daily test pieces. It is a very carefully designed item, and a crucial tool for supervision and monitoring.

(7) For supervision and monitoring we aimed to produce a system which could operate without any specialist supervision, i.e. that had specialist keyboard operator *training* skill, and with very little supervision of any sort. We did *not* aim to produce a system in which there was *no* supervision. We believed that the total absence of supervision was neither desirable nor possible.

To achieve our aim we allowed for the involvement of a supervisor — or, as we preferred to say, a coordinator — from among the employees of the organization making use of the training. This coordinator could be comprehensively briefed in a short time, and would then perform the relatively slight duties involved thereafter — amounting to only a few minutes per trainee per day. But he or she would then be *there* — on the premises, though not normally in the room — as the all-important point of personal contact.

With unskilled supervision we felt it essential to have the built-in facility for us to monitor progress off-site. The results records allow this. The top copy of each sheet on the record, plus the work actually keyed on the short exercises involved, was to be sent to us to allow us to keep in touch with each trainee's progress. If we see anything amiss we can put it right, and we can answer queries or worries. On the whole things do not go wrong, the system is designed to preclude that, but sometimes we cannot avoid playing a part. How can you expect a coordinator to adapt a system for a trainee with a missing finger without professional help? (Yes, it has happened.)

(8) The scripts were circulated among our trained Malt staff here and in the USA for comment. We then carried out photography and recording.

The first-edition cassettes and all the associated MAVIS items were put on field-test. We consequently remade several cassettes, principally because of production errors, but with improvement in content too. On the whole, however, there was little we wanted to change. The field-test did, however, allow us to clarify in our own minds the function of the coordinator, and to develop and sharpen the briefing we gave. It was only after this early experience that we were able to cut down the coordinator's briefing to one day. The coordinator's own manual was the last item we produced, after the system was already in commercial use.

[Extracts from the cassettes shown here]

Results

MAVIS has been commercially available since 1975.

How has it all worked out?

In usage terms, MAVIS has found its greatest acceptance in the UK in the printing industry where there is a continuing need for retraining. In the USA the new printing technology has already superseded the old, and the time for retraining is over. MAVIS has, however, filled a need in initial training and in upgrading: in the data prep. world as much as in the printing industry. In both countries, MAVIS has been able to bring a highly developed form of training to many who would not otherwise have received it.

Trainees did not, as we feared they might, recoil from the idea of training by, or through, a machine. In fact they have welcomed it, particularly — but not exclusively — older retrainees, because it is self-paced and non-competitive.

The hardware has proved reliable. The on-site, coordinator system and the off-site monitoring has worked smoothly.

That covers about everything except for the all-important performance results of the training itself.

As a result of the off-site monitoring procedure we have available the results in speed and accuracy for almost every MAVIS trainee through every day of training.

We think that the results are outstanding. Two weeks ago I visited two very different newspapers that had been using MAVIS. These papers between them had had experience of almost every other type of keyboard training — do it yourself, local biddy, on-site instructor, Sight and Sound. Enthusiasm for MAVIS went all the way from managing director down through production manager and father of the chapel to apprentices. One overseer told me 'We've trained ten men with MAVIS and they're all good' — and then truthfulness overcame him: 'Well one of them isn't all that good.'

I know that is not quite the kind of evidence a scientific evaluation needs. With the figures we have available it might seem easy to make some definitive assessments. Unfortunately this is not so. The figures are only comparable if there is comparability all along the line: the previous experience of trainees; the circumstances of training; the method of testing and the method of marking the tests. We have never yet laid hands on entirely comparable results from other systems.

The nearest we can get to a straightforward comparison is with our own face-to-face instruction — and that is a stiff comparison to face. Even here straightforward comparisons are difficult. We can say, though, that MAVIS stands up extremely well. Indeed if there are any excuses needed they are not from MAVIS.

The actual figures we have are meaningful only in context. If anyone wishes to see them they can be easily made available. Better still, if anyone wants to organize and finance, a proper inter-system trial we should be delighted to cooperate fully.

The figures we do have are in fact very valuable to us. The accumulation of day-to-day progress figures has enabled us to establish norms, and spot any departures from them very quickly. That helps our monitoring. Still more valuable, perhaps, are the predictions we can make. These are of three kinds:

(1) Predictions on which *group* of employees (e.g. apprentices, ex-lino operators) is likely to respond best to training. (We can predict for individuals, too, but that involves aptitude testing, which is another story.)
(2) Predictions on what level of speed and accuracy is likely to be achieved by a given group after training.
(3) Predictions on what level of improving production results will follow from what training policies — and over what period.

	Forecast	Actual			
Speed		*keystrokes per hour*			
	%	*before*	*after*	%	%
Operator 1		8,098	10,450	29	
Operator 2	50	9,624	14,091	46	69
Operator 3		8,008	19,052	138	
Accuracy		*error percentage*			
		before	*after*		
Operator 1		5.3	0.9	83	
Operator 2	75	4.1	0.5	88	85
Operator 3		0.7	0.1	88	

Table 1. *Comparison of forecast and actual improvement with MAVIS Bradford Telegraph and Argus*

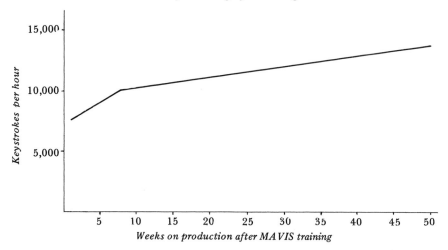

Figure 1. *Shows improving production results measured over 7 or 8-hour day predicted for a group of trainees at a London newspaper*

Conclusion

On the most general level the conclusions to be drawn from the whole MAVIS experience are as follows:

(1) The conditions and circumstances of industrial life frequently make stand-alone audiovisual training systems highly desirable — where they can be created.

(2) It *is* possible to create an audiovisual training system that is stand-alone: i.e. such that it teaches comprehensively, and without any skilled instructional staff in actual attendance, even a very complex manual skill. But it is hard work to create it!

(3) The results of training by such a system are unsurpassed by the most expert face-to-face tuition.

(4) A last conclusion that has not been argued through earlier: we foresee that, in that conveniently indefinite period, the 'foreseeable future', there will be a continuing need for *both* more or less stand-alone audiovisual systems *and* for traditional face-to-face tuition.

14. Design of Package Training Materials for Accountancy Firms

D. M. Tyrrell,
Training Services Manager, Institute of Chartered Accountants in England and Wales

Abstract: Package training materials were developed to overcome practical and economic difficulties found in meeting the training needs of accountants. These packages can be used by inexperienced lecturers when and where the training is needed. Certain design principles guide the preparation of a package which may include video, audio and print material.

Background

The first use of the term 'package courses' by the Institute was in 1972 when course speakers and supporting documentation were made available so that local district societies could run courses when and where they wanted. These 'packages' never proved very successful as district societies usually preferred the Institute to mount the course for them in their area. It was, however, the first time that while courses were developed centrally the actual presentation was left to local organizers.

The use of television arose out of a separate development in 1971 when reel-to-reel television was demonstrated to the Institute's Courses Committee. They were impressed with the possibilities of putting courses onto tape, but a subsequent cost study showed that this was impractical. Two years later, however, the introduction of video-cassettes and a number of uses of the medium by accounting firms in the United States, encouraged the Institute to explore further the idea of television package training. The first subject, 'Extraordinary Items and Prior Year Adjustments', was chosen because the ideas were relatively simple and because while there was a need for considerable training in the subject few people were qualified to speak on it. It was only when the television element had been made that the need for support material was fully recognized. Therefore, the support material was only properly integrated into the package when a second television presentation on inflation accounting was made.

Although there had been an audio-tape library of tax lectures, for a number of years the Taxation Courses Sub-Committee had serious reservations about the use of audiovisual media. In December 1974 they became concerned with the quality of presentation on Institute courses and so formed an Audio and Audio-Visual Media Working Party, under the chairmanship of a Courses Committee member. This working party visited organizations active in the field of educational technology applied to professional education and conducted a survey among professional accounting firms. They recommended that audio tape and video tape in cassette format were the most useful media for the development of multi-media package courses. They considered that there was an increasing interest in audio-tape package material and recommended that the existing audio-tape library should be extended and that a quarterly taxation bulletin be launched. This was done and the first issue of the *Quarterly Tax Bulletin* was published in June 1976.

Year	Event	Significance
1972	'Package' courses (documentation plus speakers) made available to district societies.	First complete course available when and where required. No development work required by organizers.
1974	Audio-tape lectures available for hire.	Allowed training to be conducted when and where it was wanted.
1974	'Extra-ordinary Items and Prior Year Adjustments' published.	First use of video-cassette recorded instruction.
1975	'Inflation Accounting — A Guide for Management to Current Purchasing Power Accounting' course published.	First multi-media package.
1975	Audio and Audio-Visual Media Working Party reported.	First systematic study of the possible use of available technology by the Institute.
1976/77	'Practical Auditing' series published.	Used TV in a new way with high-quality documentation. Set a new standard for package materials.
1976	'Finance Managers' Guidelines' series launched.	Use of audio cassette linked with a work book for individual study.
1977	'Basic Book-keeping' and 'CCA Proposals and Likely Effect' published.	First packages based solely on print support materials and OHP slides.

Table 1. *Development of package training materials*

Table 1 outlines the development of packages within the Institute. The largest project undertaken was 'Practical Auditing' and this was the first time material suitable for student accountants had been produced. The Audit Courses Sub-Committee, aware of package developments in other areas, had looked at the demand for auditing courses and suggested that any material had to start at the beginning of a programme of accountancy training. The series used much more television than previously as a method of introducing reality into the training situation, and integrated it with the documentation to give a fully multi-media package. The support material was also designed to be technically good and finished off to high standards. As a result further courses for students have been developed; so much so that its provision is currently the largest part of the package material production in the Institute. Although some of these courses are video-based, most consist of a Leader's Guide, with overhead projector slides, a Student's Manual, and realistic case studies.

This last approach has formed the basis for the most recent developments in the Institute's programme. From this year, Institute members are being recommended to complete 120 hours continuing education every three years and for some categories of member this will be compulsory. It is expected that there will be an increased demand for courses to update accountants or extend their professional skills. The Institute is therefore launching a series of standard package courses, which can be run by local district societies or other organizations. The first of these appeared in April 1977 and it is hoped to have a library of at least seven by April or May 1978.

Standards demanded of the Material

The Institute now has five full-time staff engaged in package production. Individual study material on audio tape is produced, but this is insignificant in comparison with the effort devoted to packages used as the basis of a conventional course. There are two main conditions set for such packages. Firstly, they should be seen to meet their training objectives, and secondly they should be capable of being used either by a non-specialist or by a subject specialist without any lecturing experience.

The first condition means that all packages are prepared according to accepted educational principles, therefore there is the input of technical knowledge through a video-tape session and/or a lecture, the consolidation of this learning by means of quizzes, group discussion, and so on, and practice at using the skills learnt through case studies or simple figure exercises. Once a package has been drafted it is validated by organizations representative of the intended market. Usually three to five organizations are selected and they have to provide the participants, a lecturer, and a venue. Most such organizations are professional accountancy firms and there is at least one validation outside London and one with a small firm. The Institute has been fortunate in the cooperation it has received from validating organizations and in most cases courses are mounted to meet genuine training needs.

The second condition is important because this is one of the prime purposes of a package. However, whether a non-specialist or a non-lecturer is likely to use the material depends on the type of course. In some subjects, for example a new accounting standard, there is a need to run many courses on basic principles over a reasonably short period, but there are only a limited number of accountants versed in the subject. In this case what is required is to provide an accountant who has a reasonable amount of lecturing experience and can work through from the lecture notes, even though the subject matter is not immediately familiar. In other subjects, such as updating on a particular tax, there is a continuing need for training and there are sufficient specialists to provide the lectures. However, such specialists are not likely to have had either much lecturing experience or the time to develop appropriate material.

Approaches used

Five training packages produced over the last three years have been chosen as representative of the approaches used in the 24 being produced by the Institute by Spring 1978. The significant differences in structure are outlined in Table 2.

As a result of the Institute's course-running experience a positive effort has been made to structure all training packages so that the key points of the subject are emphasized to participants and they have a chance to consolidate what they have learnt. But, with experience of producing packages. significant changes have been made in this overall approach. The television material, originally conceived as taped instruction, is now used to introduce as much realism as possible into a course. The video is followed by a short discussion period and then a lecture on the detailed technical points is given by the course leader. The amount of support material provided has also been extended considerably. In the first courses it was assumed that leaders only needed general guidance on the use of the package; later, lecture summaries were extended, and now detailed lecture outlines are almost always provided. Many more overhead projector slides are now supplied with each course and this reflects not only greatly reduced reproduction costs but also improved design for the lecture outlines.

Material to consolidate the learning is vitally important if a course is to achieve

Course *Year published* *Training time*	Extraordinary Items *1975* *2 hours*	Practical Auditing *1976-77* *7½ days*	Basic Book-keeping *1976-77* *5 days*	Capital Transfer Tax Updated *1977* *1 day*	Auditing Small Businesses *1978* *2 days*
Television					
As taped instructions	✓	–	n.a.	n.a.	n.a.
As a way of introducing reality into the course	–	✓	n.a.	n.a.	n.a.
Support Material					
Leader's Guide	✓	✓	✓	✓	✓
Participants' Manual	✓	✓	✓	✓	✓
OHP slides (number)	4	67	25	37	43
Audio-tape discussion material	–	–	–	–	✓
Lecture Outlines					
Summaries only	✓	✓	✓	–	–
Detailed outlines	–	–	–	✓	✓
OHP slides reproduced in Leader's Guide	✓	✓	–	✓	✓
Consolidation Material					
Case study or substantial exercise	–	–	✓	–	–
Other – quizzes, discussion problems and worked exercises	✓	✓	✓	✓	✓

n.a. = not applicable

Table 2. *The design of training packages*

its objectives. Approaches used include short question and answer sessions, discussion questions or problems, and detailed case studies or exercises. In some cases, particularly in 'Basic Book-keeping', the case study is the major part of the whole course and, in other instances, particularly where a course is an introduction to a relatively diverse subject, the consolidation material is very difficult to provide. In more recent courses efforts have been made to improve the approach to the design of consolidation material. It is also hoped to introduce some form of post-test into the material when it is validated.

Once the subject for a new course has been decided, a team of accountants and Institute staff is appointed to be responsible for the production of the material. Their first task is to draw up an outline of the course clearly indicating its objectives, its intended audience, the detailed subject matter to be covered, and the media to be employed. This is then approved by the relevant working party, after which the team produces the support material and, where appropriate, the television or audio elements.

The most important part of the support material is now the Leader's Guide and once the outline is approved it is usual to draft this document first. The main part of the guide is taken up with lecture outlines and these have become more and more detailed with each new course. At present there are three parts to its design. First, all the main points that the lecturer must get over are given in roman type. It is recognized that lecturers may well read this section verbatim, although it is not recommended. Secondly, notes and instructions to the leader are given in italics. These are so phrased that the leader would not be able to read them verbatim and they include material less essential to the understanding of the subject, instructions (such as when to show overhead projector slides), and practical examples of the application of a particular principle or idea. These examples are deliberately given in italics so that the lecturer will think about them before using them. Otherwise they could be misconstrued by his audience.

Thirdly, the visual back-up is integrated with the spoken word. This is frequently the weak link in the material because slides are often overcrowded, reproduce lists of items, or are inappropriately used by leaders. In an effort to overcome these problems original 'cartoons' have been commissioned and, wherever possible, concepts are illustrated with graphs or diagrams. Improvements have been made and it is now an important objective when the draft Leader's Guide is reviewed, to identify the total visual effect of the slides and, therefore, what cartoons or graphics are required. In 'Preparing Company Accounts', issued in 1978, mnemonics illustrated by cartoon drawings have been used to enliven those sections giving lists of items required to be disclosed by statute under the Companies Acts.

The Institute has recognized that it is not enough just to provide the package, also it is necessary to provide both an updating service and tutor training sessions. 1978 will see the first major exercise in updating when the very successful 'Basic Book-keeping' course will be revised. Selected customers have been asked to fill in a questionnaire and some of these asked to attend a working day at the Institute to comment in detail on the whole course. Another updating requirement arises from the stream of legislation and official advice from accounting bodies and its effect on existing material. 'Capital Transfer Tax Updated' was issued in September 1977 and had to have supplementary updating sheets as a result of the Chancellor's Mini Budget on 26th October 1977. This was before a single copy was sold!

Production Arrangements

The Institute require that the packages are of the highest quality from both the training and the accountancy points of view. Such expertise is often difficult and expensive to obtain although the Institute is fortunate in that many of its members very generously give their services on a voluntary basis. The way of working that has built up over the years is for the working party responsible for initiating the course to appoint a technical monitor from among its members. The monitor, in consultation with the Institute's Secretariat appoints the technical adviser who is an accountant with experience in the particular field, but not so senior that he is unable to give time to preparing and assembling the necessary technical material. The training Services Section with the adviser and monitor turns this into training material, validates the course, and edits and produces the final package.

Where video or audio material is involved in the course, an outside producer is sub-contracted by the Institute and becomes a member of the project team. Wherever possible the Institute sub-contracts its package production work, only using its own staff or facilities where this is essential for the control of quality of material. In only one case has sub-contracting not worked and this was because it resulted in a lack of control over the production process and so seriously delayed publication of already advertised packages.

Further Developments

The main activity of the Institute's Training Services Section is the preparation of training packages designed to provide all the material required to run a conventional course. Over the next few years the range of courses provided will be consolidated both for student and post-qualifying education and a policy towards updating evolved.

However, any major new departures are likely to be in the production of home study material. Audio cassettes have been available from the Institute for some time and in recent years these had always been accompanied by some form of user's guide. With the 'Finance Manager's Guidelines' series launched in October 1976 the cassette and work book were carefully linked to provide a structured learning package. However, these packages have not been tested for their learning effectiveness nor has there been much feedback on how they meet the home study needs of accountants. It is hoped to relaunch the present home study series in 1978 incorporating these ideas.

Under the Institute's proposals for members to complete 120 hours training every three years, courses and conferences run by accountancy and other bodies will be accredited. However, the Institute has said it will allow a certain proportion of the credits to be claimed through the use of home study. Research is now being undertaken into ways of accrediting such packages for those members for whom post-qualifying training will be a requirement. It is hoped that any accreditation scheme will be integrated into the Institute's proposed home study series and can be used as the basis of tutorial feedback.

15. Utilization of the Programmed Learning Technique in Management Development

C. H. Mason, *The Management Services Organization, Maryland, USA*

Abstract: Managerial excellence calls for the application of various functions and principles which constitute the whole body of the management job. Those required elements must be learned as would be any subject; in the classroom and its application. This presentation summarizes the all-encompassing theory and emphasizes its importance as a guideline in all managerial decisions.

The development of managerial personnel is one of the most critical problems facing industry today. My purpose in this paper is to explore the application of the programmed learning technique to the problem, not to discuss any details of programmed learning *per se*.

Real progress in the process of executive development has been minimal. Not that there has been a lack of activity in this respect — far from it. Fantastic amounts of money, time and energy have been expended over a period of many years. Seminars, workshops, newsletters and special courses have been legion. Participants in the various programmes have been literally buried in a mass of unrelated theories, catch phrases and gimmicks. As might be expected, however, rewards in the form of meaningful job improvement have been generally negligible.

The whole fault lies in the failure of managers to evaluate training needs, to establish clear-cut objectives and to set practical, measurable standards of performance. Training for the sake of training has been the rule. Programmes are entered into on a hit or miss basis with the thought that **some** good will rub off from **any** training. In practice, however, the reverse is often true. Ill-conceived, poorly planned programmes can do considerable harm. They serve to confuse rather than clarify. More important, they often convey a picture of management merely in terms of the various gimmicks and sleight of hand remedies currently in vogue.

They serve to obscure the broad scope of interrelationships of the basic managerial functions. Certainly, slipshod planning in a matter of such importance as the development of key personnel is, in itself, a demonstration of poor management.

The uncertainty and constant vacillation in the selection of management training methods stems from a common belief that the subject is one which cannot be defined in precise terms; that management theory is merely academic; that the management job contains too many variables to allow for practicable standards of performance.

Managerial excellence has been judged largely by the economic results rather than by the management actions *per se*. External forces have in many cases been so controlling as to completely overshadow excellence in managerial performance. By the same token, poor management is often credited with successes which are 'in spite of' rather than 'because of' its actions. We must, therefore, judge management in terms of its adherence to accepted principles, rather than merely on its success or failure in isolated circumstances. Obviously, such judgements cannot be made without a common understanding as to what constitutes the whole managerial responsibility.

Now, what is management? What are those actions the manager must take to insure the good working order of an organization? There are as many definitions as there are writers on the subject. Two rather brief ones, however, rather well sum up the overall function. Lawrence Appley defined it as, 'Not the accomplishment of things, but the development of people.' Henri Fayol saw it as, 'The application of principles, not the uncovering of some divinely endowed individual.' Suffice to say, we can conclude that the management function:

(1) is the accomplishment of things through people
(2) involves the application of certain principles, and
(3) must be learned as we would learn any subject, in the classroom and the laboratory.

Although management cannot be completely defined in precise terms, the total management job can be broken down into a number of specific tasks or duties. These can be summarized in terms of five basic functions:

Planning — A prerequisite to all managerial actions. It provides a means of anticipating eventualities, preparing for contingencies and mapping out required actions. It should be treated as a practical procedure, requiring a systematic analysis of all factors involved. It is basically essential to management at all levels.

Organizing — Involves the bringing together of all of the people required to accomplish the mission. It calls for a determination of the jobs to be performed, the selection of personnel to fill those jobs, and the relationship of one to the other. In this function we are concerned with the formal structure and the principles which must be observed in the day-to-day relationships.

Leadership — The exercise of authority in such a way as to ensure maximum effectiveness of personnel. In many treatments of management theory it is defined as commanding or directing. I prefer to treat the function in its broadest scope — encompassing the activities of training, motivation and discipline. It should provide the skill and the will to do the job.

Coordinating — The blending together of the various activities in such a way as to insure that the combined results will be greater than the total of the individual efforts. It might well be called the essence of management. Few management problems arise in which poor coordination is not a factor. An important thing to remember about this function is that it is a two-way process, not merely a passing down of information after decisions have been made.

Controlling — In order for a manager to devote maximum time to planning, coordinating and other matters requiring his personal attention, he must delegate duties and authority extensively. How to do this while upholding the responsibility which is inherent in his position is a continuing problem. The answer lies in an adequate system of control, a determination of the relationship between standards and performance, and the taking of such action as is necessary to correct any disparities. To maintain control over managerial activities, of course, calls for clear-cut, measurable, commonly understood standards of performance at every level.

In the application of these functions, it is important that there be a constant reminder that:

(1) each has a relationship to all others;
(2) they are all 'cogs' in the management 'machine';
(3) their relative importance in various situations must be determined in each

case;
(4) their proper application as a 'package' will constitute excellent management.

The time and sequence in which management carries out the various functions cannot be specified, nor is it feasible to determine their relative worth in the total job. Since management is dynamic, it must be understood that in nearly all cases the functions are carried out simultaneously and that they represent a continuous and changing process. It is important, also, to remember that in the teaching of these theories it must be emphasized that only to the extent that they can be identified with day-to-day work activities will they have real meaning.

Now, people from all levels of management have for years been made aware of these basic functions. They were first published by Henri Fayol in 1908 and have never been seriously disputed. Any management programme of consequence is designed with these guidelines in view. Certainly, no sensible person can deny their truth. Why then are they so consistently ignored in management practices? Why is fire *fighting* preferred to fire *prevention*?

It stems directly from a reluctance to take time to do the only thing which will provide time to analyse specific problems in terms of the accepted principles of good management. This reluctance is based on a fear of abandoning a management by experience, intuition, and horse sense for that which seems to represent vague theory.

Actually, once there is a recognition of the necessity of management by principle, the transition need not be a difficult one. The intuition, horse sense, and experience which proves so ineffective as the 'whole' of management can well become a valuable asset when applied as an adjunct to a solid managerial function.

Now, where can programmed learning accomplish what the multitudinous other approaches have failed to do over all these years? Treated as merely another gimmick which might be given a try, it will accomplish no more than past programmes. Given the full attention it deserves at all levels of management, however, it can provide the emphasis on objectivity which is so sorely needed. I believe it will be very useful because it:

(1) calls for clearly defined objectives and careful sequencing of subject matter as a prerequisite to all other actions;
(2) is a means of control over the student's progress based on meaningful standards of performance; and
(3) is a planned programme of instruction to fit the needs of each individual or group, considering scope and procedure in each case.

In short, the programmed learning technique, as I see it, calls for the exercise of good management in the teaching of management. That this would not be a basic requirement for *any* training process may come as a surprise to many, but such is all too often the case.

Now, in the utilization of this technique in management development, how do we proceed? Firstly, we must ensure that the programme objectives coincide with the beliefs and practices of those in authority. As the subject matter encompasses the duties of every level of management, many questions will have to be raised and many people consulted as to the determination of objectives and standards to be applied. It would serve no purpose to teach theories which might be alien to those who must finally enforce them.

The writing of the programme will, in itself, be of inestimable value to all concerned. At the same time, it will be a task of great magnitude. It will involve the breaking down of each of the management functions into its various elements and putting these elements in proper perspective for programming. Further, it will call for a determination as to standards of performance as well as appropriate controls. Beyond this there must be consideration of the work processes which will be involved in the application of classroom theories. Many of those who assist in the planning process, as well as in the implementation, will openly resist it; others will treat it as another of those training gimmicks which will soon pass, as have others in the past. At best, there will be little inclination to give the process the support it needs and deserves. At first blush the obstacles appear to be overwhelming. This fact, however, points up the need for such a step-by-step approach and the necessity for the resolving of each item of dissent as it arises.

Managers must be made to see that, today more than ever, meaningful management training is overdue; that there are no shortcuts, no secret formulae, no pat solutions to the critical problems of management development. There are no alternatives to a head-on approach. The need for better management is an overwhelming one. Business and industry are facing urgent problems which are largely a direct result of inept management. Added to the problem are the direct effects of the increasing economic, social and political influences throughout the world. Time is running out.

Programmed learning, of course, provides no panacea. It would be ridiculous to infer that it would. It does, however, offer one of the most promising approaches to the development of management know-how. Given the wholehearted, active, continuing support it requires, it can produce fantastic results. To give it less is unworthy of the effort.

16. Programmed Learning in the Footwear Industry

K. H. Westley
Manpower Research and Services Department, Shoe & Allied Trades Research Association, Kettering, Northants

Abstract: This paper outlines the application of a technology of training by the Shoe & Allied Trades Research Association (SATRA), to three jobs within the footwear manufacturing industry. The first is a technician-type job and the other two are operative jobs with particular aspects which presented some interesting problems for solution.

Introduction

The British footwear manufacturing industry has a long tradition of training. This may seem surprising for an industry which has never had an apprenticeship scheme, but the lack of such a scheme has probably been a contributory factor to the take up of new ideas and techniques in that there has been no need to change an established code of practice.

The industry operated many schemes based on the traditional educational college approach, mixing theory with practical training. Course syllabuses were organized by local colleges in footwear manufacturing areas, leading to qualifications issued by the City and Guilds or, in the case of management subjects, by the professional institution for the industry.

Before considering training in the footwear manufacturing industry, it is necessary to consider the nature of the organization of work within the industry. The industry is very operative labour intensive. Hence, the majority of the training needs are operative-based. Most of the machines used in the industry are sophisticated developments of hand tools, and operatives set and adjust the machines to cope with variations in the work, for example shoe sizes, design variations and material variations (which can occur in rapid succession during a working day). Thus the operative has to be part-technician. There are a limited number of technicians and these usually comprise those people associated with the design and engineering of the shoe plus a few maintenance engineers. Other staff are management and the usual business functional specialists.

The training need within the footwear manufacturing industry is, therefore:

(1) For management — involving the usual management and supervisory skills but with some technical knowledge of the industry.
(2) Functional specialists, e.g. production planning, work study, quality control, finance, marketing — where across-industry training is readily available.
(3) Technician training — some of which is very specialized and some (e.g. engineers) is general.
(4) A considerable variety of operative-type jobs.

Traditionally, the shoe industry was concentrated in certain well-defined areas, and local colleges catered for the needs. However, the industry has contracted over the last 20 years and several factories have been set up in the non-traditional shoemaking areas. In these circumstances, we have the classical requirement for training which could be provided by a programme-learning approach, in that the numbers are relatively small and scattered, training is required at variable times, and most would-be participants are reluctant to travel far to receive training.

In this paper, I shall outline the application of the technology of training by the Shoe & Allied Trades Research Association (SATRA), to three jobs within the footwear manufacturing industry. The first will be a technician-type job and the other two will be operative jobs, but with particular aspects which presented some interesting problems for solution.

Training the Pattern Cutter

In the footwear industry, a pattern cutter takes a design for a shoe, which may be either a drawing or a three-dimensional model, and breaks it down into suitable component parts for manufacture.

At the design stage the shoe is seen as a three-dimensional object, as it will be in its final form. However, the cut parts are two-dimensional. This means that the pattern cutter has to convert a three-dimensional shape so that pieces can be cut from two-dimensional material and again transformed, by the manufacturing processes, into a three-dimensional object. In order to do this, the pattern cutter must be able to apply knowledge and skills in the following main areas:

(1) The materials to be used and the degrees to which they can be stretched or compressed by machines and processes in order to accommodate the transition from two to three dimensions.
(2) The machines, processes and skills available in the factory for cutting pieces, joining them together, shaping them and providing a final shape which will not collapse with the pieces trying to revert to two dimensions.
(3) If natural materials (e.g. leather) are to be used, the various characteristics of the different parts of materials both in manufacture and wear.
(4) How the various patterns decided upon can be arranged with the most economic use of material.
(5) The economics of the various production processes. For example, is it better to use larger pieces with a greater material cost but with a saving in a production process, or, conversely, smaller pieces with lower material but higher production costs.
(6) Company policy concerning the range of products produced and the market.
(7) Physical skills in being able to draw, trace and cut out the necessary patterns.
(8) Diagnostic skills in conducting trials of new patterns, assessing the results and making changes as necessary.
(9) The various changes necessary in different parts of the shoe for changes in sizes and width fittings.

The job of the pattern cutter combines many types of skills covering the whole range of Bloom's taxonomy. For example, consider a typical pattern-cutting operation, adding an allowance to a pattern edge using dividers. Normally the allowance, say 13mm, is predetermined, thus making the actual operation a straightforward combination of physical skills plus procedural convention. But why the figure of 13mm and when would you vary it? Here the pattern cutter requires a knowledge of certain principles or theories and must be able to evaluate exactly the results of his efforts in order to ascertain the correct amount of allowance for a particular shoe.

Learning Analysis

Taking Bloom's taxonomy as a basis, the job of the pattern cutter covers all the main areas of knowledge, comprehension and action.

At the lower end of the knowledge section of the taxonomy, items relating to terminology, facts and conventions, for example, can be dealt with relatively easily using standard techniques. This is mainly a matter of presenting information in a suitable form, adding reinforcement, checking, and so on as necessary. Some items require no more than the Ruleg approach of programmed learning. With principles and theories, the necessary knowledge can be developed by reference to practical examples and using more of a discovery learning approach.

Comprehension can be tackled by using the knowledge related to the factory situation. Here discovery learning combined with a system of checking and correction by a superior is a suitable approach. Tackling of the action section is best done by applied guided discovery. Again, it is a question of providing a format and arranging suitable guidance and checking.

Training Strategy

From the foregoing, it is apparent that there could be no standard package for training pattern cutters throughout the footwear manufacturing industry. Our analysis showed that some of the knowledge and manipulative skill element required by a pattern cutter would be common across the industry and we could, therefore, provide a suitable learning package to cover these items. Nevertheless, many of the skills required by a pattern cutter are directly related to the very individual needs of the company.

Our next step was to tap the considerable resources already existing within the company. We therefore set about providing a framework within which the factory staff could be involved to guide the learning of the trainee pattern cutter. The trainee was provided with a series of questions to ask appropriate factory staff, who were briefed using notes in the package for the head pattern cutter. The trainee would be required to record the answers which he had 'discovered' for himself, and the system had to be such that he would record only appropriate information. By a suitable series of questions and guidelines, we were able to eliminate the all-too-familiar experience of trainees receiving the wrong amounts of the wrong type of information at the wrong time.

Although, so far, we have written about pattern cutting there are, in fact, several methods of deriving patterns for shoes. The programme deals with the two most common methods of pattern cutting. Figure 1 shows a diagrammatic representation of the system showing its modular arrangement and possible alternative strategies. Factories would choose those modules (or units) which are appropriate to the procedures used in their factory. This arrangement also allows for the trainee to spend short periods working at the programme interspersed with other work which may or may not be connected with pattern cutting. Alternatively, it is possible for a trainee to work straight through the programme. In this manner, we have brought maximum flexibility to the administration of the programme.

Media

The theoretical information is mainly presented using a Singer Caramate tape/slide machine (Figure 2). Together with the tape/slide information, most units also have work books in which the trainee records information and are retained as the personal property of the trainee for future reference. One unit, for example,

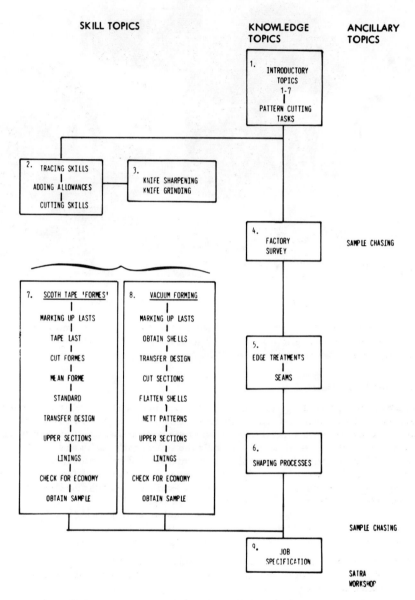

PATTERN CUTTING TRAINING PROGRAMME

SKILL TOPICS

KNOWLEDGE TOPICS

ANCILLARY TOPICS

1. INTRODUCTORY TOPICS 1-7 PATTERN CUTTING TASKS

2. TRACING SKILLS / ADDING ALLOWANCES / CUTTING SKILLS

3. KNIFE SHARPENING / KNIFE GRINDING

4. FACTORY SURVEY

SAMPLE CHASING

7. SCOTH TAPE 'FORMES' / MARKING UP LASTS / TAPE LAST / CUT FORMES / MEAN FORME / STANDARD / TRANSFER DESIGN / UPPER SECTIONS / LININGS / CHECK FOR ECONOMY / OBTAIN SAMPLE

8. VACUUM FORMING / MARKING UP LASTS / OBTAIN SHELLS / TRANSFER DESIGN / CUT SECTIONS / FLATTEN SHELLS / NETT PATTERNS / UPPER SECTIONS / LININGS / CHECK FOR ECONOMY / OBTAIN SAMPLE

5. EDGE TREATMENTS / SEAMS

6. SHAPING PROCESSES

SAMPLE CHASING

9. JOB SPECIFICATION

SATRA WORKSHOP

Figure 1. *Diagrammatic representation of the programme*

Figure 2. *Pattern-cutting programme in use*

involves a survey of the major operations within the factory and is almost entirely a guided discovery learning approach. This system is also used to develop the necessary sensori-motor manipulative skills.

Use of the Programme

The first step in using the programme is to decide which units are required for the particular factory concerned. This is carried out by the head pattern cutter or another person who will supervise the programme, with assistance from one of our training specialists. A set of notes describing the supervisor's duties and responsibilities is issued. For example, a particular section may inform the supervisor that it is necessary to supply the trainee with materials, clear a visit to a factory department, supply information on the firm's procedures and check the answers which the trainee has written in his work book.

The package received by the trainee is complete in itself in giving instructions in how to operate the equipment and use the various work books.

The general procedure then followed by the trainee is as follows:

(1) Information on a particular topic or aspect of that topic or overview, if necessary, is given to the trainee. A check is carried out to see whether the trainee has understood the information.
(2) At suitable points reinforcement with further checking is incorporated in the programme.
(3) The trainee is required to carry out some activity which is directly orientated towards the company's needs. This is usually recorded, checked

TASK 23

SEAM AND EDGE TREATMENT BREAKDOWN

You should now be well acquainted with the types of seams and edge treatments used in your factory. Demonstrate this knowledge by :

1. Selecting 3 styles from your current range of footwear

2. Examining and identifying all seams and edge treatments for each style

3. Listing your findings on the sheets overleaf and drawing a quick sketch of each seam and edge.

Example

TREATMENT : Lapped seam

WHERE FOUND : Quarters joined to vamp

SKETCH :

LAPPED SEAM

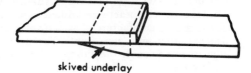

skived underlay

Figure 3. *An example of a task from the work book*

by the supervisor and then retained by the trainee as a source of reference.

After completing the programme, the Singer Caramate, slides and tapes are returned. It is possible for the programme to be used to extend these knowledge areas for different situations. For example, suppose a trainee received appropriate parts of the training programme in a particular factory. At some later time, he may change his job and be employed by another factory but his original training may not have covered some of the requirements of the second factory. In this case, he can receive the appropriate units of the programme, acquire any new knowledge and reorientate his existing knowledge to the requirements of the second factory.

Results

Results to date are very encouraging. Trials have been carried out and it appears that trainees can reach a level of competence in about two months which previously required about one year of training. The major advantage claimed by the users is the considerable flexibility of the programme, and how all knowledge is related to the firm's needs. Furthermore, should these needs change, then the programme can again be used to provide the necessary training.

This programme does not conflict with attendance at further education establishments. In fact, it forms a very useful introductory programme to advanced training in pattern cutting and design.

Operative Training involving Machine Setting

The machine involved, manufactured by the British United Shoe Machinery Co Ltd, is known as the 4A Pulling and Lasting Machine and is in common use in footwear factories. It essentially takes the upper part of the shoe, pulls it over the last to give it the shape of the foot, and fixes the front part of the upper to the insole by means of adhesive. This operation is critical because it aligns the upper correctly on the last, ensures that the design features are presented correctly, and enables subsequent operations to proceed. This machine superseded two or three previous operations.

The training situation which presented itself to us was as follows:

(1) The machine is relatively expensive. Most factories have only one or two machines of this type and maximum production is required from the machines, so no spare machines are available for training. Consequently, training can only take place on production machines when these can be made available at lunchtime, after hours, or when irregularities in the production flow mean that the machine is unused for a short period.

(2) The machine manufacturers wished to sell in the widest possible market, covering the manufacture of such diverse items as children's shoes, ladies' dancing shoes, and safety boots. The machine, therefore, has numerous adjustments to cover these eventualies — in fact a total of over 90 such adjustments.

(3) Most factories produce a variety of styles in small batches. The machine could require wiper plates and other fittings to be changed and settings adjusted for each new style of shoe, which could mean four or five changes per hour. Additionally small changes are required for different sizes of shoes — commonly three or four different sizes per dozen pairs.

(4) Some settings are calibrated but others are by eye. Added to this, the upper material is variable and different settings may be required within one batch of shoes.

(5) Once the machine is set up, the shoe is placed on the machine and performs

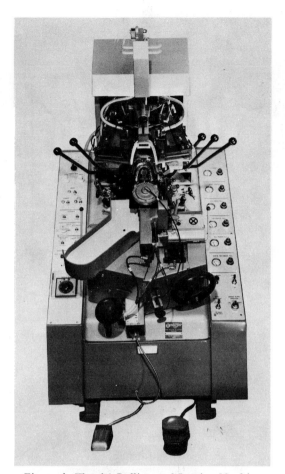

Figure 4. *The 4A Pulling and Lasting Machine*

the first part of the cycle when it stops. Adjustments can be made at this stage but, if settings are grossly out, the shoe may already have been damaged beyond repair, and in any case, this setting takes time. The machine cycle is then completed during which no remedial action can be taken and the operator only knows whether the settings have been correct when the cycle has been completed. He is then in a position to make adjustments for the next shoe.

Obviously, the cognitive and diagnostic skills associated with this operation are considerable; the amount of manipulative skill is relatively small.

This then is the situation within which we have to apply the training. We tackled the problem as follows:

The trainee is first given some general information concerning the job and its importance in the production process. An audio tape and work book are used for this purpose (Figure 5). He then observes the actions of a skilled operative while listening to the tape. The recording guides his observations by means of a series of

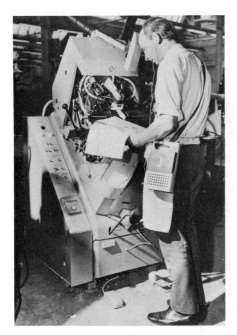

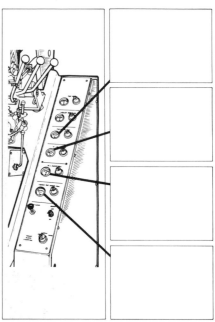

Figure 5. *The programme in use at the 4A Machine*

Figure 6. *A page from the work book*

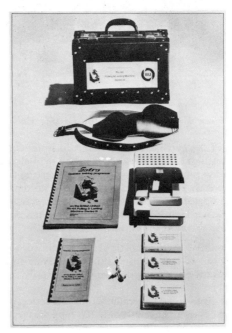

Figure 7. *The complete programme*

questions such as 'What does he do with his right foot and when?' A pattern of questions with check answers follows until the trainee has absorbed the routine cycle of the operation. He is then given instructions on operating a machine by himself, again using a guided discovery type of approach. He is rapidly introduced to some simple work and gains confidence in doing this work interspersed with further information. Gradually, he is introduced to the complexities of various styles of footwear, machine settings and adjustments, quality standards and fault diagnosis. The random servicing items are also covered.

The use of a tape player to give the instructions leaves the operative free use of hands and eyes. He records notes and machines settings in his work book, which mostly consists of outline drawings and has the minimum of printed information (Figure 6). In this way, he builds up a personalized record of the machine and the work and standards of the factory.

The whole programme is administered by the department supervisor who has only to carry out the normal supervisory arrangements of ensuring that the machine and work are available and checking quality standards and output.

The traditional time for training on this machine with an instructor is between two and four weeks. The programme develops operatives to a high standard within about five days on average. However, they are often producing satisfactory work on straightforward styles of shoes within two hours of starting the programme.

One advantage which has come to light in using this programme is that operatives prefer it because it is 'dumb'. Trainees feel reluctant to ask a human instructor to explain a point several times, but the programme keeps no record of how many times a particular section has been used. Also, many departmental supervisors have found the programme helpful to update their own technical knowledge on this machine.

A further programme was produced for a later version of this machine with the company's development engineers. The new machine and training programme were launched simultaneously.

Operative Training involving high Manipulative Skill

Most skilled operations in footwear manufacture require a high level of manipulative skill, together with other knowledge-based skills, most linked to a sensory input. One such important operation in shoe manufacture is known as roughing. In this operation, the part of the upper material which has been pulled over and fastened onto the insole, has to have its surface layer removed in preparation for an adhesive bond to the sole. This removal of the surface layer is carried out on a revolving wire brush and/or scouring band.

The operative presses the bottom of the shoe against the roughing surface and, at the same time, moves the shoe around the brush or band to produce a uniformly roughed surface. Depth of rough and the exact position of the edge of the roughened area are crucial. Obviously, considerable manipulative skill is involved. In addition, the operative has to recognize different types of materials and be able to rough them accordingly. He has a few maintenance jobs to do, one of which is periodically to sharpen the wire brush.

We attempted to see whether we could further develop training technology to cover this type of situation.

In the event, we produced a programme which can train these operatives on the following lines.

Because the operative uses both hands and needs to watch the operation carefully, we again provided instructions by means of an audio tape (Figure 8). A work book is used to record specific items for reference relating to the materials used and the factory processes. The degree of roughing and materials used must relate to the individual factory so we provided a batch of five standard materials in the programme. The supervisor selects the appropriate materials, or if he is using other materials, prepares his own standards.

Figure 8. *The roughing programme in use*

We also provide templates to assist the operator to record effective grasps and hand movements for efficient roughing.

With the pulling and lasting machines described earlier, the speed of operation is, to a large extent, governed by the machine cycle. However, the speed of operation on roughing is entirely operator controlled. Further, it is essential to develop a good working rhythm for both uniform roughing and to prevent fatigue. To help the trainee, we developed an audio-pacing device which emits bleeps (Figure 9). The trainee can have the taped instructions fed into one ear and the audio bleeps fed into the other ear. The pacing device is entirely operator-controlled and provides him with feedback of his performance; it goes some way to motivating him to increase his performance to an acceptable standard.

The supervisor administers the programme and carries out normal supervisory duties such as allocating work, checking on output and quality and advising on technical matters. However, at no time is the supervisor called upon to instruct.

Summary

In this short paper I have only been able to describe briefly some of the applications of programmed learning in the footwear manufacturing industry by SATRA. However, the three programmes outlined show the considerable range of learning situations to which training programmes of this type can be applied. One

Figure 9. *Audio pacing device*

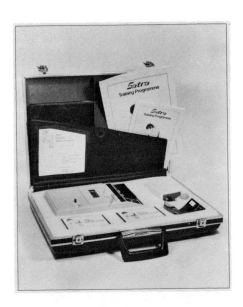

Figure 10. *The complete roughing programme*

job is that of a technician involving a considerable range of learning requirements. Another is mainly concerned with the diagnostic and procedural skills involved in machine setting, whilst the third involves considerable manipulative skills linked to sensory inputs. There is no fixed pattern of training and the learning inputs must be geared to the senses available.

In the case of the pattern-cutting technician, we have also drawn on the considerable resources within organizations. By presenting the trainee with a planned programme of learning involving standard knowledge inputs and factory practices, we have been able to cater for the individual requirements of each organization. In this respect, we have come nearly full circle in that we 'sit the trainee next to Nellie', but make sure that the information received is correctly structured.

We believe that, by using this approach, we have developed techniques which can be applied in a wide variety of industrial situations. It is possible to produce skilled technicians and operatives in a fraction of the time taken formerly. In a situation involving technological change, training and retraining for new skills is vital. Our approach is one way of tackling this problem.

Further, this approach is important to the people concerned. If we can give people skilled status in a relatively short time we not only improve their earning capability but also their self-esteem. Learning with these programmes requires effort on the part of the trainees and, when people achieve results through effort, they take pride in their expertise. Thus, if programmes of this type are appropriate, they can not only produce skilled people but also give them status. I would suggest that these two factors taken together represent an important break-through in training.

17. Some Applications of Educational Technology Technology

J.R.S. Bulford, A.R.G. Tallis and P.W.J. Howard
Agricultural Training Board, Beckenham, Kent

Abstract: The paper outlines the rapid changes taking place in agriculture and indicates some particular advantages to be gained from training in the UK. Examples of the media in the form of simulators for training in lambing and calving and a film on heat detection in cattle are shown. A call is made for a greater international interchange of information and ideas on media for training in agriculture.

Introduction

The title of our conference is 'Educational Technology in a Changing World'. Perhaps the agricultural industry in the United Kingdom can claim that its 'world' has changed more than most over recent years. The total whole-time and part-time family and hired workers in Great Britain fell from 376,366 in 1967 to 278,232 in 1976. Production of milk increased from 7,069 million litres in 1936-38 to 13,603 million litres in 1975-76; production of wheat increased from 1,678 thousand tonnes in 1936-38 to 4,488 thousand tonnes in 1975-76 and the total area of agricultural land has fallen by 641,000 hectares in the last ten years. Britain has one of the highest tractor densities in the world with a tractor on every 15 hectares of arable land and there are some 80 establishments devoted to research and development in agriculture.

The ever-increasing cost of agricultural land and the high cost of capitalization for stock and machinery have tended to mean that agriculture has changed from being a way of life to a highly efficient business operation. The constant introduction of new techniques, more sophisticated machines, material, seed varieties, chemicals and breeds of livestock has meant that the agricultural labour force has had to accept and deal with some very rapid changes.

Since its formation in 1966 the Agricultural Training Board (ATB) has had as one of its objectives the identification of possible changes and pressures on the agricultural labour force, and the design of strategies to assist the industry to deal with the resultant demand for training.

The purpose of this paper is to present a number of instances in which the ATB has applied educational technology in an attempt to help the industry with its problems in the area of skills training. Its secondary purpose is to call for a much greater exchange of ideas on applications of educational technology on an international basis. Agriculture is a world-wide industry and there must be common learning problems, many of which might be solved by the freer exchange of ideas and knowledge.

A Training System

In its early days the ATB was faced with the problem of developing a system for the production of its recommendations on training. Tradition suggested that training boards should identify the various occupations within industries and then define the skills and knowledge possessed by experienced workers in those occupations. On analysis of some of the traditional occupations of the agricultural industry it soon became apparent that job descriptions varied greatly. For example, no two herdsmen or glasshouse workers carried out identical duties. It was, therefore, decided to base recommendations on the products of the industry. We are thus able to identify all tasks that have to be undertaken in the production of milk, the rearing of calves, the production of potatoes or the production of carnations. By identifying the tasks (or activities as we call them) within the production sequence it has been possible to develop training recommendations and associated training support material for the more important activities. In this way a 'supermarket' of training material and aids is being built up which can match the training needs of any agricultural worker having regard to what is being produced on his particular farm, and according to the duties which he undertakes. As new and changing techniques are introduced so these can be slotted into the 'supermarket' at an appropriate place in the production sequence.

By way of example Table 1 gives a list of activities which may be undertaken in the production of calves — Calf Rearing.

Training material covering the activities in this list consists of Instruction Plans to help those giving instruction and Trainee Guides for trainees receiving instruction. For some activities other paper-based aids to learning are produced and, where appropriate, audiovisual media and aids. All this material is produced as a result of fairly conventional systems of analysis of skills.

Learning Difficulties

To illustrate the type of material being produced we can look at an activity which we identify as an area of particular learning difficulty. Such activities usually call for the complete range of instructional and learning material which can be produced. The example chosen is Assisting at Calving, usually shortened to 'Calving'. Calving only infrequently becomes a problem. 90 per cent of calvings take place naturally with the cow managing quite happily without assistance. Of those cows needing help, half require the expertise and experience of a veterinary surgeon. The remainder can be dealt with by the stockman. The costs to the farmer and country of calf mortality, however, makes it essential to transfer some of the skill and experience of the veterinary surgeon to the cowman. To assist with training of cowmen the Board has produced a calving simulator. This is a development from our previous lambing simulator, which owes much to an original idea from the Glasgow Veterinary School. Details of the construction of the simulator are set out in Figure 1.

For the purpose of operating the simulator a dead calf has to be obtained. This is placed inside the transparent plastic uterus in the normal, or one of the abnormal, calving positions. Various vaginal and uterine pressures can be represented by the addition of air pressure to appropriate areas.

The aims of training using the simulator are to enable cowmen to:

(1) identify when to leave well alone and when to call the vet;
(2) give appropriate assistance to a cow having problems.

The first step is for trainees to recognize the norm situation. To this end an illustrated description of the process of parturition is given. This is reinforced wherever possible by internal examination of live cows, preferably demonstrating stages of cervical dilation.

UNIT A — Basic activities
Safe lifting and carrying
Recognizing signs of health and disorder in calves
Moving and handling calves
Restraining a calf
Disposing of a dead calf
Wiring a three-pin plug
Preparing and storing veterinary equipment and materials

UNIT B — General routine activities
Washing accommodation and equipment using hand tools
Using a pressure washer
Disinfecting, whitewashing and creosoting
Fumigating livestock accommodation and equipment
Using thermometers, time switches, thermostats, dimmers
Preparing calf accommodation for restocking
Daily bedding down (calves)
Maintaining environment control equipment
Dealing with a power failure
Mixing milk substitute
Feeding milk substitute (bucket)
Training a calf to drink and bottle feeding
Feeding milk substitute ad lib (machine feeding)
Feeding milk substitute ad lib (non-mech) teat feeder
Providing hay concentrates
Weaning calves
Weighing calves

UNIT C — Veterinary activities
Ear tagging
Ear tatooing calves
Dosing
Injecting calves
Disbudding calves (hot iron)
Castrating calves (Burdizzo)
Castrating calves (knife)
Castrating calves (rubber ring)
Removing spare teats

© Agricultural Training Board

Table 1. *Calf rearing*

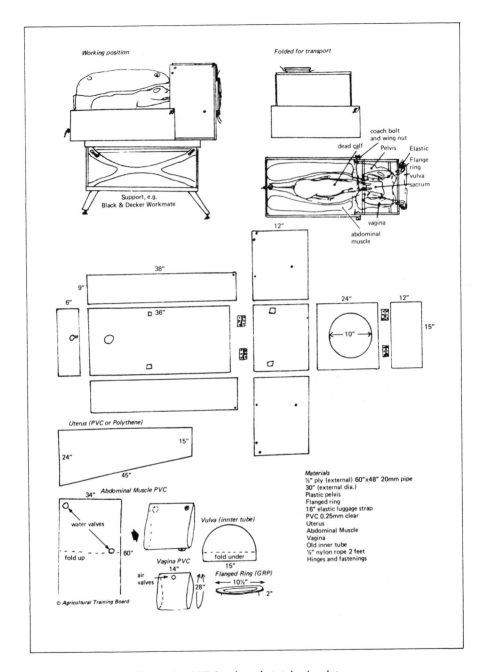

Figure 1. *ATB bovine obstetric simulator*

152

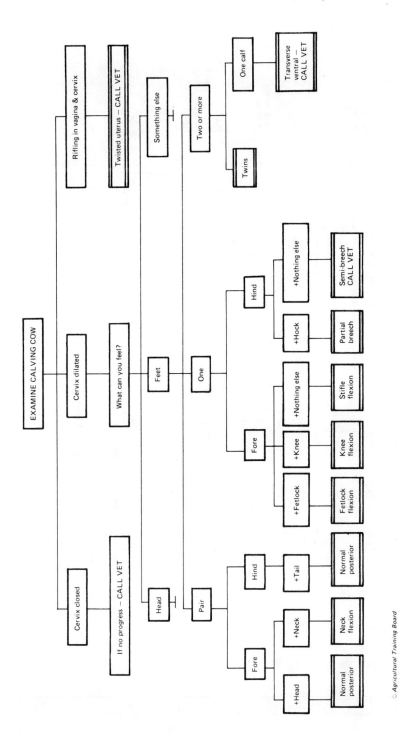

Figure 2. *Algorithm for identifying calf presentations*

© Agricultural Training Board

153

Figure 3. *Heat detection*

R3 (watch cow)			
S4.A (*Heat present*)	S_1^+ :	(*Standing to be mounted and not moving away*)	R4.1 Note No. and date
	S_2^+ :	(Mounting another *head first* — the one that mounts)	
	S_3^+ :	(*Swollen vulva*, mucous, etc)	
S4.B (*Heat future*)	S_1^- :	(*Being mounted unwillingly* when cannot evade)	R4.2 Note No. and need to look again at cow
	S_2^- :	(*Mounting other cows*)	
	S_3^- :	(*Disturbed behaviour* — bellowing, bunting*, sniffing, licking, Flehman's Grin, etc.)	
	S_4^- :	(chin resting, head to tail circling*, following other cows, being followed, etc.)	
S4.C (*Heat past*)	$S_{(-5)}$:	(*Dried mud on flanks* — from being mounted)	R4.3 Note No. and date for future observation
	$S_{(-6)}$:	(*Swollen vulva*, mucous smears on tail and flanks, blood, etc.)	
	$S_{(-7)}$:	(*Oestrus yawn*)	
	$S_{(-8)}$:		

Notes:

R3 : 4 or 5-hour intervals; *Night* and day: 30 mins plus per observation (not less or miss heats); *Undisturbed* cows.

* : stimulus conglomerates — need further analysis.

© *Agricultural Training Board*

The trainee then moves immediately onto the simulator with a normal presentation. The trainee learns to discriminate by feel between normal and abnormal presentations (see Figure 2). The simulator allows the linking of visual to tactile cues by using transparent material and a separate flip chart. After this corrective manipulations can be practised and the calf drawn out. The confidence that stockmen acquire from this training allows them to approach a real calving with fewer qualms.

Another area of learning difficulty on which work is being carried out at the present time is the 'Detection of Heat in Cattle'. This is a training problem brought about very much by the changing world. On modern intensive dairy farms the herdsman has very little time to observe his cows and to recognize when they are ready for artificial insemination or to receive the bull. The task is again a highly perceptual skill and one on which much of the financial success of the herd depends. A film has, therefore, been produced in conjunction with Bristol and Reading Universities. Dr Richard Esslemont of Reading University has been responsible for much recent research on Heat Detection while Dr Sue Long of the University of Bristol Veterinary Department has been able to offer further technical advice and obtain the help of the Audio-Visual Aids Unit of the University's Department of Drama in the production of the film. The various signs of heat — past, present and future — which have been identified and which form the basis of the training are set out in Figure 3.

16mm film was chosen, as the stimuli must be recognized among groups of moving cows. The film is divided into three segments and is designed to be stopped at the end of each segment to allow discussion, further explanation and emphasis by the instructor, usually a veterinary surgeon. The first two segments demonstrate the various signs of heat that must be recognized and when to look for them. The final segment consists of a series of film sequences which require the trainee to practise identification of cows on heat moving within a normal herd.

International Cooperation

One of the objectives of APLET is to provide a 'platform for the exchange of views and a means of communication between members'. Agriculture is practised in all countries of the world and there must be many common learning problems. Comparatively little, however, is published. The authors have put forward their own modest contribution in the hope that it will encourage others working in the field of agricultural education and training to present papers and perhaps enable a section to be devoted to agriculture at a future conference.

Conclusion

The authors submit that the agricultural industry has been forced to change more than most over recent years. We believe that educational technology has a vital part to play in both the UK and throughout the world in assisting with change and with meeting the ever-increasing demand for food production. Some applications of educational technology to particular learning problems have been presented, but we see a need for much greater cooperation in solving what must be common learning problems in many parts of the world.

Chapter 4: 'Ways and Means'
– The Instructional Media

This chapter is a chapter of differences — differences as wide ranging as those witnessed to exist by this conference between the educational needs of industrialized and 'developing' nations.

In the opening paper, Mr Stewart (18) gathers his experience as media consultant with WHO in India, Sri Lanka, Sudan and Egypt, to make a plea on behalf of the developing nations for an appropriate technology *of* education rather than more technology *in* education. The reader is further directed to McAleese (1) and Barker (Ch.11) in this respect.

In contrast, working in a country suffering the pains of de-industrialization, Mr Winfield (19) of the North Staffordshire Polytechnic presents a rationale for, and describes the design of, a mixed media course integrating a structured student work book with videotape playback facilities, for use in teaching students social-perception skills.

In the field of electrical science, Mr Rees *et al.* (20) of the Gwent College of Higher Education, describe the design of a part-time course which integrates and optimizes the advantages of team teaching, independent learning and resource-based learning.

An 'appropriate technology' certainly seems to have been found in the fourth paper of the chapter, wherein Professor Oh (21) of the University of Alberta, concisely describes the design, implementation and evaluation of a programmed multi-media course in educational graphics. Not only were course objectives achieved (to save instruction time) but also the unexpected 'bonus' of a large degree of increase in the quality of students' products.

Mr Bird (22) compares the effectiveness of teaching an aspect of film-making by traditional classroom methods or by film. A singularly thorough investigation produced no evidence that film was more or less effective than traditional classroom methods.

Of interest to readers who are yet to encounter the problems of setting up a tape/slide presentation unit, will be Dr Stephens's account (23) of such a facility, constructed by his department at the University of Reading. The paper provides useful details regarding the construction and equipping of the facility together with detailed costings.

A significant development in the use of a computer-microfiche interface is described by Dr Murza (24). The paper describes the production of microfiche from computer and camera outputs, then illustrates a typical self-instructional sequence using this system.

The Royal Navy have long been regarded as leading proponents of CCTV in education and training. In the eighth paper of the chapter, Lt Com Brooking (25) presents a comprehensive review of the Navy's activity and achievements in this area over the last ten years.

The final four papers of the chapter are grouped together quite consciously in order to allow reflection on the role of the 'high technology' media in education — particularly in 'distance learning' and its implications for a continuing education both in developed and developing societies.

Educational broadcasting is looked at by Dr Hurst (26) of the British Council. In a paper which examines attitudes to the medium, the very fact of centrally produced broadcasts is brought into question. Dr Hurst indicates that the economics of this kind of broadcasting are such that programmes have to be 'packaged for the mass, not for the individual; this being at odds with the general trend toward individualizing instruction'.

The more individualized and interactive medium of 'teleconferencing' is surveyed and evaluated by Dr Becker (27). Her detailed survey of the field will be of value to anyone investigating the medium. One can forsee existing open or non-dedicated telephone lines being utilized, together with slow scan video for instructional purposes on a large scale. This 'high technology, low cost' instructional medium could be of great significance for a planet high on technology but low on resources.

The chapter closes with two papers which deal with perhaps the most expensive medium of communication yet devised by mankind — satellite communication. Dr Daniel (28) points to some of the problems involved in using satellites for instructional communication. Not the least of these problems is cost: between $2.25m and $3.5m, depending on the system chosen. Dr Daniel offers reasoned warning 'of the danger that current educational experiments on satellites may never give rise to operational applications'.

Dr Robertson (29) led one such educational experiment in the use of the Canadian communications satellite, 'Hermes'. Dr Robertson concludes that the experiment was a success — perhaps ETIC '79 will receive an operational evaluation?

18. Appropriate Educational Technology

A.M. Stewart, *Dundee College of Technology*

Abstract: In recent years there has been great interest in the application of appropriate technology in developing countries. In the field of education this has tended to become the application of technology **in** education rather than technology **of** education. It is suggested that an appropriate educational technology will find expression in the analysis of the learning situation such that relevant objectives are derived, and in the design of instructional strategies such that available resources are utilized to bring about the achievement of these objectives.

Introduction

You need hardly be reminded of the continuing problem within the field of educational technology of having to consider technology **in** education and technology **of** education. Both are valid parts of an educational technology approach to the teaching and learning processes and the problem really only arises when one or other of these aspects is considered to the exclusion of the other.

Appropriate Technology

Appropriate technology is a term which is currently being applied in a number of fields in the developing world, and its origins can be traced to the intermediate technology ideas of Dr E.F. Schumacher.

It is all too easy to assume that the technology of the industrialized countries can, by transfer, solve problems in the developing world, and such assumption has led, in many parts of the world, to the wholesale adoption of costly and often inappropriate methods and techniques which are of benefit to only a small minority of the people.

Even in the industrialized world the appropriateness of many technologies is being questioned.

Educational Technology in Developing Countries

When we try to examine the application of educational technology in the developing world, we are very quickly forced to the conclusion that it is largely a technology **in** education which is being pursued. In country after country, millions of dollars have been spent in providing the hardware of the media and the software of alien cultures. The emphasis has always been on the use of media and visual material.

Perhaps much of this emphasis was and is due to the particular instructional forms used in developing countries, as has been pointed out in a UNESCO publication (1975): 'Teachers continue to copy from a book on to a makeshift blackboard . . . This form of teaching has become ingrained as the only way to instruct in existing circumstances.'

From this emphasis on media and visual material there has gradually evolved a new emphasis on objectives until the present state of educational technology could be said to be an objectives-based mediated instructional system.

Sam (1975) has indicated that in an educational technology approach to educational problems in developing countries 'educationists are encouraged to state objectives clearly, preferably in behavioral terms instead of the usual general principles which cannot be evaluated in any way.' He also notes that 'the choice of media may not be very great in many developing countries' and that 'even where they are available, the traditional approach is so deeply engrained that they are not used to the maximum.'

Various articles in the current issue of *Programmed Learning and Educational Technology* (1978) could be used to support this understanding of educational technology in developing countries. Essentially, teachers are becoming more precise about the learning they are trying to facilitate and they are using media in the hope that it may more readily be facilitated.

Developments in Appropriate Educational Technology

In the pursuit of mediated instruction, many educational technology centres have been established and equipped with sophisticated media systems. International funding made the supply of such equipment possible, but when this initial funding had ended and when spares were needed, the hard currency for replacements was not readily available. The problems of using this kind of technology were real — lack of suitably trained manpower; uncertain electrical supplies; non-availability of spares; and a host of other difficulties, and in response to these problems, attempts have been made to develop appropriate technologies for education and training.

For example, attempts are being made to produce, distribute, and utilize low-cost colour visual materials in the form of colour microfiche, and there is no doubt that such a system would be only a fraction of the cost of colour slide sets (it has been estimated at 5 per cent of the cost). A cheaper viewing and projection system still needs to be developed, but the system does look as if it has possibilities.

Various other appropriate technologies have been devised — some which are likely to be useful and others which are more likely to appear in a programme about 'oddball' inventions.

It has to be accepted that some sophisticated technologies will inevitably be adopted regardless of the difficulties and cost, and that there is no point in trying to dissuade governments or educational authorities. After all, such folly is quite common in the so-called developed world.

The point which has to be made, however, is that all of this, no matter how necessary, is only the application of appropriate technology **in** education, and that without an associated and appropriate technology **of** education, the educational problems of the developing world will continue.

Educational Needs in Developing Countries

What then, are the educational problems of the developing world and how can an appropriate educational technology be identified and applied?

Various writers have indicated a number of problems. For example, Dube (1976) has stated that

> Dated philosophies of education — absorbed by the educational elite some decades back in high prestige centres of learning abroad and often rejected by their progenitors after they

have outlived their utility — continued to guide the educational system.

He also claims that

the products of secondary and higher education swell the rosters of the unemployed for general category jobs. Most of them are unemployable for tasks that need specialised skills. The information packages that are doled out to them turn their minds into receptacles of knowledge rather than its creators.

And, in identifying the kind of education needed he says

To meet the challenges of the future we will need knowledge and skills of the highest order. Highly developed problem-solving capability will be needed not only in the fields of science and technology but also in the fields of human relations and management.

Cookey (1976) has identified the examination system for school and university entrance as one of the reasons why education cannot easily reorientate to meet national needs. He also cites the absence of science teaching as a serious weakness and argues that

science teaching is more than the encouragement of pupils to cram disconnected facts; it is an opportunity to establish in the pupils' minds scientific concepts and attitudes which can be applied in solving problems, and should be regarded as an integral part of a country's general education system.

These comments reinforce the views of many who have worked in developing countries. The result of the educational system is frequently an ability to remember vast amounts of information — facts, concepts, and principles — but an almost complete inability to apply such concepts and principles to solve problems. This situation is immediately obvious to anyone who has attempted to work in educational technology in developing countries — or at least to anyone who is concerned with more than just a technology in education. There is, therefore, an overall inappropriateness in what is learned.

No amount of technology in education will ever solve this kind of problem. What is also needed is a technology of education, and that cannot be applied until the teachers themselves have been oriented towards an appropriate technology of education.

In *A Systems Approach to Teaching and Learning Procedures: A Guide for Educators in Developing Countries* (UNESCO, 1975) the writers have frequently shown that the teacher has been unable to adapt. This is hardly surprising. As the teacher is a product of a system which has not emphasized problem-solving capabilities, he can hardly be expected to suddenly show such capability when he becomes a teacher. In the same book it has been stated that 'the traditional habits of teaching are so strong in the schools that no one has given much thought to changing them to meet the new situation' and that 'because of the lack of pre- and in-service training, many teachers are not aware of what may be done to change the learning environment.'

Thomas (1976) in a review of the work of UNESCO indicates that in this present decade

three new objectives received high priority in UNESCO's programmes: quality of education, teacher training, adaptation of educational systems. This amounts to saying, in plain terms, that school enrolment can, if necessary, be slowed down, provided that education is adapted to the real needs of the country and that greater care is bestowed on the recruitment, training and further training of teachers.

Application of an Appropriate Educational Technology

These emphases on adaptation to real needs and the training of teachers must go together. It is the teacher who needs to be trained to analyse the learning situation and derive appropriate objectives, and it is the teacher who needs to be trained to design appropriate instructional strategies. When the available resources for these strategies are considered, it is the teacher who is likely to be the most readily available and adaptable. Lessinger and Gillis's (1976) concept of the teacher as performer has probably great relevance in this context.

Recall the usual visual description of the learning system design process and

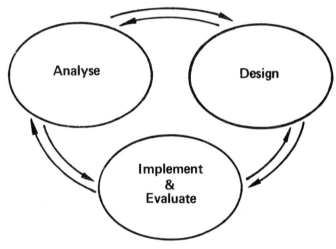

Figure 1

identify the present work of the teacher in the developing world (and many teachers in the otherwise developed world) within this system. Attention has been paid to the **design** phase, in that attempts have been made to write specific objectives in behavioural terms and to use mediated instruction when possible or desirable. The **implementations and evaluation** phase has also received attention, particularly in respect of assessment of the student's achievement of the specified objectives, but with little attention to the effectiveness and efficiency of the total system. The great weakness, as has already been pointed out, is that little or nothing has been done in the **analysis** phase, with the resulting irrelevance or in inappropriateness of the objectives chosen.

An appropriate educational technology must, of course, involve all three phases, but its application in the design phase is, above all, desperately needed at this time. An appropriate educational technology in the developing countries, therefore, at this present time, has to be one which lays less emphasis on technology **in** education (whether it be 'appropriate' or not) and more emphasis on technology **of** education, and the appropriateness of that educational technology is likely to find expression in the analysis of the learning situation such that relevant objectives are derived, and in the design of instructional strategies such that available resources are utilized to bring about the achievement of these objectives. The key person in all this is the teacher, and the urgent need is for these teachers (and their teachers) to be oriented towards an appropriate educational technology.

162

References

Cookey, S. J. (1976) The training and supply of middle-level personnel. *Prospects,* 6, 2, p.227.

Dube, S. C. (1976) Theories and goals of education: a third world perspective. *Prospects,* 6, 3, pp.350, 361.

Lessinger, L. and Gillis, D. (1976) *Teaching as a Performing Art.* Crescendo Publications Inc, Dallas, Texas.

Sam, L. R. (June 1975) The role of educational technology in developing countries. *West African Journal of Education,* 19, p.307.

Thomas, J. (1976) Thirty years in the service of education. *Prospects,* 6, 3, p.319.

UNESCO (1975) *A Systems Approach to Teaching and Learning Procedures: A Guide for Educators in Developing Countries,* pp.127, 139. The UNESCO Press, Paris.

19. Social Perception: Designing Mixed-Media Instruction in a Polytechnic

I. Winfield, *North Staffordshire Polytechnic, Stoke-on-Trent*

Abstract: The educational objective is to increase accuracy of social perception and the ability to analyse human interaction among students enrolled in higher education.

A teaching video-tape was designed and produced, which incorporated an integrated student work book. The combined instructional material of television and associated work book allowed the student to interact by actively responding.

Introduction

Patterns of employment are changing in industrially advanced Western societies. Fewer people are employed in direct manufacturing industries while more are becoming employed in the service and supply industries. There is a noticeable growth in administration, management, the recreation industries and in the helping professions.

By and large people in these occupations are concerned with managing and making judgements about people; in understanding human motives and behaviour. The corresponding training needs for these occupations are being increasingly identified as quite specific social skills of interaction. Training designers are responding to these training demands by using closed-circuit television, video-tape and video-cassette in a variety of ways.

This paper describes two things. Firstly, it details a method of task analysis the author has found helpful in identifying and describing specific social skill goals. This method assists in identifying sub-goals and enabling competencies required for these skills. Using this approach a mixed media social skills training 'package' has been designed and made. This is described. Secondly, the paper describes a pilot study and series of experiments that are currently under way at the North Staffordshire Polytechnic. These are exploring the most effective ways of presenting the teaching material.

Learning Objectives and Task Analysis in Use

Most instructional designers specify their objectives closely and undertake rigorous task analyses. In this field the major works of R. M. Gagné (1965, 1970, 1977) have been especially influential. Typically sub-goals in an overall learning task are identified according to their type or category of learning. The sub-goals are then arranged in a hierarchy of increasing complexity of learning category with the overall learning goal serving as the pinnacle.

Learning hierarchies generated this way can be validated for their teaching efficiency by a relatively easy process (White, 1973, 1974), and instructional designers now seem willing to use these techniques of learning task analysis across a wide range of mostly rule-based or analytic knowledge domains. For example, recent practical applications range from designing mathematical instruction (Kane and Phillips, 1973) to technical draughting (Lawson, 1973, 1974) and to common workshop motor skills (Dallos and Winfield, 1975). All instructional designers would, however, be cautious in specifying learning 'routes' or elaborate hierarchies for verbally based learning material, for clearly the richness of verbal associations and mediating ideas that an individual learner has for this type of material precludes a rigid, mechanical hierarchical approach. Gagné himself (1968) warned against the dangers inherent in using this approach in inappropriate subject areas.

Can there be a Task Analysis of Social Skills?

The question at first sounds preposterous — and rightly so. For, of all the human skills we learn, social skills would appear to defy inflexible programming or otherwise systematic instruction. We acquire social skills often by a sudden realization of our failings — certainly we acquire our more adult skills in non-institutional settings. These and other considerations add up to general recognition of the non-incremental nature of social skills learning in adults.

Even though there have been notable advances in our knowledge of the mechanics of interactive behaviour and social skills our knowledge of their acquisition remains relatively meagre and often controversial. To attempt the systematization of their acquisition would be to court disaster. For not only would the over-precise specification of social skill objectives attract the charge of spurious precision, the whole process of training in skills could be construed as running counter to the traditions of Western liberal education (Davies, 1976). Our awareness of the complex issues involved has been sharpened by the other social sciences, notably sociology. Berger and Luckman (1972) observe that the very notion of what we deem to call a social 'skill' or a social act worth preserving or developing embodies certain values, and hence, ideological presuppositions. These presuppositions should not be left unquestioned, but should themselves be examined openly. Smith (1972) doing this, notes two opposite extremes to which many social skills training courses are currently put — namely Machiavellian or humanistic.

Even if the instructional designer is unable to use the precise notion of 'routes' through learning hierarchies and to be able to usefully apply them to social skill goals, it might still be possible to gain benefit from undertaking a task analysis.

If we identify a particular social skill or activity the following question is a meaningful and instructive one: 'Just what kinds of social behaviour and under what circumstances might a learner demonstrate mastery of this learning material?' In attempting to answer this question all the underlying concepts, social abilities and discriminations of social activities which are enabling competencies should be thrown into focus.

As an example of this approach Pearn (1975) identified the social skill requirements of, among others, managers, nurses and prisoners. His emphasis is upon the pragmatic, immediate social skill requirements of these people. To illustrate his point he identifies a special social skill badly needed by certain categories of long-stay prisoners when released into open society. This is the ability to project the self and generally 'manage' interviews with petty officials: the social security interview, the job interview.

This is a specific skill, which has long been left unpractised by the subject. Pearn is able to see five different kinds of learning needed in this particular task.

Student Participation in Defining a Specific Social Skill Goal

A number of conversations with part-time and full-time students of management, personnel management and sociology, led to the recognition of a specific social skill need. All students acknowledged the need to understand the dynamic of small decision-making groups. The students expressed the desire to be able to identify and name processes and events as they actually happened in real-life groups. The terminal goal was therefore identified as an increase in the ability to recognize and name behaviour as it is exhibited by people interacting in a small group setting.

What can be said about the enabling competencies or sub-goals required to reach such a goal?

The first step consisted of counselling the students themselves. For instance, how did they see the learning task ahead? What range of abilities did they possess in this direction already? What did they personally see as obstacles to increasing their abilities in social perception? Issues raised by this dialogue, together with curriculum considerations generated some useful sub-goals. These sub-goals were then identified as to the category of learning they belonged to, and this was used to plan the instructional sequence (see Figure 1).

Choosing the Media of Video-Tape and Work Book

Many reviews of research on the use of television for teaching higher categories of learning (abstract concepts, principles, problem-solving strategies) show the medium as performing weakly, relative to other media of instruction (Chu and Schramm, 1967; Campeau, 1972).

Perhaps as a reaction to those unfavourable findings, researchers and programme designers now appear to be exploring ways of intervening in the actual process of learning from televised instruction. Here are a few examples:

- □ when using ETV to teach subtle visual discriminations, strong enhanced visual reminders are repeatedly inserted 'on screen' (Tidhar, 1973).
- □ programme-makers insert questions during transmission in order to elicit critical activity and student response. Student errors are corrected (Teather and Marchant, 1974).
- □ overt student participation and response can be got by designing student work books to accompany 'off air' ETV transmissions (Clay, 1974).

For the chosen goal, instruction was to be undertaken by the combined media of video-tape with a student work book programmed into the transmission. This approach was chosen because identified were two overlapping sets of student need. The students themselves, while acknowledging the need for theoretical and conceptual inputs necessary for understanding group behaviour, equally favoured some form of experiential learning: they wanted to witness, to experience and critically relate to the subject matter at a participative, emotional level.

The work book was to perform most of the former functions; the televised sequences the latter.

Making the Tape and Integrated Work Book

One guiding principle during the design and manufacture was that of careful stimulus control within the appropriate media. Consider Travers, 1966:

The common practice of filling both the auditory and visual channels with a continuous flow of information would seem to have little support, except perhaps that it may satisfy some of the compulsion of film producers . . . The silent film with the alternation of picture and print would appear to find much theoretical support as a teaching device.

166

Category of learning

Problem solving:

> Recall and use of relevant rules, concepts and discriminations when a novel problem is presented on screen (the Case Study Exercise).

Rules:

> Demonstration of behaviour associated with high participation communication pattern. Verbal statement of behaviour in the experimental condition:
>
>
>
> 'the wheel'

> Demonstration of behaviour associated unequal participation communication pattern. Verbal statement of behaviour in the experimental condition:
>
>
>
> 'the circle'

Concepts:

> Communication patterns, e.g. structured, unstructured.

> Different goals for groups: e.g. problem solving, recreation, quasi-therapeutic.

Discriminations:

> Discriminating between: verbal and non-verbal communication; non-verbal leakage; task-related and non-task-related communication, etc.

Figure 1. *Part of task analysis of learning*

A printed work book contained the following items:

- ☐ explanations of concepts that would be new to the student
- ☐ a written statement of the overall learning objectives
- ☐ advance organizers for sections of immediately following video-tape
- ☐ a detailed description of a simple experiment performed on the screen
- ☐ a display of the programme content. The students were able to see continuously where they were in relation to the whole exercise
- ☐ a 'programmed' question and answer section

The screen was used for those functions it is unashamedly good at: illustrating aspects of interactive behaviour and the nuances of human expression and forms of human communication. The dynamic 'fizz' of a small working group is eminently televisual.

The tape and work book were made to a conventional eight-point learning sequence plan (Gagné and Briggs, 1974). This consisted of:

(1) State the objectives of the instruction.
(2) Inform the learner of the objectives by providing a model of performance.
(3) Provide learning guidance.
(4) Learning guidance: providing a verbal definition.
(5) Learning guidance: providing a variety of examples.
(6) Present the stimulus and elicit the performance.
(7) Provide feedback.
(8) Assess attainment of objectives.

During the design and manufacture of the tape and work book reference was made continuously to the category of learning being undertaken by the learner at any point in the learning sequence. Prescriptions for choosing the appropriate method of instruction follow easily from this. For instance, in order to teach students to discriminate between close-appearing social behaviours (a form of discrimination learning) successive cue discrimination was used. A heightened, enhanced difference was displayed, then gradually reduced so that students learn to make fine discriminations. Similarly when students were asked to learn principles they were first invited to formulate those principles in their own words in the accompanying work book.

A Gagnérian recommendation on how to teach a problem-solving strategy would be to show its applicability to a wide variety of situations by transfer or generalizability. The student is invited to apply these in a later exercise.

The tape and work book work as follows. Students are instructed by the screen to read the work book. In this the objectives are spelt out and the programme content and types of learning involved are explained and displayed. The student is then 'cued' into the first short sequence of tape which illustrates some aspect of group behaviour. The student alternates between screen and work book answering questions posed both on screen and in their work book. Feedback on adequacy of response is provided both by the work book and screen. Teather and Marchant (1974) speculate interestingly, that the periodic shifts of attention from screen to work book and vice versa, itself enhances learning.

Testing Learned Social Perception: The Case Study Exercise

Any criterion test of learning should be appropriate to the instruction used. An audiovisual case study was devised which consisted of four minutes of group activity. This four-minute tape had accompanying sound but was without commentary in any way, and it featured a group of people engaged in a genuine problem-solving activity that the students were known to be interested in. It was chosen and edited so that it contained all the essential features of group behaviour as taught in the main teaching tape and work book.

A content analysis was made of the case study tape by independent observers. Written statements at the appropriate level of analysis were pooled and entered onto the case study exercise scoring sheet.

Students at the end of the teaching tape were invited to self-test their learned abilities by studying this case study. They were instructed to note down on their case study response sheets, what features of group behaviour they perceived as it was actually happening. They were told they could make their notes in shorthand form to be later expanded when the transmission ended. It served, in short, as a measure of their ability to transfer their learned abilities to a totally new situation — to test their social perceptiveness.

Pilot studies on the tape and work book and the use of the case study exercise so far have shown:

☐ The case study exercise can be used as a pre-test before the main instructional period. Used in this way it performs a function similar to pre-tests used in other instructional media (Hartley and Davies, 1976).

☐ Students can be given a 'structured' case study response sheet which asks them to categorize behaviour into the major areas studied on the tape (task-related communication, non-verbal communication, etc.). Total number of student responses in this 'structured' condition is higher than if no structuring of response sheet is given. This suggests that students appreciate a degree of guidance upon how to use audiovisual case-study materials.

References

Berger, P. L. and Luckman, T. (1972) *The Social Construction of Reality*. Allen Lane, The Penguin Press, London.

Campeau, P. L. (1972) *Selective Review of the Results of Research on the Use of Audio Visual Media to Teach Adults*. Council for Cultural Co-operation, Steering Group on Educational Technology, Council of Europe, Strasbourg.

Chu, G. C. and Schramm, W. (1967) *Learning from Television, What the Research Says*. National Association of Educational Broadcasters, Washington.

Clay, R. C. (1974) The influence of student participation on learning from ETV. *Visual Education*, October 23-28.

Cook, J. M. (1969) *Learning and Retention by Informing Students of Behavioural Objectives and Their Place in the Hierarchical Learning Sequence*. Maryland University, USOE Final Report ERIC: ED 036-869.

Cook, J. M. and Walbesser, H. H. (1973) *How to Meet Accountability with Behavioural Objectives and Learning Hierarchies*. Advance Educational Press, Maryland.

Dallos, R. and Winfield, I. J. (1975) Instructional strategies in industrial training and rehabilitation. *Journal of Occupational Psychology* **48**, 4, pp.241-52.

Davies, I. K. (1976) *Objectives in Curriculum Design*. McGraw-Hill, London.

Gagné, R. M. (1965) *The Conditions of Learning*. 1st Ed. Holt, Rinehart and Winston, New York.

Gagné, R. M. (1968) Learning hierarchies. *Educational Psychologist*, **6**, 1. (Presidential Address given by the Retiring President, American Psychological Association, 3 August 1968, San Francisco, California).

Gagné, R. M. (1970) *The Conditions of Learning*, 2nd ed., Holt, Rinehart and Winston, New York.

Gagné, R. M. (1977) *The Conditions of Learning*, 3rd ed., Holt, Rinehart and Winston, New York.

Gagné, R. M. and Briggs, L. J. (1974) *Principles of Instructional Design*. Holt, Rinehart and Winston, New York.

Gropper, G. L. (1966) Learning from visuals: some behavioural considerations. *Audio-Visual Communication Review,* **14,** 1, pp.37-69.

Gropper, G. L. and Lumsdaine, A. A. (1961) *The Use of Student Response to Improve Televised Instruction.* The Metropolitan Pittsburg Educational Television Station and the American Institute for Research, Pittsburg.

Hartley, J. and Davies, I. K. (1976) Pre-instructional strategies: the role of pretests, behavioural objectives, overviews and advance organizers. *Review of Educational Research,* **46,** 2, pp.239-65.

Jamieson, G. H. (1973) Visual media in a conceptual framework for the acquisition of knowledge. *Programmed Learning and Educational Technology,* **10,** 1, pp.32-9.

Kane, R. B. and Phillips, E. R. (1973) Validating learning hierarchies for sequencing mathematical tasks in elementary school mathematics. *Journal for Research in Mathematics Education,* May, pp.141-51.

Lawson, T. E. (1973) Influence of instructional objectives on learning technical subject matter. *Journal of Industrial Teacher Education,* **10,** 4, pp.6-14.

Lawson, T. E. (1974) Gagné's learning theory applied to technical instruction. *Training and Development Journal* April, pp.32-40.

Pearn, M. (1975) *The C.R.A.M.P. Approach to the Teaching of Social and Life Skills and a Glossary of Selected Social Skills Training Terms.* Industrial Training Research Unit, Cambridge.

Smith, P. B. (1972) The skills of social interaction. In Dodwell, P. C. (ed.) *New Horizons in Psychology,* 2. Penguin, Harmondsworth.

Teather, D. C. B. and Marchant, H. (1974) Learning from film with particular reference to the effects of cueing, questioning and knowledge of results. *Programmed Learning and Educational Technology,* **11,** 6, pp.317-27.

Tidhar, L. (1973) Can visual reminders increase learning from television. *British Journal of Educational Technology,* **4,** 2, pp.142-9.

Travers, R. M. W. (1966) *Studies Related to the Design of Audio-Visual Teaching Methods.* University of Utah, US Dept. of Health Education and Welfare, Office of Education Contract No. 3-20-003.

White, R. T. (1973) Research into learning hierarchies. *Review of Educational Research,* **43,** 3, pp.121-36.

White, R. T. (1974) The validation of a learning hierarchy. *American Educational Research Journal,* **11,** 2, pp.121-35.

20. An Integrated Learning System for Technician Education

P. A. I. Davies, J. F. Jarvis, J. G. Kelly, D. T. Rees and K. R. Webber
Gwent College of Higher Education, Newport

Abstract: An integrated learning system has been developed which optimizes the advantages of team teaching, independent learning and resource-based learning. Details are given of the planning of the system, its implementation and evaluation. Investigations have been carried out into the effect of the system on student attitudes.

1. Introduction

There are many examples of innovative learning systems in operation. These include programmed learning, Keller plans, simulation and gaming, team teaching, etc. There is considerable evidence of the effectiveness of these systems. In developing the system described here an attempt is made to obtain a correct 'mix' of learning strategies, appropriate to the course aims in an integrated meaningful whole, rather than use any one method.

The system was devised for the third year of a City and Guilds Electrical Technicians Course (Course No. 281), and in particular for the subject of 'Electrical Principles' and its associated laboratory work. The course as it had operated for many years has posed many problems. Students entering the course at the Gwent College of Higher Education have studied the previous two years at a variety of other colleges, and therefore their background, achievement and study methods varied considerably. They are young apprentices and attend college for one day a week of eight hours class contact. The motivation of these students was not good and their examination results at the end of the session had remained poor for many years. There was considerable dissatisfaction from both college staff and employers.

Much of the literature available on new approaches to learning relates to full-time students and there is little previous information on the success of innovative methods for part-time students. Although the course is meant to be specific for the electrical engineering technician, the relevance of it to the student's vocational need is not explicitly known. An added difficulty is that the students come from a variety of industries, often requiring different skills. It is therefore desirable to present the course so that it will provide not only for the immediate scientific and technical information required by the student, but also develop attitudes and skills that will be of longer-term value.

The system to be devised should, therefore, attempt to overcome the problems and constraints mentioned above.

2. Organization and Planning

It was decided at the outset that a team of at least three staff should investigate the problem. The group would regularly, purposefully, and deliberately work cooperatively in the planning, conducting and evaluating of learning experiences. The basic assumption is that a group of professionals whose minds are focused on a problem will arrive at solutions superior to those offered individually. In selecting a group of staff it was essential to have people who were innovative and were aware of various trends in teaching methods, and who would work together closely. The staff selected were three of the latest recruits to the faculty. The staff involved readily agreed that if they were not fully conversant with various approaches they would attend staff development courses, such as those provided at colleges of education (technical).

Early on in the planning the team became aware of the resource implications. More flexibility of time-tabling than normally available in further education would be necessary, and it was imperative that the lecturers involved were given time for cooperative planning, and that their other teaching commitments were arranged so that they were available at the same time. Space requirements would also have to be flexible. Various hardware would be required, but a very important aspect would be the design of the software, such as handouts, slide/tapes, overhead transparencies etc. It was realized that the production of these would require close collaboration with a graphics artist/photographer. Fortunately at this stage, it was possible to incorporate into the team an experienced media resources officer who was conversant with the design of learning materials.

The course was divided into eight units on the basis explained in the next section. Most of the units involved three or four weeks' work. One member of the team took on the role of coordinator for a particular unit, both for the planning and the operational stage. The units were grouped into four phases, each phase occupying seven to eight weeks. The students are tested at the end of each phase.

3. Educational Rationale

The course should meet the educational aims of most courses in the further education sector, that is it should provide for the needs of industry, commerce and society and contribute to the personal development and ambitions of the student. More specific aims are provided by the City and Guilds of London Institute, viz:

> The electrical engineering technician must be able to apply in a responsible manner proven techniques. To do this, it is necessary to have a basic knowledge of theory, be able to communicate information, be familiar with regulations and specifications, be aware of the methods of diagnosis and testing, be able to keep up to date with developments and understand the practical implications of situations.

The content of the course is provided as a traditional syllabus of a list of topics. In planning a new approach the first task was to write the syllabus in behavioural objective terms. As can be seen from the aims quoted above, the affective domain is also involved. If the learning environment is supposed to enable students to achieve these skills, then some reservations must be made on the effectiveness of many traditional teaching situations, which assume that:

(1) the group size should remain the same for all activities
(2) the lecture room is equally appropriate for all activities
(3) students learn at the same rate.

It is now well established that:

(1) Optimal class size is related to the type of learning
(2) For the mere receiving of knowledge large classes are not inferior to small classes.
(3) For the manipulation of knowledge, small classes are optimal.

(4) For complex mental exercises and development of attitudes, one-to-one tutorials are superior to small classes.

Furthermore, the activities selected for the students should be those appropriate to the objectives, and as far as possible effective use should be made of all the relevant activities that are available. In this case it was decided to use large group instruction, small group and individual work involving assignments, investigations and projects, with back-up material of handouts, audio pages and slide/tape materials. The system thus uses resource-based learning, with the teacher as a manager, in contrast to the conventional system where the teacher is often simply an information source. However, in large group instruction the role of the teacher as expositor and motivator is preserved. The division of material among the learning situations was therefore based on the criteria set out in Table 1.

Criteria	Situation
Topics of mainly knowledge/information content, basic concepts, overview of relevance to industrial scene.	Large group instruction (LGI)
Goals requiring personal interaction between students, and between student and teacher. Topics of difficult concepts, evaluation, development of desirable attitudes, and awareness of values.	Small group work (SGW)
Objectives students can achieve by themselves — comprehension, analysis, seeking and organizing information, self-reliance and self-discipline	Directed private study (DPS)

Table 1

In addition to analysing the course into objectives a conceptual map was developed in order to make explicit the relationship between each part of the syllabus. This enabled the objectives to be placed in a form of hierarchy and formed the basis of dividing the course into units.

4. Implementation

The time available for the course is four hours per week for approximately 33 weeks. The first half-hour is used for the large group instruction. This lecture is delivered by one of the team with the other members always present in a supportive role, for example, giving a demonstration or assisting with audiovisual aids. The lecture is highly visual, using slides, CCTV, and overhead transparencies and practical demonstrations. The lecture is designed for high impact, it gives the student an overview of the work for that particular unit, and touches on the relevance of the work to the industrial scene. The students are not expected to take any notes, and a 'potted' version of the lecture is always available afterwards for the student on slide/tape equipment.

The students then divide into three small groups with individual lecturers. After consultation between students and teacher each group decides on its next activities. There may be a tutorial period, or students may move into the laboratories, the library, or into a learning resources room. Individual learning material is available in print form, supported by slide/tape programmes, and audio pages which provide analytical problems, guidelines and data for assignments, and instruction on laboratory procedures and equipment.

173

In an *assignment* the attitudes demanded of a student are more than just participating in a teacher-led environment. He has to demonstrate problem-solving skills, propose solutions, and justify his approach. In total he is appreciating a set of values.

The *investigations* may be only pen and paper exercises, but often require laboratory and experimental work. The student is required to accept responsibility for his own learning and recognize the role of systematic planning.

Projects are more open-ended than the previous exercises, and frequently involve cooperation with other students. They show how the student demonstrates industry, punctuality, self-discipline, and how he participates in group activities. In total it is a good indicator of the student's attitudes and values.

5. Resource Requirements

Lecture rooms, tutorial rooms and laboratories are usually tightly scheduled and to operate the system described in an otherwise traditional environment can prove difficult. In this instance, if traditional methods of instruction had been used there would have been two, or maybe three, 'parallel' classes. In total therefore the space demands need not be any greater, except there is the constraint that they must be available at the same time. One room was permanently allocated as a 'resource centre' and served as the focus for the work. All handouts, slide/tapes, audio pages were available here, and it was fortunate that the room was in a laboratory area which made the movement of students between the various areas and the availability of staff an easy matter.

Cooperative planning and preparation of learning materials places heavy demands on staff time and effort. However, large rewards can follow if the acceptance of criticism from within the team, and shared responsibility for adopted decisions result in combining innovation and soundness. It is not essential for all the team to participate in the teaching of the course, although this offers clear advantages for its evaluation and improvement.

The availability of hardware such as CCTV, overhead projectors, slide/tape and audio equipment is an important resource, and ease of operation and reliability does much to make things run smoothly.

To optimize the advantages of an integrated learning system a continuing source of up-to-date learning materials is needed. It is essential that sufficient reprographic facilities are to hand; good layout and a well-chosen typeface, or if available a variety of suitable typefaces can do much to encourage learning.

However, it is in the generation of visual learning material such as slides, transparencies, charts and diagrams that the skills of the graphic designer are essential. His inclusion in the team from the outset ensures that the experience of a planner and manager of design and production techniques is at the service of the teaching team. The graphics artist will provide the expertise in communication, and will ensure that the visual materials meet the criteria of clarity, interest and motivation, relevance to the learning situation, and ability to convey the message in the time available.

The importance of the latter criteria to the success of a system based on resource material should be stressed. The constraints will always be skills, time, money, but they are not insurmountable and it is possible to resolve these problems by a systematic approach. Art work can be conveniently proportioned for a range of media, and production procedures can be standardized.

6. Student Assessment

In accord with the philosophy that a variety of learning activities should be used, assessment is undertaken in several ways. Phase tests, in-course assessment and end tests are used.

The phase tests, every seven to eight weeks, are objective-based and comprise multiple-choice questions and an 'open-book' examination. The pass mark is 60 per cent and one resit is allowed.

In-course assessment is based on the assignments, investigations and projects, and particular attention is given to the development of attributes in the affective domain, although it is recognized that the reliability of marking may be subject to variability.

The end test is entirely open-book and problem-centred. An attempt is made to generate problems which are relevant to the student's work situation. The pass mark is 40 per cent.

7. Evaluation

Evaluation of the system has been divided into *internal evaluation* and *external evaluation*. By internal evaluation is meant how well the system meets the short term and the more easily measurable objectives. External evaluation takes into account more long-term objectives such as how successful the course has been in creating the right attitudes and meeting the vocational objectives of the student in his industrial role. At this stage it is not possible to come to any definite conclusions. Student successes have improved compared with the previous courses, but insufficient data is available on how the students fare in the subsequent year of the course which is conducted on traditional lines and leads to a conventional external examination. The validity of any such data may, however, be questioned, as success in such an examination may not depend on the entire range of skills that have been aimed at in the present course. On a subjective basis, it has been reported by staff taking the subsequent year that the competence of the students in the laboratory is much improved.

The lack of any adverse reports from the employers is taken to indicate a considerable improvement over the previous course. At least, since students still fail it can be taken that employers and college are in agreement on the assessment. In the past there were many cases of students failing whom the employers rated as good.

To evaluate the change in students' attitude a standard attitude test has been given at the beginning and end of the course, as well as to students on other similar courses taught conventionally. So far this has failed to show any definite evidence of attitude change in terms of total personality.

Feedback from students has also been obtained by means of a questionnaire. Preliminary results show that about 70 per cent of the students favour the integrated course approach.

8. Conclusion

It has been shown that it is possible to use innovative methods with part-time technician students. The students not only readily accepted the system, but liked it. Those of us who participated also found the challenge enjoyable.

Although we have emphasized the resource implication of the scheme used, it is possible to achieve many of its main features with modest resources; the essential requirement being professional cooperation within a team.

The analysis, planning and operation can be readily adapted for other courses, especially those of the Technician Education Council.

An indirect but important advantage of the system is that it provides an

175

excellent method for staff development, by attaching an inexperienced lecturer to the team.

Acknowledgement

The authors gratefully acknowledge the support of the Nuffield Foundation and the Governors of the Gwent College of Higher Education.

21. Teaching a Graphics Course through Programmed Instruction

C. Y. Oh, *University of Alberta, Edmonton, Canada*

Abstract: The paper describes the development of video-taped individualized instruction programmes to teach students the graphics component in a course on the preparation of instructional materials. Student performance is reviewed and compared to that when conventional teaching methods were used. Reasons for a significant improvement in student performance are proposed.

Statement of Problem

Ed. AV 363* — Preparation of Instructional Materials. This course is a hand-on introduction to the techniques of preparing instructional materials, for classroom use.

The majority of the course (40 per cent) is devoted to graphics. Topics covered include lettering, visualization, mounting, and transparency production. The remainder of the course includes introductions to: 'basic' photography (25 per cent), audio recording techniques (15 per cent) and design and production of video programmes (20 per cent).

Overwhelming student interest in the course has forced the department to offer 20 sections each year. Indications are that this number will increase, as 30 to 50 students are unable to register in the course each term as a result of a limited enrolment capacity.

At present, in a regular term, six or seven sections of the course are offered simultaneously. Each section accommodates up to 22 students. This means that approximately 150 students are taking the course at one time. These large numbers create heavy demands on equipment, materials and working facilities. To distribute this demand each section follows a different instructional sequence which results in a staggering of topics between sections. This staggering reduces the problem of simultaneous demand for specialized equipment such as cameras, tape recorders, and CCTV units.

However, in the graphics section of the course there is a peak demand on certain equipment within each topic. This problem is compounded by a degree of overlap between sections in the teaching of the graphics topics, with normally half the sections covering graphics at the same time.

The above problems created a great deal of pressure on instructors and students. An innovative teaching method was necessary to reduce this problem.

* Ed. AV 363 — Preparation of Instructional Materials — the course is one of the 18 instructional technology courses offered by the Faculty of Education at the University of Alberta. This course is one of the two introductory courses to the Instructional Technology programme which leads to the diploma and Master's degree. Since these introductory courses are specifically designed for classroom teachers, they are extremely popular with students.

Instructional Design and Methodology

Totally individualized instructional segments were designed for each topic in the graphics section of Ed. AV 363. Seventeen slide/tape sets were produced for classroom instruction, and were accompanied by a student manual. The slide/tape sets were dubbed unchanged onto ¾" colour video-cassettes. Rather than cutting, slide changes were a short dissolve. Two copies of each of the 17 slide/tape sets* and one copy of each of the 17 colour video-tapes were placed in an existing carrel area for use by two of the sections of Ed. AV 363. Seven of the topics did not require any prerequisite skills. This allowed students to start in different places.

At the beginning of the course each student received a copy of the student manual and a student activity guide for the graphics section. The student manual provides detailed step-by-step production procedures and most of the necessary production materials. The student activity guide explains the topic, objectives, finished product, student manual references, media materials references and the minimum pre-entry skills for each topic.

Production facilities available to students to complete their assignments include the classroom and the CMPA (Curriculum Materials Preparation Area). Both have all the equipment needed to complete the assignments. The CMPA is a service area available to students and staff within the faculty where they can prepare their own instructional materials for use in student teaching, class projects, presentations, or any other instructional uses. Students are able to purchase small quantities of production materials required for the graphic assignments at the CMPA. Both the CMPA and the carrel area are open for extended hours, 8.30 a.m. to 9.30 p.m. weekdays, and 9.00 a.m. to 5.00 p.m. weekends.

Regular class meetings were completely cancelled for five weeks except for a one-hour seminar per week, at which time the whole class met with the instructor and discussed their activities and problems. Students were required to turn in their finished products one day ahead of the seminars so that the instructor could evaluate them and return them at the beginning of each seminar. This produced lively discussion of the procedures and any difficulties encountered.

Since seven out of 15 topics did not require pre-entry skills students were encouraged to start at any of those seven topics. This distributed the demand for equipment, both for the playback of the media materials and for production activities.

Initial implementation of this instructional method took place in 1976. Previous to this the instructional method consisted of: introduction to the new topic, live demonstration, and discussion. Student performance in 1974 and 1975 was recorded using this conventional instructional method. In 1976 the individualized instructional method was implemented and student performance recorded. In the spring of 1978 samples of all required graphics products were added to the individualized instructional packages in the carrel area.

Evaluation of student products has been consistent for all three instructional methods. Products are graded according to the following scale and conditions.

Grade		Numerical value
A	Perfect	10
B	Not perfect but usable	6
C	Poor — but just usable	3
D	Not usable or not as assigned	0
E	No work handed in	-10

* The 17 slide/tape sets are part of a complete graphics kit entitled *C. Y. Oh: Production Techniques for Instructional Graphic Materials* published by Charles Merrill Publishing

Until work has been graded and returned, any piece of work can be replaced by another attempt at that assignment.

Any assignment with a grade of C, D, or E can (and should) be repeated. The repeats are graded on a A-, B-, and C- scale (worth 8, 5 and 2 respectively). The repeat must be handed in within one week of the graded work being returned.

Both the instructor and his teaching assistant worked together on evaluation and closely followed guidelines for evaluation stated in the manual. A high degree of consistency in evaluation from year to year was therefore maintained (see Figures 1 and 2).

Findings

(1) The quality of the student products were significantly better when using the individualized instructional method than when using the conventional classroom demonstration method.

(2) A saving in time occured. All students completed the six weeks graphics unit in five weeks.

(3) Instructor time was spent more constructively in consultation with students and in revising programmes.

(4) As a result of decreased instructional load the instructor and his teaching assistant felt that the class size could be increased by approximately 30 per cent. (This would require additional lab facilities.)

Discussion

The individualized instructional segments for Ed. AV 363 were designed to save instructional time for both instructors and students without adversely affecting student learning or quality of student products. An unexpected result was the increase and futhermore the degree of increase, in the quality of students' products.

Since this improvement in quality was not the main objective for designing the individualized instructional programmes, it is important to consider a number of possibilities which may account for this finding.

(1) There is a consistency and standardization of production skills and techniques with media presentations which cannot be matched by live demonstrations.

(2) Media presentations allow repeated observation of production techniques. By contrast live demonstrations are often limited to one presentation only, due to time constraints and the irreversible nature of most processes.

(3) With media presentation each viewer sees the same demonstration from the same perspective. However, with a classroom demonstration, students' viewing angle and distance from the demonstration differ. With large classes some parts of a demonstration may be obscured for some of the students.

(4) Less time is required to view a media demonstration. With live demonstrations preparation is necessary, time is needed for equipment set up and operation, and time is spent waiting for steps in the production process to be completed, e.g. diazo development, picture lifting.

(5) A positive motivational factor was observed when using the individualized instructional method. Students enjoyed the complete freedom to schedule

Company, 1977. This package includes student manuals, an instructor's manual, 39 slide/tape sets and 35 audio-tutorial cassette tapes.

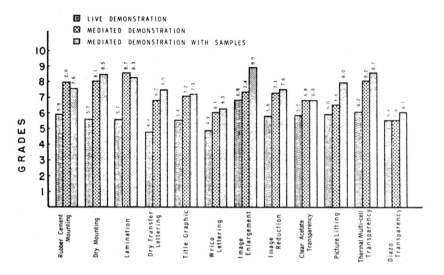

Figure 1. *Comparison of student achievement by instructional method and topic*

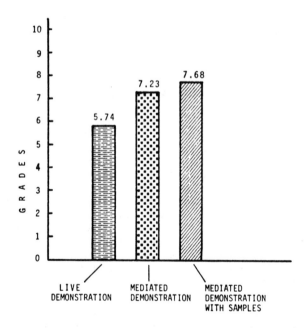

Figure 2. *Comparison of class average by instructional method*

their own working time. This freedom appeared to result in a more positive approach to assignments when they were undertaken.

(6) This opportunity for flexible scheduling reduced the frustration which usually occurs when other courses demand extra work, e.g. tests, term papers, etc.

(7) More immediate feedback was available to students concerning the quality of their products, as the decreased classroom instructional time allowed all material to be marked and returned at each class meeting.

(8) Individualized instruction allowed students to identify problem areas before coming to class meetings and before beginning production assignments. Possible problems could be discussed and solutions suggested in class before time-consuming and costly mistakes were made.

The instructor felt that all the above reasons contributed in some degree to the improvement in quality of student products. The addition of sample products to the individualized instructional packages further increased quality of student products for certain topics.

The use of individualized instructional segments is a valid means of saving instructional time and may result in improvement of learning.

22. A Comparison of the Effectiveness of Teaching: (1) In the Traditional Classroom Situation and (2) By Cine Film

C. M. Bird, *Garnett College, London*

Abstract: This study is aimed at determining, whether exposition of subject matter by a tutor in a traditional classroom situation is more, or less, effective as a method of teaching student lecturers to make 8mm cine loops, than exposition of the same subject matter by cine film.

Introduction

Context to the Problem

Garnett College, London, is one of four colleges of education in the United Kingdom which prepares teaching staff for the colleges of further and of higher education. The college trains some 600 lecturers annually, of whom about 150 attend a short course on how to make 8mm (silent) cine film loops. The objective of the course is to have the students in groups of three make a three-minute loop in colour film, so that they will be able to make other similar loops without close supervision. The students coming on the course are assumed to have no knowledge of photography.

The course runs for three two-hour periods at weekly intervals, i.e. for a total of six hours. The first 50 minutes comprise exposition concerning: the camera controls, the use of the camera and tripod; some factual information about film, the illumination of the scene, the filling in of a shooting-script form, and examples of some common faults of loops made by previous students. *It is this exposition which is the subject matter of the following study.*

The exposition until December 1976 was by traditional classroom teaching methods, i.e. the course tutor mainly lectured, there was some question and answer, demonstration and class practice with equipment. So the term 'traditional classroom situation' for the purposes of this study refers to these practices of lecturing, question and answer (both to and from the students), demonstration and student practice with equipment.

From January, 1977 a cine (sound) film titled *The Making of Film Loops (for Teachers)* which covers the above subject matter and which lasts about 35 minutes has been shown in place of the traditional classroom teaching. The students with camera, tripod and shooting-script blank forms at hand have watched the film and stopped and restarted the projector as directed. The remainder of the course has continued unaltered. So the only change in the six hours of the course procedure has been to replace the exposition of the traditional classroom situation by exposition by cine film.

The Constraints inherent within the Cine Film

In the making of the cine film *The Making of Film Loops (for Teachers)* a number of constraints were imposed for the benefit of the students.

Firstly, the length of the film does not extend beyond the normal lecture duration of the traditional classroom situation it replaces: a duration of 35 minutes seemed to be about right.

Secondly, the film does not embody (with one exception — see below) any filmic techniques that cannot be used by the students in the making of their own loops.

However, one major exception was made to this general principle. The exception is the use of sound track for commenting upon the visual. The researcher felt that a cine film of duration of 35 minutes which was silent, would not be making adequate use of the teaching time available.

The Statement of the Problem

The use of cine film to replace the traditional classroom situation immediately posed the problem as to whether in this context of teaching student lecturers how to make 8mm film loops, the cine film was as effective a teaching method as the classroom teacher; in simple terms: 'Is exposition by cine film in the context of teaching student lecturers to make cine loops more, or less, effective as a teaching method than the traditional classroom situation?'

A Review of the Literature

Research on improving the effectiveness of film as a teaching medium dates back at least a quarter of a century. For example, Twyford and Carpenter (1956) collated the findings of some seventy research studies in an attempt to distil off the essential theory for the production of effective teaching films. Vandermeer, *et al.* (1965) showed that the inclusion of captions in the form of summaries, labels and graphs improved the effectiveness of the two films that they were using as a teaching medium. Then came a change of direction. Current research (say from about 1970 onwards) seems to have centred around the problem of how effective the use of cine films as a teaching medium can be.

J. M. Foy and J. R. McCurries (1973) have examined the contention (which they think, may be held by many university lecturers) that the learning resulting from instruction by cine film is minimal. The results of the examination show that significantly more learning occurred with a group of pharmacology students who saw seven relevant instructional cine films than with a comparable group who did not see the films.

T. Smith (1972) has compared the effectiveness of two methods of presentation of (1) slides and (2) cine film as aids to the learning of a simple manipulative laboratory skill. The results show that the mean learning time for students who saw the film loop was about one-third of the mean learning time for students who used the tape/slide synchronization method of presentation. Further, students learning from the cine loops experienced in the practical situation less difficulty in anticipating the next manipulative movement and had more fluent movements than those students who did not see the film loop.

D. Gleissman and R. C. Pugh (1976) used nine cine films to teach the skill of categorizing teacher behaviour. Three films demonstrated the basic concepts of teacher behaviour within a traditional classroom situation and six films then provided examples of these concepts. The findings indicate that the use of instructional films led to increased skill in categorizing teacher behaviour in terms of specified sets of concepts.

H. Marchant (1975) examined the problems inherent in the writing of film scripts for educational films and concludes that the subject matter of the scripts should be selected with reference to predetermined objectives.

B. D. Pearson (1972) has examined how nursing students can be taught to distinguish between inferences and observations by viewing instructional films. One group of students made direct observations of a patient who at the same time was being filmed. A second group of students saw the film whilst another group saw also a film of a nurse examining the patient. The results show that while there was little difference in the test performances of the groups who viewed the film, both film groups performed better than the non-film group.

All the above-mentioned studies suggest that students *do* learn from watching cine films. The immediate question which comes to mind is: How much do they learn? The answer to such a question involves finding a means of measuring the learning which accrues to students watching cine films — a standard of comparison is required. A readily available standard is the learning which accrues to students taught in the traditional classroom. A comparison can be made between the learning that accrues to students from being taught the same subject matter (1) in the traditional classroom situation and (2) by cine film.

It is this comparison that the following study, in the limited area of teaching student lecturers to make cine film loops, aims to make.

The Statement of the Hypothesis

For the purpose of this study, the problem stated earlier was transformed into the hypothesis:

> Student lecturers learn to make 8mm film loops no less and no more effectively when the initial exposition is by cine film than when such student lecturers are taught in the traditional classroom situation.

Rationale for the Hypothesis

A cursory view of any simple expository situation suggests that a tutor's exposition can be cine filmed and the recording can be used to replace the tutor's exposition on future occasions. However, practice reveals at least two major shortcomings. Firstly, the original three-dimensional scene is represented in cine film by a two-dimensional image, i.e. solid objects become represented by flat photographic images. Secondly, this two-dimensional representation is inferior to the original scene in photographic definition, i.e. the detail available in the original scene is reduced in the photographic representation — cine film compared to the human eye is insensitive. Against these two shortcomings has to be balanced the advantage afforded by selective sitings of the camera. The camera is a privileged observer taking positions which no student in the traditional classroom occupies. The camera can 'see' from many angles; it can move nearer to or away from the exhibits; it can magnify or reduce the size of the original in the photographic representation.

Therefore, it may be that the loss of quality in cine film representations is more than compensated by the 'pride of place' views afforded by selective sitings of the camera.

Operational Definition of the Variables

With the purpose of the study (a comparison of the effectiveness of teaching by (1) the traditional situation and (2) by cine film) clearly in view, the variables are easily defined.

The *independent variable* is: Instruction in the traditional classroom situation versus instruction by cine film.

The *dependent variable* comprises the amounts of student learning that result from each of the methods of instruction.

The problem, now, was how to measure such learning.

Measurement of the Dependent Variable

Pre-test and post-test questionnaires were considered — and rejected. They were rejected because it was felt that the students (adults aged approximately 25 to 45 years) would not be prepared to spend time answering questionnaires. The questionnaires could not be incorporated into the course, for the time duration of the course (six hours) is short enough! Further, the researcher wished to avoid telling the students that a study was being made, in order to preclude a possible reactive effect (*Hawthorne: cf Brown*, 1954). Indeed, during the whole of the study, as it was eventually made, the students were unaware that a study was being made.

The problem of measuring the amounts of learning that accrue from each of the two types of exposition was solved by considering the marks awarded for the cine loops that the students made on the course. After the initial exposition, the students make three-minute loops. These loops are assessed by members of staff of the college. It is these assessments which are used in the study as measurements of student learning. Up to December 1976, all loops made by the students resulted from exposition taking place in the traditional classroom situation. From January 1977 the loops resulted from exposition made by the cine film. So comparable groups of students were selected, i.e. the assessment marks awarded for students' loops made between January and June 1976 have been compared with the assessment marks awarded for students' loops made between January and June 1977.

The Operational Restatement of the Hypothesis

In operational terms, the hypothesis now became: Student lecturers learn to make 8mm film loops no less and no more effectively when the initial exposition is by cine film than when such student lecturers are taught in the traditional classroom situation and when the measures of the effectiveness of each method of exposition are the assessment marks awarded to the students of the two groups (traditional classroom-situation group and cine-film group) for the cine loops that the students make after the expositions.

The Significance of the Study

For about the last dozen years the researcher has been tutoring up to 90 students a year in the making of 8mm cine (silent) loops. The students have come to the tutoring in groups of approximately 12 students per group. This has meant for the tutor much repetition of the initial exposition which has lasted about 45 minutes in the traditional classroom situation. It is easily seen that if a cine film of the exposition could have been used to replace the tutor's personal exposition, then he would have been free during the screening of the cine film to do those other tasks which only he as a person can do.

The Method Section

The Subjects of the Study

The student lecturers who participated in the study were all attending Garnett College of Education, London, UK and reading for a Certificate of Education in Further and Higher Education. For the purpose of this study, two groups were selected. One group consisted of 72 students who were at the college in the spring and summer terms of 1976 i.e. between 1 January and 31 May 1976 were the selected dates. The other group consisted of 81 students who were at the college in the spring and summer terms of 1977, i.e. between 1 January and 31 May 1977. These periods were selected so as to compare students who were at similar stages of their year's course within the college.

The Procedure

In 1976, the students in groups of approximately 12 students per group attended a traditional classroom situation in which the following subject matter was discussed by the tutor:

> The camera controls, the use of the camera and tripod, some factual information about film, the illumination of the scene, the filling-in of a shooting script form, and some examples of common faults made by previous students.

In 1977, the students in groups of approximately 12 students per group attended the screening of a cine film entitled *The Making of Film Loops (for Teachers)* which covers the same subject matter as that which the tutor had covered in 1976.

After the exposition by either the traditional classroom situation or by cine film, all students (i.e. both 1976 and 1977 students) for the remaining five hours of the course followed the same procedure: the students divided into teams of three students per team of like or of allied specialisms. The three members of each team then decided on a topic for their loop, put together a shooting script, made captions and exhibits where necessary and shot three minutes of film. After processing, the film was edited, if time allowed. The loop was then given to the course tutor for assessment.

The Assessment of the Loop

Each loop was assessed by the course tutor (who is an educational technologist) and also by another college tutor (not an educational technologist but chosen because he is a specialist in the subject matter of the loop). The tutors agreed a global mark (called in the results here an **Aggregate Mark**) out of a maximum of 20 possible marks.

The educational technologist in arriving at his aggregate mark did so after awarding a maximum of five possible marks for each of four areal considerations. These considerations centred around and included the points listed below. The lists are not comprehensive, nor can they be so. In practice, each loop is found to have merits and detractions of its own; but it is felt to be possible to indicate some central common areas of consideration which appertain to many loops.
Consideration One concerned the suitability of the chosen topic for a film loop

---

Course: Making 8mm Film Loops

Notes for Students

The objective of the course is that students in teams of three students per team should make a three-minute cine loop in colour film so that they will be able to make other similar loops without close supervision.

The course meets weekly for three two-hour sessions.

Session One   View (duration 35 minutes) the cine film:
The Making of Film Loops (for Teachers).
In teams of three choose very quickly a topic for a loop and write a shooting script.

Session Two   Collect exhibits; make captions; have trial runs and when satisfied, expose the film.
Give the cartridge of exposed film to the technician who will send it to processing.

Session Three   Preview and if necessary edit the loop.
Project the finished loop before the group and give relevant commentary and explanation.
Class discussion of the merits and detractions of the loop.

Session One: Viewing the film: *The Making of Film Loops (for Teachers)*

On the desk in front of you are: An 8mm cine camera
A photographic tripod
A dummy cartridge of film
Shooting-script blank forms

When you are ready, switch on the projector and then follow the screen instructions. After viewing the film, in teams quickly decide a topic for a loop and start putting together a shooting script. The course tutor will be circulating around the teams in order to give advice and check that your script writing is proceeding smoothly.

Now, switch on the projector and happy viewing!

Figure 1

and the usefulness of the particular shooting script in the making of the loop.

Consideration Two centred around the selection of aids and of captions.

Consideration Three concerned the students' use of the camera and tripod.

Consideration Four centred on how much of the loop was usable in the classroom.

The **Aggregate Mark** is the simple addition of the marks awarded under the Considerations One to Four.

The Design of the Study

The design structure of the experiment is basically one of the so-called true experimental designs often called the 'post test-only control group design' (e.g. Tuckman, 1972, p106). Course organization forced the researcher to accept constraints on the basic design. Randomization of the students consists of accepting the first 72 students as constituting one group (year 1976) and the remaining 81 students as the second group (year 1977). However, since these students are on the same course (merely a year apart) and they are at the same stage of that course, there is no reason to suppose that this grouping could affect the results in any adverse way.

Data Analysis

The t test had been applied to each of the five corresponding sets of results to ascertain if the differences of the means are statistically significant.

The data analysis shows that for each and all of the considerations, the differences of the means are not significant. To be significant, at the five per cent level of probability, the t value of 49 degrees of freedom would need to be larger than 2.011 (Tuckman, 1972, p320). The computed values of t are found to be as follows.

Consideration One $t = -.52$ Not significant
Consideration Two $t = -.77$ Not significant
Consideration Three $t = -.87$ Not significant
Consideration Four $t = 1.16$ Not significant
Aggregate Mark $t = -.36$ Not significant

Final Conclusion

From the above results and their analysis, it is concluded that this experiment does not provide any evidence from which it can be inferred that the cine film is any more, or less, effective than the traditional classroom tutor as a means of exposition in teaching student lecturers how to make 8mm cine loops.

References

Beveridge, J. A. (1969) Script writing for short films. In *UNESCO Reports and Papers on Mass Communication,* **57,**

Brown, J. A. C. (1954) *The Social Psychology of Industry.* Penguin, Harmondsworth.

Chu, G. C. and Schramm, W. (1967) *Learning from Television: What the Research Says.* Stanford University, Institute for Communication Research (ERIC No. ED 014900), Stanford, California;

Coppen, H. (ed.) (1970) *A Survey of British Research into Audio Visual Aids; Supplement.* National Committee for Audio Visual Aids in Education, London.

Films and video in education (7 January 1977) *Times Educational Supplement,* **23.**

Foy, J. M. and McCurries, J. R. (1973) Learning from pharmacology films. *University Vision*, **36**.

Gleissman, D. and Pugh, R. C. (1976) The development and evaluation of protocol films of teacher behaviour. *Audio Visual Communication Review*, **24**, 1, p.21.

Gormann, D. A. (1977) Classroom teachers use media to learn media. *Audio Visual Instruction*, **22**, 15.

Hartley, J. (1973) The effect of pre-testing on post-test performance. *Research in Education*, **10**, 56.

Homes, P. D. (1959) *Television Research in the Teacher-Learning Process*. Wayne State University Division of Broadcasting, Detroit, Michigan.

Hubalek, F. (1977) Production of 8mm films. *Educational Media International*, **1**, 18.

Marchant, H. (1975) Communicating by instructional film: a presentation strategy. In Baggaley, J. P. *et al.* (eds.) *Aspects of Educational Technology VIII*. Pitman, London.

Pearson, B. D. (1972) Applying learning theory and instructional film principles to film for learning observational skills. *Audio Visual Communication Review*, **20**, 3, p.28.

Platts, C. V. (1976) Recording science lessons on cine film and the analysis of such records. *School Science Review*, **58**, 5.

Smith, T. (1972) Selection of a method of presentation to aid the learning of manipulatory skills. In Austwick, K. and Harris, N. D. C. (eds.) *Aspects of Educational Technology VI*. Pitman, London.

Teather, D. C. B. (1974) Learning from film: a significant difference between the effectiveness of different projection methods. *Programmed Learning and Educational Technology* **6**, 328.

Tuckman, B. W. (1972) *Conducting Educational Research*. Harcourt Brace Jovanovich, New York.

Twyford, L. C. and Carpenter, C. R. (eds.) (1956) *Instructional Film Research Reports* **2**, p.924 US Naval Training Device Center, Penscola, Florida.

Vandermeer, A. W. (1950) *The Relative Effectiveness of Instruction by: Films Exclusively, Films plus Study Guides and Standard Lecture Methods*. US Naval Training Device Center, Penscola, Florida.

Vandermeer, A. W. *et al.* (1965) *An Investigation of Educational Motion Pictures and a Derivation of Principles relating to the Effectiveness of these Media*. Pennsylvania State University, Notre Dame, Indiana.

Wittich, W. A. *et al.* (1959) *The Wisconsin Physics Film Education Project*. University of Wisconsin.

23. A Facility for Self-Paced Instruction using Tape/Slide Programmes

A.G. Stephens, *University of Reading*

Abstract: A facility is described for the presentation of tape/slide programmes using the commercially available Wessex audiovisual unit. The design and construction of a self-contained area to house these units and costs are indicated.

Introduction

Self-paced instruction for teaching biochemistry and physiology was considered for a variety of reasons. The primary motivation arose from a sudden 15 per cent increase in the numbers of students requiring to study these subjects during their first year at university. This increase threw a considerable strain on the resources available for the practical classes. A reappraisal of the educational objectives for some of these classes indicated that self-paced instruction using tape/slide programmes might be a more appropriate teaching method to achieve these objectives. In addition, there was a desire to provide a wider choice of teaching methods available in the department. There appeared to be merit in having this teaching aid available to provide a wider range of learning experiences for the student.

The carrel system described by Clarke (1975) and the audiovisual laboratory described by Macqueen, Chignell, Dutton and Garland (1976) were visited in Dundee. From the latter of these two it was clear that biochemistry could be taught successfully to medical students using individualized learning techniques. One of the first-year courses taught in Reading is designed to provide physiology and biochemistry for students in the agricultural faculty. A parallel between biochemistry for medical students and physiology and biochemistry for agriculture students was drawn. It seemed that a shift of objectives away from those involving the development of manipulative laboratory skills to those concerned with analysis and critical evaluation of experimental data was desirable. Individualized learning using tape/slide programmes was seen as a suitable choice of teaching method.

The decision to set up an audiovisual unit was taken in June 1977. A minimum-sized facility consisting of six booths equipped to present tape/slide programmes was proposed. From the outset it was realized that six units would not provide sufficient capacity for the major integration of this teaching method into courses. Rather it would allow about 100 students an experience of a tape/slide presentation perhaps only once or twice a term. It was agreed that the technique should be introduced into the first-year physiology and biochemistry course for agriculture students. There would also be times when the units were available for use by students following other courses in the department and if suitable programmes were available this was to be encouraged. A use for the units was foreseen during the revision periods prior to university examinations.

The approach outlined above reflects the desire that was felt for caution and experimentation with this teaching method. On the one hand, complete reorganization of the courses was to be avoided, but on the other hand some experience in providing self-paced instruction was to be gained. Some critical evaluation of the system could then be made from this venture after a period of one year.

Audiovisual Equipment

Reliable equipment was sought. Purchase of a slide projector and a cassette player separately was considered. These two items could then be installed and linked together to provide automatic slide change synchronized to the recorded commentary. However, it was clear that there was little saving to be made in this way when the costs of the individual item plus the inconvenience of linking them together were compared to the purchase price of a complete audiovisual unit, i.e. 'Wessex A-V unit' manufactured by Elm Tech Services Ltd, distributed by George Elliot & Sons Ltd. Further, this equipment was already based upon the Phillips N2214 cassette recorder joined by compatible electronics to a Liesegang A30 slide projector; both of which were established, tried and tested pieces of equipment. These were incorporated into a robust case providing back projection onto a ground glass screen. The whole unit designed to stand on a desk was ready for use. Six Wessex A-V units were purchased. Two with record and playback facility (£298 + VAT each) and four with playback facility only (£275 + VAT each).

Location

A suitable location for six audiovisual units in individual booths or carrels proved difficult to find. The teaching laboratories could not be used as these were required for other courses and there was no other room available. There was, however, a large foyer area adjacent to the main teaching laboratories and the booths might be sited there provided adequate privacy, comfort and quiet could be ensured. The area would need to be fully enclosed and self-contained with walls extending up to the ceiling (approximately eight feet) to partition the unit adequately from the main foyer area.

Construction

The design is illustrated in Figure 1. Two parallel rows of four booths were constructed to house the six audiovisual units and provide an assessment/preparation area and a storage area. A passage was left down the middle and access was from either end.

Standard chipboard sheets (4 x 8 feet, 12mm thick) were bolted together through soft wood battens (2 x 2 inches) to make the walls and partitions. Chipboard (18mm thick) was used to construct working surfaces and shelves. These surfaces were supported on battens bolted to the walls. The top was left open although extra rigidity was provided by wooden battens secured across the front of the booths. The construction was painted and plastic edging strip fitted over the exposed chipboard edges. Electrical wiring was carried out to provide each booth with a double 13 amp power socket and indicator lamp with switch. A small strip-light was located at each access point to the area. A hard-wearing carpet was fitted and curtains hung at either end. A small desk lamp and a Wessex A-V unit was mounted in each booth.

Construction was carried out by the department's workshop and technical staff

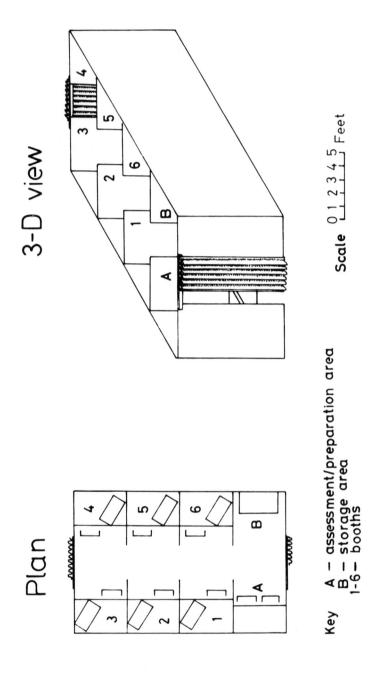

3-D view

Plan

Scale 0 1 2 3 4 5 Feet

Key A — assessment/preparation area
     B — storage area
     1-6 — booths

Figure 1. *Design of the audiovisual facility*

and was rapidly completed during the 1977 summer vacation.

Costs

The costs are presented in Table 1.

	£
Chipboard, softwood and bolts	200
Paint	50
Edging strip, signs and labels	15
Electrical fittings and wiring	100
Carpet	100
Curtains	30
Chairs	50
Desk lamps	25
Six Wessex AV units	1,910
Total	£2,480

Table 1. *Costs of materials and equipment*

The principal items of expenditure were the Wessex A-V units accounting for three-quarters of the total cost. The remaining £570 represents the cost of the self-contained area carpeted and furnished. No attempt has been made to estimate labour costs. The total cost is comparable to that which is encountered when considering purchases of scientific equipment for a biochemistry teaching laboratory, e.g. spectrophotometer or six simple colorimeters.

Observations during Use

The unit has been in use for two terms and the construction has so far proved to be rigid and robust. A questionnaire was used to evaluate the students' reaction to the use of tape/slide presentations. The results of the questions concerned with the equipment and facilities are given in Table 2.

Factor	Percentage response				
General comfort	very uncomfortable 0	uncomfortable 1	adequate 32	comfortable 52	very comfortable 15
Extraneous noise	very disturbing 0	annoying 6	did not interfere 52	quiet 22	completely unnoticed 20
Use of AV unit	did not function 0	worked with difficulty 4	satisfactory 26	easy to use 48	very simple to operate 22
Headphones	very uncomfortable 4	uncomfortable 26	adequate 34	comfortable 33	very comfortable 3

Table 2. *Evaluation of the equipment and facility.*
Student responses given as a percentage

These responses indicate that the facility provides privacy and comfort and that the equipment is easy to use. However the following comments and observations

193

have been made:

(1) It was necessary to mount the AV units on the right-hand side of the desk to allow easy access to the cassette-player keys and the socket for the headphones. The working surface remaining is therefore to the left of the AV unit. This is not convenient for right-handed users.

(2) The cassette-player controls are not readily accessible or visible from the sitting position. This is inconvenient should the student wish to rewind a small section of the tape for repetition.

(3) There is a hold switch mounted on the front of the unit to allow pauses to be made during the programme. However, if used, recovery of the commentary takes a few seconds and a few words of the succeeding section are lost.

(4) The slides cannot be set to zero automatically as they are held in a linear magazine and need to be manually aligned before the start of the programme.

These disadvantages need to be balanced against some positive features of the Wessex AV unit. The main controls for the projector are readily accessible on a panel above the screen and include a brilliance control. The unit provides manual and automatic slide operation. Pulses for automatic slide change are simply recorded. The unit can be used for large-screen projection by withdrawing the mirror from the rear. The whole unit is compact, versatile, convenient and economically priced.

Some minor mechanical and electrical faults have occurred with the equipment, but these have all been rapidly corrected by the manufacturer. One problem which proved difficult to resolve occurred during the making of copies of a programme. A pulsed master cassette was produced and copies prepared using a 'Wollensak' cassette copier. Although the commentary was perfectly reproduced the pulses were not consistently copied. This resulted in unreliable performance, sometimes the pulse on the copy was sufficient to activate slide changes and sometimes not. This problem is closely associated with the length of the recorded pulse signal and has only occurred when copies have been made. It was investigated and it is thought to have now been resolved. No problem occurs when the cassettes are pulsed individually, although for multiple copies this is tedious and time-consuming.

Future Development

Tape/slide programmes in physiology and biochemistry related to medical sciences are widely available for hire or purchase. Some of these programmes were obtained, but the success of this type of teaching depends largely on the production of material specifically designed to achieve objectives associated with a particular course. Immediate developments are to be in the preparation of such material to teach physiology and biochemistry to students with an agricultural interest. Programme writing will be much more demanding and time-consuming than the building and provision of the audiovisual units. Subsequent evaluation will then decide any further expansion of the facility.

References

Clarke, J. (1975) A carrel system for an institution for higher education. In Baggaley, J. P. *et al.* (eds.) *Aspects of Educational Technology VIII.* Pitman, London, p.140.

Macqueen, D., Chignell, A., Dutton, G. J. and Garland, P.B. (1976) Biochemistry for medical students: a flexible student-oriented approach. *Medical Education* 10, p.418.

24. Microfiche: A New Medium for Audiovisual Instruction

G. **Murza**, *IDIS, Bielefeld, Germany*

Abstract: The paper describes the microfiche format in the context of the IDIS-Microdok information system. The production of fiches by computer and camera is described together with an outline of the presentation systems required. The operation of a typical self-instructional programme using the system is illustrated.

Audiovisual Instruction as a component of a Comprehensive Information System

In 1972 IDIS (Institute for Documentation and Information on Social Medicine and Public Health) was commissioned to give an expert opinion on the development of a European-System on Industrial Security (EURISIS).

The expert opinion is described elsewhere (Nacke, Gerdel and Lange, 1973); the proposed system is called IDIS-MICRODOK which is an acronym of 'Mikrofiche-Informationsspeicher mit computererstellter Registerorganisation zum Zweck der Dokumentation' (Microfiche-Information System with registers organized by computer for the purpose of documentation). The information output of the system is based on microfiches.

A microfiche is a sheet the size of a postcard. It contains information, especially text information in a reduced form. Standard reduction ratios are 1:24 and 1:42.

In other words: a microfiche may contain information that has been reduced by ratio 1:24 or 1:42. By using a reduction ratio of 1:42 microfiche may consist of 208 frames, each of which stores a sheet the size of DIN-A-3.

There are two main methods of producing microfiches:

1. Outputs from a Computer (so-called COM)

Outputs from a computer (COM) containing information and data which is continuously stored on magnet tape; as a rule the data is organized and structured prior to being processed on microfiche.

2. Microfiches produced by a Special Camera

Producing microfiches by means of a special camera may be more time-consuming, but this is more appropriate for storing information which does not require manipulation being already in the form of journals, books, documents, etc. An advantage of this kind of microfilming technique is that it can store text and data as well as *pictorial* information.

In the meantime procedures are known which allow the production of colour-microfiches of high quality (Murza, Nacke and Strate, 1976).

The microfiche is a very inexpensive and convenient medium and it is used in conjunction with a microfiche-reader.

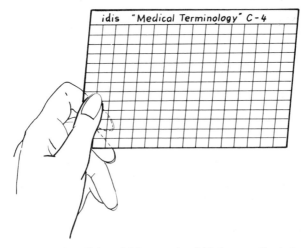

Figure 1. *A microfiche which contains 208 frames; the information is stored at a reduction ratio of 1:42*

Figure 2. *A microfiche-reader*

Since it demands no technically complicated equipment microfiche might well be used for instructional purposes to a greater extent in future. It would be beyond the scope of this paper to describe the whole information system of IDIS-MICRODOK which, as mentioned above, is a comprehensive system to provide special groups (such as physicians, engineers, psychologists, etc.) who work in the fields of public health, occupational and social medicine, with information such as scientific literature, abstracts, laws, documents, addresses and also educational materials.

An Instructional System based on the Use of Microfiche

The following is a description of that part of INDIS-MICRODOK which goes beyond the single provision of information. It is planned that those groups which make use of IDIS-MICRODOK will not only be provided with microfilms which contain different kinds of information but also with instructional material. In practice, the user of MICRODOK will not only have a file of microfiches provided (by means of which it is possible to store thousands of pages on a few microfiches which may be placed on one's desk), but he will also, in addition, regularly receive *audiovisual* information on microfiche.

To make use of this facility, it will be necessary to have a microfiche-reader and a cassette recorder at one's disposal.

The system may be used to various degrees of sophistication of comfort. The equipment for the most simple version consists of the usual microfiche-reader and a normal cassette recorder. The cost of this version is about £350.

A more sophisticated version consists of an automatic microfiche-reader which is controlled by a special cassette recorder.

Figure 3. *The comfortable equipment of IDIS-MICRODOK; pictures on the reader are automatically adjusted by impulses on the cassette*

The following is a brief outline of its functioning: all the operational information is stored on a normal cassette tape; the arrangement being schematized in the lower part of Figure 4. The diagram represents the width of a cassette tape and is divided into four tracks. The upper two tracks are reserved for mono or stereo recording, i.e. the audio information is stored here.

Track 3 contains inaudible impulses for the automatic adjustment of the microfiche-reader, allowing any frame of the microfiche to be synchronized with a section of the audio tape.

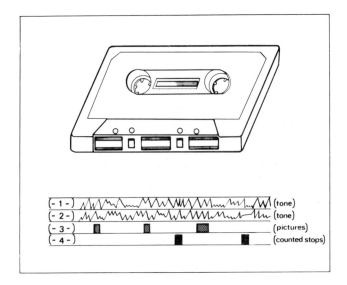

Figure 4. *Illustration of the usual cassette and the schematized impulse structure*

Thus a synchronized presentation of the audiovisual information is guaranteed at any point, regardless of whether the pictures of the microfiche are projected one after the other or whether several visual images are presented repeatedly. Another type of impulse is put on track 4. These impulses divide the presentation into frames in so much as the system stops at each of these impulses automatically and restarts only after the learner's response. Furthermore, since these stops are counted by the system, it is possible to 'by-pass' any number of these impulses by means of a key board, giving the learner random access to any information stored on the tape. In other words, by means of this system, it is possible to instruct a learner in linear as well as in branched fashion in a form of programmed instruction.

In order to illustrate how this may be achieved, a possible section of such programmed instruction is explained below, and is to be read in conjunction with Figure 5:

(a) Learner passes stop 1.
(b) He receives audio information from track 1 and 2 and simultaneously illustrations, displayed by the microfiche-reader (adjusted by impulses on track 3).
(c) At stop 2 the programme only continues after learner's response.
(d) Knowledge is controlled immediately.
(e1) In the most simple case the learner has to decide between two alternatives:
(e2) if he is of the opinion that the first alternative is the correct answer, he presses button 4; if he prefers the other alternative, he presses button 3 on the keyboard.
(f) Preferring the second alternative, the learner is informed of a wrong answer.

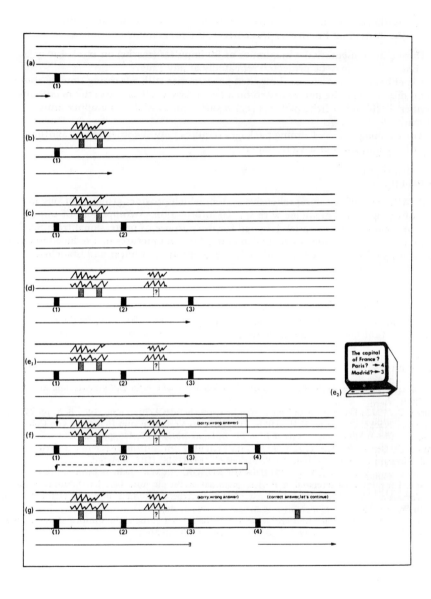

Figure 5. *Principles of programmed instruction. Technical equipment: cassette recorder and automatic microfiche reader*

Thereafter the programme returns to the beginning of the unit which has not been learned correctly.

(g) Choosing the first alternative causes the programme to run to position 4 and he learns that his answer was correct; the programme continues.

During implementation a maximum of 99 impulses (marks) on track 4 may be set. Each picture may be projected repeatedly at any time.

Experience has shown that branched programmes with a learning time of about 20-40 minutes may be implemented on a customary C-60 cassette; the maximum number of 208 microfiche pictures is also sufficient as well as the upper limit of 99 marks.

The exchange of the learning packages requires only the insertion of another microfiche and another cassette tape.

Summary

IDIS-MICRODOK is a comprehensive system which provides groups working in the area of occupational medicine with special information. A component of this system is audiovisual material designed for the purpose of professional training. The visual medium is the microfiche which stores text and pictures in a reduced manner. The most sophisticated version allows the presentation of linear and branched learning programmes.

Acknowledgement

The author would like to thank John Bonnington of Dumfries and Gallway Technical College for assistance with the English of the paper.

References

Murza. G. (1975) *Das Ausbildungskonzept des IDIS Nachrichten für Dokumentation,* 26 pp. 63-7.

Murza, G. (1975) Durch Selbsthilfe ein zweckentsprechendes Lehrsystem. *Aula,* 8, 3, pp.273-6.

Murza, G, Nacke, O., Strate, K.H. (1976) Ein eintaches Verfahren zum Herstellen von Color — und Halbton-Mikrofiches. *Nachrichten für Dokumentation,* 27, 4/5, pp.163-4.

Nacke, O., Gerdel, W., Lange, H. (1973) Gutachten über den Aufbau eines europäischen Information systems für industrielle Sicherheit (EURISIS) IDIS, Bielefed.

Nacke, O. and Winkelmeir, E. (1975) IDIS-MICRODOK. Ein Mikrofiche — Informations — speicher mit computererstellter Registerorganisation für die Aufgaben der Dokumentation. Vortrag auf der Jahrestagung der Fachvereinigung Arbeitssicherheit, Berlin 18 October 1974. In *Proceedings der Fachvereinigung Arbeitssicherheit,* Berlin.

Nacke, O. (1977) Aufgaben und Probleme des Aufbaus eines europäischen Informationssystems für Arbeitsmedizin. *Mikrodok-Informationsdienst,* 18, pp.35-7.

25. Ten Years of Closed Circuit Television in the Royal Navy

Lt. Com. B. A. Brooking, *RNSETT, Southampton*

Abstract: The Royal Navy has been using the medium of Closed-Circuit Television for the last ten years for education and training. During this time some 26 Closed-Circuit Television units have been established.

This paper aims to show the benefits which may be gained from the applications of CCTV, together with an argument for the necessary strategy, bearing in mind the strengths and weaknesses of the medium.

The aim of the Royal Naval training system is to train men and women in a cost-effective manner to do their jobs in the operational fleet and supporting shore establishments. The content of training courses is derived from a process which starts by identifying the present and future tasks that fully trained personnel will be required to perform. The learning strategies to be used in training are then selected, with reference to the training content and the requirement to use resources cost-effectively. Closed-Circuit Television is a commonly used instructional medium to help achieve our aims in training our personnel.

In the last decade, throughout the world, the use and value of instructional television appears to have aroused much suspicion. Perhaps now is an appropriate time to trace the development of the medium in an organization such as the Royal Navy in terms of:

(1) Extent of usage
(2) Equipment
(3) Nature of usage
(4) Criteria for selection and control
(5) Consideration of costs

and to evaluate its use, together with future recommendations for exploiting its potential.

1. Extent of Usage

In 1968 the first CCTV studio in the Royal Navy was opened at the Royal Naval School of Educational and Training Technology in Portsmouth. Since then the use of the medium has expanded, and over the past 10 years, 25 CCTV units have been established in Royal Naval training establishments or schools all over the country. In addition to recommending, purchasing and setting up appropriate equipment, it has been necessary to train personnel in the operation of the medium. The first internal course at the Royal Naval School of Educational and Training Technology was a 5-day Closed-Circuit Television Production Techniques Course, to train officers and senior ratings for appointments in training establishments, and over the period the number of courses available has increased. They now include a 5-day

CCTV fleet production technique course for ship personnel and a 3-day CCTV ship production techniques course for teams as opposed to individuals. CCTV maintainers' courses are available on all types of production equipment, and a CCTV component is now an integral part in the training of Wrens training support assistants.

Most training establishments in the Royal Navy now use the medium of CCTV in some form, and a corps of CCTV-trained personnel has been built up.

2. Equipment

Original production equipment used was the 1-inch video-tape recorder which was large, unreliable, inflexible and incompatible. Video-tapes produced on one video-tape recorder could not necessarily be played on another. Over the decade the quality and flexibility of production equipment improved, and the emergence of smaller ½-inch video-tape recorders gave more mobility. The portable video-tape recorder enabled producers to record on location rather than be restricted to a studio. Over the last few years developments have included cartridge and cassette systems as an alternative to open-reel tape. This has helped to establish compatibility, and given much greater flexibility in production; it has also given independence in operation to instructors and trainees. Additional facilities such as still-frame and slow-speed have provided scope for showing greater detail on particular topics such as physical training.

3. Nature of Usage

Areas of use of the medium have been wide, and have varied from postgraduate engineering training to basic seamanship, from communications to gunnery training. Obviously the nature of usage of instructional television has been closely linked with the scope and limitations of equipment, but over the last 10 years six main functions have emerged which have benefited education and training. These are:

    (1) live display
    (2) immediate playback
    (3) delayed playback
    (4) telecine
    (5) off-air broadcasts and recording
    (6) individualized learning

'Live display' uses a property unique to the medium, which is the capability of transmitting sound and vision directly to as many locations as there are outlets. This has been used in training establishments, where it has proved useful in enabling an instructor of a specialized subject to demonstrate his skill to several classes simultaneously. As a result of this the size of class is not limited to the immediate environment, and the use of the zoom and close-up facility has been effective in drawing the attention of trainees to particular details. Ships are now being fitted with CCTV, and this provides a 'broadcast' capability from a studio to many parts of the vessel which can be used for communication in a variety of topics, including education or training. 'Immediate playback' provides an opportunity to record an action or movement and replay it within seconds. This has proved an effective facility for analysis of both individual and interpersonal skills, in that material may be replayed for the benefit of subsequent instructor and trainee analysis. The main area of use in the Royal Navy has been in the training of instructors themselves, and other applications have included physical training and bandmaster conductor skills. The camera has proved a ruthless analyst. In using this function, which is unique to television — because there is no need to process the recording — not only have performances improved, but time on course has been saved. 'Delayed playback' is the production of a complete entity either as a whole lesson or part of a lesson. The main advantage of such a tape is that if it is well-planned, prepared and quality-controlled, it can be very effective in that locations, equipment or situations may be recorded and brought into the classroom. This has been used as a safety factor in areas where it is necessary to observe potentially dangerous processes, and in some cases the medium has even been able to reduce course time by condensing material. In addition, technical effects such as using split-screens and captions or superimposition can aid learning. Such productions can be cost-effective in saving travel time and cost, and have been applied to nuclear and submarine training. But appropriate investment in equipment, time and production expertise is necessary to produce an acceptable result. Experience has suggested that in using this function the medium is most effective not as a complete substitute for an instructor, but as an aid to instruction — however tempting it may be to reduce the cost of personnel.

'Telecine' is the process by which 8mm or 16mm film may be transferred to television. This has proved effective in education and training in that it enables an instructor to select, edit and use only those parts of a particular film which have relevance to his or her lesson. The application of video-cassette recorders and players has given further independence, in that instructors have greater control over replay equipment, including the use of stop/start/rewind, stop-frame and even slow-speed facilities, and there is no need to darken a classroom to show the video-tape on a monitor or monitors. Although television projectors have been researched, it is considered that such is the loss of picture quality that it is preferable to use several monitors, especially when viewing locally produced tapes. While the principle of viewing one large screen is recommended, at this time it would appear that projected television quality needs improvement before being usable.

'Off-air' broadcasts and recordings are sometimes used in Royal Naval education and training — copyright permitting — but their use is comparatively limited, as such programmes are rarely relevant for our specialized purposes.

'Individualized Learning' is very relevant to the Royal Navy, and there seems to be great potential for using CCTV as an independent learning facility. This may be used as a supplement to conventional instruction, or in providing an opportunity for learning 'on the job' in ships or establishments where an instructor may not be readily available. Video-cassettes provide a convenient and reliable learning format for trainees to use.

4. Criteria for Selection and Control

Should instructional television be suggested in the design of a course in Royal Naval education or training, the Royal Naval School of Educational and Training Technology is tasked with conducting a feasibility study to determine whether CCTV is cost-effective, and ask the simple but important question: Why Video? Such studies usually take six months, and during that time as well as applying appropriate testing and assessment procedures many criteria are evaluated. Such factors as whether there is a requirement for showing movement, whether performance is improved, whether time or equipment is saved, need to be considered. All are relevant criteria in the process of selecting the appropriate medium. Once a CCTV unit has been established, it is inspected every two years to ensure that the medium is still being used cost-effectively. It is recommended that the medium be employed as far as possible in an active rather than passive mode, and where appropriate the use of work-sheets and tests is encouraged to supplement video material.

5. Consideration of Costs

There seems little doubt that one of the reasons why instructional television has not lived up to the expectations of many organizations has been the lack of consideration of investment and subsequent expenditure. In many cases it has been kept down to a price rather than raised up to a standard — and there would appear a definite need for a policy in the setting up, application and development of the medium in terms of:

(1) Cash Expenditure — to purchase suitable production and replay equipment, and adopt a standardized format.
(2) Personnel — to be properly selected, trained and employed for periods long enough to ensure continuity.
(3) Time — to enable facilities to be used professionally and cost-effectively.
(4) Support Resources — to provide adequate back-up in terms of equipment and maintenance.

Although apparently obvious these important factors have often been neglected or ignored, and the medium has lost effectiveness.

Original policy in the Royal Navy was one of decentralization, where individual establishments were allowed to build up their own CCTV facilities within a budget, dependent on application. While this appeared satisfactory in that growth of the medium proceeded with caution, what was not appreciated was the high degree of creativity, expertise, time and support necessary to produce complete video-tapes or programmes suitable for instructional use. Much depended on the subjectivity of the television officer and the attitude of management to the medium. In the 1960s, due to equipment limitations, many programmes consisted of no more than a 'talking head' technique, and should have been produced using less expensive tape/slide facilities. Since then many viewers have tended to compare directly the quality of CCTV with broadcast standard programmes, and have failed to take account of the fact that there is an enormous difference in comparative expenditure and quality of production equipment. There is no doubt that CCTV equipment is now much improved and training is more effective, but there would still appear to be two main areas of contention at this time:

Video *v* Film
and
Colour *v* Monochrome

Film provides excellent quality reproduction and is preferable in certain contexts such as large-group viewing, but it needs processing and is expensive in production costs. Television is less expensive, may be produced more quickly, and may be updated more easily. It can provide great stimulus and interest in showing realistic and authentic settings — provided its use is balanced with other training aids; it gives greater independence to an instructor in a classroom, and can provide a very effective individualized learning facility.

The debate over colour or monochrome is a very subjective and emotive topic. In the Royal Navy our research findings have shown that in general there is no significant difference in the learning capacity of students using colour rather than monochrome video-tapes. What is certain is that colour production is several times as expensive and complex as monochrome, because it must be really 'life-like'. It is recognized that eventually its widespread use will be inevitable, and there are some subjects such as medicine where colour is essential. The short-term policy adopted by the Royal Naval School of Educational and Training Technology for this specific purpose has been to purchase the best-quality colour camera it can afford, together with an efficient automatic editing suite, to produce simple but cost-effective tapes.

In the long term it would appear that as a result of its experience in the use of CCTV over the last decade, the Royal Navy is ready for the next step, which is the move towards the setting up of a centralized colour production unit with mobile facility. In such a large and widespread organization, decentralization of equipment and trained personnel can be a hindrance, and can even set up barriers to effective communication between units. The recommended solution is to employ a small but full-time professional team using appropriate production equipment. This would not only provide experience and continuity, but should reduce CCTV machine and studio 'idle time'.

A decentralized policy relies too heavily on the subjectivity of the training establishment management and television officer. Very often such individuals do not have the aptitude, time or necessary equipment to use the medium effectively. Such units are not cheap to run — even with part-time facilities — and in practical application once a training tape has been produced, its assessment is rarely done effectively, as a remake causes so many problems. It would be more cost-effective to transfer expenditure to a centralized unit — with its target to produce not several tapes a year but a week. The requirement would not be for long, involved programmes, but short, simple and relevant aids. It is considered that individual establishments could be provided with simple but effective monochrome CCTV support for 'live display' and 'immediate playback' purposes at a reasonable cost. Production expertise, training, time and support are not so critical in these functions, and as the trainee is directly involved, it is unlikely that the stimulus of colour will be needed because motivation will be intrinsic to the learner.

The centralized unit should provide production and editing capability which would meet an increasing demand for video-tapes and give an improved service to training establishments and ships, all of whom could hold colour playback facilities. Training and manpower costs, expenditure on equipment and maintenance should be considerably reduced, and an effective working partnership could be set up to take full advantage of the specialist subject-knowledge of a training establishment, and the professional television knowledge of the centralized production team.

In the last 10 years the Royal Navy has had much experience in the application of instructional television, and is aware that it can provide the most definite benefits to education and training. But it does need to be properly used and managed, otherwise its effect will be no more than a novelty, and it will never have any practical, cost-effective value. The medium has great potential. Provided that it is well administered and fully supported it can fulfil our high expectations.

26. Levels of Use of Educational Broadcasting in Britain and West Africa: A Study of Rejection of an Innovation

P. Hurst, *The British Council, London*

Abstract: Content analysis of interviews with schoolteachers (n=50) in Britain and West Africa, indicates why educational broadcasting has had a relatively marginal impact so far, and why there are differences of levels of use between primary and secondary teachers and between industrialized and developing countries.

For more than fifteen years now the use of educational broadcasts in schools has been widely advocated in both industrialized and developing countries. These are some of the arguments that have been put forward in favour:

(1) Broadcasts can bring material and experiences not otherwise available into the classroom.
(2) Broadcasts give pupils access to experiences outside the classroom at lower cost than visits and trips.
(3) Broadcasts can present more effective teaching materials than the classroom teacher can create, and achieve economies of scale at the same time.
(4) Broadcasts can enhance teacher effectiveness by their multiplier effect; watching or hearing master teachers at work will have a spinoff effect on the classroom teacher.

In short, broadcasts were thought to offer a means of creating a major increase in the effectiveness of educational systems worldwide, plus a simultaneous lowering of per student costs — in other words, a dramatic gain in efficiency.

A decade and a half later, most commentators do not detect any such significant improvement in educational systems at all, let alone ascribe it to educational broadcasting. Tom Singleton, the former director of the Centre for Educational Television Overseas, says that: 'Few of the existing television services in developing countries can be described as an important component of the educational process. Many are not only unimportant, they are complete failures' (1973). Dave Berkman (1976), looking back at the limited spread of ETV in America, entitles his article: 'Instructional television: the medium whose future has passed?' He notes that we cannot ask whether ETV has died, for 'one cannot ascribe life to that which never lived'.

Likewise Wilbur Schramm, after years of advocating educational broadcasting, moved in his report 'Big media, little media' (1973) to urge less costly and smaller-scale innovations. Martin Carnoy (1975) has done a cost-benefit analysis of some supposedly successful ETV systems in developing countries and argues that devoting resources to teacher training would have been a far more cost-effective investment.

If these sorts of opinions about schools broadcasting are justified, is this because pupils are failing to benefit from seeing or hearing the programmes? The answer is 'no', because they are apparently not seeing or hearing very many. The reason for this is that teachers generally make comparatively marginal use of broadcasts, and a significant number make no use of them at all.

This state of affairs cannot usually be discerned from the statistics of broadcasting authorities. The Schools Broadcasting Council of the United Kingdom, for example, claimed that in 1972-73 98.8 per cent of primary schools in England, Wales and Northern Ireland used radio, and 71.7 per cent used TV; of secondary schools 70.7 per cent used radio, and 71.1 per cent used TV. But these figures cover all types of usage, from regular listening and viewing of several series to the use of a *single* broadcast in the course of a year. Similarly in the USA, Berkman has noted that advocates of instructional TV never give the 'one figure which would make or break their case', the percentage of the enrolment who regularly receive instruction via TV. One would also want to see this level of use of broadcasts expressed as a proportion of those which are available for the age-group in question.

There are, however, a small number of researchers, such as Becker (1964), Featherstone (1969) and Pursaill (1968), who have actually asked groups of teachers how many broadcasts they use, and why they do or do not use them. In addition, the study which I want to discuss here (Hurst, 1977) was an investigation into the levels of use of broadcasts by teachers in East Sussex in England, and in Sierra Leone in West Africa. I should also add that I worked as a schools TV producer in a developing country (not Sierra Leone) for a number of years. Taking all these sources together, I think the following is a fairly accurate picture of how frequently teachers use radio and TV. Of course, I am generalizing, and there are undoubtedly individual schools where broadcasts are used intensively. I also know for a fact that there are many schools where broadcasts are used infrequently, if at all.

In industrialized countries, broadcasts are generally used more in primary schools than in secondary ones. In primary schools it is not uncommon to find that some teachers use up to three or four broadcasts a week (radio and TV). I have not encountered a teacher who regularly used more than four in one week. Nevertheless, this is less than the number which are usually available and relevant to particular age-groups in most industrialized countries. Most other primary teachers use one or two broadcasts a week. There are few non-users.

In secondary schools in industrialized countries use of broadcasts is usually significantly lower, as other observers have pointed out. Radio programmes are less used than TV. It is quite normal to find that many teachers in secondary schools do not bother with broadcasts at all, and that even the minority of enthusiasts rarely exceed using one or two broadcasts a week.

In developing countries, levels of use of broadcasts are much lower. In some countries it can be quite a difficult task to locate *any* teacher who uses broadcasts, even though broadcasts are regularly transmitted. Of course, there is normally a more restricted choice of programmes than in industrialized countries, but even so the levels of use are usually minimal. One also finds a similar difference between elementary and secondary teachers in the Third World as in the West. In developing countries secondary teachers customarily make almost no use of radio and TV broadcasts, while their primary colleagues do make a little more.

I am, of course, giving an impressionistic picture, based on what I have seen myself and on what other observers have said. My version of the facts could be disputed. But, assuming that my picture of educational broadcasting is not too far from the truth, then the question we naturally ask is: why is this so? Why has educational broadcasting failed to live up to the expectations of its advocates of a decade or so ago? Why do teachers make such restricted use of it?

It is significant, I think, that this failure of broadcasting is symptomatic of a global sense of disappointment and frustration with the results of attempts to reform educational practices during the same period. It is not as though educational broadcasting fizzled out while every other innovation was a brilliant success. Therefore we ought to ask, not just why has educational broadcasting failed to deliver the goods but also why most of the attempts at reform in industrialized and developing countries have failed to bring about the dramatic improvements that were envisaged? What can we learn about how to do it better in future?

There is a family of explanations for the low level of use of schools broadcasts which are conventional among advocates of the innovation.

(1) Teachers are by nature conservative and resistant to any kind of change whatsoever.
(2) Teachers are afraid of being replaced by machines.
(3) Teachers are afraid that their students will make unfavourable comparisons between their competence and the level displayed by the TV teacher.
(4) Teachers are unwilling to surrender control of the classroom to an alien intrusion since they cling to the godlike authority they enjoy there.

These alleged motives are quite common in the literature, but I have yet to find a single piece of empirical evidence reported which bears them out. They remain completely unsubstantiated.

However, as I observed before, a few researchers have gone directly to the teachers to find out what they think. It is interesting that the study of teachers in East Sussex and Sierra Leone endorses the findings of the other earlier researchers I mentioned before, and it also contradicts the unsubstantiated explanations of conservatism, Luddism, and so forth.

The study itself was an attempt to test a model of the decision logic which people are presumed to employ when choosing whether to adopt an innovation at some level of use, or to reject it. The model consists of a set of appraisal criteria, which can be represented as the following questions:

(1) *Relevance.* Do the alleged outcomes of adoption constitute benefits?
(2) *Effectiveness.* Are the alleged outcomes of adoption likely to ensue in practice?
(3) *Feasibility.* Are all the resources necessary for adoption actually available?
(4) *Side-effects.* How do any unintended disadvantages of adoption compare with the benefits?
(5) *Efficiency.* How does the return of benefits on input compare with current practice?
(6) *Priority.* If there are a number of innovations available, what is their rank order of efficiency?
(7) *Trialability.* Can the innovation be temporarily adopted on a reduced scale for trial purposes?

This calculus assumes that the potential adopter is satisfied with the adequacy and accuracy of the data on which he is basing the decision.

This study was not by nature a wide-scale survey, but was an intensive investigation into the way people *think*. 50 teachers — 30 Sierra Leoneans and 20 from East Sussex — from four schools in Sierra Leone and three schools in East Sussex participated. Tape recordings were made of interviews with the teachers and a total of 28 hours of recordings were subjected to a content analysis. Some of the teachers had been given an earlier taped interview two years before, and some had taken part in taped group discussions two years earlier, but these recordings were used to help devise the interview schedule and were not part of the content analysis. The aim of the analysis was to discover to what extent the reasons given by teachers for using or not using particular broadcasts, or broadcasts in general, conformed to or diverged from the model of logic outlined earlier.

In fact none of the reasons given diverged from the model, and so no new types of argument were discovered. However, it was noticeable that the more experienced and trained teachers in both countries appeared to be more certain of their judgements and to have more and clearer reasons than their less experienced or trained colleagues. It was concluded that this phenomenon indicates that decision logic is learned through experience (including training) rather than being innate.

Another finding was that in both countries primary teachers made more use of broadcasting than secondary teachers, a phenomenon which has been remarked on by others in relation to this and other innovations. The analysis again indicates an explanation. Primary and secondary teachers have different types of training as a rule, and this leads to rather differing conceptions of their roles as teachers. This difference can best be described in terms of Basil Bernstein's distinction between integration and collection codes. Primary teachers tend to view the curriculum as an integrated corpus of knowledge, and to see their role as transmitters of this unified curriculum. They see themselves as generalists in relation to specific aspects of the curriculum. Secondary teachers tend to regard the curriculum as a collection of distinct disciplines, in one of which they are specialized. The effect of this is that primary teachers are apparently more willing to accept innovations which have been designed by outside specialists. Many primary teachers, for example, who have no musical training are glad to use music broadcasts in the classroom. Secondary teachers, however, are noticeably inclined to believe that their own expertise in the particular subject they teach is second to none, or second to very few at least. This makes them much more critical and discriminatory with regard to innovations which touch on their specialism. Both primary and secondary teachers alike are highly discriminatory with regard to their own students' needs. They frequently claim that innovations designed by people with no knowledge of their particular students must be scrutinized very carefully before being used regularly. In the case of broadcasts, this applies equally to individual series and programmes. Teachers who are regular users of one series may be highly critical of another. I also found teachers who reported favourably on using a series with one class but unfavourably on its use with another.

The decision calculus described above is pitched at an abstract logical level. More specifically, Table 1 lists the grounds on which teachers decide not to use broadcasts at all, to use fewer than are available, or to discontinue the use of a particular series.

Why the difference in levels of use between developing and industrialized countries mentioned before? One obvious reason is that more programmes are transmitted in the latter, but a more important factor is the more widespread use of audio and video-cassette recorders. These have, in the West, helped to overcome some of the disincentives formerly encountered, but there are still a lot of disincentives left, and moreover video-recording technology needs to be developed a lot more if educational broadcasting is to become less marginal than at present. Audio recording is now relatively cheap, reliable and compatible. But video recording is above all expensive, especially in relation to the resources available in developing countries. And the more teachers in a school who wish to record off-air and play back at convenient times, the greater the stock of recorders and cassettes that is necessary.

Another problem that needs to be tackled, this time by the broadcasters rather than the hardware manufacturers, is the question of lockstep and individualized instruction. The economics of broadcasting is such that an audience of a certain critical mass is required to justify the high production and transmission costs, and even if one could make a variety of versions of any one programme to meet varying needs, there is not sufficient air time available to accommodate them. The

- ☐ Inadequate advance information
- ☐ Inaccurate advance information
- ☐ Difficulty of controlling (selecting) content
- ☐ Content irrelevant
- ☐ Method unsuitable — encourages passivity, illiteracy and imposes lockstep
- ☐ Level too high/low
- ☐ Pace too fast/slow
- ☐ No receiver
- ☐ Receiver u/s
- ☐ Poor reception
- ☐ Competition for receiver
- ☐ Educational returns do not justify difficulties in setting up
- ☐ Syllabus overcrowded — no room for 'enrichment' material
- ☐ Ancillary materials unavailable/arrive late/too expensive
- ☐ Timetabling problems — broadcast schedule and school timetable conflict
- ☐ Recording problems — no recordist or machine required for simultaneous record and playback
- ☐ Accommodation of equipment
- ☐ Theft of equipment
- ☐ Available time devoted to other innovations
- ☐ No mains/batteries
- ☐ Poor audibility in classroom

Table 1. *Grounds of total or partial rejection or discontinuance of educational broadcasts given by teachers*

effect of this is that programmes are packaged for the mass, not for the individual, but this is at odds with the general trend toward individualizing instruction. This fact helps to explain why in the Open University, for instance, using broadcasts never amounts to more than 5 per cent of a student's time, and why in most courses broadcasts are an optional element. One solution might lie in dropping broadcasting as such, and concentrating on the surface distribution of cassettes from central libraries. Such a system might offer a number of savings on costs, as well as permit more individualized variety in programming.

To return once more to the question of innovations in general, a recent study by the Rand Corporation (Berman, McLaughlin, *et al.*, 1974-78) of the implementation of several hundred projects in the USA argues that the key to bringing about a successful level of use of an innovation lies in a process of mutual adaptation. This means that there needs to be adjustment and modification of both the adopting institution and the innovation. In the case of educational broadcasting, both here and in developing countries, I suggest that the initiative now rests with the manufacturers and the broadcasters. The schools have gone a long way and spent a lot of time and money in trying to get the best out of broadcasts. It is now time for the broadcasters and manufacturers to look very closely at the reasons why educational broadcasting is not having a major impact, and to think up some bold and radical solutions.

References

Becker (1964) The utilisation of school television broadcasts in England. University of Nottingham.

Berkman, D. (May 1976) Instructional television: the medium whose future has passed? *Educational Technology*, pp.39-44.

Berman P., McLaughlin, *et al.* (1974-78) *Federal Programs Supporting Educational Change.* 8 vols. Rand Corporation, Santa Monica, California.

Carnoy, M. (1975) The economic costs and returns to educational television. *Economic Development and Cultural Change,* 23, 2.

Featherstone, P. (1969) Report to the Independent Television Authority. Mimeographed, ITA Fellow, University of Sussex.

Hurst, P. (1977) The selection of sociocultural innovations. DPhil dissertation, University of Sussex.

Pursaill, D. (1968) The use of television in Brighton and East Sussex schools. MPhil dissertation, University of Sussex.

School Broadcasting Council (1973) *BBC School Broadcasts: Facts and Figures.* School Broadcasting Council, London.

Schramm, W. (1973) *Big Media, Little Media.* Stanford University, Palo Alto.

Singleton, T, (October 1973) Educational TV in the Third World. *Screen Digest,* p.51.

27. A Survey and Evaluation of Teleconferencing

A. D. Becker *University of Wisconsin-Madison, Wisconsin*

Abstract: Over the past ten years an expanding wave of telephone-based instruction in the United States, Canada and Europe has created a flurry of research in its wake. Teaching aids such as slow-scan television, electro-writers, 35mm slides, overhead projection and films are variously used either at the point of origin or the distant sites of the lecture. Such aids, while not unique to telephone-based instruction, are supports which tend to heighten the effectiveness of this medium.

Over the past ten years an expanding wave of telephone-based instruction in the United States, Canada, and Europe has created a flurry of research in its wake. Although the telephone was first used as an instructional medium in 1939 to assist homebound and hospitalized students (Rau and Hicks, 1972), it was not until the mid-Sixties that the idea burgeoned in the field of continuing education. The University of Wisconsin-Extension, the University of Florida School of Pharmacy, Britain's Open University, the University of Quebec and institutions of continuing higher education in Kansas, California (Parker, 1976), Illinois, Ohio, and Oklahoma are among the schools which now employ instructional telephone systems. Most of these institutions use a private, four-wire, permanently installed system leased from a telephone company on a 24-hour basis. Teaching aids such as slow-scan television, electro-writers, 35mm slides, overhead projection, and films are variously used either at the point of origin or the distant sites of the lecture. Such aids, while not unique to telephone-based instruction, are supports which tend to heighten the effectiveness of this medium.

The comparatively new area of instructional telephone research, to which the generic term 'teleconferencing' can be applied, will be reviewed and evaluated in this paper.

Definitions

There is ample confusion about the definition of terms in telephone literature over the past fifteen years, yet the word 'teleconferencing' appears to be emerging as a broad category. 'Teleconferencing' may be used as a generic term which encompasses any type of long-distance discussion in which two or more separated groups are joined through a telephone system (Parker, 1976). 'Telelecture' and 'telephone-based instruction' are specific forms of teleconferencing; the former is conferencing applied in an instructional setting which does not use a dedicated telephone line, and the latter is conferencing applied in a fixed system which uses a private, four-wire, dedicated telephone line. Additional terms such as conference calls, teleteaching and teletutoring, can be subsumed under telelecture or telephone-based instruction depending on the system at point of origin. Reports employing all the telephone terms mentioned were surveyed for this review.

The most rigorously conducted teleconferencing studies and those which can be considered in the mainstream of instructional media research are controlled experiments, yet this category yields only 15 investigations, among nearly 200 reports. On first view a reviewer might conclude that little serious research has been conducted in this area, yet closer scrutiny of the large number of experimental, descriptive and case studies reveals a serious intent to evaluate the telephone as a means of instruction.

Experimental Studies

Findings among those studies which attempt to isolate and control specific instructional variables vary from study to study. Results most often cited are from investigations conducted by Beattie and Frick (1963), Blackwood and Trent (1968), and Puzzuoli (1974). The most recent and perhaps the best experimental study is that of Flinck (1976). Closer scrutiny of the methods employed, the variables isolated and sampling procedures used in the studies which form the core of this new literature are required for evaluation purposes.

Beattie and Frick (1963), comparing two models of telelecture, concluded that one was better than the other. Students receiving a 30-minute telelecture were first given 10 minutes to formulate questions and then 20 minutes to direct these questions to the lecturer. The second group was given a 30-minute telelecture and an overnight period to formulate questions. When the second group directed their questions in a 30-minute period, their questions were considered 'more qualified'. It is interesting to note that the variable under consideration here, a unit of time, is not unique to teleconferencing.

Pitting face-to-face teaching with telelecturing, Blackwood and Trent (1968), found no significant differences among the two instructional modes. Using an intact group of 71 students, the researchers randomly assigned subjects to the two simultaneous treatments. One group remained in the studio with the lecturer while the other group received the lecture remotely by telephone. The researchers found no difference in levels of cognition nor attitude among the groups. Subjects, however, of ages 35-44 were more positive in their attitude towards remote teaching and students aged 45-64 liked face-to-face lecture better.

In another study conducted to test the effectiveness of telelecture and face-to-face teaching, Puzzuoli (1974) measured the achievement and surveyed the opinions of subjects within intact groups. Mining engineering and modern maths formed the content of the courses taught. Findings of no significant differences between control (face-to-face) and experimental (telelecture) groups emerged. It is interesting to note that Puzzuoli's only control group consisted of four subjects. Differences of attitude between experimental groups, however, were significant. Those subjects receiving telelecture with 'variations', aids such as electro-writer and 35mm slides, were more positively disposed towards telelecture than were those subjects receiving telelecture without variation.

In an experiment with distance education and conference calls in Sweden, Flinck (1976) develops a method for analysis of the content of telephone calls. Although Flinck was not testing telelecture here, he did isolate and evaluate a characteristic unique to teleconferencing in general. Further description of his analysis will appear later.

Difficulties encountered in the major experimental studies cited and in additional experimental studies begin to form patterns.

(1) Intact groups are used while statistics (t tests, ANOVAS, z tests) which assume random samples are applied (Beattie and Frick, 1963; Puzzuoli,

1974; Boswell *et al.*, 1968; Edelman, 1968).

(2) Samples are sometimes so small that errors of the second type may occur (Puzzuoli, 1974; Nunley, 1965).

(3) Studies which compare face-to-face lecture with telelecture make no attempt to account for variations across the modes of presentation (Blackwood and Trent, 1968; Puzzuoli, 1974; Boswell *et al.*, 1968; Edelman, 1968; Nunley, 1965).

(4) Studies which assess prior knowledge on pre-tests fail to use these tests to reduce unexplained variance in post-test results (Boswell *et al.*, 1968; Puzzuoli, 1974; Edelman, 1968).

It would be foolish to conclude here that the cited authors and other authors conducting teleconferencing studies were poor researchers. In fact, they are in the mainstream of instructional media research, which has for the past 20 years paid homage to 'true experimental' designs. In an effort to meet unrealistic design criteria, these researchers have, by and large, ignored the discrepancy between the instructional setting employed by teleconferencing and the setting required for true experimental design.

In the *first* difficulty cited above, inaccurate statistics were applied to intact groups. If 'true experimental' design was not the goal of these researchers, appropriate statistics for intact groups could have been employed. Stanley and Campbell (1966) give guidelines to the use of such statistics for 'quasi-experimental' designs. Focus on the structure of the instructional setting and the type of data necessary to collect must again preceed the selection of a research design.

The same argument may be employed to counter the *second* difficulty, namely, small samples. Some non-parametric procedures (Hays, 1963) are suitable for analysis of small group data, or application of observational techniques from group to group over an elongated period of time might fit the teleconferencing setting. Again limitations of samples and setting must determine research procedure.

The *third* difficulty encountered, namely, a comparison of face-to-face instruction with telelecture, presents a historical dilemma. The introduction of a new instructional medium has historically been followed by a rash of experiments which investigate the teaching effectiveness of the medium by comparing the medium with face-to-face lecture. Such was the case in early instructional film research (Knowlton and Tilton, 1929; Wood and Freeman, 1929; Sattler, 1968). It was not until the Second World War that instructional film researchers abandoned that impractical means of comparison (Hoban and Van Ormer, 1950), yet the same mistake was made when TV was introduced as a new instructional mode (Kanner, 1960). Gradually the instructional television literature began to employ more sensitive designs (Saloman, 1974). A similar evolution occurred with the introduction of computer-assisted instruction (Oettinger and Marks, 1968).

The tendency to repeat the error in which gross comparisons of medium to traditional lecture are made stems from the desire to answer the question: 'Can this medium (film, TV, CAI, telephone) teach?' But continued homage paid to and application of 'true experimental' design does not allow such gross comparisons. These comparisons do not control for intervening variables across modes of presentation, across the most important set of independent variables.

The *fourth* problem encountered is a failure to integrate assessment of prior knowledge with variance in post-test results. There was a tendency among telephone researchers reviewed here to either ignore prior knowledge or to 'go through the paces' of trying to isolate it. Again the fault stems from a desire to adhere to experimental regulations and a failure to examine the composition of the sample tested. Accurate tests for prior knowledge of content, with an adult audience ranging in age from 18-60 (this is the typical continuing education audience) must be almost impossible to construct. A more profitable exercise might be the design of instructional materials and lectures for teleconferencing, employing guidelines from the growing literature on the adult learner. A profile of this learner is emerging in the literature.

Setting

The instructional setting for teleconferencing presents unique problems and most of the difficulties cited here come from (a) a lack of consideration of the setting; and (b) the reasonable desire of these researchers to be in the mainstream of instructional media research. The telelconferencing setting, however, has some unique instructional features which recommend it as a practical teaching medium. The case studies mentioned below delineate some of these features. It is clear that there is a wide discrepancy between the instructional setting employed by teleconferencing and the setting required for 'true experimentation'. In the former instruction is carried by telephone to various settings in which there are various learners, yet the latter calls for rigorous isolation and control of the variables in the setting.

Research Questions

When reflecting on the paucity of research in the teleconferencing area, Puzzuoli (1974) posed the basic question which forthcoming literature might answer. In 1970, he wondered which subject-matter areas might best be taught through teleconferencing and some subsequent telephone studies addressed this question. Again, it was a historically inaccurate question to ask, since instructional media researchers had abandoned that question along with the research designs of early educational film studies (Sattler, 1968). By 1968 (Allen, 1969) and even earlier (Hoban and Van Ormer, 1950) attempts were being made to match learning task and medium, so the questions being posed was: 'Which learning tasks are best taught through which medium?'

With assistance from other media research, Puzzuoli's question might be refined to read: 'Which learning tasks are best taught through teleconferencing?' Yet, it may be contended, that even this question is answered in prior literature on audio instruction. Teleconferencing is basically a new delivery system for audio instruction and the question: 'Can students learn aurally?' and 'Can audio teach?' has been asked numerous times and answered in the affirmative. In a survey of instructional media research before 1969, Allen (1969) concluded that audio adequately taught informational and procedural tasks. Successful use of interactive audio techniques in language labs also attest the instructional strength of audio. When considering special learners such as slow readers (Oakan et al., 1971; Budoff and Quinlan, 1964) and students who have low verbal ability (Koran et al., 1971), audio has been an effective means of instruction. The questions, therefore, 'Will teleconferencing teach?' and 'What tasks will it best teach?' are simply redundant.

Unique Characteristics

To isolate those characteristics unique to teleconferencing and examine how they invite and hinder communication appears to be a reasonable task for telephone researchers to undertake. Puzzuoli (1974) poses additional questions which are more endemic to the teleconferencing problem. He asks about the best mix of (a) telelecture and supporting audio visuals, (b) network and audience size,

215

(c) effective use of professional talent, and (d) management system for a telelecture network. His questions and the issues addressed in the vast number of case studies found in teleconferencing suggest the formulation of new variables.

Case Studies

Records of successful teleconferencing courses have been reported in many case studies and some reporters have provided loose descriptions of classes, while others have made attempts to accurately survey and describe the settings. Without trying to isolate and control all variables in the teleconferencing setting, these reporters have applied alternate methodologies to collect what they consider and what appears in *post hoc* analysis to be relevant data.

Cooper and Lutze (1970) surveyed 550 inactive nurses enrolled in refresher courses throughout Wisconsin and the neighbouring states. The continuing education courses which were designed to activate nurses were delivered by teleconferencing. Results of the survey indicated that 12 per cent of the nurses returned to practice, and another smaller group said they planned to return sooner than they had expected.

Although the survey methods applied in the Cooper and Lutze (1970) study could be more refined, the question asked seems important. What effect did teleconferencing courses have in the decision of the adult learner to return to work? Such a question is vital to the area of continuing education and would have yielded practical information in the studies of Regan and Haasch (1970) and Nunley (1965). Survey alone would not answer this question, however. A design which employed immediate and follow-up survey, along with in-depth interview might uncover other causes for return to work, so that the influence of teleconferencing could be weighted.

In a study conducted by Hoyte and Frye (1972) one interesting variable considered was 'educational success'. The authors concluded that the instructor's view and the student's view of success were relatively independent of each other. They also indicated that the successful telelecture student was more self-reliant and independent than successful on-campus students. Again the characteristics of the adult learner are brought into focus here.

In a study where both students and instructors were interviewed, Mandelbaum (1971) reports that teachers believed teleconferencing would be successful at high levels of specialization where a lot of preparation was demanded. They also indicated that the medium was good for discussion situations. Instructors here isolated the interactive capabilities of this medium.

Flinck (1976) analysed the contents of telephone calls made on a one-to-one basis to correspondence students in Sweden. He also isolated the interactive capability of the medium. His method of recording not only the frequency and number of calls; but also the initiator, student or tutor; the topic of conversation, organizational problem, limited subject-matter problem, general subject-matter problem, study technique problem or social-personal problem, creates a distinct profile of the adult correspondence learner. The method also provides insight into the study habits and needs of adult learners in general.

Research Design

The practical literature in telephone research indicates that the unique characteristics of teleconferencing stem from its:

   (a) setting

(b) learners, and

(c) interactive audio capability.

It is not the isolation of these characteristics that will yield information helpful to telephone course designers, but the relationship of learners, setting, and interactive audio. True experimental design by its very nature relies on a stimulus-response model, which has definite limitations. It is indeed not sensitive to the gestalt of a setting, nor the intention of the learners. Alternate means of collecting interrelated data appear to be called for. Designs most sensitive to such relationships have been discussed in another paper (Becker, 1977). They are observational and survey techniques including interview. Such techniques have been loosely employed in case studies in this literature. It is the suggestion here that reliable observational and interview techniques be developed and applied to collect broad data on the key variables of setting, learner and interactive audio capability. The first stages of data collection in any field are characterized by observation and initially the collection of broad data. That stage was skipped in much of the telephone research. A return to it might yield information helpful to course designers, learners and instructors.

References

Allen, W. H. (1969) Audiovisual instruction: the state of the art. The Schools and the Challenge of Innovation, Supplementary Paper No. 28. Committee for Economic Development, New York, p.222.

Beattie, T. and Frick, P. (1963) *The Telephone Method of Teaching, ERIC* ED 036357, Denver, Colorado.

Becker, A.D. (Summer 1977) Alternate methodologies for instructional media research. *AV Communication Review,* 25, pp.181-94.

Blackwood, H. and Trent, C. (1968), *A Comparison of the Effectiveness of Face-to-Face and Remote Teaching in Communicating Educational Information to Adults.* Extension Study No. 4, Kansas State University, *ERIC* ED 028 324, Manhattan, Kansas.

Boswell, J. J., Mocker, D. W. and Hamlin, W. C. (March 1968) Telelecture: an experiment in remote teaching. *Adult Leadership,* 16, pp.321-38.

Budoff, M and Quinlan, D. (1964), Reading programs related to efficiency of visual and aural learning in the primary grades. *Journal of Educational Psychology,* 55, pp.247-52.

Campbell, D. T. and Stanley, J. C. (1966) *Experimental and Quasi-experimental Designs for Research.* Rand McNally, Chicago.

Cooper, S. S. and Lutze, R. S. (December 1970) Dial N for nursing. *Adult Leadership,* 19, pp.202-3.

Edelman, L. (October 1968) Teaching adults via telelecture and electro-writer. *Adult Leadership,* 17, pp.163-4.

Flinck, R. (1976) *The Telephone Used in an Experiment of Distance Education at the University Level.* Department of Education, University of Lund, Sweden.

Hays, W. L. (1963), *Statistics.* Holt, Rinehart and Winston, New York.

Hoban, C. F. and Van Ormer, W. (December 1950) *Instructional Film Research 1918-1950.* Technical Report SDC 269-7-19, US Naval Training Devices Center, Port Washington, New York.

Hoyte, D. P. and Frye, D. W. M. (1972) *The Effectiveness of Telecommunication as an Educational Delivery System.* Kansas State University, *ERIC* ED 070-318, Manhattan, Kansas.

Kanner, J. H. (1960) Army television research activities. *AV Communication Review,* 8, 74.

Knowlton, D. C. and Tilton, J. W. (1929) *Motion Pictures in History Teaching.* Yale University Press, New Haven, Conn.

Koran, M. L., Snow, R. E. and McDonald, F. J. (1971) Teacher aptitude and observational learning. *Journal of Educational Psychology,* 62, pp219-28.

Mandelbaum, J. D. (1971) Six experimental telelecture sites report. *Educational Screen and Audiovisual Guide.*

Nunley, B. G. (1965) A study of the effectiveness of telelecture in the retraining of elementary teachers in mathematics. An unpublished doctoral dissertation, University of Texas, Austin, Texas.

Oakan, R., Wiener, M. and Cromer, W. (1971) Identification, organization, and comprehension for good and poor readers. *Journal of Educational Psychology,* **62,** pp.77-8.

Oettinger, A. G. and Marks, S. (Fall 1968) Educational technology: new myths and old realities. *Harvard Educational Review,* **38,** p.701.

Parker, Lorne (1976) *Introduction to Teleconferencing: A Training Program.* University of Wisconsin-Extension, Madison, Wisconsin.

Puzzuoli, D. A. (1974) *A Study of Teaching University Extension Classes by Telelecture.* West Virginia University, *ERIC* ED 042-961, Morgantown, West Virginia.

Rau, P. V. and Hicks, B. L. (April 1972) Telephone-based instructional systems. *Audiovisual Instruction,* pp.18-22.

Regan, E. A. and Haasch, L (January 1970) Telelectures and tuberculosis. *Adult Leadership,* **18,** pp.215-16, 222.

Salomon, G. (1974) Sesame street in Israel: its instructional and psychological effects on children. New York Children's Television Workshop.

Sattler, Paul (1968) *A History of Instructional Technology.* McGraw-Hill, New York.

Suppes, P., Jerman, M. and Brian, D. (1968) *Computer-Assisted Instruction: Stanford's 1965-66 Arithmetic Program,* p.29. Academic Press, New York.

Wood, B. D. and Freeman, F. N. (1929) *Motion Pictures in the Classroom.* Houghton Mifflin, Boston.

28. Satellites in Education: Experimenting for Ever?

J. S. Daniel, *Athabasca University, Edmonton, Canada*

Abstract: The paper warns of the danger that current educational experiments on satellites may never give rise to operational applications. Although some successful and apparently cost-effective uses have been demonstrated, regulatory and legal constraints presently combine to keep operational satellites out of the reach of educational institutions.

Introduction

Although cynics have said that non-stick frying pans are the only tangible benefit to the ordinary man of our huge investment in space technology, communications satellites must also rank as a useful development. Their arrival has caused a steep drop in the rates for international telephone calls and greatly increased the volume of live television exchanges.

Space technology, like most expensive 'big' technologies, has been a government-sponsored development. Whilst public attention has naturally been focused on men in space, governments have also been funding, in addition to defence applications, the development of satellites and tracking systems for peaceful uses such as telecommunications, weather forecasting and geological prospecting.

Whenever a technology is evolving rapidly there is a considerable difference between the equipment in operational use and that under development. Operational systems need both reliable technology and back-ups. Thus an operational satellite communication system requires at least two satellites. Since building and launching a satellite costs up to $100 million, experimental satellites are not usually made in pairs. Operational use being thus precluded, such satellites inevitably have much spare transmission time, since the technical experiments themselves are not very timeconsuming.

Partly from a sincere desire to develop social applications of satellites, but also in order to have some publicly visible return on the vast investment of taxpayers' money, governments have encouraged experimentation on satellites by medical and educational institutions. Such was the genesis of the experiments performed in the US and India on the Applications Technology Satellites, notably ATS-6, the intercontinental exchanges on the Symphonie satellite and the Hermes experiments in North America.

In these projects the term 'experiment' is of legal rather than scientific significance. Since governments undertake not to compete with the licensed telecommunications carriers, the word 'experimental' is there to recall that such projects are not regular, operational uses which are taking business away from the carriers. Indeed, in a scientific sense 'experiments' is a misnomer for these activities, which are better described as demonstration applications.

Naturally, some of these demonstrations have been successful and useful applications of satellites in education have been identified. The institutions and participants involved tend, in such cases, to seek regular access to a satellite to continue the successful activity. It is then that they discover the gap that has to be bridged in moving from a government-sponsored project on a 'free' satellite to regular use of a commercial satellite.

This paper is about that gap. Unless it can be bridged, many experimenting institutions will justly feel that they have been the victims of a confidence trick, having been obliged, at the behest of government, to disappoint expectations and undermine their credibility.

We shall summarize satellite experiments to show what educational applications have been tried, before examining the nature of the gap between experiment and practice and suggesting how it is most likely to be bridged.

Satellite Experiments in Education

Writing in 1975, Polcyn (1975), after noting that, 'Whether the technology [of satellites] is of value for educational purposes remains to be seen', described the ATS-6 and CTS projects and concluded, 'The commitments to these experiments will exceed a quarter of a billion dollars; this . . . promises to be a major event in this decade. . . . From these experiments, educators should receive some inkling of the educational potential of satellite technology.'

Although the term inkling is somewhat modest, it is true that the experiments have not always been conducive to realistic testing of likely applications. The ATS experiments have received such generous external funding that few adjustments to economics were necessary. Although excessive funding was certainly not a characteristic of the CTS project there were also so few ground terminals available that many demonstrations lacked realism. In the case of Symphonie, the experiments were largely conducted by governments for diplomatic purposes.

The following types of communications were however tested under various conditions for educational purposes:

(1) Educational TV broadcasting to groups (e.g. India's Satellite Instructional Television Experiment).
(2) Educational TV broadcasting to groups with audio return (e.g. ATS-6 Appalachia and Rocky Mountain projects).
(3) Multipoint audio-conferencing (e.g. the Peacesat experiment with ATS-6).
(4) Tele-lecturing either with bi-directional video or one-way video with audio return (e.g. the Carleton/Stanford curriculum exchange on CTS).
(5) Research seminars with one-way video to several points with audio return (e.g. CTS electron microscopy experiment).
(6) Library consultation (both video and audio) and document transmission (e.g. Quebec CTS project).
(7) Linking cable TV stations for live interaction between communities (e.g. Quebec CTS).
(8) Multi-point videoconferencing (e.g. CTS experiment by Canadian Public Service Commission).
(9) Various types of computer communication and conferencing (e.g. Peacesat).
(10) Transmission of videodocuments for storage and later use (e.g. Symphonie France/Ivory Coast).
(11) Interactive 2 and 3 point video conferences (e.g. Symphonie France/Quebec).

Although some projects used bandwidth too lavishly to survive in a world of real costs, others did not bring out a clear need, and still others could have been better carried out on terrestrial links, some experiments suggested viable applications. Such applications usually combined some of the following characteristics: large distances, sparsely populated areas, large or high specialized audiences, interaction, dynamic consortia of institutions.

Successful experiments generate a desire for operational applications. Our evaluation (Daniel, Côté and Richmond, 1977) of the CTS experiments in Canada suggested that the factors which promote the assimilation of satellite technology by educational institutions are essentially the same as those identified by Hooper (1975) for the technology of computer-assisted learning. However, the operational use of satellites does not just depend on the institutions concerned, since major legal, political and economic hurdles have to be cleared. To these we now turn.

Access to Satellites

In the experiments conducted to date, governments have always provided free satellite time, have usually made terminals available at no cost, and have often also funded projects directly. Since this level of support is unlikely to be forthcoming for operational applications, planners of such systems should begin by estimating the cost of the type of satellite system they wish to use. Although detailed costing is impossible until negotiations with carriers and suppliers are undertaken, approximate figures can provide some guidance.

A study (Daniel *et al.*, 1977) was conducted in 1977 on the costs of a hypothetical satellite network linking 30 points across Canada. It was assumed that 10 of the sites would be able to transmit and receive in video, audio and data, whereas the 20 other sites, whilst being able to receive in all these modes, would only have a transmit capability for audio and data. The annual cost of such a system, excluding the educational and programming costs, was estimated to be around $3.5 million, made up as follows:

Lease of space segment (full-time rental of one transponder)	$2,000,000
Lease of ground terminals	$1,250,000
System maintenance and operation	$250,000

For comparison, an audio-only system which would allow interactive voice and data communication between 200 sites was also costed. The figures were:

Lease of space segment	$150,000
Lease of ground terminals	$1,800,000
System maintenance and operation	$300,000
Total	$2,250,000

These figures provide an indication of the cost of space communication. Furthermore, the assumptions which must be used to derive them highlight the main difficulties of access to satellites for educational users.

Lease of Transponders

The major item in the cost of the video system is transponder leasing at $2 million per year. Since it is unlikely, at least in the initial phase, that the system would be in use for more than a few hours per day, it might appear more appropriate to estimate this use and use an hourly lease rate. However, such a rate does not exist, since on the Canadian Telesat domestic system transponders can only be leased on an annual basis.

221

Ground Terminals

The study estimates that with current technology, ground terminals could be supplied at the following costs for the quantities required by the two systems:

1 video transmit station	$162,000
1 video receive station	$65,000
1 audio transmit/receive station	$20,000

The annual lease costs cited earlier reflect the fact that in the Canadian system only Telesat can legally own ground terminals. In such a non-competitive system the real prices charged might well be higher.

These figures reveal that if educational institutions could buy ground terminals and lease transponder capacity as required, then the costs of satellite use would be reasonable for certain applications. On the other hand, operational use is likely to remain out of the question so long as the restrictions on leasing transponders and buying terminals remain in force.

Interestingly enough, the Canadian government decided, in late 1977, to review these two aspects of policy in connection with its decision to allow a merger between Telesat and the Trans-Canada Telephone System.

This merger, the implications of which are of wider than Canadian interest, itself poses a threat to would-be satellite users. For long distances, especially where multipoint or broadband communication is involved, satellites are cheaper than terrestrial links. However, telephone companies, whose major investment is in such links, have their profits regulated as a function of that investment. Clearly they have little incentive to allow prices for satellite use to reflect the competitive costs of this form of communication.

This is not the place to discuss at length the politics of communications in a particular country. However, the Canadian case does highlight issues which will arise in each country that acquires a satellite system. Educators, and the public-service sector generally, will have to try to ensure that access to satellites is not denied to them by protective tariffs and regulations designed to shelter older technologies.

Using Satellites Efficiently

Even if unreasonable obstacles to satellite use are removed, educational institutions must still expect to pay the technological costs incurred by their use of satellites. The approximate costs we have quoted indicate that there is a considerable incentive to use satellites efficiently. In concluding this paper, we shall examine some factors which influence the cost-effectiveness of educational use of satellites.

Cooperation Between Institutions

Even if satellite time could be leased on an hourly basis, it would still be important to use the system intensively so as to make the most of the ground terminals and the skilled operating personnel. Since few institutions have needs that could absorb the full capacity of a satellite system, there are strong arguments for using a consortium approach. Several successful satellite experiments have been done on this basis (the Appalachia, Rocky Mountain, WAMI and Peacesat experiments on ATS and the British Columbia experiment on Hermes). Moreover, consortia are increasingly being formed to use other 'big' technologies in education such as CAL and cable TV.

Thrifty Use of Bandwidth

Postmen who had been used to delivering letters by car would probably be reluctant to do their rounds by bicycle or on foot, even if these means were shown to be more cost-effective in certain areas. In a similar manner, there is a danger that satellite experiments, where cost-effectiveness is not usually an issue, have created some expensive habits in the use of bandwidth. Specifically, many satellite experimenters now have the feeling that broadband TV is essential in cases where other studies on terrestrial systems have shown narrowband communication to be as effective. Fortunately the leaders of the US Public Interest Satellite Association (PISA) are actively arguing the merits of narrow-casting applications of satellites. Since hundreds of voice or data channels can be fitted into the same bandwidth as one TV channel the need for TV communication should be examined critically in every application.

The Success of the Application

Applications which are generally judged to be successful are, by definition, more cost-effective than satellite projects of which the success is dubious. This statement is not simply a circular argument. Although the satellite experiments conducted to date do not furnish directly much data about cost-effectiveness, they have highlighted factors which promote success. These factors, which are not specific to satellites, but which appear to apply generally to the use of big technology in education, were listed by Hooper (1975) and then used by him in planning the National Development Programme for Computer Assisted Learning in the UK.

Conclusion

In this brief paper we have attempted to signal the danger that satellite experimentation in education may lead, after the expenditure of millions of dollars, to a frustrating impasse. Melody (1977) goes so far as to suggest that the development of satellite communications technology is fast becoming an end in itself and that educational experiments are simply a part of the system required to keep a vicious circle turning. On this interpretation 'satellites are the twentieth century pyramids, the ultimate professional tinkertoy'.

Proving this interpretation wrong should be a matter of urgency for governments involved with satellites, for the stakes in the educational satellite game are rising all the time. The real dangers ahead are clearly implicit in a recent proposal by the Eskimo Brotherhood of Canada to conduct a pilot project on the Anik-B satellite. This project, which will test various new communications services under normal operating conditions, would appear to have every chance of success. In addition to satisfying the criteria imposed by the Canadian government for all Anik-B experiments, it also meets Hooper's criteria and fits the constraints imposed by the Eskimo Brotherhood itself. If the project is indeed successful, and Canada's northern people discover through it solutions to some of their many problems, they will wish to implement these solutions in a permanent, operational manner. Unless this passage from the experimental to the operational is going to be possible it is wrong to build expectations by encouraging such projects.

References

Daniel, J. S. *et al.* (1977) *The Costing of Two Networks.* Vol. 1 in *The Use of Satellite Delivery Systems in Education in Canada.* Télé-université, Quebec.

Daniel, J. S., Côté, M. L. and Richmond, J. M. (1977) Educational experiments with the communications technology satellite: a memo from evaluators to planners. *NATO Symposium on Evaluation and Research on Telelcommunications Systems.* Bergamo, Italy.

Hooper, R. (1975) *Two years on.* National Development Programme in Computer Assisted Learning, Council for Educational Technology of the United Kingdom, London.

Melody, W. (1977) Communication to be published in the proceedings of the Royal Society of Canada Symposium on the Hermes Satellite. Ottawa.

Polcyn, K. A. (1975) *An Educator's Guide to Communication Satellite Technology.* Andromeda Books, Washington DC.

29. The Use of a Communications Satellite and Interactive Colour Television in Simulation Teaching of Fire Suppression Skills

W. D. Robertson, *British Columbia Institute of Technology, Canada*

Abstract: Hermes, the Canadian communications technology satellite, was used as part of the experiments undertaken by the British Columbia Ministry of Education's Distance Education Planning Group to determine the feasibility of interactive television.

This paper describes how one group from the British Columbia Institute of Technology utilized satellite time to transmit a series of interactive programmes based on people and processes in the British Columbia forest industry.

Project Background

Hermes, the Canadian communications technology satellite launched in January 1976, has been used since October 1976 by Canadian and American groups in a variety of educational, medical and technical experiments (*CTS Reference Book*, 1975; Daniel *et al.*, 1977). One of the recent experiments was conducted by the British Columbia Ministry of Education's Distance Education Planning Group (DEPG). DEPG was established in 1977 'to develop a system for the delivery of educational programs and services to students throughout the province studying in a "distance learning" mode' (Carney, 1977). Hermes was used as part of the experiments undertaken by DEPG to determine the feasibility of interactive television as a component in a multi-modal education delivery system.

The British Columbia Institute of Technology (BCIT), a two-year tertiary education, diploma-granting institution, was invited by DEPG to join with the three public universities, four of the fourteen regional two-year colleges, and a number of other organizations in forming a production and delivery consortium for the duration of the experiment. BCIT was to produce eight hours of colour television programming based on some employment-related theme of broad public appeal.

The experiment was to run for eight consecutive weeks beginning 25 October 1977. The Canadian Federal Department of Communications (DOC) which controlled access to Hermes, allocated broadcast times of Tuesdays and Thursdays, 13.30 to 15.30 and 20.30 to 22.30 hours both days. In addition DOC supplied one portable earth originating station, five portable earth receiving stations, and staff to set up all six stations and to operate the originating station.

The Ministry of Education's television and film production group, the Provincial Educational Media Centre (PEMC), was responsible for some production, technical coordination and broadcasting the productions assembled by the participating organizations. DOC's staff were to transmit the studio signal to Hermes, geostationary over the equator at about 116° west longitude and at 23,000 miles altitude. Hermes would then rebroadcast the signal at 200 watts in the 12 to 14 GHz band to the five receiving stations. The PEMC studio (transmission site) is located in the greater Vancouver area; the other five stations at Campbell River,

Chilliwack, Dawson Creek, Kelowna and Pitt Lake. In three of the centres, the signal was to be fed to local television cable systems; in the remaining two centres special viewing studios were created. Characteristics of the five centres are set out in Table 1.

Centre	Distance from Vancouver in Air Miles	Cable System Viewing Populations	Regional Populations
Campbell River	100 (N.W.)	16-18,000	20,000
Chilliwack	55 (E.)	80,000	100,000
Kelowna	175 (E.)	25,000	65,000
Pitt Lake	35 (N.E.) in deep narrow valley	none	125
Dawson Creek	470 (N.N.E.)	none	13,000

Table 1

Each centre was equipped with a 25-inch colour television set to receive the high resolution colour television signal and all but Pitt Lake were able to transmit an audio signal back to the PEMC studio via Hermes simply by operating a microphone and speaking. Pitt Lake used a radio phone connected into the studio sound system. Each centre could hear all the other centres and could communicate via the PEMC studio system. Cable system viewers could communicate from their homes by telephoning into their local cablevision office where the ground station was located and having their telephone signal transmitted via Hermes to the PEMC studio.

Although the prime audience was the 10-15 persons anticipated to be at studios near each of the receiving stations, because of the connection to three cable systems, the potential viewing audience was in the tens of thousands. Approval of the experimental details was given at the end of August 1977. The first programme was to be on air eight weeks later.

The BCIT Proposal

BCIT staff decided to utilize the eight hours of provided time in a series based on people and processes in the British Columbia forest industry. The series would consist of eight connected programmes conducted in a modified photojournalism plus live interview format. Each programme would contain between 10 and 30 minutes of recorded materials drawn from library stocks and new footage obtained specially for the series, 5 to 10 minutes of live panel discussion, and the balance of time to a total of 55 minutes for live interaction among people from the five receiving sites and the central studio panel. The topics and format were carefully selected:

(1) Forestry and broadcast communications experts were on BCIT faculty and could be used as resource persons.

(2) Photojournalism and field shooting with portable television units were part of the Broadcast Communications Technology students' normal training and the project could be combined with their studies.

(3) Continuing education staff, who were managing the programme, had experience and contacts in the forest industry and in the government forest agencies, both of which could be drawn upon for support.

The primary, non-content related, objectives set by BCIT continuing education administration were:

(1) To determine the cost-benefits of institute-produced television materials.
(2) To test the interdepartmental work team concept when applied under considerable stress.
(3) To measure the acceptance of interactive television by the public as a component in a distance education system.
(4) To demonstrate the benefits of combining with government and industry in the design and production of an educational programme.
(5) To test our ability to conduct an effective forest fire suppression simulation via television and radio.

BCIT Project Organization

A project management team consisting of the Director of Business Programmes, Director of Engineering Programmes, Director of Library and Audio Visual Services, and Manager of Programme Development was given instructions to obtain resources and delegate operational responsibility. Eight production teams were created from five experienced television directors, twelve forest industry experts, three curriculum developer/writers, two professional announcers, four electronics technicians, two graphic artists, and five clerical assistants. To these BCIT staff members five forestry company employees and three provincial government forestry service senior staff were added.

Project objectives were widely discussed in a series of meetings of most of the staff involved. The project management team then assigned responsibilities through the line organization, and then decentralized responsibility to the eight production teams. The manager of programme development became functional project manager controlling finances, arbitrating disputes, obtaining special resources, and acting as liaison with the DEPG staff and PEMC production studio. All the staff members retained their normal teaching responsibilities to varying degrees.

Simulation Objectives

For the purposes of this paper, Programme Seven, the forest fire suppression simulation, will be examined in some detail because the project team consider that of the eight programmes produced, the simulation was the most challenging programme to create and has the most potential for successful interactive television teaching.

Forest fire suppression is taught as part of the training of BCIT forestry technologists. While we modified the method of presentation, the instructional objectives were unchanged:

(1) To assess those conditions which indicate forest fire hazard and difficulty of fire suppression.
(2) To organize available resources into a logical and effective pre-suppression plan.
(3) To deploy the available resources in the most effective manner possible when confronted with a forest fire.

The major programme goal is to create a pool of skilled personnel through experience gained in a controlled environment.

Normal Simulation Structure

The person or team for whom the simulation is run assumes the role of the 'fire boss'. The fire boss is provided with a set of topographical and forest inventory maps for a real forest region, weather data, fire weather index decision aids, and a list of staff and equipment resources. The fire boss is normally given 24 hours to create a contingency plan for a fire that can be expected to occur anywhere in the 250 square mile area covered by the maps.

The team creating the simulation environment consists of four role players who act out the parts of some of the fire boss's resources (e.g. central dispatcher, helicopter pilot, fire crew foreman, patrol aircraft pilot, sub-foreman), an audiovisual technician who operates the simulator, and the simulation director who controls the responses of the four role players and the audiovisual effects in response to the reactions of the fire boss. The simulator projects four superimposed coloured images onto a central screen — a static forested scene, moving smoke, moving fire, and growing char. Options exist for showing the creation of a fire break or road. The fire boss is isolated in front of the image and communicates with the role players via closed circuit microphone system. The role players are connected to the director via head sets and, as directed, reply to the fire boss's requests through individual microphones. Sound effects of aircraft, saws. pumps, and trucks are fed into the simulation at appropriate points to lend realism. Every attempt is made to almost hypnotize the fire boss into believing that the scene is real. The visual effect is of overlooking a real forest fire from a vantage point about a quarter of a mile from the fire and of communicating with a headquarters and ground team by radio phone. Depending on the fire boss's response to the fire, the director will let the fire grow out of control or will allow it to appear to be held to its initial size. The simulation can last from about 15 minutes to several hours depending on the complexity of the problem set.

Following the simulation the role players and director critique the performance of the fire boss.

Modification of Simulation for Hermes Project

The fire boss team, made up of four employees of B.C. Forest Products Limited, only one of whom had any fire experience, was located at the Pitt Lake receiving site, 35 miles from the rest of the simulation group. (The Pitt Lake site was the logging camp recreation hall which usually had between 30 and 50 people watching the programmes.) The Pitt Lake group was supplied with maps and resource information one week prior to the simulation exercise. The simulation image was projected onto a standard glass screen in front of a Philips LDK-25 colour television camera borrowed from a local television station. The role players, sound effects sources, and simulation director were located in the PEMC studio near the projected image.

When the simulation began, the audio and video signals were sent about 100 feet to a standard television control room which was out of direct line of sight of the simulation crew. The control room accepted the live signal and inserted brief film clips of aircraft and ground crews from a series of video playback units in the control room area. The choice of clips to be inserted and at what point was an almost instantaneous decision by the programme director, depending on the actions of the simulation director and the fire boss. The fire boss received the visual and audio signals from the 25-inch colour monitor provided at the receiving sites. Teams at the other four sites had been told to be prepared to assume the role of fire boss on several seconds notice if the radio phone link to the Pitt Lake crew was interrupted.

Results of the Simulation Exercise

The simulation was rated by the participants and observers as effective. Many persons experienced in such simulations commented that there was an element of realism not present in conventional fire simulations. A detailed evaluation of 37 questionnaires collected from all six sites following the simulation provided some useful data:

(1) 78 per cent rated the visual quality as good or very good.
(2) 78 per cent rated the audio quality as good or very good.
(3) 67 per cent stated the programme content was understandable to very understandable. Only 5.4 per cent rated it not understandable.
(4) 80 per cent stated the programme held their interest well; 5.4 per cent rated it low in interest.
(5) 78 per cent stated that the addition of film clips added to the effect of the simulation. No one felt they were a distraction (Yeoell and Riches, 1978).

A useful qualitative finding was that the simulation exercise preparation produced improved, relevant interaction over some of the earlier programmes that were less structured for the recipients. Considerable preparation had been requested of participants in each of the receiving sites and each had an active role to play in the programme either as part of the fire team or as critiquers.

General Conclusions

(1) The satellite transmission system and microphones were not a barrier to effective two-way communication.
(2) There was a significant acceptance of television in fire simulation.
(3) Interaction was improved when recipients were set tasks prior to broadcast dates.
(4) Communications satellite can be an effective tool for reaching isolated sites scattered over an area as large as the Province of British Columbia.

References

Carney, P. (Chairman) (1977) *Report of the Distance Education Planning Group on a Delivery System for Distance Education in British Columbia.*
CTS Reference Book (NASA) (1975) Lewis Research Centre, Cleveland. Ohio.
Daniel, J. S., Côté, M. L. and Richmond, J. M. (1977) Educational experiments with the communications technology satellite: a memo from evaluators to planners. *NATO Symposium on Evaluation and Research on Telecommunications Systems.* Bergamo, Italy.
Yeoell, B.D. and Riches, E. (1978) Unpublished Hermes project evaluation. BCIT, p.31.

Chapter 5:
Applications in Science Education

Few (if any) disciplines offer more scope for useful application of many facets of educational technology than science and engineering subjects. Often, material to be taught is intricate in detail, complex in its concepts, and complete mastery of 'prerequisite' knowledge may be quite essential for students to progress efficiently.

Dr Sutton (30) underlines the importance of evaluating the exact state of students' comprehension of physics, when the students first enter university from a variety of educational backgrounds. He presents a highly objective account of 'diagnostic testing' and its use in identifying (and subsequently helping) students needing clarification of scientific concepts.

Mr Telfer (31) expands our coverage of higher physics education with an impressive account of a 'three-tier' approach developed at Paisley College of Technology. Various media are carefully integrated into the system, choice being dependent on the nature of the subject material. Instructional objectives are found to be well received by students.

Dr Jenkins (32) describes how video-taped lectures may be used to help two categories of 'students with difficulties' in undergraduate chemical engineering courses. The causes of their difficulties in normal lessons are examined, and it is argued that the live class lesson is still by far the best way for these students to grasp conceptually difficult information. The video-tapes allow the students to extend their attention to the lesson by repetition, until satisfied with their comprehension.

Dr Race (33) considers the same classes, but from the point of view of physical chemistry laboratory work. In particular, language problems experienced by overseas students are considered, and a description is given of the development and evaluation of a series of objective-based laboratory scripts.

Turning to the teaching of biochemistry, Dr Bryce and Mr Stewart (34) give a comprehensive account of the design, development and use of self-instructional packages using the Philips PIP tape-film system. As well as cogently discussing the educational principles underlying the packages, the authors include much useful technical detail which should prove of considerable value and interest to those considering the production of similar packages for other subject areas.

Dr Ellington and his colleagues (35) argue that science-based educational games have yet to be used to their full potential in school and college curricula. They provide a detailed catalogue of games already developed and used in parts of Scotland.

Finally, Mrs Bardell (36) provides a stimulating discussion of the language used in scientific writing, in terms of effective communication versus other factors such as the 'scientist's wish to impress the reader'. It seems very worthwhile for all scientists developing educational programmes to scrutinize their own styles of writing, and ensure that the printed word (the most basic 'building-brick' of educational technology) is being used as effectively as possible.

30. Identification of Educational Needs: Diagnostic Testing

R. A. Sutton, *University College, Cardiff*

Abstract: The paper discusses an approach to the problem of determining the entry skills of first-year university physics undergraduates. It sets the work in the context of what was possible within the Physics Interface Project — a collaborative venture involving six British universities: Birmingham, Cardiff, Chelsea (London), Keele, Surrey and York. It mentions briefly the kind of follow-up activities that the project members found to be necessary.

Introduction

Almost a decade ago the Institute for Educational Technology at the University of Surrey carried out a survey of the background knowledge of a group of first-year physics students and came to the conclusion that A-level syllabuses were not a good guide as to what ground work students had actually covered by the time they arrived at university.

Since that time this finding has been reinforced many times over by investigations carried out within the Physics Interface Project (Ebison *et al.*, 1975; Sutton, 1977*a*, 1977*b*) between 1970 and 1976. This project involved the collaboration of six university physics departments — namely those at Birmingham, Cardiff, Chelsea (London), Keele, Surrey and York — who, with a grant from the Nuffield Foundation, came together with the aim of helping students in the transition from school to university.

With the benefit of hindsight, looking back over the project's investigations, it is clear that any formal differences and any apparent content differences between the physics syllabuses that are published by the various A-level examining boards are very much less significant than are the differences between what individual sixth-formers **learn** at school. These latter differences are even greater than the differences between what the sixth-formers are **taught.** For the most part teaching syllabuses are not exact reproductions of the respective published syllabuses, since these have to be **interpreted** by the teachers and translated into what they consider to be necessary and sufficient for imparting an adequate grasp of the various topics and concepts.

What is more, because of the nature of physics, mathematical competence is also important; there is growing concern at the present time that there may be even more serious problems in that area than in physics!

How then is the university teacher to know the background levels of knowledge and understanding of the subject, so that he or she can determine what is an acceptable starting point for the university course? One way would be to simply ask the students what they had or had not covered at school, or what they had not been able to cope very well with, if at all. This of course seems to be no more than commonsense, yet my experience has shown it to be a very unreliable method — especially since one has to resort to questionnaires if a large number of students

233

Subject Area Omitted from A-level work	Percentage of student sample in 1972 (N=371)	Percentage of student sample in 1973 (N=180)
Alternating current	16.2	3.3
Amplifiers	1.6	—
Angular momentum	—	0.6
Atomic/nuclear physics	5.1	1.1
Capacitors	1.6	1.1
Colour	0.3	—
Cyclotron	—	0.6
Diode rectifier	0.3	—
Doppler effect	—	1.1
Electricity	4.9	1.7
Electrochemistry	4.6	3.3
Electrical instruments	0.3	—
Electric motors	—	0.6
Electromagnetism	0.8	—
Electronics	1.3	—
Electrostatics	3.2	1.1
Electric/magnetic fields	0.3	—
e/m	0.3	—
Gas laws	0.3	0.6
Gravitation	1.1	—
Heat	1.4	1.1
Inductance/reactance	1.3	0.6
Induction	0.3	—
Inertial mass	—	0.6
Kinetic theory	4.0	1.1
Kirchhoff's laws	—	1.1
LCR circuits	0.3	—
Lenses	—	3.3
Magnetism	3.0	1.7
Magnetic properties	0.8	0.6
Mechanics	3.2	2.8
Mirrors	—	0.6
Moment of inertia	1.3	1.1
Optics	3.5	2.8
Optical instruments	1.1	1.1
Photoelectricity	0.3	—
Photometry	0.3	—
Physical optics	0.3	—
Rotation of rigid bodies	—	1.1
Spectra	0.3	—
Thermal radiation	1.3	0.6
Thermodynamics	2.2	—
Transformer	0.3	—
Transistors/valves	2.7	2.8
Viscosity	0.3	1.7
Wave motion	4.3	—
X-rays	—	0.6

Table 1. *Subject areas which students in 1972 and 1973 claimed* **not** *to have studied at A-level*

Difficult topic	Percentage of student sample in 1972 (N=371)	Percentage of student sample in 1973 (N=180)	Difficult topic	Percentage of student sample in 1972 (N=371)	Percentage of student sample in 1973 (N=180)
Alternating current	18.9	7.8	Magnetism	8.6	7.8
Adiabatic/isothermal			Mass/weight	0.3	—
expansion	0.5	0.6	Mechanics	4.0	12.2
Amplifiers	0.3	—	Moment of inertia	1.3	—
Atomic/nuclear			Motion of charge		
physics	2.4	3.3	in a magnetic		
Black body radiation	1.1	0.6	field	0.3	—
Boltzmann's constant	—	0.6	Motor principle	0.5	—
Capacitance	1.3	—	Newton's rings	0.3	—
Circular motion	0.3	0.6	Optics	3.5	9.4
D.C. circuits	1.6	0.6	Optical instruments	0.3	—
Diffraction/			Permittivity	—	0.6
interference	2.2	2.8	Polarization	0.3	—
Diffraction grating	0.3	—	Potential	—	0.6
Doppler effect	0.5	1.1	Potentiometer	—	0.6
Electricity	10.0	14.4	Prévost's theory	0.3	1.1
Electrochemistry	0.3	—	Probability	—	0.6
Electromagnetism	4.9	7.2	Projectiles	0.3	—
Electronics	0.3	0.6	Properties of		
Electrostatics	11.6	10.0	materials	0.5	—
Electric fields	0.3	2.2	Quantum theory	—	0.6
Electric instruments	0.5	—	Rectification of A.C.	0.3	—
Electrical units	0.3	—	Relative velocity	0.5	—
e/m	—	0.6	R.M.S. value	0.3	0.6
Electromagnetic waves	—	0.6	Rotation of rigid		
Entropy	—	0.6	bodies	—	0.6
Force on a conductor	0.3	—	Simple harmonic		
Gas laws	0.3	5.0	motion	0.8	1.7
Gravitation	0.3	1.1	Sound	1.3	0.6
Geometric optics	0.8	—	Standing waves	—	0.6
Heat	1.9	8.3	Surface tension	0.8	0.6
Huyghens' principle	—	0.6	Thermodynamics	0.8	0.6
Inductance/reactance	1.3	1.1	Thermometry	0.3	—
Induction	3.8	1.1	Valves/transistors	1.3	—
Inertia	0.3	0.6	Vectors	0.3	—
Kinematics	0.3	—	Viscosity	—	1.1
Kinetic theory	2.2	2.2	Wave motion	5.4	7.2
Lasers	—	0.6	Wave-particle		
LCR circuits	—	0.6	duality	0.3	—
Lens formulae	0.3	1.1			

Note: It should be noted that these subject designations were those adopted by the students themselves. They are not all mutually exclusive since, for example, 'electronics' might be considered to include 'valves' and 'transistors'. The term 'inertia' may have been confused with 'moment of inertia'; 'lens formulae' might be synonymous with 'geometric optics', and so on.

Table 2. *Subject areas which students in 1972 and 1973 claimed to have found* difficult *at A-level*

have to be surveyed. The responses one gets depend very much on the way the questions are framed and it is not always obvious what any individual student means by his or her answer.

Tables 1 and 2 show the kinds of free responses obtained when students were asked to list the topics that they or their teachers omitted from their A-level studies and those topics that they found difficult. Leaving aside the thorny question of what we might mean by 'difficult', a major problem is to accurately interpret the **content** of the responses. For example, it is not at all self-evident what might be included under any one of the proffered subject headings: 'wave theory' or 'electronics' to name only two, might mean almost any number of things, and certainly might mean different things to different students. What is more, some students were found to be quite unaware of topics having been left out by the teacher, simply because they were not aware of what was in the syllabus anyway.

This means that, short of interviewing each student individually, a more objective 'diagnostic device' is required if we really do want to discover which students are unable to do what. Consequently, a great deal of the project's efforts went into devising and developing diagnostic objective tests that would be as reliable as could be obtained, and that would not only enable students in need of help to be identified, but would also pin-point subject areas where difficulties of one kind or another might arise in the future. These criterion-referenced tests were standardized on the conventional 'stem + four alternative answer options' format, only one answer being correct in each case.

Prior Knowledge Tests

The decision to adopt the simple 'four-option' test format was based on the need for a scheme that would be straightforward to operate, without much in the way of procedural instructions and which would be similar in structure to the kind of objective test questions that were coming into increasing use in O-level and A-level examinations. There is clearly no advantage to be gained by baffling the students with questions that are structurally complicated, as some of the more sophisticated objective test items can be. Moreover, it is not too difficult to devise items which can test comprehension of basic concepts and principles and at the same time offer a reasonable range of distracters based on typical misunderstandings of the subject matter.

The first of these tests contained thirty-five items ranging over a wide spectrum of subject topics in physics — mechanics, properties of materials, electricity, optics, sound, atomic physics — together with items testing essential mathematical skills. The test was surprisingly well received by the students on its trial run, although the results served more as a lesson in how not to construct diagnostic tests than as a source of useful data. The outcome was that all future tests concentrated respectively on specific subject areas and were limited in scope to what the university teachers collectively regarded as prerequisites for their courses. The first single-subject test, however, was not on physics but on mathematics.

This test was first tried on second-year sixth-formers in about May 1971 and again with first-year university physics students in the following October. The results of these two trials are interesting because they revealed that the university students scored significantly less well than the sixth-formers. This is illustrated by Figure 1 which shows the score distributions superimposed. Figure 2 shows the proportions of students and sixth-formers answering each question correctly, and the proportions of those who for one reason or another failed to answer any given question. The average score obtained by the sixth-formers was 68.8 per cent while that for the students was 56.1 per cent.

236

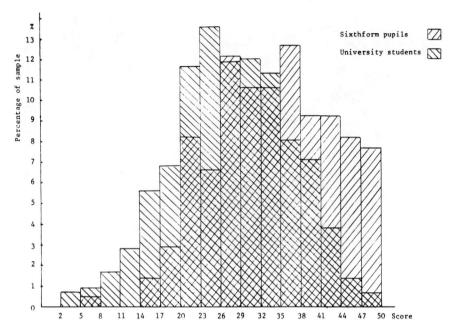

Figure 1. *Comparison of scores obtained on the 1971 Mathematics Test by sixth-form pupils and by first-year university students*

Although the sixth-formers seemed able to cope well enough with 50 questions in the space of a double-lesson period, many of the university students failed to reach the items towards the end of the test. Because of this, future tests were limited to not more than 30 items to be completed within about 50 minutes.

At first the tests were supervised by a member of staff but later on supervision was found to be unnecessary — provided that a proper explanation of what the tests were for was given to the students beforehand. A comparison of the results of tests in mathematics and in optics that were given to comparable groups of students — one group being supervised, the other being allowed to work through the test where they liked — showed no significant differences. Both groups showed the same kind of fundamental misunderstandings of the subject matter. The following Optics question (see Figure 3) offers a typical example of the pattern of results from the two groups.

The 'S' column shows the percentages of supervised students selecting each option and the 'U' column shows the percentages from the unsupervised group. The sample sizes were 63 (supervised) and 70 (unsupervised). The average scores on the whole test were 54.8 per cent (supervised) and 69.7 per cent (unsupervised).

It is also interesting to compare the results on the mathematics test between, say, 1971 and 1975. To illustrate how the results differ, two items have been chosen which remained identical in content and structure. These are as shown in Figures 4 and 5, the figures in the two columns indicating the percentages of students choosing each answer option on the two occasions.

The mean score on the whole test in 1971, obtained with a sample of 424 first-

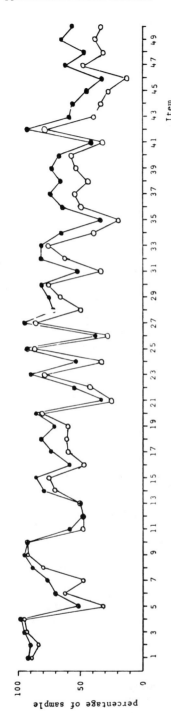

Figure 2(a). *The percentages of sixth-formers (●) and first-year university students (○) selecting the correct answer for each item in the Mathematics Prior Knowledge Test (1971)*

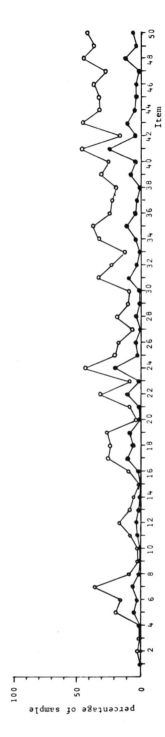

Figure 2(b). *The percentages of sixth-formers (●) and first-year university students (○) selecting no answer for each item in the Mathematics Prior Knowledge Test (1971)*

238

A man with defective eyesight can only focus objects clearly at distances between 0.2m and 1.0m from his eyes. What kind of spectacles should he wear in order to see distant objects?

		S percentage	U percentage
(A)	Converging lenses of focal length 1.0m	15.9	15.7
(B)	Diverging lenses of focal length 1.0m	39.7	57.1**
(C)	Converging lenses of focal length 0.2m	12.7	5.7
(D)	Diverging lenses of focal length 0.2m	20.6	15.7
	[None]	11.1	5.7
	N	(63)	(70)

** = correct response

Figure 3

If $\dfrac{a}{b} = \dfrac{c}{d}$ then

		1971	1975
(A)	$\dfrac{a + c}{b - d} = \dfrac{a}{b}$	4.7	3.8
(B)	$\dfrac{a - c}{b + d} = \dfrac{a}{b}$	6.8	5.9
(C)	$\dfrac{a + 2c}{b + 2d} = \dfrac{a}{b}$	48.1	58.6**
(D)	$\dfrac{a + c^2}{b + d^2} = \dfrac{a}{b}$	5.0	2.1
	[None]	35.4	29.5

** = correct response

Figure 4

The limiting value, as $x \to 0$, of $\dfrac{\sin x}{x}$, where x is measured in radians is

		1971	1975
(A)	0	23.3	16.0
(B)	1	50.9	54.4**
(C)	∞	10.4	12.7
(D)	Indeterminate	7.3	13.5
	[None]	8.0	3.4

** = correct response

Figure 5

year students was 56.1 per cent compared with a mean of 63.1 per cent with a sample of 237 students in 1975.

It would seem therefore that even on the basis of just two questions, the misconceptions that showed up in 1971 were still manifest in 1975 in roughly the same proportion of the student population. Indeed, if we analyse every item in the project's tests in this way, the same inferences can be made. What is more the test results tend to point to the failure to understand or fully grasp fundamental

239

concepts and principles as the main reason for obtaining wrong answers. What the implications of that finding might be are another matter.

Of course students get wrong answers for any number of reasons, but for the most part these can be put into three groups, i.e. temporary forgetfulness, not having been taught a particular topic, or not having fully mastered a particular concept or principle. Any student may demonstrate any or all of these in any one area of subject matter, and it is when we get to the stage of having to decide which applies that we have to look to the tutors for further help. There is absolutely no doubt that the cooperation of tutors in sympathetically following up test results is vital in making the whole scheme not only viable but credible. In my experience those students who thought the scheme was most worthwhile and most helpful were those whose tutors took the most care about follow-up.

Of necessity follow-up procedures were generally left for individual departments to decide for themselves, since whatever was to be done had to be acceptable to the staff. It might, however, be appropriate just to mention that to supplement what the tutors and lecturers might wish to do themselves, the project produced a number of concise self-teaching units that link up with the tests, but which can be made use of in almost any number of ways — either singly or in combination. These are now available from the project's publishers, University College Cardiff Press. Again the success or otherwise of these materials depends very heavily on the attitudes of the staff, since if the staff do not like them for any reason, the students do not receive them!

Acknowledgements

I am grateful to the Editorial Board of University College Cardiff Press and to *Physics Education* for freely permitting me to make use of published material, and in particular for permission to reproduce Tables 1 and 2.

References

Ebison, M. G., Sutton, R. A. and Taylor, C. A., (1975) Entry to physics courses at the tertiary level. *Royal Society-Institute of Physics Joint Committee on Physics Education.* Royal Society, London.

O'Connell, S. (1970) From school to university. *Universities Quarterly,* **24,** pp.177-85.

Sutton, R. A. (1977a) *Physics Interface Project Resource Booklet.* University College Cardiff Press, Cardiff.

Sutton, R. A. (1977b) The interface between school and university. *Physics Education* **12,** 5, pp.304-11.

Sutton, R. A. (1977c) Diagnosing prior knowledge levels of first-year university physics students. *Programmed Learning and Educational Technology,* **14,** pp.92-5.

31. A Three-Tier Approach to First-Year Physics

W. S. Telfer, *Paisley College of Technology*

Abstract: The paper outlines the development of a first-year physics course to accommodate a wide ability and background range, without needing to increase substantially on staffing or spending. A prerecorded three-tier system is described.

Introduction

The problem at Paisley College was not only how to produce and implement a first-year physics syllabus which would cater for a wide variation in student entry qualifications (Milson, 1975), but also to find an answer which would not involve an initial increase in costs (Larkin and Reif, 1977) or staff. A prerecorded three-tier system was flexible enough to allow a student movement between different capability levels and also to allow him to decide his readiness to take advantage of this mobility. This paper is a description of the teaching method and an intermediate assessment of the problems and successes.

General

The content of the alternative first-year physics syllabus at Paisley College has been developed for students of biology. It must therefore be considered terminal and must stand complete in itself. Qualifications for entry into a degree course in biology do not require the student to be qualified in physics, and the minimum requirement in mathematics is 'O' grade in the Scottish Certificate of Education. In the present group of 46 students, 10 fall into this category and the remainder vary in qualifications up to having passes at the Higher grade in physics and mathematics.

The course must therefore take into account this wide variation in entry qualifications and must provide a proper understanding of the principles of physics where these apply to biology and to the instruments which will be in common and constant use by biologists. The classical university college approach of lectures and tutorials was considered to put the less-qualified student at risk and also leave the very well-qualified student underemployed with its attendant risks. The three-tier approach overcomes both of these difficulties. The content was placed in three sectors: Basic, Course and Development and in order that these sectors should interact properly, complete reliance on the lecture approach was abandoned and replaced by prerecorded programmes with their back-up of slides, film strip, overhead transparencies and printed handouts. (Postlethwait *et al.*, 1972; Abercrombie, 1974).

At the beginning of the academic session 1977–78 the latest phase of building construction was completed on the college campus, this to be shared between the biology and physics departments. Eighteen months previous to this the author received permission from the college planning group to commission a learning unit in this building in an area originally designed for class teaching. The total area thus being determined, 130 square metres, the immediate problem was to plan an efficient layout. The total area was divided into two parts, the learning unit proper with 35 student places which provided tape players, tape/slide and tape/film strip facilities where the students could study either individually or in pairs using individual viewing screens and headphones, and a viewing room, sufficient in size for up to 15 students and equipped with chalkboard, marker board, screen, tape/slide projector, overhead projector and loudspeaker system. It was hoped that the viewing room would greatly encourage the interactive element in student learning and although this has been found to be the case it must be reported that it does not often take place without the active encouragement of the author.

The Three Tiers

The Basic Sector was designed to enlarge and explain the basic assumptions that are made in the course. Each basic topic was covered by an individual programme. They were either audio tape or tape/slide and, as was the case with all programmes in the learning unit, the Basic Sector programmes were available on request giving the student immediate access when he needed to revise a specific topic. It was initially considered that a relatively small number of basic programmes would be sufficient for the student's needs, but it has been found necessary to enlarge this sector considerably and it is indeed in a state of constant expansion. Most of the programmes were concerned with mathematical theorems and problems, e.g. the basic principles of algebra and trigonometry but there were also programmes on basic measurement, errors and accuracy.

The Course Sector was the major sector. It contained the standard material found in a syllabus written for biology or premedical students. All students must have satisfactorily completed this sector upon which the final examination was based. There were five subject headings: optics, mechanics, electricity, modern physics and heat. The programmes on heat were prepared by Professor L. W. Barr, Head of the Department of Physics. All the others were prepared by the author. Each subject contained an average of 23 programmes, usually a mixture of audio tape, tape/slide and tape/overhead depending on the programme content and the most effective form of presentation. Five weeks were allocated to each subject heading, usually five programmes to each week, the fifth one being a solutions tape concerned with the problems raised by the previous four. In this way problems directed to a specific topic could be attempted by the student in the first instance. The revision tutorials available at the completion of each subject heading contained more general questions, and questions requiring a more extended range of competence for their solution. It was considered that the emphasis in this sector should be given to both the general principles of physics and also to the basic principles, the operation of, and the general limitations of the measuring instruments extensively used by biology students and graduates.

There were six Development Sector packages ranging from the Microscope to the Health Physics problems encountered in a radiation environment. In this sector the able student could study five or six programmes in a specific package, each of which developed a theme introduced in the Course Sector. Again the form of presentation used was that considered most suitable to the material presented. The author of this short report was fortunate in persuading five colleagues in his department to agree to provide a Development Sector package in his own specialist area, bearing in mind the content of the Course Sector, the different objectives of the two sectors and the academic level of the students. By making use of this sector a student could, for example, learn of oil-immersion, phase-contrast and polarizing microscopes after having studied the simple and compound microscope in the Course Sector. Hopefully he would also be able to highlight the limitations and discuss some of the important advances in science made with the use of the microscope.

Final Points

Instructional objectives (Bloom, 1956; Davies, 1971) were available and these were well received by the students.

On average one hour of the student's weekly timetable was allocated to laboratory work; one hour in small group tutorials, about seven students in each group; three hours in the learning unit; and a single mass lecture taken by the author of the Course Sector programmes.

The doubts and fears concerning every aspect of this undertaking experienced by everyone concerned have been well documented elsewhere (Bingham, 1976).

Possible modifications to the methods of presentation of the course material have become apparent, indeed small additions and refinements have already been made, this will undoubtedly be a continuing process.

A comprehensive series of results will be necessary before any final assessment of the method can be reported but the response of the students has been considered sufficiently encouraging to stimulate the inclusion of the laboratory experiments into the teaching programmes as the next step in the course development.

References

Abercrombie, M. L. J. (1974) *Aims and Techniques of Group Teaching,* 3rd ed. Society for Research into Higher Education, London.

Bingham, E. G. (1976) Skills for the occasion. In Clarke, J. and Leedham, J. (eds.) *Aspects of Educational Technology X.* Kogan Page, London.

Bloom, B. S. (ed.) (1956) *Taxonomy of Educational Objectives: Cognitive Domain.* McKay, New York.

Davies, J. K. (1971) *The Management of Learning.* McGraw-Hill, New York.

Larkin, J. H. and Reif, F. (1977) Better instruction with lower costs: some practical suggestions. *American Journal of Physics,* 45, 2.

Milson, A. (1975) A self-learning scheme in applied science (physics and chemistry) for students of widely varying background knowledge. *Programmed Learning and Educational Technology,* 12, 6.

Postlethwait, S. N., Novak, J. and Murray, H. T. (1972) *The Audio-Tutorial Approach to Learning,* 3rd ed. Burgess, Minneapolis.

32. The Use of Video-Tape Recordings as an Aid to Teaching in an Undergraduate Course

B. G. M. Jenkins, *Polytechnic of Wales, Pontypridd, Mid-Glamorgan*

Abstract: The development of a library-housed collection of video-taped lectures is described, in terms of the particular problems experienced by some overseas students studying a chemical engineering course. The choice of the medium is explained and justified, and initial student reaction described.

The chemical engineering department runs two BSc degree courses and a Higher National Diploma (HND) course. The entry qualifications for the degree course are two appropriate GCE A-level subject passes, and for the HND one appropriate A-level pass or the equivalent of the above entry qualifications. Students enter the courses though with a wide variation in entry qualifications, from those with the bare minimum outlined above to those with very good passes indeed, often industrially based in this case. The group therefore represents a mixed ability group from the teaching point of view and has to be treated as such.

From experience in teaching first-year courses to these students over the last ten years, it has become evident that the student intake into both BSc and HND courses can each be divided into four groups.

Firstly, there are those students who are very able, can work on their own, know what has to be done and will get on with it. Students falling into this category will survive whatever system embraces them. The next group possesses sufficient ability, and with encouragement and work is capable of succeeding. A third group is in the borderline area, but is capable of succeeding given a lot of attention and encouragement and hard work on its part. Finally we have a group of overseas students whose mother tongue is not English and who are slowed down by language problems.

The first two groups are not of great concern from the teaching point of view. When taught in the normal way, appropriate to their particular course, these two groups are capable of succeeding in their work and obtaining their degrees and diplomas without many problems or difficulties. It is the latter two groups which give cause for concern.

The most obvious solution to the problem and probably the best answer is to provide more teaching and tutorial time for these students. However, this is not usually possible. Staff shortages and substantial teaching loads, together with research and administrative activities mean that there is very little time available over and above the allotted timetabled hours as approved in the original degree and diploma submissions to the appropriate bodies for approval.

More effective use of the allotted time available is an alternative solution. This, of course, is carried out to a large extent. Time for copying notes off the board is minimized by providing notes in handout form. The overhead projector is used so that slides can be prepared in advance, again saving time otherwise used for writing on the board. Prior information of the lecture topics also helps so that the students have a chance to read up on the topic beforehand and hence they have some knowledge of the topic being discussed. These methods all help to make the lecture and tutorial periods more effective and allow more time for teaching and individual contact with the class.

However skilfully the lessons have been presented, however well written the handouts, and however good the students' own notes there comes a time when the student is on his own; when he sits down at his own desk in his own place and gets down to learning the material he has collated from various sources. It is at this time that problems and difficulties arise. Points which seemed quite simple and straightforward when explained in class now appear difficult to understand, and in fact are quite often incomprehensible.

In this situation, what does the student do? The usual solutions are to ask a classmate to explain it to him or to see the lecturer concerned and ask him for assistance, and here a bottleneck in the system occurs. Whilst the lecturer is almost certainly very willing to help there are often practical problems involved. He might be away, too busy for a day or two, or otherwise engaged. Hence valuable time is lost; the student gives up that particular piece of work and gets on with something else he can cope with. Too often, of course, the student never returns to that particular topic and it gets shelved, never to be fully understood.

Now, in a class lesson one can talk a lot around the main topic or lesson objective being covered. It can be approached from many angles and explained in many ways. There is feedback from the class and this often determines the direction which the lesson takes. Points of difficulty can be explained neatly and clearly through verbal and visual communication which are almost impossible to explain in writing or would literally take reams of paper to do so. Thus, however good notes and handouts are, it is impossible to replace the live class lesson.

If the live class lesson cannot be replaced because it is the best teaching situation, but resources are such that there is insufficient time to repeat the lesson, or conduct sufficient tutorials based upon it, the next best thing must be a video-tape recording of the class lesson. Now, though whilst watching a television recording there is no opportunity for direct feedback most of the good points are still retained. This is the method being tried out as a pilot scheme for the process principles course in the first years of the HND and BSc degree courses in chemical engineering.

The scheme is directed particularly at the two groups singled out earlier, the less able students and some overseas students. The latter group contains some very able students, but because of lack of familiarity with the English language they sometimes have difficulty in picking up everything that is said in class. Their written English and understanding of written English is good, but the problems occur with spoken English in this case. The lecturer talks too quickly, has an unfamiliar accent, uses colloquial phrases with which they are not familiar and in my own particular subject uses technical terms which are new to them. Hence they miss a lot of what goes on in a lesson, which as I have already stated is the most important means of communicating information. They are thus at a disadvantage. However often the lecturer is prepared to explain things and repeat himself, there comes a point when there is simply not sufficient time available to do so.

For a student such as this there are undoubted advantages in using a video-tape recording of a particular lecture. First of all it is effectively a live teaching situation. He can see and hear what is going on and if he cannot pick up a particular point can repeat the recording several times until he does so. He thus has a substantial degree of control over his rate of learning. Additional question sheets are available for use with the particular programme being viewed so that there can be some feedback and interaction during the session.

245

The scheme is operated in the following way. The original lesson is given to the class as one would normally do. The same lesson is then recorded in the television studios of the Polytechnic. It covers the same material as the original lesson but one can learn from the class presentation and spend more time on the points which caused difficulty in class. The tape is of 30 to 40 minutes duration. After any editing which may be necessary it is transferred to the main library for filing. It is kept in the main library and the students have access to it during normal library hours. They have to sign for it when using it and this gives an indication of the use made of it.

It must be emphasized that it is in no way intended to replace the normal lecture but is intended only to reinforce the material which has already been covered in class. The object of this project is to help the student improve his learning by the provision of additional material which he can use in his own time. It is intended to clarify points already covered in lessons and tutorials, for revision and recapping on work already covered. It would not at this stage be used for the introduction of new material.

The effectiveness of the scheme in improving a student's learning and understanding will probably be almost impossible to assess, unless there is a dramatic and immediately obvious change in the ability of the class. There are so many other parameters involved in teaching a class of students, from the students themselves, the lecturer, and differences in examination papers from year to year that it is going to be very difficult to pinpoint an improvement in the class performance as directly attributable to this project.

Television is not new in teaching. But this particular exercise is not at present being carried out in any engineering department in the country as far as is known, certainly not in any chemical engineering department.

Student reaction to the project has been very favourable so far. They maintain that it has helped them considerably already. Whilst this might be no more than an initial flush of enthusiasm for what is for them a novel method of learning, it appears to bode well for the future of the project.

33. Teaching Physical Chemistry Objectively – Extension to Laboratory Work

W. P. Race, *Polytechnic of Wales, Pontypridd, Mid-Glamorgan*

Abstract: An account is given of the development of an objective-based laboratory scheme in physical chemistry. The factors behind the design of structured laboratory scripts are discussed, and related to the special needs of first-year students in a polytechnic. Details are given about the assessment of the laboratory work, and the management of the laboratory.

Introduction

In most higher education courses containing physical chemistry, students spend well over half the time allotted to the subject in a laboratory. Normally, much careful planning is directed into the content and organization of the theoretical part of a course. However, the many hours spent by students performing and writing up practical work are seldom exploited to provide maximum opportunity for students to develop crucial knowledge and skills. This paper reviews the development of the laboratory component of a course in the context of the particular needs of typical first-year science and chemical engineering classes at the Polytechnic of Wales.

In the theory course (with which the laboratory course is designed to be integrated closely) the complete physical chemistry syllabus is divided into a series of one-hour 'units'. In each of these, the student is issued with a structured handout comprising three to six pages, with the 'unit objectives' formulated at the start of the first page. Accomplishment of these objectives is designed to serve as the prerequisite necessary for progress to the next unit. The handouts involve the students in a variety of participatory activities during each lecture period, including applications of the theory, revision exercises. and elicitation of concepts. The students are also required to fill in on the handouts important diagrams, equations and graphs. Towards the end of each lecture period, class members are tested orally on the unit objectives.

The need for a complementary objective-based laboratory course became increasingly apparent during the first two-year development of the theory course. Information gathered from students by questionnaire confirmed their wish for the style of laboratory script described below.

Specific Requirements of the Laboratory Course

Students responded enthusiastically to having clearly formulated objectives present throughout the theory course, often commenting on how useful they found it when they saw clearly exactly what they were required to know. The particular needs of the classes for which the objective-based laboratory course was developed are discussed below.

Language Difficulties

The first-year chemical engineering HND and degree classes consist largely of overseas students. A wide range of nationalities includes Malaysian, Greek, Indian, Middle Eastern, African and South American origins. For many such students, the first year of study in higher education presents a considerable level of difficulty with the use of English, even when they have studied for several years in the language. The difficulties are such that typically about half the members of a class are virtually unable to set up and perform any moderately complex physical experiment, if only a standard laboratory instruction sheet is issued to them. Not surprisingly, the ability of such students to write even a coherent descriptive account of procedure is very limited. Therefore, most of their energies are dissipated simply in trying to perform and describe an experiment, leaving little in reserve for the much more valuable tasks of interpreting their experimental data, and assessing the significance of factors limiting experimental accuracy.

Class Size

Typically, 20 students may attend a laboratory together, working independently or in pairs. Since it would be prohibitively expensive to duplicate sophisticated instruments and apparatus to allow each class member to perform the same experiment in any one laboratory session, it is normal in any physical chemistry laboratory for 10 or more different experiments to be in operation at any point in time. A rota is devised so that each student has the use of each experiment during a series of laboratory sessions. Since it is impossible and undesirable to postpone the whole of the laboratory course until after the completion of the theory course, it is inevitable that the situation frequently arises where a student will be confronted with an experiment 'ahead' of the current state of the theory he has been taught. Therefore sufficient directly relevant theory must be presented concisely and quickly to the student for him to understand the principles demonstrated by the experiment. It is not possible for a lecturer to give a 'mini'-lecture to each student at the start of a laboratory session, so a way has to be found to present in written form carefully judged theoretical background to enable the student to understand the experiment without unduly limiting the time at his disposal for the actual measurements and investigations.

Integration with Theory Course

The relevance of practical work to 'in-depth' theory has to be made self-evident if students are to appreciate laboratory work as a crucial part of the course as a whole. It is necessary to design experiments so that the understanding of selected theoretical concepts and their applications and consequences is furthered. The relevance of the experiments may best be demonstrated to students if the objectives to be achieved in the laboratory are carefully formulated and presented. In particular, the objectives can be used to show students the importance of interpreting the meaning of their data, rather than simply leading them to present descriptive accounts of the measurements and instrumentation.

Continuous Assessment

A first-year class consisting of students from many nations and backgrounds inevitably shows a wide range of abilities. This makes the need for each student to receive immediate and repeated feedback on his individual level of competence critical. Rowntree (1977) discussed the need to use assessment procedures to provide encouragement to students, and to minimize inhibiting side-effects which are only too easily produced by a detailed assessment system. The laboratory provides a more informal and intimate climate to give individual attention and help to students than the lecture situation. To optimize the value of this aspect of laboratory work requires careful planning of the management of assessing and reviewing experimental work.

Structure of Laboratory Scripts

With due consideration of the factors mentioned above, it is proposed that the potential benefit of the laboratory course is optimized by producing for each different experiment a duplicated structured script. This is used by the student in carefully planned ways before, during and after the actual performance of the experiment. A script is issued to each student one week before the (fortnightly) laboratory session, and is required to be handed in for assessment one week after the session. The marked script is then discussed directly with the student during the next laboratory session. The general structure adopted is summarized as follows:

- ☐ 'Objectives' — a list to be achieved by the student during the experiment and subsequent writing up.
- ☐ 'Theory' — a concise presentation related directly to the particular experiment.
- ☐ 'Experimental Procedure' — a numbered set of operations to enable the average student to proceed through the setting up and performance of the experiment without needing further direct assistance.
- ☐ 'Results' — grids and spaces for data to be recorded directly into the script as measurements are made.
- ☐ 'Treatment of Results' — a list of calculation instructions and graphical treatments for the student to perform on his data.
- ☐ 'Supplementary Questions' — a set of up to 10 questions probing many specific aspects of the student's comprehension and interpretation of his work.

It is of value to consider separately in some detail the format adopted for each of these sections, and the objectives underlying their design and use.

'Objectives'

Apart from a grid to contain the dates of issue, performance and assessment of the experiment, the front page contains the title and a list of objectives (see Figure 1). The first of these, labelled 'Principal Objective of Experiment', is intended to give the student a clear, unambiguous idea of the main purpose of the experiment. If he fails to achieve this objective he may regard his attempt at the experiment as unsuccessful.

Next there follows a list of between five and eight 'Other Objectives'. These are intended to make the student aware while he is doing the experiment of subsidiary (but collectively very important) aspects of the work. He need not necessarily achieve all of these to receive a favourable grade of assessment.

Sometimes these other objectives serve as pointers for particular aspects of the experiment which the student should be anticipating. On occasion, where a series of repetitive measurements is necessary, these can be linked with an objective such as 'to gain practice in the rapid and accurate use of a precision balance'. In the absence of such an objective, students would often find such measurements tedious; when the objective is stated they are conscious that such practice is

Phase Equilibria	Name
Experiment 6	Date Assigned
	Date Performed
Phase Diagram of a	
Simple Eutectic System	Date to Submit
(Theory: Phase Equilibria Unit 13)	Date Assessed
	Assessment

Principal Objective of Experiment: to construct the phase diagram of the tin-lead system

Other Objectives:

1. To practise the use of thermocouples to monitor temperature

2. To construct a thermocouple calibration graph from data supplied

3. To record cooling curves for different tin-lead compositions starting at temperatures where the system is completely liquid, and finishing below the temperature by which complete solidification has occurred

4. To analyse the cooling curves to determine the temperatures at which pure components or eutectic mixture begin to solidify

5. To observe and account for the differences in form of the cooling curves at different compositions

6. To assess the precision of the determination of points on the phase diagram

7. To practise quantitative use of the phase diagram

Figure 1. *An example of the first page of a typical objective-based laboratory script*

useful, and a significant improvement in the standard of measurements is produced. The 'other objectives' do not relate only to skills. They often relate also to aspects of the analysis of the data, and its interpretation.

'Theory'

When essential for the adequate understanding of the experiment, this section presents a very concise summary of the relevant theory. The section is specifically designed to help students to understand the experiment before class coverage of the related theory. It also serves as a rapid revision exercise if the experiment is attempted after general coverage of the theory. Where feasible, the section duplicates material directly from course theory units, so that the close interdependence of laboratory and theoretical work is emphasized. The section is omitted entirely where experiments can be done satisfactorily from basic knowledge; this takes advantage of the situations where direct experimental work is a valuable 'way in' to theoretical considerations.

'Experimental Procedure'

As noted recently by Harris (1977), reducing the load on laboratory supervisory and technical staff is often closely related to the production of a well-thought-out operation schedule. Often, too much staff time is taken up simply showing students how to begin experiments. The students may well learn more (and find the work more rewarding) if they are able to start without direct help.

The 'experimental procedure' section is designed to take the student step-by-step through the setting up of apparatus and instruments, and continues in the same manner through the main part of the experiment. The language is kept as direct as possible, and the steps are numbered making it easier for the student to recall exactly what stage he has reached in the procedure. It is intended that the *average* student can work right through the experiment without having to call on the technician or lecturer for direct help. This allows much more time for the staff to help weaker students. Also, it is possible to give more explanation of more complex refinements to the most able students, preventing them from finding the work unchallenging. Students are encouraged to work at their own pace; the section often contains additional (but optional) work for faster students to attempt.

One of the fundamental long-term aims of any science laboratory course is to train the student to write accurate and comprehensive reports, which necessarily include fluent accounts of experimental procedure. The numbered operations presented in these scripts are designed to show by example how to describe clearly and simply the consecutive steps in a complex sequence of operations. Later in the course, after the student has used several such scripts, he is given ones with this section omitted, and asked to supply a 'procedure' section. At a given time, perhaps two or three students are using scripts without procedure instructions, and it is easy to find staff time to start them off on their experiments by demonstration or instructional talk, while the majority of the class work unaided from complete scripts.

'Results'

Measurements are entered directly into spaces and tables in the scripts. At the start of the course it is emphasized that recording data on 'scrap' paper has serious disadvantages, such as the probability of losing data between measurement and writing up. A more serious disadvantage of 'loose' results is that if anything 'goes wrong' with an experiment it is seldom possible to conduct a 'post-mortem' if the original measurements are no longer available. Students readily appreciate that if all original readings are preserved in the script, such a post-mortem can often indicate that the error occurred in the handling of the data rather than in the measurements. It is much more acceptable to students to be asked to 're-work' some data, than to repeat a whole experiment.

Inevitably, while recording data into a script, the student will sometimes enter 'mistaken' measurements and need to correct the entry; also results may be misplaced in tables. This means that sometimes the 'results' section may appear rather untidy. Some students are concerned by this, and would rather hand in for assessment a 'fair copy' of the section. This wish is accommodated when necessary by issuing an extra copy of the 'results' section, on condition that the original untidy data section is included in the script as an appendix.

'Treatment of Results'

In physical chemistry experiments, the work is usually far from finished when all the measurements have been recorded. Almost always, graphical or numerical handling of data is required, followed by interpretation of the behaviour observed. This section consists of a numbered list of operations to be done on the measured data. The faster students often perform these operations directly as they do the experiments. The slower students can catch up on these steps after the laboratory session, where in the absence of this section they may have abandoned further progress with the interpretation of their results. Discouragement of the competent-but-slow student is avoided, and the fast student is not allowed to become bored. The section usually leads towards a numerical, tabular or graphical presentation of the main conclusions of the experiment.

'Supplementary Questions'

At the start of the course, it is explained to the class that this section carries a substantial weighting in the assessment of scripts. The questions are posed with spaces left for the insertion of answers, the sizes of the spaces deliberately intended to show the students approximately how much detail is expected.

This section is primarily designed for completion after the laboratory session, when it is intended to stimulate the student to think critically about the interpretation and accuracy of his data, and about possible modifications to the experimental apparatus and procedure. The section always includes direct questions to make the student assess the nature and relative importance of different sources of experimental error. Often, questions are included to give the student practice at quantitative applications of the results of the experiment.

Sometimes, two or three of these questions may be quite advanced, and detailed knowledge of the relevant theory may be prerequisite. To avoid discouraging students reaching these questions before class coverage of the theory, these questions are qualified by instructions such as 'do not attempt this question until after class coverage of phase equilibria unit 13'.

The final question (with unlimited space for answer) is always of the form 'write any additional comments, observations and criticisms so that this script is a comprehensive record of the experiment'. The response produced by this question is of considerable value during assessment. Much useful feedback about areas of undue difficulty is received, with interesting suggestions for modification of equipment and procedure. The most able students write freely about additional interpretative detail of their data, and improvements in methodology. Lazier students concentrate on the factors outside their control on which they can blame any shortcomings in the results! Students with pronounced language problems can be identified from the lack of fluency of their discussion, or from severe brevity in their response to this question.

Management and Assessment

Careful consideration was given to the timing of issue and collection of scripts. The student performs an experiment at fortnightly intervals, and the timing is such that he is always in possession of just one script. This avoids any chance of him bringing the wrong script to the laboratory or for assessment. Having the script for seven days before the laboratory session allows the conscientious student to read through the experiment, and do any revision which could be useful. It also means that at the start of the laboratory session, each student can begin work as soon as he enters, avoiding almost all of the 'chaos' which would prevail if experiments were assigned at the start of the laboratory sessions.

PRACTICAL PHYSICAL CHEMISTRY COURSE

Report Assessment

Student's Name:

Date Expt. Performed: 16th Feb. 1978
Date Assessed: 24th Feb 1978

Experiment Code (P6)

Grade	Excellent	Very Good	Satisfactory	Poor
entry of data				
graphs				
calc. values				
actual results				
suppl. questions				
discussion				

Overall assessment (%) (75)

If further work required: details

Take more care in future with phase field labelling — otherwise very good.

To be re-submitted by (date)

Reassessment: ( )

Figure 2. *Example of the use of an assessment grid*

Scripts are marked using an 'assessment grid' so that each student receives feedback on his competence in various aspects of his work (see Figure 2).

Each script is discussed individually with the student at a convenient point during his next experiment (i.e. two weeks after he performed the experiment being assessed). At this interview, general explanations and suggestions are made, but more specialized discussion (often relating to the more advanced of the supplementary questions) is deferred until all the students have attempted the experiment concerned. Otherwise, other students would inevitably overhear correct answers being discussed, and would be at an unfair advantage. From time to time, a class session is used to run through two or three experiments completed by the whole class. The scripts are then returned to the students, and detailed discussion of correct data (and answers to questions) occurs. This procedure provides useful revision of the work.

After the initial interview, the student is given the assessment grid, but the script is retained until a class review session.

Adaptation to more Advanced Course Work

It may well be argued that to continue to use such scripts late into a degree course would be to 'spoon-feed' students and stunt their report-writing development. However, in view of increasing concern about the difficulties concerning language of scientific reports, for example Cooper (1964) and Bardell (1978), it can be argued that these laboratory scripts may well help towards effective report writing. Students can be 'broken-in' gently by issuing isolated experiments with only a sketchy instruction sheet, and asking for a report to show what might have been the objectives, treatment of data, and supplementary questions in a 'full' script.

O'Connell and Penton (1975) discussed 'self-teaching' and 'independence-in-learning' situations in science laboratory classes. By careful planning of the progress towards advanced work, the student can be gently moved from the 'self-teaching' frame of reference offered by very detailed laboratory scripts, towards the 'independence-in-learning' situation so essential if the student is to progress effectively into scientific research later in his career.

For experiments involving advanced instrumentation (such as polarographic analysis and automatic electrometric titration techniques) replacement of the 'experimental procedure' section by video-taped demonstration is planned. Howland (1975) reported this medium most effective in such situations. The advantage anticipated is that the individual student should be able to spend as much time (or as little) as he needs to familiarize himself with the operation of complex instruments.

Evaluation of the Laboratory Course

In the two terms that these scripts have been in use, several trends have already been noticed. Laboratory attendance has improved to over 90 per cent. Previously, particularly towards the end of a course, attendance of poorer students often dropped, leaving the able and conscientious students (who were in some respects 'penalized' by having more work to do than their less motivated colleagues). The increased attendance seems to be part of a general increase in the students' satisfaction with the laboratory course as a whole.

A dramatic improvement in the 'keeping-up-to-date' regarding writing up and assessment has occurred. Less than 3 per cent of scripts were handed in 'late'. Previously, typical behaviour was that about half of any class would run several weeks behind in writing up towards the end of a course.

A healthy and amicable competitiveness has grown among class members. Students quickly realize that a good report will earn them between 90 and 100 per cent, and that a poor one may earn less than 20 per cent. Many students strive to beat 'personal bests'. This situation is in marked contrast to the apathy which sets in with the all-too-common system where a 'good' report earns maybe 8 out of 10, and an indifferent one earns 6 out of 10.

The students developed a considerable interest in the objectives of the experiments. In some trials, experiments were issued without their objectives, and the students asked to compile lists of objectives for the experiments. Most students elicited at least two-thirds of the objectives which had been formulated for the experiments, and one or two new ones were produced.

Finally, a questionnaire has been designed to be issued to students during the last term of the year. It is anticipated that useful information about the students' attitudes to the organization and content of the laboratory course may be collected from the responses.

Although the course described above was developed specifically for physical chemistry laboratory classes, it would appear that the method may be used with advantage for practical work in many other science and engineering disciplines. It is applicable to 'limited budget' situations, since the savings in staff time and the much more effective use of student time more than offset the relatively minor costs of producing duplicated scripts. The method is also appropriate for use in developing countries, where advanced education is often conducted using English language, and where the design considerations related to language problems are particularly applicable.

(The author will be pleased to supply specimen laboratory scripts on request).

References

Bardell, E. (1978) Communication of scientific information. In Brook, D. and Race, W.P. (eds.) *Aspects of Educational Technology XII.* Kogan Page, London.

Cooper, B.M. (1964) *Writing Technical Reports.* Penguin, Harmondsworth.

Harris, N.C.D. (1977) *Programmed Learning and Educational Technology,* 14, 4, pp.280-8.

Howland, R.J. (1975) Videotaped instructional material in laboratory teaching. In report of symposium *Educational Techniques in the Teaching of Chemistry and Other Sciences* at Surrey University. Chemical Society, London.

O'Connell, S. and Penton, S.J. (1975) Independent learning in the laboratory. In Furniss, B.S. and Parsonage, J. R. (eds.) *Indepenaent Learning in Tertiary Science Education.* Thames Polytechnic/Chemical Society, London.

Rowntree, D. (1977) *Assessing Students: How Shall We Know Them?* Harper and Row, London.

34. Design and Production of Self-Instructional Learning Packages in Biochemistry using the Philips PIP System

C. F. A. Bryce and A. M. Stewart, *Dundee College of Technology*

Abstract: A number of learning packages have been produced for the Philips PIP system and are discussed in terms of their effectiveness as resource-based learning material. The educational benefits derived from the choice of such mixed media are discussed and methods for improvement in the presentation are outlined.

Introduction

Resource-based learning in biochemistry in Dundee College of Technology has, over the past two years, developed significantly as a result of close cooperation and interaction between subject specialists in biochemistry and the educational technology staff of the college.

The implementation of specific learning packages was initially carried out and encouraged for essentially three reasons:

(1) They provided the lecturer with 'extra' curriculum time for revision, tutorials etc.
(2) They were effective in increasing student motivation.
(3) Initial validation indicated that they facilitated learning of specific objectives.

With respect to the sometimes large difference in student ability within a class, the design and production of programmes which were self-paced was essential.

Choice of Media

Owing to the fact that a number of the structures dealt with in biochemistry and molecular biology are particularly complex, a media format which allowed gradual build-up of such structures and also facilitated animation where necessary was desirable. For these reasons, the Philips PIP tape/film system was chosen. The programmes involved the production of an audio-control cassette, a film cassette and a printed work book in which the student responded to objective test questions. In a recent article, Hunt (1977) pointed out that perhaps the most important factor governing the effectiveness of the media was the teacher himself, and there appears to be a number of other studies which confirm this view (Tobias, 1969; Dodge, Bogdan, Brogden and Lewis, 1974). Certainly the experience which we obtained from the design and production of our first PIP programmes gave us high expectations on the potential usefulness of the system and feedback from the students involved in the teaching packages and from other staff involved in their implementation have confirmed these early hopes. Only a more extensive use of this media will indicate whether or not we are observing the 'Hawthorne effect' as described by Parsons (1974). This can best be considered as an increase in student learning performance resulting from exposure to a new educational system which they perceive as being special to them. Clearly, as more and more programmes are produced and a wider student audience is exposed to them then, if it exists, such an effect would be short-lived.

Systems Approach

A systems approach was used in the design and production of each package, and student feedback was achieved from response to questions raised within the course of the programme and to objective tests at different stages in the presentation.

In evaluating the use of learning via the media, a number of people believe, particularly in the current stringent economic climate, that an important factor to be considered is not just if it is effective but also if it is cost-effective (Cumming and Dunn, 1971; Spencer, 1977). There are, however, a number of inherent problems in assessing educational packages solely on the basis of 'outcome' since the outcome is itself, in many cases, difficult to define.

Multi-level Programming

With respect to the variation in students' abilities within a class and between similar classes, some packages were designed using multi-level programming — multi-level in terms of both subject level and student level.

In biochemistry it is not unusual to cover the same topic at different levels in successive years of a course, thus an audio-control tape was pulsed in such a way that a topic for year one of a particular subject matter (which is usually a general overview of the material) was covered (see Figure 1).

In the second year, the same topic is covered in greater depth, so a second audio-control tape was produced to take the students through the same film cassette, utilizing a different frame sequence but still having a fair proportion of the visual material common to both programmes (see Figure 1).

Once the students have mastered the material they have access to a revision tape which rapidly covers the main points in the topic. These presentations are distinguished, therefore, at the subject level.

The programmes are also variable for student ability level in that students can be taken through the subject slowly in small steps or relatively quickly in larger steps (see Figure 1).

This aspect of multi-level programming has a potential usefulness in school teaching in light of the new N and F level proposals (2 levels) in England, and the proposals arising from the Munn and Dunning Reports in Scotland (3 levels: Credit, General and Foundation).

Technical Aspects of Design and Production

Production of Artwork

PROBLEMS ASSOCIATED WITH IMAGE POLARITY. At the outset of the study, it was decided to use negative image artwork for the visual material of the different learning packages, but this decision was initially based on a purely subjective basis of aesthetic appeal. For this reason we undertook a critical appraisal of the objective comparison of the use of either positive or negative images in visual display systems.

A review of the extent to which a student's learning performance is dependent on aspects of the physical environment, in particular the standard of projection, has recently appeared in the educational technology literature (Wilkinson, 1976). In this study, a number of possible projection variables which affected student performance were identified. For many of these parameters there exists a set of reasonably well-established standards and recommended practices to help the programme designer obtain the maximum benefit from the teaching package (American National Standards Institute, Association of Education Communications and Technology, Council for Educational Technology for the United Kingdom, Eastman Kodak Company, etc.). One aspect of perception on which there does not appear to be general agreement is whether or not one should use positive images or negative images in a teaching package.

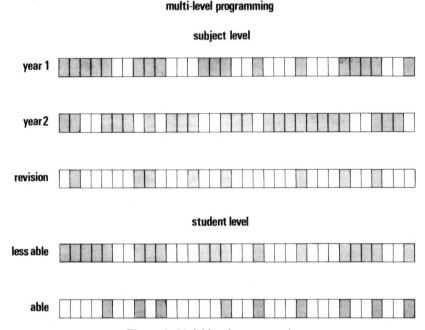

Figure 1. *Multi-level programming*

Objective comparisons of the two are scarce, but opinions concerning their relative effectiveness (usually supported by logic or personal experience) are common and frequently contradictory. Several studies have investigated differences in reading (or search) speeds, comprehension and subjective preference under both polarities, however, a disparity of polarity recommendations has resulted (Rubin, 1957; Nelson, 1965; Judisch, 1968; Block, 1968; Lee, 1975 and Desrosiers, 1976).

What then is the problem associated with this area which results in independent groups arriving at widely divergent conclusions? It appears that analysis of the various environmental parameters show these to be so interrelated and interdependent that it makes a study of any one, in theory at least, extremely difficult, if not impossible.

In addition to these problems associated with the physical variables that can be manipulated by the designer, there is also an important problem associated with the response of the individual viewer, and this is far more difficult to measure than many of the physical variables. The type of 'performance measures' chosen as appropriate for this application are, in general:

(1) the time required to complete lessons in a programmed instruction course and

(2) the number of errors made during the sessions.

In addition to these objective measures, some subjective preferences for positive or negative images can also be obtained for different viewing conditions. It would appear that as a result of the considerable complexity and interrelatedness of each of the physical parameters affecting student performance, an objective assessment of such a topic as image polarity is probably not feasible and one must therefore rely on subjective judgements although it should be borne in mind that such criteria usually show high variability and are often misleading.

The use of negative images in the present study was of particular benefit to us in that it greatly facilitated the production of visual material since we could simply make use of an IBM composer for the majority of the artwork, and also it greatly facilitated the unmasking of complex or detailed visuals and easily allowed animation where required.

The artwork, if textual, was typeset using an IBM composer; otherwise the material was produced by a graphics artist. As far as was possible the artwork was contained within a grid (10cm x 8cm). A lith negative enlargement (21.5 x 16cm) was then produced from each piece of artwork and the image was coloured using a variety of self-adhesive transparent colouring materials.

PROBLEMS ASSOCIATED WITH COLOUR DENSITY. The self-adhesive colouring materials, obtained from a variety of commercial sources, were found on use to give wide variation in light transmission.

This problem was circumvented by first taking densitometer readings of each of the coloured materials in turn. A 'working range' was decided on and all those with densitometer readings in excess of this were discarded. With those colours, particularly the yellow, giving high light transmittance additional layers were added until the densitometer reading fell within the working range.

Programme Production

The camera assembly used in the present study is shown in Figure 2. A Beaulieu R16 16mm cine camera was positioned on a horizontal assembly as shown and gearing allowed it to be easily moved vertically, horizontally and laterally relative to the image area. The lith artwork was positioned accurately on the image area using a transparent grid overlay. This overlay, marked with both vertical and horizontal lines, was hinged such that once the artwork was 'squared' within the image area it could be swung out of the field of view. The artwork was routinely fixed in place using black masking tape. The lighting was, as shown in the illustration, achieved by back illumination through the transparent image area. Once positioned single shot filming of each image was carried out, masking and unmasking areas with black masking tape as required. This approach prevented any problems with accurate registration that may have occurred had we used positive artwork at the production stage.

Multiple 8mm copies of the 16mm master were produced by reduction printing. The audio component was produced on a master tape which was then pulsed using the Philips LCM 2025 pulse generator, as described by the manufacturer. These synchronizing pulses could be anything from a single pulse to a series of pulses for animation varying from 1 frame/second (or less) to 24 frames/second. The pulsed master tape could then be dubbed on to four audio cassettes using the high-speed copier.

Figure 2

Improving the Presentation

For the reasons given earlier, in the production of learning packages in biochemistry, one of the most appropriate characteristics of stimulus configuration is motion. The motion, however, is not meant to represent simulated or real motion, but instead is used as a means of generating complex visual components in a step-by-step process.

In terms of appropriateness, level of sophistication, cost, availability and technical quality, it was possible to reduce the alternative modes of presentation to four:

(1) print (programmed)
(2) tape/slide (lap-dissolve)
(3) tape/OHP (overlays and masking)
(4) tape/film (PIP system)

Using supplementary criteria of efficiency and effectiveness, it was felt that tape/OHP would be inappropriate (poor for cues, time-consuming for complex overlays, etc.).

Similarly, it was felt that print on its own would be less effective for some of the visual materials since *small* changes were often introduced from frame to frame which would be difficult to identify unless some form of cueing device was used (bold type, colour, etc.).

Using criteria and guidelines as described above, we were left with the mixed-media tape/slide (lap-dissolve) or tape/film (PIP system).

From our own college situation, the expected difference in cost-effectiveness of these media was probably insignificant, and so the final mode of presentation was a matter of personal choice. Since it was intended that some programmes be used in the lecture-room situation, 35mm slide format was chosen for these as this provided better projection properties for group viewing than the 8mm film of the PIP system. For those programmes designed for individualized study, the PIP machine was the more appropriate choice. It was felt that those programmes produced for lap-dissolve could be easily converted to PIP format and the latter could be used in the independent study area on an individual basis for revision, etc. In carrying this out we discovered that the use of such techniques as lap-dissolve and TV fades, etc. (see later) within the programme improved the technical quality of the learning packages and also the continuity of the programme and so helped to maintain the student's interest and hence motivation.

The major technical problem which we encountered in converting lap-dissolve 35mm slide format to 16mm film format was one of exposure, and to achieve the desired exposure we were required to use high-speed film (Video News film, HS 7250 with a rating of ASA 400).

As before, multiple 8mm copies of the 16mm master were produced by reduction printing.

As a consequence of this work, we felt we could also make use of the various fade/wipe facilities, etc. which were available in our TV studio. The major problem in this area of work was the presence of a 'roller-bar' or 'scan-bar' when we carried out the filming. To eliminate this distractive feature efficiently it was found necessary to use a precision crystal control system with the cine camera.

Use of a combination of these various styles of presentation has resulted in the production of a number of programmes which are effective in significantly stimulating greater subject interest with the students using them.

Initial validation of these programmes has been carried out using objective test procedures and it appears that they do facilitate the learning of specific objectives.

The college is committed to the provision of self-instructional facilities and has recently added to this by providing 15 PIP units in the learning resources area of the library.

Encouraged by our early success with the students' performance in this field, we are continuing with the design and production of still more learning packages and hopefully learning a little more from each unit as it is produced.

Acknowledgements

We would like to thank the Nuffield Foundation for an award under the Small Grants Scheme for Undergraduate Teaching for support of part of this study.

We would also like to thank Mr Ron Stewart of the British Broadcasting Corporation for his most helpful advice and interest.

References

Block, G. A. (1968) Two studies on the effect of film polarity on patent examiners performance. Study 1. Simulated search. Study 2. Ability to discuss fine details. National Bureau of Standards, Washington, D.C.

Cumming, C. and Dunn, W. R. (1971) The application of cost-effectiveness techniques to educational technology. In Bajpai, A. C. and Leedham, J. F. (eds.) *Aspects of Educational Technology IV*. Pitman, London.

Desrosiers, E.V. (1976) The effect of image/surround brightness contrast ratios to student preference, attention, visual comfort, and visual fatigue. PhD dissertation, Boston University School of Education.

Dodge, M., Bogdan, R., Brodgen, N. and Lewis, R. (1974) How teachers perceive media. *Educational Technology* 14, p.21.

Dunning, J. (1977) *Assessment for All: Report of the Committee to Review Assessment in the Third and Fourth Years of Secondary Education in Scotland.* HMSO, Edinburgh.

Hunt, G. J. F. (1977) Educational technology: cream or salt in the classroom? *Programmed Learning and Educational Technology,* 14, 1, p.74.

Judisch, J. M. (1968) The effect of positive — negative microforms and front — rear projection on reading speed and comprehension. *National Micrographics Association Journal,* 2, 2, p.58.

Lee, D. R. and Buck, J. R. (1975) The effect of screen angle and luminance on microform reading. *Human Factors,* 17, 5, p.461.

Munn, J. (1977) *The Structure of the Curriculum: in the Third and Fourth Years of the Scottish Secondary School.* HMSO, Edinburgh.

Nelson, C. E. (1965) *Microfilm Technology.* McGraw-Hill, New York.

Parsons, H. M. (1974) What happened at Hawthorne? *Science,* 183, p.922.

Rubin, J. (1957) The viewing characteristic of positive vs negative images as they effect visual fatigue. *National Micro News,* 29, p.1.

Spencer, K. (1977) An evaluation of the cost-effectiveness of audio-taped and video-taped self-study media presentations. *British Journal of Educational Technology,* 8, 1, p.71.

Tobias, S. (1969) Effects of attitudes and prepared instruction and other media on achievement. *Audio Visual Communication Review,* 17, p.3.

Wilkinson, G. L. (1976) Projection variables and performance. *Audio Visual Communication Review,* 24, p.413.

35. Building Science-Based Educational Games into the Curriculum

H. I. Ellington, F. Percival and E. Addinall,
Robert Gordon's Institute of Technology, Aberdeen

Abstract: The main body of the paper is divided into two sections. The first reviews the various ways in which the authors have promoted the use of science-based games and simulations in secondary schools during the last few years, and then describes how they are currently collaborating with Grampian Region Education Authority, the Association for Science Education and the Scottish Education Department with a view to building such games into the school curriculum. The second discusses present and future uses of science-based games and simulations in the authors' own college.

Introduction

During the last five years, the authors have been heavily involved in the development and exploitation of science-based educational games and simulation exercises. Until now, such exercises have not generally been built into the main curricula of schools and colleges, however, their role being that of 'optional extras'. The authors believe that this strictly limited use of games and simulations does not allow their full educational potential to be exploited, and that this potential will only be realized once such exercises are fully integrated into the curriculum. This paper presents a case for such integration, and describes a number of recent developments which are helping to bring it about.

Educational games and simulations, whose large-scale use was initially limited to areas such as military training, business management and the social sciences, are now finding an increasing number of applications in a wide range of other areas, including the pure and applied sciences (Taylor and Walford, 1972). In the latter area, multi-disciplinary simulation games which demonstrate the relevance of science and technology to the real world have proved to be of great potential value in the general education of both scientists and non-scientists, since they can be used to achieve a wide range of educational objectives (particularly in the affective domain) that are not easily attainable using traditional methods of teaching (Percival, 1976). A case for the much more widespread use of such exercises in our schools and colleges is presented in detail elsewhere (Ellington and Percival, 1977a, 1977b; Ellington et al., 1978a).

At the moment however, science-based games and simulations are largely confined to the periphery of the curricula of our schools and colleges, being employed as useful but optional 'extras' and 'time-fillers'. In addition, only a relatively small number of enthusiastic teachers and lecturers make use of such exercises even to this limited extent. The authors believe that science-based games and simulations will never realize their full educational potential until they (a) are incorporated into the basic curriculum and (b) achieve general rather than isolated use. The former will allow the undoubted educational strengths of games and simulations (Ellington and Percival, 1977a) to be put to optimum use as a complement to more traditional teaching methods; the latter will allow much larger numbers of pupils and students to benefit from these educational strengths. This paper describes a number of ways in which the authors are working towards these ends.

Part 1 Promoting the Use of Science-Based Games and Simulations in Secondary Schools

1. Present Uses

During the last five years, the authors have been involved in the development of a large number of science-based games and simulations of different types, and have been active in promoting their use in secondary schools. The exercises have been of two basic types, namely, inter-school competitions run on a regional or national basis and self-contained educational packages designed for use within a single school.

THE COMPETITIONS. The authors have been involved in the organization of three large-scale inter-school competitions in recent years, namely, 'The Bruce Oil Management Game', 'Hydropower 77' and 'Power for Elaskay', and are currently preparing the material for a fourth ('Project Scotia').

The 'Bruce Oil Game', originally developed by staff of RGIT and Aberdeen Journals Ltd during 1974, is based on a computerized simulation of the development and exploitation of a hypothetical offshore oilfield, and involves the competing teams in making a wide variety of technical, geographical and economic decisions (Ellington, Addinall and Langton, 1977). It has been run every winter since 1974-75, and over 120 school teams from all parts of Britain have now taken part.

'Hydropower 77' was based on a multi-disciplinary design project developed by two of the authors in collaboration with the North of Scotland Hydro-Electric Board (NSHEB) during the summer of 1976. The competing schools (all from the Hydroboard's area) had the task of first choosing the most suitable site for and then designing a hydro-electric pumped storage scheme in a hypothetical highland area, and had both to submit a written 'consultant's report' and prepare a multi-media presentation of their final scheme. It was run during the winter of 1976-77 (Addinall and Ellington, 1978).

Because of the great success of 'Hydropower 77', the NSHEB decided to run a similar competition during the following winter. This competition ('Power for Elaskay') involves the competing schools in appraising the alternative energy resources of a hypothetical offshore island, planning a rolling programme for the generation of electricity over the next 50 years, and preparing a multi-media presentation of their proposed programme (Ellington, Addinall and Smith, 1977). At the time of writing, the competition is still in progress.

The fourth competition, which will be run on a national basis during the winter of 1978-79, is currently being developed by RGIT staff in collaboration with the Institute of Electrical Engineers, BBC and IBA. It will be based on a competitive design project similar to that used in 'Hydropower 77' and 'Power for Elaskay'.

All the above competitions were designed to show the relevance of science and technology to the real world and to demonstrate the need for inter-departmental cooperation within schools when working on a major multi-disciplinary project (features of science-based simulation games which the authors believe to be particularly important from an educational point of view — Ellington and Percival,

1977a). Feedback received from teachers who have been involved in the various competitions has given strong support to the authors' beliefs in this regard (see Addinall and Ellington, 1978, for example).

THE SELF-CONTAINED PACKAGES. The various science-based packages in whose development and exploitation the authors have been involved during the last few years have all been primarily designed for use in the senior forms of secondary schools, although they can also be used at tertiary level. As in the case of the various competitions described above, they are all of a highly multi-disciplinary nature and are designed to show the relevance of science and technology to the real world. In addition, each exercise is designed to achieve a specific set of educational aims and objectives, many of which are non-cognitive in nature.

For convenience, the packages can be classified under three headings, namely: 'physics-based packages', 'chemistry-based packages', and 'other science-based packages'.

PHYSICS-BASED PACKAGES. The first physics-based game with which the authors were involved was 'The Power Station Game', developed on behalf of the Scottish Education Department between 1973 and 1975 (Ellington, Langton and Smythe, 1977). 'The Power Station Game' has since given rise to a large number of related projects (Ellington et al., 1978b) which have produced a number of further physics-based packages. These have included 'Hydropower' (Ellington and Addinall, 1977a), 'The Central Heating Multi-Project Pack' (Cowking, Ellington and Langton, 1978) and 'Power for Elaskay' (Ellington and Addinall, 1978). Note that both 'Hydropower' and 'Power for Elaskay' are based on scenarios first used in two of the competitions described above.

CHEMISTRY-BASED PACKAGES. During the last five years, the Science Education Group at Glasgow University (in which one of the authors worked from 1973-76) has been involved in the development and evaluation of several chemistry-based simulation exercises designed for use in schools and colleges (Johnston, Percival and Reid, 1978). These have included 'Proteins as Human Food' (Percival, 1977), 'The Amsyn Problem' (Ellington and Percival, 1977a), 'What Happens When the Gas Runs Out . . .?' and 'The Alkali Industry'. Another chemistry-based exercise in whose development the authors have recently been involved is 'Point Fields Public Enquiry' (Ellington, Garrow and Muckersie, 1978).

OTHER SCIENCE-BASED PACKAGES. The authors have produced two further science-based packages which have been used in schools, namely, 'Fluoridation?' (Percival and Ellington, 1978) and 'North Sea' (Ellington and Addinall, 1977b).

2. Possible Future Uses

All the exercises listed above have been field-tested in schools, and many (e.g. 'The Power Station Game' and 'The Amsyn Problem') have achieved fairly extensive usage. The enthusiasm with which they have been received by both teachers and pupils has reinforced the authors' belief in the educational value of such exercises, and has encouraged them to promote their use on a much wider scale. Three specific ways in which this is being done are described below.

INCORPORATION OF GAMES AND SIMULATIONS INTO THE MODERN STUDIES CURRICULUM. The authors are currently collaborating with Grampian Education Authority with a view to building suitable games and simulations into the modern studies school curriculum at all levels from S1 to S6. The widespread use of several of the science-based exercises listed above (e.g. 'Point Fields Public Enquiry' and

'Fluoridation?') is being actively encouraged by the modern studies adviser, who also plans to organize a residential course for senior pupils around these exercises. In addition, a joint RGIT/Grampian Education Authority Working Party has recently been set up in order to develop a number of new exercises designed specifically for use within the modern studies curriculum. The first of these exercises will be a simulated case study into the siting of a new school.

INCORPORATION OF GAMES AND SIMULATIONS INTO THE NEW 'SCIENCE IN SOCIETY' COURSE. During the last few years, the Association for Science Education has been working on a major curriculum development project designed to produce an A/O-level physics course (entitled 'Science in Society') for use throughout England and Wales. The main aim of this course is basically the same as that of the various games and simulations described above, namely, to broaden the education of both scientists and non-scientists by showing the relevance of science and technology to the real world. Because of this, the Chairman of the ASE recently invited the authors to join the 'Science in Society' Project Team with a view to building suitable games and simulations into the structure of the new course. Several of the exercises described above are to be so used, and a number of new exercises, designed to fit into specific parts of the course, are to be developed.

USE OF SIMULATIONS AND CASE STUDIES IN THE SCE O-GRADE PHYSICS COURSE. A working party comprising staff of RGIT, Aberdeen teachers and members of the School Inspectorate has recently been set up in order to develop and evaluate small-scale simulation exercises suitable for use in the SCE O-grade physics course. The work will complement similar work recently carried out from Glasgow University in O-grade chemistry by Norman Reid.

Part 2 The Use of Science-Based Games and Simulations at RGIT

1. Present Uses

For some years, gaming and simulation techniques have been extensively used in a number of schools within RGIT, particularly the Schools of Business Management Studies, Social Studies and Architecture. It is only during the last two or three years, however, that science-based games and simulations have started to find a place in the Institute's courses, albeit in a peripheral role. For example, 'The Bruce Oil Management Game' is now used as a case study with students on the post-diploma-level course on offshore engineering run by the School of Mechanical and Offshore Engineering, and 'Fluoridation?' is used in a similar manner with students of the School of Health Visiting. In addition, several of the physics- and chemistry-based exercises listed above are now used as case studies in the Institute's physical science degree courses.

2. Likely Future Uses

This relatively limited use of science-based games and simulations in RGIT is likely to increase considerably during the next few years as a result of recent developments regarding the various CNAA degree courses in physical science that are run by the Institute. In the course of a recent visitation regarding these degrees, the CNAA Party were extremely impressed by the various science-based simulation games that had been developed in RGIT, since the philosophy behind these games appeared to be in close harmony with the Council's Regulations regarding the balance and general aims of a degree course (CNAA, 1974).

The Visiting Party also expressed a wish that such games should be made an integral part of the curricula of the Institute's physical science degrees in order to help achieve these general aims.

It was subsequently decided that the associated studies content of the above degree courses should be completely revised in such a way as to include science-based simulation games and case studies as an integral part of the curriculum. Each student will now be required to devote a minimum of ten hours to such exercises in each of the first three years of the various courses. It is expected that a similar policy will eventually be adopted in respect of other courses operated by RGIT.

Note: Many of the games and simulations mentioned in this paper are now generally available from the following sources:

'Fluoridation?', 'Hydropower', 'Point Fields Public Enquiry', 'Power for Elaskay', 'The Power Station Game'. Institution of Electrical Engineers, Station House, Nightingale Road, Hitchin, Herts, SG5 1RJ.

'Proteins as Human Food', 'What Happens When The Gas Runs Out. . .?'. The Secretary, Education Division, The Chemical Society, Burlington House, Piccadilly, London W1V 0BN.

'The Amsyn Problem'. Science Education Group, Department of Chemistry, The University, Glasgow, G12 8QQ.

References

Addinall, E. and Ellington, H. I. (1978) 'Hydropower 77'. In McAleese, R. (ed.) *Perspectives on Academic Gaming and Simulation 3.* Kogan Page, London.

Council for National Academic Awards (1974) Regulations and Conditions for the award of the Council's First Degrees, Clause 4. CNAA, London.

Cowking, A., Ellington, H. I. and Langton, N. H. (1978) The central heating multi-project pack. *Physics Education* (in press).

Ellington, H. I. and Addinall, E. (1977a) The multi-disciplinary multi-project pack — a new concept in simulation gaming. *PLET,* 14, 3, pp.213-22.

Ellington, H. I. and Addinall, E. (1977b) North Sea — a new board game based on the offshore oil industry. In Gibbs, G. I. and Wilcox, J. (eds.) *Perspectives on Academic Gaming and Simulation,* SAGSET, Loughborough, pp.81-3.

Ellington, H. I. and Addinall, E. (1978) Power for Elaskay — a learning package on alternative energy resources for use by science teachers. *School Science Review* (in press).

Ellington, H. I., Addinall, E. and Langton, N. H. (1977) The Bruce Oil Game — a computerised business management game based on the North Sea oil industry. In Gibbs, G. I. and Wilcox, J. (eds.) *Perspectives on Academic Gaming and Simulation,* SAGSET, Loughborough, pp.107-12.

Ellington, H. I., Addinall, E. and Smith, I. H. (1977) Power for Elaskay — the Hydroboard's new competition for secondary schools. *Bulletin of Scottish Centre for Maths, Science and Technical Education,* 12, pp.21-3.

Ellington, H. I., Langton, N. H. and Smythe, M. E. (1977) The use of simulation games in schools — a case study. In Hills, P. and Gilbert, J. (eds.) *Aspects of Educational Technology XI.* Kogan Page, London, pp.399-406.

Ellington, H. I., Addinall, E., Langton, N. H., Percival, F., Smith, I. H. and Smythe, M. E. (1978a) Science-based simulation games for the high school. *Proceedings of 16th NASAGA Conference,* Boston, USA, 1977 (in press).

Ellington, H. I., Addinall, E., Langton, N. H., Smith, I. H. and Smythe, M. E. (1978b) The Power Station Game family of technological/environmental simulations. *Proceedings of 16th NASAGA Conference,* Boston, USA, 1977 (in press).

Ellington, H. I., Garrow, A. G. and Muckersie, J. R. (1978) A simulated public inquiry for use in schools and colleges. In Megarry, J. (ed.) *Perspectives on Academic Gaming and Simulation 1 & 2.* Kogan Page, London.

Ellington, H. I. and Percival, F. (1977a) Educating 'through' science using multi-disciplinary simulation games. *PLET,* 14, 2, pp.117-26.

Ellington, H. I. and Percival, F. (1977*b*) Science-based simulation games — a means of bridging the 'two culture' gap. *Proceedings of 8th ISAGA Conference,* University of Birmingham, section 1, no. 1.

Johnstone, A. H., Percival, F. and Reid, N. (1978) Simulations and games in the teaching of chemistry. In Megarry, J. (ed.) *Perspectives on Academic Gaming and Simulation 1 & 2.* Kogan Page, London.

Percival, F. (1976) A study of teaching methods in tertiary chemical education. PhD Thesis, University of Glasgow.

Percival, F. (1977) Development and evaluation of a structured scientific communication exercise. In Hills, P. and Gilbert, J. (eds.) *Aspects of Educational Technology XI.* Kogan Page, London, pp.255-61.

Percival, F. and Ellington, H.I. (1978) Fluoridation? — a role-playing simulation game for schools and colleges. *SAGSET Journal,* **8,** 3, pp.93-9.

Taylor, J. L. and Walford, R. (1972) Simulation in the class-room. Penguin, Harmondsworth.

36. Communication of Scientific Information

E. Bardell, *University of Wales Institute of Science & Technology, Cardiff*

Abstract: The effectiveness of communication in science depends largely on the readability of scientific prose. Yet many scientists are reluctant to write in simple language for fear of losing credibility. However, a study of attitudes to scientific prose has shown that authors of simple, direct active styles enjoy higher credibility than those whose writing is unreadable.

Scientific study of human communication is a relatively new discipline which originated in the USA and is now gaining popularity in Britain. Many people may associate the term 'communication studies' with the study of the mass media, as this has been a favourite subject for some time now. However, in recent years a lot of research has been done on various aspects of human communication in many other areas too, including communication in science.

Communication as a Process

In all acts of communication the same process takes place: someone passes some information to someone else, in speech or in writing. Thus the process of communication always involves a sender of information, the piece of information itself, a person who receives it, and a medium through which it is passed. In his book on communication David Berlo (Berlo, 1960) names these 'ingredients' of the process: the source, the message, the receiver, and the channel, respectively. In addition, he distinguishes two other elements, the encoder and the decoder, but these are really part of the source and the receiver: the encoder is the source's vocal mechanism or his writing hand which enables him to send out the message, and the decoder is the receiver's hearing or eyesight through which he receives the message.

We always communicate for a purpose. When we send out a message, we expect it to achieve something for us, whether it is to get more money for a project or just to draw attention to ourselves. Therefore we want to make our communication effective. The way to do this is to make sure that all the necessary 'ingredients' of communication work. If anything goes wrong with one of them, communication will be impaired or will break down completely. To take an obvious example, if we attempt to write to someone who cannot see, our message will not be received; communication will break down because of a fault in the decoder. Again, if you told me that radiation had a packet property as well as a wave property, you would not communicate anything to me, because my knowledge of the properties of radiation is non-existent. In this case communication would break down because of faults in the receiver and in the source: I, the receiver, would have insufficient knowledge to understand your message, and you, the source, would have made an incorrect assumption about me. Various faults can also occur in the message itself (e.g. a clumsy sentence construction), in the encoder (e.g. loss of

269

voice), and in the channel (e.g. illegible handwriting).

As these faults can prevent our communication from achieving its purpose, we must try and avoid them by assessing the conditions of each communication situation correctly and making the right choices. This is not an easy task. Although all the 'ingredients' are present whenever we communicate, they vary from situation to situation: we talk or write to different people, about different things, in all sorts of circumstances. Therefore each communication situation is unique and has to be considered on its own merit.

Communication in Science: The Need for Readability

Of course, all I have said above about communication in general applies to communication in science, too. However, all acts of scientific communication have certain features in common which distinguish them from communication in other areas. Firstly, the people who take part in them, i.e. the sources and the receivers, are scientists who may be involved in research, production or education. Secondly, the contents of their communication are special — the messages convey scientific information. Thirdly, the purposes of communication in science are characteristic of this area: scientists communicate with one another in order to report on the progress of scientific research, inform about new developments in theory, give advice on practical problems in production, etc.

Some scientific information is presented in speech, for example at conferences, lectures or discussion groups. But much more is communicated in writing, in books, manuals, company reports and numerous theoretical, practical and general interest journals. Writing is definitely the most important channel for communication in science as it crosses the barriers of space and time, enabling scientists to benefit from the work of others before them, as well as to compare their findings with those of other scientists all over the world.

However, it will not do so, if it is clumsy and difficult to understand. Scientific writing, more than any other kind of writing, needs to be readable. One reason for this is that the primary purpose of communicating in science is to inform, not to annoy or confuse the readers. Another reason, pointed out by Reginald Kapp in his excellent book on presenting scientific information, is that most of the information we communicate in science is new and often conceptually difficult, so it should not be made even more difficult by bad presentation (Kapp, 1948).

Yet another reason why scientific writing should be easy to read is that it helps the working scientist. Nowadays so much scientific information is being published, especially in journals, that, in order to keep up with new developments, a scientist has to get through a lot of articles rather quickly, and the more readable they are, the easier his task becomes.

Unfortunately, a great deal of scientific prose today is very difficult to read. In books and articles we often come across sentences, or even whole passages, that are almost impossible to understand on first reading. Here is an idea of what an unreadable sentence might look like:

> Nevertheless, since adrenalectomy is followed by an increase in the release of adrenocorticotrophic hormone (ACTH), and since ACTH has been reported (J. Founder, 1972) to decrease the aggressiveness of intact mice, the possibility exists that the effects of adrenalectomy on aggressiveness are a function of the concurrent increased levels of ACTH.

The situation in scientific speaking is not much better; in fact, it can be worse. Because spoken presentations are often prepared as written articles, they do not take into account the specific conditions which affect communication in speech, such as the listeners' short-term memory limitations, noise, visual distractions etc. Owing to these, sentences which would be just manageable when seen on paper become completely incomprehensible when heard.

The Causes of Unreadability

What makes some sentences difficult to grasp immediately? Readability has been studied for some time now and we have a fair idea of what affects it. For example, Rudolf Flesch in his book on the art of readable writing gives a good account of the causes of unreadability (Flesch, 1949, pp.162-75, and *passim*).

One of the main causes of poor readability is the length of sentences. Long sentences often have to be re-read because by the time you reach the end of the sentence you forget what it said at the beginning.

Long, unfamiliar words are another source of difficulty. Of course, scientists cannot avoid using technical terms, many of which are long and strange-sounding words, but for readability's sake these should be kept to a minimum. If there is no danger of misunderstanding, common, ordinary words should be used instead. For example, we need not say that something 'exhibits' a certain property when 'shows' or 'has' would do just as well.

Abstract words are more difficult to understand than concrete words, especially as they also tend to be longer and less familiar. The use of negatives can be confusing, too, particularly when two or more are found in the same sentence.

Another cause of unreadability is nominal style, in which sentences contain no active verbs, but are built up of nouns, adjectives and nominalized verbs linked by prepositions and forms of 'be'. This style is difficult to read because it uses long words and produces complex sentences (Wells, 1960). What is more, it allows the writer to pack a lot of information into relatively few words, which then take a long time to understand. For example:

> Lunar and tidal cycle dependent egg-laying rhythms are evident in numerous marine animal species.

Flesch suggests (Flesch, 1949) that there is more to readability than just reading ease: to be readable, a piece of prose should also have what he calls 'human interest'. This is achieved by using personal pronouns, quotations, sentences addressed directly to the reader, etc. Most scientific prose has little or no human interest in this sense; it is usually written in a dry and impersonal style. Moreover, such style affects the reading ease too, because scientists, in trying to write in an impersonal manner, use many complex and roundabout constructions. For instance, many scientists like to write almost exclusively in the passive voice, e.g. 'samples were collected', 'an experiment has been conducted', etc. Using the passive voice is not, in itself, a crime, but the over-use of any type of sentence construction or stylistic device makes the style monotonous and can be irritating in a long article.

Apart from general studies of readability, a lot has been written specifically about good communication in science. The authors of such publications generally follow the principles of readable writing and adapt them to the particular conditions that apply in scientific communications. I have already mentioned Kapp's book on how to present scientific information (Kapp, 1948). Another book for technical writers by Robert Gunning (Gunning, 1968) postulates ten principles of clear writing which advocate simplicity, directness and individualism in style. There are many other books devoted to this subject, as well as shorter publications such as Booth's *Writing a Scientific Paper* (Booth, 1971) and Kirkman's *What Is Good Style for Engineering Writing?* (Kirkman, 1971).

271

Why do Scientists Write Unreadably?

In spite of all the good advice from experts on readability and scientific writing, much of scientific prose remains highly unreadable. Obviously, scientists are not prepared to follow this advice. Why is this?

There could be many reasons why scientists are reluctant to write plainly. One of them emerged quite clearly from the pilot work I did in preparation for my study of scientific prose: it is tradition. Scientists have been brought up to write in a formal, dry and impersonal style. In my interviews with scientists they told me that, for them, writing this way was 'like wearing a black tie at a funeral', it was 'the done thing'. They have been taught that, as scientists, they have to be objective, so they do not like to use personal pronouns such as 'I' or 'we', although it should be clear to anybody who cares to think about it that being objective does not consist in saying 'It has been discovered' when you actually mean 'I have discovered'.

Another reason why scientists write unreadable prose may be that writing readably requires more effort. For example, nominal style is easier to write than the more active and direct verbal style, particularly for people who, like scientists, are more concerned about what they say than about how they say it (Wells, 1960, p.217).

However, these reasons are not sufficient to explain why so many scientists write unreadably. After all, traditions change — in everyday life new ways are replacing old ones all the time. Also, an author will be prepared to put more effort into his writing if he starts losing his readers on account of his difficult style. And this may well happen; my pilot interviews have shown that, when it comes to reading, scientists themselves prefer readable styles.

Enquiries by John Kirkman (private communication) have brought to light what is, probably, the most important reason why scientists hesitate to use simple language and plain style in their writing. They are afraid of losing credibility and esteem in the eyes of their readers, that is, they think that writing plainly may make them appear less knowledgeable, and may take away some of the respect accorded to them by other scientists.

A Study of Attitudes to Scientific Prose

To find out whether these fears were justified, last year I began a study of attitudes to the language and style of scientific prose. My aim was to discover how scientists see other scientists through their writing, i.e. how they judge an author's credibility on the basis of the language and style he chooses for presenting scientific information.

What is involved in judgements of credibility? American research has shown (see, for example, McCroskey, Larson and Knapp, 1971, p.81; and Whitehead, 1968, pp.60-2) that people generally assess other people's credibility by making judgements about their

- competence in the subject;
- trustworthiness;
- dynamism;
- objectivity;
- intention toward the readers/listeners;
- personality in general.

The interviews in the pilot stage of my study confirmed that similar factors were involved when scientists judged the credibility of other scientists. They showed also that, in assessing an author's credibility, scientists based their judgements on two more factors,

— the author's communicative abilities;
— the appropriateness of his language and style to the situation.

The findings of my pilot study, as well as the results of earlier research on credibility, provided the basis for the questionnaire which formed the main part of my study. The questionnaire contained two samples of scientific prose which were introduced as different authors' versions of the same passage taken from the middle of a scientific article. Thus the information conveyed by the samples was identical, and they differed only in the way they were written. 'Brown's version' was difficult to read; it consisted of one long paragraph with long sentences, unfamiliar words and plenty of technical jargon. Its style was formal, stiff, impersonal and indirect. On the other hand, 'Smith's version' was written in a fairly informal and direct manner, using simple language with the very minimum of technical terms. It had three logical paragraphs, and was generally very readable.

Following the samples were two sections of questions. Those in the first section asked about the respondents' reactions to the two samples. The questions in the second section were designed to test the respondents' attitudes to the authors of the samples as seen through their writing. Each section closed with an 'open' question which allowed the respondents to add their own comments about the authors or the samples.

As the samples had identical contents, the order in which they appeared in the questionnaire was important. After reading one sample, the readers would be familiar with the topic and would therefore find the second sample easier to understand than it would have been if read on its own. This would bias the responses towards whichever sample appeared second. To cancel out the effects of such biases, I introduced two versions of the questionnaire: version BS, where Brown's sample was followed by Smith's, and version SB, where the samples appeared in the reverse order. With kind help from several learned Societies, these were distributed to scientists employed in both industrial and academic establishments.

General Responses to the Questionnaire

The tables below summarize the results of the survey. The figures in the tables are based on 338 questionnaires, of which 163 were BS versions and 175 SB versions. About 70 more questionnaires were added later but, as all of them were BS versions, I did not include them in the general results. However, I used them in the age and the type of employment analyses (see below), where the two versions of the questionnaire were scored separately.

As Table 1 shows, the majority of respondents stated that they preferred reading scientific articles written in a style similar to Smith's. His style was also considered to be more appropriate for scientific writing by three times as many respondents as was Brown's.

Although both samples contained exactly the same information, the majority of respondents found Smith's version more interesting to read than Brown's. Smith's version was judged to explain things better by three times as many respondents as Brown's. It was also found to be more precise by twice as many respondents as Brown's, although the majority thought that neither sample was better in this respect.

The great majority of respondents agreed that Brown's sample was more difficult to read than Smith's.

273

Question	Smith's version %	Brown's version %	Neither %	No answer %
1. prefer this style for scientific writing	76	20	2	2
2. more appropriate style for scientific writing	54	18	26	2
3. more interesting to read	58	15	26	1
4. more precise	28	14	56	2
5. more explanatory	52	17	30	1
6. more difficult to read	15	75	10	0

Table 1. *Judgements of the samples*

Question	Smith %	Brown %	Neither %	No answer %
1. a more competent scientist	23	15	59	3
2. communicates his thoughts more successfully	68	17	12	3
3. inspires more confidence	32	19	46	3
4. has a more dynamic personality	38	15	42	5
5. has more consideration for his readers	72	10	14	4
6. has a better-organized mind	49	15	31	5
7. is more stimulating	51	14	32	3
8. is more objective	29	17	50	4

Table 2. *Judgements of the authors*

Question	To inform his readers %	To impress his readers %	Other or no answer %
Smith's main intention	81	5	14
Brown's main intention	35	38	27

Table 3. *Judgements of authors' intentions towards their readers*

The figures in Table 2 show that the majority of respondents could not decide, on the basis of style alone, which author was a more competent scientist; but of those that did decide, a greater number favoured Smith. Similarly, many respondents found it difficult to decide which author inspired them with more confidence, which author was more objective, and which author was more dynamic; but of those that made the decision, considerably more chose Smith.

The great majority of respondents felt that Smith had more consideration for his readers and communicated his thoughts more successfully than Brown. Also, Smith was found to be more stimulating and better organized in his thinking by over three times as many respondents as Brown.

Table 3 shows how the respondents saw the authors' intentions towards their readers. The overwhelming majority felt that Smith's main intention was to inform his readers. As for Brown, opinions were divided almost equally between those who thought he wished mainly to inform his readers, and those who thought he wanted to impress them.

These results show that judgements of credibility are influenced by language and style. In answers to all the questions Smith, the author of the readable sample, received many more votes than Brown, even if, in some questions, the majority went to neither of them. This indicates that scientists consider an author who writes in simple language and plain, active style to be more credible and worthy of esteem than one whose writing is complex and highly jargonized.

The Influence of Age and Type of Employment on Responses

Two further analyses of the scores, which I did separately for BS and SB versions of the questionnaire, showed that the age of the respondents and their type of employment affected their responses to the questionnaire.

In the age analysis, which included 419 questionnaires, I compared the responses of scientists of four age groups: under 25, 25 to 35, 36 to 45, and over 45. The results were obscured by very small numbers of respondents in the 'under 25' groups in both versions of the questionnaire, as well as by uncontrolled factors such as type of employment, occupation and field of experience.

However, both the BS and the SB scores showed one tendency which might well be due to age. It occurred in the answers to three questions:

(1) Which author's style is more appropriate to scientific writing?
(2) Which author is more competent as a scientist?
(3) Which author inspires more confidence in what he says?

In these questions the percentage of votes given to Smith went up with age, i.e. it was at its lowest in the 'under 25' group, higher in the '25 to 35' group, higher still in the '36 to 45' group, and highest in the 'over 45' group.

This is, perhaps, surprising as older people might be expected to be more conservative and traditional in their attitudes than the young, and therefore might find it harder to accept informality and directness in scientific writing. On the other hand, having had more experience of communication in science than younger people, they may be more aware of the value of readability in scientific prose.

The type of employment analysis was based on 392 responses, of which 148 were by industrial scientists and 244 by academic scientists. The scores of both versions of the questionnaire showed that, in several questions, industrial scientists gave more of their votes to Smith or his sample than did academic scientists. Thus, compared with academic respondents, a higher percentage of industrial respondents preferred Smith's style to Brown's and thought it was more appropriate for scientific writing. Similarly, a higher percentage of industrial respondents found Smith's sample more precise than Brown's, and stated that he inspired them with more confidence in what he said than did Brown.

Yet another difference emerged from the question concerning Brown's intention towards his readers: compared with academic respondents, a higher proportion of industrial respondents felt that Brown's aim was to impress his readers. Also, in the two 'open' questions, industrial scientists made a greater number of favourable comments about Smith than did academic scientists.

Why did industrial scientists favour Smith more than did academic scientists? People involved in industry might, possibly, have a more direct and practical approach to science than academics, which would make them prefer Smith's down-to-earth style of writing. They may also be less accustomed to formality and stiffness in style which is, perhaps, more characteristic of academic writing.

Conclusions

This study has shown that scientists need not be afraid to use simple language and plain style. It has also shown that they themselves actually prefer to read scientific papers written in a direct and active manner. Therefore there seems to be no reason, other than tradition, why scientific authors should not write more readably.

How can scientists ensure that their writing is easy to understand? I have mentioned earlier several publications which give detailed advice on how to present scientific information; reference to these should be of great help to any scientific author. The main principle of good, effective communication in science, as indeed in any other area of human experience, is close regard for the communication situation. What to say and how to say it, depends entirely on the purpose, the target and the circumstances of our communication. To bear this in mind when preparing written or spoken presentations is the surest way to successful communication.

Obviously, it is the scientist himself who can do the most to make scientific prose easier to read. But the situation can also be improved by the people who, by virtue of their jobs, are in a position to influence the shape of scientific prose, for example:

- editors of scientific journals who advise contributors on how to write papers for publication;
- university lecturers and tutors who read and correct students' papers and dissertations;
- industrial research managers and others who are responsible for internal company reports.

References

Berlo, D. K. (1960) *The Process of Communication: An Introduction to Theory and Practice.* Rinehart Press, San Francisco.

Booth, V. (1971) *Writing a Scientific Paper.* Koch-Light Laboratories Ltd, Colnbrook, Bucks.

Flesch, R. (1949) *The Art of Readable Writing.* Harper and Row, New York.

Gunning, R. (1968) *The Technique of Clear Writing.* McGraw-Hill, New York.

Kapp, R. O. (1948) *The Presentation of Technical Information.* Constable, London; reprint 1964.

Kirkman, J. (1971) *What Is Good Style for Engineering Writing?* The Institution of Chemical Engineers, London.

McCroskey, J.C., Larson, C.E. and Knapp, M.L. (1971) *An Introduction to Interpersonal Communication.* Prentice-Hall, Englewood Cliffs, New Jersey.

Wells, R. (1960) Nominal and verbal style. In Sebeok, T. A. (ed.) *Style in Language.* The MIT Press, Cambridge, Mass., pp.213-20; reprint 1966.

Whitehead, J. L. Jr. (1968) Factors of source credibility. *Quarterly Journal of Speech,* **54,** pp.59-63.

Chapter 6:
Applications in Medical and Paramedical Education

The medical and paramedical fields embrace a vast range of education, ranging from the complexities of training doctors to the communication of basic family-planning information in undeveloped rural communities.

In the paper from Southampton (37), the authors give a penetrating account of issues arising in the training of doctors. They look in particular at the objectives and practice of 'clinical attachments'. An interesting comparison is drawn between 'the science and art of medicine', contrasting 'training to think objectively' with the build-up of experience giving an intuitive approach to diagnosis.

Mr Fieldhouse and Mr Shaw (38) provide an excellent example of the use of educational technology in a training situation. They describe the training of dietitians, using video-recorded interviews, games, and student self-assessment. Their account examines in detail the communication of interview technique, and the training of dietitians in the design of appropriate resource materials.

Ms Taylor (39) examines in detail the use of simulation in the training of nursing staff. Simulation is proposed as an alternative methodology to direct clinical experience, suitable for achieving many specified objectives, particularly considering economic constraints. An example of a court-case simulation exercise is described, involving training in some of the legal aspects associated with nursing.

Mr Hancock (40) presents an account of the use of behaviour modelling to train family-planning field-workers in Rhodesia. This example of health education training in a developing country is illustrated with examples of the interview-content models produced to train the field-workers to handle typical situations. Such training is found to be faster and more effective than when field-workers were allowed to build up experience gradually during actual practise.

Mr and Dr Zelmer (41) conclude this chapter with an illuminating study of low-technology resourcing applied in community health work in the Canadian Arctic and in Asia. They include a series of basic recommendations, which appear very realistic and practicable in the context of community health work in underdeveloped and developing countries.

37. Relevance in Medical Education: An Evaluation of Students' Introduction to Clinical Medicine

C R Coles and B Mountford, *University of Southampton*

Abstract: Medical teachers share a number of problems with teachers in all other professions. Firstly they have to decide what knowledge is necessary for their students to become competent and then they have to achieve some sort of balance between theoretical study and practical experience. The course which they 'design' reflects these deliberations. Students, on the other hand, have to take on trust that the theory they learn will be of value later on and that the sequence in which it is being learned is the most effective. However, many of them either realize early on that this trust is not altogether well placed or find themselves 'overloaded' with masses of apparently unrelated knowledge. As a consequence many of them 'lower their sights' and concentrate on the only reality — passing the next examination. They quickly learn to 'play the system'.

One major problem seems to be that it is easier to decide what knowledge a competent doctor needs to have and even to describe the necessary skills and attitudes, than it is to devise situations through which the necessary 'experience' and 'confidence' can be gained. And attempts to design courses principally by defining terminal behavioural objectives have failed to take account of this: it is a *non sequitur* to assume that the knowledge needed should become the 'content' of the courses — teaching and learning are quite different activities. The undergraduate medical curriculum, particularly in the clinical years, is still rather like attempting to teach people to swim by sitting them round the pool watching the instructors swimming up and down!

In 1967 the General Medical Council (GMC, 1967) updated its guidelines for the planning of undergraduate medical courses with a view to righting these wrongs. The principles it advocated reflected a number of trends and certainly influenced the curriculum planning of newer schools. Southampton is within this tradition (Acheson, 1976) with its integrated approach to the teaching of the basic medical sciences, early medical contact, a blurring of the distinction between pre-clinical and clinical studies, etc. Each of these 'innovations' has been adopted in order that students might not only see the relevance of their work but would begin to integrate their theoretical learning with their practical experience. This paper examines these claims against the evidence of evaluative studies of courses in the medical school to see how these novel features influence students in their first major contact with patients.

The Southampton Medical Curriculum

Two innovations, in particular, might appear to contribute towards increased relevance. The first became known as the *systems courses* which are the major vehicle for teaching the basic medical sciences. Rather than conventional 'discipline'-based courses these are presented as topics which focus on bodily systems such as the cardio-vascular system, the respiratory system, the renal system, etc., the

279

rationale being that patients suffer from illnesses which relate to bodily systems rather than academic disciplines.

Secondly, there has been an attempt to blur the traditional distinction between pre-clinical and clinical studies. Indeed a major change occurs at the start of the third year when students attend their first clinical attachments although, even then, nearly half their time is spent attending other courses. This study looks at how students cope with their third-year clinical attachments and whether these innovations appear to be beneficial to them in this task.

Third-Year Clinical Attachments

At the beginning of the third year students are allocated to a group of about 10 students and timetabled throughout the year to be rotated between different areas of clinical medicine in 5 or 10-week blocks. Groups of students are attached to clinical 'firms'. Normally these are Health Service units headed by a consultant and staffed by housemen, senior housemen, and registrars, although occasionally a firm may be a mix of university and NHS staff. The two objectives of the clinical attachments have been carefully worked out and explicitly laid down. The first states that, by the end of the year, students are expected to be competent in 'taking a history' and 'carrying out a thorough physical examination'. These terms are important to this discussion and need some amplification.

'Taking a history' means first questioning a patient about the signs of his present illness and then about the illnesses he has suffered in the past. It can also involve eliciting information about the patient's home circumstances, social background and even interpersonal relationships, all of which may be important in the management of the case. A 'physical examination' is a routine set of procedures which gives the physician information about the condition of the various bodily systems. The whole process of history taking and physical examination — known as 'clerking a patient' — might take one or two hours and during this time the student is encouraged to make notes which are written up afterwards.

The second objective is less explicit. During the third year it is hoped that students will acquire some knowledge of clinical medicine and the management of cases. As we suggested at the outset this raises two important questions: 'How should this come about?' and 'To what depth at this stage?'

The Studies

Pilot evaluations had been carried out of a systems course (Coles, 1976a) and of a clinical attachment (Coles, 1976b). Evidence from these has been reported elsewhere relating to course designing (Coles, 1977a). However, with the appointment of a research assistant (BM) it was decided to undertake full and intensive evaluation of third-year clinical attachments.

The methodology of the investigation, too, has been written up elsewhere (Coles, 1977b) but requires a brief mention as it embodies a number of the assumptions we are making. We begin by collecting any documentary evidence relating to the courses (timetables, prospectuses, course descriptions, lecture notes, etc.), attend as many planned sessions as possible making notes of our observations, and we interview, informally and non-directively, the people involved (students, staff, administrators, doctors, nurses, patients, etc.). The raw data is sifted for 'issues' (features within a course which appear to be acting for or against its success) and reports are written. In the first instance these are directed at the course coordinator or consultant in charge of an attachment and are essentially descriptive in nature, although they do contain some 'comments' of our own based on our perception of the issues. These reports, and indeed our own observations, are, admittedly, impressionistic, but we take care to exchange our own views and opinions before submitting reports. Staff appear to welcome these reports, are interested in our ideas, and seem to appreciate suggestions. Our aim, however, is rather more covert: it is to generate a discussion amongst the staff in order that *they can see for themselves* the reasons for modifications to the course and possible ways of achieving greater efficiency. Our approach is based on the belief that staff come to a teaching situation holding a complex set of assumptions, attitudes, values and expectations which influence their teaching and of which, frequently, they are unaware. Moreover, the courses on which they are teaching also contain a number of assumptions and values which are hardly ever made explicit and which may or may not articulate with their own. Thus, in our opinion, one important feature of a course evaluation is to expose some of the 'hidden' features in an attempt to facilitate a greater shared understanding of them. Course development and staff development are closely interrelated (Coles, 1977c).

Observations

Over a period of about six months four firms have been intensively studied. We informally interviewed teaching staff before, during and after the attachments, 29 interviews in all. We also talked with staff at planned sessions for students on the attachments and attended five staff meetings. Of the planned sessions we attended 56 ward rounds, 12 outpatient clinics, 30 tutorials/seminars, 13 tape/slide sessions, 6 X-ray meetings, 8 case demonstration meetings and 9 assessment sessions. We spoke with all students many times either individually, in small groups or in a full group of between six and ten students. Reports have been written and discussions are currently proceeding. Although much of this must remain confidential at this stage, we feel that we are in a position now to make three generalized comments that appear unrelated but which, as we shall argue, are probably closely connected.

1. The 'Arrangement' of Clinical Attachments

One feature that struck us was the marked difference between those firms who seemed to concentrate on 'teaching' clinical knowledge and others who simply allowed students to clerk patients. Staff justified the former by saying 'You need a considerable amount of knowledge in this area of medicine before you can make any sense of the clinical situation', whilst the latter said 'Knowledge comes later — we just want students to make contact with patients'. We found it useful to distinguish between these two approaches by characterizing the former as a move from 'general to specific' and the latter as 'specific to general'. In educational terms the former is didactic, the latter heuristic. Clearly either 'arrangement' carries with it a number of implications for both staff and students. For example, didactic teaching requires the teacher to be an efficient 'transmitter of information' and the student must 'take on trust' that this information will be of value later. Heuristic teaching requires the teacher to 'set up' situations through which the student will learn, whilst the learner must develop powers of observation, an enquiring mind and the ability to seek out information to account for his observations. What did we find when we observed these different arrangements?

On a firm which was arranged didactically students started out by feeling pleased to be so well organized. Their timetables were detailed and explicit — they knew what they were doing, when and where. Later on, however, they seemed rather less certain, appearing to have difficulty in 'applying the knowledge' and all wanted more contact with patients. In the wards they felt more like 'observers' than learners whilst some even reported feeling superfluous and a nuisance.

On a 'heuristic' firm student-reaction was quite different. At first they felt insecure, 'lost' and 'thrown in at the deep end'. Later, however, they appeared able to cope with the uncertainty and even began to feel as though they were contributing to the work of the firm. Certainly, the staff sensed that a number of the students had improved during the attachment and some felt that the end of attachment grading should reflect improvement rather than 'terminal standard'. This threw up all sorts of problems concerning the role of assessment and the grading of 'in-course' work such as the patients' notes written by students. Above all it pointed to a need for staff to 'monitor' each student's experience and for a closer control of the allocation of patients to students.

In short, the 'heuristic' approach seemed to be more beneficial for the *development* of the student than the 'didactic' one, but it has to be acknowledged that it carries all sorts of new roles and responsibilities for both staff and students of which neither seemed totally aware and for which they were ill equipped.

2. The Relevance of Previous Experiences

As we suggested earlier, one fundamental principle of the Southampton curriculum is that it attempts to integrate theoretical knowledge and practical experiences. In the two years leading up to the student's first major clinical attachment a number of its courses might be described as 'enabling' in that, in a sense, they have been designed to prepare students for what is to come later. In the main these are 'early medical contact', the 'systems courses' and an 'introductory course in clinical medicine'. We do not propose to comment on the content of these courses (that is the information which, on paper, they contain and its apparent relevance to clinical experiences), but rather to present students' views on how relevant they felt them to have been in retrospect.

From the views students express it appears that the value of 'early medical contact' — in which students are attached to a general practitioner from their very first week — depends largely on the individual situation. At best they report being made welcome and specially catered for. They felt they were given an appropriate amount of responsibility, clear guidance and a variety of specially chosen patients. At worst, students reported feeling that they were being tolerated, fitted in, accommodated as observers, given no responsibility, little guidance, and shown patients that may or may not have been appropriate. Now it has to be said that this is how students saw their 'early medical contact' in the light of later work and in discussions with their peers. The people responsible for organizing this experience expect students to hold the former rather than the latter view since this is the view they themselves hold. Nevertheless it seems fair to say that students' experience of 'early medical contact' is variable.

The 'systems courses', too, came in for their share of comment. When we evaluated one particular clinical attachment which has a systems course which refers closely to it we detected a number of problems relating to its relevance. Generally, all students felt that the systems course had been of little value to them when they commenced their clinical attachment. About a quarter of them felt that it ought to be relevant partly because they were frequently told so by their tutors, and partly because they appeared to appreciate the medical school philosophy of integration. However, they ended their attachment still seeking personal confirmation of this. Indeed, one or two students were even apprehensive because they felt pressure on them by the staff to link their theoretical knowledge with practical experience, but found themselves unable to do so. About half the students were rather more positive and approached their attachment accepting that there were important links with its relevant systems course. However, as time went on, even they reported that their previous learning seemed irrelevant to what they were now doing. Indeed all of the students felt that the reciprocal was happening: rather than the systems course benefiting the clinical attachment, the clinical attachment helped the students to understand the systems course more fully. This observation strengthened our claim that, from the learners' point of view, a 'feed-forward' view of relevance — theory before practice — is inappropriate.

The 'introductory course' takes place at the end of year 2. It consists of a concentrated fortnight in which students are introduced to clinical procedure, and this is followed up on two afternoons a week when they are attached to two clinicians in small groups to practice history taking and physical examination. When we talked with students at the start of their attachments we were surprised to find it rare for them to report that this experience had been of much value to them. The reasons were complex and, like 'early medical contact', depended on individual experiences. Where students had not been very well 'catered for' they gained very little experience, but even when their 'introduction' had been closely structured they felt that it could have been more valuable. In the latter case it seems that this was not to do with the techniques or skills they had acquired, but rather with the expectations that had developed concerning 'what clinical attachments were all about'. This seems to suggest that clinical work is more than a set of skills — a fact supported by our final set of observations.

3. The 'Science' and 'Art' of Medicine

Frequently, experienced doctors make a distinction between the science and the art of medicine. By this they seem to be suggesting that on the one hand medicine consists of a systematic and methodological approach to diagnosis whilst, on the other hand, it requires making intuitive and apparently 'non-logical' decisions. The 'science' of medicine is encouraged in the third year by ensuring that students become competent at taking a full history and making a thorough physical examination. The emphasis is on sharpening up the skills — doing things properly, systematically and thoroughly.

The 'art' of medicine, however, is never made explicit. Students see it happening in outpatient clinics, when a doctor clerks a patient on admission, and when they sit-in on routine case-history discussions. Some are baffled by it. We observed a group of students discussing the notes made by a doctor who had clerked a patient on admission. One commented that the notes contained more information than might have been expected from the questions that the patient had been asked. Another student said 'He couldn't . . . you can't put down anything that you haven't asked about'. Clinical tutors, too, sometimes feel this discrepancy. Some refuse to allow students in their clinics whilst others are reluctant saying, 'We are rather sloppy in our clinics' rationalizing this as '. . . because of the pressures on time'. In short, when students seem confused it is because they appear to have been asked to do one thing — thoroughly adopt particular skills and routines — whilst they observe doctors behaving in quite a different way. It seems to the student to be a case of 'do as I say, rather than as I do'.

The science/art debate seems to be something of a challenge and is worth further investigation. The research so far seems to suggest that the diagnostic 'thought process' of *senior* clinical students does not differ qualitatively from that of qualified doctors — it follows a pattern of hypothesis generation and testing (Campbell, 1976). To the observer this 'thought process' must appear more of an art than a science — apparently more related to 'intuition' than to 'thoroughness'. The point is that the doctor does not gather all the information there is to collect and then sift out what is relevant to the case, but asks three or four pertinent questions to test hypotheses that he is formulating. This raises at least two important questions in relation to the education of the doctor, although, at present, we have no simple solutions.

(1) Does this 'thought process' only develop with experience or can it be taught? It rarely seems to appear in the undergraduate medical curriculum.

(2) Is the best preparation for this 'thought process' a thorough grounding in history taking and physical examination?

In other words, does one teach students 'the long way round' and let them discover (or even teach them) the 'short cuts'? It might be wrong, for instance, to call the thought processes of the experienced clinician 'short cuts'. How much 'insight' might the student be allowed *before* he acquires appropriate skills and techniques? Some schools (MacMaster is the best example — see Barrows, 1976) claim that it is possible to teach hypothesis generation and testing from the outset. Clearly more research is vital.

Suggestions

Obviously we would not be so imprudent as to make sweeping recommendations at this stage without a fuller evaluation. However, it seems to us that a number of points might be made even now. For example, students might have some experience of *clinical* medicine very early on in their first year, possibly in addition to 'early medical contact', in which they attempt to take a history and make a physical examination in the way that they are expected to in their third year. In this way they might see what a clinical attachment 'was really like' before they undertook very much theoretical study. The knowledge they acquire might then be set against a clearer perception of clinical medicine. The introductory clinical course, coming before the first major attachment, could then take on a much more important 'bridging' role of linking theoretical knowledge and practical experience. Rather than introducing the students to clinical attachments it might prepare them for understanding clinical thinking. This might be the best time to introduce the diagnostic thought processes used by experienced clinicians. However, this presupposes that clinicians *are aware* of the processes which they employ routinely but which they seem to regard as 'sloppy'. It might be that they are not being 'sloppy' at all but are acting quite appropriately. Perhaps, too, they are wracked with guilt that they are not being as 'thorough' as they, themselves, were taught to be! Any course development programme would seem to first require some self-analysis on the part of the tutors.

Conclusions

At the outset we must say that any apparent criticism we make has to be set against a general feeling of confidence with the new medical school and that its curriculum is 'on the right lines'. There have now been graduates for two years and these doctors are taking up posts as housemen both in the Region and elsewhere. Generally their supervisors are giving glowing reports about them: in terms of its product the Southampton Medical School has little to worry about and a great deal of which to feel proud. However, as educational researchers we have been concerning ourselves more with the *processes* of courses rather than the products. These are a few generalized comments which we feel able to make so far.

(1) Innovations such as the ones reported here may have been *adopted* but they may still be a long way from being *implemented*. Frequently it has appeared to us that the courses are only nominally novel. Many staff are still teaching

as they were taught. Moreover, the students' expectations are no different — they still see themselves as having to swat up the facts in order to pass their exams. As our studies have shown, innovations frequently carry many more implications than staff or students seem to realize and their successful implementation may require a positive and planned strategy, probably including some changes of thinking on the part of both staff and students.

(2) The ways in which courses are *organized* seem to be dependent on the assumptions, attitudes, values, and expectations of the staff rather than on the explicitly stated aims of the curriculum. If staff see their role as 'transmitters of information' then the course will tend to be didactic in nature. If they see themselves as the 'managers of learning situations' then it will become heuristic. This decision seems to be quite independent of the subject-matter content of the teaching (and of the objectives) and appears to be made unconsciously or with little 'thinking through' of the reasons for and implication of making it. Yet the implications of this decision can be widespread, influencing not only *how* the course is organized but even *what* is taught and learnt. More insidiously it can even 'influence' courses coming before and after — for good or ill.

(3) Problems may arise when there is a 'mismatch' between the principles underpinning a course and the assumptions being made by individual teachers and learners on the course. Some students and staff, whether in didactic or heuristic firms, felt uneasy probably because they appeared to be making discordant assumptions about teaching and learning. Whether an innovation succeeds or fails seems to depend less on how well it has been designed or how appropriate it may appear or how carefully the objectives have been defined, but more on how its underlying assumptions articulate with those held by staff and students.

(4) Relevance is a very real problem in professional courses. It may seem 'logical' to teach knowledge before its application, but learners in real life rarely learn in this way. Situations need to be devised through which relevant knowledge will be acquired almost as a 'planned accident'. Learning starts at the specific, moves to the general and then oscillates between the two: fundamentally it heuristic.

(5) We need to question over-emphasizing thoroughness of technique. Do 'Being a doctor' and 'Becoming a doctor' need to be more alike? Does it need to be taught 'like it is'? Problems seem to arise because professionals are unaware of the principles by which they routinely function — probably because they themselves were never taught these principles: they just acquired them. Principles *can* be identified and situations *can* be devised through which they may be acquired. But the 'logical approach' to the design of these situations seems to be something of a red herring.

References

Acheson, E. D. (1976) About Southampton's medical school. *British Medical Journal,* 2, pp.23-5.

Barrows, H. S. (1976) Problem-based learning. In Clarke, J. and Leedham, J. (eds.) *Aspects of Educational Technology X.* Kogan Page, London.

Campbell, E. J. M. (1976) Basic science, science and medical education. *The Lancet,* 17.1.76, p.134.

Coles, C. R. (1976*a*) Integration and concentration: an evaluation of the cardiovascular systems course at the University of Southampton Medical School. *Medical Education.*

Coles, C. R. (1976*b*) Developing professionalism. MA thesis (part) unpublished, University of Sussex.

Coles, C. R. (1977*a*) Course designing: some suggestions following evaluation of undergraduate medical courses. In Hills, P. and Gilbert, J. (eds.) *Aspects of Educational Technology XI.* Kogan Page, London.

Coles, C. R. (1977*b*) Curriculum evaluation: the Southampton perspective. Paper given at ASME/SRHE Conference, London. November. 1977.

Coles, C. R. (1977*c*) Developing professionalism: staff development as an outcome of curriculum development. *PLET,* 14, p.4.

GMC (1967) *Recommendations as to Basic Medical Education.* General Medical Council, London.

38. Applications of Educational Technology to Dietetic Education

P. Fieldhouse and M. Shaw, *Leeds Polytechnic*

Abstract: The development of communication skills by the student dietitian is essential if she is to be effective in clinical practice. An interview model is proposed as an aid to teaching interpersonal skills, and a short course concerned with resource design is briefly described.

We were recently asked: 'What has educational technology to do with dietetics?' The answer extended to quite considerable proportions and it is that answer which forms the basis of this paper!

Much of the dietitian's working day is taken up with talking: whether this is to individual patients or to groups, the ability to communicate effectively is essential for professional success. Surprisingly, the skills of communication have been largely neglected in academic courses and whilst dietitians have been competent in both natural and behavioural sciences, many of them have found great difficulties in 'putting it across' to the patient. With the support of the staff and resources of the Educational Technology Unit at Leeds this deficiency is now being tackled. The success of efforts made so far is reflected in the enthusiastic acceptance by students of the two short communication courses which form part of their curriculum. These can essentially be labelled 'interview technique' and 'resource design'. On both the pre- and post-clinical courses, educational technology has made possible the development of new teaching methods, centred on student activities.

Interview Technique

The main tasks of the dietitian are to collect information on eating habits in order to assess the nutritional adequacy of diets, and to give sound dietary advice. For the individual patient this is usually accomplished by means of a personal and confidential interview. However, it is unfortunately well recognized that much dietetic advice goes unheeded, and poor dietary compliance is a major problem. This has been traditionally ascribed by the frustrated dietitian to poor motivation and lack of will power on the part of the patient. The work of Ley and Spelman (1967) in particular, would suggest that much of the fault could be due to poor communications. If dietary advice is to be followed, it must first of all be understood and secondly remembered. It is up to the dietitian to promote understanding and retention in her interactions with patients.

Until recently, a dietetic student would not normally have the opportunity to interview a patient until she reached the third year of her training, when she commenced clinical training. She was expected to 'pick up' this skill by sitting in on a few interviews, then trying it for herself. Proficiency thus became a matter of experience with much 'hit and miss' activity in between. In an attempt to prepare the student for this type of interaction and to maximize the 'hit' activity, the development of student interview skills has been incorporated into a pre-clinical course on communications. The aims can be stated thus:

(1) To show the student what can and should be achieved in an interview situation.
(2) To allow the student to experience the interview situation in a 'safe' setting.
(3) To allow the student to develop confidence in her own verbal abilities.
(4) To allow the student to review and assess her own interview performance.

Video-tape recordings have proved to be an effective means of promoting these aims and have led to a high degree of commitment and enthusiasm on the part of the students.

The main objective of giving dietetic advice, is that the patient will make the necessary changes to his diet to achieve optimal nutrition. This is facilitated by the following points of comprehension and cognition.

(1) The patient will understand that he has a need for a special diet or for dietary modification.
(2) The patient will understand the principles on which his diet operates.
(3) The patient will be conversant with the dietary modifications required, i.e. what it means in terms of food.

This implies certain essential activities must take place in the dietetic interview.

Initially, an interview model was proposed (Figure 1) and a set of criteria of satisfactory performance defined (Figure 2). These were based partly on clinical experience and partly on published literature (Byrne, 1976; Maguire and Rutter, 1976).

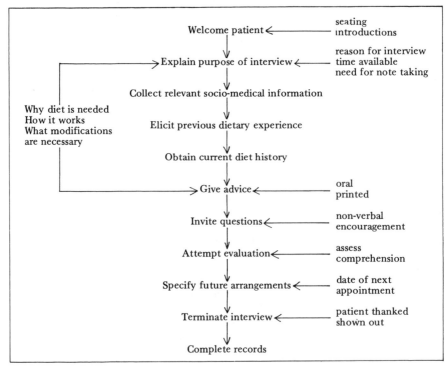

Figure 1. *Proposed dietetics interview model*

□ Patient ease
□ Purpose explicit
□ Dietary and socio-medical information elicited
□ Response clarification and follow-up
□ Question style
□ Interview control
□ Advice quality
□ Evaluation of patient comprehension
□ Interview termination

Figure 2. *Criteria used to assess interview performance*

With the cooperation of experienced dietitians from a local hospital several recordings were made, illustrating some of the principles of dietetic interviewing. Examples were made of a 'good' and 'poor' interview, and a session where the dietitian had to deal with an uncooperative patient. Viewing of these recordings is followed by group discussion, when the class attempt to identify the reasons for success and failure, and this in itself is a valuable exercise.

The next step is for each student to carry out her own interview. The 'patients' are role-played by other students who are given brief role guidelines with some scope for development *in situ*.

The interviews are recorded in the Educational Technology Unit studios, and are later played back and discussed individually with each student, their performance being assessed by a 'checklist' method. Two examples of interview analysis are shown (Figures 3 and 4) with the patient guideline in each case. One student was obviously more effective in her attempt to carry out a successful interview.

Patient guidelines

Mrs Jones, Age 70 yrs. Diabetes Mellitus

Rather deaf — but anxious to please: was put on diet many years ago, but has forgotten the details. Lives alone — but daughter visits regularly: still active — loves baking: cooks for grandson when he is at school — tends to finish off leftovers. Doctor wants to try diet modifications before using oral hypoglycaemic drugs.

Interview Description

1. Interview Procedure:	Not presented in logical sequence. Purpose of interview not adequately explained at beginning.
2. Information Gathering:	No information gained on previous diet. Very sketchy diet history obtained.
3. Question Style:	Leading questions suggest the 'right' response to the patient.
4. Clarification:	Vague responses are acceptable, without attempt to obtain more precise information.
5. Information Giving:	Unqualified advice given, e.g. 'not too much potato'.
6. General Manner:	Pleasant: attempts to maintain calmness in a stressful situation. Tendency to condescension. Non-verbal clues of despair and exasperation.
7. Conclusion:	Unsatisfactory: dietitian not able to cope with patient's inability to understand.

Figure 3

Patient Guidelines

Mrs White, Age 30 yrs. Diabetic, 2-3 months pregnant. 2 other children age 2 yrs. and 4 yrs. Husband is bank clerk.

No previous problems with diet, but wants general advice — cannot afford luxuries — and sometimes tends to skimp own meals.

Interview Description

1. Interview Procedure:	Good: Dietitian introduces herself attempts to find out previous history.
	Logical presentation. Dietitian controls interview throughout.
2. Information Gathering:	Good attempt: follows up patient's responses.
3. Question Style:	Leading questions suggest meal patterns to the patient.
4. Clarification:	Tries to obtain precise information though doesn't always follow up a good start.
5. Information Giving:	Good summary of dietary needs of patient: tries to identify with patient, but advice given is rather vague.
6. General Manner:	Quite efficient, but inclined to be offhand.
	Criticism of patient — both direct ('The trouble with you is . . .') and implied ('it should be quite easy') are made.
	Non-verbal indications of boredom are easily picked up.
7. Conclusion:	Dietitian, still in control, indicates end of interview: offers further help: but not too enthusiastically!

Figure 4

Later on, the student has the opportunity to interview a real patient, under supervision of her tutor, and a similar, though unrecorded, assessment session follows.

An analysis of recordings shows, at this early stage, the most common interviewing faults made by students (Figure 5). Many of the faults are similar to those encountered in medical interviewing by student doctors (Maguire and Rutter, 1976), suggesting that communication and relationship difficulties are common problems, throughout the medical and para-medical fields.

Common Interviewing Faults

☐ Failure to explain purpose and procedure
☐ Biased and leading questions asked
☐ Insufficient information obtained
☐ Advice given too vague or general
☐ Overdeference to patient
☐ Inaccurate information accepted
☐ Inability to terminate interview smoothly

Figure 5

The material recorded is being used to refine the interview model in relation to the dietetic student. It is intended ultimately to quantify the criteria of satisfactory performance, and to evaluate the usefulness of the refined model in clinical practice.

An extension of this work is the current development of a number of short dietitian/patient interaction episodes, designed to illustrate different aspects of the interview processes, and to portray various situations which the dietitian may have to cope with, for example the domineering patient who will not listen to advice; the elderly patient who keeps wandering off the point; the depressed patient who bursts into tears. These episodes will be used in formal teaching sessions, and will also be available on a self-access basis to students for closer study.

Part of the communication course focuses on non-verbal communication, and video recordings provide rich source material for this. In an interview, a patient's non-verbal behaviour can give valuable information to the dietitian, for example an excessively nervous patient is unlikely to attend fully to what is said (see Pietroni, 1976). A silent interaction is shown to the students, who are asked to note non-verbal behaviour, and to judge the patient's emotional state and reaction to the dietary advice. The tape is re-run, with sound, and discussion follows on the reliability/usefulness of non-verbal clues.

It is, of course, impossible to fully prepare a student to meet all contingencies, but the teaching of standard interview procedure and the identification of common pitfalls is seen to be a useful and valid exercise.

Resource Design

Whilst the pre-clinical course concentrates on communication skills, the post-clinical course is more concerned with resource design and production. The aims of this course are:

(1) To familiarize students with the principles involved in the systematic development of teaching materials.
(2) To give students an opportunity to relate these principles to teaching and learning situations with which they are likely to be involved.
(3) To allow students to apply these principles in the design and production of a teaching/learning experience.

The activities in which the students become involved are numerous and varied: typical examples are tape/slide presentations; poster production; game development. Although the end products of this short course are not (nor intended to be) in themselves sufficiently sophisticated or professionally produced for actual usage, they do act as a stimulus for the student, once qualified, to produce her own teaching materials. Some of the ideas generated could certainly find application in clinical practice. For example, an audio tape and booklet, giving a simple explanation of the principles of a diabetic diet, promises to be of value in teaching diabetic in-patients. A tape/slide on breast feeding is to be shown in ante-natal clinics, whilst another dealing with 'Food for Health and Happiness' has enjoyed success in primary schools.

Games

The Educational Technology Unit, in consultation with the authors, has produced a children's nutrition game, based on snakes and ladders. The concept of 'good nutritional practice — up the ladder', 'bad nutrition — down the snake' is exploited to illustrate some principles of healthy diet. The game has enjoyed immense success in local schools, but as yet there has been no attempt to evaluate its long-term effect on dietary behaviour. Nutrition lends itself to gaming, and there is a wide scope for further developments in this area. Students on the resource-design course have recently produced a board game for teaching diabetic children, which is being evaluated in a local hospital.

At undergraduate level there are many ways in which games can be utilized to teach aspects of nutrition. The authors have designed a game which attempts to simulate one day in the working life of a hospital dietitian. Movement is on a game board representing the plan of a hospital: players must reach specified points on the board, in order to carry out preassigned tasks. Their performance is rated by fellow students who role-play patients and other hospital staff.

Although we are only just beginning to explore the application of education technology to dietetic education, it is apparent that there is much of value to be accomplished. The benefits are seen in two main ways: (1) By the introduction of new and more effective teaching methods into dietetic courses within the Polytechnic; (2) By the training of dietitians who are enthusiastic and capable enough to devise and use new instructional methods in their work. This in turn implies benefits to the patients in terms of better communications and more effective dietary advice, and sums up our developing answer to the question posed at the beginning.

References

Byrne, P. (1976) Teaching and learning verbal behaviour. In Tanner, B. (ed.) *Language and Communication in General Practice.* Hodder and Stoughton, London.

Ley, P. and Spelman, M. S. (1967) *Communicating with the Patient.* Staple Press, London.

Maguire, P. and Rutter, D. (1976) Training medical students to communicate. In Bennet, A. E. (ed.) *Communication between Doctors and Patients.* Nuffield Provincial Hospitals Trust, OUP, Oxford.

Pietroni, P. (1976) Non-verbal communication in the general practice surgery. In Tanner, B. (ed.) *Language and Communication in General Practice.* Hodder and Stoughton, London.

39. Simulation in Health Education

A. Taylor, *John Abbott College, Quebec, Canada*

Abstract: The author focuses upon the use of simulation as an alternative to actual clinical experience in health education. Clinical experiences tend to be very costly endeavours and the educational technologist has the challenge of designing appropriate learning alternatives. Simulation is one methodology where the student can develop and use the decision-making or problem-solving skills which are so necessary in the actual practice of health-care workers.

Introduction

It can be said that the vital purpose, function and responsibility of a health profession rests upon the clinical practice of its membership. Clinical education of health professionals must, therefore, be planned and implemented by health science practitioners who are able to serve as role models for their students as well as to provide appropriate learning activities for them. The clinical setting provides the critical milieu for the student to integrate classroom theory with the development of professional skills and attitudes. However, clinical education is a costly item and with budgets being cut or kept in a steady state, the health educator is faced with the challenge of using available resources in a manner that assures the quality of student performance and at the same time recognizes the financial constraints.

The use of simulation as an alternative methodology to actual clinical experience in health education holds a great deal of appeal. Simulation can be used to meet a number of learning objectives. It allows for a very complex real-life situation to be simplified in order that its essence may be studied in a meaningful way. Simulation, then, can provide a sort of protected learning environment where students can become participants in making decisions and yet be allowed to make mistakes without injury to actual clients.

The author does not subscribe to the concept that all clinical experience can be eliminated with the use of simulation as an alternative. However, it is suggested here that simulations can be successfully developed to provide appropriate learning activities for students in meeting many programme objectives. Simulations should be linked to a larger curriculum content and be intended to contribute directly to the objectives of that curriculum. They can, in fact, be used to precondition the student to reach as high a level of ability as possible in order to maximize their experiences in the clinical area during any given semester.

Gagné and Briggs (1974) suggest that the events of instruction related to a given performance objective are external to the learner and include:

(1) Gaining attention
(2) Informing the learner of the objective
(3) Stimulating recall of prerequisite learnings
(4) Presenting the stimulus material

(5) Providing 'learning guidance'
(6) Eliciting the performance
(7) Providing feedback about performance corrections
(8) Assessing the performance
(9) Enhancing retention and transfer

Thus, instruction is planned for the purpose of supporting learning.

In order for instruction to be effective, however, there are several internal events of the learner which are extremely important. These are the capabilities which the learner has previously attained such as factual information, intellectual skills and cognitive strategies.

Simulation — a Methodology

In a simulation those who take part move from the role of the observer to the role of the participant who may act out past, present, or future concerns. Another important aspect of simulation surrounds the notion that the participant can examine his attitudes and those of others.

Simulation gives the learner an opportunity to formulate and voice opinions in an environment that is punishment-free and to discover rather than be told. An advantage for the teacher is that simulations may be developed in a relatively short period of time. However, conducting a simulation is a far different method from lecturing. It demands more expertise and confidence on the part of the teacher before beginning such an activity.

The method seems, nevertheless, to have a particular value where the clinical conditions are complex and, therefore, difficult for the student to understand. Where conditions are too dangerous for the student to learn a skill through practice with actual clients is another indication for the use of simulation. In the case of learning a complex skill the use of computer simulations is extremely valuable.

Dr P. David Mitchell's 'EDSIM: The Classroom in a Computer for Practice Teaching' is a simulation in which the participant is provided with the opportunity to practice instructional decisions within the context of a responsive but simulated environment: a computer-based simulated classroom. This concept of simulation could certainly be developed in the area of health-related technologies.

Real performance in a simulated situation is the type of simulation which most closely approaches the real on-the-job performance. One might say that carrying out cardiopulmonary resuscitation on a Recording Resusci Anne Doll would represent real performance in a simulated situation. Feedback from the doll's readout would indicate if the rescuer had saved a life. This type of learning situation reduces the consequences of mistakes and allows the participant to learn under less stress than the actual clinical situation would present.

Another example might be the 'programmed or simulated patient' as an educational simulation. In this example, the designer assists an individual to act out the behaviour of a patient with a given medical record. The programmed patient must develop complete verbal and non-verbal cues in preparation for the simulation. Then, in the classroom setting the learners can, given specific learning objectives, be expected to relate to the programmed patient's presentation in an appropriate manner. This version of simulation seems to hold some very valuable possibilities for the preparation of health-care professionals. There is no risk for an actual client. The learner's anxiety about possibly causing an individual harm is reduced. The learner can even call for a 'time out' during the simulation and have a discussion with the instructor or fellow learners before proceeding again.

Simulated performance in a simulated situation might be said to be 'two steps' away from actual clinical experience. An example of this type of simulation would involve role-playing and/or problem solving. In this type of simulation there is no risk and minimal stress.

The environment is a protected one. An example of this type of simulation is a court case simulation such as the one developed by the author and presented here.

Simulation — a Design

Simulation as a methodology uses one or more of three types of presentation. They are the case study, role-playing, and problem solving. In designing a simulation for third-year diploma nursing students at John Abbott College the author has attempted to incorporate all three types of presentation into one simulation. It was the hope of the designer that the participants would become so immersed in their roles that they would essentially become the person they were playing for the time of the simulation. Since the simulation was to be developed around the programme objectives related to legal and ethical responsibilities of nursing practitioners, the designer also hoped to prepare the participants for their future roles and to shape their attitudes in respect of their responsibilities to their clients. The manner in which this simulation was developed made allowance for giving particular participants separate or confidential information. With the problem-solving or decision-making aspect incorporated, it was also intended that participants would be forced to make decisions against the pressure of time. In the nursing programme of John Abbott College the faculty attempts to use the problem-solving approach as a teaching strategy. Using this simulation, the learner is confronted with a problem situation which he has not previously dealt with. Verbal 'cues' should be kept to a minimum as the learner engages in discovery learning while he invents a solution. Internally, the learner is, therefore, forced to recall relevant information and previously learned capabilities. He then uses this to problem-solve in the novel situation.

The Simulation — a Court Case

In designing this three-hour classroom activity for approximately 48 third-year students the author attempted to use Gagné's hierarchy of functions served by various instructional events as a guideline. In the area of gaining attention, the designer allows for the teacher to meet with all the participants one week in advance of the actual simulation. At that time the following list of required readings, statement of the case, and list of roles were distributed to the participants as advanced organizers. Ausubel suggests giving this sort of information prior to the instructional activity in order to enhance the learner's ability to organize the new material, and consequently to learn and to remember it. The required readings, including two self-instructional packages, serve as reminders to the learner of concepts that are important in terms of their relationship to new material to be presented in the simulation itself. The pre-simulation handouts inform the learner of the objectives of this activity in relation to the total curriculum as well. As the learner prepares for the learning activity he/she is stimulated to recall prerequisite learning.

The teacher is responsible for preparing the classroom in the form of a courtroom as much as resources will allow. It is suggested that the 'typical' courtroom arrangement be used.

Briefing given only to the judge includes the fact that should the jury report other than a unanimous decision the procedure should be as follows:

(1) 10-2 acceptable.
(2) Otherwise, a new trial would be ordered.
(3) Judge to decide the sentence and amount of damages payable to the plaintiff should the defendant(s) be found guilty.

A 30-minute debriefing session is an integral part of the simulation. There is also an opportunity to provide feedback about the performance. Hopefully, retention and transfer of knowledge are enhanced. It is the responsibility of the teacher to assist the students in dealing with aspects related to the objectives. That is, further exploring attitudes and feelings regarding legal and ethical aspects of nursing practice and referring to their application of problem solving throughout the activity in terms of assessment, planning, interventions and evaluation. This is followed by assessing the simulation as a learning activity. The students are asked to complete the simulation evaluation form as shown in Figure 1.

STUDENT EVALUATION OF COURT CASE SIMULATION

Please circle the number of the rating you feel is most appropriate (1 — poor, 2 — below average, 3 — average, 4 — above average, 5 — very good).

Rating Scale

1 2 3 4 5

---

1. Did you feel this simulation stimulated you to ask questions?   1 2 3 4 5

2. How would you rate the trial as a learning experience?   1 2 3 4 5

3. Did you feel that the 'simulation' characters covered all possible aspects of the case?   1 2 3 4 5

4. Did the simulation give you an objective concept of the real-life situation of malpractice?   1 2 3 4 5

5. Did you agree with the final verdict?   1 2 3 4 5

6. Did you feel this simulation technique was an effective way to present information?   1 2 3 4 5

Comments

Figure 1. *Student simulation evaluation form*

EXAMPLES OF HANDOUT MATERIALS GIVEN TO CLASS

SIMULATION — COURT CASE

Objective I   — To explain attitudes surrounding legal and ethical aspects of nursing practice

Objective II — To apply the problem-solving process in a novel situation

Pre-Class Assignments:

I   *Required Readings**

    (1) Wood, L. *Nursing Skills for Allied Health Services,* Vol. I, W. B. Saunders, Toronto.

    and (a) 'The Health Worker and the Law', pp.1-9,

         (b) 'Introduction to Ethics and the Healing Arts', pp.11-25.

    (2) Creighton, H. *Law Every Nurse Should Know,* 3rd ed., W. B. Saunders, Toronto 1975. Ch.11: 'Canadian Law and Legal Practice', p.207.

    (3) *Code of Ethics* (The Order of Nurses of Quebec), from the *Quebec Official Gazette,* 22 Sept., 1976.

II *Suggested Readings**

    (1) Kerr, Avice, 'Nurses Notes: That's Where the Goodies Are!', *Nursing '75,* 5, 2, p.34.

    (2) The Order of Nurses of Quebec, 'Résumé of answers given to nurses requesting information concerning certain nursing acts, care techniques and medical acts', February, 1977.

*Copies to be given out in class one week prior to simulation.

III *Simulation Game — A Court Case*

Information about the courtroom proceedings is attached as well as a statement of the case in question. Each student will select a role from the list being circulated in the class. Please write your name and phone number below the role you wish to play. (A copy of this list will be available to you at the end of this afternoon's class in order for you to plan your part in the case with others.) You are encouraged to prepare for your roles so as to represent reality as much as possible. You are also encouraged to 'dress' your part as much as is possible.

Please Note: Observer #1 and #2 are asked to meet with the teacher prior to the simulation for briefing.

Objectives

One of the terminal objectives to be met by graduates of the John Abbot College Nursing Programme is to 'act in accordance with the legal and ethical responsibilities of a graduate nurse'.

In order to successfully meet this objective, the graduating student must be able to demonstrate competence in the following areas while practising clinically:

(1) Hold in confidence personal information and use judgement in sharing this information.

(2) Record and report information in accordance with legal and ethical requirements.

(3) Provide nursing care in accordance with provincial legislation governing nursing practice.

(4) Identify the legal implications of recording, reporting, doctor's orders, narcotic administration and act accordingly.

(5) Demonstrate and maintain a professional appearance and behaviour in the clinical setting.

It seems possible that you as students will reflect your opinions and attitudes regarding professional legalities while taking part in this simulation courtroom lawsuit.

PROCEEDINGS

Object of simulation — to present the various aspects of the case and come to a verdict.

The judge will conduct the proceedings — *all* comments should be directed towards 'his' bench.

All witnesses must remain outside the courtroom until called in.

Plaintiff's case — heard first

(approx. 30 minutes) — his counsel will call their witness and the defendant's counsel has the opportunity to cross-examine each person put on the stand

— the plaintiff's counsel may re-examine witnesses after their cross-examination. There is then closure of the plaintiff's case.

Next — the defendant's case is presented in a similar manner (approx. 30 minutes).

When the defendant's counsel closes their case, the judge will ask the jury to meet for their deliberations (privately but *so all others in the courtroom can hear*).

The jury is to have 20 minutes to come to a unanimous decision. In any case, they must return to their places in the courtroom within 20 minutes at which time the judge will ask the jury for its decision.

Following this simulation a post-game discussion or debriefing session will take place led by the teacher (approx. 30 minutes).

A short evaluation form about the court case simulation will be circulated for completion in class. Your comments will be helpful in planning future use of the game.

You will be informed as to the results of the real-life situation which occurred in New Brunswick.

Note: This case is based upon a real-life situation which occurred in New Brunswick in January, 1971.

'In January, 1971 a patient at the Saint John General Hospital had part of the fingers and thumb of his left hand amputated. The amputation became necessary when gangrene developed after the patient received an intramuscular injection of Bicillin in his left arm from a Saint John nurse. The patient sued the nurse for negligence in administering the injection.'

STATEMENT OF THE SIMULATION GAME CASE

Mr Jack Lumber, a 45-year-old labourer arrived at the Emergency department of the Luckyship General Hospital. After a three-hour wait he was seen by Dr Ronald Doodle. Mr Lumber spoke of having had a sore throat and congestion in his lungs. Upon examination, Mr Lumber was found to have a very sore throat and a temperature of 38.3 $^{\circ}$C. After taking a throat culture, the doctor ordered 1,000,000 I.U. of Bicillin I.M. stat.

Miss Nancy Nuckle, being the nurse in the examination room at the time Dr Doodle ordered the medication, proceeded to prepare the I.M. dosage of Bicillin. Having calculated the dosage and drawn up the medication into a syringe, Miss Nuckle asked Mr Lumber to unbuckle his belt and slip his pants down over his hips in order for her to give him an injection in his buttock. Mr Lumber refused to do so. Miss Nuckle, therefore, decided to give the I.M. injection into the deltoid muscle of the left arm. This she did and then recorded the medication as given.

Mr Lumber went home having some discomfort in his left arm. By the time he reached home he noticed his left arm was very uncomfortable. 'Guess that nurse hit a tender spot when she gave me that shot', said Mr Lumber to his wife.

Two Weeks Later:
Mr Lumber was unable to use his left hand very well. He phoned Dr Doodle's office saying 'I'll sue you for this!' In the week that followed, Mr Lumber had part of his fingers and thumb of his left hand amputated owing to the gangrene that had developed after his intramuscular injection of Bicillin. He filed a litigation against Dr Doodle, Nurse Nuckle, and the Luckyship General Hospital for a sum of $2,000,000.00.

Question:
Were Dr Doodle, Nurse Nuckle and/or the Luckyship General Hospital negligent in Mr Jack Lumber's care and, therefore, responsible for the loss of his fingers and thumb?

Summary and Conclusions

The author has had the opportunity to use this simulation with two groups of students for which it was designed. The participants seemed to find it useful as a learning activity. Certainly, it can be said to be an enjoyable way of learning material which one is required to know.

Professionalism demands that the nurse and other health-care workers have knowledge and understanding of legal and ethical aspects of one's profession. Practitioners have not always understood the legal implications of their actions and the reporting and recording of them. It seems, therefore, essential that the attitudes surrounding these issues be explained in depth with students throughout their programme. Simulation is one method of doing just that.

Evaluation of a simulation should ideally include a comprehensive examination of individuals' relevant performance in the clinical setting prior to the instructional event. Then, in addition to measuring the internal effectiveness of the simulation, one could compare pre-simulation and post-simulation measures. The challenge here is to identify elements which are both measurable and relevant in terms of the curriculum objectives.

The author feels that the sort of questionnaire used in this case as an evaluation of the simulation at least provides immediate feedback and seems useful in terms of making instruction decisions regarding future use of the activity. Certainly it is a simple technique, and often very valuable comments are obtained with respect to providing a more satisfying experience for future participants.

The author feels that simulation is a useful tool to be used as one of the alternatives in the selection of appropriate learning activities. Simulations can certainly be developed as viable and exciting alternatives to actual clinical experience and used by teachers who enjoy working as facilitators. This method allows the student to achieve effective and skill growth as well as cognitive gain.

References

Adams, Dennis (1973) *Simulation Games: An Approach to Learning.* Charles A. Jones, Ohio.

Armstrong, R. H. R. and Taylor, John (1970) *Instructional Simulation Systems in Higher Education.* Cambridge Monographs on Teaching Methods No. 2., Cambridge Institute of Education.

Boston, Robert E. (1972) *How to Write and Use Performance Objectives to Individualize Instruction,* Vol. 4 — 'How to develop performance instructional activities and evaluations'. Educational Technology Publications, Englewood Cliffs, New Jersey.

Cruickshank, Donald (1977) *A First Book of Games and Simulations.* Wadsworth Publishing Co., Belmont, California.

Drumheller, Sidney J. (1971) *Handbook of Curriculum Design for Individualized Instruction — A Systems Approach.* Educational Technology Publications, Englewoods Cliffs, New Jersey.

Fletcher, J. and Dobbins, A. (1971) An approach to evaluating learning in simulation games. *Educational Technology Research,* No. 24. Educational Technology Publications, Englewood Cliffs, New Jersey.

Gagné, Robert and Briggs, Leslie (1974) *Principles of Instructional Design.* Holt, Rinehart and Winston, New York.

Gibbs, G. and Howe, A. (1975) *Academic Gaming and Simulation in Education and Training.* Kogan Page, London.

Glazier, Ray (1969) *How to Design Educational Games,* 5th edn. Abt Associates, Massachusetts.

Heitzmann, Wm. Ray (1974) *Educational Games and Simulations.* National Education Association, Washington, DC.

Kidder, Steven and Nafziger, Alyce (1972) *Proceedings of the National Gaming Council's Eleventh Annual Symposium.* Johns Hopkins Press, Baltimore.

Levine, Allan (1974) *A Study of Cognitive and Affective Outcomes of a Chemistry Learning Game.* Sir George Williams University, Montreal.

Maidment, R. and Bronstein, R. (1973) *Simulation Games Design and Implementation*. Charles E. Merrill, Ohio.

Megarry, Jacquetta (1977) *Aspects of Simulation and Gaming — An Anthology of SAGSET Journal Volumes I-IV*. Kogan Page, London.

Mitchell, P. D. (1972) A simulated classroom to study pre-instructional decisions. Paper presented to the National Gaming Council's Eleventh Annual Symposium.

Sillier, K. and Erving, G. (1971) *Environmental Simulation*. Educational Technology Publications, Englewood Cliffs, New Jersey.

Stadsklev, Ron (1974) *Handbook of Simulation and Gaming in Social Education — Part I: Textbook*. Institute of Higher Education Research and Services, The University of Alabama.

Tansey, P. J. (1971) *Educational Aspects of Simulation*. McGraw-Hill, London, p.2.

Tansey, P. J. and Unwin, D. (1969) *Simulation and Gaming in Education*. Methuen Educational, Toronto.

40. Training Family Planning Field-Workers by Behaviour Modelling

P. M. J. Hancock, *Institute of Adult Education, University of Rhodesia*

Abstract: The importance of field-workers in family planning diffusion is emphasized, and behaviour modelling is proposed as a method for improving their communication abilities. A process model and 12 content models for training purposes are presented.

Introduction

Most developing countries have accepted family planning as an essential concomitant of development for some time, yet there remains concern over the limited progress made in spite of considerable financial expenditure on diffusion, social research and medical support.

In the Innovation-Decision process:

KNOWLEDGE → PERSUASION → DECISION → CONFIRMATION (Rogers, 1973, p.79)

the initial knowledge gained by the target population may be from a wide variety of sources including mass media, neighbours or change agents. The next stage, persuasion, is probably the most difficult and the most important, and Rogers (1973, p.122) considers this stage to be almost entirely dependent on face-to-face contact between the client and the field-worker:

> The moment of truth in any national family planning programme occurs in the interaction between a change agent and a client, for this contact is where the change agents' appeals result in either adoption or rejection of the family planning innovation being promoted. The relative success of this persuasion process depends, in some part, on how the change agent is perceived in the eyes of the client.

Rogers considers that home visits to clients by para-professional field-workers are one of the most effective and often the most efficient communication strategies to secure the adoption of family planning methods.

In an address at the David Owen Centre, University College, Cardiff, Sales (1977) expressed similar views:

> The trend is to bring family planning services closer to clients by using local groups and people, by using networks already in place and integrated with the culture of their societies.

Increasingly, he continues, family planning services are supplied by a variety of carriers — midwives, health visitors, housewives, commercial outlets — and for a programme to be sustained it is essential to obtain the participation of the community, right down to the smallest social units.

These comments highlight the field-worker as a key person in family planning diffusion, as the main link between the clients and the whole family planning service. It seems that in many countries the task of overcoming the manpower problems for family planning communications has not been met (Bogue, 1973).

It is hoped that this paper may make a contribution to this problem by outlining a method of training which should improve the field-workers' interaction behaviour.

Factors affecting the Training of Field-Workers

Before devising training for the field-worker the factors which go to make her an important link must be considered, so that the training can develop these factors rather than weaken them.

Rogers (1973) in common with other authors in diffusion considers that for a change agent to succeed he must not be too different from his clients, i.e. he must be homophilous rather than heterophilous with the population to whom the innovation is directed, whether it be agriculture, health or family planning.

If the change agent is too heterophilous she will not have credibility with the client; for example, the average family planning officer might be too highly educated to 'reach' a rural peasant population. At the opposite extreme the change agent may be too homophilous to effect change; for example in Pakistan where an attempt was made to use traditional midwives as family planning aides their failure was attributed to their similarity in attitudes, lack of innovativeness and technical inability, with the groups from which they were selected. A further problem is that such aides may be too different from the trainers for them to be able to communicate with each other.

The generally agreed solution seems to be to develop a para-professional field-worker who is sufficiently homophilous with the population to have credibility, but who is sufficiently educated to be trainable in the technical aspects of the job, and is therefore also likely to have attitudes favourable for innovation. She is thus likely to have the potential for developing the two main factors giving her credibility: (1) competence in the job, (2) safety credibility, i.e. Is she sufficiently like the client to serve as a role model, or more simply, can she be trusted by the client?

Rogers (1973, p.123) summarizes the position as shown in Figure 1.

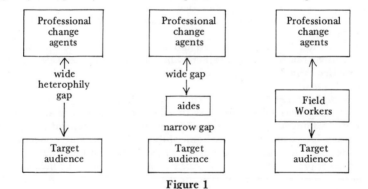

Figure 1

The field-worker must therefore be selected for potential technical ability, and for homophily. If the target population is totally illiterate then it may be difficult to reach a compromise between these two selection criteria, but the average black community in Rhodesia is marginally literate, and the problem therefore is not acute.

The task of the trainer is to develop methods to make the field-worker technically competent, and to increase her apparent homophily with the clients by improving her ability to communicate at this level. Training in the technical aspects of the work is relatively straightforward, provided three-dimensional models are

303

used; the second and more difficult task of improving communication abilities is the subject of this paper.

Behaviour Modelling

Behaviour modelling has been used with some success for the training of family planning field-workers in Rhodesia. Although no precise evaluation has been carried out, the method is recommended with confidence because of its good standing in training for interaction in management, industry and commerce.

Behaviour modelling is not particularly new and the principle is well established in primary and secondary schools, but in adult education it has received wide attention only recently, and with new developments in educational technology, particularly video- and audio tapes, it has become increasingly popular.

The principles and techniques of behaviour modelling have been well documented and supported (Bandura, 1969; Goldstein and Sorcher, 1974). The main steps are:

(1) Analysis of the behavioural requirements of the interaction concerned.
(2) Development of a model depicting the desirable features of the interaction.
(3) Presentation of the model, either by film, video-tape or audio tape, or by role-playing, to the trainees.
(4) Discussion of the model by the trainees to identify the key points.
(5) Imitation and practice of the model by the trainees.
(6) Reinforcement of the new behaviour by the trainer and peers.

Behaviour modelling has similarities with role-playing, but it has more discipline and precision, and because the objectives are clearly stated the training can be more thoroughly evaluated than can traditional open-ended role-playing. The learning principles applied in behaviour modelling are discovery learning (Step 4), imitation (5), learning by doing (5), intensive practice leading to overlearning (5) and social reinforcement (6), all of which have a body of sound research data and knowledge to support them.

Training is conducted in small groups and the main function of the trainer is to develop a positive, reinforcing atmosphere which increases the confidence of the trainees. Practice should be intensive with many well-spaced repetitions so that overlearning leads to transfer.

Goldstein and Sorcher (1974, p.65) show that behaviour modelling leads to increased empathy (defined as sensitivity to others' feelings plus an ability to communicate this understanding in language the others comprehend). Empathy is obviously a key factor in establishing homophily, and is a difficult concept to communicate. Behaviour modelling aims to change such attitudes indirectly; underlying the approach is the behaviouristic principle of changing behaviour first, which will then lead to a change of attitude if the new behaviour is reinforced.

An additional advantage of using behaviour modelling for the training of field-workers who may not have a high level of education is that it largely obviates direct training in subjects such as communication and motivation. These constructs are difficult to follow in the abstract and even if the theory is understood there is no guarantee that this will lead to transfer to the work situation. It is possible that such knowledge may even disrupt a person's natural ability to communicate with others. With behaviour modelling there is no need for the trainee to work out how to apply the new knowledge: the actual behaviour required is imitated and practised, the motivational and communication components of the interaction having been worked out and incorporated into the models by the trainer.

A possible disadvantage of this approach is that it may lead to rigid behaviour where flexibility will be important. To counter this the trainer should occasionally place herself in the role of the client, once the trainees have developed confidence, and deliberately depart from the patterns shown in the models. Also, different personality types may have different ways of behaving, and the trainer needs to be sensitive to the manner in which trainees prefer to achieve their interaction goals.

Models for Training Field-Workers

Objectives

The general objectives of the field-worker at the 'persuasion' stage will depend on the knowledge and attitudes of the client, but will probably fall into the following hierarchy:

Minimum objective: leave client on friendly terms.
Intermediate objectives: arouse awareness or interest.
Maximum objective: client makes some kind of commitment to family planning.

Content and Process

Following Bales (1970) interaction may be analysed according to content (what is said) and process or style (how it is said). For the interaction under discussion neither content nor process have been closely analysed, and the models recommended below are based on the experience of African family planning officers and field-workers (Hancock, 1977).

Process Model

The steps shown here apply to each content model:

(1) Use customary greetings, observe formalities of manners, language, dress.
(2) Find something to praise, e.g. health of child, crops, garden, house.
(3) State your role clearly.
(4) Avoid disparaging remarks, and maintain (increase) self-esteem of client,
(5) Allow client to speak fully.
(6) Listen carefully to client's views.
(7) Avoid arguments.

Content Models

1. With a Peasant Farmer or Couple

(i) Preserves health of the mother.
(ii) Assures healthy children.
(iii) Improves children's lives, giving them a better education and helping them to get a better start.
(iv) Lessens worry and overwork on the part of the mother and father.
(v) Farm produce is not all consumed by the family therefore the remainder can be sold.
(vi) Avoids overcrowding, ensures happy family life, more companionship and lessens tension.
(vii) Helps to reduce the burden of poverty and welfare which the community has to bear.

(viii)   Farm cannot be subdivided into small sections for children to inherit.

2. With a Remote Couple who have never heard about Family Planning

(i)   Family planning and tradition accepted in the area.
(ii)   Advantages of breast-feeding and how this is interfered with by an untimely pregnancy.
(iii)   How spacing will help improve health of the children.
(iv)   How family planning helps to preserve health of the mother.
(v)   How family planning will help lessen worry and overwork.

3. With a Newly Married Couple living in an Urban Area

(i)   Congratulate them on their newly married life.
(ii)   Advantages of a small family:
        — easily accommodated and modern furniture,
        — can easily provide all necessities — food, clothing and education,
        — can save for the future and secure a decent future for the children.
(iii)   Urban financial pressures and how a large family can intensify such pressures.
(iv)   Time for mother to regain her health, and have more leisure and time for herself.

4. With a Man who believes Family Planning causes Immorality

(i)   Immorality has plagued mankind since time immemorial.
(ii)   Not caused by availability of contraceptives.
(iii)   Depends on one's character and up-bringing.
(iv)   Modern pressures contribute towards this problem.
(v)   Immorality among men who are never on family planning.
(vi)   Basic cause of this fear is lack of trust of wife.
(vii)   Family planning improves marital relationship.

5. With a Wealthy Man who says he can afford Many Children

(i)   Everyday general expenses are lessened.
(ii)   Preserve the high standard of living.
(iii)   Avoid subdividing property or savings among many children.
(iv)   Lessen worry and overwork on part of mother and father.
(v)   Children need more than material things.
(vi)   Preserve health of the mother.

6. With a Church Leader/Member who believes that planning a Family is Wrong

(i)   'Multiply and replenish the earth' — Genesis 1:28; Genesis 9:1.
(ii)   Onan — Genesis 38:8 — 10.
(iii)   Jesus encouraged planning. Luke 14:28.
(iv)   Paul on support of family. I Timothy 5:8.
(v)   All churches approve of family planning.

7. With a Person who has Political Opposition

(i) Family Planning Association is not a government organization and is not a political issue.
(ii) It is a health service started by our ancestors.
(iii) Today it is encouraged at United Nations and accepted worldwide.
(iv) All countries in Africa have family planning.
(v) In Rhodesia family planning is for all races.
(vi) It will never reduce African numbers — compare African and European numbers and rate of increase.
(vii) Immigration of little or no effect on numbers and selective immigration necessary for every country.

8. With a Person who wants Many Children for Cheap Labour or Old Age Security

(i) Children are not parents' servants, they are no longer an asset but a liability.
(ii) Parental responsibility in this modern world.
(iii) Quality more important than quantity.
(iv) Nowadays parents can plan for old-age security.
(v) Mother's health ruined by frequent pregnancies.
(vi) Lessen worry and overwork on part of mother and father.

9. With Council Chairman, Secretary, Chief or the Council

(i) Helps to avoid over-population in their area and famine.
(ii) Helps community to meet its responsibility in providing education, health and other services.
(iii) Helps to keep down delinquency and youth problems.
(iv) Helps to reduce welfare burden of the community.
(v) Helps to preserve their non-renewable resources.

10. With a Group of Men

(i) Ability to choose number of children according to his means.
(ii) Less financial worry and it permits savings for the future and for retirement. Worsening of present financial condition is avoided.
(iii) Disadvantages of further overcrowding in the home are avoided and there is more comfort in the home.
(iv) Provides husband and wife with more leisure, opportunity to enjoy each other's companionship. They experience happier marital relationship.
(v) Gives both husband and wife time to take part in the life and development of their community.
(vi) Preserves wife's health.
(vii) Improves children's future in life.

11. With a Group of Women, e.g. Women's Club

(i) Helps preserve health of the mother.
(ii) Offers opportunity to do a better job of rearing children.
(iii) Lessens worry and overwork on the part of the mother.
(iv) Gives the wife more time to develop her personality and talents.
(v) Improves the sexual adjustment by eliminating fear of unwanted pregnancies.

12. With Ante-Natal, Post-Natal Mothers

(i)   Helps mother to restore her health.
(ii)   Gives her time to attend to the new baby.
(iii) Baby receives better care and love.
(iv) Gives wife more time to develop herself and enjoy her family ties.

Conclusion

The above models were derived logically by experienced personnel, and a more systematic analysis of actual interactions may produce more useful suggestions. The models were developed specifically for the Rhodesian African socio-cultural milieu, and will not necessarily apply to other situations. Nor can they be expected to provide the field-worker with a complete set of answers for the Rhodesian situation. Attitudes and behaviour are contingent upon many factors, cognitive, affective and connative, and there will be wide differences between individuals in any culture, and within individuals over time.

Where this approach has been used, the new field-workers have stated that it has enabled them to start work with immediate confidence, whereas experienced workers often say that it took them a long time to develop the correct repertoire of behaviour and the necessary confidence. Even experienced workers say that behaviour modelling has given them new insights into their own interaction behaviour.

Acknowledgement

The assistance of the Family Planning Association of Rhodesia in the development of the models is acknowledged.

References

Bales, R. F. (1970) *Personality and Interpersonal Behaviour*. Holt, Rinehart and Winston, New York.

Bandura, A. (1969) *Principles of Behaviour Modification*. Holt, Rinehart and Winston, New York.

Bogue, D.J. (1973) Communication research and evaluation. In Johnson, W.B., Wilder, F., Bogue, D.J. *et al.* (eds.) *Information, Education and Communication in Population and Family Planning*. Community and Family Study Centre, University Chicago.

Goldstein, A. P. and Sorcher, M. (1974) *Changing Supervisor Behaviour*. Pergamon, Oxford.

Hancock, P. M. J. (1977) *Report on Training Methods for Field Educators*. Family Planning Association of Rhodesia, Salisbury.

Rogers, E. M. (1973) *Communication Strategies for Family Planning*. Free Press, New York.

Sales, R. M. (1977) *The Implications of Change*. David Owen Lecture, University College of Cardiff.

Viarstra, G. A. (1974) Some thoughts about the attitude concept in relation to family planning. In Jongmans, D. G. and Claessen, H. J. M. (eds.) *The Neglected Factor*. Van Goreum, Netherlands.

41. Applications of Educational Technology for Community Health Workers in Developing Countries

A. C. L. Zelmer and A. E. Zelmer, *International Communications Institute, Edmonton, Canada*

Abstract: The paper describes the system constraints on developing training materials in South East Asia and the Canadian Arctic. Five typical methods of design and production are outlined, and recommendations given for producing materials. Design with and for users, simplicity and visualization are stressed, based on field experiences.

The authors are adult educators who have been involved in health education activities in both Canada and South East Asia. Dr (Mrs) Amy E. Zelmer was a public health nurse in rural Canada, a health educator for the Province of Alberta, and has worked as a consultant to the Community Health Programme in the Arctic. More recently she was a consultant in health education with the Regional Office of the World Health Organization in New Delhi. Mr Zelmer's field is the production and use of low-cost media. In addition to working with the federal Ministry of Health and Welfare in the Canadian Arctic he has served as a consultant to government and non-government health and family planning projects in India and Sri Lanka, primarily under the auspices of UNESCO and UNICEF.

Although the authors of this paper have been employed by agencies of the United Nations, the opinions expressed in it are personal and do not necessarily coincide with the views officially held by the UN or its agencies.

Introduction

To a Canadian, used to an abundance of media resources, it is a sobering experience to work in an educational programme in Asia. Resources such as projection bulbs which are taken for granted in Southern Canada were a small problem in the Arctic — it was merely necessary to budget a year in advance and remember to place the order. In India bulbs were available but often cost as much as a month's salary to purchase. In Sri Lanka, unless the bulbs were supplied by an international agency, you might wait forever to obtain 'currency control' permission to place an order, and another year for the bulbs to arrive. Obviously under these circumstances it was necessary to explore other resources, basically the use of local materials for communication support materials. This paper will look at some of the developments that we have observed both in Northern Canada and South East Asia.

First, let us look at the Canadian Arctic where health services are the responsibility of the federal government. Health personnel are almost all white; often, however, they are non-Canadians. They almost always have very different cultural perceptions of their role in the health services than do the indigenous Indians and Eskimos. In the conflict that follows the native peoples are mainly the losers. Since they do not understand, they reject both the medical services and the personnel involved.

To counter this rejection the government began a programme of community health workers, recruited jointly by the village councils and the local health personnel. The community health workers received a six-week training course which included first-aid, preventative health measures, basic community organization techniques, and the preparation and use of basic audiovisual materials. The audiovisual portion of the training included the use of projection equipment, half inch television recorders, tape recorders, local production of slide sets, posters, puppets and other simple visual aids. Each worker was supplied with a basic kit of materials: an Instamatic camera, film and flash bulbs, razor blades, scissors, ruler, T-square and triangle, paints, paste and paper. On-going support included an irregular newsletter with new programme ideas and recognition of work accomplished. In addition, the regional health educator makes periodic visits to the community health workers, many of whom work in very isolated communities.

As might be expected the programme has met with mixed success, however, it is significant that almost four years later several of the original workers are still in the programme and they have become very sophisticated at producing simple posters, slide sets, puppets, etc. They have become an integral part of the health care team in their own community and use audiovisual materials in their day-to-day village teaching.

In Asia the community health workers, variously called primary health workers, village level workers, auxiliary workers, etc. and the special purpose workers for family planning, malaria control, etc. have much the same basic purpose. They serve to extend the primarily urban-based national medical system to the neglected slums and rural villages. In rural areas less than 15 per cent of the population will have access to Western-style medical services, although there may well be practitioners of various indigenous medical systems. The community health worker normally provides health education and preventative medical services. In some areas they are also trained in first-aid, basic curative medicine or midwifery. With an objective of providing one such worker for every village, the governments of the region are faced with the task of recruiting and training several hundred thousand such workers over the next decade or so. This task alone is formidable. In addition, if the programmes are to succeed, it would appear essential to regularly provide support services in the form of motivation, equipment and supplies, and on-going training.

Incidentally, while we are primarily discussing village health workers it should be remembered that much the same problems face the other extension workers in education, agriculture, social services, cooperative development, etc.

System Constraints

The staffing and physical facilities for any programme obviously depend to a certain extent upon government priorities and here, health has generally done quite well at least at the national levels. Western-style medical services are high priority for most Asian governments. Most cities have large hospitals and the capital cities usually boast of intensive-care units and medical research facilities. Many of these urban institutions were built during the time of colonial administrations to serve the foreign population. At that time village and rural health services were often neglected. Today many countries continue the same pattern of services without any evaluation of its effectiveness. In addition, the people of these countries may assume that better health care is provided in the urban institutions and pressure the government to expand them at the expense of the rural services. As a result the recurring expenses for large urban health institutions consume a large portion of the national health budgets.

In a similar manner national and regional training centres have electricity and at least a moderate selection of audiovisual equipment. Bulbs, audio tape, film and other supplies will not likely be readily available. For status and other reasons an electrician or technician will usually be required to operate the equipment. The need for safe keeping of the equipment may well leave it unused. After all if the replacement cost of a bulb equals a month's salary and every blown bulb will be deducted from your salary, you wouldn't use a projector either!

Occasionally field-workers are issued projection equipment but since they usually travel by bus, bicycle or on foot this equipment will not be used even if available. It is also unlikely that electricity would be available in a village and batteries are expensive. The field-worker, in this case the community health worker, must therefore depend upon a few hand-carried flip charts or posters and the occasional visit of a mobile cinema van. Often she gives up and merely talks with her clients.

We recognize that this is a somewhat pessimistic picture, however, among the best programmes the lack of resources need not be a hindrance. A well-motivated field-worker, knowing that she is part of a smoothly functioning health team, uses the scarce resources of paper and other materials to assist a basically interpersonal communication programme. She teaches by example, by demonstration. Her enthusiasm more than overcomes her constraints.

What of production facilities: Is there no way to produce materials centrally for distribution to the field? Yes, in many cases there are very adequate workshops containing silk-screen presses, roneo machines, offset presses, dark rooms and other facilities. However, as with projection equipment, the maintenance of these machines is hampered by the lack of training and spare parts. Sophisticated machinery requires expensive printing plates, inks or chemicals for operation. This means scarce foreign exchange, or the machines sit idle. As well, as we will discuss shortly, there is usually a lack of coordination between the field-workers and the production centre. Materials that the field-workers need cannot be produced because of absolute budgetary constraints or because the budget is already committed to more prestigious projects. Prestigious films, posters and the like are seldom field-tested and almost invariably have been developed by the head office 'specialist' in response to administrative needs rather than to solve field-workers' problems. Except for a major field-testing project in Nepal and isolated cases elsewhere, it is normal for materials to be developed without any reference to the audience and users in the field. The materials produced may look good but fail to be used by field-workers.

Materials Design and Production

In the midst of these bureaucratic structures, complete with some of the most tangled red tape imaginable, there is a reasonable amount of media production. It is true that most production facilities are under-utilized (and likely to remain so for some time). It is true that it may take five or more years to produce a local translation of an encyclopaedic 'manual' adapted from an overseas model. It is true that many of the materials produced do not get used. However, it is also true that in other projects useful materials are emerging. Field-testing, both pre- and post-production, is becoming more common. Field-workers, especially in non-government projects, are beginning to fund more realistic, i.e. smaller, shorter-term, media projects such as brochures and leaflets rather than just the encyclopaedia-style manuals.

From our experiences and those of our colleagues it would appear that there are about five different strategies for the design of educational materials. Each method has its advantages and disadvantages, all of them take considerable time and only two of the five methods involve the eventual user — the field-worker.

311

First we have prototype materials prepared at a specially convened conference, often internationally. Programme staff from a number of countries, with subject specialists and technicians, artists and writers, are typically gathered together for one to three months to prepare guidelines and/or the completed draft for a manual, or a radio series, a handbook, or a media kit, on a specific topic. The materials produced may be very useful but will usually require extensive adaptation for use in individual countries. In addition, they often use expensive reproduction techniques and set a standard that most local production centres cannot hope to match.

Next, we have the committee-produced manual, developed within a single country, usually in the capital city. In a typical production a number of specialists, MD's, PhD's, etc. will be hired to write individual chapters in their own speciality. The results are very inconsistent, highly technical and almost never visual. At the very least extensive editing is required to achieve consistency and readability. Since the specialists must usually do the work in their spare time, coordination is difficult and delays frequent. Usually no one assumes overall responsibility for the completed production. Unfortunately most materials seem to be prepared in this way. These high-status projects satisfy the head office and are good additions to the doctor's bookshelf.

To overcome the problems of a committee, a number of publications have been prepared by having a single 'expert' prepare materials based upon his previous experience. If this person works closely with field staff the results can be highly useful. Often however field visits are neglected and the results, however consistent and logical, are irrelevant to the field needs. Film scripts and radio programmes are particularly prone to this method. Often an administrator or a writer has 'the script' firmly fixed in his head and no amount of field-work or committee supervision will change the result. Many so-called training films end up as mini Hollywood epics this way.

The fourth method, and one of the most reliable, is for the training officer or field-worker to prepare teaching materials on an on-going basis as part of regular training programmes. These materials can be tested with several classes of field-workers or groups of clients, revised and improved with every use. Over a period of months or years the training officer or field-worker can build up a collection of short, simple training aids — flip charts, posters, flash cards, slide sets, leaflets, models and other materials. Eventually the best materials can be duplicated and compiled for wider distribution. Ideally, several persons at more than one centre could cooperate in the project. By exchanging their results, they can cut down on the individual effort required. Coordination, while obviously necessary, is equally obviously difficult.

Finally we come to the fairly common situation where the individual worker, whether at the training centre or in the field, prepares her own materials for limited use. Because of lack of supervision and encouragement these materials are never seen outside of the workers' immediate work situation.

As you can see, duplication of effort often exists since there seldom are communication links up and down an administrative chain, let alone across agencies. Worse still the production units, charged with producing certain materials in their project work plans, often get tired of waiting for the content to be prepared and set about producing their own materials. They themselves may use any or all of the above methods but seldom coordinate efforts with the field-level service units.

Recommendations

On the basis of our observations then, what would we recommend as a system for the development of educational materials in a developing country?

(1) Design and prepare materials at the lowest possible administrative level in response to field-level problems. It is absolutely crucial that top-level administrators recognize the need for communication materials for the lowest-level workers.

(2) Involve the eventual users of the materials from the very beginning.

(3) Think small. It is much easier to prepare and test a simple leaflet than it is to develop a complete training manual.

(4) Think simple. A slide set is much less complicated, both in design and use, than a film. Hand-drawn or roneo flash cards or booklets are much easier to produce and revise than are letterpress or offset publications.

(5) Field-test. Work with the eventual users of the materials to check readability and utility. Don't ask if it looks good. Ask instead 'What does it mean to you?'

(6) Whenever possible work in the language of use. This will prevent translation problems.

(7) Visualize. Many field-workers are poor readers. Use visuals to maintain interest and amplify the text.

(8) Be positive and direct. Show what should be done, not the situations that you don't want to occur.

(9) Be active rather than passive. Instructions should tell the field-worker what she personally should be doing to solve a problem.

(10) Use plenty of photographs as source materials for your visuals. For reproduction, however, whether by roneo, letterpress or offset, the quality and understanding will be optimized with line drawings.

(11) Revise materials as often as conditions change or as usage indicates. For visual materials this suggests slide sets or display prints rather than films or film strips. For print materials this suggests a loose-leaf format to facilitate exchanging pages.

(12) Visit field-workers in their work situations regularly. Follow-up visits with a periodic newsletter which exchanges programme ideas, supports and encourages individual initiative, and provides a medium for maintaining the field-worker's interest.

(13) Above all be realistic. Educational materials production takes much more time, money and effort than is usually anticipated. The physical appearance and technical quality of locally prepared materials is seldom as high as professionally prepared audiovisual or print materials from a central agency. However, the locally produced materials will often fill a direct programme need and be much better utilized than anything produced at the central facility.

References

Fuglesang, Andreas (1973) *Applied Communication in Developing Countries.* Dag Hammarskjöld Foundation, Sweden.

Harnar, Ruth *et al.* (1978) *Teaching Village Health Workers: A Guide to the Process.* Voluntary Health Association of India, New Delhi.

National Development Service (1976) *Communicating with Pictures in Nepal.* NDS and UNICEF, Kathmandu.

Varma, Ravi *et al.* (eds.) (1973) *Action Research and the Production of Communication Media.* The University of Reading, Reading.

Chapter 7:
The Computer and Educational Technology

The computer continues to hold a key role in educational technology, and is applied to a wide variety of uses. The May 1978 issue of *PLET* contains a selection of relevant papers; five more are included here. A further paper, though connected with computing, has much wider implications.

Professor Rahmlow (42) examines the advantages and drawbacks of computer-based education from three viewpoints: students, teachers developing educational programmes and teachers administering such programmes. He then describes the application of computer-based education in the teaching of economics, accounting and mathematics connected with life-insurance courses at the American College, Pennsylvania, USA.

Dr Hawkins (43) presents a wide-ranging survey of computer-based learning in higher education in Britain, USA, Canada and the Netherlands. The paper summarizes a report produced at the University of Utrecht, and it is useful that in the present form the main conclusions of the report can reach a wider cross-section of educationalists. Dr Hawkins is critical of the frequent 'isolation' of computer aspects compared to the broader field of educational technology, and she analyses reasons for this situation having arisen. She makes penetrating suggestions about how computer-based learning may be better integrated in education.

Dr Leiblum (44) provides a timely account of the factors leading to the initiation and development of computer-assisted learning programmes in university environments. The paper provides useful financial and administrative details of university CAL systems, and refers in some detail to the results of Dr Hawkins's survey above.

Dr van der Mast (45) provides an in-depth functional analysis of computer-assisted instruction, followed by an outline of the development of a modular CAI system and its use at Delft University of Technology.

Mr McCulloch (46) presents a detailed account of a computer-aided instruction programme in economics, developed at the Northern Ireland Polytechnic. His paper describes how students responded well to voluntary use of the programmes to help in their studies of economics and a section of the programme is presented and explained. The paper led to a workshop session including on-line demonstration and use of the programme.

Next, moving away from 'mainstream' use of computing in educational technology, Mrs Brew (47) provides a fascinating account of the use of educational technology in the teaching of computing. She describes the adaptation and use of an Open University course on 'The Digital Computer' directly into a 'traditional' university (Essex). The paper presents valuable considerations generally relevant to the use of OU material in traditional institutions. By including this paper in the 'computer' chapter, we hope to bring it to the notice of those directly involved in computer-based learning.

42. Opportunities and Pitfalls in Computer-Based Education Networks

H. F. Rahmlow, *The American College, Bryn Mawr, Pennsylvania*

Abstract: The paper examines advantages and limitations of computer-based learning. The emphasis is on large-scale computing networks. The American College's use of PLATO for distance education is offered as an example.

Computer networks offer a significant opportunity for improving the educational climate, especially in situations calling for teaching at a distance in settings which are either primarily educational or primarily business oriented. The reliance on computer networks is not, however, without pitfalls. If viewed as an opportunity, the potential for computer-based education networks is great. But if viewed as a panacea. the potential for disappointment and failure is even greater. This paper looks at computer-based education networks from three aspects. First, a brief description is given of the characteristics of a computer network. Second, advantages and limitations of computer-based education networks are discussed. Third, a specific application of the use of a computer-based education network by The American College.

Characteristics of a Computer-Based Education Network

Computer-based education networks are characterized by a large-scale central computer connected by a communications link to remote terminals. Students work at the remote terminals either individually or in groups. The students' interaction with the system is through a terminal, which typically consists of a typewriter-type keyboard and either a hard copy or cathode ray tube (CRT) type display. Non-educational examples of such systems are well known in business, with especially heavy use being given to systems by commercial airlines and financial service institutions. It is difficult to imagine the operation of the world's airlines without highly sophisticated computing systems.

A specific example of an education-based network is the Control Data PLATO Network. The system, operated by Control Data Corporation, is run from Minneapolis, Minnesota. Student terminals are linked to the central computer by a phone and satellite connections. The system is dedicated to educational and training purposes. The central processing unit is a Cyber 73-28. Two types of terminals are used with the system, both of which are equipped with a touch-sensitive display screen. The screen presents information to the user and can be programmed to accept touch responses. Printed copies of displays can be made available and an optical reader can be interfaced for data entry.

Advantages and Limitations of Computer-Based Education Networks

The advantages and limitations of computer-based education networks will be discussed as they apply to three groups of people. Although these three aspects overlap, for clarity of presentation it will be useful to make distinctions. The three groups are:

Students
Teacher/Authors
Teacher/Administrators

First we will consider the advantages to the student. The major advantage of computer-based systems to the student is the potential for individualizing instruction. Student progress can be continuously evaluated and the student can be assigned to appropriate learning activities.

Individualization of instruction is possible because of the one-to-one interaction between the educational system and the student. As far as the student is concerned, this is a confidential interaction between himself or herself and the system. The fact that the student is one of many persons using the system at the same time, and the fact that a record is often made of the student's progress, do not seem to detract from the feeling of individuality and confidentiality on the part of the student.

It is important to point out that, although many lessons call for one-to-one interaction between the student and the system, there are also a number of lessons that call for interaction between two or more students using the computing system. Drill and practice exercises may call for students to compete with one another in solving problems, and simulations can call for students to compete among each other or with the computer. In addition, the author has observed highly significant interactions between two adults using a program originally designed for individual use. It is my feeling, and the feeling of my colleagues, that this mode of operation should be investigated in greater detail.

Geographic and time flexibility also benefit students using computer-based educational systems. Within the constraints of the availability of hardware, students can learn at remote locations and at a time that best fits their schedule. This geographic and time flexibility is especially important for businesses having widely dispersed locations. In the United States, for example, many insurance companies have agents in field offices located in all 50 states. Persons in the field are often in need of the same training program. The computer offers flexibility in the delivery of this training.

An additional advantage to students is the record-keeping capability of large-scale computing systems. A student's progress through educational materials can be noted, and this information can be provided to each student.

A computing system offers students access to experts that they would not normally be able to interact with. For example, an educational program dealing with the complicated tax system can be developed by a team of experts and used simultaneously by students throughout the United States.

Finally, validated learning materials can be available to students. Using the data collection and editing capabilities of large-scale computing systems, which will be described later, it is possible to replicate high-quality educational experience for large numbers of students. Used appropriately, educational programs are continually improved.

There are also some significant disadvantages of a computer-based education network. Even though the student has one-to-one interaction with the computer, it is possible for a student to have a feeling of isolation and of not being part of a larger group. If one objective of an educational program is to enhance the student's interpersonal relations on a face-to-face basis, the computing system is not an ideal way to learn.

A significant problem for many students, especially adults, is the typing ability required for the use of most systems. The need for typing can be minimized by the use of programming techniques that limit the complexity of responses. However, it has been our experience that some students are still uncomfortable at having to interact with the system through the typewriter.

System malfunctions are another disadvantage of computing networks and are very frustrating to the individual student. Malfunctions can occur either in the computing system itself or (as is more often the case) in the communication links between the computer and the terminal. It is suggested that, in evaluating malfunctions of computers, these be treated in the same light as malfunctions of other hardware or instructors (for example, failures of bulbs in overhead projectors and illness or labour disputes with instructors).

The next three disadvantages or potential problems with computer-based learning systems are counterparts of advantages that were mentioned earlier. While the geographic and time-scheduling of computer-based systems can be an advantage, it can also be a limitation. The terminals themselves and communications links are not inexpensive. At present they cannot be universally located throughout the world. The distribution of other educational materials, such as books, can be accomplished with considerably more ease.

Finally, the confidentiality of student system interaction is not absolute. There is currently no foolproof method for assuring that only authorized persons have access to student data. Furthermore, the student may not know which persons do in fact have authorization to observe directly or indirectly his or her performance.

Next, we will turn to a consideration of advantages and limitations from the point of view of the teacher/author. The teacher/author is defined as a person or a group of persons with responsibility for developing educational programs.

The developmental features of many computer-based education systems are outstanding. Text-editing capabilities allow authors to revise and re-configure educational materials with relative ease. The record-keeping capability of large-scale systems also enables authors to make use of student experience for the development and revision of programs. Diagnostic testing and observation of students during development are among the more significant features of any computer-based education system and — because of the potential for geographic dispersal of students — are of special importance in networks.

The communication capability of computer-based networks is also of special importance to authors. Authors may communicate via the network with students and other experts using the system. The capability of being able to communicate with other experts on a system-wide basis should not be underestimated. The capability provides an opportunity for a community of scholars to exist in spite of geographic dispersal and time discontinuities.

Now let us look at the other side of the coin. In order for an author to effectively use a computer-based education system, a period of training and acclimatizing is necessary. With most systems, an author can obtain a superficial understanding of system capability and operation relatively quickly. However, to use a system to its fullest extent and to capitalize on the advantages of a system require considerable sophistication — sophistication with respect to both programming skill and instructional design capability. This last point leads directly to a potential pitfall of all computer-based education programs, whether they be on the network or in a stand-alone system. The development of sophisticated materials requires individuals with expertise in educational technology and systems capability. An educational program that is implemented on a computer is not necessarily sophisticated. Trash and trivia can be disseminated by sophisticated computer-based education networks just as they can through any other educational media.

Authors need to have good typing skills in order to effectively utilize current computing networks. This skill is important both for entering and for editing materials. I do not mean to imply that the author must be a conventional typist or use orthodox methods, but rather that he or she be a competent typist.

In spite of the highly sophisticated record-keeping capability of computer-based education networks, there is danger in not seeing a student face-to-face. It has been the experience of my colleagues and myself that much can be gained from direct observation of students, especially during the developmental stages of educational programs. To rely only on a computer interface with students is to lose considerable valuable data.

Next, computer-based education networks will be discussed from the point of view of the teacher/administrator. The teacher/administrator is defined as a person or a group of persons responsible for administering educational programs to students.

In theory economies of scale can be highly significant in computer-based education networks. Once developed, a program can be used by thousands of students in remote locations at different times. Through the use of a single educational experience by large numbers of students, the economy of the system can be realized.

Large-scale computing networks can also offer a rich curriculum to students. Since administrators are not constricted by a lack of instructors, they can offer their students a broader range of programs.

Finally, the record-keeping capability of large-scale systems enables administrators to carefully monitor student progress.

In looking at the limitations, the first that must be carefully evaluated is that dealing with economies of scale. To date, the economies of scale touted for computing networks do not normally exist. Unless educational programs can be developed and used by large audiences, it is a false economy to utilize networks.

To reiterate a limitation mentioned earlier, system accessibility may be a problem. In order for the system to operate effectively there must be terminals and communications links to a large number of locations.

Two related problems need to be considered in looking at the introduction of large-scale computer systems: there is a normal resistance to innovation, and the roles of individuals may have to be modified. The common resistance to innovation among students, teachers, and administrators is well documented and will not be elaborated on. It is important to note that the traditional role of the instructor or faculty member is significantly modified through the use of large-scale computer-based education networks. As in other large-scale education developments, the instructor no longer can act alone but must operate as a team member. The instructor's skill in non-face-to-face communication becomes critical. In addition to these communications and interpersonal-relations problems, the administrator must be keenly aware of the reward system for various personnel. If a professor develops a high-quality instructional program that can be used by many persons on a computing system, what is the perceived value of this work as contrasted with face-to-face teaching, publication, and other research?

An Application

The remainder of the paper will deal with the use of a computer-based education network by The American College. The American College is an institution of higher learning with a campus in Bryn Mawr, Pennsylvania. The College's primary mode of interaction with students is teaching at a distance. Its 60,000 students are located in all 50 states and some foreign countries. Nearly two-thirds of the students range in age from 26 to 40 and 20 per cent are 41 years of age or older. Sixty per cent of the students are college graduates, and less than 20 per cent have only a high school diploma. Students in The American College's graduate program are typically highly educated before beginning their master's study. Over 95 per cent of the College's students are employed full-time and are pursuing their education on a part-time basis. Approximately 60 per cent are life underwriters.

There is no prescribed method of study for American College programs. Students can obtain from the College a study guide, which is cross-referenced to specified textbooks. These textbooks are usually acquired by students independently. Students generally study in one of three modes of instruction: in classes (over 1,100 classes met in 1976), in study groups, or as self-studiers. Students are given credit only for courses in which they pass examinations, which are administered at approximately 290 examination centres throughout the United States and at selected locations overseas. Exam development and grading is carried out by The American College faculty on its campus.

The diverse background of its students, their need for effective educational programs, and their geographic dispersion lead the College to investigate computer-based education networks. The College has developed and is using — on an optional basis — the Control Data PLATO network for educational programs in selected sections of three of its courses, which cover content in economics, analytic accounting, and the mathematics of life insurance. The courses utilize the computing system where it can be most advantageous and also incorporate existing audio, video, and print materials where they are most appropriate.

Common characteristics of the lessons developed by the College for use with the computing system are:

(1) Diagnostic testing
(2) Record-keeping for students and administrators
(3) Incorporation of existing audio, video and printed materials
(4) Drill and practice exercises
(5) Interactive instruction
(6) Assistance for both logistics and academic problems

The economics course is comprehensive including pre-tests, a printed work book, supplemental on-line instruction, on-line simulation review exercises and post-tests. Selected portions of the course can be used to supplement classroom instruction or the material can be used on a stand-alone basis.

The analytic accounting course is designed for practice and review for the person who interprets financial statements rather than for the accountant or book-keeper who must prepare statements. Students are presented with problems requiring application of principles. For detailed instruction students are referenced to off-line material.

The mathematics of life-insurance course is a comprehensive course including diagnostic tests, instruction and practice, quick reference to important concepts, and drill. A practice examination is provided and students are given feedback on both their knowledge and their pace in taking the examination.

Development of the three courses was carried out by teams of faculty, professional staff, and students at The American College. The basic team members were a designer, subject-matter expert, systems expert, and student subjects. A minimum of four persons were involved in the development of each section of the courses, although more persons, especially students, were involved in most instances.

Different modes of development were used for each course. In all cases, preliminary instruction design was done without using the computing network. The development of curriculum materials was done for some courses using the network itself (on-line) and for other courses off-line. In some cases the material was written out virtually verbatim prior to coding into the computer. In other cases the general outline was given to the system's expert, who wrote the material on-line.

The materials that have been developed are currently being used by The American College students on its campus in Bryn Mawr and at various sites on the Control Data PLATO Network. Initial student attitude and performance is highly positive. However, the College still views its work as experimental.

Reference

Fratini, Robert C. (1978) Computer-based education for professionals in the financial sciences. Presented to Association for the Development of Computer-Based Instructional Systems (ADCIS). To be presented at 1978 Winter Conference, Dallas, Texas.

43. A Survey of the Development, Application and Evaluation of Computer-Based Learning in Tertiary Education in the UK, the USA,the Netherlands and Canada

C. A. Hawkins, *State University of Utrecht, the Netherlands*

Abstract: A survey of CAL in tertiary education in the USA, Britain, Canada and the Netherlands is given, based on a questionnaire about (1) siting and scale of work in CAL centres, (2) purposes of CAL, (3) consultancy and training, (4) procedures for developing courseware, (5) the future. Certain aspects influencing the organization, goals and financing of projects are discussed.

The Project on which this Summary is based

The survey was undertaken as part of the experimental project in computer-based learning established in January 1975 in the State University of Utrecht. It was directed in the first instance to meet certain immediate objectives of the project, to ascertain likely trends of development. Over 60 project leaders from a number of countries participated in the survey, many of them from major American projects of long standing. All the British NDPCAL (National Development Programme in Computer Assisted Learning) tertiary level projects are represented in the study, and most of those sited in Dutch universities. The proportion of Canadian projects represented is lower, probably because there was a postal strike at the time, but they nevertheless make an important contribution to the final report.

The report of this survey has been published in full by the Department of Research and Development in Higher Education of the State University of Utrecht under the title 'Computer-Based Learning — a Survey of the Factors influencing its Initiation and Development'. It is in two parts. Part 1 provides an overview of the origins and contributing sources of computer-based instructional systems and the present situation in the UK, USA, the Netherlands and Canada, together with a rationale of the survey, the general conclusions and recommendations. Part 2 has been printed in four sections, one for each of the countries surveyed. The present summary refers to Part 1, the general observations of the survey and the conclusions and recommendations based on them.

Important Aspects of the Survey

It was an important feature of the survey to assume that, in view of its diversity of origin and application, a consensus view of computer-based learning is out of reach at the present time. What was looked for was an impartial charting of the range of practice and opinion. This is in contrast with the approach of the frequently quoted previous study by Anastasio and Morgan (1972).

The most striking aspect of computer-based learning is its separateness. It still stands somewhat apart from other manifestations of educational technology. Also, within computer-based learning itself there are subdivisions that stand just as apart from each other. There is a lack of cross-fertilization between the different types of computer-based learning, and there is little use as yet of computers in a multi-media environment. Computer-based learning is at times associated appropriately with some specific educational needs, such as those of deaf students, remote students, areas of the curriculum that demand simulation, and so on.

But it is only too often developed and promoted quite apart from or even in a spirit of competition with other educational modes. There is little attempt to align computer-based learning with concurrent educational development. It is suggested that it is this separateness, rather than its alleged technical difficulty or expense, that is preventing computer-based learning from making a full contribution to educational development. This situation is to be regretted, and the better integration of computer-based learning should be sought. Three general areas of development can be identified which could benefit from and host computer-based learning activities:

(1) Curriculum development
(2) Exploitation of audiovisual aids and self-instructional materials
(3) Organizational change associated with the individualization of instruction.

Analysis of the responses to the questionnaires indicated that, while participants rated some of these areas highly as, in their view, providing important possible reasons for utilizing computer-based learning, there was little accompanying evidence that such priorities were reflected in their projects' objectives. Projects have evidently developed in computer-based learning without benefit or hindrance from what is now generally accepted as the systems approach. They have been established prior to the formation of agreed, clear-cut objectives, and without feasibility studies, so that placement of projects and coordination with concurrent educational development is haphazard.

A second important feature of the report was a consideration of this integration, and an examination of the concept of 'institutionalization' that has been central to the NDPCAL funded projects, its definition, appreciation and application. The NDPCAL makes an important differentiation between 'soft' money, which comes from government and other outside funding agencies, and 'hard' money, which comes from the budget of the project's host institute. The NDPCAL has an operational definition of 'institutionalization', equating it to matched funding. It was conditional to their sponsorship.

The use of 'soft' money in the USA context also benefits from examination, since its usefulness is differently perceived, and since it was in the light of the American experience that the NDPCAL directorate and others made their distinction between 'hard' and 'soft' money. In Anastasio and Morgan's (1972) analysis of the factors inhibiting the use of computers in instruction, a model was established to explain why materials were not forthcoming. It was, in short, a vicious circle, in which potential authors were refraining from production in the absence of financial reward and other recognition, which potential sponsors, publishers and employers were withholding because of the lack of paradigm materials and evidence of their success It is here suggested that computer-based learning is no different from other educational innovations in this respect. They have had to break out of the same circle.

Anastasio and Morgan suggested that a suitable injection of funds would break the circle. But educational innovators are only too aware of what can occur when the 'soft' money is withdrawn, and the costs of a new enterprise are re-calculated. The project which succeeds in obtaining long-term support from its host institute can be expected to be demanding resources which finally are on a scale in line with those of similar enterprises with similar objectives.

Further, a project that is likely to feed other concurrent developments would be expected to be more likely to succeed than one which is isolated. Sadly, the responses to the questionnaire reflected no such overall vision of computer-based learning. Respondents firmly rated high goals such as 'individualization of instruction', and moderately 'mastery learning', and yet 'effecting organizational change' is rated extremely low. Surely, where these things occur, they will occur together. Can it not be that this present lack of perception of the effect of one change on another development is just a reflection of how projects at present are placed and operate? They seem usually to be in a position where they can develop some quite small part of the curriculum and the manner in which it is learnt, and possibly do this very well; but there is no impact on the main stream of events. The contrast that most immediately comes to mind is the language laboratory. In its time also considered to be relatively expensive and technically complex, language laboratory hardware was available long before good software. When the new technology could be used so that large numbers of students could obtain verbal fluency in a foreign language in a way that had previously not been possible, the whole of language teaching was changed.

In contrast with language laboratories, the potential contribution of computer-based learning to educational development is much more complex and far-reaching, as would be expected from its diverse origins. The various forms of computer-based learning, their roots and their particular characteristics are described in the full report, from which Table 1 is taken. The CAI aspects are divided into (a) the tutor, or teaching machine mode, and (b) the laboratory mode. The management aspects of computer-based learning, CMI, have been divided into (a) straightforward automation of existing administrative procedures in scoring and recording student progress, and (b) the prescriptive use of CMI, providing feedback on which guidance can be based during learning. There is a further category in which computers are envisaged as research instruments in cognitive science.

The NDPCAL gave considerable attention to institutionalization of projects, not only through their insistence on matched funding, but also in the manner in which projects were selected and established. The strategies of the NDPCAL for institutionalization in terms of close involvement with the curriculum as already taught and studied will surely be regarded by APLET members as misdirected, ensuring the relevance of final products to present classrooms at the expense of possibly more fundamental and/or broadly based change. The following quotation shows how such choices were made.

> Aiming for institutionalisation has, of course, a number of implications for project selection and design. As a result of the aim, the Programme has got directly involved with, for example, university teaching departments and not just educational technology units or computing centres. Two of the tertiary education projects are directed by heads of teaching departments, significantly. The three current schools projects are all based in local education authorities (not universities) (Hooper, 1975).

Such a policy has led to a very minor input from educational technologists and psychologists concerned with the research and development in teaching and learning at the present stage.

What is also of interest in this respect is the common manner of growth of new projects, particularly in the United States. Understandably, rather than re-invent the wheel, many are latching on to established projects and networks. Thus the responsibility undertaken by the major projects in the direction they give to computer-based learning has increased, and is increasing. The questionnaire responses from the major projects showed an awareness of this responsibility. The supra-institutional nature of development is now a major feature of computer-based learning. Inevitably, it will now be difficult for a new project to develop independently.

325

	Role	Title	Source	Explanation
CAI	Teaching machine	'Classical' CAI	Programmed learning, educational technology	Text followed by question, to which student responds and receives feedback
	Laboratory	Adjunct use of computer in 'hard' sciences	Availability and use in computer-linked subjects	Simulation Modelling Problem solving
		Knowledge-based systems in the 'soft' sciences	Attempts to achieve the advantages of laboratory-based subjects in other subjects.	
CMI	Testing	Use of computer in administration of testing procedures	Use of standardized objective tests	Test making, record keeping, test-item banking, test production
	Prescription	Individualized instruction	Mastery learning, requirements of formative as well as summative evaluation and rapid feedback	Routes student through study materials on the basis of his achievement and individual characteristics
Research Tool	Research instrument in the cognitive sciences	Artificial intelligence	Artificial intelligence Machine translation and cognitive psychology	Attempts to achieve a precise under-standing of the mechanisms capable of mediating intelligent behaviour by specifying such mechanisms in formal terms

Table 1. *Computer-based learning systems*

It is considered imperative that a general forum for review and consideration of computer-based learning should come at the present time, to permit a fundamental stock-taking and a planned appreciation programme.

Situated in Britain as we are, with the recent publication of the final report of the NDPCAL, it is appropriate to give some attention to the situation in this country. But this is an international conference, with an international theme — educational technology in a changing world — and these remarks draw upon an international survey. There follows a brief summary of the main report's conclusions, which it is hoped will promote a wider discussion, how computer-based learning may be better appreciated and more closely aligned with other educational development, and how a closer *rapprochement* of potentially interested parties might best be achieved, for the benefit of all concerned.

The General Conclusions of the Survey

These are summarized qualitatively under the headings and sub-headings of the questionnaire.

I. General Development and Scale of Work

1. BASE OF OPERATIONS. Projects in the UK, the Netherlands and Canada were usually centred in one academic department. In the USA, many more projects were established centrally, and provided a university-wide service.

2. MAIN STIMULUS TO ESTABLISH A UNIT. The importance of individual initiative is universally acknowledged, although the NDPCAL has been an important factor in the UK. In the USA high-level administrative support was often important at the initiation stage.

3. MAIN SOURCE OF INNOVATIVE EFFORT. Almost all the Netherlands projects report a major initiative from individuals, and almost none of the UK projects do so. In the USA, more recent projects were more likely to acknowledge individual initiative. There was a predominance of projects based on education and educational technology faculties among the Canadian entries.

4. STAFFING. In Canada and the USA projects characteristically have some educationists, rather more computer scientists, subject-matter specialists, and many more graduate assistants. The UK has fewer educationists or graduate assistants.

5. DIRECTION OF PROJECTS. UK projects are most likely to be directed through committees, which include extra-institutional members and project evaluators.

6. MAIN TYPES OF RESISTANCE. As would be expected, *cost* is perceived as a major obstacle. But in all countries, *inertia* was rated at least as important. *Lack of knowledge and self-confidence* equalled cost as a factor in North America, and was more important in the UK and the Netherlands. *Lack of time for faculty to reconstruct courses* was a greater problem than *lack of time to learn the necessary computer techniques.*

7. MAIN SOURCES OF RESISTANCE. Resistance is mainly perceived as *competition with other projects,* that is, research equipment in science subjects, and less expensive, research and development elsewhere. Fear and ignorance of technology, and a fear of embarking on expensive projects with no guarantee of success are all also cited.

The greatest difficulty was in the order of importance attached by university teachers and their administrators. Teaching is a poor second to research, and the improvement of teaching falls even further behind.

8. OBSTACLES TO TEACHER COOPERATION. *Learning to construct self-instructional packages* is a greater problem than *learning a computer language. Lack of incentives* is a universal problem. It was evident that recognition for promotion and tenure was more important than financial gain. *No training, or follow-up of training* was less of a difficulty than getting teachers to make an *initial* involvement.

9. USE OF MATERIALS FROM ELSEWHERE IN THE INITIAL STAGE OF A PROJECT. Most USA projects used materials from elsewhere in the early stages of work, but the tendency for UK and Netherlands projects to use extraneous materials is less.

10. USE OF OWN MATERIALS ELSEWHERE, LEVEL OF ADAPTATION AND SUCCESS. The *level* of use was under-reported, some large-scale projects summarizing activity very briefly. In contrast, *level of adaptation and success* were reported more optimistically than would be expected from item 9.

11. THE EXTENT TO WHICH OTHER MATERIALS ARE USED WHEN INDIGENOUS MATERIALS ARE AVAILABLE. This is low in both Canada and the Netherlands. In the UK, there is extensive exchange of materials between NDPCAL projects.

USA projects refer repeatedly to a few major sources of well-known, tried and tested materials.

12 & 13. LENGTH AND STABILITY OF ESTABLISHMENT. In the UK, the number of projects predating the NDPCAL is small, and the continuation of projects beyond the life of the Programme was expressed uncertainly. The more independent Netherlands projects express longer-term security, and the Canadian projects attached to education and educational technology departments seem to have their future assured.

The American projects have been grouped into long-established, mid-term (from about 1970) and new (commencing since 1974). The long-established projects are independent of each other, but newer projects frequently show dependence on older developments.

14, 15 & 16. MATERIALS AVAILABLE AND THEIR UTILIZATION. In the UK, this is mainly confined to maths, engineering and the hard sciences. These subjects also feature strongly in North America, together with medicine and computer science, although most subject areas are represented.

17. FACTORS CONTRIBUTING MOST TO SUCCESS.
Technical: A reliable, dedicated system, fast response times, computer graphics were reiterated.
Organizational/sociological: An energetic, dedicated central figure who could give leadership over a range of activities, and an enthusiastic, cooperative group prepared to work long hours. Top-level administrative support, hard funding, a 'core' of interested colleagues, and an innovative setting were also cited.

II. The Purposes of Computer-Based Learning Projects

PROJECT OBJECTIVES. The full range of objectives is given in the main report under the following sub-neadings:

   (a) *Research,* e.g. artificial intelligence.
   (b) *Educational,* e.g. course enrichment, and the individualization of instruction.
   (c) *Implementation and Innovation,* e.g. within traditional courses for large numbers of students, and off-campus CAI for non-traditional students.
   (d) *Technological,* e.g. to facilitate reliability, transferability, editorship and authoring, analysis of student performance, enrichment of terminal sites.
   (e) *Financial,* e.g. design of a comprehensive system for institutional and home use at a low cost.

III. Rated Importance of Suggested Reasons for Developing Computer-Based Learning

Most popular were the individualization of instruction, mastery learning and improving teacher effectiveness. Somewhat lower was interest in increasing educational capacity. Facilitating organizational change, and reducing teaching loads were ranked low.

IV. Training of Non-Specialists and Consultancy Services

There is a high level of informal advice for beginners. Many projects give courses in computer languages, few in instructional design. Demonstrations were often given, but there was little mention of appreciation courses.

V. Courseware Development

1. CRITERIA FOR DECISION. At present, there is an understandable tendency to encourage any efforts. Projects that can be selective have drawn up checklists of criteria, such as relevance to current educational problems, amenability to transfer, and conformity to preferred instructional models. They also assign priority in a way that maximizes scale and efficiency of use.

2 & 3. CONSTRUCTION OF THE PACKAGES AND SETTING THEM IN COURSEWARE. Only in the USA is there a clear differentiation between these tasks, where programming is frequently done by graduate assistants.

4. COURSEWARE EVALUATION. External evaluation is only a feature of the UK projects. Only a minority of projects reported that acceptance or revision of materials was based on evaluation procedures. Most comments were of a general, impressionistic nature.

VI. Expectations of Computer-Based Learning

CONFIGURATION, TERMINALS AND SYSTEMS SOFTWARE. Few respondents felt able to make clear-cut choices between big, stand-alone computers, dedicated minis, or computers in networks. Some suggested that a modern educational environment will have access to all of these. The major trend among terminals is VDU's (visual display units). The plasma panel has many devotees, but there is disappointment over the failure to reduce its cost. Few expect author languages to take the main burden of computer-based learning, most expect a heavy use of standard languages and mixed development.

LESSON STYLE DEVELOPMENT AND INTERCHANGE. Test administration, drill and practice, simple techniques and complex learning are all expected to be utilized, but there is a clear expectation that the importance of computers in facilitating complex learning will increase. A greater proportion of programmes are expected to be produced by teams. Interchange of materials remains a major problem. Many respondents indicate that the next five years will continue to be unstable, and systems should be chosen and materials developed with that expectation in mind.

References

Anastasio, E.J. and Morgan, J.S. (1972) *Factors Inhibiting the Use of Computers in Instruction.* EDUCOM, Interuniversity Communications Council, Princeton, New Jersey.
Hooper, R. (1975) *Two Years On. The National Development Programme in Computer Assisted Learning.* Report of the Director. Councils and Education Press, London.

44. Structuring Computer-Assisted Learning in a University Environment

M. Leiblum, *Computer-Assisted Instruction Project, University of Nijmegen, the Netherlands*

Abstract: The paper provides a broad review of the place of computer-assisted learning in university environments, and reviews several factors leading to its initiation and successful development.

1. Introduction

The field of computer-assisted learning (CAL) is relatively new. One should therefore not be surprised to find great variation in the organizational structure of CAL services. A service group may be found hidden in a faculty of music, located within a department of education, part of a learning resource centre, or under the control of a computing centre. Some larger CAL service agencies have independent support, receiving funds from outside agencies.

This paper reviews and offers commentary on the external organizational structures of CAL services in a university environment. Major factors affecting the placement of such services include the type of service to be provided, the available computer system, the needs of courseware development, the location of financial support, the curriculum area and user population.

2. CAL Placement, a Review

A review of the literature reveals very few articles or reports dealing specifically with placement of CAL services or how they are administered. This information can be located, however, by studying reports from individual projects, a time-consuming task, since there are hundreds of projects throughout the world. A number of surveys have been made which do contain information regarding 'structure' (Anastasio and Morgan, 1972; Weather and Williams, 1976; Hunter *et al.*, 1975) but few present a general overview or analysis of possibilities. These publications also contain very few, if any, references to the structure of CAL outside the United States. A recent study by Hawkins (1977) is more international in character. Questionnaires were sent to prominent CAL projects located mostly within English-speaking countries. Fifty-nine of the 112 28-page questionnaires were returned with most correspondence coming from the United States, Canada, the UK, and the Netherlands. One item specifically asked:

> How is your unit or project in CAI established?
> (a)   Based on an academic faculty or department.
> (b)   Based on a computing center.
> (c)   Directed by a committee, if so, to whom answerable?
> (d)   Other . . .

More than 25 per cent of the respondents (17) represented specialized health service agencies, e.g. medical and dental schools, schools of nursing or pharmacy. Since this paper seeks to study CAL location in a general university environment, this data was not studied further. It is clear, however, that the health sciences are one of the most active users of computer-assisted learning, and the study of CAL organization within this area may be useful. A summary based on the 42 remaining responses indicated 27 per cent of the projects were part of an academic faculty/ department. Among those mentioned were: psychology, mathematics, education, artificial intelligence, physics, astronomy, educational technology, digital techniques, etc. Twenty-four per cent of the projects asserted that they were supported or administered through a computer centre. Fifty per cent stated that they were part of a special institute or directed by a committee. It was here that the greatest variety of answers appeared, and it is difficult to classify them. Among the groups mentioned were: educational research centre, centre for research and development, computer-based educational research laboratory, division of educational services, institute for mathematical studies, department of self-paced learning materials, etc. Many of the respondents in this group specified that they were also responsible to an outside *ad hoc* committee.

Hawkins included another item related to external organization in her questionnaire, specifically,

> Describe in detail the constitution of the administrative body or steering committee that directs or oversees policy and activity.

Analysis shows that less than half of the American and Canadian projects are directed through formal committees. In comparison almost all of the British projects are so directed, while few of the Dutch projects are (because of the typically smaller group size). The size of the committees vary (between 3 and 15), but tend to be larger for British projects. The average size committee consisted of between 8 and 10 members, but this clearly is a function of the size and breadth of activities of the CAL group itself. Hirschbuhl (1974) and others (Christopher, 1974; Sharry, 1975; Muston and Wagstaff, 1975; Held, 1976) describe the importance and responsibilities of such committees.

A small sampling follows briefly indicating the external organizational structure of some well-known CAL projects. Lower (1972) describing the structure of CAL at Simon Fraser University (Canada), indicated that their CAL centre reports directly to the academic vice-president whose offices provide necessary funding. The role of the computing centre is to furnish the physical equipment and support services, which they do under a 'faculties management agreement'. He also reported that many CAL services are operated by local computing centres with fewer run by departments or faculties of education.

At Florida State University (1974), the CAL project was absorbed into a laboratory in the College of Education called the Computer Applications Laboratory and is administered by the College of Education. The laboratory participates in the design and development of prototype courses using computers, conducts workshops, training seminars, etc.

Ohio State University (1973) houses one of the most active and well-known CAL centres in the United States. Here also administration falls under the jurisdiction of the office of academic affairs. In 1973, the staff provided services to developers/ designers, training for programmers, system maintenance, information dissemination, coordination of operations, research assistance, demonstrations, and control of the student CAL centre. Although developers and users share a central computer and coordinate their activities through a central staff, development of materials and immediate control over student access remains in the hands of faculties.

At the University of Nijmegen, Netherlands, Leiblum (1977) reported that the CAL project evolved from an *ad hoc* special interest group. Initially, split informal support was provided by the computing centre and an educational research institute. Finally in late 1974, the university's governing council recommended that a 'formal' CAL project should be created and placed under the administrative umbrella of an educational research institute; however a separate budget was granted as well as the affirmation that policy and operational decisions should rest within the CAL project itself.

If located within a faculty, research and development will usually be limited to applications for that curriculum area. By divorcing a CAL service from any single department and placing it under a more centralized agency, the development and utilization of CAL may be more easily integrated into the overall university environment.

From a study of available literature, one can eventually isolate four main 'external' structures of CAL projects or services. They are generally affiliated with an academic faculty, a computer service agency, an educational R & D type institute, or finally, established as an independent unit reporting to an academic office or committee. It appears that a majority of projects fall under or within an educational R & D type agency, with those falling within a faculty forming the second largest group.

2.1 Factors affecting Organizational Placement

While the preceding findings are descriptive, they provide little insight into the problem of determining just where a CAL service belongs. CAL is a hybrid field, a cross between computer technologies, educational theories, and specific application (curriculum) areas. A study of the goals or objectives of the CAL service is of primary importance in determining appropriate location. Rather than trying to determine whether CAL is 50 per cent computer related, 25 per cent curriculum related, and 25 per cent educational theory related, one can study the factors that more operationally affect organizational placement.

2.1.1 TYPE OF SERVICE.

Centralized versus Decentralized. A CAL group can be initiated with the intent of providing a general service to the entire academic community or to provide a more localized service to one or more defined faculties. The former intent usually implies a sharing of computer facilities, and necessitates greater planning and cooperation among intra-university agencies. Lowering of expenses, increase of potential user population, efficiency of operations, etc. are usually the advantages cited for establishing a centralized service. In Europe, the tendency is to operate a centralized system rather than to use a 'dedicated' computer located within a faculty. In America, the abundance and low cost of mini- and midi-computers has made decentralized services more common. If there is sufficient interest, personnel, funds, and a large enough student population to warrant it, location of a CAL project within a faculty area can be justified.

Application versus Research Orientation. A CAL project can be established with a service more oriented towards performing basic research (learning about learning, testing didactical theories, etc.) or more inclined to develop application materials. A project tied to a computer service agency, or specific faculty (not Education), is more likely to be applications oriented. Those centred within educational research institutes, or departments of psychology frequently have an opposite orientation. Of course overlapping orientations exist.

Courseware Development. A CAL project may produce no new instructional materials itself, but may only join an existing network that supplies and distributes programmes. Most projects, however, even if they are part of a network, have some kind of instructional development responsibilities. A centralized facility is more likely to have the expertise necessary (aside from subject-matter specialists) to produce quality materials. A faculty-placed CAL project will have easy access to master teachers, etc. but may lack individuals with specific training and timely experience with CAL techniques. A high-quality programme product usually reflects a close cooperation between subject-matter specialists and educational technologists. A faculty-located project, if intending to stimulate material preparation (authoring) by internal staff, will also require a CAL system that provides specialized features to simplify authoring (prompting, built-in error diagnostics, some built-in instructional logics, etc.). Of course the faculty can hire specialists or advisers for guidance, but this places an additional load on a usually overworked budget. The question then of who will develop courseware and how, has a direct bearing on the organizational placement of CAL.

Training and Dissemination. If the service objectives of a project include: training of CAL authors, preparation of demonstration programmes, maintenance of programme and documentation libraries, short courses/seminars, preparation of handbooks, manuals, and other administrative tasks (e.g. student performance record collection) then location of a project within a faculty would be unusual.

2.1.2 COMPUTER SYSTEM. Aside from the type of service to be provided, the computer system (or lack of it) is a dominant factor in the placement of a CAL project. A relatively large number of projects were initiated from a computing centre, thus the mere existence of in-house computers plays a role in organizational structure. Faculties making heavy use of computing facilities, such as mathematics, physics, and computer science, are popular instigators of CAL activity, partly because of the highly structured and more objective nature of their subject matter, and partly because of the presence of computers. After a project is initiated by one agency, it is more likely that it will remain there.

In the first decade of CAL (roughly 1958-68), hundreds of specially developed systems were created. Because of the technology and computer expertise required, a CAL project usually was located within a technical or science/engineering location. Now that more general CAL systems are available, and computing costs are lower, there is a greater tendency to find CAL agencies scattered throughout a university. CAL systems can be purchased 'off-the-shelf' from major manufacturers, can be freely obtained from some government agencies or universities, can be delivered or developed by commercial educational software houses, and can be plugged into by joining an existing network (PLATO, Lister Hill Medical, NDPCAL). These possibilities now simplify initiation and increase the likelihood of finding CAL projects at non-science locations.

CAL systems have been developed for mini, midi, and large-scale computers but are more likely to be found on the latter. If wide-scale CAL services are offered, greater demands (space, response times, CPU usage, etc.) are made on the computing system, and more terminals are needed. It thus becomes more difficult and expensive for one faculty to bear the burden. CAL (as opposed to CMI) systems require a time-sharing environment, not usually available on small computers (but many exceptions exist). If located within a faculty, these small computers can support CAL applications, but at the expense of using the computer for other non-CAL work. Most smaller faculties, already financially hard pressed, could not support such 'dedicated' systems, thus a shared approach is preferable. This has implications for a more centralized administrative set-up.

2.1.3 FINANCIAL AND ADMINISTRATIVE SUPPORT. The organizational placement of CAL is obviously affected by the agency financially supporting it. Support can come directly from university resources (general or research budgets), or from government or other private funding agencies. Funds obtained through outside grants (soft money) are attractive but do carry restrictions and obligations and sometimes outside indirect control. This means of support has an annoying way of drying up quickly, leaving a toll of wasted development time and negative feelings towards the medium.

CAL projects usually require long start-up periods, dedicated personnel, and a time-consuming effort to break the conservatism and resistance to innovation found at most institutions. Temporary funding, such as a two or three-year grant from an outside agency, produces the pressure for a quick result and can inadvertently reduce the probability of long-term CAL success. Obtaining university financial support, although difficult, seems preferable. It allows for continuity, provides the time necessary to correct faults, to make liaison with staff interested in supporting CAL. Using internal funds will usually involve high administrative and academic officials in the CAL picture, a requisite for permanence.

The origins of a considerable number of CAL projects point to the initiative taken by one or two faculty members who struggle to catalyze interest in the medium for their particular curriculum area. If successful a 'physics' or 'biology' CAL project is initiated. Quite often other faculty members are drawn to the possibilities, and the potential for expansion exists. If the decentralized location persists, growth is limited and redundant efforts may follow. If incentive for CAL is generated by top-level administration or university councils and a centralized agency is created, there will be less duplication of effort and improved cooperation among faculty. Thus while grass-roots level support is initially required, CAL projects should look towards firm administrative support and involvement for longer-term successes.

2.1.4 CURRICULUM AREA AND USER POPULATION. Although the uses of CAL cross almost all curriculum areas, the literature shows its major imprint on the sciences, especially the health sciences. This may be due to the generally greater financial resources, the more structured subject matter, the lowered resistance to innovation, or the instructional needs associated with these disciplines. A study of the 1976 edition of the *Index to Computer-Based Learning* (Wang, 1976) reveals that the greatest number of programmes deal with mathematics (30 per cent of the 1,324 listings), while health sciences, chemistry, computer science, biological sciences and physics combined form 55 per cent of the total. The remaining 15 per cent deals with a diversity of subjects, too numerous to mention. Those institutions stressing 'teaching' above pure research seem more likely to sponsor CAL activities.

Districts, schools or departments having large student populations are more likely to have active CAL projects. Larger student populations make for more cost-effective CAL, but not necessarily higher-quality instructional materials. Larger numbers mean broader administrative and financial support — a goal of most CAL groups. This deters housing a CAL service within a small faculty.

References

Anastasio, E. and Morgan, J. (1972) *Factors Inhibiting the Use of Computers in Instruction.* EDUCOM, Interuniversity Council, Princeton, New Jersey.

Christopher, R.(1974) An administrative perspective on CAI. In *Viewpoints, Bulletin of the School of Education,* 50, 4. Indiana University.

Hawkins, A. (1977) *Computer-Based Learning: A Summary of the Factors Influencing its Initiation and Development.* Department of Research and Development, Maliebaan 5,

Utrecht, the Netherlands.

Held, T. (1976) The selling of a network. Paper presented at the ADCIS Winter Conference, Santa Barbara, California.

Hirschbuhl, J. (1974) Starting up and justifying CAI at the university level. Paper presented at the ADCIS Winter Conference, Washington, DC.

Hunter, B. *et al.* (1975) *Learning Alternatives in U.S. Education: Where Student and Computer Meet.* HumRRO, Educational Technology Publications, Englewood Cliffs, New Jersey.

Leiblum, M. (1977) A pragmatic approach to initiating a CAI service. In Hills, P. and Gilbert, J. (eds.) *Aspects of Educational Technology XI.* Kogan Page, London.

Lower, S. (1972) *Making CAI Make a Difference in College Teaching.* Simon Fraser University, Burnaby, British Columbia, Canada.

Muston, R. and Wagstaff, R. (1975) Introducing the computer to teacher education: an integration of human and hardware technology. Paper presented at the ADCIS Winter Conference, Charleston, S.C.

Ohio State University (1973) *CAI Users Manual,* 2nd edn. Ohio State University, Columbus, Ohio.

Sharry, J. (1975) CAI from one administrator's viewpoint. Paper presented at ADCIS Winter Conference, Charleston, S.C.

Weather, L. and Williams, R. (1976) *Survey to Determine the Status of Computer-Based Instructional Systems.* Aeronutronic Ford Corp., Houston, Texas.

Wang, A. (1976) *Index to Computer Based Learning.* Instructional Media Laboratory, University of Wisconsin at Milwaukee.

45. A Modular CAI System

C. van der Mast, *Delft University of Technology, Delft, the Netherlands*

Abstract: Many developments are occurring in the field of computer-assisted instruction (CAI). To be able to respond in a flexible way to new possibilities and requirements, a new kind of CAI system is needed. This paper describes how a system consisting of isolated modules can be integrated into a flexible, modular CAI system.

Introduction

Computer-assisted instruction (CAI) has become popular in the last 10 years, throughout the world. Courseware has been presented to tens of thousands of students, mostly in an experimental stage. CAI has not proved to be as widely accepted, practised and disseminated, however, as was expected in the initial period. This may be due to the problems encountered in creating high-quality lessons, which must be able to demonstrate the advantages of the new medium in such a way that people other than the creators can be convinced. A second reason may be the fact that there have been no obvious financial advantages of CAI in comparison to conventional educational methods (Fielden, 1977). Another reason is probably the unnecessary creation of many different author languages and CAI systems. This hampered the dissemination of CAI to all levels in education. Within 20 years there have been some tens of author languages developed for convenient and problem-oriented programming. Many CAI systems have been specially designed, some are small systems, whereas others are large. Some have specially designed terminals to present the teaching materials with those systems.

At the Delft University of Technology, Department of Informatics, a CAI project was initiated several years ago. The objective of the project was research concerning the implementation of CAI, using the most recent technological, organizational and educational developments. A few comparative studies (Bode and Dütting, 1972; Leiblum, 1974; Zinn, 1969) show that the art of CAI has been sufficiently developed in order to integrate several fundamental aspects of different streams.

For such an enterprise a first stage would be to enumerate the common aspects of both courseware and of the different author languages, including the systems and methods used to practise CAI.

This has led to the formulation of a new concept in the practical realization and organization of CAI. This will be termed 'Modular CAI'. An experimental CAI system was designed following this concept to evaluate advantages against disadvantages. This paper will discuss the concept, its implementation and the present modest experience in using this experimental CAI system.

Functional Analysis of CAI

Our starting point is an analysis of the most important functions of a CAI system in operation.

In CAI the lesson is stored in the memory of the computer. The computer's main task is to entertain a dialogue with the terminal. This should lead to a certain transport of information from and to the student. This two-way system of transportation is quite essential in CAI, both in order to maintain a good functioning of the dialogue during all sessions and to record the performance of the students for the measurement by the teacher of the impact of the lessons on the student. This means that except for **presenting** lessons, a **record** of the activities of the students also must be kept for analysis later.

The teacher who **designed** a lesson, whether on his own or in a team, should be able to **evaluate** continuously the quality of the lesson on the basis of the registered activities of the student.

The fact that many teachers and students are involved in the same CAI process means that one of the most important functions of CAI is the **distribution** of data.

Management of all mentioned activities is also one of the main functions in CAI. This takes place partially in the computer. The functions mentioned above are depicted schematically in Figure 1.

A closer examination of the functions shown in Figure 1 shows that each function consists of a whole class of activities.

For example we mean with the **design** the completion of the process of making a lesson, i.e.:

— formulating the objectives;
— structuring the course material;
— choice of the educational strategy;
— programming;
— compilation or translation into a final shape;
— testing.

With the **presentation** of a lesson we mean:

— presenting the instructional material;
— analysis of the responses from the students;
— deciding on the proceeding of the lesson.

Recording consists of the storage of:

— all responses of students;
— the response times;
— the path followed through the lesson.

These three elements form the 'historical data'.

Evaluation concerns the analysis of the recorded historical data of students and lessons and of interviews. The objective of this evaluation process is the improvement and adaptation of the lessons.

Distribution takes place in two directions, i.e. the lesson moves from the teacher to the student, whereas historical information is given the other way around.

Management of the whole process includes a multiplicity of activities, such as the administration of all data, which should be distributed, and storage and distribution of all identification codes of students and teachers, each with their own authorizations within the CAI system. In the management function also, that storage of data is included which is required to restart a lesson after a system failure or other disruptions caused by the student.

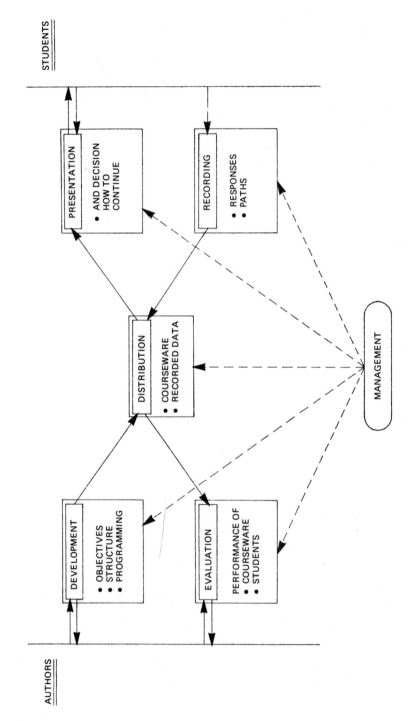

Figure 1. *Functional characteristics of the implementation of computer-assisted instruction*

Note that the above enumeration is far from complete, e.g. the contact between teacher and student on a conventional basis has not been taken into consideration.

In the technical realization of CAI we can observe two developments in two opposite directions, against the background of Figure 1. On the one hand large operational CAI systems with up to 500 terminals per computer are in existence, such as PLATO and IIS of IBM.

One advantage of this approach is that the lesson, or at least the experience in writing a lesson, is easily exchangeable. A disadvantage is the technical and organizational dependence on one central machine, in which all data of students, teachers and lessons are stored. An entirely different trend is the usage of small computers which can locally present lessons via terminals. The lessons are usually developed somewhere else and distributed mechanically.

An advantage of this approach is that its small scale allows the involvement of local computers, already in use for other purposes before CAI is introduced. This is why the costs are seen to be low. One other advantage is the larger flexibility when new technological developments take place. A disadvantage is that one does not have the power of a large computer at one's disposal.

It is still an open question, however, as to what advice to take when the advantages and disadvantages of small versus large CAI systems are considered. For example, the necessity of centralization is questionable for course materials which have taken more or less firm shape after some years of experimentation, and which are virtually self-supporting. The power of a large system is convenient in the early stage of the design of a lesson, when many changes still have to be made.

A Concept for a Modular CAI System

In our search for a modular CAI system it was deemed important that a system should have:

- well-defined interfaces;
- simple possibilities for adding or modifying modules.

The latter possibilities are required in view of technological advancement and changes in user demands. For a system as described above two issues are important:

(1) The large diversity in terms of languages and systems for which many and mostly good teaching materials are available.
(2) The rapid pace of development of performances versus prices, which differ for all sorts of machines. For example, compare the price and performance of very large computers, of microprocessors with floppy or video discs, of intelligent graphical terminals, of communication lines, etc.

In the near future technological innovations could have great influence on the possibilities of the realization of several functions shown in Figure 1.

These considerations were the reasons why this concept was formulated. The six main functions mentioned before could possibly be executed independently by using different computers. The only condition is that the data to be transferred should have a well-defined structure. Therefore the distribution, in particular the characteristics and the form of what has to be distributed is central in the concept, as shown in Figure 1.

The functions which should be carried out are in principle assumed to be independent of each other. In other words, the operation of a CAI system is in principle independent of the manner of implementation of the different functions. It is even possible that different ways of implementation of one and the same function can exist simultaneously in one and the same CAI system. We refer to the possibility that some lessons can simultaneously be followed by using a large computer in a time-sharing system and by using stand-alone intelligent terminals. This is considered as important, both with respect to the technological developments to be expected in the near future and to the different demands made by the users concerning hardware and software in the CAI environment. The courses should be distributed in such a form that their execution can be carried out without too many readjustments, even at different local computers. This form should have the nature of a code in which all necessary CAI actions are represented as a set of instructions. This means that this representation has to be some type of assembler code, executable and interpretable by a hypothetical machine (e.g. an interpreter in a particular computer). This implies that teaching material which is written in an author language should be susceptible for analysis and transfer by a compiler into this CAI assembler code.

Hence, this code should not be more detailed than is required for the complete description of the features of the different author languages. The design of the code should not be limited by the restricted possibilities of certain computers, but should meet as well as possible, the conditions imposed by fundamental CAI actions.

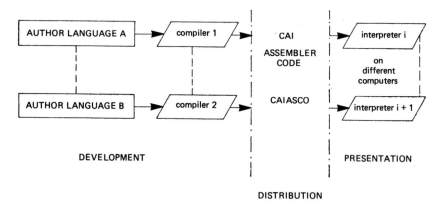

Figure 2. *The main principle of the modular CAI system: isolation of the development and the presentation of courseware*

We defined such a code and termed it CAIASCO (CAI ASsembler COde) as set out in Figure 2. The compilers and interpreters can be situated in various kinds of computers. One compiler is necessary for each author language and one CAIASCO interpreter is necessary for each type of computer. The CAIASCO code is always identical. In this way the courses which are written in one author language can be executed by various kinds of computers. We shall now give a brief description of this CAIASCO code.

CAIASCO

Analysing the different kinds of author languages we found that their facilities consist of a chain of actions which are all part of a limited set, such as:

(1) send a text to the terminal;
(2) move the cursor on the display panel;
(3) send a picture to the terminal;

  (4) execute a calculation;
  (5) set a clock;
  (6) wait for a response from the student;
  (7) switch the response processor;
  (8) analyse a response;
  (9) test a condition;
(10) jump to another part of the lesson.

Some actions have a quite broad and general significance, like action (1), while others are rather technical or apply only to the features of one author language, such as action (7). The number of such elementary CAI activities necessary to describe most of the author languages turns out to be no larger than about 100. The actions involved in these activities are so elementary that it is only from their appearance or from characteristic sequences of such actions that we can recognize what author language is in use.

Due to the elementary nature of these actions it is not simple to write a lesson in such a code. In the structure of the CAIASCO code we took more account of the possibilities of making an interpreter than of the readability for users. However, the code remains as readable as normal assembler codes.

Another important starting point was that the code had to be such that the description of a course in a new author language should not require changes in the code: the code will at most undergo some extensions. (Cf. Wiechers, 1975 and van der Mast and van der Valk, 1976 for a complete description of CAIASCO.)

The Modular CAI System in Delft

A CAI system has been designed and implemented for our research in order to try out the new concept (van der Mast, 1977). The system is functionally split up over several computers, see Figure 3.

Firstly we use an IBM 370/158 to transpose the courses which are fed by batch or interactively in an author language into CAIASCO code. This CAIASCO code is stored on tape or floppy disc for further distribution to the presentation computers. The presentation of the courses can take place in two ways:

(1) By using a dedicated PDP11/45 (28 kw) with eight terminals. The courses are interpreted in this computer. The interpreter is part of an experimental system (CAISYS), which enables users to follow courses in a multi-access way. The CAIASCO code is stored on disc before interpretation takes place. Historical information is recorded on tapes. The content of these tapes can be sorted and analysed by the IBM 370/158 (see Figure 3). An interactive graphics package for the design of static pictures and texts is available at the PDP11/45. The pictures are stored in a device-independent picture code during the stage of design, so that the use of pictures does not depend greatly on the use of certain computers or types of terminals. These pictures may be called by name from the lesson.

(2) We started during the past year with the implementation of an interpreter for a microcomputer. This microcomputer is a stand-alone small computer system with a dual floppy disc unit (LSI11). We decided on microcomputers because of the steep decrease of their prices and their growing possibilities in usage. The distribution to and from this system has to take place by means of floppy discs.

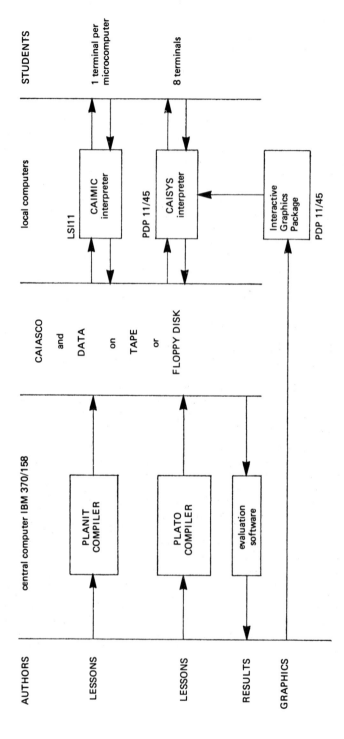

Figure 3. *Overview of the experimental modular CAI system of Delft University of Technology*

The Development of Teaching Materials

The design of a course is carried out in the same way as elsewhere. During the stages of programming and input in the computer, differences can arise compared to other systems. As the author language PLANIT was popular in the Netherlands around 1975 it is natural that we first built a compiler for this language. This compiler was written in ALGOL and has been operational for two years. The compiler informs us not only of syntactical but also of a certain number of semantical errors. Various courses designed elsewhere using a PLANIT system could be transformed into CAIASCO without any difficulty. At the moment a compiler for a subset of TUTOR language of the PLATO system is being developed. For this purpose the CAIASCO code has to be extended with some new actions. This is especially interesting because these two languages which do not resemble one another can be derived into one and the same CAIASCO code.

The Presentation and Registration

CAISYS. The experimental CAI system, CAISYS, contains a CAIASCO interpreter and also software for managing and monitoring lessons in a multi-access way. Special measures have been taken to keep response times of the system below two seconds. After technical failures or after interruptions of courses, one can proceed with the courses without difficulties. Four of the terminals have a wide variety of graphical possibilities.

During sessions students can make use of simple calculating facilities. They may always evaluate only one arithmetic expression. Besides they can define variables and functions necessary for their calculations.

The path followed through a course is monitored by CAISYS for use during the lesson. This information is not the same as the historical data on tape, which is for evaluation afterwards.

In the CAIASCO code, reference can be made to pictures. These pictures can be inserted during the loading of the CAIASCO code. The pictures can be designed by using an interactive graphics package and can be stored in libraries (see Figure 3).

CAIMIC. As a consequence of the latest technical developments in microcomputers we are now in the process of developing a CAIASCO interpreter for a microcomputer (CAIMIC). The possibilities of presenting courses will be similar to that in CAISYS. Students receive a floppy disc with a course recorded on it. Historical data will be stored on another floppy disc which is not available to the student. These stand-alone microcomputers can be easily transported.

The Use of the System

We can distinguish three categories of users of the system:

(1) teachers, authors and programmers;
(2) the manager;
(3) students.

The set up of the system makes an interactive design of courses impossible, so that the **author** cannot follow the course in a student-mode in order to test it.

Experience shows that writing a course is not as simple as we thought, and it is not advisable to present the courseware on the display in a too early stage of the design: the actual design and structuring process should not take place at a terminal. Experience also shows that programming should be carried out by programmers

343

in the design team. In our case, the task of the programmer is not to make a good run of a lesson but to write parts of a lesson in the author language and to convert it into CAIASCO, using the appropriate compiler: the **manager** of the CAI system can then take care of the CAIASCO code so that the course can be followed at terminals. A course in such a design phase should be evaluated as to its correctness, should be judged didactically and tried out by other members of the design team. The necessary changes and corrections can then be communicated to the programmer.

The task of the manager of the system is to insert the CAIASCO code into the CAISYS sub-system. It is also his task to do the accounting of students and lessons in CAISYS and to distribute passwords to students. He should take care of all tapes containing historical data and it is his duty to see that all evaluation programs are available at the large computer. The **students** are the most important users of the system. The objective they have to take place at the terminal is simple: they want to learn something from the courses. The CAI system itself can contribute to the learning process by being as inconspicuous as possible to the student. The characters should be easily read and the response time should not be too long. The terminal must be simple to use. Also the in- and out-logging procedures should be simple. In this respect the CAI system will not differ too much from other CAI systems.

Concluding Remarks

The modular CAI system here described was built in order to check the fundamentals of the underlying concept in practice. Research in this project is being carried out, particularly in the area of computer technology. In line with this approach the organization and planning were not meant to produce a large number of courses.

Experience with large numbers of students and authors has also not been available to date. Technically the system is functioning in accordance with our expectations, however.

In the near future the system will be used more intensively by lecturers and students at the Delft University of Technology. The extension the system will undergo with the compiler for the TUTOR subset and the CAIASCO interpreter for a stand-alone microcomputer system will enable us to test the changeability and the flexibility of this modular CAI system.

References

Bode, A. and Dütting, M. (1972) *Computer-Unterstutzter Unterricht: Probleme, Autorensprachen, Systemvergleiche, Dokumentation.* Diplomarbeit, Karlsruhe.

Fielden, J. (1977) The financial evaluation of NDPCAL. *British Journal of Educational Technology,* **8,** 3, pp.190-200.

Leiblum, M. D. (1974) *An Analytical and Comparative Study of Computer-Assisted-Instruction Programming Languages, their Characteristics and Usage.* Katholieke Universiteit, Nijmegen.

Mast, Charles van der and Valk, Martin van der (1976) *Voortgangsrapport 1976, CAI-project.* Delft University of Technology, Delft.

Mast, Charles van der (1977) *Voortgangsrapport 1977, CAI-project.* Delft University of Technology, Delft.

Wiechers, G. (1975) *Design and Implementation of a System for Computer Assisted Instruction.* University of South Africa, Pretoria.

Zinn, K. L. (1969) *Comparative Study of Languages for Programming Interactive Use of Computers in Instructions.* University of Michigan, Center for Research on Learning and Teaching, Ann Arbor.

46. The CAIPE Project – Aims, Development and Assessment; Computer-Aided Instruction Programs in Economics at the Northern Ireland Polytechnic

D. W. McCulloch, *Northern Ireland Polytechnic, Co. Antrim*

Abstract: The paper describes a mode of CAI where three programs are used as back-up to conventional teaching methods. First, the programming approach is discussed, and this is followed by a description of the project's recent progress, with an exposition on specific programs. Finally, the project is assessed and some consideration given to its implications and possible future developments.

My main objective is to describe and assess the CAIPE project, which has been running at the above polytechnic since September 1977. Accordingly the paper is divided into three sections, the first of which discusses the aims of the project and the programming approach adopted. This gives a basis for the description of the CAIPE project itself in the second part, and the final section is devoted to an assessment of the project, some of its implications, and future developments.

1. Aims

Essentially the problem specification adopted was as follows:

> Using BASIC, write a program which will teach a basic understanding (of demand theory, for example) to one-year students, using a conventional typewriter terminal in conjunction with an ordinary mainframe computer, as a reinforcement of lectures, tutorials, and independent study.

(The computer used is an ICL 1900, with a MAXIMOP multi-access system available for 23 hours a week.)

Two aspects of this specification are noteworthy:

(1) It is couched in relatively vague terms with no detailed definition of what the student should be able to do after having completed the program.
(2) No special teaching materials are to be developed; only the typewriter terminal is to be used.

While a detailed specification of end-behaviours would have permitted an objective assessment (of a kind) of the programs' success, the vagueness of the specification enabled the writer to program in much the same way as he prepares lectures, using his experience as a teacher to design effective teaching strategies. Consideration (1) is therefore a liberating factor, in contrast to (2) – every word printed out has to be included in a 'PRINT' instruction and therefore, to save time, effort and computer space, it was necessary to reduce the number of words and sentences to the minimum consistent with successful learning. In addition to the lack of the student feedback normally available, this puts more pressure on the writer to be concise and effective than does the need to be clear in a spoken presentation. In sum, therefore, like the prospect of hanging, this method of design 'concentrates the mind wonderfully' – in this case, upon the achievement of effective teaching strategies. Using only the terminals also makes the use of these programs feasible on most computer systems, including those incorporating visual display units (if a 'hard copy' is not required).

2. The CAIPE Project

(1) Chronological Development

We begin by defining briefly the facility which is available now, and continue by describing the events which led up to it. A total of 72 students have available to them, for terminal use during time specified by the MAXIMOP timetable, three programs which teach demand theory (DIP1), elasticity theory (ELO1), and which test demand, supply, and elasticity (TST1). All the students were given an introductory talk, a user guide, and in most cases a demonstration run, to introduce them to the mechanics of getting 'on-line'; the programs have been used, with varying degrees of enthusiasm, on a voluntary basis — such use is not a course requirement for any of the students.

The idea that computer programs could help students with some of the important ideas of economics had been with me for some time before writing began in earnest at the start of January 1977. My teaching experience seemed to show that economics was a problem area for many accountancy and business studies students, and that difficulties began with the introduction of the economists's basic analytical tools, functions, and the idea of *ceteris paribus*. Clearly, 'the quantity of a good demanded varies inversely with its price, if nothing else affecting demand changes'— this is perhaps the simplest example of economic analysis, and the one students are usually taught first. A closely related idea is price elasticity of demand, the degree of responsiveness of demand to a change in price, which is measured by the percentage change in quantity demanded divided by the percentage change in price, again assuming nothing else affecting demand changes. The program to teach demand therefore teaches the idea of a function, in the context of an introductory course. The elasticity program gives students assistance in understanding, at a point in their course when their confidence comes under greatest stress — just after coping with the demand curve (if they have) here is elasticity, which seems even tougher. It has been my experience that students can give up trying to understand economics after basic demand theory has proved to be over-taxing.

Having decided to write one program each for demand and elasticity, writing began in January 1977; in the course of this activity, the need for some sort of test program made itself felt — since the program (administering and marking a multiple-choice test) would be relatively easy to write, one felt impelled to give the students an opportunity to self-test as well as to self-instruct. A new set of problems arose when the time came to get the programs tested and running in a mode accessible to students; the help of our computer services department was invaluable at this stage, and our joint efforts got the programs running and available to students by the start of term in September 1977. To date (31 March 1978), we have recorded 117 log-ins to all three programs; about 10 of these must be discounted, as demonstrations, so we have had at least 107 runs made in their own time by individuals from a population of 72 students.

(2) Programming

The following shows, first, a sample of output from DIP1, and second, the BASIC instructions which produced it. The program is more or less self-explanatory, except for lines 724 and 866, which read 'IF T = 999 THEN 7000'. This is a 'get-out' provision which enables students, at any point where input is normally required, to jump the remainder of the program by typing in '999' instead of a normal response. The same question and answer format is common to DIP1 and ELO1, though the length of the text between questions varies; the 999 procedure is common to all three programs. What follows, therefore, illustrates the programming technique fairly well. However, in order to shed light on the programming process, those specific techniques which have emerged so far are listed and described below.

(a) LOOPING. This is a standard programming technique — in this context, the student is asked a question with (for example) four possible answers. Each time he makes a wrong answer he is asked (with or without a special text for his 1st, 2nd or 3rd mistake) to try again; in order to ensure that computer time is not wasted, a maximum number of tries is set, whether there are four possible answers, or where the student is required to type in a word. (Used in all programs.)

(b) SCORING. We must tally a student's score in a multiple-choice test; the allocation in TEST is 4 for the first answer being right, 2 for the second and 1 for the third, but this allocation may be altered as desired.

(c) RETURNING. After completing the whole program, it is possible to return the student to the beginning or to other appropriate sections of the program. (Used so far in DIP only.)

(d) STUDENT TEXT. When the student is asked to construct a figure, (e.g. a demand curve), his comprehension or otherwise of the preceding text will show itself, and will be demonstrated by his answer to a computer question about the figure (e.g. 'Does it slope downwards and to the right?' [Type in 'Yes' or 'No']). This is one solution to the problem of organizing and obtaining visual displays which draw graphs, and is used in DIP.

(e) GET-OUT. It is necessary to enable the student to end the program quickly — whenever input is required in the normal course of the program, provision has been made so that the student may type in 999 instead of the answer asked for. This will automatically terminate the program after an appropriate message, and is used in all three programs.

(f) BRANCHING. The correct answer to a question produces one text, the wrong answer another, though the wrong answer returns the student to the common stream of the program eventually. This is used to some extent in both DIP and ELO1.

3. Assessment, Implications, and Future Developments

The main cost was the time taken to write the programs; the computer time required is not extensive, especially when compared to sort programs or statistical packages. It has been reckoned that one hour of instruction in programmed learning normally takes 200 hours to prepare; at a rough estimate, I would guess that the three programs, about one hour's instruction in all, took approximately 160 hours to prepare and implement. The faster time is largely the result of the vague specification described in the first section.

The benefits are not easily measurable, though I would argue that the voluntary use of the programs over 107 times, by students from a population of 72, is good evidence that the programs are successful in assisting learning. Further, unlike members of staff, programs do not get tired, and are always available during the

347

```
IF THE PRICE OF BEER
FELL TO 25 PENCE A PINT,
WHAT WOULD HAPPEN
TO THE DEMAND FOR IT?

  RISE:1  FALL:2  STAY THE SAME:3
  CAN'T TELL:4    (TYPE IN 1, 2, 3, OR 4)
← 1
    YOU MIGHT EXPECT IT TO,
    BUT WOULD IT?

  THIS IS A SNEAKY QUESTION -
  HAVE I SAID ANYTHING
  ABOUT O.T.R.E.?

    AND IF I HAVEN'T
    CAN YOU TELL (PREDICT)
    WHAT WOULD HAPPEN?

TYPE IN THE RIGHT ANSWER.
← 3
DO YOU REALLY THINK SO?
THINK AGAIN,
AND TRY ANOTHER ANSWER.
← 2
DO YOU REALLY THINK SO?
THINK AGAIN,
AND TRY ANOTHER ANSWER.
← 4
    QUITE RIGHT;

    ALL THAT IS STATED
    IS THAT PRICE HAS FALLEN
    --IF, ALSO, INCOMES HAD BEEN HALVED,
    AND/OR THE PRICE OF WHISKY CUT BY 60%,
    THEN THE OUTCOME WOULD HAVE BEEN
    QUITE DIFFERENT FROM THAT EXPECTED.

IN JANUARY,
THE PRICE OF COD IN BIRMINGHAM FISH MARKET
WAS 90 PENCE PER POUND.
IN FEBRUARY, THE PRICE ROSE
TO £1.10 PER POUND.
    ASSUMING O.T.R.E.,
    DID THE QUANTITY OF COD DEMANDED:
RISE:1  FALL:2  STAY THE SAME:3  CAN'T TELL:4
    (TYPE IN 1, 2, 3, OR 4)
← 4
  THIS IS *** NOT *** A SNEAKY QUESTION;
  READ IT AGAIN,
  AND TYPE IN THE CORRECT ANSWER.
← 3
  NO - THINK AGAIN,
  AND TRY ANOTHER ANSWER.
← 1
  NO - THINK AGAIN,
  AND TRY ANOTHER ANSWER.
← 2
  CORRECT.
```

```
680   PRINT"IF THE PRICE OF BEER"
682   PRINT"FELL TO 25 PENCE A PINT",
684   PRINT"WHAT WOULD HAPPEN"
686   PRINT"TO THE DEMAND FOR IT?"
688   PRINT"   "
690   PRINT"  RISE:1  FALL:2  STAY THE SAME:3
      CAN'T TELL:4"
692   PRINT"    (TYPE IN 1, 2, 3, OR 4)"
720   INPUT T
724   IF T = 999 THEN 7000
726   IF T = 1  THEN 760
730   IF T = 4  THEN 800
734   PRINT"DO YOU REALLY THINK SO?"
736   PRINT"THINK AGAIN,"
738   PRINT"AND TRY ANOTHER ANSWER."
750   GO TO 720
760   PRINT"   YOU MIGHT EXPECT IT TO,"
761   PRINT"   BUT WOULD IT?"
762   PRINT"   "
763   PRINT"  THIS IS A SNEAKY QUESTION-"
764   PRINT"  HAVE I SAID ANYTHING"
765   PRINT"  ABOUT O.T.R.E.?"
766   PRINT"   "
767   PRINT"   AND IF I HAVEN'T,"
768   PRINT"   CAN YOU TELL (PREDICT)"
769   PRINT"   WHAT WOULD HAPPEN?"
770   PRINT"   "
772   PRINT"TYPE IN THE RIGHT ANSWER."
790   GO TO 720
800   PRINT"   QUITE RIGHT;"
802   PRINT"   ALL THAT IS STATED"
803   PRINT"   IS THAT PRICE HAS FALLEN"
804   PRINT"   --IF, ALSO, INCOMES HAD
      BEEN HALVED,"
805   PRINT"   AND/OR THE PRICE OF WHISKY
      CUT BY 60%,"
806   PRINT"   THEN THE OUTCOME WOULD
      HAVE BEEN"
807   PRINT"   QUITE DIFFERENT FROM THAT
      EXPECTED."
830   PRINT"   "
831   PRINT" IN JANUARY,"
832   PRINT" THE PRICE OF COD IN
      BIRMINGHAM FISH MARKET"
833   PRINT"WAS 90 PENCE PER POUND."
834   PRINT" IN FEBRUARY, THE PRICE ROSE"
835   PRINT" TO £1.10 PER POUND."
836   PRINT"   ASSUMING O.T.R.E.,"
837   PRINT"   DID THE QUANTITY OF COD
      DEMANDED:"
840   PRINT"RISE:1  FALL:2  STAY THE
      SAME:3  CAN'T TELL:4"
842   PRINT"    (TYPE IN 1, 2, 3, OR 4)"
860   INPUT T
866   IF T = 999 THEN 7000
870   IF T = 2  THEN 900
874   IF T = 4  THEN 888
880   PRINT"  NO - THINK AGAIN,"
881   PRINT"  AND TRY ANOTHER ANSWER."
884   GO TO 860
888   PRINT"  THIS IS *** NOT *** A
      SNEAKY QUESTION;"
889   PRINT"  READ IT AGAIN,"
890   PRINT"  AND TYPE IN THE CORRECT ANSWER."
895   GO TO 860
900   PRINT"CORRECT."
```

Figure 1

Figure 2

specified MAXIMOP periods, so that students having difficulty with economics can try to set things right on their own.

So far as implications are concerned, to me the most important feature of DIP1 and ELO1 is that here we have two explicit statements of teaching strategies; in this way, I teach demand, and in this way, I teach elasticity, for reasons, more or less formal, drawn from my teaching experience — design of such programs therefore enables discussion of teaching strategies which would not take place otherwise, quite apart from giving the programmer increased insight even when he works on his own. If there are definable principles of learning, discussion of such programs may help towards their discovery; this is at least in part the result of the fact that when the student is using a program he is not being taught by another person directly.

Finally, there are two directions for future developments — firstly, a program is already in the process of being written which teaches the rules for banking business required by the UK monetary authorities. The process of deposit expansion via banks' lending activities and the significance of the ratios specified by the Bank of England are both difficult areas for students, though they are fundamental to an understanding of money in our economy. The program seeks to remedy this by giving students the task of buying and selling a banker's assets to maximize profits; when a transaction is made which contravenes one of the necessary ratios, the student is given the reason for his sale or purchase being disallowed, and is asked to make a new transaction.

Evidently there are various difficult aspects of economics for which one could write programs; it is reasonable to suppose however that there are key problem areas in other subjects which have the significance (to the learner) of demand and elasticity. The second direction of development therefore is to examine other subjects to discover those areas in which the design of programs will give the greatest pay-off, and such an examination has already begun, in collaboration with one of my colleagues at the polytechnic, within the accounting subject area. It is worth noting that DIP1 and ELO1 have been relatively easy to write because they teach analytical techniques, not facts or specific procedures, and this will have to be borne in mind when topics are chosen and learning objectives specified (if appropriate) for programs in subjects other than economics.

Bibliography

Hooper, R. (ed.) (1975) *Computer Assisted Learning in the UK — Some Case Studies.* Council for Educational Technology, London.

Lumsden, K.G. (ed.) (1967) *New Developments in the Teaching of Economics.* Prentice-Hall, Englewood Cliffs, New Jersey.

Lumsden, K.G. (ed.) (1970) *Recent Research in Economics Education.* Prentice-Hall, Englewood Cliffs, New Jersey.

Noble, H.M. (1973) *Presenter: An Author Language for Computer Assisted Instruction.* Bionics Research Laboratory, School of Artificial Intelligence, University of Edinburgh.

Self, J.A. (1974) Student models in computer-aided instruction. *International Journal of Man-Machine Studies,* **6**, 2.

47. Resources for an Independent Study Course

A. **Brew**, *The Open University, Cambridge Office*

Abstract: The paper discusses the facilities which are required to implement an Open University course in a conventional university and illustrates the extent to which various resources and facilities were used when an OU course was introduced into the electrical engineering degree programme at Essex. Attention is drawn to the decisions involved, and it is argued that the amount of time spent on preparing and running the course compares favourably with other independent study courses.

Introduction

Present-day innovation in higher education has to take account on the one hand of the growing demand for individualization of learning, while being subject on the other to various resource constraints. These two factors tend to pull in opposite directions. Individualized learning can be costly in terms of staff preparation or supervision time, and can require greater resources than more conventional forms of teaching. (Roach and Hammond, 1976; Yorke, 1976; Unsworth, 1976.) Open University courses provide traditional universities with the potential for using carefully designed multi-media independent learning courses without increasing staff time, and this paper considers the factors which have to be taken into account in assessing the cost-effectiveness of using an Open University course within a conventional university setting.

The paper draws on information from an evaluation of the use by the Department of Electrical Engineering Science at the University of Essex of one second-level half-credit Open University course (Zorkoczy and Matheson, 1976). The evaluation is 'illuminative' in its approach (Brew, 1978). MacDonald (1973) has defined illuminative evaluation as 'the process of conceiving, obtaining and communicating information for the guidance of educational decision making with regard to a specified programme'. This view of evaluation involves, in the context of the present paper, the presentation of information relating to the cost of using an Open University course in one conventional university, but carries with it in recognition of the uniqueness of particular situations, the impossibility of judging the general cost-effectiveness of such schemes.

Comparing the costs of Open University teaching methods with those of traditional teaching, Laidlaw and Layard (1974) argue that there is a strong case for using existing Open University packages in conventional universities due to the fact that the variable cost per student-course is generally substantially lower for Open University courses. This assumes, however, that the cost to the user institution of putting on an Open University course can be estimated on the cost of producing that course. What it does not take into account are the additional facilities and resources, including staff time, required to adapt an Open University course to suit particular circumstances. The costs of using an Open University course in a

350

conventional university must be calculated on the basis not only of the costs of producing the course package and the consequent costs per student, but must also take into account additional costs of implementation.

The costs of introducing a new course into a traditional setting are clearly tied to local conditions, for example, the facilities and resources which are available, the possible alternative uses of these facilities and the local cost of such facilities. Evaluation of cost-effectiveness depends on such things as the size of local budgets and, of course, on who is paying. Indeed, consideration of the cost to the user institution of one Open University course shows that there is potential flexibility in the way in which the course may be used, i.e. the user can to some extent tailor the course to fit his budget. This paper therefore draws attention to the resources and facilities required to put on an Open University course and, using evidence from the Essex evaluation, discusses the extent to which they are likely to be needed.

Bearing in mind that each innovation is a unique situation, the aim of the discussion is to provide information to enable potential users of Open University courses to make realistic cost assessments. It should be noted that this paper is not concerned with large-scale innovations involving the setting up of Open University style institutions, but is concerned with the introduction of Open University courses within pre-existing conventional university frameworks. I shall distinguish resources and facilities specific to the course which was introduced at the University of Essex, and those required for the majority of Open University courses.

The Adaptation of an Open University Course to meet Local Conditions

A discussion of how the Open University course was used at the University of Essex provides an illustration of the way in which such a course can be adapted to suit local conditions, while at the same time retaining its original character as a multi-media independent learning course.

The course in question is the Open University course *The Digital Computer* (The Open University, 1975). As used by Open University students, the course comprises 16 separate units, each representing approximately 10-15 hours of work and each designed to be studied over a two-week period. These 16 units comprise 15 written texts and one collection of papers, or 'file unit'. There are 11 television and 16 radio programmes.

A special home-kit mini-computer (Opus 1) was developed for use with the course, and each Open University student is loaned one of these to use at home. Students perform a series of experiments on the Opus 1 computer, and a series (called Opus 2) using computer terminals located in local Study Centres and linked to the Open University Computing Service.

In the Open University, the course is assessed by four Tutor Marked Assignments (TMA's) and four Computer Marked Assignments (CMA's). There is in addition a three-hour examination. Marks for the best three TMA's and the best three CMA's count approximately 50 per cent towards the final grade. There is a series of 'mock' TMA's and CMA's, the answers to which are discussed in radio programmes. The course is backed up by approximately 12 hours of local or regional tutorials or day schools.

The Open University course 'package' was introduced into the second year electrical engineering degree scheme at the University of Essex. The greater part of this programme is made up of conventional lecture courses backed up by laboratory work. At the outset of the experiment at Essex, a fundamental decision had to be taken concerning the way in which the Open University course material was to be used. One alternative would have been to give a series of lectures on topics of importance and to require students to treat the Open University textual material as background or additional reading. This idea was rejected in favour of using the units for the purposes for which they were intended, namely as material for independent study. Staff putting on the course felt that in this way they would be able to combine the advantages of the Open University in terms of careful preparation and presentation of course materials for independent study, with those of the conventional university in being able to provide face-to-face tutorial support. During the academic year, 48 hours of tuition time were, therefore, scheduled for the course. This was used to provide additional material on the electronic hardware of computers which is not covered in the Open University material, to play radio and television programmes and to discuss difficult concepts, note important points, link ideas and discuss assignments.

The traditional way of assessing the electrical engineering degree programme at Essex was by end-of-year examinations for all courses and a progress examination at Christmas for courses followed in the Autumn term. In the first year of the Open University experiment, assessment remained unchanged. In the second year, however, it was decided to introduce CMA's for the Open University course and to allow these to count for 10 per cent of the students' final grade. The fact that there were only two members of staff involved in running the course with 95 students following it, was felt to make continuous tutor-marked assessment impracticable.

Some of the radio and television programmes were found to be unsuitable for use at Essex, because their content was too general or because they related specifically to the Open University situation. Moreover, it was felt that lectures were a better medium for discussions of the 'talking heads' type. Therefore, although almost all of the broadcast material was used in the first year of presentation, in the second year only three radio and five television programmes were used.

Arrangements were made in the first year for students to complete the Opus 1 experiments on an Opus 1 emulator to a PDP8 computer. In the second year, this facility was supplemented by one Opus machine, and for the third year a second one is being supplied. Opus 2 experiments were performed on a terminal linked to the PDP11/45 computer in the department. The equipment is located permanently in a laboratory.

Materials and Facilities required for the Course

As mentioned in the introduction, the cost of the physical resources required to put on an Open University course depend very much on what is locally available and the use to which these resources would otherwise be put. It is hoped that by drawing attention to the extent to which the resources are likely to be needed, potential users will be able to make their own estimations based on knowledge of local conditions.

The decision to use the Open University course as material for independent study at Essex meant that each student needed a copy of the textual material and it was decided to loan students a set of course materials for the duration of the academic year. An alternative would have been to require students to buy the material, but the staff did not favour this idea. They estimated that the units should last about five years, which is the lifetime originally planned for many Open University courses. Loaning the units does, however, tend to influence the way students study the material. It means, for example, that they need to make notes on points to be remembered and that they cannot comment in the large margin provided for this purpose in the Open University texts. It also means they cannot record answers to self-assessment questions which are set throughout the course in places provided in the text itself. The self-study task is therefore made somewhat more irksome than it might be, and places greater reliance on note-taking skills.

When and how to distribute the textual material and where to store it in vacations is an important question with which the potential user needs to concern himself. Distributing sets of course units to the 95 students following the course at Essex and collecting, checking and storing the sets at the end of the academic year was clearly quite a considerable task.

Experience with the broadcast material suggests that each Open University programme needs to be considered with respect to the particular contribution it makes to the course and its suitability for use outside the Open University. Facilities were not available at the University of Essex for students to watch and listen to broadcast material individually. Recordings were, therefore, played to the whole group in the lecture theatre at scheduled times. Television programmes were played under licence using closed circuit television monitors and a Philips video-cassette recorder. The cost to the user institution of showing films in this way is the cost of the video-cassettes plus fees for each showing, plus the cost of technician time for the recording of the programmes. An alternative would have been the purchase or hire of 16 millimetre film. The advantages of tapes are that if it is decided not to use all of the programmes, the tapes can be put to another use. They are also cheaper to buy than film. The disadvantages are that recording the programmes at scheduled viewing times may be inconvenient and depends on having access to BBC television. In addition, the quality may not be as good and, importantly, tapes are less durable than film.

Radio programmes may similarly be recorded onto cassettes or tapes by the user institutions from scheduled broadcasts, but if the cost of paying technical staff to record the programmes is taken into account, there is no saving in cost over purchasing pre-recorded tapes from the Open University.

In addition to the books of units, there are also for each Open University course varying amounts of supplementary material. This refers to written material which adds to and enhances the course, and includes course guides, broadcast notes, experiment booklets (e.g. for Opus 1 and Opus 2), assignment booklets and may also include reproduced articles.

The original Open University course guide for TM221 was inappropriate for use at Essex, since much of the material it contained was relevant only to Open University students. In the first year of the Essex experiment, no substitute was provided. However, during the course of that year it became apparent that there was a need for students to know how the component parts of the course related together, for advice on how to study and for instructions concerning the different kinds of assessment. This accords with Bridge's (1976) finding that in the initial stages of an independent study course, teachers felt it important to make clear to students what they were expected to do and what they should learn. For the second year of using the Open University course, a guide to it was written by the Essex staff. In addition, the experiment and broadcast booklets required modifications to suit the particular circumstances at Essex.

Although they were not required to complete the TMA's for formal assessment purposes, students at Essex were supplied with the assignment booklet containing the TMA's and CMA's, which were used for class discussion. As mentioned earlier, facilities for CMA's were provided by using the Opus 2 system linked to the PDP11/45 computer. There were four CMA's throughout the academic year. Students fed their answers into the computer at a terminal in the laboratory and after the deadline for a particular assignment were able to receive their grade and a model answer, again from the terminal. The CMA's were the same ones as set in the

Materials	Cost per set of materials (1978 prices)	Additional facilities/resources	Extent of use
Textual material Books (one set per student required)	£16.95	Storage space required during the Summer vacations	378,000 cu cm of space for 100 sets of Units
Broadcast material Radio programmes: audio tapes	£18.30	Audio cassette player	Used for 8 hours approximately
Television programmes: *either* Films To buy	£1,362.00 (complete set)	16 mm projector	Total projection time 4 hours 35 minutes
To hire — black and white	£8.80 (per film) + VAT + Carriage (£1)		
Total cost	£115.54		
— colour	£10.80 (per film) + VAT + Carriage (£1)		
Total cost	£139.30		
or Video-cassettes (11 x ½ hour tapes)	£141.35	Closed circuit television monitors and video-cassette	Assuming each recording is played to students once. These are used for approximately 4½ hours viewing per year
with: Licence fees per annum	£77.00	Technical staff to record programmes 5 hours approx.	If recordings are made on site, 4½ hours recording time in addition is used
Supplementary materials (Open University supplies one set)	£5.00	Secretarial services Printing: experiment booklet course guide broadcast notes	Typing of material. Approximately 14 hours 40 sheets printed back to back and bound (£37.00 per 100) 19 pages back to back and bound (£20.40 per 100) 23 sheets printed, collated and stapled (£18.60 per 100) Prices in brackets are those at the University of Essex and are included as a guide.

Materials	Cost per set of materials (1978 prices)	Additional facilities/resources	Extent of use
Opus mini-computer	£170.00	PDP8 (Opus emulator)	Computer resources estimated at: Connect time = 4 hours per student
		PDP11/45 (Opus 2)	Disc storage space for all Opus 2 programmes = 256 blocks of 512 bytes
			It was not possible to separately estimate processor time used for Opus 2 but a small allowance should naturally be made for this.
		Technical help	Depends on reliability of Opus, but not more than 3-4 hours per year.

Table 1. *Summary of materials and facilities needed for the Open University course TM221*

Open University, so resources required were simple extra computer and terminal time.

A number of Open University courses include a 'home experiment kit'. In the case of TM221, the kit is a 'cheap' mini-computer (Opus 1). Although Opus 1 is cheap in computer terms, to have supplied every Essex student taking the course with one of these would have greatly added to the overall cost per student. (They cost £170.) As mentioned earlier, in the first year of using the course at the University of Essex, the mini-computer was emulated on an existing PDP8 computer; one which was not used exclusively for the purposes of this course. The emulation did not, however, prove satisfactory and so one Opus machine was supplied in the second year. As the machine was available 12 hours a day, there were few problems regarding the sharing of this machine by 95 students. However, it is felt to be advantageous to have a second machine in case of failure. Facilities for the Opus 2 experimental work, as for the CMA's, were provided on the department's PDP11/45 computer.

The experimental work also required laboratory space where students could have access to a computer terminal. Technical help was also needed when machines did not function properly or when students experienced problems.

The cost of the Open University course materials and the extent to which the facilities required to implement the course were used at the University of Essex, are summarized in Table 1.

Time Spent Preparing and Running the Course

Two members of the academic staff were responsible for the Open University course. One of these was familiar with the course through having worked on the course team and did not, therefore, have to spend time initially reading it. In the initial stages of the experiment the strategic aspects of how to implement the course were a major preoccupation for him, although the actual amount of time spent drafting detailed proposals amounted to little more than one afternoon. In preparing for lectures and classes, he said he spent a couple of days working out the kinds of things he was going to concentrate on (e.g. difficult concepts, linking things in different parts of the course), and then used these categories as he went along, picking out before each lecture the relevant points of the appropriate unit. The other member of staff responsible for the course had not read the units prior to becoming involved in the experiment, and so was initially involved in an estimated 60 hours of reading and preparation for lectures and classes.

The major preparatory work in the first year was in relation to the Opus 1 emulator to the PDP8 and the Opus 2 programme for the PDP11/45. For the second year, the major task was the preparation of the guide to the course and the revision of the broadcast, the assignment, and the experiment booklets. Other preparatory work involved checking and testing the Opus machine and preparing the computer programme for the CMA's. It was not necessary to do any other work in relation to the PDP8 and PDP11/45 computer systems. Preparation for lectures included extending notes to include points of difficulty which emerged during the first year.

The amount of time estimated to have been spent on the course is summarized in Table 2.

This Table ignores the amount of time staff spent dealing with individual problems and queries raised by students. It was felt that the amount of time spent was largely at the discretion of the lecturer, but did not amount to more than an hour a week on average.

There is ample research evidence to suggest that independent study courses in

	Lecturer A	Lecturer B
First year of presentation		
Initial preparation: reading, preparing classes, etc.	25 hours	60 hours
Preparing experimental work	120 hours	—
Running time		
Classes — electronic hardware lectures given by other staff	(8 hours)	(8 hours)
Playing radio and television programmes	(6½ hours)	(5 hours)
'Lecturing' time	9½ hours	12 hours
Preparing and marking examination papers	24 hours	24 hours
Total time spent in first year	193 hours	109 hours
Second year of presentation		
Preparation	80-120 hours (shared)	
Running time		
Lectures on additional topics by other staff	(8 hours)	(8 hours)
Playing radio and television programmes	(2½ hours)	(2 hours)
'Lecturing' time	13½ hours	14 hours
Preparing and marking examination papers	24 hours	24 hours
Total time spent in second year	108 hours	108 hours

Note: Figures in brackets refer to times when the staff running the Open University course were present in an audience rather than participatory capacity

Table 2. *Summary of amount of time estimated to have been spent on the Open University course by the academic staff responsible for it*

general tend to involve large amounts of preparation and running time (Bridge, 1976; Roach and Hammond, 1976), and it is against such evidence that the experience at Essex needs to be assessed. The amount of time spent by the academic staff on preparing and running the Open University course compares very favourably with other independent study courses.

Whether the amount of time that was spent is more or less than that spent preparing and running a traditional lecture course is a matter for each individual lecturer to decide for himself. At the University of Essex, the lecturers' perceptions were that the amount of time spent preparing the course was a little more than a conventional lecture course and the running time was less. The following quotation by one staff member exemplifies the character of the work involved in putting on an Open University course:

Because people are going at different speeds you've got to have everything ready pretty well before you start, because you've got to tell the students what they're going to do. If they're going to answer CMA's they've got to know about that to begin with, because that's going to affect the whole way they do their self-paced instruction, if they're going to do it properly. So you've got to have the CMA system set up, you've got to have the broadcasting all ready, preferably a timetable for lectures and broadcasts, deadlines for CMA's, etc. The only scope for modification on the way through is probably the things like you could produce an addendum to the study guide which would make a few extra points about sensible study methods. But anything that's a component of the course proper, you have to get it all sorted out down to the last nut and bolt before you start. Therefore, because it's done in the abstract, as it were, or ahead of the event, you've got to take more care, be more precise about how you do it.

Summary and Conclusions

This paper has discussed the facilities which are required to implement an Open University course in a conventional university and has illustrated the extent to which various resources and facilities were used when an Open University course was introduced into the electrical engineering degree programme at the University of Essex. The paper draws attention to the possibilities for choice in implementing such a course and the decisions which have, therefore, to be taken. In addition, it has been argued that the amount of time spent on preparing and running the course compares favourably with other independent study courses.

The demand for resources and the financial cost of materials are clearly of significance in deciding whether to use an Open University course in a traditional university. However, in conclusion, mention should perhaps be made of two significant achievements of the Open University course which was used at the University of Essex. These were firstly, a noticeable improvement in student attainment compared with the course it replaced and secondly, a large measure of satisfaction in teaching the course. It is achievements such as these which justify the introduction of an Open University course into a conventional university environment.

References

Brew, A. (June 1978) Developing a methodology for an evaluation. *Assessment in Higher Education*, 3, 3.

Bridge, W. (1976) Self-study courses in undergraduate science teaching: the report of a survey. *Higher Education*, 5, pp.211-24.

Laidlaw, B. and Layard, R. (1974) Traditional versus Open University teaching methods: a cost comparison. *Higher Education*, 3, pp.439-68.

MacDonald, B. (1973) Educational evaluation of the National Development Programme in Computer Assisted Learning. A proposal for consideration by the CAL programme Committee. In *The Programme at Two*, University of East Anglia, Norwich (Centre for Applied Research into Education).

Roach, K. and Hammond, R. (1976) Zoology by self-instruction. *Studies in Higher Education*, 1, 2, pp.179-96.

The Open University (1975) *TM221, The Digital Computer*. The Open University Press, Milton Keynes.

Unsworth, P. (1976) The Keller Plan: costs and benefits of self-paced study. Paper presented at the Conference on Efficiency in Higher Education, University of London, UTMU, April.

Yorke, D. M. (1976) Microteaching versus lectures: a case study in cost-effectiveness. Paper presented at the Conference on Efficiency in Higher Education, University of London, UTMU, April.

Zorkoczy, P. and Matheson, W. S. (1976) The use of an Open University course in a conventional university environment. *Proceedings of the Conference on the Teaching of Electronic Engineering in Degree Courses*, University of Hull, April.

Chapter 8:
Learning and Perception

Educational technology is concerned with everything leading to the improvement of learning. It is appropriate that educational technologists should pause from time to time, and consider what psychologists can tell them about the learning process, and the learner himself.

Mr Fleming (48) argues the need for a more realistic image of the learner. He provides a detailed psychological argument of why careful assessment of the learner may be of much more significance than exclusive consideration of the teaching process. He outlines the assumptions behind a technological approach to teaching, and argues instead for a 'shared understanding of human action' where the learner is 'a socially responsible being who takes action', rather than someone who is passively taught.

In the next paper (49) the same author is joined by Mr Coles, and the effects of students' attitudes to learning on their actual progress are examined. The authors argue that 'how to study' instruction can only be really useful if it is related directly to the subject matter and 'professionalism' relevant to each specific field of study considered.

Dr Kirschner and Dr van der Brink (50) delve even deeper into the psychology of learning in their assessment of aspects of learning from video-taped lessons. It may well be 'sobering' to those developing educational materials to read the degree of statistical and psychological detail which may be analysed from careful investigations of students' performance using such materials.

After 'in-depth' psychology, it may appear a trivial question to ask 'Is it easier to read *across* or *down* tables?' However, considering the universality of 'searching for data in tables', it must surely be of value to find out what layout of tabular data is easier to search. Dr Hartley and his colleagues (51) report an interesting initial study of the situation, with scientific analysis of exactly *what* occurs during a search, and timings of successive searches of the same data table. If at present the conclusions of the initial survey may be found (to say the least) surprising, it will be interesting to see further work on this subject. Maybe before long, an additional recommendation in the 'notes for authors' will prescribe the more effective of the possible layouts for tabular information!

48. The Shared Understanding of Human Action: A More Appropriate Goal for Educational Technology?

W. G. Fleming, *Department of Teaching Media, University of Southampton*

Abstract: The paper examines the effects of implementing a technological approach to education, focusing particularly on the implied image of the learner. It outlines an alternative, more realistic image, and examines its implications for the conception and practice of educational technology.

Introduction

We are becoming increasingly aware of current discontent with our educational system. Many pupils dislike school and their teachers claim little job satisfaction. While some 10 to 15 years ago educational technology might have been seen as the answer to these problems, this is no longer so. The fond hopes of the past have faded. Both inside and outside educational technology the validity of a technological approach to educational issues is being questioned. While we may have thought a systematic approach seemed reasonable, we have become increasingly distrustful of the systems to which it gives rise. Where an educational technology approach is implemented, 'the system' can so easily take over. There is evidence of this in the Open University — an institution designed particularly with a technological approach in mind. Andrew Northedge (1976), who is close to Open University student reaction, comments that students feel 'courses are not so much something to do, as something done to them'. They feel the course is controlled, and course decisions are made not by them, nor their tutors, but by the system. By and large, the student must 'fit in' or 'get out'. Even the designers of the course are constrained by numerous explicit and implicit expectations inherent in the technological approach. This increases the distance between those at the teaching/learning coal-face and the point of decision-making about what will be learned where, when, how and why. Programmed learning and individualized instruction are other examples of this type of 'cling-wrap' teaching system in which learner-determined movement is minimal.

The Assumptions of a Technological Approach

This approach carries within it a number of assumptions which need to be made explicit. The overriding assumption is that the application of technological systems by the experts familiar with them is most likely to achieve the desired results. The best we can do is to adhere to the supposedly objectively determined probabilistic conditional (McAleese, 1977) principles and practices our scientific research has generated. From this a number of other assumptions emerge.

Firstly, educational ends become defined, not in the learner's terms, but in the terms of the educational technologist and his technology. What is to count as valid educational experience and achievement is determined by the system rather than by the persons wanting education. The political function of problem definition and solution has been transformed into technical and technological manipulations.

Secondly, teaching rather than learning is seen as *the* fundamental activity of education. The focus of our attention has become how the teacher can arrange an environment so that the learning will be optimized — the manipulative system to which Rowntree (1974) refers. Despite protestations to the contrary, such systems are not about the conditions of learning but they are about the conditions of teaching. They tell us little about how learners can manipulate their environment to achieve their own learning purposes. Even the implicit analogies for learning processes described by Northedge (1976) are strictly from a teaching perspective. They describe alternative conceptions of teaching, not autonomous learning.

Thirdly, this emphasis on teaching has distorted our image of the learner. While within the constraints of the system teachers are seen to be planners and decision-makers, learners are seen as recipients and reactors whose responses are determined completely by the teaching system. What we claim is 'helping learners to learn' in practice becomes 'ensuring learners cannot but learn'. They are seen as characteristically incompetent.

Alternative assumptions are possible, more realistic and more in accord with our conceptions of what education is all about.

Our image of the learner is a point at which we might start. Any change in such an image will have major ramifications for other assumptions we make about teaching and learning. The image of man dominant in educational technology and made explicit in Skinnerian psychology is quite inappropriate to education. It is an image stripped of any congruence with reality, generated by a narrow and confined view of what counts as valid scientific explanation. Neither have the information processing and cognitive process models of man demonstrated their adequacy. What we need is an image of man which is more realistic, i.e. can cope with the sort of beings we feel we are. Any explanation of our educational endeavour must heighten our understanding of reality as we perceive it, not deny it or ignore it.

Alternative Assumptions — Action Man

But what image of the learner would be more realistic? Shotter (1975) and Gauld and Shotter (1977) have started to map out for psychology an image of man which avoids the manipulative implications of Skinnerian and information-processing theories. Central to this image is the concept of human action — movements we make in order to fulfil our intentions. This conception focuses on our ability to control what we do. In a learning situation we are able to determine our own goals be they very broad and vague or very precise. We are able to select appropriate strategies to achieve our goals and can judge when we have achieved them. We can, in retrospect, think about our experiences clarifying their meaning and significance. We do not think of our own learning experiences as things which just happen to us, we feel we are in control, that we are doing our own learning. We feel ourselves to be characteristically competent. Bruner (1974) makes similar points when considering the findings from studies of early childhood learning. He concludes, 'Human intelligence is active and seeking. Action and the search for meaning are guided by intention, self-directive.'

There seems no good reason to suppose that in any learning situation, the learner will be any less self-defining and self-determining. Yet our technological approach has consistently denied this image of the learner. It has reflected back to him an image of himself as a learner which denies the autonomy and self-determination he experiences outside his formal schooling.

This concept of action, or at least activity, is not new in educational technology.

We have long advocated the involvement of the learner with the learning material. We have devised elaborate schemes mostly of a questioning variety, to galvanize the learner into such involvement. But, in essence, we have confused 'being active' for 'taking action'. We have foisted on learners our activities with our goals assessed in our terms, taking little account of the intentions and purposes, expectations, goals and values of the learner. Significant control has largely remained in the clutches of the system. This is particularly so within structured packaged material. The meaningfulness of the activity to the learner is severely restricted because he is denied any share in understanding the reasons for it. It is assumed that doing is what is important rather than knowing the reasons for doing. This form of active involvement is rather like playing a game, knowing the rules but not knowing what counts as winning. Yet, as we know, learners often perceive hidden cues which signify the system's goals — goals which are often at odds with explicit statements of the aims of the teaching system.

Towards an Understanding of Human Action

This alternative assumption and interpretation is much more realistic. It construes the learner as a socially responsible being who takes action — rather like us, in fact. Let us develop it a little further to give us a clearer understanding of the alternative assumptions we might make.

Firstly, human actions are explained by discovering the reasons agents have for doing them. To understand why a person acted as he did, we must do more than describe his observable behaviour. Neither will an explanation in terms of biological reactions, schedules of reinforcement or cognitive processes suffice. They cannot cope with the reality of our own everyday understanding of why we act. To understand the meaning of a learner's action, we must understand his intentions.

Secondly, actions are socially situated. A learner's actions relative to a particular task can only be understood by elucidating his conception, perceptions, reasons, beliefs and wishes relating to his learning milieu (Parlett and Hamilton, 1972). To understand the individual's action within the learning milieu, we must also understand the social, cultural and psychological determinants of the learning milieu. This is what Eisner (1977) calls 'thick description' — describing the meaning or significance of behaviour as it occurs in a cultural network saturated with meaning.

Thirdly, by becoming more aware of our reasons for action, a greater range of possible actions becomes open to us. In many of our actions, we do not formulate specific reasons or consciously follow explicit rules and principles when we act. We act spontaneously, as circumstances require. We do not attempt to make explicit our own processes. Studying is, perhaps, a prime example of this. In coping with the particular study task, we are unaware of the assumptions, expectations, intentions, rules, principles etc. we use to guide our actions. Yet an understanding of these actions requires reference to these intentions and rules. Being able to deliberate on these reasons and rules increases the range of possibilities open to us. We can use the rules and principles to achieve alternative goals. To the extent to which learners are not helped to become aware of their reasons for action, they are denied access to a range of possible action and thereby denied autonomy and responsibility.

These elaborations of the concept of action are an inadequate summary of the arguments presented by Shotter (1975) and Gauld and Shotter (1977). But they do serve to highlight an alternative conception of the learner which has a number of implications for educational practice and research.

Towards a Shared Understanding

What are these implications? How might we interpret the goal of educational technology in the light of this conception of the active learner?

The essence of the business is the development of a shared understanding of our actions. If what goes on in teaching/learning situations is governed by the socially situated reasons, intentions, values, expectations and assumptions of participants, and if making these reasons explicit opens up possibilities for choice, then our task is to help the participants make such reasons explicit and open to each other.

This avoids the prescriptive stipulations of a technological approach whilst at the same time being intensely practical. We do not need to argue, as Rowntree (1976) does, that understanding is not enough, that our understanding is meant to lead to change, indeed to improvement. Firstly it is not our understanding which is the focus of attention. We are only one party to the teaching/learning situation. Secondly, awareness and shared understanding of intentions, assumptions, purposes and expectations reveals possibilities for change.

Again, these ideas have appeared in our literature, although in a somewhat different form. Coles (1977) makes a case for professional development through 'sharing part of a colleague's experience and by doing so helping him to become more aware of his own professionalism'. Rowntree (1976) catches a similar perspective in acclaiming evaluation as the critical ingredient of educational technology. He writes:

> All parties feed back their descriptions and interpretations identifying the good, the bad and the problematic. We can see where the teaching needs to be improved and on the basis of specific experience, not general principles, we may see ways of improving it that would not hitherto have occurred to us. And by 'us', I mean educational technologists, teachers, students, anyone else who is paying attention to the situation.

Towards a Method of Achieving Shared Understanding

Participation

Firstly, if the meaning of an action can only be understood in its cultural context, then only those who are party to that context stand much of a chance of reaching an adequate understanding of the action. A participatory mode of enquiry is therefore fundamental.

Now the recent growth of interest in this style of evaluation (see Hamilton *et al.* (1977) for a selection of readings on 'new styles' of evaluation) is a very strong move in this direction. As Coles (1977) puts it when discussing staff development:

> Professional development is something that occurs when a professional sees his task in a new light. I believe this can be brought about when outsiders become insiders and get involved as curriculum developers with colleagues in their professional job of teaching and learning.

Coles elaborates on how the outsider can become an insider without promoting an image of himself as the answer to the client's problem. The benefits are clearly not only to the outsider but also to the insider — the development of the shared understanding of action.

Similar participatory strategies have been developed by Dr Laurie Thomas at the Brunel Centre for the Study of Human Learning. By using George Kelly's repertory grid, individuals are able, together or on their own, to make explicit their personal construction of meaning through learning conversations, developed in shared understanding of that meaning with colleagues (Thomas and Augstein, 1977):

The learner has to assume joint responsibility with the tutor for bringing his or her own learning processes under review. Together they learn to negotiate the purposes of learning from the learner's personal needs, to develop more effective strategies and tactics in learning and to review the criteria by which they would judge the effectiveness of the enterprise. As the learner moves into greater self-organisation, he takes more of the tutor's activities into himself. He becomes his own tutor and the learning conversation continues within his head.

Now, this is a far cry from much of our standard educational practice, especially in higher education. The purposes of learning may be negotiated between curriculum developers and teachers, but as Farnes (1973) points out 'the learner is the recipient of these considered opinions'. It is one thing to advocate, as has been done here, that such conversational techniques are the giving away of educational technology, but quite another to be persuaded that the relinquishment of control which it would involve is acceptable.

Conceptual Analysis

A second but related technique is that of conceptual analysis. We have already argued that to understand human action is to explicate its meaning in terms of the agent's intention within a culture. This involves careful analysis of the ways in which we use intentional terms to indicate our reasons for action. Now, the dividing line between the elucidation of the important concepts by which we regulate our daily lives and the 'outsider becoming insider' or a 'learning conversation' is very blurred. When we are exploring personal meaning or developing shared understanding, we will be elucidating the concepts by which we regulate our lives. For example, the concept of learning is central to educational technology but no less central to learners and teachers. How and what learners learn depends upon how they construe learning. A repertory grid analysis of learning events will explore the personal meaning the construct has for the learner. Similarly, an analysis of the way in which we use the term in daily life would elaborate the meaning surrounding the concept. In educational technology, we have tended to deny the validity of such common usage, preferring the supposedly more scientific definitions offered by learning theorists. Unfortunately, these definitions fail to articulate with our day-to-day conceptions and therefore can hardly serve as a basis for the elucidation of our own learning experiences. The concept of learning is a prime candidate for our skills of conceptual analysis. Starting with our day-to-day usage, we need to clarify and elaborate its meaning, because such elaboration clarifies for us what learning is all about. Only when we have a clear, shared understanding of what learning is for us all about can we make responsible decisions about how and what we learn. For example, do we view learning as an activity, an achievement, or an acquisition of something? What is the relationship between action and learning? Is action in some sense an outcome of learning? How are intentional and unintentional learning related? Is unintentional learning passive? Our answers to these questions will have implications for how we assess learning. For instance, if we conclude that action is an outcome of learning, then assessment of learning requires not only the measurement of performance but determination of the associated intentions, purposes, expectations and commitments of the learner. Current conceptions of criterion reference measurement — the purpose of which is to develop a measurement of what is learned, cannot begin to deal with learning as an inference from action.

Conclusion

The argument here has been that the assumptions underlying the conception of a technology of education are educationally inappropriate. To make a scientifically devised system, the arbiter of teaching and learning decisions is to deny the political rights of those being educated. Man has, himself, developed such systems. He is not obliged to become their slave. To give primary significance to teaching is to degrade learning and thereby degrade and distort the image of the learner.

An antidote to these assumptions is to examine an image of the learner which is more realistic, in that it is concerned with what we feel ourselves to be. Such an image centres on the conception of a socially responsible being in control of his own actions. Such actions are to be understood by reference to the reasons, intentions, expectations, principles and values given by the agent. The shared understanding of human action within the learning milieu is radically enabling, clarifying as it does the possibilities open to us.

References

Bruner, J.S. (1974) *Relevance of Education.* Penguin Education, Harmondsworth.

Coles, C.R. (1977) Developing professionalism: staff development as an outcome of curriculum development. *Programmed Learning and Educational Technology,* 14, 4, pp.315-19.

Eisner, E. (1977) Thick description. Reprinted in Hamilton, G. V. *et al. Beyond the Numbers Game.* Macmillan, Basingstoke.

Farnes, N. (1973) Student centred learning. *Teaching at a Distance No. 3,* pp.2-6. The Open University, Milton Keynes.

Gauld, A. and Shotter, J. (1977) *Human Action and its Psychological Investigation.* Routledge and Kegan Paul, London.

Hamilton, D., Jenkins, D. and King, C. (1977) In MacDonald, B. and Parlett, M. (eds.) *Beyond the Numbers Game.* Macmillan, Basingstoke.

McAleese, R. (1977) editorial. *Programmed Learning and Educational Technology,* 14, 2, pp.101-2.

Northedge, A. (1976) Examining our implicit analysis of learning processes. *Programmed Learning and Educational Technology,* 13, 4, pp.67-78.

Parlett, M. and Hamilton, D. (1972) Evaluation as illumination: a new approach to the study of innovatory programmes. *Occasional Paper 9.* Centre for Research in the Educational Sciences, Edinburgh University, Edinburgh.

Rowntree, D. (1974) Two styles of communication and their implications for learning. In Baggaley, J., Jamieson, G.H. and Marchant, H. (eds.) *Aspects of Educational Technology VIII.* Pitman, London.

Rowntree, D. (1976) Evaluation: the critical ingredient of educational technology. *Programmed Learning and Educational Technology,* 13, 4, pp.7-9.

Shotter, J. (1975) *Images of Man in Psychological Research.* Methuen, London.

Thomas, L. and Augstein, S.H. (1977) Learning to learn: the personal construction and exchange of meaning. In Howe, M.J.A. *Adult Learning.* Wiley, London.

49. Understanding Learning: A Case Study in Student and Staff Development

C.R. Coles and W.G. Fleming, *University of Southampton*

Abstract: This paper examines the assumptions about teaching and learning processes underlying the skills approach to 'how students learn'. It rejects this approach on the evidence of course evaluations which have focused on how staff and students in higher education 'cope'. It is argued here that a more appropriate strategy is to consider learning ability as a *developmental phenomenon* relating to the actual *subject a learner is studying.*

Introduction

Recent years have seen the publication of a considerable number of texts on how to learn. Indeed 'study skills' seems to be big business. The approach seems to suggest that coping with learning is simply a matter of 'getting organized'. The learner needs to acquire a set of appropriate skills and to apply them in relevant situations. He can be given hints on how to read, how to take notes in lectures, how to write essays, how to prepare for examinations. No teaching situation is left unturned.

However, the skills approach contains a basic fallacy which makes its ultimate effectiveness, to say the least, questionable. This fallacy can be detected in the assumptions it makes. In the first place it suggests that a student's prior learning experience is either non-existent or at least irrelevant to his present study tasks. Whilst a number of features of his earlier education may require 'modification' it is wrong to assume that a student comes along with a *tabula rasa*. Indeed he will come with a complex set of assumptions, attitudes, values and expectations, many of which may not match those made by the courses he is about to study. Above all, a number of students will be *unaware* of how influential these are.

A second assumption made by the skills approach is that once techniques have been acquired and mastered they can be successfully applied by the student to any situation – they are generalizable from one study task to another. It is perhaps no wonder that the student, finding that this does not work, becomes disillusioned by 'all this educational mumbo jumbo' – a perception he may carry through until he himself becomes a teacher. Study skills are not once-and-for-all; they develop over time. There is no panacea. Indeed, learning to learn 'courses' are frequently run with interdisciplinary groups of students and it is assumed, without evidence or argument, that the skills involved are quite suitable for any subject being learnt. This may well not be so.

A different and rather insidious set of assumptions is that learning is all about 'fitting in' with the teacher's 'view' of the course. He determines what skills are needed to cope with his course and expects the good student to adopt them. There seems little room for manoeuvre. In reality the good student frequently is the one who 'kicks over the traces'. Following on from this is another assumption that courses consist of a number of quite different and independent activities such as lectures, seminars, practicals, essays, examinations, etc., each requiring its own special skills. This implies, in a sense, that courses consist of 'bits' which automatically weld together to form a whole. But there seem to be no study skills available to effect this 'integration'.

When the educationist 'looks at' courses a quite different view of teaching and learning becomes evident, particularly when the research focuses on teaching and learning processes (Hamilton *et al.*, 1977). Certainly it seems true to say that the sorts of difficulties learners experience cannot be construed as due to poor technique. There is plenty of evidence to support this (GRIHE, 1976*a*). Snyder (1971), in his analysis of the Hidden Curriculum, helps higher education to recognize the importance of an 'undercurrent' within courses which students identify as the most important and *only* reality. It seems that when faced with so many confusing demands, an overload of information, and a welter of ambiguity, the student 'lowers his sights' and 'plays the system'. He develops his own 'coping skills' towards achieving this end. As Miller and Parlett suggest some students develop acute powers for seeking out the cures (Miller and Parlett, 1974). More particularly, the work of Perry (1968) suggests that students' cognitive abilities 'develop' during their courses. They move from a dualistic view of their subject in which they believe there are right and wrong answers, through a period of relativism in which they see knowledge as conditional on its context, to a state of commitment to a particular approach. In other words, the view a student has of his subject, and of himself in relation to his subject, moves from *unrelated* knowledge to a complex *system of values* (Coles, 1977*a*).

Much of our own evaluative studies parallels this. Medical students studying integrated courses in basic medical sciences were more successful when they cut lectures and worked on their own. The courses seem to contain too much teaching and not enough learning (Coles, 1976). Electronics students studying circuit analysis were more successful when they perceived their task as understanding the principles of problem solving (Coles, 1977*b*). First-line managers found an experiential course more appropriate when they had a clearer perception of their own managerial task at their place of work (Fleming, 1977). Medical students entering clinical attachments developed greater confidence when confronted with patients rather than when taught about the management of cases (Coles and Mountford, 1978).

In short, looking at courses from the viewpoint of their processes — how people are coping — seems to suggest that improving skills (whether of teaching or learning) is not going to help. Indeed, the adjustments some people make to courses might be described as 'pathological'. They set out to pick up the 'vibes', or 'play the system'. This is neither what is required nor what is desired. In fact 'getting organized' or acquiring a few techniques, or even demanding tips for teaching and learning, is more likely to help them 'play the system' more effectively. But what is more likely to help is some *increased understanding* between all the people involved.

The evidence from these sorts of studies calls for a rather different approach to understanding learning and, inevitably, is set against a different set of assumptions. Firstly, it suggests that there are a number of implicit (yet crucial) features within courses which *can* be detected if you look for them but require the learner (or the teacher) to be more aware of his own expectations and those of the course. Secondly, it assumes that what a learner construes as the intention of a course may not be shared by other students or by his teachers. Some articulating and *sharing* of assumptions, attitudes, values and expectations is required. Following on from this it assumes that the acquisition of this sharing is developmental — it is not once and for all but occurs over a (sometimes considerable) period of time.

Fourthly, understanding learning assumes that all this is a function of the subject being studied, not simply its contents but more particularly its processes.

Fifthly, it also assumes that the staff teaching the course must be involved in this shared understanding — it cannot happen without them. Staff and students need to talk more to each other about the 'processes' of the course (GRIHE, 1976b). Finally, it makes assumptions about the role of the outsider — the educational 'expert' who is attempting to improve learning understanding on the part of the student. He should not remain an outsider but needs to become an 'insider' for a period (Coles, 1977a). Moreover, he has to 'negotiate' his position with the students but more particularly with the staff. This approach assumes that student development and staff development are an integral part of the development of the course itself. It is conceivable (and in our experience quite natural) that the course will also change as a result of such an exercise (Coles, 1977a).

The Course

Two years ago, one of the writers (WGF) gave a series of occasional public lectures at the university on the topic of 'studying'. He was attempting to establish that, whereas there were a number of study techniques which students might acquire, purposeful studying requires a more positive and planned strategy. In the audience was a member of the engineering faculty who felt that his first-year undergraduate students would benefit from this. His department invited the speaker to construct a course to be included within the students' induction to their university course. Three lectures were given and two seminars held aimed at increasing students' understanding. A subsequent evaluation (based on an 'interactive' methodology — see Coles, 1977c) of the course by the other writer (CRC) tended to suggest that it had not altogether been successful. Generally students did not report a changed attitude towards study, and staff were divided on whether they felt the course had been of any value. What emerged was that the reaction by members of staff closely matched their own view of the purpose of undergraduate engineering courses. Those who believed that engineering education should provide a 'foundation of knowledge' were sceptical about the value of a learning to learn course. Some even dismissed it as irrelevant. They saw their task as being one of 'communicating what they knew' to the students. Consequently, they saw the students' role as being rather passive — to acquire all the knowledge they could whilst they were at university. Other members of staff, however, saw engineering rather more in terms of a 'method of enquiry' or 'the solving of human problems' and welcomed the learning to learn course. One member of staff said 'It's absolutely essential'. They tended to relegate the acquisition of knowledge and 'getting the answers right' as less important than the development of an approach to understanding problems. They saw students as having to assume some responsibility for their learning, but felt them to be ill-equipped for, what might be to many, a new role.

From this evaluation one issue seemed clear. If these course seminars were to be led by tutors holding varying attitudes and assumptions, there would be more success if the staff themselves were uniformly more 'aware'. It was recognized, then, that the course itself would need to be developed hand in hand with some form of staff development. In other words, it would not succeed until the staff themselves saw their own teaching, and perhaps even their subject, in a new light. It was decided, therefore, that before the course was re-run a positive development strategy would need to be adopted in which the staff who would be taking the seminars should become actively involved in its design and implementation.

A small working group of four (two engineers and two educationalists) was appointed and produced a draft course in consultation with other members of staff which was presented to tutors for discussion, criticism and modification.

369

The resultant course not only embodied tutors' ideas but, because of the new design strategy, acted to modify some of the tutors' attitudes and assumptions.

The course consisted of one lecture and one seminar and it was decided to include some form of follow-up activities during the year. The lecture was planned to move from factual knowledge relating to the psychology of learning, through research work on individual student differences, to the more fluid view of teaching and learning emerging from recent evaluative studies at the university and elsewhere. Seminar material was devised which was built around comments about teaching and learning made by staff and students during the evaluation of the first course. Those comments that appeared to be opposites (or at least incompatible) were paired, eight of the most suitable selected and they were presented in the form of a checklist for students to indicate their 'preference'.

The working party produced two sets of notes, one for students outlining the points being raised in the lecture and indicating how to complete the checklist. The second, for staff, suggested how the seminars might be run and indicated the sorts of issues staff might care to raise.

The course was run during the first week of term, the lecture being given by one of the writers (CRC), the seminars being held the following day by tutors with groups of four or five students. Discussion centred around the differences between the varying perceptions of the people involved. Eight weeks later a revised checklist based on perceptions of the engineering course itself was issued and renewed seminar discussion held.

An evaluation of this course is currently under way but initial responses appear to support the claims made for it.

Discussion

The course described above illustrates two major points. The first relates to the intention of providing students (and, as a prerequisite, staff) with an opportunity to gain a greater insight into teaching and learning. The second, more generally, concerns fundamental principles for curriculum development which the project embodies. Both points will be examined independently although, of course, they are closely interrelated.

It is felt that this 'learning to learn' course was more appropriate than conventional approaches because it focused on students developing an 'awareness' of teaching and learning issues *within a specific subject context.* At the outset it was argued that the professional development of the student as a learner is inextricably bound up with his professional development as a subject specialist. This is not to deny that the professionalism of learning can be generalized across subject boundaries, indeed there is even greater insight to be obtained when, say, an engineering student sees that his subject shares many of the characteristics of, say, history or medicine. However, this step necessitates acquiring, as it were, a 'threshold' of perceptiveness on the part of the student which cannot be assumed in the neophyte learner. Developing 'awareness' is thought to occur when the learner begins to understand his own attitudes, assumptions, values and expectations concerning the teaching and learning of his subject. This may then lead to an understanding of those that are embodied within courses and the ones held by other staff and students. The ultimate goal is for the student to be able to account for and adjust to the discrepancies and mismatches he perceives.

But the project also embodies a number of principles fundamental to curriculum development which traditionally have been described as separate activities, such as evaluation, design, implementation, and staff development. Over the years these have acquired their own styles and strategies as well as their advocates and champions — it is not uncommon for people to describe themselves as being 'in' curriculum evaluation, course design or staff development. What appears to emerge from this case study, however, is that all of these activities are essential components of *planned* curriculum development. Evaluation helps all of the participants to identify the issues, the design embodies these and the implementation involves some form of staff development as a necessary prerequisite. What the case study also shows, however, is not just that these activities are essential for curriculum development but, more particularly, that they share certain characteristics. In particular they are 'low key', 'interactive', and founded upon negotiation between the participants. In short, they are based on a common methodology sometimes known as 'action research' which differs from the rational planning model for development, not because this is 'wrong' but because it is inappropriate for *curriculum* development. For an innovation to be successfully implemented it needs to be based on a negotiation between those who will be called upon to operate within it (MacDonald and Walker, 1976).

Conclusions

A 'learning to learn' course was devised and implemented based on the development of the student as a 'professional' learner and embodying fundamental principles concerning curriculum development. The following issues appear to have emerged from the project:

(1) Students approach a learning task with a well-established (if unconsciously held) complex 'set' of attitudes, assumptions, values and expectations.

(2) A student's 'set' does not always articulate with the 'set' embodied within his courses, or with that held by his teachers. Mismatches or inconsistencies cause learning difficulties.

(3) A student's learning improves when he sees his task in a new light.

(4) Students who become 'aware' in this way are able to adopt appropriate behaviour to suit the particular circumstances of any teaching and learning situation.

(5) This 'awareness' can be acquired in a developmental sense. It should be related to a student's changing view of his subject and should be a naturally occurring part of the course. Staff and students need to talk more with each other about the process as well as the content of their courses.

(6) Courses on understanding learning (like all other courses) embody assumptions which need to be articulated, and they contain issues (which act for or against their success) which may not be predictable at the planning stage.

(7) Whether an innovation succeeds or fails depends less on how 'good' it is (that is, how well it has been designed, how relevant it may appear, or how well its objectives have been defined). Its success depends more on how well it articulates with the attitudes, assumptions, values and expectations of those involved with it.

(8) Courses need to be designed by negotiation with those who will implement them.

(9) Staff development (particularly involving an understanding of one's assumptions, attitudes, values and expectations) is a necessary prerequisite for the successful implementation of an innovation. Paradoxically it can arise as a result of staff becoming involved in a curriculum development project.

References

Coles, C.R. (1976) Integration and concentration: an evaluation of the cardiovascular systems course at the University of Southampton Medical School (Abstract). *Medical Education,* **10**, 6, p.524.

Coles, C. R. (1977a) Developing professionalism: staff development as an outcome of curriculum development. *Programmed Learning and Educational Technology,* **14**, 4, pp.315-19.

Coles, C.R. (1977b) Gains and losses in a guided self-study engineering course: towards a problem-solving approach. In Hills, P. and Gilbert, J. (eds.) *Aspects of Educational Technology XI.* Kogan Page, London.

Coles, C.R. (1977c) Curriculum evaluation: the Southampton perspective. Paper presented at ASME/SRHE Conference, London, November 1977. (To be published)

Coles, C.R. and Mountford, B. (1978) Relevance in medical education: an evaluation of an introduction to clinical medicine. In Brook, D. and Race, P. (eds.) *Aspects of Educational Technology XII.* Kogan Page, London.

Fleming, W.G. (1977) An evaluation of an experiential course for first line managers. (Private communication)

GRIHE (1976a) Up to expectations. A study of the students' first few weeks of higher education. Simons, H. and Parlett, M. with Jaspan, A. Group for Research and Innovation in Higher Education, Nuffield Foundation, London.

GRIHE (1976b) Learning from learners. Parlett, M. and Hewton, E. Group for Research and Innovation in Higher Education, Nuffield Foundation, London.

Hamilton, D. *et al.* (1977) *Beyond the Numbers Game: A Reader in Curriculum Evaluation.* Macmillan, London.

MacDonald, B. and Walker, R. (1976) *Changing the Curriculum.* Open Books, London.

Miller, G.M.L. and Parlett, M. (1974) *Up to the Mark: A Study of the Examinations Game.* SRHE, London.

Perry, W.G. (1968) *Forms of Intellectual and Ethical Development in the College Years: A Scheme.* Holt, Rinehart and Winston, New York.

Snyder, B. (1971) *The Hidden Curriculum.* Knopf, New York.

50. The Effect of Adjunct Question Position, Type and the Presence or Absence of Feedback on Learning from a Video-Taped Lesson

P.A. Kirschner and H.J. van der Brink, *University of Amsterdam*

Abstract: The effects of adjunct questions on learning from a fixed-pace video-taped lesson are explored. A general facilitative effect for both total learning and relevant learning is found, along with two possible Trait-Treatment Interactions. One interaction (compensatory) was found for student ability and adjunct questions, the other (preferential) for prior education and adjunct questions.

Within the past ten years, there has been much conclusive evidence as to the positive effects of the interspersing of questions (adjunct questions) throughout written texts. These positive effects arise, according to Rothkopf (1966), from the adjunct question's ability to stimulate mathemagenic activities within the reader. Mathemagenic activities refer to those activities which give rise to learning and consist of (a) the relatively overt activities of attending to and scanning the text (i.e. eye movements, subvocal articulation), and (b) the more internal processes accompanying reading (i.e. mental review, drawing inferences). Although there has been much research as to the factors which affect the efficacy of adjunct questions in written prose, factors such as question location, question type, question pacing, response mode and presentation mode of the questions and the presence or absence of feedback, there has been relatively little research done on the effects of these factors on the utility of adjunct questions with video-taped learning materials (Bertou *et al.*, 1972; Michael and Maccoby, 1961).

The crux of the problem lies in whether or not the results obtained in research with written prose texts may be generalized to learning from video-tapes presented in a group or in a broadcast situation. A video-tape, when presented to a group is non-stop, whereas written texts are not. With a written text, the reader may proceed at his/her own pace and may pause to think about or reflect upon the subject content or the adjunct question until he/she decides to proceed further. With a video-tape such as the one used in this experiment, the pace is predetermined and when the allotted time to think has elapsed, the video-tape proceeds, regardless of the viewer. For adjunct questions in a written text, the reader can review that which he/she has just read to try to find the correct answer to the question posed, whereas the viewer of a video-tape cannot. Research on adjunct questions in a written text concludes that their effect is greatest when they are placed every paragraph or two (Frase, 1968a; Frase *et al.*, 1970) and that performance declined sharply as the amount of material between adjunct questions increased (Eischens *et al.*, 1972). If these guidelines were followed for video-tapes, one would probably end up with a discontinuous mass of interruptions rather than a continuous whole. Whereas written texts are spatial in form and involve only the visual modality, video-tapes are temporal and involve both the visual and auditory modalities. These two modalities may at times present congruent information while at other times incongruent and even dissonant information. These are but a few of the major differences between written prose texts and video-tapes, but are enough to show that one must be cautious in trying to generalize the results of research in one to the other.

The following is a report on the results of a combined field and laboratory experiment designed to explore the following questions:

(1) Do adjunct questions have a facilitative effect on general learning, question specific (relevant) learning and question incidental learning from video-taped learning material?

(2) If so, what is then the optimal combination of the following three factors: question position, question type and the presence or absence of feedback?

(3) Are the results found in a laboratory situation for adjunct questions generalizable to the educational setting (field)?

(4) Are the results found for the effects of adjunct questions generalizable from written texts to fixed-pace video-taped learning materials?

Method — Field Experiment

Subjects

The experimental sample consisted of 78 second-year university students enrolled in an education course in the education department of the University of Amsterdam.

Materials

The experimental materials consisted of a 75-minute video-tape about Jena-plan education which was divided into ten approximately equal segments. After each segment, a comprehension-type adjunct question was inserted in a combined aural and visual mode. These questions concerned subject content contained in each preceding segment. Five of these ten questions were included as relevant learning items (they were transformed into multiple-choice items) on a criterion test, along with 15 incidental learning items (five comprehension-type and ten knowledge-type). A questionnaire containing 15 items was also developed to determine the prior education, prior knowledge of Jena-plan education, attitudes towards the video-tape and the subject matter, and attitudes towards the adjunct questions (experimental group only) of the subjects.

Procedure

Following a short introductory statement, the subjects viewed one of the two versions of the video-tape. The group which viewed the version without adjunct questions (control group) was told only to view the video-tape carefully. The group which viewed the video-tape containing the ten comprehension questions, each one inserted after the relevant segment (post-questions) without feedback, were in addition informed of the presence and the format of the adjunct questions.

The experiment was run in two shifts. Subjects were randomly assigned to each group on the basis of the first letter of their family name. Both groups were informed that they would have to answer a questionnaire at the completion of the viewing. No mention was made of the criterion test.

After viewing the video-tape, each subject received a test booklet containing the criterion test and the attitude questionnaire, so that upon completion of the criterion test, the subjects could proceed directly to the questionnaire.

SCORE	STATISTIC	CONTROL	EXPERIMENTAL	TOTAL
Total	Mean	13.25	13.37	13.28
(TOTSC)	S.D.	2.45	1.80	2.30
$X_{max}=20$	Range	0-18	10-16	6-18
Incidental	Mean	9.90	10.21	9.97
(INCSC)	S.D.	2.06	1.51	1.93
$X_{max}=15$	Range	5-14	7-13	5-14
Relevant	Mean	3.56	3.16	3.31
(RELSC)	S.D.	1.08	1.02	1.06
$X_{max}=5$	Range	1-5	1-5	1-5
Comprehension	Mean	6.59	6.78	6.64
(COMPSC)	S.D.	1.50	1.32	1.45
$X_{max}=10$	Range	2-9	4-9	2-9
Knowledge	Mean	6.66	6.58	6.64
(KNOWSC)	S.D.	1.53	1.02	1.41
$X_{max}=10$	Range	3-10	5-8	3-10

$N_{con}=59$ $N_{exp}=19$ $N_{tot}=78$

Table 1

Results — Field Experiment

A primary analysis of the results obtained from the criterion test showed that there were no significant differences between conditions with respect to the total score (TOTSC), relevant score (RELSC), incidental score (INCSC), knowledge item score (KNOWSC), and comprehension item score (COMPSC), nor were there any

375

differences between RELSC and INCSC or KNOWSC and COMPSC within experimental treatments.

A secondary analysis of the results with respect to student aptitude and prior education showed that when each condition was divided on the basis of those scoring above the median (Good Students) and those scoring below the median (Poor Students), the poor students in the experimental group significantly outscored the poor students in the control group ($p < .05$). There were no significant differences, however, between the conditions for good students (see Table 2).

	Good Students n=40		Poor students n=38	
	n=32 Control	n=8 Experimental	n=27 Control	n=11 Experimental
TOTSC	15.06	15.13	11.11	12.09
COMPSC	7.41	7.88	5.63	6.00
KNOWSC	7.66	7.25	5.48	6.09
RELSC	3.72	3.75	2.93	2.73
INCSC	11.34	11.38	8.19	9.36

TOTSC:EXP > CONTR $t=2.15$ $p < .05$

INCSC:EXP > CONTR $t=2.52$ $p < .05$

Table 2

When each condition was divided on the basis of prior education, it was found that although the three groups (Academic High School — AHS, Teachers College — TC, and Other — OTH) did not differ with respect to achievement on the criterion test, there were significant differences and noteworthy trends within the groups between conditions. Within the AHS group, the results show that those in the control condition outscored those in the experimental on all five scales (TOTSC, RELSC, etc.), though not significantly. Within the TC group, those in the experimental condition outscored those in the control condition on all five scales, with TOTSC, INCSC, and COMPSC being significant ($p < .05$). There was no definite trend within the OTH group (see Tables 3 and 4).

From these results one is tempted to conclude that the adjunct questions had a differential effect with respect to the aptitude or the prior education of the subject. In other words, what may exist here is a Trait-Treatment Interaction (TTI).

Method — Laboratory Experiment

Subjects

The experimental sample consisted of 134 first-year psychology students at the

	AHS n=44		TC n=17		OTHER n=17	
	n=32 Control	n=12 Exp.	n=13 Control	n=4 Exp.	n=14 Control	n=17 Exp.
TOTSC	13.84	12.75	12.62	15.25	12.50	13.33
COMPSC	7.09	6.42	6.08	7.75	5.93	7.00
KNOWSC	6.75	6.33	6.54	7.50	6.57	6.33
RELSC	3.63	3.08	3.00	3.50	3.07	3.00
INCSC	10.22	9.67	9.62	11.75	9.43	10.33

AHS = Academic High School
TC = Teacher College

TOTSC TC.-EXP > TC -CONTR $t=2.63$ $p < .05$
COMPSC TC -EXP > TC -CONTR $t=2.42$ $p < .05$
INCSC TC -EXP > TC -CONTR $t=2.56$ $p < .05$

Table 3

	CONTROL n=59			EXPERIMENTAL n=19		
	n=32 AHS	n=13 TC	n=14 OTHER	n=12 AHS	n=4 TC	n=3 OTHER
TOTSC	13.84	12.62	12.50	12.75	15.25	13.33
COMPSC	7.09	6.08	5.93	6.42	7.75	7.00
KNOWSC	6.75	6.54	6.57	6.33	7.50	6.33
RELSC	3.63	3.00	3.07	3.08	3.50	3.00
INCSC	10.22	9.62	9.43	9.67	11.75	10.33

(a) for the Control Group

TOTSC(AHS) > TOTSC(OTHER) $p < .05$ $t=2.08$
COMPSC(AHS) > COMPSC(OTHER) $p < .005$ $t=3.20$
COMPSC(AHS) > COMPSC(TC) $p < .05$ $t=2.03$

(b) for the Experimental Group

TOTSC(TC) > TOTSC(AHS) $p = .005$ $t=3.76$
KNOWSC(TC) > KNOWSC(AHS) $p < .025$ $t=2.02$
INCSC(TC) > INCSC(AHS) $p = .01$ $t=3.35$

Table 4

University of Amsterdam who must participate in a certain number of experiments as part of a course requirement.

Materials

The same video-tape was used here that was used in the field experiment. Adjunct questions were again inserted, but this time before the relevant segment (pre-questions) in four copies of the video-tape and after the relevant segment (post-questions) in four copies of the video-tape. A copy of the video-tape without adjunct questions was also made.

The criterion test was enlarged to 40 items of which ten measured relevant learning (multiple-choice versions of the adjunct questions) and 30 measured incidental learning (ten of the same question type as the adjunct questions and 20 of the other question type). For example, if a subject viewed a video-tape with knowledge-type questions in it, for that subject there would be ten relevant knowledge items, ten incidental knowledge items, and 20 incidental comprehension items. The reverse of this is true for a subject who views a video-tape with comprehension adjunct questions.

The questionnaire was also revised so as to help gain an insight into how those in the feedback conditions experienced the feedback.

Procedure

Following a short introductory statement, the subjects viewed one of the nine versions of the video-tape. The experiment had a 2 x 2 x 2 design with the factors being question position (pre-questions and post-questions), question type (knowledge and comprehension) and feedback (with and without) along with a view-only control group. The treatments can be best seen in Table 5.

All nine groups were instructed to view the video-tape carefully and were informed that a questionnaire would follow the viewing. All eight experimental treatment groups were informed of the presence, position and format of the adjunct questions. The experimental treatment groups viewing a video-tape with feedback were also informed of the presence, position and format of the feedback.

The experiment was run in nine shifts. The selection of subjects for this experiment was accomplished through the use of a subscription list. Assignment to treatment groups was dependent upon which of the nine subscription lists the subject chose to sign.

There were eight experimental treatment groups of 13 subjects each and a control group containing 30 subjects.

Following the viewing, each subject received a test booklet containing the criterion test and the questionnaire. Upon completion of the criterion test the subjects proceeded directly to the questionnaire.

Results — Laboratory Experiment

A primary analysis of the results obtained for the criterion test showed that the interspersing of adjunct questions had a facilitative effect on total learning ($t=2.20$, $p<.05$). The mean scores for all of the treatment groups for TOTSC, RELSC, and INCSC can be found in Table 6.

In a test comparing each experimental treatment with the control group, only the group receiving knowledge pre-questions with feedback scored significantly higher ($t=2.77$, $p<.01$). No group did worse than the control group.

QUESTION POSITION	QUESTION TYPE	FEEDBACK MODE
Prequestion	Knowledge	Without
Prequestion	Knowledge	With
Prequestion	Comprehension	Without
Prequestion	Comprehension	With
Postquestion	Knowledge	Without
Postquestion	Knowledge	With
Postquestion	Comprehension	Without
Postquestion	Comprehension	With

Table 5

A three-way analysis of variance yielded neither main effects nor interaction effects.

Relevant learning, for both the knowledge question and the comprehension question conditions, was facilitated. The knowledge question groups outscored the control group ($t=4.79$, $p < .001$) and the comprehension question groups outscored the control group ($t=3.94$, $p < .001$). Both differences were highly significant. A two-way analysis of variance yielded a significant main effect for feedback in relation to relevant learning for both the knowledge and comprehension groups ($F=35.19$, $p < .0001$ and $F=9.65$, $p < .01$) respectively). In other words, the presence of the feedback had a score-enhancing effect on relevant learning. Incidental learning, however, was unaffected.

There were unfortunately not enough TC or OTH students in the laboratory experiment to perform any secondary analysis on the influence of prior education on the effectiveness of the adjunct questions. In the analysis of good and poor students, the results proved to be similar to those obtained in the field experiment. The poor students in the experimental treatment groups significantly outscored the poor students in the control group on TOTSC ($t=1.65$, $p < .05$), relevant knowledge learning ($t=4.61$, $p < .001$) and relevant comprehension learning ($t=3.62$, $p < .001$). Incidental learning was unaffected. As in the field experiment, there were no significant differences for the good students.

Discussion

Primary Analysis

The results of the laboratory experiment show that adjunct questions have a facilitative effect on both total learning and relevant learning from video-taped

379

	WITH FEEDBACK		WITHOUT FEEDBACK		
	PRE-QUESTION	POST-QUESTION	PRE-QUESTION	POST-QUESTION	
K N O W L E D G E	28.85	27.92	28.00	27.46	
	9.54	9.31	8.23	7.85	
	19.31	18.62	19.77	19.61	KNOWLEDGE
	28.39		27.73		28.06
	9.42		8.04		8.73
	18.96		19.69		19.33
C O M P R E H E N S I O N	26.46	27.31	27.92	26.31	
	7.85	8.08	6.62	6.46	
	18.61	19.23	21.30	19.85	COMPREHENSION
	26.89		27.12		27.00
	7.96		6.54		7.25
	18.92		20.57		19.75
	WITH FEEDBACK 27.63		WITHOUT FEEDBACK 27.42		
	8.69		7.29		
	18.94		20.13		TOTAL
	PRE-QUESTION 27.80		POST-QUESTIONS 27.25		27.54
	8.70		7.16		7.93
	18.96		19.73		19.54

	CONTROL
TOTSC	25.73
RELSC	7.40* 5.60+
INCSC	18.33*20.13+

$N_{each\ exp.\ treatment} = 13$ $N_{control} = 30$

$N_{with\ feedback} = 52$ $N_{total} = 134$

$N_{without\ feedback} = 52$

$N_{pre-questions} = 52$

$N_{post-questions} = 52$

$N_{all\ exp.\ treatments} = 104$

* The RELSC and INCSC are composed
+ of different items for the knowledge and comprehension groups.

* Knowledge RELSC and INCSC
+ Comprehension RELSC and INCSC

Table 6

learning material intended for presentation to a group. The adjunct questions had no effect on incidental learning. These results generally agree with those results obtained in research on written prose texts.

The optimal combination of factors appears to be that of knowledge pre-questions (regardless of whether feedback is present) for total learning. For relevant learning, the determining factor appears to be the presence of feedback. These results are in agreement with Frase (1968b, 1973) and Rothkopf and Kaplan (1972), who found that total and relevant learning were facilitated by specific questions, which are roughly comparable to our knowledge questions, but that incidental learning was unaffected by such questions. Frase (1970, 1973), Rothkopf (1966) and Rothkopf and Billington (1974) found that pre-questions, while facilitating relevant learning, could not improve performance on incidental learning items. None of these eight combinations could be said to have a clear effect on incidental learning.

The question of whether results obtained in a laboratory situation are generalizable to the educational setting cannot be conclusively answered in this study. The comprehension post-question without feedback (the field treatment) was also ineffective in the laboratory where it was actually the lowest experimental treatment group with respect to total learning and relevant learning.

The question of whether results obtained for adjunct questions in one medium (written texts) may be generalized to another medium (video-tapes) has also been only partially answered. On the one hand, a general facilitative effect was found for total learning and relevant learning, while no effect was found for incidental learning. This is in agreement with the literature relating to the use of adjunct questions in written prose. On the other hand, the treatment which in our study had the least effect (comprehension post-questions without feedback) has been generally accepted to be the treatment which is not only beneficial for relevant learning, but also for incidental learning.

The question that must be asked at this point is whether this difference is inherent to the video medium or whether it is inherent to the learning situation, that is, fixed-pace instruction to a group. Would the results obtained in these two experiments differ very much from an experiment in which a lecturer used adjunct questions while lecturing a large group; or a tape/slide presentation with adjunct questions presented to a whole class; or an educational radio programme with adjunct questions that is broadcast to different schools? The possible answer is 'no', since each of these experiments involves a fixed-pace learning situation.

Secondary Analysis

It appears from the secondary analysis of the results found for the criterion test, that the use of adjunct questions may have had a differential effect on the learning of the subjects. This is known as a Trait-Treatment Interaction. In both the field experiment and the laboratory experiment it seems that individuals who might be classified as having lower mental ability may have benefited more than those of higher mental ability from the posing of adjunct questions. This is in support of the results found by Koran and Koran (1975) who also found such an interaction (they call it an Aptitude X Treatment Interaction — ATI).

They reason that frequent selective reinforcement of the subject's attention (through the use of adjunct questions) to specific aspects of, for them, the prose passage 'may reduce the burden of semantic processing and capitalize on the role of associative memory'. They go further to say that by 'selectively reinforcing attention to question related types of material in the learning material, a reduction in the (verbal) processing requirements may be expected to accrue'. Being that the

381

questions serve to reinforce and maintain mathemagenic activities appropriate to the nature of the task, (increased) pacing of the questions should ensure more efficient maintenance (Frase, 1968c) thus primarily benefiting less able subjects. Koran and Koran go further to say that it is possible that 'lower-ability subjects are weak primarily in attentional and discrimination skills. Accordingly, the insertion of questions may compensate for this lack through their attention-directing and attention-controlling features, thus accounting for their beneficial effect upon low-ability subjects' (p.80). Berliner (1971) also has reported that the use of adjunct questions inserted into a video-taped lecture may help subjects low in memory ability while even possibly impairing the performance of subjects high in this ability. In our experiments, there was no evidence of impairment in these subjects.

A further example of a possible TTI may be seen in regard to the different effects that the questions had on subjects who had attended different types of secondary schools. This effect may lie in the fact that the adjunct questions used in the field experiment were of the comprehension type and therefore required deeper processing of the material than would knowledge questions (Anderson, 1970; Craik and Lockhart, 1972). Being that 'teacher's college' subjects are probably familiar with both the problems encountered in the school, and also with various different school systems (even if the system discussed in the learning material is not one of them), they may have the theoretical and practical foundations which are necessary for this deeper processing. 'Academic high school' subjects, however, probably lack this foundation. Thus, when asked to process the information presented in the video-tape on a deeper level, through the introduction of comprehension questions, this lack of foundation may actually inhibit learning.

These two apparently different explanations of the effects found in the secondary analysis may be clarified by referring to the heuristic models for the generation of aptitude-treatment interaction hypotheses as described by Salomon (1972). Salomon distinguishes three complementary models: the remedial approach model, the compensatory model and the preferential model.

The *remedial approach* is designed for the low aptitude scorer; i.e. the one who shows poor mastery of subordinate task specific skills by making up for his/her deficiencies by exposing him/her to more of the same type of treatment. To quote Salomon: 'When learners are spoon fed with an externalized representation of the covert visualizations they ought to activate on their own (in our research it is the making of connections between theory and practice) it is mainly the poor visualizers who benefit.'

The *compensatory model*, rather than making up for deficiencies, compensates for each learner's deficiency by providing the mode of presentation that the learner cannot provide for him/herself. One is not trying to fill in gaps within the limits of specific performances, as is the case in the remedial approach, but rather only to circumvent their debilitating effects.

The *preferential model* tries to capitalize on what the student is already capable of doing. It exploits available strong points in the student's characteristics. It is preferential in the sense that the treatment plays to the learner's preferred style or information-processing strategy.

In the case of the poorer students, it is possible that the enhancement of their score may be due to the fact that the information in the video-tape is reviewed through the use of the adjunct questions (the remedial approach), or that via the use of the adjunct questions, the connections between theory and practice are provided, thus compensating for the poorer student's inability to make those connections alone (the compensatory model). Since the scores of the better students are unaffected (the remedial approach predicts interference for better students) the compensatory model seems the more plausible explanation. However, further research is necessary before any definite conclusions can be made.

In the case of the TC-students, one is tempted to opt for the preferential model, whereby the interspersing of adjunct questions capitalizes on and utilizes the learner's strong points; in our study, the knowledge of different forms of education both in theory and practice. This approach does not explain the downward trend found for the AHS-students. This is at least partially in agreement with Cronbach and Snow as cited in Koran and Koran (1975) who state, 'Thus, Aptitude X Treatment Interactions may be viewed as arising from a compensatory-conciliatory process in which a treatment may remedy a particular deficiency while capitalizing on another well-developed characteristic of the learner.'

References

Anderson, R.C. (1970) Control of student mediating behavior during verbal learning and instruction. *Review of Educational Research*, **40**, 3, pp.349-69.

Berliner, D.C. (1971) Aptitude-treatment interactions in two studies of learning from lecture instruction. Paper presented at the meeting of the American Educational Research Association, New York.

Bertou, P.D., Clasen, R.E. and Lambert, P. (1972) An analysis of the relative efficacy of advanced organizers, post organizers, interspersed questions and combinations thereof in facilitating learning and retention from a televised lecture. *Journal of Educational Research*, **65**, 7, pp.329-33.

Craik, F.I.M. and Lockhart, R.S. (1972) Levels of processing: a framework for memory research. *Journal of Verbal Learning and Verbal Behavior*, **11**, pp.671-84.

Eischens, R.R., Gaite, A.J.H. and Kumar, V.K. (1972) Prose learning: effects of question position and informational load interactions on retention of low signal value information. *Journal of Psychology*, **81**, pp.7-12.

Frase, L.T. (1968a) Effect of question location, pacing and mode upon retention of prose material. *Journal of Educational Psychology*, **59**, pp.244-9.

Frase, L.T. (1968b) Some data concerning the mathemagenic hypothesis. *American Educational Research Journal*, **5**, pp.181-9.

Frase, L.T. (1968c) Some unpredicted effects of different questions upon learning from connected discourse. *Journal of Educational Psychology*, **59**, pp.197-201.

Frase, L.T. (1970) Boundary conditions for mathemagenic behaviors. *Review of Educational Research*, **40**, pp.337-48.

Frase, L.T. (1973) Integration of written text. *Journal of Educational Psychology*, **65**, pp.252-61.

Frase, L.T., Patrick, E. and Schumer, H. (1970) Effects of question position and frequency upon learning from text under different levels of incentive. *Journal of Educational Psychology*, **61**, pp.52-6.

Koran, M.L. and Koran, J.J. (1975) Interaction of learner aptitudes with question pacing in learning from prose. *Journal of Educational Psychology*, **67**, pp.76-82.

Michael, D.N. and Maccoby, N. (1961) Factors influencing the effects of student participation on verbal learning from films; motivating versus practice effects, feedback, and overt versus covert responding. In Lumsdaine, A.A. (ed.) *Student Response in Programed Instruction.* National Academy of Sciences — National Research Council, Washington, DC.

Rothkopf, E.Z. (1966) Learning from written instructive materials: an exploration of the control of inspection behavior by test-like events. *American Educational Research Journal*, **3**, pp.241-9.

Rothkopf, E.Z. and Billington, M.J. (1974) Indirect review and priming through questions. *Journal of Educational Psychology*, **66**, pp.669-79.

Rothkopf, E.Z. and Kaplan, R. (1972) An exploration of the effect of density and specificity of instructional objectives on learning from text. *Journal of Educational Psychology*, **63**, pp.295-302.

Salomon, G. (1972) Heuristic models for the generation of aptitude-treatment interaction hypotheses. *Review of Educational Research*, **42**, pp.327-43.

51. Searching Tables in the Dark: Horizontal vs Vertical Layouts

J. Hartley and K.L. Davies, *Keele University;* and **P. Burnhill,** *Stafford College of Further Education*

Abstract: This paper is concerned with the layout of materials presented in tabular formats, and in particular with whether or not there is an advantage for a horizontal or a vertical layout of the same data. The question, simply put is, is it easier to read across or down tables, particularly large and complex ones?

An examination of the available research concerning the design and layout of tables is not particularly revealing on this question. There are a fair number of comparison studies (tables vs line-graphs vs barcharts, etc.), and there is some research on typographic cueing within tables (e.g. the use of bold typefaces), but there are only two or three experiments which bear on the horizontal/vertical issue. Macdonald-Ross (1978) ably summarizes almost all of this research on tabular — and other graphic — materials and the interested reader can consult this paper for detailed references.

In most of these experiments, participants are required — individually or in groups — to utilize the tables in laboratory situations and to locate or write down the answers to written or oral questions. Speed and accuracy are the two measures usually recorded. No investigator known to the authors has reported on the eye-movements of searchers employed in the different tasks, although in a sense the most obvious behaviour that one sees when someone scans a table is a movement of the eyes.

The use of eye-movement recorders is, however, to some extent controversial. The devices that have been developed impose restraints on the reader (with head clamps, bite bars, etc.); they impose restraints on the material that can be used (often material is presented on slides); and, generally speaking, they are expensive.

The recently developed Whalley Reading Recorder (Whalley and Fleming, 1975), however, is not expensive and, although it does impose restraints on the reader, these are a rather different kind. Essentially the Whalley Reading Recorder involves the searcher in guiding a small hand-held torch in a darkened environment. The torch is attached by a rod to a joystick control-assembly and thus the recorder looks and acts like a torch on a pendulum that can swing in any direction. The movement of the torch is translated into electrical resistance by two potentiometers arranged orthogonally in the joystick assembly, and the movement can be recorded for subsequent (or on-line) computer analysis.

In this paper then, we describe the results that we obtained when we used the Whalley Recorder to assess the difficulties found by readers when they were asked to search for information in tables. In Experiment 1 searchers were asked to locate information directly. In Experiment 2 searchers were asked to make comparisons between two items of information presented in the table. Again, therefore, explicit information was being asked for (the readers did not have to interpolate data), but this task was more difficult than that in Experiment 1.

Materials

Three levels of table complexity were developed, and a horizontal and vertical layout was designed for each. These tables were typed in either a horizontal or vertical format on a standard A4-size page. Copies of them are available from the authors.

Sets of questions were devised and written on separate cards in order that in the experiments the searchers would not receive the same search tasks in the same order.

The question cards for each table layout were determined before each student's arrival, and were placed in a small box whose illumination did not interfere with the display features of the Whalley Recorder.

Experiment 1

The participants in this experiment, 12 women and 7 men university students, were tested individually. Each student was shown the Whalley Recorder and its method of operation. A practice study with a table of the least complex design was then employed to familiarize them with the procedure.

In brief this was as follows. Each student was presented with a table (the horizontal or vertical layout of one of the levels of complexity) with the light spot centred on the centre of the table. The experimenter then asked the student a question (e.g. How many boys are there in School C who are left-handed?). The student searched the table with the recorder and called out the answer. The light spot was then re-centred, and the next question presented. Each student was asked eight questions on each table.

Two recordings were made: (1) a tape recording of the experimenter's questions and the student's answers; and (2) a recording of the tracking movements of the student.

Experiment 2

The procedure in Experiment 2 was essentially the same as that in Experiment 1, except that the students were asked to locate and compare two figures in a table rather than to locate one figure. In this experiment 19 students again acted as participants, 15 women and 4 men. In Experiment 2, the participants answered 12 questions on each table.

Results

Time Taken

For each student we were able to measure from the audio-tape recording the time taken from the end of the experimenter's question to the calling out of the answer by the student. To assess the time taken per layout we calculated the mean time taken for the students to give the correct answers. In doing this we excluded the time taken to answer the first question on any one of the layouts. We did this because the first question for each layout usually took the longest time to answer, for in order to answer it the students had to explore the whole 'map' of the table. We also ignored trials on which the students made errors, i.e. we used only the times taken to give correct answers.

There were in fact very few errors, especially on the least complex tables: on the most complex tables the most common 'errors' arose because the students forgot the question and asked for it to be repeated.

The results obtained in Experiment 1 are shown in Table 1 and those obtained in Experiment 2 are shown in Table 2. Because in both studies the variances obtained were not homogeneous between the three groups it was not possible to carry out an analysis of variance. However, the results quite clearly indicated in both studies that the complexity level of the table affected the results, but that the arrangement of the layout did not.

| | | Levels of complexity | | |
		Least complex	More complex	Most complex
Horizontal layout	$\bar{x}$	3.4	5.8	9.4
(N=19)	s.d	1.7	2.6	3.3
Vertical layout	$\bar{x}$	3.6	5.8	10.0
(N=19)	s.d.	1.5	2.3	3.9

Table 1. *The mean times (and standard deviations) taken in seconds to retrieve items from tables of different levels of complexity set in horizontal and vertical formats (Experiment 1)*

| | | Levels of complexity | | |
		Least complex	More complex	Most complex
Horizontal layout	$\bar{x}$	5.6	8.8	12.1
(N=19)	s.d.	1.7	2.7	4.5
Vertical layout	$\bar{x}$	5.8	9.1	14.9
(N=19)	s.d.	1.7	4.3	10.5[1]

[1] One person took 42 seconds in this group

Table 2. *The mean times (and standard deviations) taken in seconds to compare items from tables of different levels of complexity set in horizontal and vertical formats (Experiment 2)*

Search Strategies

The search strategies employed by the students are difficult to discuss because it is not possible to condense a pile of varied drawings into a neat statistic and because, in a paper of this nature, it is not possible to illustrate all the paths traced by the 38 students across the six tables.

Figure 1 shows as an example the responses of a female student in Experiment 1. Figure 1a shows her first response to the very first question she was asked. This was 'How many right-handers in School B are girls?' It took this student 45 seconds to find the answer. Her answer to question 8 in this series 'How many boys in School B are right-handed?' took 6.6 seconds and the path taken is shown in Figure 1b. She found the school, then boys, and gave the answer. Both these questions were asked of the more complex tables in the vertical layouts.

These traces show two things (which were common to both experiments). The first of these is the rapid amount of learning that took place. Items were recovered much more rapidly after the initial search trial till by the end of a series of questions on one layout the movements were quite swift. The second of these is that the sequence of the search path was *not* clearly dictated by the question. Thus the question 'How many boys in School C are left-handed?' did not always lead to the sequence (1) boys, (2) School C, (3) left-handed. The format of the initial question in a series did seem to direct the sequence of the search more than later

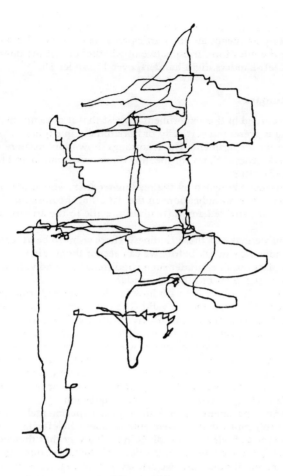

Figure 1(a)

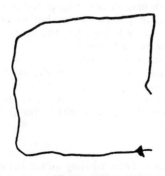

Figure 1(b)

ones in the series, but by and large the dominant features in the tables were soon mastered and the search was directed by these. For example, in the most complex tables most, but by no means all, the participants went to the school column first when answering the questions, irrespective of whether or not the question started with boys, girls, left-handers, right-handers, over 15, under 15.

Concluding Remarks

The time data recorded in this experiment suggest that it does not matter much whether material is presented vertically or horizontally in explicit tables of the kind explored in this experiment. The recordings show rapid mastery of table layouts and speed-retrieval times for locating direct information and for making comparisons within tables.

The search strategies revealed by the reading-recorder were more varied. Nonetheless, there were no indications in the data that the horizontal or vertical layouts of the tables provided any difficulties specific to the arrangement of the table.

What then can we make of these findings? There seem to be at least two important questions we can ask before we can accept them. First of all how far can we trust the data obtained under such conditions? Secondly, how far do the data simply reflect the decisions that we made?

The first question is concerned with how far data obtained from the Whalley Reading Recorder can be regarded as valid. The recorder certainly slowed down the searchers, and made it possible to observe both the time taken and the search strategies used by each participant. It seems likely to us that the lack of significant differences between the layouts with respect to time would probably be replicated in natural conditions (with these materials), but we are not so sure that the search strategies would be similar. We are not really able to assess the validity of the recorder unless the data it produces reveals or reflects known differences. This leads us to consider our second question.

In planning this experiment we took the typical experimental approach of simplifying the problem so that we were able to assess the effects of one particular variable. We constructed our table headings in such a way that they could be easily remembered, and we fabricated the data for the table contents. In essence (and with the wisdom of hindsight) we can say that our tables were constructed so as to be equally easy to use in either layout, and this is what the data in Tables 1 and 2 reflect.

In natural situations, of course, many tables are like the ones that we constructed and our research may simply suggest that in such cases it does not matter much whether or not they are presented horizontally or vertically. However, when the data in the table are related to each other in more complex ways then these conclusions may not apply.

We now intend to use the recorder to look at some of the other differences reported in the terms of table usage (e.g. see Wright and Barnard, 1975; Wright, 1977; Ehrenberg, 1977) to see if in fact these differences can be replicated and whether or not the recorder can illuminate their cause. This research will use more meaningful materials and will throw more light on the validity of our approach.

Acknowledgements

We are grateful for advice from Peter Whalley on the construction of the Recorder and to Stuart Forrest for building it. Our thanks are also due to the students who took part in the experiments, and to the Social Science Research Council who financed this research.

References

Ehrenberg, A.S.C. (1977) Rudiments of numeracy. *Journal of the Royal Statistical Society A,* 140, 3, pp.277-97.

Macdonald-Ross, M (1977) How numbers are shown: a review of the research on the presentation of quantitative data. *Audio-Visual Communication Review,* 25, 4, pp.359-409.

Whalley, P.C. and Fleming, R.W. (1975) An experiment with a simple recorder of reading behaviour. *Programmed Learning and Educational Technology* 12, pp.120-4.

Wright, P. (1977) Decision making as a factor in the ease of using numerical tables. *Ergonomics,* 20, pp.91-6.

Wright, P. and Barnard, P. (1975) Effects of 'more than' and 'less than' decisions on the use of numerical tables. *Journal of Applied Psychology,* 60, pp.606-11.

Chapter 9:
Resourcing Educational Technology

Whether 'resourcing' is taken to mean the acquisition and storage of materials as in libraries, or the provision of finance to execute a project: it is often of crucial importance in educational technology and its applications. In this chapter both meanings of the word may be considered.

Dr Anderson (52) provides a splendid account of 'Low-Budget Assessment Procedures'. In our original 'Call for Papers' one of the suggested aspects of educational technology in a changing world was 'Limited Budget' work. However, though many authors thought that their papers could be classified under such a heading, Dr Anderson's is the only one which hit the topic 'bang on'! His account of the use of low-budget assessment in schools will give inspiration and ideas to many teachers feeling the effects of economic constraint. Much of the work could be related to further and higher education with beneficial results.

Libraries in educational institutions rarely have a surplus of funds to initiate and execute the training of librarians in developments in teaching methodology. Dr Hills (53) describes the design and production of a teaching package for use by librarians.

From Heriot-Watt University's Civil Engineering Learning Unit (54) 'Encouraging Freedom in Learning' provides a stimulating account of careful attention being paid to the student's needs. A 'Decision Card' information system is recommended for the retrieval by students of resource materials when courses offer considerable freedom in the selection of content.

Finally, Dr Leedham (55) returns us to the school sector of education with a review of the development of the Longman Group Reading Programme over the last ten years.

52. Some Low-Budget Assessment Procedures

E. W. Anderson, *University of Newcastle-upon-Tyne*

Abstract: a variety of simple and inexpensive assessment procedures has been tested in schools. Feedback was obtained (a) directly from the children, (b) through the children's use of material, (c) from the teaching, (d) through the school organization, and (e) from experience beyond school. Examples from each source are described.

In discussing strategies for the evaluation of curriculum materials, Eraut (1972) identifies five main sources of feedback: (1) students, (2) teachers, (3) classes, (4) institutions and (5) experts. A teacher wishing to assess the overall effectiveness of his programme must consider evidence which can be obtained from these different sources. This paper examines a number of simple and inexpensive techniques which have been used successfully in local schools and which illustrate the variety of evidence available. While the basic ideas have general validity, the individual teacher may need to adapt them according to the type of children with whom he is dealing and the institution in which he is working.

The work originated through requests from a number of probationary year teachers who wanted to examine their own classroom performance in a more structured manner. They were all concerned with the same broad field which includes aspects of geography, environmental studies and social studies, although the ages of children taught ranged from 9 to 18 years. The main criteria for designing the procedures were that:

(1) They should be capable of use with children throughout the age range.
(2) They should require only limited preparation by the teacher.
(3) The materials required should be inexpensive.
(4) They should allow operation by one teacher only.
(5) The interpretation of results should be comparatively simple.

It was decided that feedback should be obtained: (1) directly from the children, (2) through the children's use of material, (3) from the teaching, (4) through the school organization, and (5) from experience beyond school. Examples from each of these areas are described.

1. Children

The normal rapid method of assessment from children is by question and answer, but this process has several limitations. Only one child is involved at any one time and natural reticence may preclude many from taking part. It is at best usually a crude sample of responses which can be taken. In many ways the ideal system is seen in the language laboratory in which each child is linked directly to the teacher. However, for everyday use in studying subjects other than languages, this is obviously too costly to install and maintain.

An inexpensive and simple procedure can be established with the Cosford Responder (Hawkins and Hawkins, 1973). This consists of a solid triangle of card having a different colour on each of the four faces (Figure 1). By moving the responder so that a particular colour faces the teacher, the child can communicate directly. As, during teaching and testing sessions, the responder is held and virtually enclosed within the child's hands it can be moved without the knowledge of the other children. Thus the problem of shyness can be overcome. By oral testing, the teacher can not only assess immediately what proportion of the class has understood the topic under discussion, but also diagnose weaknesses shown by individuals.

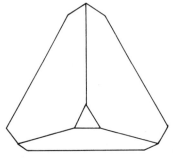

Figure 1. *Cosford Responder*

Each teacher can refine his own method of using the responders, but during the trials, lasting several months in comprehensive schools, the following procedure was adopted. When points were being explained, the children held the responders with the yellow side facing the teacher. If they did not understand, they turned the red side and it was then possible to clarify the explanation. For tests, there was a known code of colours so that, for example, agreement was signified by the green face and disagreement by the red. However, the main questions to be posed were carefully planned before each lesson so that the usual categories of objective test question involving selection. identification, discrimination, matching, etc., could be employed. The questions were written on a test sheet, chalkboard, or overhead projector transparency, together with the possible answers, each having its colour code.

The method was assessed at various levels including comparing the results obtained with those from classes tested in a more conventional manner. Unobtrusive measures included the obvious interest of the children and also the fact that other teachers showed interest and in some cases adopted the procedure. Success can also be measured by the number of child responses. For a normal 35-minute period, this might approach 30, but with every child involved, the figure with responders is near to 900.

The responder facilitates testing in groups and also assessment of groups, but other methods for evaluating group discussion have also been investigated. Recording by tape recorder, with and without the knowledge of the participants, is comparatively familiar. Similarly, the use of games, including role playing, has provided useful feedback but is well documented. A further group technique developed for problem solving was brainstorming, which involves producing as many hypotheses as possible without, initially, evaluating them. The full procedure consisted of the following stages, each taken in order round the group:

(1) Make alternative statements of the problem.

(2) Repeat (1) but with knowledge of what other people have said.
(3) Choose selected statement(s).
(4) Identify the wildest ideas put forward.
(5) Use reverse-brainstorming to see in how many ways the ideas put forward can be criticized.
(6) Analyse what has gone on in the sessions.

The sort of problems considered were deliberately either of a very broad compass, or else controversial topics. This was to minimize the knowledge component so that answers received could be used for attitude recognition.
To the very broad question:

Discuss the advantages and limitations of contour maps in the recognition and study of landforms

(1) Statements were made about the precise wording of the question, attempts were made to rephrase the question to bring out the most important assumptions that lie behind the original question. This was a most productive 10 minutes devoted to clarifying what the question really involved.
(2) Under the specific headings extrapolated from the question the pros and cons of contour maps were examined and many factual points and regional examples mentioned.
(3) This led to a synthesis, which produced a qualified acceptance of the usefulness of contour maps. Other techniques were also discussed.

The notes taken of this session, which lasted about half an hour, revealed on analysis that 40 distinct and relevant statements had been made about the question. An examination candidate with more time at his disposal might be expected to produce perhaps one-third of this total. Thus in terms of the main areas of the question and the generation of ideas, the brainstorming session proved to be far more efficient than other methods of problem solving.

2. Material

Apart from the verbal methods described, learning can also be assessed directly through children's use of material. This normally takes the form of written tests, essays, or practical examinations. However, except in the case of objective tests, this type of assessment is rarely structured. The request to produce a programme for remedial classes provided an opportunity to design more precise evaluation methods. The children involved, although backward in basic subjects, were mostly manually dextrous and motivated by practical and particularly art work. Therefore it was decided to use these visual and spatial abilities centrally in the learning structure so that arithmetic, writing and reading were developed through them.

The graphicacy programme which was developed continues in several schools and is now complex. However, the basic apparatus for assessment remains the geogboard. It consists of a square of pegboard with a framework keeping it just above the surface of a desk and thereby allowing it to hold pegs. The size commonly used houses 15 x 15 holes, which gives sufficient scope for manipulation but means that it is small enough to be handled comfortably by one child. Therefore each child has his own geogboard on which he can plot patterns or play as required and each can have exactly the same representation irrespective of his own artistic ability. A large range of plotting symbols is available, varying in colour, shape and size, and it is a simple matter to adapt others, while it may be useful to superimpose or combine symbols, thus adding a third dimension. If symbols with heads, such as golf tees, are employed, areas can be enclosed by string or rubber bands in the same way as happens with nailboards but without the inherent risks of the latter. Shapes can also be constructed by stitching directly through the holes in the board. Plotting with symbols can be supplemented by drawing and by the use of overlays so that temporary marks can be made and also the whole board can be adapted for games playing. It is clearly possible with suitable colouring or overlays to play most board games.

As the programme progresses from the concrete to the abstract, so the geogboard allows increasing use of imagination and flexibility in investigating problems. An example of a simple progression which has been used can be cited (Figure 2):

(1) Draw from life or imagination a sketch of an approximately square field with a river flowing across the middle. Draw in some cows and a clump of trees.
(2) Draw an aerial view of the same scene.
(3) Using symbols for the cows and trees convert the scene to a pattern on the geogboard.
(4) Visualization: How does the same scene appear from various viewpoints, etc?
(5) Interpretation: problems concerned with density, patterns and dispersion involving alterations in the spatial arrangement.
(6) Application: simple problems, e.g. How could the cows be distributed at the hottest part of the day?

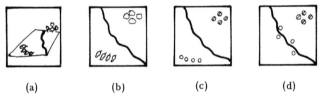

(a)	(b)	(c)	(d)

Figure 2. *Geogboard sequence*

This programme has been run in four schools including a community home. Results have been encouraging, indeed in the community home with the regular pattern of ability testing, very significant gain scores were recorded.

Another rather less restricted but nonetheless rigorous method of assessment through material was developed with algorithms and logical trees (Lewis and Woolfenden, 1969). These are normally considered as learning devices and were initially used as such in a school where a range of programmed material was tested. After using programmed books, information maps, work cards and algorithms, the children expressed a preference for the last two. They were therefore familiar with the approach when it was decided to employ algorithms as an assessment method. Many relationships can be shown in diagrammatic form, but the most interesting development so far has been in classification. To construct a Yes/No dichotomous algorithm requires logical thought, and is an excellent test of real understanding. For example, having discussed how coastlines might be classified or how rock types may be distinguished on a topographic map, the children, in this case sixth formers, were asked to produce an algorithm summarizing the information. This obviously tests not only the learning of material but also a more fundamental appreciation of the subject.

3. Teaching

Apart from through the learning achieved, the teaching performance can also be assessed directly. Most easily, but probably least accurately this might be through the use of a checklist or catechism concerning points varying in level from adequacy of introduction to quality of voice. However, this demands a good memory and a facility for objective self-criticism. Micro-teaching techniques, particularly those using closed-circuit television (e.g. Brown, 1975), can be far more revealing and provide a more faithful evaluation. However, these techniques can only be employed occasionally or the learning environment is disrupted by the assessors and equipment. Interaction analysis (e.g. Cohen, 1976) provides another series of procedures which allow assessment of teaching effectiveness. Again the situation is artificial, particularly with the recorder in the classroom. Once any such distraction appears, the normal atmosphere is disturbed and, when the stress for the teacher is taken into account, it can be appreciated that the situation is rather unrealistic. This could be overcome by the regular appearance over a period of such distractions, but the expenditure of manpower would not be possible in most schools.

In an attempt to overcome these difficulties, the meso-analysis disc was designed (Figure 3). This has the great advantage that it is operated by the teacher himself, and in general, the children remain unaware of its use. However, only comparatively major events can be recorded and it therefore lacks the detailed precision of interaction analysis. The disc is inscribed with a series of concentric circles and is then stuck over the dial of the teacher's wristwatch, leaving the end of the minute hand visible. Each teaching activity required is assigned to one circle. At the start of the period, a mark is made along the line of the minute hand; then as each activity ends, a mark is made on the appropriate circle again indicating the position of the minute hand. Within the centre circle a mark is made for every question asked so that a record of the total number can be obtained. For the tests completed in six schools, the circles were used to denote administration, exposition, question and answer, visual aids and the children's own work.

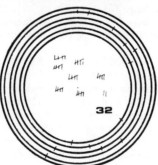

Figure 3. *Meso-analysis disc*

The completed discs allowed the pattern of different types of lesson to be analysed. For example, the proportion of time spent on question and answer sessions could be related to such factors as class control, quality of work produced, class enthusiasm and the teacher's own level of satisfaction with the period. Clearly there can be no fixed pattern for a lesson, but meso-analysis discs allow an assessment which can be used as a guide.

4. School Organization

Feedback through school organization may be obtained on a number of levels and stages. For example, the organization involves both people and facilities and it might be examined with regard to the stated aims of the school. Several schools have produced such catalogues of aims but it is more difficult to construct guidelines which allow progress towards the aims to be assessed. Rather than consider procedures which must be necessarily somewhat subjective, it was decided to concentrate on the physical arrangements of the school. Work study techniques (International Labour Office, 1968) provide a basis for analysing the benefits and limitations of spatial organization. They also present a logical analytical exercise for children, and therefore selected techniques of method study were used to provide feedback for assessment.

The flow process chart is constructed from five symbols (Figure 4) signifying: (a) operation, (b) inspection, (c) transport, (d) storage, and (e) delay. Using the symbols, the children were able to draw up charts recording the daily activities of their classes. These provided a detailed diary allowing delays and excessive movement to be clearly identified.

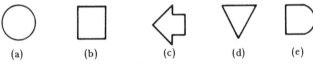

(a)   (b)   (c)   (d)   (e)

Figure 4. *Work study symbols*

As the school most involved with this project was on a split site, movement could be plotted on a plan of the school using the same symbols and producing a flow diagram. Again it was possible to locate difficulties and suggest improvements to the timetable. On a smaller scale the arrangements for taking the daily meteorological readings were analysed (Figure 5), and an improved layout suggested. The operations shown are: (1) barometer reading, (2) maximum and minimum thermometer readings, (3) wet and dry bulb thermometer readings, (4) cloud and visibility readings, (5) wind measurements, (6) rain gauge reading, (7) grass minimum thermometer readings, (8) calculations, and (9) fill in daily weather chart.

Movements can also be recorded by lengths of string attached to the plan by pins. Repeated journeys thus have more strands between the pins than infrequent movements and the completed string diagram provides a basis for producing a more efficient arrangement. For a laboratory or classroom the benches, desks, etc., can be represented by templates loosely attached to the plan. The positions of these can then be altered, the string rewound and any saving of movement measured.

The results from this particular programme have been very encouraging. It has been possible to suggest improvements to the school organization on a variety of scales and the children involved have also benefited. However, it is realized that the organization of a school is extremely complex and the examples given only touch upon the subject.

5. Beyond the School

There are obvious difficulties in obtaining feedback beyond the school but without it, long-term aims cannot be assessed. For the Durham schools, the immediate problem was to monitor work-experience projects, but it was hoped

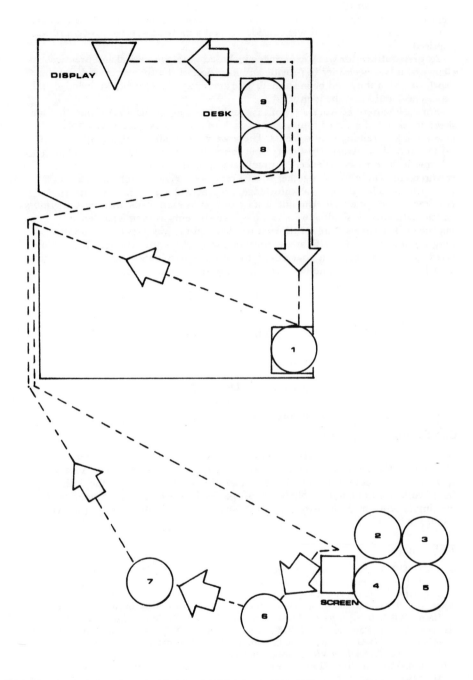

Figure 5. *Flow diagram*

to extend this later to include the early stages of the job itself. One method employed with some success in this type of situation has been the writing of diaries. For this project, however, it was considered that a more structured procedure was required.

As preparations for work experience included both theoretical and practical elements, it was necessary to provide an indication of the topics covered and the depth to which they had been studied. The areas requiring further knowledge and experience could then be identified.

For each variety of work a set of task and recording sheets was produced. Each sheet consisted of a list of topics against each of which was a set of symbols indicating the training requirements. There were six symbols (Figure 6): (a) theoretical: acquaint, (b) theoretical: more detailed, (c) practical: no experience, (d) practical: some experience, (e) practical required, (f) practical: priority requirement. These fitted together form a rectangle. Figure 6 (g) shows a set indicating detailed theoretical knowledge, no practical experience and priority requirement for practical. The initial state of preparation was shown by the symbols and adjustments by shading were made by the students as their knowledge improved. The sheets were scrutinized regularly and it was possible to monitor progress and also to identify areas requiring more school preparation. The scheme was so successful that it has been used for probationary year teachers in schools, allowing heads of departments to check on job training and progress.

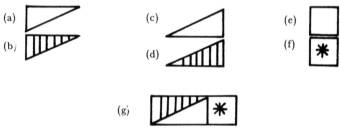

Figure 6. *Training symbols*

Conclusions

Five main sources of feedback related to schools have been examined and examples of programmes in each area have been described. Assessment is a wide ranging and developing subject and clearly a full consideration of it even within the defined framework would be impossible in a short paper. However, it is contended that the simple procedures discussed are effective and can be easily and inexpensively established.

References

Brown, G. (1975) *Microteaching: A Programme of Teaching Skills.* Methuen, London.

Cohen, L. (1976) *Educational Research in Classrooms and Schools: A Manual of Materials and Methods.* Harper and Row, London.

Eraut, M. (1972) Strategies for the evaluation of curriculum materials. In Austwick, K. and Harris, N.D.C. (eds.) *Aspects of Educational Technology VI.* Pitman, London.

Hawkins, P.F. and Hawkins, R.E. (1973) The application of the systems approach to training in the Royal Naval Supply School. In Budgett, R. and Leedham, J. (eds.) *Aspects of Educational Technology VII.* Pitman, London.

International Labour Office (1968) *Introduction to Work Study.* International Labour Office, Geneva.

Lewis, B.N. and Woolfenden, P.J. (1969) *Algorithms and Logical Trees: A Self-Instructional Course.* Cambridge Algorithm Press.

53. Librarians' Needs in Relation to Teaching and Learning in Higher Education

P. J. Hills, *Institute for Educational Technology, University of Surrey*

Abstract: This paper describes the work of two projects concerned with librarians' needs in relation to teaching and learning methods. After a preliminary investigation involving some 253 librarians a teaching package has been designed to give information on methods of teaching and learning now available. It is now in the trials stage.

Since September 1975 a small working party consisting of representatives from the North London Polytechnic, University of Surrey and Hatfield Polytechnic examined the needs of librarians in relation to teaching and learning methods. This included a survey of courses on teaching and learning offered to librarians in the UK, attendance at the teaching and learning course of the University of Surrey, a survey of librarians' opinions in the field of user education and a 'Delphi' exercise, which involved questioning a number of experts in this field.

At the beginning of the project there were a number of questions concerned with the need to consider librarians in relation to the range of teaching and learning methods now coming into use in academic courses and being considered for their user-education courses.

After preliminary discussions the main aims of the project were agreed to be:

(1) To consider the need to acquaint librarians with a range of teaching and learning methods and methods by which this might be carried out.
(2) To consider the ways in which the librarians might apply such methods to the provision of instructional material for library users.
(3) To consider ways in which the whole area of possible library use by students might become a recognized part of normal course work.

The Survey of Librarians' Opinions

In an attempt to investigate librarians' 'needs in relation to teaching and learning methods', a questionnaire was sent out in 1976 to librarians concerned with user education, to which 253 librarians responded.

The central aim, or focus, of the questionnaire was to find out what teaching methods were in current use and in what context (subject matter and level). It was also intended to determine what teaching methods the librarians would like to know more about so as to improve their quality of teaching.

Results of the Questionnaire

The results indicated that librarians, whether talking about basic orientation to the library or advanced subject literature instruction, relied heavily on the normal lecture method.

A lot of interest was shown in learning more about audiovisual methods, in

401

particular tape/slide, and in the use of practical exercises. Librarians concerned with user instruction apparently feel that these techniques are needed to supplement their oral presentations. One librarian made the observation that audiovisual techniques are very popular with librarians because they tend to dislike any form of public speaking. Techniques such as tape/slide take direct attention away from the librarian and focus it on the screen. If this observation is generally true, it could lead to encouraging more librarians to participate in user instruction. But it should also be recognized that there are librarians who do not, under any circumstances, regardless of teaching method, want to teach.

From the results, it is apparent that there is interest among many librarians to find out more about teaching methods which would assist them in their instruction of students.

Other general conclusions can be summarized as follows:
Librarians who engage in library instruction need much more support from:

(1) Library administrators (i.e. people who control time and funds needed to support active and effective programmes).
(2) Teaching staff in the various departments (without their support widespread course-related user instruction is virtually impossible).
(3) Professional librarian colleagues (reader instruction is not a burning issue among many librarians in academic librarianship; there are librarians who do not believe in it and/or do not want to teach).

The Delphi Exercise

The working party decided to consult a number of experts. The technique decided upon to elicit expert opinion was a version of what is known as the Delphi exercise. Altogether, six people agreed to participate in the exercise, all of whom were experts either in the field of librarianship or teaching and learning methods in higher education.

Methodology

This was accomplished by a series of posted 'rounds'. For the first round, each expert received a list of assumptions and ideas which resulted from the working party's preliminary findings. Each expert commented in writing and returned the results. The second round circulated to each participant a copy of the first-round document which included everyone's comments (names were deleted to preserve anonymity), for each expert to react to the other experts' comments. Following the return of the second-round results, the working party contacted a few of the participants and requested that they clarify, or expand upon, certain responses which other experts found unclear. After the return of these amplifications, a final report was drawn up, summarizing the total Delphi exercise.

Results

The first part of the exercise asked for experts' opinion on the three aims previously given. Everyone agreed that the three aims were important. They also felt that librarians will first have to define exactly what it is they want to teach, before settling on teaching methods. In order to determine this, it will be necessary to ensure that, as one respondent put it, 'library staff have adequate access to the activities of course planning committees and academic standards review bodies'. In short, librarians will have to leave their libraries and find out what courses students are taking, how these courses are taught, and talk to teachers to find out how library skills can be integrated into course work.

Getting actively involved with the rest of the academic community, after so many years in apparent isolation, will not be easy. One of the Delphi participants described the present situation as follows:

> The power structure of universities gives an almost unhealthy freedom of action to lecturers and places librarians in a very subservient role. If the lecturers are prepared to continue with their inefficient ways of teaching it is difficult to see how the librarians can force them to change their ways.

In addition to whether or not there is a need to acquaint librarians with teaching and learning methods, the Delphi exercise also asked the experts to go one step further and comment on how this should be accomplished. In this connection, two questions were asked:

(1) What is the best way of acquainting practising librarians with the range of teaching and learning methods available?

(2) What are the practical constraints which have to be overcome in order to achieve 'the best way'?

In the case of practising librarians, most felt that short courses were the best way of acquainting them with teaching and learning methods. The practical constraints were few in number, but very strong. One was concerned with the personalities of librarians: there are librarians who hate teaching. As one expert put it: 'It is a difference basically between librarians who regard themselves as guardians of repositories and librarians who see themselves as information providers.'

Another major constraint was lack of support for such short course work for librarians from library administrators. If the head of a library refuses his staff either funding or time off, short course attendance is impossible.

In addition to librarians and teachers, the exercise also scrutinized library schools. Everyone agreed that library schools should play a more active role — but how? The consensus was that they should be offering full course work with library school students and short courses for practising librarians. But easier said than done. Two problems emerged out of the Delphi exercise comments. The first was with the problem of offering short courses to practising librarians:

> On the post-experience side, library schools can only do more if libraries and librarians will let them. The resistance to the idea of releasing staff for continuing education is remarkably strong in some places. It seems almost ridiculous the way in which librarians will claim to be leading agents in the life-long education of the community and then put all manner of barriers in the way of their own staffs.

The other problem is with the level of competence of library school staff in the realm of teaching and learning methods. How many staff members themselves have received training in this area? As one expert saw it, library schools should not attempt to teach teaching and learning methods to students unless 'they have the staff experienced to do so. If staff were not experienced then there should in the first instance be courses in learning and teaching techniques for staff in library schools.'

The Next Step

From this work it became apparent that there was a real need to develop methods to acquaint librarians with the large variety of teaching and learning methods that now exist, both so that they know about the work of their academic colleagues and so that they can apply these methods to their user education programmes. It is not immediately apparent whether this should be in the form of conferences, courses, seminars or self-teaching packages but it would seem that there are certain features which this training should cover. These include the use of audiovisual materials, the effectiveness of specific teaching aids and methods which can be applied to user education.

In the design of conferences or short courses there are many problems, not the least of these being the lack of financial support for delegates, due to the rising cost of transport and accommodation. Where members of library staffs are not being replaced, an additional burden may be thrown on those remaining, who may find it difficult to take off time during normal working days in order to attend a conference. The working party has come to the conclusion that what is needed is not just more short courses of the normal type, which reach only a relatively small number of people, but some form of teaching package. If this provided the basis for local group action and individual study, it could be more effective and reach far more people than a conventional course.

The British Library has now funded a project, based at the University of Surrey, entitled: 'Development of a Teaching Package on Teaching and Learning Methods for Librarians'. A working party has been formed consisting of Miss Ann Aungle and Miss Nancy Hammond from North London Polytechnic, Miss Sarah Green from South Bank Polytechnic, myself (as director), Professor Elton and Mr Reg Carr from the University of Surrey. The working party is being coordinated by Mr Bob Elliott, on sabbatical leave with the University of Surrey from the University of Windsor, Ontario, Canada. This project develops further this idea, producing a package of materials that should fulfil the need for information in the area of teaching and learning methods.

The Teaching Package

In Part One of the package, information is given about important teaching methods in use today in higher education. The methods were chosen because of their possible relevance to a user education programme. My own contribution describes teaching methods which can be effective with individual or small groups of students. With the exception of packaged learning, very few of the techniques described are used in any known user education programmes; but they could be. Professor Elton's description of the lecture method demonstrates that the lecture does not have to be passive; the lecture audience can be encouraged to participate to some degree. In short, there are many teaching methods in higher education which could be, with some adaptation, applied to a user education programme.

Part Two of the package outlines teaching methods which are presently employed in user education programmes. The most popular methods are apparently lectures, printed handouts, the traditional tour and, the most recent innovation, the tape/slide package. To a limited degree, there is some overlap between teaching methods as discussed in Part One and Part Two. Thus, some librarians are already using and experimenting with teaching methods which are used in higher education in general.

Part Three presents the issues of objectives and evaluation.

Next, in Parts Four and Five, audiovisual and printed materials are covered. Most teaching today relies on some form of printed and audiovisual materials. In fact teaching often uses a mixed-media approach (e.g. the lecture and the overhead projector, handout, etc.).

The Sixth, and final, part summarizes the package and also suggests follow-up activities which actively involve the librarians with material covered in the package.

Trials of the package are at present in progress and it is hoped to make the package available to librarians later in 1978.

For further information on the package, please contact Dr P.J. Hills, Institute for Educational Technology, University of Surrey, Guildford GU2 5XH.

Further Reading

Adams, R.J. (Winter 1976-7) Teaching packages for library user education. *Audio-visual Librarian,* 3, 3, pp. 100-6.

Bradfield, V. *et al.* (March 1977) Librarians or academics? User education at Leicester Polytechnic. *Aslib Proceedings,* 29, 3, pp. 133-42.

Fjällbrant, N. (1976) Teaching methods for the education of the library user. *Libri,* 26, 4, pp. 258-9.

Hammond, N.R. (1975) Teaching library use. In Cowley, J. (ed.) *Libraries in Higher Education,* Bingley, London, pp. 92-101.

Hills, P.J. (ed.) (1977) *Tape/Slide Presentations and Teaching Packages for Library User Education.* SCONUL.

Hills, P.J., Lincoln, L. and Turner, L.P. (1977) *Evaluation of Tape-Slide Guides for Library Instruction.* British Library Research and Development Department report no. 5378 of the Tape/Slide Evaluation Project, University of Surrey, Guildford.

Revill, D.H. (February 1970) Teaching methods in the library: a survey from the educational point of view. *Library World,* 71, pp. 243-9.

Review Committee on Educational Technology for Information Use (1977) *Final Report.* British Library Research and Development Report 5325.

Stevenson, M.B. (1976) *User Education Programmes: A Study of their Development, Organisation, Methods and Assessment.* British Library Research and Development Report 5320.

54. Encouraging Freedom in Learning: Implications for Cataloguing and Retrieval of Resource Materials

A. L. Barker and E. G. Bingham, *Heriot-Watt University, Edinburgh*

Abstract: Any innovation, however well organized, is likely to encounter stumbling blocks of one kind or another in the early stages; not all of these can be anticipated. Often the secondary problems which are inadvertently created at the beginning may well threaten the complete effectiveness of the new development. This paper reports and discusses one such side-effect of an educational innovation, which relies for its solution on the field of information science.

Background

The Civil Engineering Learning Unit at Heriot-Watt University has been in operation now for some seven years, offering its students pre-recorded instruction of various kinds with the underlying premise that this provision means that lecturers are freed for closer contacts with individual students. A basic aim is to offer students freedom in learning. This is achieved to a greater or lesser extent depending on timetabling and syllabus constraints by making it possible for students to work as individuals or in small groups, which allows them freedom of pace in learning, and by providing a range of materials so that they also have some choice of study method. In practice, it is also possible sometimes to offer freedom of content, when students are able to choose for themselves topics for more detailed study or even to organize a substantial part of a course in one subject for themselves (Cowan, 1978). Students are further encouraged to consider objectively their own level of mastery of a subject and in some instances to share in the evaluation of their performance in particular assignments, which allows them to enjoy some freedom of assessment. Thus although the courses are necessarily reasonably structured and classes are formally timetabled in groups for the various Learning Unit activities, a fair amount of independence and freedom is engendered (Bingham, 1977).

Early Administrative Problems

In seeking to improve and extend the opportunities for students to exercise this freedom a large collection of structured and interrelated resource materials has been gradually built up. Problems began to arise when efforts were made to communicate to the students the range of materials on offer to them at any particular point within the course of their study.

In an effort to curtail these difficulties, materials were structured to fit within a predetermined pattern of options (Figure 1) to which students soon became accustomed and which they came to expect.

The materials for a particular week could then be displayed on racks on a trolley for easy self-selection even if sometimes one type of item was omitted from a particular set. The only problem then remaining was that the materials which still

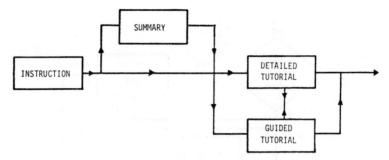

Figure 1. *Standard pattern*

lay outside this standard pattern often remained virtually unused because students failed to explore options which sounded unfamiliar to them, even when they were informed of their existence.

Students quite often sought advice from the Learning Unit staff about available materials when they had a particular learning difficulty or interest which prompted them to explore the potential of the collection. But these students often found it hard to explain their needs adequately and the staff were hard pressed to interpret them accurately. Besides, the collection of resource materials was by now so large that it was impossible for any one person to be familiar enough with all the available resources to be able to advise students effectively on an individual basis. The 'cataloguing system' such as it was, provided only operational details such as accession number, title, physical format and run-time for tapes. Another means of providing the necessary advice and information was sought.

Basis for a Solution

In turning this weakness into a strength it seemed advantageous to base the information system around the student seen as an agent of choice, aware of his responsibility in exercising this freedom. It could conceivably be made possible for each individual to plan his own study route through his course. Thus the provisions for offering students freedom of study method, pace and content would be enlarged and there would be greater opportunity for the staff to add to the collection new types of materials and activities which had formerly been outside the system capabilities.

Operational Environment

Before considering possible solutions to the problem, several constraints had to be taken into account.

Because of the conditions imposed by class sizes and timetabling, anything between 20 and 100 students may well arrive at the Learning Unit at about the same time, all wanting to know immediately what they should be studying during the next hour. This means that any retrieval system must come up with the answers to their questions speedily, efficiently and with a minimum of effort from the user within, say, five minutes of the start of the period so that time is not wasted. Obviously, multiple copies of the catalogue are needed so that physical access is not restricted and queues of frustrated students do not build up.

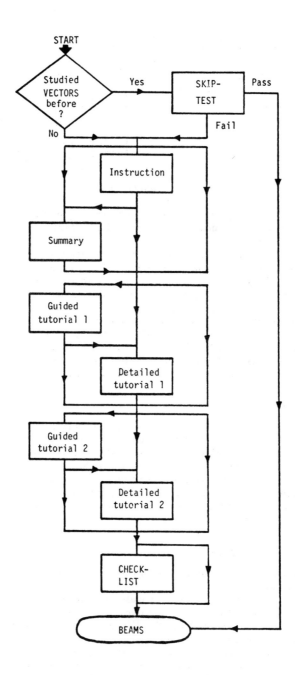

Figure 2. *'Vectors' flow chart*

Since finance, staff time and resources are also limited, the retrieval system must be fairly straightforward to set up, operate, administer and update. Pressures and demands on staff time must be kept to a tolerable level.

Initial Experimental Developments

A small study was undertaken to investigate the information needs of the student users of the Learning Unit and also the requirements of the information retrieval system as seen by the teaching and administrative staff. Experimental developments included the use or adaptation of existing library cataloguing codes such as the LANCET Rules (Library Association, 1973), and also the design of rather stylized flow charts (Figure 2).

A fair representation of 'either/or' choices and 'main stream' items could be incorporated in these diagrams. But 'both/and' routes (where several items are all to be studied eventually but in any order) and 'skip-routes' (where not all items need to be studied if the student is confident or has previously been taught the topic) called for subtleties which the writers were hard-pressed to express clearly in this diagrammatic form.

It was appreciated that the user needs to be informed not only about each separate item by details such as title, coverage, physical form, run-time and so on, but also where this particular item fits in to a 'block' or package of instruction. These interrelationships were as much a vital characteristic of the item as its own unique features which would be described in a conventional catalogue.

Pilot Schemes

In the summer term of 1977 two parallel trial retrieval systems were designed, operated and modified (Barker and Cowan, 1978). They both covered revision materials for the first-year 'structures' course, a neatly self-contained sector of the total collection. For the one day per week there was no formal timetable, and students were able to come and go as they pleased. There were no constraints on the amount of study, content, length of time to spend, topics to be covered or the order in which to tackle them. There was also no other means by which the students might find out about the available materials, apart from the two trial systems which were displayed on noticeboards in the circulation space outside the Learning Unit.

Information Sheets

One system of 'Information Sheets' was basically a rearranged catalogue-type description of each item together with notes, listing the items which preceded, were direct alternatives to or followed the item in question. This cross-referencing proved rather confusing to the students, since it was also not always easy for them to pick out a particular detail from among the rest. From an administrative point of view, the Information Sheets involved a lot of repetitive writing and took a long time to fill out. They were therefore not popular with the academic staff who had to supply the necessary information.

Decision Cards

The other system of 'Decision Cards' grew out of the flow chart representation and considerations of frame progression and linkages in programmed learning. Attention

409

NUMBER 1/301	TITLE Cranked beams tutorial
BLOCK Beams Revision	
PRE-REQUISITE ITEMS Competency check test 1/278	
STUDY TIME 1 - 3 hours	
RECORDED TIME 40 mins	
INTENDED USE (INDIVIDUAL) / GROUP / CLASS	
PHYSICAL FORM Cassette tape + question sheet (A4) + answer sheet (2 pages A4)	
AUDIENCE: YEAR CI COURSE Structures	
AUTHOR J. Cowan DATE MADE April 1977	
DESCRIPTIVE NOTES ON STYLE AND APPROACH Straightforward questions, graded difficulty	
SUMMARY OF MAIN TEACHING POINTS Cranked beams only, as per objectives list	
RECOMMENDATION FOR USE Selective approach to choice of questions, depending on performance in 1/278	

NOTES ON ORDER AND CHOICE BETWEEN ITEMS

PRECEDED BY   1/141 Beams revision (2) deflection + cranks
              1/157 Beams revision (3) hinged beams
              1/317 Beams tutorial
              1/209 SF + BMD tutorial
              1/278 Competency Check Test

PARALLEL TO   1/209 SF + BMD tutorial
              1/302 Beams Post-test
              1/317 Beams tutorial

FOLLOWED BY   1/209 SF + BMD tutorial
              1/302 Beams Post-test
              1/317 Beams tutorial

Figure 3. *Information Sheet*

was focused on the points in the flow chart where decisions between several alternatives had to be made. These options were then grouped on one Decision Card (Figure 4).

```
┌────────────────────────────────────────────────────────────────────────┐
│                                                                          │
│   INFLUENCE LINES REVISION                                    CARD A      │
│   ─────────────────────────                                              │
│   If wishing to start immediately by tackling revision tutorials  Card E │
│                                                                          │
│   For routine revision of main teaching points (leading eventually       │
│     to tut 1/213)                                                1/212   │
│                                                                          │
│   For a remedial summary, with an elementary approach, covering          │
│     beam reactions only                                          1/228   │
│                                                                          │
│   For a mixture of remedial teaching and guided calculation of a         │
│     worked example concurrently.  (Intended for someone needing          │
│     to start almost from the beginning again)                    1/231   │
│                                                                          │
│   For a brisk remedial summary, quickly revising all aspects             │
│     including complications, snags and dodges                    1/232   │
│                                                                          │
│   If wishing to check competence immediately in Post-test        1/335   │
│                                                                          │
└────────────────────────────────────────────────────────────────────────┘
```

Figure 4. *Decision Card*

Depending on which of the alternatives was followed up, the 'sequence list' of materials in numerical order (Figure 5) signalled which other Decision Card pinpointed the next decision point.

```
┌────────────────────────────────────────────────────────────────────────┐
│ CI : STRUCTURES                                                          │
│                                                                          │
│ TERM 3 : Revision Materials                                              │
│ ──────────────────────────────────────────────────────────────────────  │
│                                                                          │
│ Chosen from decision card:        Item No.        Next decision card:    │
│                                                                          │
│     Influence Lines E             1/114           Influence Lines F      │
│     Equilibrium A                 1/127           Equilibrium B          │
│     Vectors A                     1/132           Vectors B              │
│     Beams A                       1/137           Beams B                │
│     Beams A,B                     1/141           Beams C                │
│     Beams A,C,B                   1/157           beams D                │
│                                                                          │
│     Equilibrium A                 1/206           Equilibrium B          │
│     Equilibrium B                 1/207           Equilibrium C          │
│     Beams A                       1/208           Beams D                │
│     Beams D                       1/209           Beams E                │
│     Pin-jointed Frames A          1/210           Pin-jointed Frames B   │
│     Pin-jointed Frames B          1/211           Pin-jointed Frames C   │
│     Influence Lines A             1/212           Influence Lines E      │
│     Influence Lines E             1/213           Influence Lines F      │
│     Pin-jointed Frames A          1/216           Pin-jointed Frames B   │
│                                                                          │
```

Figure 5. *Extract from sequence list*

One criticism of this system was that very little information about the actual items was provided beyond a brief 'cryptic' descriptive phrase or recommendation.

Full-Scale Trials

Drawing on experience so far and the lessons learnt from the initial trials it was decided to experiment further with two full-scale trials over the next academic term (Barker, 1978).

All the possibilities were again carefully considered and further views on user and staff requirements sought. The two retrieval systems given the full trial were both based on Decision Cards which were to be duplicated so that a set of the relevant Decision Cards could be given to each student.

'Hybrid' Scheme

Since it had been observed during the pilot trials that some students used both the Information Sheets and Decision Cards in conjunction, a 'hybrid' system was initiated. Decision Cards similar to those of the pilot scheme were drawn up (Figure 6) and a back-up system of amended Information Sheets provided the more typical catalogue description of each item (Figure 7).

E	RELATIONSHIP BETWEEN PROPERTIES AND USE OF MATERIALS		
E1	1/246 AT	Introductory outline of this block, including programme and objectives	E2
E2	Both the following should be studied:		
	1/118 TS	Argument for the existence of a relationship	E2
	1/119 TS	Argument against the existence of a relationship	E2
	STUDY OF BOTH THE ABOVE COMPLETED		E3
E3	1/202 AT	Introduction to follow-up activity : debate	E4
E4	Prepare your own argument for or against the existence of a relationship		E5
E5	"Debate" Arrange discussion with course tutor		E6
E6	Check programme and objectives listed on h/o 1/246		E6
	STUDY IN THIS BLOCK COMPLETED		B

Figure 6. *POMAS Decision Card*

This trial scheme covered a small collection of third-year 'enrichment' materials and the first part of a special experimental course 'Properties of Materials: Alternative Syllabus' (POMAS). In the latter case, extensive and problem-free use was made of the Decision Cards, although the Information Sheets were relatively neglected, partly because some of the class maintained they were unaware of their existence, and partly because of the effort required on the part of the user to search the file.

'Expanded' Decision Card Scheme

The second scheme consisted of 'expanded' Decision Cards giving fairly full descriptions of each item (Figure 8). This was used to cover the first term of the first-year 'structures' course.

NUMBER	TITLE	POMAS
1/153		Practice identification of serviceability failures

STYLE AND APPROACH

Question, response, answer

SUMMARY OF MAIN TEACHING POINTS

Practice in identifying modes of serviceability failure in everyday and civil engineering examples

SPECIAL INSTRUCTIONS

NONE

RECORDED TIME   15 MINS

STUDY TIME   15 mins

PHYSICAL FORM   Tape/slide

INTENDED FOR USE BY   (INDIVIDUAL) / GROUP / CLASS

TOPIC   Serviceability

AUDIENCE: YEAR CI	COURSE POMAS

AUTHOR   John Cowan   DATE MADE   Sept. 1975

Figure 7. *POMAS Information Sheet*

<table>
<tr><td colspan="3"><h1>VECTORS</h1></td><td>Week 4
1 of 1</td></tr>
</table>

A	1/229 AT h/o solns qns, solns	Vectors Skip-test (self-marking) If you have studied 'Vectors' before you may not need further instruction - attempt diagnostic test 8 min (40 min)	B
	NOT STUDIED VECTORS BEFORE/NOT CONFIDENT ON THIS TOPIC		C
B	PASSED SKIP-TEST		J
	FAILED SKIP-TEST		C
C	1/172 T/OH h/o	Vectors 1 Instruction - Obj. 1,2,3,4,5 (2(a), 2(b), 4 graphically) 33 min (40 min)	D
	REMINDER OF MAIN TEACHING POINTS		D
	CHOICE OF TUTORIALS		E
D	1/173S AT h/o	Vectors 1 Summary 10 min (10 min)	E
	CHOICE OF TUTORIALS		E
E	STRAIGHTFORWARD TUTORIAL covering main points of Vectors 1 Instruction		F
	COMPREHENSIVE TUTORIAL with further material content beyond Vectors 1		G
	QUICK TEST OF COMPETENCE		H
F	1/173G AT h/o qns	Vectors 1 Guided tutorial 4 min (20 min)	H
	1/173D AT h/o solns	Vectors 1 Detail tutorial 18 min (30 min)	H
	MORE DEMANDING TUTORIAL		G
G	1/219G AT h/o qns	Vectors 2 Guided tutorial 10 min (30 min)	H
	1/219D AT h/o solns	Vectors 2 Detail tutorial 4 min (20 min)	H
H	1/234 AT h/o solns qns	Vectors Checksheet 5 min (15 min)	J
	READY TO MOVE ON TO NEXT TOPIC		J
J	1/176 AT h/o	Beams Introduction - highly recommended as 'scene-setter' before Beams 1 Instruction 10 min (10 min)	BEAMS

Figure 8. *Decision Cards — 'expanded'*

It seemed that because the 'standard pattern' of options still prevailed in the early stages of the course it was recognized as such by some of the students who felt no need to use the Decision Cards and hence missed out on various alternatives or optional materials.

Review

As a result of these two full-scale trials it was decided to standardize on the 'expanded Decision Card' scheme (Figure 8) as the best means of making most of the information directly available to individual students. Work is also in progress on compiling an 'authority file' to give cataloguing details of the separate items and a record is being kept of the albeit rough and rather 'ad hoc' flow charts which are drafted when drawing up the Decision Cards.

Evaluation

Evaluation of the schemes described has been carried out by observation, interviews, student questionnaires and random checking. The criterion has always been the success of the scheme in meeting the needs of the student users of the information system when they are genuinely exercising a meaningful freedom of choice in decision-making, in accordance with the educational aims of the teaching staff.

Observations to date indicate that extensive and problem-free use has been made of all the systems based on Decision Cards, except that where some students expected and recognized the established standard pattern (for which the materials were usually on open access, displayed week by week as appropriate) they chose not to consult the Decision Cards and hence missed out on various alternative or optional materials. This reluctance to use the schemes on the part of some students, despite initial instruction, staff available for consultation, and reminders illustrated with examples of what has been missed was probably the major difficulty faced while introducing the information system, but this declined noticeably towards the end of the second term when the range of choices proliferated so as to obscure the standard format.

On the other hand, students who have conscientiously studied the Decision Cards before attending their classes have exercised considerable freedom in choosing what to do; and there is evidence that individuals have followed widely differing study paths and at different rates.

In general the lecturers have been able to add to the collection a wider range of materials than was formerly feasible because an adequate means of describing them to the students now exists (Figure 9).

Alternative approaches that had not even been contemplated before have been offered and well used, in addition to those that were previously in the realms of 'wishful thinking'. Thus the capability of the collection to provide individualized learning facilities has been extended.

Conclusions

(1) If the materials held in a resource collection are not deliberately structured to be interrelated in a study course, then the Decision Card information system is not applicable since its framework is built upon these linkages. Conventional cataloguing and indexing techniques can cope in this type of situation (Beswick, 1975).

415

Styles of audio-tutorial tape offered or developed during the period 1971-1976

Detailed tutorial tape	— a complete worked example solution
Guided tutorial tape	— assisting the student to carry out his own detailed solution
Summary	— a review of the main teaching points
Revision	— a review tape intended for people who have already had the instruction, presumably sometime previously
Remedial	— prepared for those who had difficulty with the subject matter, and examples based on it, when they first encountered it
Initial instruction	— provided on audio-tutorial when it was anticipated that each learner would wish to go at his own pace from the outset
Self marking tape	— for drawings or tests, to enable the student to form his own assessment of his own work

A total of seven different tape types, in six academic sessions, finishing at Easter 1977.

New types of audio-tutorial tape developed or put in to regular use during the period March 1977 — March 1978

Routine post-tests	— intended for use by students at the end of each block of instruction, to check their progress
Quickies or checklists	— short tutorials of a multiple-choice type, where the answers are discussed on the audio tape
Supplementary tutorials	— offered in parallel with the standard programme of tutorials, but generally to a different standard being either more difficult or more straightforward
Introductory commentaries	— to explain to the student the content of a forthcoming block of instruction, and the administrative arrangements associated with it, or to provide similar such information.

A total of four new tape types in one academic session.

Thus it will be seen that there has been an increase of almost 60 per cent in the types of materials offered, and that this increase has occurred in a period which represents about 14 per cent of the life of the Unit.

Figure 9. *Table of additional materials offered*

(2) A Decision Card information system (or something similar) will usually be necessary for the effective operation of courses such as the POMAS course described earlier (Cowan, 1978) which offers considerable freedom in the selection of course content.

(3) If the inter-institutional exchange of materials which normally fit into a structured course is envisaged at some time in the future, it would be essential for standard description formats to be drawn up to allow comparisons to be made between very similar materials, taking into account their original and intended learning contexts so that effective use can be made of them.

References

Barker, A.L. (1978) A retrieval system for learning resource materials in the context of individualised instruction. Paper to be presented at the 1978 Annual Conference of the Institute of Information Scientists.

Barker, A.L. and Cowan, J. (1978) Cataloguing and retrieval of interrelated resource materials. *British Journal of Educational Technology.*

Beswick, N.W. (1975) *Organising Resources: Six Case Studies.* Heinemann Educational, London.

Bingham, E.G. (1977) Free format timetabling revisited. In Hills, P. and Gilbert, J. (eds.) *Aspects of Educational Technology XI.* Kogan Page, London.

Cowan, J. (1978) 'Offering freedom in the choice of course content'. To be published.

Library Association, Media Cataloguing Rules Committee (1973) *Non-Book Media Cataloguing Rules.* NCET Working Paper 11. National Council for Educational Technology and the Library Association, London.

55. Progress with Programmed Learning 1968-78: The Development of the Longman Group Reading Programme

J. Leedham, *Rothley, Leics*

Abstract: The Liverpool Conference in 1974 published in its proceedings, an account of six years of work with reading programmes. During the intervening five years the material has been widely published and accepted. The reported results have led to further work in interrelating concept, perception and language. Current trials have indicated very warm acceptance for the methods used and the controls employed.

Programmed Learning in 1978

The principles of programmed learning have provided the guideway for applied systems of education and training since 1960. The by-ways of educational technology, algorithmic-heurism systems methodology, simulation and micro-teaching and so on, have branched off from this principal road. The signpost on this main road now reads:

> *Define* the Task
> *Ensure* the learning population
> *Organize* learning material
> *Confirm* the learning situation
> *Test* the result
> *Revise* the Task

This simple statement of principle embraces most reported deviations. *Ensuring* the learning population indicates that learners need the programme, are ready for it and have had preliminary adjustments made so that they can use new techniques. *Organizing* the material means using media and systems which are appropriate and economical. *Confirming* the situation is the practice of making adjustments for individuals as learning progresses. *Testing* and *Revising* the Task are self-explanatory terms.

DEFINING: ENSURING: ORGANIZING: CONFIRMING: TESTING: REVISING

These are human attributes and this is what contemporary programmed learning is all about. Any system of programmed learning which has progressed must have taken greater account of the inclusion of human endeavour. The following details indicate one successful scheme especially developed over ten years in accordance with these principles.

The 1968 Reading Programmes

The 1974 Liverpool Conference of APLET published an account of six years' work with reading programmes (Leedham, 1974a). In particular, a scheme just then published by Longmans, 'Reading Routes', was examined as an example of

418

programmed material likely to be successful after several years of preparation. The simplest way to review this material is to see a film clip which states the aims and shows the content. (A three-minute film extract was shown to Conference [Eds.].)

The scheme relies particularly upon the use of controlled vocabulary, interrelated text and illustration: titles were scheduled to develop concepts progressively; but at that time little was understood of such schedules. The grading of the scheme was in small steps, folder by folder in a linear pattern. A skip-branching programme was built into the scheme to enable pupils to advance at their own speed. The scheme and its development is described in the appropriate teachers' guide (Leedham, 1974b) and the other descriptive literature of the date (Leedham, 1974c).

The programme had been extensively tested and it is now well received in the UK and overseas. It has already been said that the idea of developing concepts on the basis of title, content and vocabulary was not very thoroughly grasped. In the event complete success for the scheme was perhaps denied because of failure to be simple enough despite the editorial motto of *KISS*. This stands for *Keep It Simple Stupid*. Doubtless the experience is a common one that the achievement of simplicity comes by much effort and frequent failure. Nevertheless the relatively high level of acceptance of the scheme in English-speaking countries led to the establishment of further trials, first undertaken in 1973. These trials in turn led to an extension of the programme now to be described. Although five years in trial and production it is not yet published but should be by the autumn of 1978 or spring of 1979.

The Development of an Improved Programmed System

In considering how to improve on success authors of programmed schemes need first to debate how to retain those elements identified with this success and to avoid developing over-clever schemes lacking these elements. It seemed apparent from observation that the linear skip-branch format with well-illustrated folders proceeding along a carefully graded path was a reasonably successful formula. This graded path relied upon vocabulary control, linguistic control and a topic development extended to match concept development. For example, the simplest folder on the 'animal routeway' is entitled 'Brave Dogs' and the title of an advanced folder 100 steps onward is 'The Language of Fish'.

By examining the scheme and its results in the light of our programming formula it was possible to define areas for improvement (see Figure 1).

The Reading Routes Blue Box

It will help to refer to the most recently developed programme under the title of Blue Box by which it will eventually be known. The following detail explains how revision has been achieved on the basis of the preliminary analysis so far quoted.

Trials

It is fortunate that the publishers share the very healthy view that theory without practice is only half the story. They supported trials on 50 schools throughout the UK to test if the following revisions were effective.

	Observation
Define Task:	Task too difficult for poor readers. Teacher help often needed. Concept forming provision inadequate.
Ensure Population:	Preparatory Scheme needed to overlap present programme.
Organize Materials:	General format acceptable. Illustrations need programming. Programmed progress to be consolidated by using BLOCK-STEPS rather than small steps.
CONFIRMING:	Alternatives to be possible at teacher's discretion. Story or fictional elements in each BLOCK as recapitulatory elements.
TESTING:	Scoring and checking system to be simplified. Less questions to be asked.
REVISING:	Use of 'BLOCK-STEPS' to achieve this.

Figure 1

(1) DEFINE TASK

Revision needed
Rewrite complete scheme for lower age groups dovetailing into existing programme. Use teacher support from the start. Develop a title list keyed to known conceptual development.

How achieved
The scheme was redefined for reading ages of six years upwards and was programmed for children or others starting to read or lagging in progress. An audio component involving the teacher was included to cover the first 20 folders. The titles were put in blocks of five with four blocks to a 'theme'. These titles matched the accepted identities of concepts for age (examples were shown to Conference).

(2) ENSURE POPULATION

Revision needed
Describe population more exactly in terms of reading ages. Indicate in teacher's guide the need for learner to start where the textual and illustrative 'mix' is comprehensible to him. From a reading age of 8.0 years ensure that the reading material matches to previous programme but is shorter and simpler.

How achieved
The table of reading ages was graded in four and five monthly intervals. A test was devised using text and illustration to place learners who were starting the programme. Length of passage and number of questions were kept below that of the comparable original scheme folders.

(3) ORGANIZE MATERIAL

Revision needed
Simplify colour coding of folders. Relate illustration and text so that pictures or photographs support text stage by stage. Devise such a scheme that learners can consolidate learned material from several folders.

How achieved

Colour coding reduced to four colours. Sequenced photographs were taken covering a preliminary scenario. Texts were written under controlled conditions as to vocabulary and structure so that illustrations supported comprehension. Drawn illustrations were used for each revisory folder. Themes using 20 folders each matched the concept development of each reading age. Within each theme, four 'BLOCK-STEPS' on linked topics consisted of five folders each. Of these five folders, the fifth was a revision folder covering the preceding four folders. Each revisory folder was associated with audio or printed support.

(4) CONFIRMING

Revision needed

Introduce more teacher participation in early stages. Include revision items at frequent intervals. Maintain interest with revisory story.

How achieved

The first 20 folders were matched to an audio component. The teacher could use this in various ways. A smaller question component enables teachers to supervise self-checking more adequately. The fifth or revisory folders of each 'block' were written in story form as against the non-fiction content of the preceding four folders.

(5) TESTING AND REVISING

Revision needed

A simpler scoring system and work book to be produced. (Revision system to be teacher-linked.)

How achieved

The work book and scoring system were matched to the age range by experimental investigation. Each revisory folder was matched to a work card which involves the learner with the teacher at some time.

When the revised programme was eventually drawn up — it took some two years — a 10 per cent black and white print-off was done in order to test the material in schools. (Examples of the folders and associate illustrations were screened at this stage.)

Trial Results

PARTICIPATING SCHOOLS. 55 schools were supplied with the materials. They were distributed as follows:

Clackmannan	1 Primary	Leicestershire	3 Primary
Derbyshire	1 Primary		1 Infant
Dundee	1 Primary		3 Remedial
Dudley	1 Primary		2 Middle
Isle of Wight	1 Primary	Leeds	1 Remedial
Lancashire	15 Primary	Lincolnshire	3 Primary
	8 Junior	Norwich	1 Infant
	1 Middle		3 Primary
Stirling	2 Primary		1 Middle
West Bromwich	1 Primary		1 Remedial

421

Nottinghamshire	1 Primary	(Infant 5–7 years)
	1 Remedial	(Primary 5–10+ years)
	1 Middle	(Middle 10–14 years)
Peterborough	1 Middle	(Remedial 10–17 years)

A special distribution was made to the Home Office Studies Unit for use with adult retardees.

Of the 55 schools, 48 made effective returns. Of these 48 schools 39 made comprehensive returns. It will be seen that the coverage was geographically wide and ranged over the age span 5–14+ years with major emphasis at the primary level.

QUESTIONNAIRE ANALYSIS. The reporting schools gave details of 70 different age groupings. Table 1 was arrived at by a very conservative assessment of each response.

The main input from the trials was the examination of responses from the learner. From this it was quickly evident that 25 per cent of the printed trial material was not achieving its target. This, again, appeared to be because of the over-complex treatment of topics outside the conceptual ability of the learner. For example, a well-illustrated folder on 'DEER' was responded to below the required level. In the view of most teachers this was because 'a deer' was not a distinctly appreciable idea as compared with a dog or a horse. The considerable detail from the responses and teachers' comments led to very much alteration of some of the distributed folders, and the cancellation of others. With the revised 10 per cent sample it was then felt safe enough to brief the team of five authors who would produce the revised Blue Box Programme. The results will be seen in the finally published versions late in 1978 or early in 1979. As the scheme was produced during the compilation of the Bullock Report on reading standards, it was natural that it would be influenced by it. Fortunately, the Bullock tenets and the scheme run well together (Bullock, 1975).

Summary

It is obvious that, even after years of careful planning, learning material can fail to achieve its goal. The essential elements for successful programming at this (or quite probably any) level are simplicity, teacher inclusion, trial and revision. Perhaps it is of note that the seven photographs sequenced in an early folder were the result of hundreds of trial photographs. This was typical of much of the revision. In most cases it was clear that children today have visual reference concepts much in advance of their literary concepts. After 15 years' experience with systems and programming it appears to the author that progress is best ensured by the formulae KISS and DEOCT (Define, Ensure, Organize, Confirm, Test).

References

Bullock, A. (ed.) (1975) *A Language for Life.* HMSO (The Bullock Report), London.

Leedham, J. (1974a) The development of a programmed reading system for primary education. In Baggaley, J.P., Jamieson, G.H., and Marchant, H. (eds.) *Aspects of Educational Technology VIII.* Pitman, London.

Leedham, J. (ed.) (1974b) *Reading Routes Red Scheme. Teacher's Guide.* Longman, Harlow.

Leedham, J. (1974c) *Educational Technology. A First Look.* Pitman Education Library, London.

Leedham, J. (ed.) (1978) (due) *Reading Routes Blue Box.* Longman, Harlow.

Age Group (Chronological)	Years					
	6 to 7	7 to 8	8 to 9	9 to 10	10 to 11	11+
Number of Groups	10	21	20	11	4	4
Assessed						
Very Good	1	4	4	5		
Good	5	11	9	2		1
Satisfactory	2	5	5	2	2	1
Fair (less than satisfactory)	1	1	1	2	1	1
Useless	1		1		1	1

School Groups assessing Hard or Easy

Age Range	6 to 7	7 to 8	8 to 9	9 to 10	10 to 11	11+
Hard	3	15	8	5	1	
Easy	7	6	12	6	3	

The following detail is compiled from 39 reporting schools:

School groups indicating teachers necessary support diminished	27
School groups indicating teachers necessary support continued	12

Matching of reading ages to those stated on folders

Matched	Did not match	Partly matched
22	7 (too high)	10

Was cassette useful?
Yes   26
No   13

Was cassette recorder available?
Yes   29
No   10

Did illustration help reading?
Considerably   26
A little   12
Not at all   1

Were photographs more help than drawings?
Yes   30
No   9

Should a 70% score be achieved before child goes on?
Yes   44
No   5

Table 1

Chapter 10:
Additional Contributions
and Delegates' Forum Review

Additional Contributions

An extra perspective was added to the conference by the welcome addition to the programme of some films and talks (often on subjects rather more remotely connected to educational technology). Some of these contributions allowed delegates to observe a view of educational technology from a completely different frame of reference to their own (for example Philip Kogan's most interesting and informative account of the publisher's view). Others described initial ideas, and these may well be discussed in more detail after development and evaluation of the ideas. The additional contributions are summarized below.

P. Kogan, the managing director of APLET's publishing house, gave a most interesting presentation entitled 'The publishing decision'. An account was given of the economic aspects of publication, and the factors leading to a publisher specializing in particular subject areas (such as the accumulation of back-up expertise). Typical educational technology publications would be costed on the basis of between 1,250-2,500 copies being sold, maybe over an initial two-year period. It was noted that the situation regarding the publication of journals was different in many respects from book production. R. E. B. Budgett (General Editor of APLET Publications) who chaired the ensuing lively discussion, made the point that the standard of copy submitted by many distinguished colleagues was far from good, and bad copy caused serious problems (and much increased costing) to the publisher. (It must be added that in editing these proceedings, we could hardly fail to notice that the more distinguished the author, the further away from the suggested format and deadlines the submissions were!)

A. P. W. Gardner of Queen's College, Glasgow gave a presentation entitled 'The importance of examining educational models prior to management decision about needs'. The presentation examined basic models of the educational process, and the relevance of these models in the establishment of priority needs for teachers and managers. It is to be hoped that in due course the topic of this stimulating presentation will be expanded on and will appear at a future conference or in publication.

R. Delpak and W. M. Hague of the Polytechnic of Wales presented an account of the teaching of an interdisciplinary subject (vibrations) to civil engineering students. A teaching programme was outlined, including details of the roles of tutorial and project work. The work described included detailed consideration of the syllabus material involved. It may be profitable for a future paper to provide an educational assessment of the course, and details of the structure and objectives of teaching programme components.

J. Melia, Training Adviser of T.A.C. Construction Materials, Ltd, presented a description of a plan to use programmed learning techniques for the instruction of asbestos cement operatives. After outlining the cement-making processes, the aims of the planned programmes were given, including improving operatives' expertise maintaining quality and production levels, and generating a team spirit among operatives. It may be hoped that after implementation of the programme, an interesting evaluation of its effectiveness may be presented at a future conference.

P. M. J. Hancock, of the Institute of Adult Education, University of Rhodesia, presented work done in collaboration with A. P. Petasis, on 'Deriving interaction models for training supervisors in industry'. The work described the results of 342 operatives completing a questionnaire to provide information about elements of effective supervision. The results illustrate the effect on operators of approaches ranging from polite to 'threatening dismissal'. Four interaction training models were derived, one recorded on video-tape was used to illustrate the study. P. M. J. Hancock also introduced a film 'Savings for life in rural Africa'. This was concerned with basic adult education and 'savings clubs' to enable peasant farmers to meet their subsistence and cash needs, relevant to the development of farming areas in Rhodesia and 'third world' countries.

P. Hurst, of the British Council, introduced a film, 'A communication strategy for development' produced jointly with the Indian television service. It presented work done during a one-year experimental lease by NASA (USA) to the Indian government of an 'Applications technology satellite'. The film illustrated programmes being recorded and viewed in villages and schools, and considered research and evaluation of the satellite experiment.

Delegates' Forum Review

In the 'Delegates' Forum', provision was made for the presentation of post-deadline papers, as well as for any impromptu presentations or discussions arising out of the conference in general. The 'Delegates' Forum' was organized by Dr D. I. Trotman-Dickenson (Polytechnic of Wales). In fact, only two papers were presented in the Forum (partly because some other post-deadline contributions were accommodated in the main conference streams where a number of cancellations had occurred). Abstracts of the two papers are given below.

New Techniques in Industrial Training for Illiterates

Y. Jordan, *Manager, Industrial Training Unit, Natal College for Advanced Technical Education, Durban, South Africa*

There is an urgent need for operator training for the labour-intensive industrial concerns in South Africa. Although this was recognized some time ago, progress has been slow owing to the following problems:

(1) trainees' lack of sufficient formal education
(2) language difficulties
(3) lack of success of conventional teaching methods
(4) training officers being either academics or technicians.

L. C. Cowie of Durban, South Africa, proposed a solution to the problem by devising an industrial training officers' course which was packaged and implemented this year at the Natal College.

The presentation covers very briefly the sets and subsets contained in this course, viz. the training officer is taught to do the following:

(1) Analyse
    (a) what to analyse
    (b) how to analyse using general systems theories, and Parets principle (20/80)
(2) Build his course of training for a selected occupation
    (a) using programmed instruction
    (b) using visual and sound tracks in the language of the learner
    (c) packaging the course (practical work)
(3) Implement his course training
    (a) selecting training and evaluating a course controller having the same

cultural and occupational background as trainees
(b) evaluating the course programmes and the students' progress.

Although it is argued that literacy before vocational training is the ideal, it is not possible in terms of time, numbers involved, and economics. This attempt to solve the problem starts at the other end of the scale: 'training the father so that he may educate his son'.

Some Effects of Educational Technology on Curriculum Reform

D. J. Magin, *University of New South Wales, Australia*

The university's Tertiary Education Research Centre had been established to improve teaching and learning within the university. The presenter described evidence (with examples mostly from engineering courses) of the impact of educational technology on various curricula and on projected reforms.

Of recent origin as an instructional tool, interactive computing could be considered as the most dramatic and significant of the innovations mentioned. The availability of a Wang desk-top mini-computer in an undergraduate engineering laboratory led to investigations of using it to improve teaching. The use of automated marking was also seen as a desirable innovation. Introduction of on-line remote computing facilities opened up new areas of syllabus, and new sets of course objectives that had not been included in the traditional engineering curricula.

The concept of the 'missing curriculum' in engineering courses in the University of New South Wales is significant. Examples presented illustrate that there are many chances to use educational technology which go beyond improvement of efficiency. The new tools can be used to extend learning experiences and to change the curriculum.

Chapter 11: Workshop Sessions

Workshop Review

D. M. Wharry, *University College, Cardiff*

Introduction

The provisional programme of workshops included in the conference booklet indicated that seven delegates wished to provide workshops. By the end of the introductory session (in which some details were given about forthcoming workshops) the organizers were pleased to accept two further proposals for workshop activities.

The purpose of these notes is to indicate to those who were unable to participate, an outline of the content of each workshop. One session has been transcribed fairly completely (J. G. Barker) and the transcript (along with a summary of his conference paper) has been included after this review. It is hoped that the inclusion of this detailed conference will be useful to 'undecided' delegates at future conferences, who may opt to participate in workshops as a result of the transcript providing them with information about what actually is involved in attending a typical workshop.

One of the problems facing delegates at these conferences is the choice of activity at a particular time; opting for a 1 to 3 hour-long workshop session could entail missing up to four lectures of the programme. However, an alternative solution of placing all the workshops at one time and holding no normal presentations during that time, would have meant a dozen or so fewer papers being given a presentation at the conference (and also have meant that a delegate could only attend a single workshop). A further difficulty arises when a workshop needs to be given in two parts (an introductory talk to be followed later by some practical or feedback activity). The presenter may be disappointed to find fewer (or even none) of the original 'takers' for the second session.

It was possibly for the reason indicated above that the well-attended opening workshop **A Proposal for Analysing Lecture Styles in Higher Education** showed a rather disappointing response to the presenter's request that participants bring back data accumulated during the conference to the second session (at the end of the conference). The workshop proposed to participants that each should learn a system of interaction coding (proposed by D. M. Wharry) and should then apply it to several lectures during the conference. They were then to bring back the results at the end of the conference. It was hoped that this would yield some interesting (and I hasten to add: anonymous!) information on the possibility of making quantitative descriptions of various lecturing styles. In the event, the request probably was too daunting — to learn a new system, employ it, and at the same time get the most out of the lectures attended seemed a near impossibility. Because of the interest expressed, however, the initial part of this workshop is presented formally, at the end of this chapter.

433

R. Clements (Insight Training Ltd) presented the second workshop **The Effects of Attitudes, Behaviour and Teaching Style on the Teacher/Student Relationship.** This was based on a system of psychotherapy known as translational analysis (T.A.) which was brought to the attention of the public in Berne's well-known book *The Games People Play*. During the session, some of the more common psychological games played out between the teacher and the taught, were discovered and discussed. Each participant was involved in exercises designed to uncover games which he initiated and others into which he was drawn. This need for awareness was borne out by the observation that we play out our games from a position of unawareness, although the feeling of discomfort at the termination indicates some sense of manipulating or being manipulated.

The concepts of Berne, which were dealt with during the workshop, were broken down into four main areas:

(1) Structural analysis — dealing with the structure and functions of the personality of the individual.
(2) Transactional analysis — analysing and classifying the elements of communication between individuals.
(3) Game analysis — identifying and breaking up repetitive and destructive patterns of ulterior behaviour.
(4) Script analysis — identifying the prohibitive and permissive messages around which children make life-long decisions for living.

Mapping the Field of Educational Technology was the title of the third workshop run by J. Green (Middlesex Polytechnic) and A. Morris (South Thames College) as a sequel to one on the same theme at ETIC '77. Participants were asked to comment on and add to a conceptual model of the functions and competencies of an educational technologist when filling five discernable roles, viz.

resource manager
systems developer
learning consultant
materials producer
innovator.

After 30 minutes, pairs of participants reported back their amendments and opinions, which were further discussed in open forum.

By way of a plan for action the group thought it would be possible to produce a document that would survey the competencies required to perform the various tasks within a number of discernable roles involving the use of educational technology. It was anticipated that such a survey would probably involve some 35 experts — ideally at an international level — and the group recommended that a pilot exercise be set up. This would initially involve only the following (who were participants in the workshop): P. Baker, J. Coffey, J. A. Davies, W. J. K. Davies, E. Howarth, G. Hurley, M. A. Lezer, C. Neville, F. O'Reilly, C. Teall and J. Twining. They would carry out a 'paper exercise' and perform a task analysis of the role of VALIDATOR. The workshop leader (J. Green) would coordinate the pilot scheme, issue a report on the paper exercise, and arrange a follow-up meeting.

Summary of Amendments and Opinions

Group I   ☐ suggested that NEGOTIATOR for resources be added to the list.
             ☐ pointed out that in the school environment there are two sets of aims

	— those directed towards EXAMINATIONS	
	— those concerned with the development of the individual (not obligatory)	
Group II	☐ related the roles to people in colleges and schools	
	☐ observed that there was no reference to LEARNER	
	☐ remarked that in most institutions there existed a network of relation for 'getting things done'	
	☐ asked . . . who had the job of looking at existing materials?	
Group III	☐ asked if there was a 'central role' of systems development manager?	
	☐ observed that the decisions made by a materials producer were cyclic not linear	
Group IV	☐ linked the given roles with institutions	
	— Resource manager — Head of Resource (School)	
	— Systems developer — Staff Development (School)	
	— Learning consultant — Adviser LEA	
	— Materials producer — MRO/LEA (teacher centre leader)	
	— Innovator — general global plans	
Group V	☐ distinguished between competencies and functions	
	☐ commented that it would be possible to identify 'core competencies' and thus produce the necessary training scheme.	
Group VI	☐ suggested that VALIDATOR be added to list.	

D. I. Trotman-Dickenson (Polytechnic of Wales) conducted a workshop entitled **The Use of Data Response in the Teaching of Economics and for Examination Purposes.**

The use of Data Response in the teaching of economics and for examination purposes is relatively new and so far had not been widespread in universities, polytechnics and schools in the UK.

In future it will have to be used more extensively. The University of London introduced for the first time in June 1977 a compulsory paper in Data Response for the General Certificate of Education examinations in economics at the advanced level. Consequently several thousand candidates who are entered each year for this examination, by secondary schools and colleges of further education in the UK and by overseas centres in the developing countries, will have to be familiarized with Data Response.

D. I. Trotman-Dickenson devised and experimented for some years with the Data Approach Method (DAM) as a method of teaching, programmed learning, and as a basis for examinations. She became aware of the need for DAM from her experience of teaching at the University of Manchester, University of Edinburgh, University College of Wales, Aberystwyth and the Polytechnic of Wales. Many students studying economics at a foundation level have little knowledge of mathematics. They are put off courses in statistics for economists or in quantitative methods because they find them difficult. A high proportion of the students in their subsequent careers will not be called upon to compile economic statistics, but some may have to be able to analyse and interpret them.

The object of DAM is to familiarize students with economic data and to give them some quantitative knowledge of economic problems as a first step to analysis and evaluation of statistical material.

The purpose of her workshop was to:

(1) Demonstrate the use of DAM with the aid of her *Economic Workbook and Data* (Pergamon Press) on which DAM is based.

(2) Discuss preparation of DAM material and its adaptation to specific requirements
   (a) for schools and universities or polytechnics
   (b) for different courses or sections of syllabus
   (c) to illustrate various aspects of the economy of the UK and of other countries.
(3) Evaluate DAM in the light of her experience in using it for
   (a) seminar work
   (b) tutorial exercises
   (c) written work
   (d) assessment of students' performance and progress.
(4) Compare her findings with those of other users of Data Response as a method of teaching and as a basis for examinations.

H. I. Ellington and F. Percival (Robert Gordon's Institute of Technology) had intended to start a workshop with a short paper outlining the educational advantages of role-playing simulation games, and then to involve participants in a game having a public enquiry format **Point Fields Public Enquiry**. Unfortunately this workshop had to be cancelled at the last moment.

J. G. Barker ran a well-attended workshop **The Design of Training Packages for Developing Countries**. This dealt with some of the practical problems found in the design of group instructional materials destined to be used in training situations in developing countries. A transcript of this workshop is included later in this chapter. The complete session lasted some two hours and the script given is necessarily somewhat abbreviated, but it does serve to give readers some insight not only into the topic but also into the style of a typical ETIC workshop.

One of the very welcome later additions to the workshops programme was made by G. Frewin (Essex) with the title **Writing a Management Game**. At the outset the basic intention of the exercise was defined. A basic business exercise was then played, and this was followed by the writing of an exercise. The basic ideas which were developed during the session were:

(1) a provisional checklist for defining games and certain other items of educational technology, and
(2) some specifications against which teaching could be measured.

As a sequel to his presentation, D. McCulloch (of the Northern Ireland Polytechnic) arranged with the Computing Centre of the Polytechnic of Wales to make available his BASIC programmes DIP 1, E 10 and TST 1. The title given to his workshop was **Computer Aided Instruction Programmes in Economics (CAIPE)**. Participants were firstly shown the very simple operating procedures used to log-in on a computer terminal and call up these programmes, and then they were able to put themselves in the position of students using the programmes to learn something of some of the fundamental concepts of economics. A detailed account of the inception and development of these programmes together with an appreciation of the assessment, implications and future development of the project appears in Chapter 7 (paper 45).

As a finale to the workshop sessions, J. Megarry (Jordanhill College of Education) undertook to conduct a brainstorming session. Participation in such an activity at the end of the conference was useful in assisting delegates to consolidate and internalize the ideas presented in previous papers. It helped them to react to, criticize and illuminate these ideas with their own background experience and opinions. One hopes that as a result of this workshop, delegates will find inspiration and develop ideas which will result in the presentation of papers and workshops at future ETICs.

Editorial Note

In the preceding pages Dr Wharry gives an informative survey of the content to the conference's complete workshop programme. In general, it seems that workshops offer a very valuable means of delegates 'getting inside' new areas of educational technology. We fear, however, that many delegates do not venture into a workshop, partly out of uncertainty about 'what they may be letting themselves in for'. To help future delegates see the value of the detailed searching a workshop usually produces, we present next a detailed transcript (prepared by J. G. Barker) of his workshop. Moreover, to illustrate further the typical connection of workshops with mainstream conference presentations, we precede the transcript with a shortened version of Mr Barker's conference presentation. Inevitably, it may be argued that some of the 'micro-detail' of the workshop transcript is only of passing interest, but the illustration of exactly what happens at a workshop may be of great value in encouraging delegates in future to 'dip into' the workshops provided (and thereby make the success of the workshops more certain).

56a. Semi-Programmed Group Instruction: An Appropriate Technology for Developing Countries

J. G. Barker, *Tecmedia Ltd, Loughborough, Leics*

Abstract: This paper describes the development of a series of export training packages being produced for International Trade Centre UNCTAD/GATT. The project is at the frontier of educational technology — paradoxically because no 'technology' in terms of physical hardware can be assumed to exist in the learning situation.

The approach is called 'semi-programmed group instruction' because the instructor must modify and adapt the modular units of instruction to suit the needs and ability of his audience.

The theme of this conference is the development, application and evaluation of educational technology related to the needs of industrialized and developing countries, within their respective resource constraints. Now this seems to me to be an entirely proper subject for a conference. Indeed, it seems to be a somewhat overdue subject for a conference, which brings me to the point of this paper which is to describe my own experience in the design of learning systems for developing countries.

It is not, unfortunately, a story of cool scientific method — rather one of blood, sweat and tears.

I founded Tecmedia in 1972, offering a specialized design and production service to educational publishers. However, we were gradually drawn away from conventional books towards media packages — not because they were more profitable but because they seemed to be more exciting. I think we are the only commercial outfit in the world exclusively dedicated to the production of packages. And it is not difficult to see why we are alone in this field.

The market is so small and specialized and the commercial production of packages is fraught with so many problems, that educational publishers shy away from them and concentrate on products with spines — good old money-making books. They have left the multi-media field to the audiovisual specialists: tape/slides, films, video or audio cassette oriented packages with support material. Tecmedia stands alone, somewhere in between the two sides. Its product is neither book oriented, nor audiovisual oriented. It is (I hope) need oriented.

We were dragged kicking and screaming into the production of packages by David Barnett of BP Educational Service some five years ago, when he commissioned us to re-design the 'Decisions' packs; a series of decision-making simulations for schools. We developed a particular design approach based on the concept of a large plastic portfolio which opened up to reveal all its contents in a methodical way.

We soon discovered that, due to the hundreds of separate items, coherent design was only possible by working hand in glove with the writers at Bath University and the various experts. Integrated mixed-media packages are impossible to produce by conventional linear publishing methods. You literally have to all climb into bed together and create a multi-disciplinary team. Writers, editors, graphic designers

438

and production people have to work together from the beginning.

The Export Training Project

In 1974, following the success of the first 'Decisions' pack *West Oil Distribution*, we were approached by Dr Malcolm Harper of Cranfield School of Management. He had been commissioned by International Trade Centre UNCTAD/GATT to develop a range of training packages which would improve the quality and quantity of export training in the developing countries.

The problem could briefly be stated thus:

(1) There is an urgent need for increased export training in developing countries.

(2) Many more instructors are needed and it is uneconomic and impractical to fly people to the West for training. Training packages could help to train people *in situ*.

(3) Textbooks existed — they had been tried and had failed. An approach was needed which broke away from the traditional textbook.

(4) A bright and attractive 'audiovisual' approach was required — although no audiovisual equipment could be assumed to exist in the training situation.

(5) The packages would have to work in any one of a hundred or more developing countries. No clear information was available about the target population. Almost by definition we knew nothing about its learning ability.

(6) No equipment could be guaranteed (other than a chalkboard and a classroom) and yet a modern audiovisual approach was required. Only four elements could be assumed to be present in the learning situation: instructor, students, chalkboard, classroom.

(7) Because the subject was export marketing we might also make guarded assumptions about the likelihood of additional resources being available such as: duplicating facilities (photocopying or typing), cassette recorder, overhead projector or slide projector.

(8) Because of postal and customs problems it is impossible to rely on delivery of supplementary materials, so any solutions would have to be self-contained.

Each pack had therefore to stand on its own, without any further supplies from external sources. We needed a solution where it would be possible to utilize the most modern reprographic facilities and audiovisual display equipment if available, but where it would still be possible if necessary to run each session with the minimum of facilities. Because instructors might be reluctant to use the materials, it had to be easy to use within existing resources.

We evaluated a number of alternative audiovisual approaches. Film was out of the question on cost grounds. Slide/filmstrip was economically possible but unlikely to be widely used. Overhead projectors were still rare although more likely to be present in institutions teaching exporting, e.g. in the urban areas. Cassette recorders were still a novelty but likely to increase in the wake of consumer demand.

We were faced with a frightening battery of constraints including the knowledge that potential instructors would be unfamiliar with both the subject area and participative learning methods. Nevertheless we were convinced that a traditional approach — (lecture + dictation = textbook) was doomed to failure from the start.

The approach which we eventually developed with Cranfield is a hybrid system — a marriage of the lecture method with modern participative learning techniques. It has some interesting characteristics which seem to be relevant to a much wider field than export training or indeed developing countries. I have called the approach 'semi-programmed' group instruction (SGI):

439

This information must frequently be given in the language and weights and measures of the importing country.

Countries also have their own regulations concerning the marking and labelling of dangerous substances such as explosives.

Shipping marks

All cases and crates have to be marked for shipping or other transportation. Often a customer will have his own shipping mark so that consignments due for him are more easily recognizable at the port of destination.

Shipping marks must always be large enough and legible enough to be understood by the people handling the goods.

Several types of information are included in shipping marks:

— *essential data.* Including the name of the exporter and his address, the name of the customer and his shipping mark. There may also be a case or crate number.

— *other data.* Including the weight of the packages, the name of the ship, the port of shipment and destination and the origin of the goods.

— *handling instructions.* Including a mark showing the centre of gravity of the case, the proper position of slings and any warnings such as 'fragile' or 'this side up'.

Shipping marks such as those shown on E2 should be clearly stamped on each case. The marks are often a distinctive shape with the customer's initials inside them. Underneath the mark the destination is given as well as the number of cases in the shipment and which case that particular one is of the set. For example, the first case of ten cases would be signified 1/10. The weights and measurements of each case should also be indicated.

To indicate that goods should be handled with care there is an international sign of a wine glass. Other internationally recognized symbols are shown on E2.

Most national handling symbols are based on those recommended by the International Organization for Standardization.

SHIPPING MARKS EXERCISE

Ask CMs to write down what they think the various handling marks mean?

Answer:

1 'handle with care'	2 'use no hooks'
3 'this way up'	4 'sling here'
5 'keep away from heat'	6 'centre of gravity'
7 'keep dry'.	

DISCUSSION

Issue **H1** and discuss the procedures that must be followed when packaging goods ready for export.

Ask
What information do CLs think should be on the outside of shipping crates? Go through these after they have replied.

Display E2 (top half)

Display E2 (bottom half)

Issue H1

Figure 1. *Typical page from Course Leader's Guide, export training pack*

— Group instruction because it emphasizes group, rather than individual, learning.
— Semi-programmed because it gives the course leader a completely self-contained package of resources and step-by-step framework for a complete course and because it allows for continuous adaptation to the local situation.

The whole subject of exporting has been divided into 12 subject areas — each covered by a simple self-contained pack. Each pack contains a discrete course covering the subject area, broken into a number of sessions. Clear instructions are given with each session as to exactly what material is required, so that instructors are not frightened by the management task in using material of this sort.

Each session starts with a brief talk by the instructor, but these are constantly broken by marginal instructions to the course leader (see Figure 1). Ask course members . . . Display transparency . . . Issue handout . . . We then move into a group learning activity.

Despite our forebodings about the experience of potential instructors we opted for a participative learning approach. We reckoned that this would have the added benefit of harnessing the collective knowledge of the course members (which might well exceed that of the course leader). We therefore opted for a limited lecture format interspersed with and followed by 'blueprints' for learning activities. These include exercises, case studies, simulations and games. The temptation to give a monologue is guarded against by the presence of constant reminders to 'Ask' and 'Elicit' the 'following points . . .'.

All the materials are housed in a 'triptych' — a three-fold plastic wallet which holds and protects all the materials. The wallet opens first at the Course Leader's Guide, which gives full details of each session, and reproduces the course members' handout and the exhibits.

In the middle compartment are masters of the 'handout' materials printed on long-lasting plastic paper and held in a ring mechanism so that these can be copied individually. This compartment also contains an audio cassette and game accessories.

Visual exhibits are provided in the next section, along with overhead transparencies which can also be copied for other forms of display. Some packs also contain multiple copies of an exercise materials booklet. The aim throughout is to achieve maximum flexibility and adaptability.

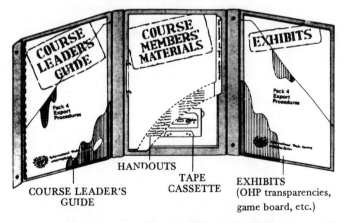

Figure 2. *The design solution: a typical pack*

The course leader may wish that he had a tape recorder or an overhead projector, and may even be motivated to try and obtain one, but he must be able to use the packs without such equipment. Audio cassettes are provided but transparencies were given with suggestions as to how these should be used if a cassette player were not available.

Overhead transparencies are included in each pack, but the course leader is invited to copy these onto flipchart or chalkboard if an OHP is not available. Alternatively he can photocopy, duplicate or make slides of them.

Does the Solution Work?

We are heavily committed, personally as well as commercially, to the concept of training packages as a useful resource for developing countries, but we do not have all the answers. In the light of the resource constraints there are still some fundamental paradoxes in our 'solutions'. Take, for example, in the case of the export training packages, the presence of 'photocopyable' masters of handout materials. This is contradictory to the view that photocopiers are a scarce resource and that the material should be adapted for the local audience.

The problem is that if we reject the conventional wisdom of 'chalk and talk', any design solution will create supply problems. The packs themselves may be viewed as a potential threat by the insecure or incompetent teacher. To the good teacher they may be irrelevant. The packs, it can be argued, will be of greatest benefit in a para-teaching situation, e.g. where a potential course leader exists who has some subject knowledge but lacks the experience and courage to teach. If he has attended a course, he can be the ideal medium for extending the training programme downwards. But getting the course mounted in the first place will be inhibited because, in the present system, training is likely to take place in an academic institution — precisely the place where new teaching approaches and external help are most likely to be ignored.

Then there is the paradox of evaluation. How do you evaluate a project such as this? Certainly, it is easy to be critical of the amount of field-testing, monitoring and evaluation which has taken place.

A recent postal survey of users revealed a high level of appreciation of the packs — but the survey did not really tell us how useful they had been or whether the level of export training had been enhanced. There are enormous time delays in international communication. There is also a 'conspiracy of kindness' which makes all answers suspect. My own experience in using the packs on Instructors' Workshops in the developing countries is that they meet with unstinted delight and approval. However, it will be difficult to overcome institutional barriers overnight.

The packs may achieve their objectives in devious ways. We have one firm piece of positive evidence. The programme continues to be supported by contributions from numerous governments. French and Spanish versions of the packs are being produced. Government Export Training Programmes are actually paying for the packages they request. A reprint of our first pack has just been delivered. Despite the lack of feedback we feel mildly optimistic that we have actually done something useful.

Conclusions

The project I have described appears to be at the frontiers of educational technology precisely because no 'technology', in terms of physical hardware, can be assumed to exist.

The production of training packages is certainly an art rather than a science. People talk glibly about the importance of validation. But they do not tell you how you can validate a mixed-media package before it is produced, or how you can afford to modify it when your validation reveals weaknesses.

The solutions we have developed and which I have described are the result of thousands of man hours of effort (50 per cent of it wasted — but we do not know which half). The glossy packages we produce are the tip of an iceberg. We do not talk about the generations of revised manuscripts and all the false starts.

To produce training packages for a defined target audience in a Western country is difficult enough. So how can a team of people in the West produce packages for an ill-defined target audience in any one of a hundred developing countries?

The cost of developing specialized training packages is quite enormous. Few developing countries would have either the time, the money or the expertise to do it themselves. It makes sense for international agencies like the UN to fund the production of such packages, especially when they replace or supplement existing training which often takes place in the West — at enormous cost in air travel.

The pooling of expertise and production economics which result from international funding in this way has a price. It means that the subject content must be general rather than specific. The course leader is essential because he must modify and adapt the material to his local situation. We may compose the score, but he is the musician interpreting the score and adapting it for his audience.

In relation to the theme of this conference I believe that there is need for a greater realism when talking about educational technology for developing countries. I am well aware of the dangers of generalization and the existence of many exceptions. Nevertheless my travels in India, Sri Lanka and Africa confirm the view that comparison of resources has some value. Television, radio, tape/slides and Western textbooks are not appropriate educational technologies for the vast majority of learning needs. Yet Western solutions are exported. Indeed, as the London publishers, the British Council and the Open University will confirm — we do very nicely at exporting our 'run-ons' to the East.

I believe that the West has an enormous contribution to make in knowledge transfer to the less developed countries. The United Kingdom is in a particularly strong position in this respect. Yet no one is prepared to admit that Western educational technology is usually inappropriate.

Where is the research being carried out which will find ways of training specialists and managers *in situ*? You cannot train a marketing manager in India by lecturing him from American textbooks c. 1950. That does not produce wealth. It merely produces academic theorists who are able to teach theory to future academics. Neither should we continue to indulge in the lucrative practice of posting professors or importing students.

I may be biased, but I believe that teaching packages have the most profound potential for the developing countries, precisely because they encapsulate a subject area, yet thrust the responsibility for its dissemination firmly back into the hands of the people who should be teaching it.

The resources available in the developing countries are clearly very different from those in the West. One thing that developing countries have a surfeit of is bright people; highly trained and intelligent people who are underemployed or unemployed. Unfortunately the skills they possess are not in the practical subjects which the countries need. Packages of the type described, placed in the hands of such people, could provide a powerful catalyst for rapid change; an appropriate technology for developing countries.

56b. Workshop Transcript: Problems in the Design of Training Packages for Developing Countries

Presenter: **J. G. Barker**, *Tecmedia Ltd, Loughborough, Leics*

Participants	Institution	Objective in attending workshop
BEAZER, Ann	Home Office Unit for Educational Methods	To look at ways of communicating information to learners via 'packages'.
BOURMISTENKO, V. LAMAZOUADE, A.	International Telecommunications Union, Geneva	To further the development of training systems in the telecommunication field for the benefit of developing countries.
BULFORD, J. R. S.	Agricultural Training Board (UK)	To seek thoughts and ideas in light of need to develop material for an overseas country.
BHUSAN, S.	University of Birmingham	To learn effective techniques of preparing training packages. To be aware of problems faced by package producers in preparing packages for developing countries. To share experience on how difficulties can be overcome.
HURLEY, Geoffrey	ILO, Turin Centre	To listen to other people's successes and failures in cross-cultural resource production.
MELIA, Jim	TAC Construction Materials Ltd	To learn the problems my company can expect to face apart from lack of equipment in introducing programmed learning techniques for operatives and supplying materials, books and visual aids to our associate companies in Nigeria and India.
REMINGTON, J. C.	Royal Navy CINCNAV Home, Portsmouth	To gain insight into problems of training overseas personnel for use within the Royal Navy.
SUTTON, Tony	Home Office Unit for Educational Methods	To exchange ideas on the packaging and presentation of learning material.
ZELMER, L.	Consultant to UNICEF, UNESCO and International Communications Institute	To exchange ideas (?) on development of materials to support training programmes in developing countries.

John Barker began the workshop by asking each participant to write on a slip of paper their objectives in coming to the session. All the participants agreed to this and their responses are shown above. (A few other participants attended the workshop, but unfortunately their names and objectives were not recorded as they arrived when the session was under way.)

The workshop kicked off with a brief summary of the stated objectives: to exchange ideas, see how information is communicated, examine cross-cultural resourcing problems, share experience.

The common thread was the exchange of ideas on the problems of designing packaged materials for use in developing countries. He suggested that we might see if these objectives had been achieved at the end of the 90 minutes.

He queried Mr Zelmer's inclusion of a question mark after the words 'to exchange ideas' on his written objective. Mr Zelmer pointed out that he was referring to his previous experiences of workshops of this type which inevitably degenerated into a monologue from the chairman. John Barker promised to try and avoid this happening (a promise not entirely fulfilled).

About half the participants had attended Mr Barker's morning paper. For the benefit (?) of the rest Mr Barker proceeded to give a short résumé of it. Participants were able to examine examples of export packages produced by Tecmedia on behalf of UNCTAD/GATT for use in developing countries and a package for nutrition workers produced on behalf of FAO.

In contrast, Mr Zelmer produced examples of simple packages — materials for the training of village health workers, produced for rural development in Sri Lanka. These included simple flannelgraphs, posters, picture story cards, six slides. He gave examples of the need for simple, low-cost solutions.

Mr Barker displayed an OHP comparing the severe resource constraints of a typical developing country. He said that the somewhat sombre picture created by such an assessment could well lead one to conclude that instructional resources other than a traditional textbook are out of the question.

Here was the paradox: we know that the traditional textbook is not the answer. The package approach was attractive. But as soon as we start to explore the possibility of employing media other than printed images on paper we are faced with the problem that equipment can never be *assumed* to exist. This raises almost insurmountable problems. Yet ways had got to be found. We could not just throw our hands in the air in despair.

The problems are well illustrated by the following extract from Mr Zelmer's paper.

> Resources such as projection bulbs which are taken for granted in Southern Canada were a small problem in the Arctic — it was merely necessary to budget a year in advance and remember to place the order. In India, bulbs were available but often cost as much as a month's salary to purchase. In Sri Lanka, unless the bulbs were supplied by an international agency you might wait forever to obtain 'currency control' permission to place an order, and another year for the bulbs to arrive.

Mr Barker suggested that training packages needed to be defined: there were two types:

— teaching packages — resources for use by a trainer
— learning packages — mainly self-instructional packages for the trainee.

He thought that in terms of defining packages in the West for use in the developing countries the emphasis should be on the former. Teaching packages could be a powerful resource if their limitations were recognized.

It seemed that there were two main strands in analysing the place of training packages in relation to their acceptance by the trainer:

— teaching confidence
— subject confidence.

445

This led him to conclude the following:

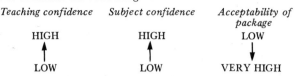

Teaching confidence	Subject confidence	Acceptability of package
HIGH	HIGH	LOW
↑	↑	↓
LOW	LOW	VERY HIGH

Example: A teacher with high perceived confidence in both teaching and subject is unlikely to accept a complete course package from external sources (although he may select bits from it).

Mr Hurley said that it was difficult to get a subject specialist on to the rostrum and packages had been found to be very useful in this respect.

Mr Barker expressed the view that in the hands of the right people, even though they might have low teaching confidence and low subject confidence, training packages could provide a rapid catalyst for change in the developing countries.

He said: Developing countries had a surplus of bright, intelligent people who had been academically trained and as a result were virtually unemployable. He thought that packages in the hands of such people could have a significant effect.

Mr Hurley said that he thought Mr Barker was insulting the intelligence of people in the developing countries by presenting them with material that it was very difficult to modify and adapt to their individual needs. He said that the package had yet to be invented which could be used by all of us quite happily in our own situation. He thought the packages described were very inflexible and should be designed perhaps with more thought for the intelligent man on the spot. He should be able to adapt them, use what he wants, add what he wants and take away what he wants, and finish up with something useful.

Mr Zelmer said it was very important to make extremely clear how to use the package, how to change it. Every package designer should build this into his package.

Mr Barker agreed entirely that a package was a resource which the trainer should adapt to his own requirements. He reiterated the point made at the start that the task of writing a package for use in any one of a hundred developing countries ranked as an impossible problem. It was impossible to talk about specifics, for example the unit of monetary measurement had to be dollars, one couldn't talk about rupees.

He stressed that throughout the packs there was emphasis on the need to adapt the materials to the local situation. But here was another paradox. Although they emphasized the need for adaptation, it was done with some cynicism that this adaptation would actually take place. For example, master 'handout' materials had been printed as separate A4 sheets printed on plastic paper in a ring mechanism for easy extraction and reproduction.

The trainer should ideally rewrite the handout material. But in practice, how many will have the resources to do this and then get it typed and duplicated?

Mr Hurley said that in his experience typing and duplicating was cheap and secretaries were usually available. He got the impression that the packs were difficult to adapt from the statement by Mr Barker that it had been decided to adopt the overhead transparency for the visual media and the cassette for the audio media.

He didn't think an overhead transparency was a very flexible medium and an audio cassette certainly wasn't.

Mr Barker said: OK, so here is the paradox. Are you saying we shouldn't provide transparencies or a cassette?

Mr Hurley: I'm suggesting we should be discussing what kind of media we should be supplying for use in packages for use in the developing countries. I'm not sure you've come up with the right answer.

Mr Barker pointed out that in the case of the audio cassette, in the event of wanting to adapt the material or in the absence of a cassette recorder, instructions were given on the need to re-record the material locally or enact it to the class using two or three course members in front of the class.

They were deliberately using the audio cassette as an additional resource. But it was not, in general, *essential*. The same was true of the overhead transparencies. If an OHP did not exist the images could be drawn on to chalkboard or flip chart, made into slides or even photocopied. They were not *essential* — they were enhancements. In his view coloured OHPs were an ideal visual resource — they were so adaptable.

He emphasized that the subject was exporting — adding value and getting goods moving from the developing countries to the developed countries. The subject matter was thus somewhat *external* to the countries; for example Western exporting requirements. It was not as localized as, say, nutrition training.

In the FAO work a completely different approach had been adopted. Tecmedia had said: OK, it's impossible to produce generalized packs, let us produce only 50 prototypes and then let us wage a 'hearts and minds' campaign to persuade individual governments to support the production of bespoke tailored packs adapted to the local situation. Thus the 'combined wisdom' of all the best experts could be brought together into one package and then adapted to one country's individual needs.

Participant: You see I like the story from WHO about the man who went to Africa with a package containing overhead transparencies. They had no OHP and no electricity. The transparencies were being used as window glass, they made very attractive stained glass windows!

Participant: Exactly the sort of problem you run the danger of. The International Planned Parenthood Federation have done some very interesting work with portable flip charts for many developing countries, at very low cost. I feel you're on the wrong lines with the media you're planning to use.

John Barker: The trouble with flannelgraphs is they don't fit into a pack. They are generally large (20x30 inches) and don't fit into a pack. There are also cost problems. It's no use supplying just the flannelgraph. You would have to supply the bits and pieces that go on it.

Question: Why can't you just supply the information for them to construct their own?

Mr Zelmer: You can print them on material and fold them up to go in the pack.

Mr Barker: Let's be clear about what we are talking about. In the case of the export training packs we are talking about training at graduate level, probably in an academic institution or a chamber of commerce type of organization. A flannelgraph would be laughed out of the room.

Participant: Ah, you didn't say that, that makes a difference.

Mr Barker: I'm sorry, I thought I'd made it clear that the packs were designed to teach exporting to government officers and businessmen.

Question: Are we talking about solving problems in the design of your export training packs? I thought we were talking more generally about packages for developing countries.

Mr Barker: You said you thought we were on the wrong lines. Maybe I'm defending too strongly.

Mr Bhusan: The solutions you outline are fine for businessmen but for the general masses they are inappropriate.

Mr Barker: We agree on that.

Participant: There is the danger that the people you give these packages to are also going to be the people involved in future package construction. This will be the experience they have of the instructional package. The materials they are going to have to use for rural development are not going to be of the same sort. They are going to be able to differentiate between the needs of the different populations.

Mr Hurley: Yes, even our managerial courses do non-projected aids as part of their programme for this exact reason — to make them realize the existence of media other than the sophisticated ones. Because they are going to have to go into the field and talk to people at a lower level and in the rural areas.

Mr Bulford: As far as the audience we are talking about is concerned a flip chart or flannelgraph has its place if your audience is six or ten people. But it's no use with a large audience.

Mr Zelmer: In practice it is. An A2-sized poster or a small chalkboard will suffice for a class of 100 people. In India one 12-inch TV will serve 600 people in an instructional situation. [There was some surprise at this statement.]

Mr Zelmer: I don't think it's being patronizing to say that if institutions like FAO and WHO provide some material it will never get translated into usable form for local circumstances. If WHO provided a filmstrip on hygiene for use with sanitation people in New York City hotels it would be used to train people on how to clean up the village market in Sri Lanka — merely because the WHO supplied it!

In the case of your FAO materials it will be the same. You might as well print 20,000 copies of it. The prospect of getting governments to make reasonable adaptations are slim precisely because it's got the FAO insignia on the front cover.

Mr Barker: No I'm sorry — I may be as bewildered as anyone else in this room on how you tackle the developing country problem. But we are suggesting the production of only 50 copies of a prototype to be trialled extensively in Asia and Africa. It would then be adapted to the needs of the particular country.

Mr Barker then described the various elements of the proposed FAO pack and demonstrated the pack.

It is a prototype only. We will try to persuade governments to adapt it as their own.

Mr Zelmer: I agree that would be nice. It would be the best. But I've seen many examples where this has not happened because of the FAO symbol on the front cover. And adaptation to the local situation means transliterating it to the local situation — not even translating it.

Mr Barker: I'm suggesting we *don't* have the FAO symbol on the front cover.

Mr Zelmer: But you already have. Once it gets to the government that's effectively prevented its adaptation.

Mr Barker: We are going to trial the prototype in a wide range of developing countries. After revisions we are going to persuade governments to back the project and then *help* them to convert it to their needs. You are cynical, but I think that that is at least one possible way out of the dilemma.

Frankly there are so many problems that we could well all go home if we think too hard about them. We've got to do something. Let's be *positive*.

Participant: I think Mr Zelmer *is* overstating the case. I agree that there is a tendency for packages to be used indiscriminately. But I think you have got to give guidelines on how they can be adapted. We've got to make it relatively easy.

Mr Barker: Well, Instructors' Workshops are being organized. A pack is being produced on running Instructors' Workshops as part of the Export Training Programme.

Mr Hurley: I notice with the FAO packages that you are using some very sophisticated techniques such as role play and case studies. These are very difficult things to use in cross-cultural situations. We have found, particularly in Africa, and also in Iran, that it is not easy to persuade people to use role plays. I'm surprised that you are building it in as such a large integral part of your package.

Mr Barker: Here is another very ambivalent situation. My experiences in India and particularly Sri Lanka suggest that if you can get the people over the initial hurdle they jump with delight into participative learning methods — it's a release from 20 years of chalk and talk. Once you've got them to realize that they are allowed to let their hair down things work out fine.

Mr Zelmer: I agree, once you get over that big hurdle. Personally I made myself a guinea pig and trained two people who were not part of the group to enact a role play activity. But it was ten days before we got the group doing it.

Mr Barker: Yes. There is a learning curve. The first time it may be a failure. The next time is a bit better . . . and so on. You get better at it as people's defences come down.

You say that participative learning activities such as role plays and case studies are too sophisticated. Well, we have made them very simple. And again, what is the alternative? How can you teach subjects like management and communication skills without two-way communication?

Ann Beazer: I keep asking myself whether we should be sitting here designing solutions to developing country problems.

Mr Barker: Quite! This is supposed to be an international conference. There aren't enough black faces around the table. Only two people at the conference are from developing countries.

Mr Bhusan: It's OK to import technology from the West if it's needed. We just change and adapt it to our needs.

Mr Zelmer: A package of learning materials imported to meet a particular need is fine too, providing you explain clearly how to adapt the materials. They can't be sophisticated. They have to be things like flannel, printed and ready to be cut up. But in India, for example, you'd need 40 different packages and maybe 10,000 copies of each one. I have difficulty in understanding how India could adapt them when they haven't even adapted them to India — let alone the regions.

Mr Barker: Should the West be meddling at all in the education problems of the developing countries?

449

Mr Zelmer: My government (Canada) spends a lot of money on training materials for developing countries. Although I'm an independent, one of the reasons I work as I do is to try and make better use of the materials. If you are going to spend millions in supplying materials it makes sense to try and make sure that at least some of it does some good.

Mr Bourmistenko: I wish to stress the importance of adaptation. ITU have been involved in these problems in the field of telecommunications training. Even in Western Europe the problem of adapting material is a serious one. The cost of adaptation can be as much as one-tenth. In the case of developing countries adaptation costs can be low but in any case it must be built in as an essential part of any international project. These packages seem very useful. Simplicity is the keynote — and adaptability.

[Mr Barker then demonstrated the development of page format away from a straight text narrative towards a more open format, utilizing a lecture note, information mapped, type of format for the Export Training Course Leader's guides.]

Mr Barker: The theory of adaptation is *great*. But we all know even from our own experience that it seldom happens. Often we mug up a session the night before rather than plan it weeks in advance. In a developing country the reality is it's probably much easier to just use what you've got.

We can talk about the essential need to *adapt*. But it isn't all that easy in the field. We've got to find some way round it. Our solution of bespoke tailoring to the country's needs is one way. But Mr Zelmer says it is impossible.

Mr Zelmer: Not impossible. Improbable!

Mr ?: You then run the risk of reading the material out verbatim.

Mr Barker: We've tried to avoid that with the new format. Breaking the material up into talking points, etc. It may be a better approach. But we're not yet sure.

Mr ?: Yes but we have had experience of people reading out exactly as written . . . italics in the left-hand column.

Mr Barker: I've heard of an instructor playing a tape right through including bleeps and instructions to stop the tape. What can you do? We're getting into a negative posture now.

Mr ?: Can I introduce another dimension. Jack Hurley has left but I wonder about the function of a body like ILO which takes people from their country and ostensibly runs courses . . . (tape ran out)

Discussion on need to internalize training, not white people telling black people how to do it. Packages can help technology transfer, enabling black people to train black people.

Urgent need to differentiate between:

- **rural**
- **urban rich.**

Decision about the sophistication of the media is dependent on this. Need to create perception of *need*. Motivation. Training packages should be sucked into the country not imposed on it or handed out at field level. Governments must be convinced at high level so that channels can be cleared and priority given. Stricter régimes in developing countries can sometimes ordain that training will (or will not) take place.

The meeting ended with some concerns that individual objectives had been achieved, so far as they could be in light of the problems. The lack of any forum for discussion of such problems was noted. The lack of the anticipated Third World attendance at the conference and hence the workshop mitigated against any deep and positive conclusions.

Note for future workshops:

(1) The idea of stating objectives at the start was acceptable and gives opportunity to structure towards needs of participants.

(2) The free form discussion led to limited participation. Mr Zelmer and Mr Hurley were the predominant participants, but they were outvoiced by the organizer despite his expressed intent.

57. Analysing Lecture Styles

Presenter: **D. M. Wharry**, *University College, Cardiff*

Abstract: A set of categories is suggested which can be used to describe the style with which a lecture is given in behavioural and non-evaluative terms. The categories broadly take account of both verbal behaviour and the use of visual aids and demonstrations. A feature of the system is the use of a variable, experimental category.

A computer program in FORTRAN IV has been developed which prints out a 10 x 10 matrix derived from the observation record. A time-line display can be printed, and the program also presents information concerning the frequency and length of strings of sequential occurrences of the same category.

Introduction

One of the major deterrents against using a system of classroom interaction coding and analysis, such as that of Flanders (1968; 1962), is the time and effort needed to process the results to obtain the interaction matrix. Typically, this may take about three-quarters of an hour for a 20-minute recording, if done by hand. This may account in part for the lack of use of this method in staff development in higher education. The use of such instruments has been reviewed by Tribe and Gibbs (1977) who describe an investigation into lecturing styles, in low-inference terms, currently being carried out at Hatfield Polytechnic. This approach is somewhat different from the subject of this paper in that recording by Tribe and Gibbs was performed from video-tape, the behaviours being noted at 30-second intervals with the playback being stopped while the recording is done, whereas in the present work a single category is noted at 3-second intervals by an observer in the lecture itself. This method can also be applied to video recordings.

In the present workshop, which took place during the first sessions of the conference, the aim was to describe this system for the analysis of lecturing styles and to invite participants to criticize, discuss and propose amendments. It was hoped that participants would try to apply this new system during the mainstream presentations of the conference and return to part 2 of the workshop with recordings they had made; that they would be able to pool their experiences and come up with firmer definitions of each of the nine specified categories, and that they would be able to make suggestions for possible uses of the experimental category. In the event, participants felt that the process of categorizing a talk might interfere with their understanding and retention of the content. The author said that in his own case, over the past three years, coding his education students while observing their teaching practice lessons had in fact heightened his perception and attention — it is difficult to take microsleeps when having to write a code number every three seconds! Perhaps this effect is a result of being very familiar both with the method and with the lessons being observed.

The Categories

The categories have already been published as a proposal for analysing lecturing styles (Wharry, 1978) and some details of how each may be interpreted are given in that reference, however for convenience they are summarized below in Table 1. Unlike Tribe and Gibbs (1977), who generated some 100 descriptions by repeated analysis of video recordings of lectures, the present author had in mind some stereotypes of university lecturers when creating these categories. He asked himself, and others, the question, 'What sorts of behavioural, low inference observations might be made during a lecture which would describe and distinguish these extreme caricatures?'

0	*Pauses* by lecturer
1	*Reading aloud* of information verbatim
2	*Spontaneous information giving* (spoken)
3	*Personal opinion* or criticism of others' work given by lecturer
4	*Questions/directions* aimed at eliciting a response from the audience
5	*Humour* — by word or other means, whether or not successful
6	*Static visual aids* or playback of audio tapes without visual aids
7	*Moving audiovisual aids or demonstrations,* with or without spoken commentary. May also include chalkboard or OHP work 'live'
8	*Active audience participation,* by verbal or other means
9	*Experimental category* to be defined by the observer/lecturer, before or during observations

Table 1. *Categories for WALS*

Some of the original models or caricatures from which these categories were drawn may easily be deducted from Table 1, for example 'The Reader' who buries his head in notes and reads solidly (but oh so beautifully!) for the whole of the next 50 minutes and then bows and walks rapidly out of the lecture hall. It must not be assumed from this, however, that the author thinks reading is out of place in a lecture, since well-chosen extracts from one's own or others' works can have a stimulating effect on the listener.

It is expected that the pattern of the proportions by which each category is used, the number of codings or tallies in total combined with the duration of each string of a given tally, will yield a useful description of his style. This description could be given words, but being quantitative in nature, it should be susceptible to analyses by statistical methods. This may be attempted when more data has been accumulated and the final form of the categories 0-8 finalized. It is too early to say yet if unambiguous descriptions of styles are possible, but preliminary results are encouraging as one may see from the two examples quoted below.

So far about 40 sets of codings from various sources — university lectures, public lectures, evening talks to professional associations and televised broadcasts — have been obtained. Except in the case of public and broadcast lectures the author has been careful to obtain prior permission to make the observations during a lecture, and he has undertaken to maintain the anonymity of the speakers and to attempt no evaluation nor offer any criticism on the basis of his observations. It was felt that this might overcome the reluctance of lecturers to admit one to their teaching sessions.

Use for In-Service Training

Tribe and Gibbs have demonstrated (1977) that even in the early stages of such a

453

project, it is not impossible to persuade colleagues to admit peer or student evaluations of their teaching for attempts to be made to relate these to the observations being made. In the context of staff development and in-service training one hopes that lecturers may find this a useful means to obtain a descriptive feedback about their own lecturing styles. They may care to define their aim and objectives in advance of the teaching session, and hence, on the basis of one of the models theoretically advanced about learning, describe the sort of teaching styles they think would best suit their subject, surroundings and audience. Too often, it would seem from discussions with colleagues, a person's lecturing style appears nearly invariable and unrelated to the particular circumstances, and, moreover, the speaker himself is usually unable to evaluate this for himself, even when viewing a video recording. Perhaps extended experience of using some such system as this may demonstrate whether or not a lecturer's style is a very personal attribute or whether it is related strongly to faculty, topic and/or audience.

Workshop Activity and Discussion

During the workshop the participants were asked to try their hands at coding a short extract of a lesson on colour given in a home economics class. Some discussion then developed concerning the interpretation of the categories, and also of how fine or coarse a description of style one might expect to derive from the observations. During the extract, the lecturer was making some observations, apparently not of a contentious nature, but these remarks, made in answer to a student's question, were prefaced by the words 'I think'. This was taken by about half of the participants to indicate a statement of opinion (category 3) and by the remainder as a general piece of spontaneous information-giving (category 2). In the ensuing discussion a member of the audience, who has considerable experience of this kind of work, suggested that a much clearer signal might be needed before this category was used. He suggested that some such phrase as 'In my opinion . . .', indicating a question about which experts might disagree, could be taken as a clear signal for the use of category 3. This is, in fact, in line with one of the author's original models from which these categories were drawn. The occasional use of somewhat provocative statements of personal opinion could act on the audience in a positive manner. One can, however, have too much of a good thing and many will be familiar with the caricature of the 'blunt north-country man' who succeeds in completely alienating his southern audience.

Use of the Experimental Category 9

The use of the experimental 'catch-all' category, 9, was discussed. In a later part of the video recording used for this session, although not actually shown, the lecturer called upon a student to act as a laboratory assistant during a demonstration of dyeing. The author used category 9 for coding this action and has found such a definition useful on other occasions. Such decisions about assigning a specific behaviour to this category often have to be made on the spot during coding, although prior consultation with the lecturer about his aims and possible teaching strategies may suggest a use for this experimental category in advance. If one finds that a particular invention needs to be used during several coding sessions it may be considered worthwhile including this as one of the permanent categories and dropping one that is less frequently used. In fact, the category 1 of Flanders (1968), 'Accepts feelings expressed by pupils' has been found not to be used at all frequently during teaching sessions in further education colleges, and the author has adopted this procedure in order to introduce a category defining a particular

454

behaviour he wished to investigate with his teaching-practice student.

This is, perhaps, one criticism that might be made of the original Flanders system in that it did not allow for the investigation of slightly differing aspects of teaching behaviour and interaction. It is hoped that users of this system will always include an experimental category in order to keep alive to the possibility of observing an unpredicted but valuable aspect of teaching strategy or behaviour.

Another suggestion made by a participant regarding category 9 was that it might be used for recording the audience's assumed internal response. However, it is argued that this would be of such a subjective nature as to be nearly incapable of definition or objective description. It is, moreover, not a low inference, physical description of style, but lies very much in the affective domain. Of course, something similar might be said about category 5 (humour) it was then suggested, but in reply the speaker indicated, and with fairly general assent, that it is possible to pick up fairly accurately a speaker's verbal or physical attempts at humour, but unless actually roaring with laughter, or rolling in the aisles, the reaction of the audience is very difficult to judge. In the case of the TV broadcast, audience reaction can only be judged by the observer actually present in the studio.

It was pointed out by a participant that it frequently might be possible for two or more categories to be assigned to the same three-second period — what should be done then? That the basic ground rules must be clearly laid out in advance was generally accepted, and the author's general procedure was to give precedence to the highest category number. Thus, if an active demonstration is being observed in silence for a few moments then category 7 would be written down in preference to category 0, although if the demonstration continued in silence for such a period that the audience showed by physical reactions — facial expressions, muttering and/ or restless movements — that attention was falling considerably, the observer might consider replacing his 7's with 0's. Another possibility would be to generate a new category 9 if this became a frequent occurrence, and category 9 was not already in use for some other behaviour of the lecturer or his audience.

The Computer Program

A computer program has been developed in FORTRAN IV on a System 4 computer in the South West Universities' Computer Network, in which the data, in the form of initial comments and the series of code numbers recorded during the observation, is entered via punched cards. An interactive, rather simpler program has also been developed which may be run on the network computer or on a smaller PDP 11 machine.

The program first outputs some literal strings identifying the lecturer, date, institution and topic and then the whole data in a series of lines each of which represents one minute of observations. The present program allows for up to 9,999 tallies to be entered at one time (about 8 hours and 20 minutes of continual observation), and for strings of a repeated category of up to 400. Simple changes in dimensioning in the program will permit these values to be extended to about 100,000 tallies and strings of 4,000 identical codings. This output is shown in Figure 1.

The program then goes on to process the data in groups of 20, so as to obtain the interaction matrix described by Flanders (1968), and this is depicted in Figure 2. This is essentially a record, in tabular form, of sequential action-reaction pairs. For example, if category 2 (spontaneous talk) is followed by category 6 (AVA) and then by category 3 (opinion), the first pair would result in incrementing store (2,6). This results in the value at the junction of line 2 column 6 being increased by one unit. The next pair in this series of three codings is 6 followed by 3 and this

455

```
LECTURER: DR. CARL SAGAN(BBCTV)

DATE: 5.1.78

INSTITUTION/DEPT.: ROYAL INSTITUTION CHRISTMAS LECTURE


6  6  6  6  6  6  6  6  6  6  6  6  6  6  6  6  6  6  6  6
6  6  6  6  6  6  6  6  6  6  6  6  6  6  6  6  6  6  6  6
6  6  6  6  6  6  6  6  6  6  2  2  2  2  2  2  2  2  6  6
6  6  6  6  6  6  6  6  6  6  6  6  6  6  6  6  6  2  2  2
2  2  2  6  6  6  6  6  6  6  6  6  6  6  6  6  2  2  2  6
6  6  6  6  6  6  6  6  5  2  2  2  2  2  2  2  2  2  2  2
2  2  2  2  2  2  2  2  2  2  2  2  2  2  2  2  2  2  2  2
2  2  2  2  2  2  ?  2  2  2  2  2  6  6  6  6  6  6  6  6
2  2  2  2  2  2  2  2  2  5  2  2  2  2  2  6  6  6  2  2
2  2  6  6  6  6  6  6  2  2  6  6  6  6  6  6  2  2  2  2
2  2  5  5  2  2  2  6  6  6  6  6  6  6  6  2  2  2  2  6
6  6  6  6  6  6  6  6  6  6  6  2  2  2  2  2  2  6  6  6
6  6  6  7  6  6  6  6  6  6  2  2  6  6  2  2  2  6  6  6
6  2  2  2  2  2  6  2  6  6  2  2  2  2  2  2  2  2  2  2
2  2  6  6  6  7  2  6  6  6  3  8  2  2  2  2  6  6  6
2  2  4  4  0  4  4  2  4  4  4  4  2  2  2  7  7  7  7  7
4  7  8  7  4  8  4  7  8  5  0  0  2  2  2  2  7  7  7  7
7  7  7  7  7  7  7  7  7  7  7  7  7  7  7  7  7  7  7  7
7  7  7  7  7  7  7  7  2  2  2  2  2  7  7  7  7  7  2  2
2  2  2  2  2  2  0  2  2  2  6  6  6  6  5  6  6  6  2  2
```

Figure 1. *Print-out of data set (block form)*

would result in location (6,3) being incremented by one unit, and so on through the whole data set. The matrix thus indicates clearly a series of steady states (boxes (6,6), (2,2) and so on) and of transitions (boxes (2,6), (6,3) etc.), and from this a pattern of interactions developed during the class may be derived, as indicated by Flanders (1968).

An alternative to the data print-out of Figure 1 is currently being developed so as to present the data set in the form of a time-line display. In this, the sequential code numbers are printed, one to a line, in columns which indicate their actual numerical values. A graphical indication of style as the lecture progresses is thus obtained. For example, one would be able to see at a glance if the lecturer's style is mainly confined to talk, when the line of figures or dots would lie to the left of centre, or if to the right, one sees that he has employed visual aids, demonstration or invoked audience participation during that part of the session. A comedian would be expected to yield a vertical central line under category 5.

Another option in the program is shown in Figure 3. This gives a basis for analysing the teaching session in terms of the number of strings of the same code number used in uninterrupted succession. The left-most column indicates the category being considered (0-9). The second column gives the number of strings in which that category occurs by itself, and these can vary in length in the present form of the program from 1 to a string of 400 — it seems unlikely that an observer would be tempted to write the same number once every three seconds for 20 minutes! In the third column will be found the average length of the strings used in that particular category, rounded to the first place of decimals; this gives some indication of the frequency with which the lecturer changes from one activity to another, and the duration of a single activity. It is also of interest to be able to inspect the actual number of times a string of a given length is used, and this can be

	0	1	2	3	4	5	6	7	8	9
0)	1	0	2	0	1	0	0	0	0	0
1)	0	0	0	0	0	0	0	0	0	0
2)	1	0	128	0	2	2	18	3	0	0
3)	0	0	0	0	0	0	0	0	0	0
4)	1	0	2	0	6	0	0	2	1	0
5)	1	0	3	0	0	1	1	0	0	0
6)	0	0	16	0	0	2	152	2	1	0
7)	0	0	3	0	2	0	1	37	2	0
8)	0	0	1	0	1	1	0	1	1	0
9)	0	0	0	0	0	0	0	0	0	0

ACTUAL NUMBER OF TALLIES: 400

Figure 2. *Print-out of interaction matrix*

seen from the three lines of figures which follow on from the values described above. These figures are to be read from left to right in vertical groups of three. The upper digit gives the hundreds value, the middle the tens and the lower the units. It can thus be seen that the lecturer in Figure 3 used category 2 in 26 strings of average length 6.0; his shortest string was of 3 seconds duration and he used three of these, and his longest string lasted 43 x 3 seconds (just over 2 minutes).

Comparison of Styles

The format in Figure 3 was designed to make the print-out appear as a histogram, and if the details of the individual strings are not required the analyst can select another option which suppresses the string lengths display and substitutes a plain line of dashes. The length of this line is proportional to the number of strings and inversely proportional to the total number of tallies made during the whole observation session. Thus if a greater number of observations is made in one session than in another the length of the line from one to the other should not alter significantly, if the style remains the same. The use of this type of display, it is hoped, will enable the investigator to gain an immediate visual impression of these particular aspects of a speaker's style and to compare it side by side with another's. This is exemplified in Figure 4 where two eminent astronomers, Professor Carl Sagan and Professor Sir Fred Hoyle, are shown side by side in profile, so to speak.

```
LECTURER: DR. CARL SAGAN(BBCTV)

DATE: 5.1.78
0     3    1.3
                  000
                  000
                  112
1     0



2    26    6.0
         0000000000000000000000000000
         00000000000000000000000010014
         1112223333344445555556638923
3     0



4     6    2.0
                  000000
                  000000
                  111225
5     5    1.2
                  00000
                  00000
                  11112
6    21    8.2
         00000000000000000000000
         00000000000000000001114
         122333344406667839239)
7     8    5.6
                  00000000
                  00000003
                  11111451
8     4    1.3
                  0000
                  0000
                  1112
9     0
```

Figure 3. *Print-out of strings analysis*

Lecturer: Dr Carl Sagan (BBCTV)			*Lecturer:* Sir Fred Hoyle		
Date: 5.1.78			*Date:* 18.1.78		
0	3	1.3 --	0	6	1.0 ---
1	0		1	12	11.9 ------
2	26	6.0 -----------	2	25	7.2 ------------
3	0		3	3	5.0 --
4	6	2.0 ---	4	0	
5	5	1.2 --	5	0	
6	21	8.2 ---------	6	11	4.0 ------
7	8	5.6 ----	7	0	
8	4	1.3 --	8	0	
9	0		9	0	

Figure 4. *Comparison of lecturing profiles*

It will be seen that their styles appear very different, although the broad fields of their lectures — the effect of bodies from outer space on mankind — were the same. At this stage one has only one example of Sir Fred giving a public lecture (of talk and slides) to an adult audience of about 400 in the university's Sherman Theatre in Cardiff. The data on Professor Sagan's lecturing style was gathered by coding his series of televised Christmas lectures from the Royal Institution. There would, of course, be a difference in aims, of resources and of audience for these two lectures and so one cannot infer any effects of the various variables, nor whether the style is a personal one. It may be significant that the category 3 appears in Sir Fred's lecture but not in Professor Sagan's.

Conclusion

It is hoped that efforts will be made to collect data from individuals in a variety of settings so that estimates of the effects of such variables as:

☐ size and type of audience
☐ aims of the lecturer
☐ subject matter
☐ available technical resources
☐ lecture room environment, etc.

can be made. Already similar methods have been used allied with micro-teaching in the in-service training of university lecturers (Brown, 1977) and it is hoped that the special features of this 'Analysis of lecturing styles', that is to say:

> continual modification of categories by the use of category 9, recording both verbal and non-verbal transactions, and the use of the computer in preparing the matrix and other displays,

will make this system a useful and attractive method for staff development programs.

The author will gladly supply program listings in FORTRAN IV to enquirers, and would be glad to cooperate with those interested in gathering and analysing data referring to the analysis and development of lecturing styles in higher education.

Acknowledgements

The author would like to acknowledge the many discussions and helpful criticisms contributed so readily by his colleagues and by participants in this workshop. He is also greatly indebted to Mr Colin Draper, now at Brunel University, for taking the major burden of developing the programs mentioned in this article.

References

Brown, G. A. (1977) Some myths and methods of staff training and development. In Trott, A.J. (ed.) *Selected Microteaching Papers.* Kogan Page, London.

Flanders, N.A. (1962) in Amidon, E. J. and Hough, J. B. (eds.) *Interaction Analysis: Theory, Research and Application.* Addison-Wesley, Reading, Mass. and London.

Flanders, N. A. (1968) Interaction analysis and inservice training. *Journal of Experimental Education,* 37, pp.126-32.

Tribe, A. J. and Gibbs, T. A. (1977) Analysing lecturing in low influence terms. *Research Intelligence,* 3, 2, pp.32-5.

Wharry, D. M. (1978) A proposal for analysing lecturing styles in higher education. *Impetus,* 8, pp.26-31.

Appendices

List of Exhibitors

Trade Exhibition

Company

Unichart/Buckley Displays Ltd
Cumbermay Ltd
Polaroid (UK) Ltd
Management Games Ltd
PTS (Derby) Ltd
Eos AV Electronics Ltd
Philips Electrical (Video) Ltd
Radio Rentals Contracts Ltd
Western Sound Visual Ltd
Drake Video Services Ltd
Rediffusion Industrial Services Ltd
Wyeval AV Ltd

Gordon AV Ltd
F.W.O. Bauch Ltd
E. J. Arnold Ltd
Tandberg (UK) Ltd
Kenro Photographic Products Ltd
Macmillan Film Productions Ltd
BP Educational Enterprises Ltd
Kogan Page Ltd
HTV Ltd
Focal Press Ltd
AV Distributors Ltd

Members' Exhibition

Science Department, Polytechnic of Wales
Agricultural Training Board
Gwent College of Higher Education
Hendershot Programmed Learning Consultants
Dundee College of Education
Robert Gordon's Institute of Technology
Royal Naval School of Educational and Training Technology
Educational Foundation for Visual Aids
Council for Educational Technology
Hamilton College of Education
The British Council
Geographical Association Package Exchange (GAPE)
Society for Academic Gaming and Simulation in Education and Training (SAGSET)
Kogan Page Publishers
Jordanhill College of Education
Network of Programmed Learning Centres (NPLC)
Association for Programmed Learning and Educational Technology

Sponsorship

Our grateful thanks are due to:

Eos AV Electronics Ltd, for donating wallets.

Mid Glamorgan Adult Training Centre for the Mentally Handicapped, for producing and supplying the coat-hangers.

Polaroid (UK) Ltd, for supplying conference badges.

PTS (Derby) Ltd, for donating audio and video recording tape.

Rank Xerox Ltd, for the loan of additional reprographic facilities.

Spicer Cowan Ltd, and John Dickinson Ltd, for donating paper for conference printing.

Staedtler (UK) Ltd, for donating pens to the Conference.

Transatlantic Plastics Ltd, for donating the plastic wallets for meal-tickets.

List of Delegates

NOTE: **Bold** print denotes contributor. * conference chairman. † delegate forum participant or workshop contributor.

Adamson, R. M., England.
Adderly, K., England.
Allaway, B. A., England.
Allen, Sqn Ldr N. E., England.
Anderson, Dr E. W., England.
Baker, P. J., England.
Baldwin, L., England.
Bardell, Mrs E., England.
Barker, Miss A. L., Scotland.
Barker, J. G.† Ch.11, England.
Barnes, Lt Col B., England.
Barnett, Comdr M. M., England.
Baxendale, Lt Comdr R. D., England.
Bearden, R. J. L., England.
Beazer, Ms A. J., England.
Becker, Dr A. D., USA.
Bhushan, S., England (visiting fellow, India).
Bingham, Ms E. G., Scotland.
Bird, C. M., England.
Bourmistenko, V., Switzerland.
Brandenburg, Prof Dr W. J., The Netherlands.
Brew, Mrs A., England.
Britton, R. J., England.
Brook, D., Wales.
Brooking, Lt Comdr B. A., England.
Brower, R., The Netherlands.
Bryce, Dr C. F. A., Scotland.
Budgett, Comdr R. E. B.,* England.
Bulford, J. R. S.,* England.
Buxton, Ms A., England.
Carson, J., Scotland.
Clarke, J. L.,* England.
Clarke, Dr W. D.,* England.
Clements, R.† Ch.11, England.
Coates, Ms J., England.
Coffey, J.,* England.
Coles, C. R., England.
Conn, Miss M., England.
Cooke, P. A., Hong Kong.
Coombes, M. G., England.
Cooper, Ms J., England.

Cooper, R., England.
Cramer, G. J., The Netherlands.
Crapper, Ms S., England.
Cropper, Comdr T. K.,* England.
Dalton, K. G., N. Ireland.
Dando, Miss A., Wales.
Daniel, Dr J. S., Canada.
Davies, J. A.,* England.
Davies, Miss K. L., England.
Davies, Dr P., Wales.
Davies, P. A. I., Wales.
Davies, W. J. K.,* England.
Day, H., England.
De Feny, Mlle M., France.
De Potter, R., The Netherlands.
Dear, Comdr B. D., England.
Delpak, Dr R.† Ch.10, Wales.
Devillebichot, Ms A., England.
Dippel, Dr R., W. Germany.
Dodd, B. T., England.
Duguid, Gp Capt A. G., England.
Edney, P. J., England.
Ellington, Dr H. I.,* Scotland.
Ellis, P., England.
Evans, L.F., England.
Fagan, D. V.,* England.
Farmer, R. G., England.
Farrow, R. J., Wales.
Feest, Comdr F. M., England.
Fieldhouse, P., England.
Fleming, W. G., England.
Forrest, Ms A., Wales.
Fox, G., England.
Francis, J. L., Wales.
Fraser, Sqn Ldr G., England.
Freeman, Lt D. J., Canada.
Frewin, Ms G. † Ch.11, England.
Gardner, A. P. W.† Ch.10, Scotland.
Gay, K., England.
Gelder, J. M., England.
Gensch, Dr G., W. Germany.

465

Ghose, Prof A., England.
Gibbs, G. I.,* England.
Giddings, Lt Comdr A. P., England.
Ginn, D. V., Wales.
Goose, Major R., England.
Grady, Lt Comdr J., England.
Green, D. J., Wales.
Green, Dr E. E., USA.
Green, J.† Ch.11, England.
Guns, Dr N., The Netherlands.
Hague, W. M.† Ch.10, Wales.
Hall, Sqn Ldr K., England.
Hammond, Dr D., England.
Hancock, P. M. J., Rhodesia
Hanson, J.,* Wales.
Harris, Dr N. D. C., England.
Hassall, R. D., England.
Hawkins, Dr C. A., The Netherlands
Hawkridge, Prof D. G., England.
Heath, Ms J., England
Hills, J. E., England.
Hills, Dr P. J., England.
Hilton, Lt Col B., England.
Holstead, D., England.
Howard, P. W. J., England.
Howarth, E.,* England.
Howe, Ms A., England.
Howe, Lt Comdr C., England.
Hubbard, G., England.
Hudson, H., England.
Hurley, G., England.
Hurn, Major B., England.
Hurst, Dr P., England.
Jarvis, J. F., Wales.
Jenkins, Dr B. G. M., Wales.
Jenkins, G., Wales.
Jones, B., England.
Jordan, Ms Y., S. Africa.
Kebby, Ms P. A., England.
Kelly, J. G., Wales.
Kirkwood, R., England.
Kirschner, P. A., The Netherlands
Kitchin, Lt Comdr M. J., England.
Kogan, P.† Ch.10, England.
Kole, Dr A. P., The Netherlands.
Koning, Dr S., The Netherlands.
Koorn, W. H., The Netherlands.
Lamazouade, A., Switzerland.
Leedham, Dr J., England.
Leiblum, Dr M. D., The Netherlands.
Lewis, P. G. J., England.
Lezer, Dr M. A., The Netherlands.
Lincoln-Smith, J., England.
Lloyd-Jones, E., Wales.
Loy, B., England.
McAleese, R.,* Scotland.
McCulloch, D. W.† Ch.11, N. Ireland.
Macdonald, A., Scotland.

McDowell, Lt Comdr W. R., England.
McLuckie, I. F., Scotland.
McPherson, I. N., Scotland.
Magin, D. J.† Ch.10, Australia.
Manton, D. J., England.
Marson, Ms S. N., England.
Mason, Col C. H., USA.
Megarry, Dr J.,*† Ch.11, Scotland.
Melia, J. † Ch.10, England.
Mëyling, T. C. G., The Netherlands.
Moffat, J. M., England.
Moore, Lt Comdr J. D. S., England.
Morris, Mrs A.† Ch.11, England.
Morris, R.,* England.
Moss, Dr G. D., Wales.
Murza, Dr G., W. Germany.
Neville, C., England.
Newton, Ms J. C., England.
Nichol, N., Scotland.
Nielson, Major W. R., Canada.
Noiroux, R., Belgium.
Nwana, Prof O. C., Nigeria.
Oakley, J., England.
Oh, Prof C. Y., USA.
O'Reilly, Ms F., England.
Ormerod, D. H., England.
O'Sullivan, K., England.
Owens, R. D., Eire.
Page, G. T., England.
Paice, J., England.
Payne, Capt T. W., England.
Percival, Dr F., England.
Phillips, E.,* England.
Prestley, Wing Comdr D. E., England.
Pritchard, D. F. L., England.
Race, Dr W. P., Wales.
Rahmlow, Prof H. F., USA.
Read, Ms P. M., England.
Redfern, D., England.
Rees, D. T., Wales.
Rees, E., Wales.
Reeves, J., England.
Remington, Lt Comdr J. C., England.
Robertson, Dr W. D., Canada.
Romiszowski, A. J., Brazil.
Rowatt, R., Scotland.
Rushby, N. J., England.
Ryan, Miss B., Wales.
Schellekens, Dr A. M. H. C., The Netherlands.
Shaw, Mrs B., England.
Shaw, M., England.
Shingler, Sqn Ldr F. J., England.
Sinclair, J. K.,* Scotland.
Spear, J. H., USA.
Staples, Wing Comdr D. H., England.
Steele, A. M., England.
Stephens, Dr A. G., England.
Stewart, A., Scotland.

Sumpter, Lt Comdr D., England.
Sutton, A. H., England.
Sutton, Dr R. A., Wales.
Tallis, A. R. G., England.
Tan, T. L., Singapore.
Taylor, Ms A., Canada.
Teall, Lt Col C., England.
Telfer, W. S., Scotland.
Thomas, Lt Comdr R., England.
Townsend, I. J., England.
Tucker, R. N., Scotland.
Twining, J. P., England.
Tyrrell, Dr D. M., England.
Van Holten, C., The Netherlands.
Van der Sandt, Dr M. A. J., The Netherlands.
van der Mast, C., The Netherlands.
Walker, D. R. F., England.
Ward, R., England.
Ward, Ms S., England.
Ware, Sqn Ldr M., England.

Watkins, Sqn Ldr T., England.
Webber, K. R., Wales.
Webster, R., England.
Welchman, M. M., England.
West, Lt K., England.
Westley, K. H., England.
Wharry, Dr D. M.† Ch.11, Wales.
Whitlock, Q. A.,* England.
Wiliam, Dr A. R.,* England.
Wilkinson, G. M., N. Ireland.
Willems, Dts H., The Netherlands.
Williams, A., Scotland.
Willmore, F. R., England.
Wilson, Ms B. E., Switzerland.
Winfield, I., England.
Winterburn, R., England.
Wood, A., England.
Wright, Ms M., England.
Zelmer, Ms A. C. L., Canada.

Closing Address

J. Hanson, *Polytechnic of Wales, Pontypridd, Mid-Glamorgan*

It is difficult to summarize even the broad areas of the more than 70 papers and workshops of this conference. All the papers have been concerned in one way or another with various problems in teaching and learning. Some have expounded new approaches and developments in the technology, while others have recorded and initiated discussion of applications of that technology.

The aim of the conference was to set these expositions and discussions within the theme of educational technology in a changing world. Once again the papers offered have covered the broad spectrum of educational technology, not specifically the chosen conference theme. Perhaps this can be examined in the future. It seems that papers and presentations aimed at a narrower theme leading to discussions in greater depth might be beneficial.

The broad aims of the organizing committee were:

1. to bring together experts in and practitioners of educational technology in such an atmosphere and setting as to encourage an exchange of views and ideas.
2. to provide a forum for practising educational technologists to bring the members up-to-date on what they have been doing.
3. to extend a warm Welsh welcome to members.

Did the conference succeed in any way in achieving its aspirations? Geoffrey Hubbard, in an admirable opening address, outlined the various aspects of change in the changing world and examined their effects on educational technology. He went on to make four propositions, one of which, particularly in the world of the British polytechnics, seems to provide a challenge to would-be innovators and developers. This is that educational technology is in many ways too far in advance of its use. To put this another way, educational technologists should be spending more time putting their technology to use in meeting the everyday teacher's teaching problems and the everyday student's learning problems. This is substantially a matter of disseminating ideas and developing enthusiasm for educational technology among teachers. It is a pity that the ideas and the techniques are embraced by only a few enthusiasts among teachers. To be seen using modern educational technology is to be unusual. For those facing the economic constraints of the developed world and for those struggling with the challenging and exciting task of establishing an education service, it is essential to come to a conference like this. The real proof of their worth, however, will be the measure of their success in persuading their teaching colleagues to use new ideas and techniques.

If some members leave this conference with a determination to concentrate on motivating and encouraging their teaching colleagues to experiment with modern educational technology, the goals of the conference will have been reached.

Keyword Index

adjunct questions 50
agriculture 17
algorithms 52
appropriate educational technology 1, 18, 56
appropriate technology 18, 56
assessment 33, 52
audio page 20
audiovisual equipment 23
audiovisual package 13, 14, 56

behaviour modelling 40
biochemistry 34
brainstorming 52

carrel 23
case study 2
CCTV 25
CET 10
CGLI 7, 8
chemical engineering 32
chemistry 33
cine film 22
civil engineering 54
communication, scientific 36
computer-aided instruction (learning) 42,
    43, 44, 45, 46
computer-microfiche 24
computer systems 42, 57
conceptual analysis 48
course development 4, 7, 8, 31, 49
course development teams 11
courses in educational technology 7, 8

decision logic 26
design of training packages 10
developing countries 1, 18, 41, 56
diagnostic testing 30
dietetics 38
dissemination networks 6
distance learning 27, 29, 42

economics 46
education
    — in-service 7

— medical 37, 39
— in United States 6
educational
    — broadcasting 26, 28, 29
    — innovation 6
    — media 1
    — needs 18
entry skills 30
evaluation 3, 5, 6, 47

family planning 40
field-workers 40
film loop 22

gaming 38
graphics 21, 52
guided discovery learning 16

health education 38, 39, 41
Hermes 29

IDIS-Microdok 24
independent study 47
individualized instruction 5, 21
industry 13
information retrieval 54
information systems 24
innovation 6, 26
    — in developing countries 1
in-service education 7, 8, 9, 12, 53, 57
    — two-tier strategy 10
instructional design 3, 14
integrated learning system 20
interaction 27
interaction analysis 57
interviewing 38

keyboard 13

laboratory 33
language difficulties 32, 33, 36
learner-cued instruction 16
learner-paced instruction 31
learning 48, 49

learning materials 11
lecturing styles 57
librarians' needs 53
libraries 53
low cost media 12, 33, 41, 52

management development 15
mathematics 5
mature student 5
MAVIS 13
media consultant 1, 56
media
   − educational 1, 56
   − low cost 12
medical education 37, 39
meetings 2
microfiche 24
   − computer 45
mixed ability 31, 32
modularization 4
modular system, computer 45
multi-level programming 34

nursing 39
nutrition 38

objectives 33
Open University 47
operative training 16

packaged dissemination 6
package learning 11, 13, 17, 31, 53, 56
   − training materials 14
perception 51
personnel training 25
physics 30, 31
PIPs 6
PLATO 42
professional education 14
programmed learning 5, 16, 21, 55
propagation 6
psychology 48, 49, 50

questions − adjunct 50

readability 36
reading programmes 55
remedial teaching 12, 32
resource-based learning 20

resource design 38
resource retrieval 54
resources 47
re-training 13
Royal Navy 25

satellites 28, 29
science 33
   − games 35
scientific writing 36
self-assessment 38
self-instruction 5
simulation 2, 39
simulation and gaming 35
skills analysis 13
slide/tape 20, 21, 23
small groups 20
social perception 19
social skills 19
space technology 28
staff development 49
stand-alone systems 13, 45
strategies 9, 12
student development 49
support materials 7
syllabus 8

tables 51
teaching aids 21
team teaching 20
TEC 10, 11
TELEBRAS 4
telecommunications 4
telecommunications systems 28
teleconferencing 27, 28
telephone-based instruction 27
training
   − by objectives 4, 33
   − identification of needs in 17
   − materials 41
   − workshops 10

understanding 48

video-tape 19, 21, 32, 50
vocational training 3

work book 19
writing − scientific 36

Author Index

(alphabetical list of authors, including co-authors not present as delegates)

Author	Paper	Page
Addinall, E.	35	263
Anderson, E.W.	52	393
Bardell, E.	36	269
Barker, A.L.	54	406
Barker, J.G.	56	438, 444
Becker, A.D.	27	212
Bingham, E.G.	54	406
Bird, C.M.	22	182
Brew, A.	47	350
Brooking, Lt Comdr B.A.	25	201
Bryce, C.F.A.	34	256
Bulford, J.R.S.	17	149
Coffey, J.	11	100
Coles, C.R.	37, 49	279, 367
Cooper, J.	12	108
Daniel, J.S.	28	219
Davies, K.L.	51	384
Davies, P.A.I.	20	171
Davies, W.J.K.	7	67
Ellington, H.I.	35	263
Evans, L.F.	2	21
Fieldhouse, P.	38	287
Fleming, W.G.	48, 49	361, 367
Green, E.E.	3	29
Hancock, P.M.J.	40	302
Hanson, J.	Closing Address	469
Hartley, J.	51	384
Hawkins, C.A.	43	323
Hawkridge, D.G.	6	61
Hills, J.E.	8	76
Hills, P.J.	53	401
Howard, P.W.J.	17	149
Hubbard, G.	Keynote Address	11
Hurst, P.	26	206
Jarvis, J.F.	20	171
Jenkins, B.G.M.	32	244
Kelly, J.G.	20	171
Kirschner, P.A.	50	373
Leedham, J.	55	418
Leiblum, M.D.	44	330
McAleese, R.	1	17
Machado, N.H.S.	4	39
McCulloch, D.W.	46	345

Author	*Paper*	*Page*
Mason, C.H.	15	132
Moffatt, J.M.	13	119
Mountford, B.	37	279
Murza, G.	24	195
Neville, C.	9	85
Oh, C.Y.	21	177
Percival, F.	35	263
Race, W.P.	33	247
Rahmlow, H.F.	42	317
Rees, D.T.	20	171
Robertson, W.D.	29	225
Romiszowski, A.J.	4, 5	39, 48
Shaw, M.	38	287
Stephens, A.G.	23	190
Stewart, A.M.	18, 34	159, 256
Sutton, R.A.	30	233
Tallis, A.R.G.	17	149
Taylor, A.	39	293
Telfer, W.S.	31	241
Tyrrell, D.M.	14	126
van der Brink, H.J.	50	373
van der Mast, C.	45	336
Ward, R.	10	94
Wharry, D.M.	57	433, 452
Webber, K.R.	20	171
Westley, K.H.	16	136
Winfield, I.	19	164
Zelmer, A.C.L.	41	309
Zelmer, A.E.	41	309